ACCA
STUDY TEXT

Paper 3.3

Performance Management

IN THIS JUNE 2004 EDITION

- Targeted to the syllabus and study guide
- Quizzes and questions to check your understanding
- Clear layout and style designed to save you time
- Plenty of exam-style questions with detailed guidance from BPP
- Chapter roundups and summaries to help revision

FOR EXAMS IN DECEMBER 2004 AND JUNE 2005

BPP Professional Education
June 2004

First edition 2001
Fourth edition June 2004

ISBN 07517 1669 3 (previous ISBN 07517 1158 6)

British Library Cataloguing-in-Publication Data
A catalogue record for this book is available from the British Library

Published by

BPP Professional Education
Aldine House, Aldine Place
London W12 8AW

www.bpp.com

Printed in Great Britain by W M Print
45-47 Frederick Street
Walsall, West Midlands
WS2 9NE

We are grateful to the Association of Chartered Certified Accountants for permission to reproduce past examination questions and questions from the pilot paper. The answers have been prepared by BPP Professional Education.

Page

INTRODUCTION

PART A: MANAGEMENT ACCOUNTING FRAMEWORK

PART B: DESIGN OF MANAGEMENT ACCOUNTING SYSTEMS

PART C: PERFORMANCE MEASUREMENT

PART D: PLANNING AND CONTROL

PART E: DECISION MAKING

THE BPP STUDY TEXT

Aims of this Study Text

To provide you with the knowledge and understanding, skills and application techniques that you need if you are to be successful in your exams

This Study Text has been written around the **Performance Management** syllabus.

- It is **comprehensive**. It covers the syllabus content. No more, no less.

- It is written at the **right level**. Each chapter is written with the ACCA's **study guide** in mind.

- It is targeted to the **exam**. We have taken account of the **pilot paper and all sittings so far**, questions put to the examiners at ACCA conferences and the assessment methodology.

To allow you to study in the way that best suits your learning style and the time you have available, by following your personal Study Plan (see page (viii))

You may be studying at home on your own until the date of the exam, or you may be attending a full-time course. You may like to (and have time to) read every word, or you may prefer to (or only have time to) skim-read and devote the remainder of your time to question practice. Wherever you fall in the spectrum, you will find the BPP Study Text meets your needs in designing and following your personal Study Plan.

To tie in with the other components of the BPP Effective Study Package to ensure you have the best possible chance of passing the exam (see page (vi))

Recommended period of use	Elements of the BPP Effective Study Package

From the outset and throughout	**Learning to Learn Accountancy** Read this invaluable book as you begin your studies and refer to it as you work through the various elements of the BPP Effective Study Package. It will help you to acquire knowledge, practise and revise, efficiently and effectively.

Three to twelve months before the exam	**Study Text** Use the Study Text to acquire knowledge, understanding, skills and the ability to apply techniques.

Throughout	**Big Picture Posters** Display these where you're studying and give yourself a feel for the overall shape of the paper and the connections between syllabus areas. Examiners have stressed that you will need to be able to link up different areas when you take the exam. The visual stimulation the posters provide will help you remember the key areas of the syllabus.

Throughout	**Virtual Campus** Study, practise, revise and take advantage of other useful resources with BPP's fully interactive e-learning site with comprehensive tutor support.

Throughout	**i-Pass** **i-Pass**, our computer-based testing package, provides objective test questions in a variety of formats and is ideal for self-assessment.

One to six months before the exam	**Practice & Revision Kit** Try the numerous examination-format questions, for which there are realistic suggested solutions prepared by BPP's own authors. Then attempt the two mock exams.

From three months before the exam until the last minute	**Passcards** Work through these short, memorable notes which are focused on what is most likely to come up in the exam you will be sitting.

One to six months before the exam	**Success Tapes and CDs** The tapes and CDs cover the vital elements of your syllabus in less than 90 minutes per subject. They also contains exam hints to help you fine tune your strategy.

HELP YOURSELF STUDY FOR YOUR ACCA EXAMS

Exams for professional bodies such as ACCA are very different from those you have taken at college or university. You will be under **greater time pressure before** the exam – as you may be combining your study with work as well as in the exam room. There are many different ways of learning and so the BPP Study Text offers you a number of different tools to help you through. Here are some hints and tips: they are not plucked out of the air, but **based on research and experience**. (You don't need to know that long-term memory is in the same part of the brain as emotions and feelings – but it's a fact anyway.)

The right approach

1 The right attitude

Believe in yourself	Yes, there is a lot to learn. Yes, it is a challenge. But thousands have succeeded before and you can too.
Remember why you're doing it	Studying might seem a grind at times, but you are doing it for a reason: to advance your career.

2 The right focus

Read through the Syllabus and Study guide	These tell you what you are expected to know and are supplemented by exam focus points in the text.
Study the Exam Paper section	Past papers are likely to be a reasonable guide of what you should expect in the exam.

3 The right method

The whole picture	You need to grasp the detail – but keeping in mind how everything fits into the big picture will help you understand better. • The **Introduction** of each chapter puts the material in context. • The **Syllabus content**, **Study guide** and **Exam focus points** show you what you need to **grasp**. • BPP's Big Picture Posters will help you see the links here.
In your own words	To absorb the information (and to practise your written communication skills), it helps **put it into your own words**. • **Take notes.** • Answer the **questions** in each chapter. As well as helping you absorb the information you will practise your written communication skills, which become increasingly important as you progress through your ACCA exams. • Draw **mind maps**. We have an example for the whole syllabus. • Try 'teaching' to a colleague or friend.

BPP
PROFESSIONAL EDUCATION

Give yourself cues to jog your memory	The BPP Study Text uses **bold text** to **highlight key points** and **icons** to identify key features, such as **Exam focus points** and **Key terms**. • Try **colour coding** with a highlighter pen. • Write **key points** on cards.

4   **The right review**

Review, review, review	It is a **fact** that regularly reviewing a topic in summary form can **fix it in your memory**. Because **review** is so important, the BPP Study Text helps you to do so in many ways. • **Chapter roundups** summarise the key points in each chapter. Use them to recap each study session. • The **Quick quiz** is another review technique to ensure that you have grasped the essentials. • Use the **Key term** index as a quiz. • Go through the **Examples** in each chapter a second or third time.

Developing your personal Study Plan

One thing that the BPP Learning to Learn Accountancy book emphasises (see page (iv)) is the need to prepare (and use) a study plan. Planning and sticking to the plan are key elements of learning success.

There are four steps you should work through.

Step 1. **How do you learn?**

First you need to be aware of your style of learning. The BPP Learning to Learn Accountancy book commits a chapter to this **self-discovery**. What types of intelligence do you display when learning? You might be advised to brush up on certain study skills before launching into this Study Text.

> BPP's **Learning to Learn Accountancy** book helps you to identify what intelligences you show more strongly and then details how you can tailor your study process to your preferences. It also includes handy hints on how to develop intelligences you exhibit less strongly, but which might be needed as you study accountancy.

Are you a **theorist** or are you more **practical**? If you would rather get to grips with a theory before trying to apply it in practice, you should follow the study sequence on page (x). If the reverse is true (you need to know why you are learning theory before you do so), you might be advised to flick through Study Text chapters and look at questions, case studies and examples (Steps 7, 8 and 9 in the **suggested study sequence**) before reading through the detailed theory.

Step 2. **How much time do you have?**

Work out the time you have available per week, given the following.

- The standard you have set yourself
- The time you need to set aside later for work on the Practice & Revision Kit and Passcards
- The other exam(s) you are sitting
- Very importantly, practical matters such as work, travel, exercise, sleep and social life

Note your time available in box A.

A | Hours [ ]

Step 3. **Allocate your time**

- Take the time you have available per week for this Study Text shown in box A, multiply it by the number of weeks available and insert the result in box B.

B [ ]

- Divide the figure in Box B by the number of chapters in this text and insert the result in box C.

C [ ]

Remember that this is only a rough guide. Some of the chapters in this book are longer and more complicated than others, and you will find some subjects easier to understand than others.

Step 4. **Implement**

Set about studying each chapter in the time shown in box C, following the key study steps in the order suggested by your particular learning style.

This is your personal **Study Plan**. You should try and combine it with the study sequence outlined below. You may want to modify the sequence a little (as has been suggested above) to adapt it to your **personal style**.

BPP's *Learning to Learn Accountancy* gives further guidance in developing a study plan and deciding when and where to study.

BPP
PROFESSIONAL EDUCATION

Suggested study sequence

Tackle the chapters in the order you find them in the Study Text. Taking into account your individual learning style, you could follow this sequence.

Key study steps	Activity
Step 1 **Topic list**	Each numbered topic is a numbered section in the chapter.
Step 2 **Introduction**	This gives you the **big picture** in terms of the **context** of the chapter. The content is referenced to the **Study Guide**, and **Exam Guidance** shows how the topic is likely to be examined. In other words, it sets your **objectives for study.**
Step 3 **Knowledge brought forward boxes**	In these we highlight information and techniques that it is assumed you have 'brought forward' with you from your earlier studies. If there are topics which have changed recently due to legislation for example, these topics are explained in more detail.
Step 4 **Explanations**	Proceed methodically through the chapter, reading each section thoroughly and making sure you understand.
Step 5 **Key terms and Exam focus points**	• **Key terms** can often earn you *easy marks* if you state them clearly and correctly in an appropriate exam answer (and they are indexed at the back of the text). • **Exam focus points** give you a good idea of how we think the examiner intends to examine certain topics.
Step 6 **Note taking**	Take brief notes if you wish, avoiding the temptation to copy out too much.
Step 7 **Examples**	Follow each through to its solution very carefully.
Step 8 **Case examples**	Study each one, and try to add flesh to them from your own experience – they are designed to show how the topics you are studying come alive (and often come unstuck) in the real world.
Step 9 **Questions**	Make a very good attempt at each one.
Step 10 **Answers**	Check yours against ours, and make sure you understand any discrepancies.
Step 11 **Chapter roundup**	Work through it very carefully, to make sure you have grasped the major points it is highlighting.
Step 12 **Quick quiz**	When you are happy that you have covered the chapter, use the **Quick quiz** to check how much you have remembered of the topics covered.
Step 13 **Question(s) in the Question bank**	Either at this point, or later when you are thinking about revising, make a full attempt at the **Question(s)** suggested at the very end of the chapter. You can find these at the end of the Study Text, along with the **Answers** so you can see how you did. We highlight those that are introductory, and those which are of the standard you would expect to find in an exam.

Short of time: *Skim study technique?*

You may find you simply do not have the time available to follow all the key study steps for each chapter, however you adapt them for your particular learning style. If this is the case, follow the **skim study** technique below (the icons in the Study Text will help you to do this).

- Study the chapters in the order you find them in the Study Text.

- For each chapter:

  ○ Follow the key study steps 1-3, and then skim-read through step 4. Jump to step 11, and then go back to step 5.

  ○ Follow through steps 7 and 8, and prepare outline answers to questions (steps 9/10).

  ○ Try the Quick Quiz (step 12), following up any items you can't answer, then do a plan for the Question (step 13), comparing it against our answers.

  ○ You should probably still follow step 6 (note-taking), although you may decide simply to rely on the BPP Passcards for this.

Moving on...

However you study, when you are ready to embark on the practice and revision phase of the BPP Effective Study Package, you should still refer back to this Study Text, both as a source of **reference** (you should find the list of key terms and the index particularly helpful for this) and as a **refresher** (the Chapter Roundups and Quick Quizzes help you here).

And remember to keep careful hold of this Study Text – you will find it invaluable in your work.

More advice on Study Skills can be found in the BPP **Learning to Learn Accountancy** book

SYLLABUS

Aim

To ensure candidates can apply judgement and technique in the analysis of relevant data to provide management with the information required to contribute to a range of strategic planning, control and decision-making situations.

Objectives

On completion of this paper candidates should be able to:

- understand the objectives of preparing management information and the need to adapt techniques in a changing commercial environment

- identify the information needs of management and contribute to the development of appropriate systems

- evaluate the strategic performance of a business and recommend appropriate performance measures

- understand the significance of the relationship between financial and non-financial indicators of business performance

- apply techniques to evaluate management decisions in relation to costing, pricing, product range and marketing strategy

- identify and apply appropriate budgeting techniques to enable management to control the business

- demonstrate the skills expected in Part 3.

Position of the paper in the overall syllabus

Paper 3.3 builds on Paper 2.4 *Financial Management and Control.* Candidates are expected to have a thorough understanding of the Paper 2.4 syllabus. In addition, candidates will also be required to apply the principles and techniques covered in Paper 1.2 *Financial Information for Management.*

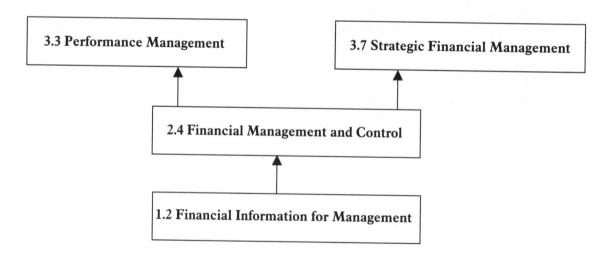

SYLLABUS

1 Developments in management accounting

(a) Objectives of management accounting information in relation to:

    (i)   short-term planning and strategic planning

    (ii)   control and decision making

    (iii) effective use of management accounting techniques

(b) Changes in management accounting

    (i)   Contingency theory

    (ii)   Institutional theory

(c) Trends and developments in management accounting techniques and methods

    (i)   Evaluation and promotion of change in techniques and methods used

    (ii)   Evaluation of the effect of the rate of change of technology and products on management accounting

    (iii) Current issues in management accounting principles and their relevance and application

(d) Impact of changes in business structures

    (i)   Appraisal of continued use of management accounting techniques (eg standard costing)

    (ii)   Impact on management accounting of changes in business processes and management techniques

    (iii) Changes in business structure and management accounting (eg team/project focus)

2 Design of management accounting systems

(a) System objectives and the uses of information in relation to:

    (i)   short-term and strategic planning

    (ii)   control and decision making

    (iii) effective use of management accounting techniques

(b) Sources of information

    (i)   From within the organisation

    (ii)   From suppliers and customers

    (iii) By comparison with competitors

    (iv) From government and other statistical sources

(c) Recording and processing methods

    (i)   Collection and recording of monetary and non-monetary information

    (ii)   Identification of requirements for different purposes

    (iii) Influence of management accounting principles and techniques

    (iv) Influence of IT systems

    (v)   Effect of type of business entity

(d) Format of reports

    (i) Analysis and dissemination to relevant individuals/groups
    (ii) Effect of management structure and style
    (iii) Frequency, timing and degree of accuracy
    (iv) Influence of trend, materiality and controllability issues.

3 Performance measurement

(a) Performance hierarchy

    (i) Mission statement and the fulfilment of a vision
    (ii) Corporate planning and the achievement of strategic objectives
    (iii) The accomplishment of operational plans
    (iv) The attainment of specific departmental targets

(b) The scope of performance measurement

    (i) Financial performance - profitability, liquidity, activity and gearing

    (ii) Non-financial business indicators

    (iii) Performance measurement for non-profit seeking organisations

    (iv) Performance measurement for pubic sector service provision

    (v) Long and short run performance

    (vi) Performance measurement models such as the balanced scorecard (to improve the range and linkage between performance measures) and the performance pyramid (to relate strategy and operations)

(c) External considerations

    (i) Economic/market conditions

    (ii) Financial, environmental and service quality regulation from government agencies

(d) Management impact on performance measurement

    (i) Accountability issues
    (ii) Benefits and problems of performance measurement
    (iii) Reward schemes and performance measurement
    (iv) Management style and performance measurement

4 Planning and control

(a) Strategic management accounting

    (i) Corporate v operational strategy
    (ii) Life cycle issues
    (iii) SWOT analysis
    (iv) Benchmarking
    (v) Consideration of risk and uncertainty
    (vi) Strategic management accounting in the context of multinational companies

(b) Budgeting and budgetary control

    (i) The appraisal of alternative approaches to budgeting - incremental, rolling, ABB etc
    (ii) Budgeting as a planning and control device
    (iii) Quantitative aids and risk analysis

(iv)   Behavioural aspects

(v)   Current developments in budgeting

5   Decision making

(a) Pricing strategies and the evaluation of pricing decisions

    (i)   Price/demand relationships

    (ii)   Relevant costs and pricing decisions

    (iii) Pricing and product life cycles

    (iv) Target costing and pricing

    (v)   Transfer pricing and decision making

    (vi) Transfer pricing in the context of multinational companies

(b) Information for decision making

    (i)   Relevant cost analysis

    (ii)   CVP analysis and profit maximisation

    (iii) Product profitability and limiting factor analysis

    (iv) Customer profitability analysis, including activity based

    (v)   Theory of constraints and throughput accounting

    (vi) Accounting for uncertainty

    (vii) DCF techniques

Excluded topics

The syllabus content outlines the areas for assessment. No areas of knowledge are specifically excluded from the syllabus.

Key areas of the syllabus

The key topic areas are as follows.

- The contribution of management accounting systems towards the achievement of corporate objectives

- Identifying appropriate performance indicators for particular business situations

- Abstracting relevant information from financial reports to assess performance

- Identifying and processing costs as an aid to decision making

Introduction

Paper 3.3

Performance management
(United Kingdom)

Study Guide

1 STRATEGIC PLANNING AND DECISION MAKING

Syllabus reference 1a

- Identify the characteristics of strategic planning and decision making

- Contrast strategic planning with short term/operational planning

- Identify the areas of management accounting information which are of importance in strategic management

- Evaluate the relevance of discounted cash flow principles in information for strategic decision making

- Select and analyse costs and revenues relevant to strategic planning and decision making in a range of situations

2 SHORT RUN DECISION MAKING AND CONTROL

Syllabus reference 1a

- Explain the significance of endogenous information sources in relation to short run decision making and control

- Identify the characteristics of short term non-strategic activities

- Identify the areas of management accounting information appropriate for short term decision making

- Explain the differences between management control and operational control in the context of short run decision making and control

3 CHANGES IN MANAGEMENT ACCOUNTING

Syllabus reference 1b

- Explain the contingency theory of management accounting: Otley

- Explain how institutional theory presents a framework for understanding changes in and the implications for management accounting: Powell and Di Maggio

- Explain and demonstrate activity based management

4 TRENDS IN MANAGEMENT ACCOUNTING TECHNIQUES AND METHODS

Syllabus reference 1c

- Discuss the expansion in the scope of management accounting in the last 40 years

- Identify and discuss some recently adopted management accounting techniques

- Explain how new techniques may be evaluated

- Discuss the ways in which management accounting practitioners are made aware of new techniques

- Illustrate how an organisation's structure, culture and strategy will influence the adoption of new methods and techniques

- Assess the continuing effectiveness of traditional techniques within a rapidly changing business environment

5 TECHNOLOGICAL CHANGE AND MANAGEMENT ACCOUNTING

Syllabus reference 1c, 1d

- Discuss the changing accounting information needs of modern service orientated business compared with the needs of traditional manufacturing industry

- Discuss how modern IT systems provide the opportunity for instant access to management accounting data throughout an organisation

- Discuss how modern IT systems facilitate the remote input of management accounting data in an acceptable format by non-finance specialists

- Explain how modern information systems provide instant access to previously unavailable data that can be used for benchmarking and control purposes

BPP
PROFESSIONAL EDUCATION (xvi)

- Discuss the need for businesses to continually refine and develop their management accounting systems if they are to prosper in an increasingly competitive and global market

6 CHANGES IN BUSINESS STRUCTURE AND MANAGEMENT ACCOUNTING

Syllabus reference 1d

- Identify the particular information needs of organisations adopting a team/project focus

- Discuss the concept of business integration and the linkage between people, operations, strategy and technology

- Explain the influence of Business Process Re-engineering on systems development

- Identify and discuss the required changes in management accounting systems as a consequence of empowering staff to manage sectors of a business

7 SYSTEM DESIGN AND SYSTEM OBJECTIVES

Syllabus reference 2a

- Identify the accounting information requirements for strategic planning, management control and operational control and decision making

- Describe, with reference to management accounting, ways in which the information requirements of a management structure are affected by the features of the structure

- Evaluate the objectives of management accounting and management accounting information

- List and explain the attributes and principles of management accounting information

- Explain the integration of management accounting information within an overall information system

- Define and discuss the merits of, and potential problems with, open and closed systems

- Suggest the ways in which contingent (internal and external) factors influence management accounting and its use

- Illustrate how anticipated human behaviour will influence the design of a management accounting system

- Explain and discuss the impact of responsibility accounting on information requirements

8 INTERNAL SOURCES OF INFORMATION

Syllabus reference 2b, 2c

- Identify the principal internal sources of management accounting information

- Illustrate how these principal sources of information might be used for control purposes

- Identify the direct data capture and process costs of internally generated management accounting information

- Identify the indirect costs of producing internal information

- Explain the principal controls required in generating and distributing internal information

- Discuss the factors that need to be considered when determining the capacity and development potential of a system

- Explain the procedures that may be necessary to ensure security of highly confidential information that is not for external consumption

9 EXTERNAL SOURCES OF INFORMATION

Syllabus reference 2b, 2c

- Identify common external sources of information eg suppliers, government, trade associations, customers, database suppliers

- Identify the costs associated with these external sources

- Discuss the limitations of using externally generated information

- Identify the categories of external information that are likely to be a useful addition to an organisation's management accounting system

- Illustrate how the information might be used in planning and control activities eg benchmarking against similar organisations

10 RECORDING AND PROCESSING INFORMATION

Syllabus reference 2c, 2d

- Identify the stages in the information processing cycle in the context of accounting information

- Identify how the collection and analysis of information is influenced by management accounting principles and techniques being used by the organisation

- Describe the systems involved in the collection and recording of monetary and non-monetary information

- Illustrate how the type of business entity will influence the recording and processing methods

- Explain how IT developments eg spreadsheets, accountancy software packages and electronic mail may influence recording and processing systems

- Discuss the difficulties associated with recording and processing data of a qualitative nature

11 PERFORMANCE HIERARCHY

Syllabus reference 3a

- Discuss the purpose of a mission statement and the pursuit of a vision

- Discuss the structure and content of a mission statement

- Explain how high level corporate objectives are developed

- Identify strategic objectives and how they may be incorporated into the corporate plan

- Explain how strategic objectives are cascaded down the organisation via the formulation of subsidiary objectives

- Identify any relevant social and ethical obligations that should be considered in the pursuit of corporate objectives

- Discuss the concept of the 'planning gap' and alternative strategies to 'fill the gap'

- Identify the characteristics of operational performance

- Contrast the relative significance of planning as against controlling activities at different levels in the performance hierarchy

12 FINANCIAL PERFORMANCE IN THE PRIVATE SECTOR

Syllabus reference 3b, 3c

- Explain why the primary objective of financial performance should be concerned with the benefits of the shareholders

- Discuss the crucial objectives of survival and business growth

- Discuss the appropriateness of differing measures of profitability eg ROCE, EPS, ROI, sales margin, EBITDA, Residual Income, NPV, IRR

- Explain why indicators of liquidity and gearing need to be considered alongside profitability

- Compare and contrast short and long run financial performance and the resulting management issues

- Contrast the traditional relationship between profits and share value with the long term profit expectations of the stock market and recent financial performance of new technology/communication companies

13 NON-FINANCIAL PERFORMANCE INDICATORS FOR BUSINESS

Syllabus reference 3b, 3c

- Discuss the interaction of NFPIs with financial performance indicators

- Discuss the implications of the growing emphasis on NFPIs

- Identify and comment on the significance of NFPIs in relation to employees eg staff turnover, sickness rates

- Identify and comment on the significance of NFPIs in relation to product/ service quality eg customer satisfaction reports, repeat business ratings, customer loyalty, access and availability

- Discuss the difficulties in interpreting data on qualitative issues

- Discuss the significance of brand awareness and company profile

14 PERFORMANCE MEASUREMENT FOR NON-PROFIT SEEKING ORGANISATIONS

Syllabus reference 3b, 3c

- Discuss the potential for diversity in objectives depending on organisation type

- Comment on the need to achieve objectives with limited funds that may not be controllable

- Identify and explain ways in which performance may be judged in non-profit seeking organisations

- Comment on the difficulty in measuring outputs when performance is not judged in terms of money or an easily quantifiable objective

- Explain how the combination of politics and the desire to measure public sector performance may result in undesirable service outcomes

- Comment on 'value for money' service as a not-for-profit sector goal

15 PERFORMANCE - A BROAD PERSPECTIVE

Syllabus reference 3c

- Comment on the need to consider the environment in which an organisation is operating when assessing its performance eg What are the prevailing market conditions? Is funding relatively easy or difficult to secure? Does the strength of the national currency impact on the organisation's performance? Is the prevailing political climate particularly favourable or unfavourable towards the organisation currently? How have these issues changed over time?

- Consider the impact of governmental regulation on the performance measurement techniques used and the performance levels achieved (for example, in the case of utility services and former state monopolies)

16 ALTERNATIVE VIEWS OF PERFORMANCE MEASUREMENT

Syllabus reference 3b

- Discuss the 'balanced scorecard' as a way in which to improve the range and linkage of performance measures

- Discuss the 'performance pyramid' as a way in which to link strategy and operations

- Discuss the work of Fitzgerald and Moon that considers performance measurement in business services using building blocks for dimensions, standards and rewards

17 MANAGEMENT BEHAVIOUR AND PERFORMANCE

Syllabus reference 3d

- Explain the relationship between performance measurement systems and behaviour

- Discuss how performance measurement systems can influence behaviour

- Consider the accountability issues arising from performance measurement systems

- Identify the ways in which performance measurement systems may send the 'wrong signals' and result in undesirable business consequences

- Comment on the potential beneficial and adverse consequences of linking reward schemes to performance measurement

- Explain how management style needs to be considered when designing an effective performance measurement system

18 STRATEGIC PLANNING AND CONTROL

Syllabus reference 4a

- Compare strategic with operational planning and control

- Explain how organisational survival in the long term necessitates consideration of life cycle issues

- Identify the role of corporate planning in clarifying corporate objectives, making strategic decisions and checking progress towards the objectives

- Explain the structure of corporate planning

- Discuss the combining of strategic planning with freewheeling opportunism in a fast changing business environment

- Comment on the potential conflict between strategic plans and short term localised decisions

- Explain the principles of SWOT analysis

- Explain how SWOT analysis may assist in the planning process

- Comment on the benefits and difficulties of benchmarking performance with best practice organisations

- Explain how risk and uncertainty play an especially important role in long term strategic planning that relies upon forecasts of exogenous variables

- Explain aspects of strategic management accounting in the context of multinational companies

19 BUDGETING AND BUDGETARY CONTROL I

Syllabus reference 4b

- Describe the internal and external sources of planning information for an organisation

- List the information used in the preparation of the master budget and in its functional components

- Contrast the information used in the operation of zero based budgeting and incremental budgeting

- Explain and illustrate the use of budgeting as a planning aid in the co-ordination of business activity

- Explain and illustrate the relevance of budgeting in the co-ordination of business activities

- Explain and quantify the application of positive and negative feedback in the operation of budgetary control

- Explain and quantify the application of feed-forward control in the operation of budgeting

20 BUDGETING AND BUDGETARY CONTROL II

Syllabus reference 4b

- Identify quantitative aids which may be used in budgetary planning and control

- Discuss and evaluate methods for the analysis of costs into fixed and variable components

- Give examples to demonstrate the use of forecasting techniques in the budgetary planning process

- Explain the use of forecasting techniques in the budgetary planning process

- Describe the use of learning curve theory in budgetary planning and control

- Implement learning curve theory

- Identify factors which may cause uncertainty in the setting of budgets and in the budgetary control process

- Identify the effects of flexible budgeting in reducing uncertainty in budgeting

- Illustrate the use of probabilities in budgetary planning and comment on the relevance of the information thus obtained

- Explain the use of computer based models in accommodating uncertainty in budgeting and in promoting 'what-if' analysis

21 BUDGETING AND BUDGETARY CONTROL III

Syllabus reference 4b

- Identify the factors which affect human behaviour in budgetary planning and control

- Compare and contrast ways in which alternative management styles may affect the operation of budgetary planning and control systems

- Explain budgeting as a bargaining process between people

- Explain the conflict between personal and corporate aspiration and its impact on budgeting

- Explain the application of contingency theory to the budgeting process

- Discuss the impact of political, social, economic and technological change on budgeting

- Critically review the use of budgetary planning and control

- Enumerate and evaluate the strengths and weaknesses of alternative budget models such as fixed and flexible, rolling, activity based, zero based and incremental

- Identify the effects on staff and management of the operation of budgetary planning and control

- Identify and appraise current developments in budgeting

22 SHORT RUN DECISIONS I

Syllabus reference 5b

- Distinguish between relevant and irrelevant information using appropriate criteria

- Identify cost classification(s) in decision making

- Explain how quantitative and qualitative information is used in decision making

- Evaluate and assess the frequency, timing, format, and degree of accuracy in the provision of decision making information

- Describe the basic decision making cycle for business decisions

- Classify problems for the purpose of modelling into simple, complex and dynamic problems

- Explain the relevance of endogenous and exogenous variables, policies and controls, performance measures and intermediate variables in model building

- Explain the nature of CVP analysis and name planning and decision making situations in which it may be used

- Compare the accounting and economic models of CVP analysis

- Explain the assumptions of linearity and the principle of relevant range in the CVP model

- Prepare breakeven charts and profit-volume charts and interpret the information contained within each, including multi-product situations

- Comment on the limitations of CVP analysis for planning and decision making including multi-product situations

23   SHORT RUN DECISIONS II

Syllabus reference 5a, 5b

- Explain the use of avoidable cost, incremental cost, marginal cost and variable cost in decision making

- Describe the relationship between fixed cost and the time horizon used in a decision situation

- Explain how opportunity cost is used in making decisions

- Identify and calculate relevant costs for specific decision situations from given data

- Explain the meaning of throughput accounting and its use in decision making

- Explain and illustrate the impact of limiting factors in decision making

- Solve problems involving changes in product mix, discontinuance of products or departments

- Implement make or buy decisions using relevant costs

- Explain and demonstrate activity-based customer profitability analysis

- Make decisions as to whether to further process a product before sale using relevant costs and revenues

- Use relevant costs and revenues in decisions relating to the operation of internal service departments or the use of external services

24   PRICING I

Syllabus reference 4a

- Identify and discuss market situations which influence the pricing policy adopted by an organisation

- Explain and discuss the variables (including price) which influence demand for a product or service

- Explain the price elasticity of demand

- Manipulate data in order to determine an optimum price/output level

- Calculate prices using full cost and marginal cost as the pricing base

- Compare the use of full cost pricing and marginal cost pricing as planning and decision-making aids

25   PRICING II

Syllabus reference 4a

- Calculate prices using activity based costing in the estimation of the cost element

- Contrast and discuss the implications of prices using the activity based costing technique with those using volume related methods in assigning costs to products

- Take informed pricing decisions in the context of special orders and new products

- Discuss pricing policy in the context of skimming, penetration and differential pricing

- Explain the problems of pricing in the context of short life products

- Explain the operation of target pricing in achieving a desired market share

26   RISK AND UNCERTAINTY

Syllabus reference 5b

- Define and distinguish between uncertainty and risk preference

- Explain ways in which uncertainty may be allowed for by using conservatism and worst/most likely/best outcome estimates

- Explain the use of sensitivity analysis in decision situations

- Explain the use of probability estimates and the calculation of expected value

- Explain and illustrate the use of maximin, maximax and minimax regrets techniques in decision making

- Describe the structure and use of decision trees
- Apply joint probabilities in decision tree analysis
- Illustrate the use of decision tree analysis in assessing the range of outcomes and the cumulative probabilities of each outcome

27 TRANSFER PRICING I

Syllabus reference 5a

- Describe the organisation structure in which transfer pricing may be required
- Explain divisional autonomy, divisional performance measurement and corporate profit maximisation and their link with transfer pricing
- Formulate the 'general rule' for transfer pricing and explain its application
- Describe, illustrate and evaluate the use of market price as the transfer price
- Assess where an adjusted market price will be appropriate for transfer business
- Assess the impact of market price methods on divisional autonomy, performance measurement and corporate profit maximisation
- Calculate an appropriate transfer price from given data

28 TRANSFER PRICING II

Syllabus reference 5a

- Describe the alternative cost based approaches to transfer pricing

- Identify the circumstances in which marginal cost should be used as the transfer price and determine its impact on divisional autonomy, performance measurement and corporate profit maximisation
- Illustrate methods by which a share of fixed costs may be included in the transfer price
- Comment on these methods and their impact on divisional autonomy, performance measurement and corporate profit maximisation
- Discuss the advantages which may be claimed for the use of standard cost rather than actual cost when setting transfer prices
- Explain the relevance of opportunity cost in transfer pricing
- List the information which must be centrally available in order that the profit maximising transfer policy may be implemented between divisions where intermediate products are in short supply
- Illustrate the formulation of the quantitative model for a range of limiting factors from which the corporate profit maximising transfer policy may be calculated
- Analyse the concept of shadow price in setting transfer prices for intermediate products that are in short supply

- Illustrate the corporate maximising transfer policy where a single intermediate resource is in short supply and a limited external source is available and explain the information which must be available centrally in order that the transfer policy may be formulated
- Explain and demonstrate the issues that require consideration when setting transfer prices in multinational companies

29 DECISIONS

Syllabus reference 5b

- Define and illustrate the concepts of net present value and internal rate of return
- Calculate the net present value and internal rate of return in the evaluation of an investment opportunity
- Explain the use of DCF techniques for decisions involving cash outlays over long periods
- Explain the relationship between net present value and residual income where annuity depreciation is used in the residual income calculations
- Compare and contrast net present value with payback and accounting rate of return in the evaluation of investment opportunities

THE EXAM PAPER

- The examination is a three-hour paper constructed in two sections.

- The two compulsory questions in Section A may or may not be based on the same scenario.

- Section B questions will comprise at least one question that is purely discursive.

- In viewing the paper as a whole, the balance between computational and discursive questions will not vary significantly from diet to diet.

- Each examination paper will comprise at least one element from within each of the five main syllabus headings.

- Core areas will be examined regularly in Section A. The more peripheral areas will be examined in Section B.

- The 'rotation' of topics within successive examination diets will reflect the relative importance of these topics.

		Number of marks
Section A:	Two compulsory questions (no single question will exceed 45 marks)	60
Section B:	Choice of 2 from 3 questions (20 marks each)	40
		100

Additional information

The Study Guide provides more detailed guidance on the syllabus.

Analysis of past papers

The analysis below shows the topics which were examined in all sittings to date of the current syllabus and in the Pilot Paper.

June 2004

Section A

1   Profit, RI and ROCE calculations; decision making (including qualitative issues); transfer pricing (including in a multinational organisation); product life cycle and pricing
2   Customer profitability analysis (including ABC)

Section B

3   Relevance of traditional management accounting control systems
4   Zero based budgeting
5   Non-profit seeking v profit-seeking organisations

December 2003

Section A

1   Profit/loss calculation; use of two-way data table; joint probabilities and expected values; performance measurement (quality of service); strategic management accounting
2   Performance appraisal of service organisation using Fitzgerald and Moon's building blocks

Section B

3   Relevance of traditional management accounting techniques (based on discussion of standard costing and quality improvement programmes)
4   Benchmarking
5   Critical assessment of a long-term decision; target costing

Introduction

June 2003

Section A

1   Financial analysis; profit forecasts; gap analysis; sensitivity analysis; impact of environmental factors
2   Profit, RI, ROI and NPV calculations; discussion on ROI, RI and NPV; non-financial issues to consider in project evaluation

Section B

3   Learning curve theory, its impact on prices (calculations) and other areas of management accounting, and its limitations
4   Public service performance
5   Behavioural issues in relation to management accounting systems, performance monitoring, budgeting and transfer pricing

December 2002

Section A

1   Public versus private sector: pricing (including ABC); decision making; provision of additional information; NFPIs
2   Financial performance appraisal (including provision of additional information and inter-country comparison); NFPIs

Section B

3   Impact of the external environment on budget preparation; sources of information; external environment information systems
4   Mission statements
5   Profit maximisation; algebraic models

June 2002

Section A

1   Performance appraisal of national breakdown recovery service; decision making with uncertainty (40 marks)
2   Performance appraisal of service business using Fitzgerald and Moon's key areas of performance; information required for performance comparison purposes (20 marks)

Section B

3   Transfer pricing
4   Budgetary control systems
5   Costs and quality

December 2001

Section A

1   Comparison of public and private sector operational and financial performance

(40 marks)

2   Decision making (pricing, limiting factors, profit maximisation) (20 marks)

Section B

3   Financial performance appraisal
4   Strategic planning and management v operational issues
5   MIS and changes in the business environment.

Pilot Paper

Section A

1   Financial performance measurement (40 marks)
2   Risk and uncertainty in decision making (20 marks)

Section B

3   The impact of budgetary planning and control systems on business performance
4   Transfer pricing
5   MIS design

OXFORD BROOKES BSc (Hons) IN APPLIED ACCOUNTING

The standard required of candidates completing Part 2 is that required in the final year of a UK degree. Students completing Parts 1 and 2 will have satisfied the examination requirement for an honours degree in Applied Accounting, awarded by Oxford Brookes University.

To achieve the degree, you must also submit two pieces of work based on a **Research and Analysis Project.**

- A 5,000 word **Report** on your chosen topic, which demonstrates that you have acquired the necessary research, analytical and IT skills.

- A 1,500 word **Key Skills Statement**, indicating how you have developed your interpersonal and communication skills.

BPP was selected by the ACCA and Oxford Brookes University to produce the official text *Success in your Research and Analysis Project* to support students in this task. The book pays particular attention to key skills not covered in the professional examinations.

> THE OXFORD BROOKES PROJECT TEXT CAN BE ORDERED USING THE FORM AT THE END OF THIS STUDY TEXT.

OXFORD INSTITUTE OF INTERNATIONAL FINANCE MBA

The Oxford Institute of International Finance (OXIIF), a joint venture between the ACCA and Oxford Brookes University, offers an MBA for finance professionals.

For this MBA, credits are awarded for your ACCA studies, and entry to the MBA course is available to those who have completed their ACCA professional stage studies. The MBA was launched in 2002 and has attracted participants from all over the world.

The qualification features an introductory module (*Markets, Management and Strategy*). Other modules include *Global Business Strategy, Managing Self Development,* and *Organisational Change & Transformation.*

Research Methods are also taught, as they underpin the **research dissertation**.

The MBA programme is delivered through the use of targeted paper study materials, developed by BPP, and taught over the Internet by OXIIF personnel using BPP's virtual campus software.

For further information, please see the Oxford Institute's website: www.oxfordinstitute.org.

CONTINUING PROFESSIONAL DEVELOPMENT

ACCA is introducing a new continuing professional development requirement for members from 1 January 2005. Members will be required to complete and record 40 units of CPD annually, of which 21 units must be verifiable learning or training activity.

BPP has an established professional development department which offers a range of relevant, professional courses to reflect the needs of professionals working in both industry and practice. To find out more, visit the website: www.bpp.com/pd or call the client care team on 0845 226 2422.

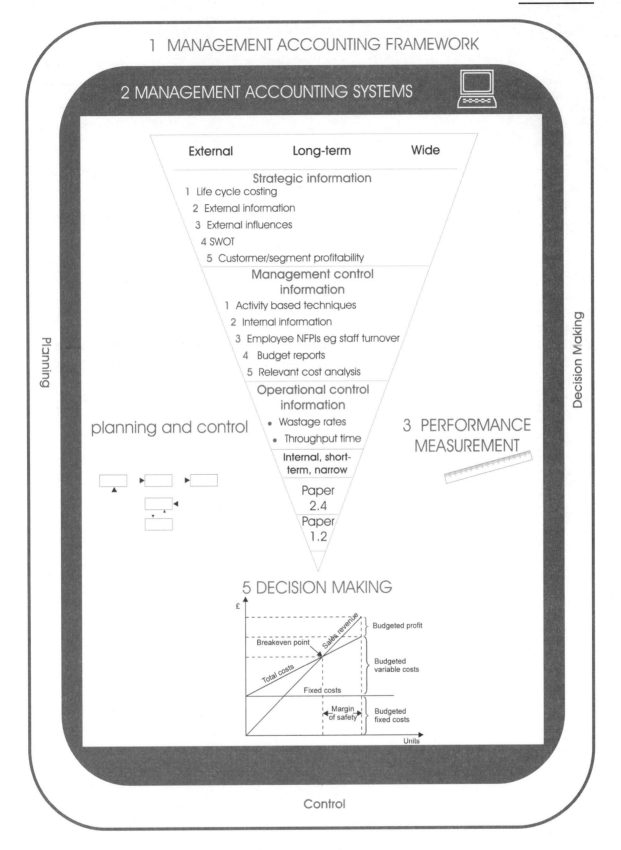

Part A
Management accounting framework

Chapter 1

STRATEGIC PLANNING AND DECISION MAKING

Topic list	Syllabus reference
1 Planning, control and decision making	1(a)
2 Characteristics of strategic planning and decision making	1(a)
3 Strategic planning versus operational planning	1(a)
4 Management accounting information for strategic planning, control and decision making	1(a)
5 Strategic decision making and discounted cash flow	1(a)
6 Costs and revenues for strategic decisions	1(a)

Introduction

The first six chapters of this text (Part A) look at the **management accounting framework**. Chapters 1 and 2 consider the **objectives of management accounting information** in relation to **planning, control** and **decision making.**

This chapter concentrates on **long-term strategic planning and decision making,** the subject of other papers at this level, and their implications for the management accountant. Chapter 2 looks at short-term non-strategic decision making and control activities.

Study guide

Section 1 – Strategic planning and decision making

- Identify characteristics of strategic planning and decision making

- Contrast strategic planning with short term/operational planning (see also Chapters 2 and 16)

- Identify the areas of management accounting information which are of importance to strategic management

- Evaluate the relevance of discounted cash flow principles in information for strategic decision making

- Select and analyse costs and revenues relevant to strategic planning and decision making in a range of situations

Section 6 – System design and system objectives

- Identify the accounting information required for strategic planning

Section 17 – Strategic planning and control

- Compare strategic with operational planning and control (see also Chapters 2 and 16)

Exam guide

The examiner is keen on the uses of management accounting information in practice so you could face a question on the use of information in strategic decision making.

1 PLANNING, CONTROL AND DECISION MAKING

1.1 Within an organisation, and at all levels of the organisation, **information** is continually flowing back and forth, being used by people to formulate **plans** and take **decisions,** and to draw attention to the need for **control** action, if the plans and decisions are not working as intended.

KEY TERMS

Planning means formulating ways of proceeding. **Decision making** means choosing between various alternatives. These two terms are virtually inseparable: you decide to plan in the first place and the plan you make is a collection of decisions.

Control is used in the sense of monitoring something so as to keep it on course, like the 'controls' of a car, not (or not merely) in the sense of imposing restraints, or exercising tyrannical power over something. We have more to say about control later in this Study Text.

Question: planning, control and decision making

This simple scenario may help you to understand how these terms are interrelated.

Mr and Mrs Average need to go to Sainsbury's to buy food and other household items. They make a list beforehand which sets out all the things they need. As they go round the supermarket they tick off the items on the list. If any particular item is not available they choose an alternative from the range on the shelves. They also buy a bottle of wine and two bars of chocolate. These were not on their original list.

(a) What part or parts of this activity would you describe as planning?
(b) There are several examples of decision making in this story. Identify three of them.
(c) What part or parts of this activity would you describe as control?

Answer

We would describe making the list as planning, but making the list is also an example of decision making, since Mr and Mrs Average have to decide what items will go on the list. Ticking off the items is control and choosing alternatives is 'control action' involving further decision making.

You should be able to answer the various parts of this question without further help.

Information for planning, control and decision making

1.2 Robert **Anthony,** a leading writer on organisational control, suggested what has become a widely-used hierarchy, classifying the information used at different management levels for planning, control and decision making into three tiers: strategic planning, management control and operational control.

KEY TERMS

Strategic planning. The process of deciding on objectives of the organisation, on changes in these objectives, on the resources used to attain these objectives, and on the policies that are to govern the acquisition, use and disposition of these resources.

Management control. The process by which managers assure that resources are obtained and used effectively and efficiently in the accomplishment of the organisation's objectives. It is sometimes called tactics or tactical planning.

Operational control (or operational **planning**). The process of assuring that specific tasks are carried out effectively and efficiently.

1.3 We look at strategic planning in this chapter. Management control and operational planning/control are covered in Chapter 2.

Exam focus point

An explanation and comparison of the features of operational and strategic management was worth a relatively easy seven marks in the December 2001 exam.

2 CHARACTERISTICS OF STRATEGIC PLANNING AND DECISION MAKING

2.1 The **strategic planning** process could include such matters as the selection of products to make and markets to sell them to, the required levels of company profitability, the purchase and disposal of subsidiary companies or major fixed assets, and so on.

2.2 **Characteristics of strategic planning**

(a) Generally formulated in **writing**, after much after discussion by committee (the **Board**)

(b) **Circulated** to all interested parties within the organisation, and perhaps to the press

(c) Does not trigger direct action but rather a series of **lesser plans** for sales, production and so on.

2.3 **Strategic information**

(a) Used to **plan** the **objectives** of the organisation and to assess whether the objectives are being met in practice

(b) Generally **externally** sourced

(c) **Summarised** at a high level

(d) Relevant to the **long term**

(e) Concerned with the **whole organisation**

(f) About competitors, customers, suppliers, new technology, the state of markets and the economy, government legislation, political unrest and so on

(g) Includes:

- Overall profitability
- Profitability of different business segments
- Future market segments
- Availability and cost of raising new funds
- Total cash needs
- Total manning needs
- Capital equipment needs

      (h) Prepared on an **ad-hoc** basis

      (i) Both **quantitative** and **qualitative**

      (j) Often **approximate** and **imprecise**

3   STRATEGIC PLANNING VERSUS OPERATIONAL PLANNING

3.1   Decisions are taken at all levels in an organisation.

    (a) **Strategic level**

      Decisions taken at the strategic level **set or change the objectives or strategic targets** of an organisation. They include decisions about the selection of products and markets, the required levels of company profitability, the purchase or disposal of subsidiary companies or major fixed assets, whether there should be an employee share of company profits and so on.

    (b) **Tactical level**

      Tactical-level decisions are concerned with the **efficient and effective use of an organisation's resources** (sometimes referred to as the '4Ms': men, materials, machines and money). Tactical-level decisions therefore include setting budgets for the next period for sales, production, stock levels and so on and setting measures of performance by which departmental results can be gauged.

    (c) **Operational level**

      Operational-level decisions are concerned with ensuring that **specific tasks are carried out effectively and efficiently**. They might include decisions concerning the allocation of particular staff to particular tasks and jobs or the action to take over customer complaints.

Question: decisions at different levels

What strategic-level, tactical-level and operational-level decisions might an organisation take in relation to sales?

Answer

Here is our suggestion. Your answer is likely to be somewhat different.

    (a) At the strategic level, senior management may decide that the company should increase sales by 5% per annum for at least five years.

    (b) At the tactical level, the sales director and senior sales managers may decide to increase sales by 5% in the next year, with some provisional planning for future years. This would involve making decisions about direct sales resources, advertising, sales promotion and so on. Sales quotas could be assigned to each sales territory.

    (c) At the operational level, the manager of a sales territory may make a decision regarding the weekly sales targets for each sales representative.

Question: strategic planning v operational planning

What do you think are the salient differences between the plans/decisions outlined below?

Decision A: Blackett & Webb

Vera Chang is the managing director of Blackett & Webb, an import/export business based in Hong Kong. The firm imports manufactured goods from overseas, principally for resale in the People's Republic of China (PRC). At a meeting on 6 June 2001, the Board is going to vote on a proposal from Langfield & Co that the two firms embark on a joint venture. The joint venture will involve the purchase by Langfield and Blackett & Webb of a small manufacturing plant in Shenzhen, just over the border with the PRC. The manufacturing plant will supply hardware components to electronics firms in Hong Kong, at a significantly lower cost than imports from overseas, thereby increasing profitability. The factory buildings will be let for a 25 year period. The initial cost of the joint venture includes machinery purchase and the hiring and training of a total labour force.

Decision B

Matthew Sparkes is a supervisor of a call centre in Darlington, in the north of England. The call centre services a major credit card company. Matthew is in charge of a team of six people. Every day he receives performance data as to the speed of response and his staff's adherence to the 'script' the firm has designed to enable staff to deal with most questions. The call centre runs on flexi-time system. Staff, within certain guidelines, have some discretion over their hours of work. On Tuesday, two members of the team have approached Matthew with holiday requests which clash. Matthew can only spare one member of his team and so has to accept one request and turn down another.

Answer

Comparisons	Decision A 'Strategic'	Decision B 'Operational'
Time frame	Long term	Immediate
Scope	The whole direction and future of the operation, its products and markets	Circumscribed to the day-to-day workings of each section
Environment and focus (internal or external)	Reflects issues relating to the external environment of the organisation, such as the economy, competition etc	Not relevant to the environment of an organisation
Capability and resource allocation	The company is changing how it resources its activities, and has decided to manufacture rather than import	Concerned merely with the deployment of resources in the team
Impact	Strategic decisions impact on the company's activities in many different ways	In the short term, this decision will have no impact on the strategy of the organisation
Complexity and programmability	The decision is complex involving significant uncertainties and there is not a simple 'rule book' for following it	The decision is a relatively simple one and arguably could be date ruled by the requirements of a procedures manual

4 MANAGEMENT ACCOUNTING INFORMATION FOR STRATEGIC PLANNING, CONTROL AND DECISION MAKING

Future uncertainty

4.1 Much strategic planning is uncertain.

(a) Strategic plans may cover a **long period** into the future, perhaps five to ten years ahead or even longer.

(b) Many strategic plans involve big changes and **new ventures**, such as capacity expansion decisions, decisions to develop into new product areas and new markets, and so on.

4.2 Inevitably, management accounting information for strategic planning will be based on incomplete data and will use **forecasts** and **estimates.**

(a) It follows that management accounting information is unlikely to give clear guidelines for management decisions and should incorporate some **risk and uncertainty analysis** (eg sensitivity analysis).

(b) For longer term plans, **DCF techniques** ought to be used in financial evaluation.

(c) The management accountant will be involved in the following.

- Project evaluation
- Managing cash and operational matters
- Reviewing the outcome of the project (post implementation review)

External and competitor orientation

4.3 Much management accounting information has been devised for internal consumption.

- Strategic planning and control decisions involve **environmental considerations**.
- A strategy is pursued in relation to **competitors**.

The challenge for management accountants

4.4 **Traditional accounting systems** have had a number of **perceived failings**.

(a) **Direction towards financial reporting**. Historical costs are necessary to report to shareholders, but the classifications of transactions for reporting purposes are not necessarily relevant to decision-making.

(b) **Misleading information** - particularly with regard to overhead absorption.

(c) **Neatness** rather than **usefulness**.

(d) **Internal focus**. Management accounting information has been too inward looking, whereas the focus should be on customers and competition.

(e) **Inflexibility** and an inability to cope with change.

4.5 The challenge lies in providing more relevant information for strategic planning, control and decision making. Traditional management accounting systems may not always provide this.

(a) **Historical costs** are not necessarily the best guide to decision making. One of the criticisms of management accounting outlined by Kaplan, Bromwich and Bhimani is that management accounting information is biased towards the past rather than the future.

(b) **Strategic issues** are not easily detected by management accounting systems.

(c) **Financial models** of some sophistication are needed to enable management accountants to provide useful information.

What is strategic management accounting?

KEY TERM

Strategic management accounting is a form of management accounting in which emphasis is placed on information about factors which are external to the organisation, as well as on non-financial and internally-generated information.

External orientation

4.6 The important fact which distinguishes strategic management accounting from other management accounting activities is its **external orientation**, towards customers and competitors, suppliers and perhaps other stakeholders.

Future orientation

4.7 A criticism of traditional management accounts is that they are **backward looking**.

- Decision making is a forward- and outward-looking process.
- Accounts are based on **costs**, whereas decision making is concerned with **values**.

4.8 Strategic management accountants will use **relevant costs** (ie **incremental** costs and **opportunity** costs) for decision making. We return to this topic later in the text.

Goal congruence

4.9 Business strategy involves the activities of many different functions, including marketing, production and human resource management. The strategic management accounting system will require **inputs from many areas of the business**.

(a) Strategic management accounting translates the consequences of different strategies into a **common accounting language for comparison**.

(b) It **relates business operations to financial performance**, and therefore helps ensure that **business activities** are **focused on shareholders' needs** for profit.

(c) It **helps to ensure goal congruence**, again by translating business activities into the common language of finance.

What information could strategic management accounting provide?

4.10 Bearing in mind the need for **goal congruence**, **external orientation** and **future orientation**, some **examples** of strategic management accounting are provided below.

Item	Comment
Competitors' costs	What are they? How do they compare with ours? Can we beat them? Are competitors vulnerable because of their cost structure?
Financial effect of competitor response	
Product profitability	A firm should want to know not just what profits or losses are being made by each of its products, but why one product should be making good profits whereas another equally good product might be making a loss
Customer profitability	Some customers or groups of customers are worth more than others
Pricing decisions	Accounting information can help to analyse how profits and cash flows will vary according to price and prospective demand
The value of market share	A firm ought to be aware of what it is worth to increase the market share of one of its products

Item	Comment
Capacity expansion	Should the firm expand its capacity, and if so by how much? Should the firm diversify into a new area of operations, or a new market?
Brand values	How much is it worth investing in a 'brand' which customers will choose over competitors' brands?
Shareholder wealth	Future profitability determines the value of a business
Cash flow	A loss-making company can survive if it has adequate cash resources, but a profitable company cannot survive unless it has sufficient liquidity
Effect of **acquisitions and mergers**	
Decisions to **enter or leave a business area**	
Introduction of **new technology**	

Exam focus point

An explanation of the term 'strategic management accounting' and the benefits of its introduction to a particular organisation were required in the December 2003 exam.

IMPORTANT POINT

Most strategic decisions are unique, so the information needed to support them is likely to be ad hoc and specially tailored to the decision.

5 STRATEGIC DECISION MAKING AND DISCOUNTED CASH FLOW

5.1 You will already have encountered the principles of discounted cash flows used to evaluate investments (for example, in new machinery) in your earlier studies.

5.2 Discounted cash flows can be used in strategic decision making – arguably they *should* be used in strategic decision making for a business. Why?

(a) The **share price** of many businesses is determined by **investors' expectations** of the likely future dividends. The value of a business is how **cash-generative** it is. Investors, therefore, monitor **cash flow** as a **key performance indicator**.

(b) Investors have an **expected return**, for any investment, **adjusted according to the risk** of one investment. Effectively, this is the '**cost of capital**' and can be used as the discount rate for evaluating investments.

5.3 **Strategic decisions are often hedged with uncertainty,** so it is not possible to predict or to quantify **every risk,** every **environmental factor,** or the responses of **competitors**. The **future** is inherently uncertain.

5.4 **DCF** is therefore better seen not as a device that will give the right answers, but as a **modelling device** to assess the **impact** of different strategic factors. **Try this question.**

Question: financial evaluation of strategy

A relatively small number of detergent companies own many of the brands offered to the market. This deters competitors. How do you evaluate, financially, a strategy such as this?

(a) The **expenditure** to **maintain market share** and **sustain brands** is a **known cost**. However the benefit is not known exactly.

(b) There might be a variety of **assumptions about market size**, market shares and the profit assumptions of a number of the scenarios identified.

(c) There are problems with forecasting the future cash flows of market share estimates.

Answer

A useful approach would be to analyse the anticipated loss caused by not undertaking a particular course of action: the present value of this loss becomes, effectively, the maximum size of any investment. For example, suppose A Ltd is worried that a competitor will shift the market dynamics from I to II.

	Market state	
	I	*II*
A Ltd's market share	20%	15%
Present value of future cash flows	£1m	£800,000

(a) There is a present value loss of £200,000. If a marketing manager suggested that an expenditure of £100,000 would see off the competitor, this would be worth doing. Yet there is still the problem of estimating the difference between market states I and II: after all, the marketing campaign might deter other competitors, too, or create an increase in demand. It is also impossible to be certain that the competitor will in fact be deterred by an advertising campaign.

(b) The strategic management accountant can assist by treating (for decision-making purposes only) certain of the firm's strategies as intangible assets. An exclusive distribution system (eg car dealership) can be an asset, as it works as an entry barrier.

5.5 Other examples of using DCF

(a) Assessing the 'value' of a 'brand' in terms of future cash flows

(b) Modelling competitors cost and assumptions

(c) Modelling the effect of a new competitor who effectively raises the industry's capacity, thereby exerting downward pressure on price

5.6 We return to DCF at the end of the text.

6 COSTS AND REVENUES FOR STRATEGIC DECISIONS

Useful cost categories for strategic management accounting

6.1 At an operations level, costs can classified as follows.

Item	Comment
Behaviour	Fixed, variable, mixed, step and so on
Function	Production, administration, distribution and so on
Type of expense	Electricity, salaries and so on
Relevance	Future cash flows against sunk costs, for example
Controllability	Advertising expenditure against corporation tax, say

Each of these classifications can be examined in terms of how useful they are as information for planning, control and decision-making information. For **strategic** decision making, however, we are particularly concerned with **behaviour, relevance** and **controllability.** The concept of relevant costs is covered in depth in Chapter 20.

Success factors for a strategic management accounting system

6.2 Strategic management accounting has to bridge a gap between financial reporting on the one hand and the uncertainties of the future on the other. Here are the success factors of a strategic management accounting system (as outlined by Ward).

- Aid strategic decisions
- Close the communication gap between accountants and managers
- Identify the type of decision
- Offer appropriate financial performance indicators
- Distinguish between economic and managerial performance
- Provide relevant information
- Separate committed from discretionary costs
- Distinguish discretionary from engineered costs
- Use standard costs strategically
- Allow for changes over time

Many of these tie in with the issue of costs and revenues and so they are now discussed in more detail. For convenience we shall use the abbreviation SMAS to mean Strategic Management Accounting System.

Aid strategic decisions

6.3 The SMAS will operate on the assumption that strategies are in place and that there is goal congruence across the business.

As part of a strategic management system, the SMAS will provide one-off information to support and evaluate particular strategic decisions and information for strategic management, in order to monitor strategies and the firm's overall competitive position. Changes in the external environment and competitor responses should be easily incorporated into the system.

Close the communication gap

6.4 The SMAS **converts financial data into information for strategic decision making**. Financial data is off-putting to many people and so the preparer of such information should make sure that it is tailored.

- Ask the recipient how he or she would like the **format** of the report
- Provide only the **relevant** supporting financial data
- Identify the **key assumptions** on which the information is prepared

Identify the types of the decision (functional)

6.5 Ward states that, despite the one-off nature of many strategic decisions, it is possible to identify the following types of financial decision.

(a) **Changing the balance of resource allocation** between different business areas, for example by increasing spending in one area. There may be a choice between investing in new production equipment, or an advertising campaign.

(b) **Entering a new business area** (eg new product development, new markets). Some account will have to be taken of the timescale in which the strategy is expected to consume resources, as benefits may be some time in coming.

(c) **Exit decisions** come in two forms.

  (i) **Closing down** part of the business and selling off the assets.

(ii) Selling the business as a **going concern**. The closure costs might be avoided if the business were sold.

6.6 To support such decisions, the SMAS should incorporate **future cash flows** rather than historic costs and include only those items which will be changed by the particular decision.

Suitable financial performance measures

6.7 These form the heart of the syllabus.

(a) **Financial data is not enough**. Customers drive a business, and competitors can ruin it, so performance measures which ignore key variables of customer satisfaction or competitor activity ignore critical strategic issues.

(b) **The financial information must suit the competitive strategies**. A report complaining about the expense of an advertising campaign ignores the fact that failing to advertise will lead to loss of market share.

Economic versus managerial performance (controllability)

6.8 A business's **overall economic performance** results from both controllable factors and uncontrollable factors.

(a) **Risk**. Shareholders may be happy with the risk, if it is balanced by suitable return, but a manager may be unhappy if his or her career is at risk from pursuing a strategy whose success is outside his or her control.

(b) **Performance**. Judging a manager's contribution on the basis of the overall economic performance of the business may not reflect his or her contribution at all. Managers should therefore be judged on their contribution over areas over which they have control.

Provide relevant information

6.9 **Relevant financial information** should be provided, which presents strategic decisions from the organisation's viewpoint. Specific, tailored reports should support individual decisions and activities, perhaps with **profitability analyses** for each market segment. Ward mentions that decision makers require supporting financial information which shows **how the economic returns of the business will change** as a consequence of any particular decision. This clearly requires the use of **incremental or avoidable** costs.

Separate committed from discretionary costs (relevance)

6.10 **Ignore sunk costs**. This has a number of ramifications for the making of business strategies.

- A cost may be **committed** even though it has not actually been incurred.
- **Discretionary costs** are those over which the decision-maker still has choice.

Distinguish between discretionary and engineered costs (relevance)

6.11 Ward refers to **engineered costs:** these are costs which derive from a relatively predictable relationship between input raw materials and output units of production.

Use standard costs strategically

6.12 **Standard costs** consist of a physical usage element (eg volume of materials) and a price element.

(a) Standard costs can indicate **operational efficiency**.

(b) The split between the **price** and **usage** elements is indicative.

- The extent to which the firm is **vulnerable** to suppliers raising prices
- The possible impact of **trade-offs** between, say, labour and materials

6.13 **Trade-offs.** If the relationships between the input material and output quantities are known, or variable, then standard costing can show the financial effects of different mixes.

(a) For example, if there is a trade off between labour and raw materials, changes in the relative costs of these factors can indicate a suitable mix: more expensive labour would result in less of a valued raw material being used.

(b) If the price of a raw material escalates suddenly, the standard costing system can be amended with the new price, and a new mix analysis calculated which takes it into account.

Exam focus point

A requirement in one of the December 2001 exam questions was to look at the benefits of a Management Information System (MIS) that provided both operational and strategic information for a particular organisation. In terms of strategy, a good answer would need to cover the value of considering strategic issues and at the types of strategic information that the MIS would need to provide.

Chapter roundup

- **Strategic planning** is the process of deciding on objectives of the organisation, on changes in these objectives, on the resources used to attain these objectives, and on the policies that are to govern the acquisition, use and disposition of these resources.

- **Management control** is the process by which managers assure that resources are obtained and used effectively and efficiently in the accomplishment of the organisation's objectives. It is sometimes called **tactics** or **tactical planning**.

- **Operational control** (or **operational planning**) is the process of assuring that specific tasks are carried out effectively and efficiently.

- **Strategic planning** does not trigger direct action but a series of lesser plans for sales, production and so on.

- **Strategic decisions** are long-term decisions and are characterised by their wide scope, wide impact, relative uncertainty and complexity.

- **Operational decisions** are short-term decisions which have a narrow focus, with little immediate impact on strategy.

- **Management accounting information** can be used to support strategic planning, control and decision making, providing it displays an external orientation and a future orientation.

- **Discounted cash flow** techniques can be used as a modelling device to assess the impact of different strategic factors.

- **Costs and revenues for strategic decisions** should be relevant and controllable.

Quick quiz

1   *Choose the correct words from those highlighted.*

Information for strategic planning is generally **externally/internally** sourced, relevant to the **short term/long term** and concerned with **individual departments/the whole organisation**.

2   Which of the following management accounting applications would not be suitable for strategic decision making?

A   DCF analysis
B   Relevant costing
C   Cost bookkeeping
D   Preparation of contract accounts

3   Traditional management accounting information has been too outwards looking, whereas the focus should be on customers and competition. *True or false?*

4   *Fill in the blanks.*

For strategic decision-making purposes:

•   Contrast economic versus .... performance

•   Separate .... from discretionary costs

•   Distinguish between .... and engineered costs

Answers to quick quiz

1   externally
       long term
       whole organisation

2   C and D, as they have no future or external orientation

3   *False.* It has been inwards looking.

4   managerial
       committed
       discretionary

Now try the question below from the Exam Question Bank

Number	Level	Marks	Time
1	Exam	20	36 mins

Chapter 2

SHORT-RUN DECISION MAKING AND CONTROL

Topic list	Syllabus reference
1 Short-run decision making	1(a)
2 Management control	1(a)
3 Operational control	1(a)
4 Management control and operational control compared	1(a)

Introduction

In Chapter 1 we looked at the first level or tier of Anthony's decision-making hierarchy, that of strategic planning. In this chapter we turn our attention to the other two tiers, **management control** and **operational control.** Whereas strategic planning is concerned with long-term decision making, management control and operational control focus on **short-run**, **non-strategic** decision making and activities.

At the end of the chapter you should have some idea of the **objectives** of management accounting information in relation to **planning, control** and **decision making.**

Short-run decision making is considered in greater depth in Chapters 20 and 21.

Study guide

Section 1 – Strategic planning and decision making

- Contrast strategic planning with short term/operational planning (see also Chapters 1 and 16)

Section 2 – Short run decision making and control

- Explain the significance of endogenous information sources in relation to short run decision making and control

- Identify the characteristics of short term non-strategic activities

- Identify the areas of management accounting information appropriate for short term decision making

- Explain the differences between management control and operational control in the context of short run decision making and control

Section 6 – System design and system objectives

- Identify the accounting information requirements for management control and operational control and decision making

Section 17 – Strategic planning and control

- Compare strategic with operational planning and control (see also Chapters 1 and 16)

Exam guide

One of the aims of Paper 3.3 is to ensure that you can identify the information needs of an effective management accounting system, so you could have to answer questions about the management control and operation control information needs within a particular organisation.

1 SHORT-RUN DECISION MAKING

1.1 Short-run decisions are normally the concern of lower-level managers and are concerned with making the best use of existing physical, human and financial resources. These are, to an extent, determined by the quality of an organisation's long-term decisions.

1.2 **Main features of short-run decisions**

- Usually based on a given level of assets and resources
- Rarely involve the entire range of the organisation's activities
- Do not usually involve major or organisational change
- Unlikely to involve a high level of uncertainty (and techniques can be employed to limit this uncertainty)

1.3 **Examples of short-term decisions**

- What price should be charged for a special order?
- What is the most profitable product mix?
- How can we make the best use of limited resources?
- Should we make product X or buy it in?

IMPORTANT POINT

Short-term decisions do **not** impact on fundamental aspects of an organisation.

1.4 Approaches to short-term decisions are covered in Chapters 20 and 21 and involve techniques you will have encountered in your earlier studies such as CVP analysis and limiting factor analysis.

1.5 Using the terminology of Anthony's decision-making hierarchy introduced in Chapter 1, short-run decision making is management control and operational control decision making.

2 MANAGEMENT CONTROL

2.1 **Management control**, which we introduced in Chapter 1, is at the level below strategic planning in Anthony's decision-making hierarchy. Whilst strategic planning is concerned with setting objectives and strategic targets, management control is concerned with **decisions about the efficient and effective use of an organisation's resources to achieve these objectives or targets.**

    (a) **Resources**, sometimes referred to as the '**4 Ms**', are men, materials, machines and money.

(b) **Efficiency** in the use of resources means that **optimum output is achieved from the input resources used**. It relates to the combinations of men, land and capital (for example how much production work should be automated) and to the productivity of labour, or material usage.

(c) **Effectiveness** in the use of resources means that the **outputs obtained are in line with the intended objectives or targets.**

The time horizon involved in management control will be shorter than at the strategic decisions level (commonly one year), there will be much greater precision and the focus of information will be narrower.

2.2 Management control activities are **short-term non-strategic activities**.

2.3 **Examples of management control (or tactical) planning activities**

(a) Preparing budgets for the next year for sales, production, stock levels, overhead cost centres, purchasing and cash

(b) Establishing measures of performance by which profit centres or departmental results can be gauged

(c) Developing a product for launching in the market

(d) Planning advertising and marketing campaigns

(e) Establishing a line-of-authority structure for the organisation

2.4 **Examples of management control control activities**

(a) Ensuring that budget targets are reached, or improved upon

(b) Ensuring that other measures of performance are satisfactory, or even better than planned

(c) Where appropriate, changing the budget because circumstances have altered and it is now irrelevant or out of date.

2.5 Management control is an essentially routine affair in that it tends to be carried out in a series of **regular** planning and comparison procedures, that is annually, monthly or weekly, so that all aspects of an organisation's activity are systematically reviewed. For example, a budget is usually prepared annually, and control reports issued every month or four weeks. Strategic planning, in contrast, might be irregular and occur when opportunities arise or are identified.

Information requirements

2.6 **Features of management control information**

- Primarily generated **internally** (but may have a limited external component)

- Embraces the **entire organisation** (and so a system must exist for planning, measuring, comparing and controlling the efforts of every department or profit centre)

- **Summarised** at a relatively **low level**

- **Routinely** collected and disseminated

- Relevant to the **short** and **medium terms**

- Often **quantitative** (labour hours, quantities of materials consumed, volumes of sales and production)

- Collected in a **standard** manner

- Commonly expressed in **money terms**

18

2.7 Types of information

- Productivity measurements
- Budgetary control or variance analysis reports
- Cash flow forecasts
- Manning levels
- Profit results within a particular department of the organisation
- Labour turnover statistics within a department
- Short-term purchasing requirements

2.8 Source of information

A large proportion of this information will be generated from **within the organisation** (it has an **endogenous source**) and it will often have an accounting emphasis. Tactical information is usually prepared regularly, perhaps weekly, or monthly.

Management control and strategic planning compared

2.9 The dividing line between strategic planning (covered in Chapter 1) and management control in **not a clear one.** Many decisions include issues ranging from strategic to tactical. Nevertheless, there is a basic distinction between the two levels of decision.

(a) The decision to launch a new brand of calorie-controlled frozen foods is a strategic plan (business strategy), but the choice of ingredients for the frozen meals involves a management control decision.

(b) A decision that the market share for a product should be 25% is a strategic plan (competitive strategy), but the selection of a sales price of £2 per unit, supported by other marketing decisions about sales promotion and direct sales effort to achieve the required market share, would be a series of management control decisions.

2.10 **Management control** tends to be carried out in a series of **regular** planning and comparison procedures (annually, monthly, weekly). For example, a budget is usually prepared annually and control reports issued every month or four weeks. **Strategic planning**, in contrast, might be **irregular** and occur when opportunities arise or are identified.

> ### Exam focus point
>
> The **sources and uses of management information** is a core syllabus area and has featured in a number of exam questions. So note carefully the information sources and uses we have described in this chapter.

Conflict between strategic planning and management control

2.11 It is quite common for strategic plans to be in conflict with the shorter term objectives of management control. Examples are as follows.

(a) It might be in the **long-term** interests of a company to buy more expensive or technologically-advanced machinery to make a product, in the expectation that when market demand for the product eventually declines, customers will buy from producers whose output is made on better machinery and is therefore of a slightly better quality. In the **short run**, however, new and expensive machinery will incur higher depreciation charges and therefore higher unit costs for the same volume of production. Since higher costs will reduce profit, considerations of 'management control' would suggest the existing old machinery should be worn out before replacement.

(b) Similarly, it is in the **long-term interests** of a company to invest in training, research and development, in spite of the costs and loss of profits in the **short term**.

2.12 **Reasons for the conflict**

(a) Inadequate appreciation of strategic imperatives at middle management level, if these have not been properly communicated.

(b) Performance measures and control measures that do not take the organisation's strategic direction into account. In this case, middle managers are actively discouraged from taking decisions which make strategic sense. (For example there is sometimes a trade off between cost and quality.)

(c) Control information only measures items that are *easily* measurable, such as accounting information. That a certain type of information is hard to measure does not make it less valuable or important.

In fact, **if there are conflicts** between strategic objectives and management control, this indicates that **something has gone seriously wrong in the planning and control process. Management control should support strategic imperatives: the strategy should be flexible enough to accommodate short-term control issues.**

> ### Exam focus point
>
> You would have needed to consider these sorts of issue (communication, new performance measures) if faced with a requirement in the December 2001 exam which asked students to consider the changes in attitude and approach that would be required if an organisation were to implement strategic management.

3 OPERATIONAL CONTROL

3.1 The third and lowest tier in Anthony's hierarchy of decision making consists of operational control decisions. Just as 'management control' plans are set within the guidelines of strategic plans, so too are 'operational control' plans set within the guidelines of both strategic planning and management control.

3.2 EXAMPLE: LINK BEWEEN STRATEGIC PLANS AND OPERATIONAL/ MANAGEMENT CONTROL DECISIONS

(a) Senior management may decide that the company should increase sales by 5% per annum for at least five years - **a strategic plan.**

(b) The sales director and senior sales managers will make plans to increase sales by 5% in the next year, with some provisional planning for future years. This involves planning direct sales resources, advertising, sales promotion and so on. Sales quotas are assigned to each sales territory - **a tactical management control decision.**

(c) The manager of a sales territory specifies the weekly sales targets for each sales representative. This is an **operational control decision:** individuals are given tasks which they are expected to achieve.

3.3 Operational control decisions are therefore much **more narrowly focused** and have a **shorter time frame** than tactical or strategic decisions.

Operational control activities

3.4 Although we have used an example of selling tasks to describe operational control, it is important to remember that this level of decision making **occurs in all aspects of an organisation's activities**, even when the activities cannot be scheduled nor properly estimated because they are non-standard activities (such as repair work, answering customer complaints).

3.5 The scheduling of **unexpected or 'ad hoc' work** must be done at **short notice**, which is a feature of much operational decision making. In the repairs department, for example, routine preventive maintenance can be scheduled, but breakdowns occur unexpectedly and repair work must be scheduled and controlled 'on the spot' by a repairs department supervisor.

3.6 Operational control activities can also be described as **short-term non-strategic activities.**

Information requirements

3.7 **Features of operational control information**

(a) **Operational information** is information which is **needed for the conduct of day-to-day implementation of plans.**

(b) It will include much '**transaction data**' such as data about customer orders, purchase orders, cash receipts and payments and is likely to have an **endogenous source**.

(c) Operating information must usually be **consolidated into totals** in management reports before it can be used to prepare management control information.

(d) The amount of **detail** provided in information is likely to **vary with the purpose for which it is needed**, and operational information is likely to go into much more detail than tactical information, which in turn will be more detailed than strategic information.

(e) Whereas tactical information for management control is often expressed in money terms, operational information, although quantitative, is more often **expressed in terms of units, hours, quantities of material and so on.**

3.8 In the payroll office, for example, operational information relating to day-rate labour will include the hours worked each week by each employee, his or her rate of pay per hour, details of deductions, and for the purpose of wages analysis, details of the time each person spent on individual jobs during the week. In this example, the information is required weekly, but more urgent operational information, such as the amount of raw materials being input to a production process, may be required daily, hourly, or in the case of automated production, second by second.

Exam focus point

Operational matters and information were examined in the December 2001 exam.

4 MANAGEMENT CONTROL AND OPERATIONAL CONTROL COMPARED

4.1 The dividing line between management control and operational control is **not always clear-cut**. For example, production planning begins as an attempt to establish a plan of production for the next week in order to conform to budget/planned requirements (management control). It then attempts to provide detailed schedules of work to be done and resources required (operational control).

4.2 **Characteristics which distinguish management control from operational control**

(a) Operational control focuses on individual tasks, whereas management control is concerned with the sum of all the tasks.

(b) Management control decisions are generally taken by managers senior in the organisation to those who take operational control decisions.

Question: management control v operational control

How might management control and operational control of repair work differ?

Answer

Management control of repair work might include the regulation of total preventive maintenance time and use 'machine hours lost through breakdown' as a measure of performance and control. Operational control would be concerned with individual breakdowns and the time taken on each repair job.

Chapter roundup

- **Short-run decisions** are normally the concern of lower-level managers and are concerned with making the best use of existing physical, human and financial resources. These are, to an extent, determined by the quality of an organisation's long-term decisions.

- **Management control** is at the level below strategic planning in Anthony's decision-making hierarchy and is concerned with decisions about the efficient and effective use of resources to achieve objectives.

- **Operational control**, the lowest tier in Anthony's hierarchy, is concerned with assuring that specific tasks are carried out effectively and efficiently.

- Management control and operational control are concerned with **short-term, non-strategic** decision making and control activities.

- Management control and operational control rely on **endogenous information sources.**

- The **dividing lines** between management control/strategic planning and management control/operational control are not always clear cut.

Quick quiz

1 What are the 4Ms?

A Men, materials, mechanisms, money
B Management, mechanisms, money, manufacture
C Men, materials, machines, money
D Management, machines, manufacture, materials

2   *Classify the following characteristics as those of either management control information or operational control information.*

	Management control	Operational control
Consolidated into totals		
Detailed		
Embraces the entire organisation		
Expressed in monetary terms		
Expressed in terms of hours, units, kgs		

3   *Choose the appropriate words from those highlighted.*

The time horizon involved in management control will be **shorter/longer** than at the strategic decision level, there will be much **less/greater** precision and the focus of information will be **wider/narrower**.

4   *Fill in the blanks.*

Using the terminology of Anthony's decision-making hierarchy, short-run decision making is ………… ……………….. and ……………………… decision making.

Answers to quick quiz

1   C

2

	Management control	Operational control
Consolidated into totals	✓	
Detailed		✓
Embraces the entire organisation	✓	
Expressed in monetary terms	✓	
Expressed in terms of hours, units, kgs		✓

3   shorter, greater, narrower

4   management control
    operational control

Now try the question below from the Exam Question Bank

Number	Level	Marks	Time
2	Introductory	n/a	

Chapter 3

CHANGES IN MANAGEMENT ACCOUNTING

Topic list	Syllabus reference
1 Contingency theory	1(b)
2 Institutional theory	1(b)
3 Activity based approaches	1(b)
4 Activity based management	1(b)

Introduction

This chapter provides you with detail about changes in management accounting.

Organisations cannot stand still. Their management accounting systems must evolve to suit the changing environment in which they operate. An understanding of this concept is vital to accountants who work in this evolving situation.

Contingency theory (**Section 1**) offers a conceptual framework for changes in management accounting, based on internal and external influences. Its foundation is an understanding that there is no single management accounting system that is suitable for all organisations.

Institutional theory (**Section 2**) offers a framework for understanding change and implications for management accounting, again based on internal and external influences.

The basic principles covered in **Section 3** should be familiar to you from your studies for Paper 2.4. Knowledge from this section is built upon in **Section 4**, which examines activity based management, a cost management application of ABC.

Study guide

Section 3 – Changes in management accounting

- Explain the contingency theory of management accounting: Otley

- Explain how institutional theory presents a framework for understanding changes in and the implications for management accounting: Powell and Di Maggio

- Explain and demonstrate activity based management

Exam guide

You are unlikely to face a full question on the topics covered in this chapter. Instead you might have to answer a part question on the relevance of one of the theories or approaches to a particular organisation.

The issues covered in this chapter are useful background to the Oxford Brookes degree Research and Analysis Project topic 1, which requires you to analyse the efficiency or effectiveness of a management accounting technique in an organisational setting.

1   CONTINGENCY THEORY

The historical development of management accounting

1.1   As you must certainly be aware by this stage of your studies, the forerunner of management accounting as the term is presently understood was cost accounting. **Cost accounting** (essentially, determining product costs, particularly for the purpose of stock valuation) emerged in the early years of this century and remained the main concern of internal accounting until the late 1940s.

1.2   A classic study in the 1950s by **Simon** *et al* was typical of the general agreement at that time that the **management process was one of decision making, planning and control**. Simon identified **three attributes** of what could by now be called **management accounting information** as follows.

    (a)   It should be useful for **scorekeeping** – seeing how well the organisation is doing overall.

    (b)   It should be **attention-directing** - indicating problem areas that need to be investigated.

    (c)   It should be useful for **problem-solving** - providing a means of evaluating alternative responses to the situations in which the organisation finds itself.

1.3   Robert Anthony made what could be the most important contribution in his 1965 book *Planning and Control Systems*. He suggested the are **three levels or tiers within an organisation's decision-making hierarchy** that we looked at in Chapter 1.

1.4   The **next phase** of development reveals what seems to be an increasing desire on the part of accounting academics to **escape from the narrow confines of their discipline**. Already in the 1950s **Argyris** had written a seminal essay that connected management accounting and psychology ('The impact of budgets on people', discussed in more detail in Part D of this Study Text). However, research into the behavioural aspects of budgeting did not begin in earnest until the late 1960s. Particularly influential was the work of Anthony **Hopwood**, who carried out empirical studies of the interaction between people and budgets.

1.5   Hopwood's 1974 book *Accounting and Human Behaviour* identified three distinct styles of evaluating managers. There is more on this in Part C of this Study Text but the important point is that although Hopwood favours the profit-conscious style he recognises that:

> 'the precise balance of costs and benefits associated with these three styles might well be different for the control of a stable technologically simple situation ... than for an uncertain and highly complex situation'.

1.6   This as another way of saying 'it all depends', 'there is no "one best way"'. In other words this is the **marriage of accounting and contingency theory**. This school of thought has featured prominently in academic writings on accounting control issues ever since the mid 1970s.

Contingency approach to management accounting

> ### KEY TERM
>
> The **contingency approach to management accounting** is based on the premise that there is no universally appropriate accounting system applicable to all organisations in all circumstances. Efficient systems depend on awareness of the system designer of the specific environmental factors which influence their creation.

1.7 The major factors that have been identified by Emmanuel, Otley and Merchant in *Accounting for Management Control* are classified as follows.

(a) **The environment**

- Its degree of predictability
- The degree of competition faced
- The number of different product markets faced
- The degree of hostility exhibited by competing organisations

(b) **Organisational structure**

- Size
- Interdependence of parts
- Degree of decentralisation
- Availability of resources

(c) **Technology** (the way in which an organisation organises its production processes, such as mass production or batch production)

- The nature of the production process
- The routineness/complexity of the production process
- How well the relationship between ends (finished output) and means (production process) is understood
- The amount of variety or complexity in each task that has to be performed

For example, the level of detail and accuracy that is possible when costing individual jobs cannot be replicated in mass production environments. Production technology is therefore argued to have a significant effect on the type of management accounting information that can be provided.

A simple example

1.8 The following example is a highly **simplistic application of the theory** but it may help you to grasp ideas that are generally presented in a highly abstract way by accounting academics.

1.9 Stable Ltd makes three different products, X, Y and Z. It has **never had any competitors. Every month** the managing director receives a **report** from the management accountant in the following form (the numbers are for illustration only).

	£
Sales	10,000
Production costs	5,000
Gross profit	5,000
Administrative costs	1,000
Net profit	4,000

1.10 A few months ago **another company**, Turbulence & Co, **entered the market** for products X and Y, **undercutting** the prices charged by Stable Ltd. Turbulence has now started to **win some of Stable's customers.**

1.11 The managing director asks the management accountant for **information** about the profitability of its own versions of products X and Y. Sales information is easy to reanalyse, but to analyse production information in this way requires a **new system of coding** to be introduced. Eventually the management accountant comes up with the following report.

	X	Y	Z	Total
	£	£	£	£
Sales	3,000	3,000	4,000	10,000
Production costs	500	500	4,000	5,000
Gross profit	2,500	2,500	-	5,000
Administrative costs				1,000
Net profit				4,000

1.12 As a result of receiving this information the MD **drops the price** of Stable's products X and Y. He **divides the production function into two divisions**, one of which will concentrate exclusively upon reducing the costs of product Z while maintaining quality.

1.13 The management accountant is asked to work closely with the division Z production manager in designing a **system that will help to monitor and control costs**. He is also to work closely with the **marketing** managers of products X and Y so that the organisation can **respond rapidly to any further competitive pressures. Reports are** to be made **weekly** and are to include as much information as can be determined about Turbulence's financial performance, pricing, market penetration and so on.

1.14 This **example may be explained in terms of contingency theory** as follows.

   (a) **Originally** the **design of the accounting system** was determined by the facts that Stable Ltd faced a **highly predictable** environment, and that it was a **highly centralised** organisation.

   (b) The design of the **new system** is the **result of a new set of contingent variables:** the entry of Turbulence into two of Stable's markets requires the system to adopt a product-based reporting structure with more externally-derived information in the case of products X and Y and more detailed analysis of internal information in the case of product Z. This is matched by a change in the structure of the organisation as a whole.

1.15 To recap, **contingency theorists' aim is to identify specific features of an organisation's context that affect the design of particular features of that organisation's accounting system.**

Contingent variables

1.16 In Emmanuel *et al's* book there is a review of the major studies in the contingency theory tradition up until that time. These are classified under the headings 'environment' and technology' (as before), with 'organisation' being sub-divided into 'size', 'strategy' and 'culture'. Here we give a summary of the main points made in this discussion.

1.17 Many of the points made in the following paragraphs will seem quite stunningly obvious and unsurprising. Some are capable of quite different interpretations. Some contradict others. None of them should be regarded as universal truths: they are simply **observations made by different researchers in the light of investigations into particular cases.**

Environment

1.18 Emmanuel *et al* identify **uncertainty as the major factor in the environment affecting the design of accounting control systems.**

(a) The **sophistication** of an accounting system is influenced by the intensity of **competition** faced. Accounting system that can produce information that allows for the preparation of an extended trial balance will be insufficient for an organisation that needs to make pricing decisions, analyse market size and market share and so on.

(b) Organisations use accounting information in different ways depending upon the **type of competition faced** (for example competition on price as opposed to product rivalry).

(c) **Budget information is evaluated** by senior managers **rigidly in 'tough' environments**, but more flexibly in 'liberal' environments.

(d) The **more dynamic** the environment (that is the more rapidly it changes), the **more frequently accounting control reports** will be required.

(e) The **larger the number of product markets** an organisation is in, the **more decentralised its control system** will be, with quasi-independent responsibility centres.

(f) The more **severe** the **competition**, the **more sophisticated the accounting information system** will be, for example incorporating non-financial information.

(g) The design of an organisation's accounting system will be affected by its environment. An organisation's **environment** will be somewhere **between** the **two extremes simple/complex** and somewhere between the **two extremes static/dynamic**.

(h) The **more complex the structure** of an organisation the **more accounting control 'tools'** (such as flexible budgeting and variance analysis) it will have.

(i) **'Turbulence'** or discontinuity in an organisation's environment (say overseas expansion or the acquisition of a major subsidiary) often requires the **replacement of control tools** (say flexible budgeting) which have been rendered obsolete by new ones.

(j) Control systems are not determined by organisation structure: **both structure and control systems are dependent on the environment.** In an **uncertain environment** more use will be made of **external, non-financial and projected information**.

(k) In conditions of **uncertainty, subjective methods of performance evaluation** (such as a manager's opinion) are more effective because they rely more on qualitative, as opposed to quantitative, information.

(l) Accounting systems are **affected by** the extent to which the organisation is **manipulated by other organisations** such as competitors, suppliers, customers or government bodies. For example, large supermarkets often insist their (smaller) suppliers adopt particular policies, procedures and techniques.

Technology

1.19 (a) The nature of the **production process** (for example jobbing on the one hand or mass production on the other) determines the **amount of cost allocation** rather than **cost apportionment** that can be done.

(b) The **complexity of the 'task'** that an organisation performs **affects the financial control structure**. It does so via organisation structure, however. (For example, a railway operator's 'task' of getting people from A to B involves keeping them fed via a catering division that is accounted for differently to the transport division.)

(c) The **amount of data** produced, **what** that data is **about** and **how it is used** closely correlates with the **number of things that go wrong in a production process and the procedures used to investigate the problems**. (This correlation exists but the research does not consider whether there is an optimum correlation between data availability and use and problem solving.)

(d) The **more automated** a production process is, the **more** 'formality' there will be in the use of budget systems.

(e) The **less predictable** the production process is, the more likely production managers are to create **budgetary slack**. (The evidence for this is weak, however, as the proponent of the view (Merchant) admits.)

(f) The structure and processes of (and so, presumably, the method of accounting for) **operational units** tend to be related to **technological variables** while the structure and processes of **managerial/planning units** tend to be related to **environmental variables**.

Size

1.20 (a) As an organisation grows it will initially organise on a **functional basis**. If it diversifies into different products or markets it will re-organise into **semi-autonomous divisions**. The **same accounting system** that is used to measure overall performance can then be **applied en bloc to each individual division**.

(b) In larger organisations the greater degree of **decentralisation** seems to lead to greater **participation** in budgeting.

(c) In **large organisations a bureaucratic** approach to budgeting produces the best performance; in **small organisations** a more 'personal' approach gives better results. (Note that this finding was reported in 1981 when bureaucracies were less unfashionable: few modern commentators associate bureaucracy with efficiency.)

(d) Organisations may grow by acquisition: when this occurs, differences in the accounting system used by the **acquired company** disappear, and it **conforms to the practices used by the acquiring company**.

Culture

1.21 (a) Control systems which are inconsistent with an organisation's value system or with the language or symbols that help to make up its culture are likely to create **resistance**: typically people would develop informal ways to get round controls that were regarded as intrusive.

(b) New control systems that **threaten to alter existing power relationships** may be **thwarted** by those affected.

(c) Control processes will be most **effective** if they operate by generating a corporate culture that is **supportive** of organisational aims, objectives and methods of working, and which is **consistent** with the demands of the environment in which the organisation operates.

Caveat

1.22 Remember that the above points are simply observations made by different researchers in the light of investigations into particular cases. They are not universal truths.

The limitations of contingency theory

1.23 Logically, one would expect those researching into the field of contingency theory and management accounting to have put forward suggestions as to how accounting systems could be improved by demonstrating what systems work well in what circumstances. So far, however, **contingency theory** seems to have **provided no more than a framework for describing existing accounting systems.**

1.24 There has been no better summary of the pros and cons of contingency theory than the conclusion to Otley's 1980 article 'The contingency theory of management accounting: achievement and prognosis' (*Accounting, Organizations and Society*) on which much of the relevant chapter in the later book by Emmanuel, Otley and Merchant is based. Otley's conclusion is quoted below, with divisions and emphasis added by BPP for clarity.

> 'A contingency theory of management accounting has a **great deal of appeal**. It is in **accord with practical wisdom** and appears to afford a **potential explanation for the bewildering variety of management accounting systems actually observed in practice**. In addition, the **relevance of organization theory to management accounting is being increasingly recognized** and contingency formulations have been prominent in organization theory. There thus appears to be a **prima facie** case for the development of a contingency framework for management accounting.
>
> However, despite the strong arguments for pursuing this line of research, a number of **reservations** need to be expressed.
>
> - Firstly, the nature of appropriate **contingent variables** has not yet been elucidated and requires greater theoretical, as well as empirical, attention.
>
> - Secondly, explicit consideration of **organizational effectiveness** is a vital part of a true contingency theory of control system design. This has been a much neglected topic from a theoretical stance and its development is urgently needed.
>
> - Thirdly, the **contingency theory of organizational design is weaker than some of its own literature suggests**, its links with organizational effectiveness being, at best, tentative. As the same contingent variables are likely to affect both organizational structure and accounting system design, it appears unwise to use structure as the sole intervening variable between contingent variables and the choice of the accounting information system.
>
> - Finally, the highly **interconnected nature of the components** that make up an organizational control package suggests that the management accounting information system cannot be studied in isolation from its wider context.'

1.25 Some further objections may be added, as follows.

(a) Most, if not all, of the writing on contingency theory and management accounting is written in a **highly abstruse style** and aimed at **fellow academics rather than practising accountants**. A good contrast is provided by the way in which Activity Based Costing has been popularised by the writings of management consultants.

(b) As Otley implies, it is by **no means clear how the various contingent variables** proposed **affect the management accounting system.** In several of the observations listed above, for example, it seems that it is the organisation structure that adapts to its environment and the management accounting system simply reflects the organisation structure.

(c) As Fincham and Rhodes point out (*The Individual, Work and Organisation*, 1987), contingency theory **plays down the importance** of power, both the **power of the strategically-placed managers and the power of the organisation itself.** An example of the former would be the influence of the MD in our simple example. An example of the latter would be the acquiring company in a take-over imposing its own accounting system on its new subsidiary.

(d) For **financial accounting** purposes accountants are expected to accept the idea of 'best practice' and to follow the rules and regulations of accounting standards and company law. Although financial accounting does not go quite so far as to insist upon one best way, it does not allow many alternatives for external reporting purposes. This is quite at **odds with the contingency approach**.

(e) The theory tend to **ignore the influence of aspects of an organisation's context which are more difficult to quantify**. It fails to recognise the impact of the people within an organisation, of management structure, managerial style and, particularly, organisational culture - those factors that make an organisation unique.

Conclusion: vive la différence

1.26 In spite of the many reservations, it is evidently true that there is not 'one best way' of designing an organisation or its accounting system: otherwise all successful organisations (and their accounting systems) would be identical. Even if this is the only real insight that contingency theory has to offer it is a very valuable one.

2 INSTITUTIONAL THEORY

The institutional view

2.1 Just as a manufacturing organisation must have an efficient production system in order to survive, the institutional view argues that **organisations need legitimacy from stakeholders** to survive. Organisations succeed when there is congruence between the view of the organisation presented to the wider environment and the expectations of its environment.

2.2 The **institutional environment** is composed of **norms and values of stakeholders** (customers, investors, government, collaborating organisations and so on). It reflects what the larger society views as **correct ways of organising and behaving**.

2.3 The institutional view is therefore that **organisations adopt structures and processes to please outsiders,** and these come to take on **rule-like status** in organisations.

2.4 **Legitimacy** (from stakeholders) is the general perspective that an **organisation's actions are desirable, proper and appropriate within the environment's system of norms, values and beliefs. Institutional theory is concerned** with the **intangible norms and values that shape behaviour,** as opposed to the tangible elements of technology and structure (so important in contingency theory).

2.5 Organisations must therefore **fit with the perceived and emotional expectations of stakeholders.** Consider the following example offered by Daft (*Organisation Theory and Design*).

> 'The Soviet Union collapsed and communism quickly disappeared because communism held little legitimacy in the minds of citizens in Russia and Eastern Europe. Just as important, when Westerners tried to construct a market-based economy in Russia, those efforts failed because citizens did not have a mental framework that saw competitive organisations as legitimate. Gradually institutions will grow and flourish in Russia consistent with the values held in the larger culture.'

The impact on structure, behaviour and activities

2.6 The institutional view sees organisations as having **two essential components.**

(a) The **technical component** is the day-to-day working technology and operating requirements. This is **governed by norms** of **rationality** and **efficiency**.

(b) The **institutional component** is the part most visible to the outside public. This is **governed by expectations from the external environment**. It therefore includes those members of staff who interact with customers and suppliers, its finished products that customers buy, its recruitment policies, the organisation's image in the community (does it raise money for charity?) and so on.

2.7 As a result of **pressure** to do things in the **proper** and **correct way**, the **formal structures** of many organisations therefore **reflect the expectations and values of the environment rather than the demands of operations**.

2.8 This means that an organisation might **establish roles or set-up activities** (Daft quotes an equal employment officer and an e-commerce division) because these are **perceived as important by society** and so increase its legitimacy and survival prospects, although such roles and **activities do increase efficiency**. An organisation's formal structure, design and behaviour may not therefore be rational in terms of the flow of work and the products/services produced or provided, but it will assure survival in the larger environment.

Institutional theory and homogeneity

2.9 So why is there so much homogeneity in the forms and practices of established organisations? Building societies, primary schools, hospitals, local authorities or companies in similar industries, in any part of the country, will appear very similar. When an industry is in its early stages, such as e-commerce, then diversity is the norm. But once that **industry becomes established**, there is an inevitable roll towards **similarity**.

> ### KEY TERMS
>
> **Isomorphism** is the term used to describe this move towards similarity.
>
> **Institutional isomorphism** is 'the emergence of a common structure and approach among organisations in the same field'. (Daft)

2.10 So how does this increasing similarity occur? **Powell and Di Maggio** identify **three mechanisms through which institutional isomorphism occurs**.

Coercive forces

2.11 All organisations are subject to **formal and informal pressures exerted** by **organisations upon which they are dependent**, and from **government and regulatory agencies**, to adopt structures, techniques and behaviours similar to other organisations. For example, large supermarkets often insist that certain policies, procedures and techniques are used by suppliers. We will see examples of the impact of pressures from regulatory agencies on systems of performance measurement in Chapter 13.

Mimetic forces

2.12 **Uncertainty** (poorly understood technologies, uncertain environment) **encourages imitation**. Organisations tend to **model** themselves on similar organisations in their field that they **perceive to be successful**, often **without proof that performance will be improved**.

2.13 Techniques such as **activity based management** (see Section 4 of this chapter), **total quality management** (see Chapter 4) and the **balanced scorecard** (see Chapter 14) have been adopted by many organisations without clear evidence of improvements in efficiency or effectiveness.

2.14 **Benchmarking** (see Chapter 8) is a legitimate technique to facilitate copying.

2.15 Adoption of such techniques will **reduce management's feelings of uncertainty**, however, and will **enhance the organisation's image** because it will be seen to be using the latest management/management accounting techniques

Normative forces

2.16 These forces mean that organisations are expected to **change to achieve standards of professionalism**, and to **adopt techniques** that are considered by the professional environment to be **up to date and effective**. Such changes may be in information technology, say, or in financial accounting or management accounting techniques.

2.17 We will see in the next chapter how new techniques are brought to the attention of management accounting practitioners and how norms are established. People are exposed to similar training and standards and adopt shared values, which are implemented within the organisations in which they work.

Institutional theory and management accounting

2.18 Di Maggio and Powell argue that **management** typically try to **ensure** an **organisation complies with the prevailing accepted logic** within any aspect of an organisation's operations.

2.19 This argument is easy to apply to management accounting, as the management accounting examples mentioned above testify. Institutional theorists would argue that **established management accounting systems and practices such as activity based costing have become widely accepted in many situations through a process of isomorphism towards the accepted 'norm'.**

2.20 Taking a wider view, most theorists agree that management accounting practices are deeply involved in the creation, diffusion and change of organisational culture and values.

3 ACTIVITY BASED APPROACHES

3.1 A focus on the **activities** that a business carries out, as opposed to how its activities have traditionally been organised into separate **functions,** lies behind much modern thinking. For instance it has been found to be more fruitful to think of what may have once been called the **warehousing** department (function) in terms what that department *does*, such as **inspection of goods**, **stock control** and **materials movement** (activities).

3.2 Depending what subject you are studying or who wrote the article you are reading you might find that this modern development has different names.

(a) **Business Process Re-engineering** might be the term used, for instance, if you are looking at how **information technology** can help to eliminate non-value added activities or co-ordinate two previously separate activities, or replace one way of doing things with a completely new, quicker and cheaper way.

(b) **Activity based** analysis might be the term used if you are looking, say, at how **costs** can be calculated in a more meaningful way.

3.3   The key point, whatever terminology is used, is that this modern development entails finding new and better ways of doing existing things so as to give greater satisfaction to customers at less cost to the business. This in turn means that **new and better information** is needed.

3.4   For instance, **activity based costing (ABC)** was developed because it was realised that older methods such as absorption costing using labour hours as the basis for absorbing overheads, did not provide useful information about what was causing the overheads to be incurred in the first place: the **cost drivers**.

Knowledge brought forward from earlier studies

ABC

You have studied basic ABC and the rationale behind it at earlier levels.

New **technology** means that **overheads** are now likely to represent a far larger proportion of overall costs than in the past.

The proponents of ABC argue that **traditional cost accounting** techniques result in a **misleading** and inequitable division of cost between low value and high value products, and that ABC provides a more meaningful allocation of costs which make unit costs more accurate. This in turn is part of a **shift** in emphasis **away** from costing merely for **stock valuation** towards costing of products made to meet actual **customer demand**.

Most overhead costs can be analysed between **short-term** variable costs, that vary with the **volume** of production, and **long-term** variable costs, that do *not* vary with the volume of production, but do vary with a different measure of **activity**.

The ABC approach is to relate overhead costs to the activities that cause or 'drive' them to be incurred in the first place and to change subsequently.

3.5   **Merits of activity based approaches**

(a)   The **complexity** of many businesses has increased, with wider product ranges, shorter product life cycles, the greater importance of quality and more complex production processes. Activity based analysis recognises this complexity with its **multiple cost drivers**, many of them **transaction-based** rather than volume-based.

(b)   In a more **competitive** environment, companies must be able to assess **product profitability** realistically. To do this, they must have a good understanding of what drives overhead costs. Activity based analysis gives a meaningful analysis of costs which should provide a better basis for pricing decisions, product mix decisions, design decisions and production decisions.

(c)   In modern manufacturing systems, **overhead** functions include a lot of **non-factory-floor activities** such as product design, quality control, production planning, sales order planning and customer service. Activity based analysis is concerned with all overhead costs, including the costs of these functions, and so it takes cost accounting beyond its 'traditional' factory floor boundaries.

(d)   **Service** businesses have characteristics very similar to those required for the successful application of activity based analysis in modern manufacturing industry.

    (i)   A highly **competitive** market

    (ii)   **Diversity** of products, processes and customers

    (iii)   **Significant overhead costs** not easily assigned to individual products

    (iv)   Demands on overhead resources related to products/customers, **not volume**.

(e)   Cost **control** may be improved because the **causes of increases** in costs can be more readily identified (poor use of storage space, for example) and means of reducing costs

34

can be investigated (extra shelving, perhaps, or automated packing procedures). We look at this in more detail in Section 4.

(f)   ABC techniques can be used in **customer profitability analysis** (see Chapter 21).

Case example

As a result of an ABC study, a FMCG manufacturer discovered that three of its top five customers in terms of gross profit using traditional techniques were in the bottom five and loss making when ABC was used.

3.6   Criticisms of activity based approaches

(a)   The **costs** of obtaining and interpreting the **new information** may be considerable. Activity based analysis should not be introduced unless it can provide additional information for management to use in planning or control decisions.

(b)   Many overheads relate neither to volume nor to complexity and diversity. The ability of a **single cost driver** to fully explain the cost behaviour of all items in its associated pool is **questionable**. What drives the cost of the external annual audit? What cost pool could it be placed in?

(c)   Some measure of **arbitrary** cost apportionment may still be required at the cost pooling stage for items like building depreciation. If an activity based system has many cost pools the amount of apportionment needed may be greater than ever.

(d)   Some people have questioned the fundamental assumption that activity **causes** cost, suggesting that it could be argued that **decisions** cause cost or the passage of **time** causes cost or that there may be **no one clear cause** of cost.

Question: criticisms of ABC

One of the directors of the company that employs you as a management accountant observes wryly that the thing that drives sales administration costs is customers ringing up and ordering things, and that if only they did this less often sales administration costs could be dramatically reduced!

How would you respond to this implied criticism of ABC?

Answer

The director is correct after a fashion, but what this really means is that the company needs to find more cost-effective ways of taking orders, not that it needs to take fewer orders. Activity analysis, if properly directed, is likely to identify the customers who take up the most time and encourage investigation of alternatives such as EDI links.

3.7   We will be looking at activity based management (ABM) in detail in Section 4.

4   ACTIVITY BASED MANAGEMENT

4.1   Recently the emphasis has switched away from using activity based approaches for product costing to using it to improve cost management. The terms **activity based management (ABM)** and **activity-based cost management (ABCM)** are used to describe the **cost management applications of ABC**.

4.2   There are a great many different **definitions** of activity based management.

4.3   Here is Drury's (from *Management and Cost Accounting*), with BPP's emphasis.

'ABM views the business as a set of linked activities that ultimately add value to the customer. It focuses on managing the business on the basis of the activities that make up the organisation. ABM is based on the premise that activities consume costs. Therefore **by managing activities costs will be managed in the long term**. The **goal of ABM is to enable customer needs to be satisfied while making fewer demands on organisation resources**. The measurement of activities is a key role of the management accounting function. In particular, activity cost information is useful for prioritising those activities that need to be studied closely so that they can be eliminated or improved.

In recent years ABM information has been used for a variety of business applications. They include cost reduction, activity-based budgeting, performance measurement, benchmarking and business process re-engineering.'

4.4   Horngren, Foster and Datar in *Cost Accounting: A Managerial Emphasis* 'define it broadly to **include pricing and product-mix decisions, cost reduction and process improvement decisions,** and **product design decisions**'.

4.5   In *Managerial Accounting*, Raiborn, Barfield and Kinney include **activity analysis, cost driver analysis, continuous improvement, operational control and performance evaluation** as the concepts covered by activity based management. 'These concepts help companies to produce more efficiently, determine costs more accurately, and control and evaluate performance more effectively.'

4.6   Clark and Baxter (*Management Accounting*, June 1992) provide a description which appears to include every management accounting buzzword. The emphasis is BPP's.

'The aim of activity-based management (ABM) is to provide management with a method of introducing and **managing** '**process and organisational change**'.

It focuses on activities within a process, decision-making and planning relative to those activities and the need for continuous improvement of all organisational activity. Management and staff must determine which activities are critical to success and decide how these are to be clearly defined across all functions.

Everyone must co-operate in defining:

*   cost pools
*   cost drivers
*   key performance indicators

They must be trained and **empowered** to act; all must be fairly treated and success recognised.

Clearly, ABM and employee empowerment take a critical step forward beyond ABC by recognising the contribution that people make as the key resource in any organisation's success.

*   It nurtures good communication and team work
*   It develops quality decision-making
*   It leads to quality control and continuous improvement

Some accountants do not appear to understand that ABM provides an essential link to total quality management (**TQM**) and its concepts of 'continuous improvement'.

ABM helps deliver:

*   improved quality
*   increased customer satisfaction
*   lower costs
*   increased profitability

It provides accountants and other technical managers with a meaningful path into the business management team.'

4.7   Perhaps the clearest and most concise definition is offered by Kaplan *et al* in *Management Accounting*. The emphasis is again BPP's.

KEY TERM

Activity based management (ABM) is '...the management processes that use the information provided by an activity-based cost analysis to improve organisational profitability. Activity-based management (ABM) includes performing activities more efficiently, eliminating the need to perform certain activities that do not add value for customers, improving the design of products, and developing better relationships with customers and suppliers. The goal of ABM is to enable customer needs to be satisfied while making fewer demands on organisational resources.'

4.8 In the following paragraphs we examine some of the aspects of ABM mentioned in the definitions above.

Cost reduction and process improvement

4.9 Traditional cost analysis analyses costs by types of expense for each responsibility centre. ABM, on the other hand, analyses costs on the basis of cross-departmental activities and therefore provides management information on why costs are incurred and on the output of the activity in terms of cost drivers. **By controlling or reducing the incidence of the cost driver, the associated cost can be controlled or reduced.**

4.10 This difference is illustrated in the example below of a customer order processing activity.

Traditional analysis

	£
Salaries	5,700
Stationery	350
Travel	1,290
Telephone	980
Equipment depreciation	680
	9,000

ABC analysis

	£
Preparation of quotations	4,200
Receipt of customer orders	900
Assessment of customer creditworthiness	1,100
Expedition of orders	1,300
Resolution of customer problems	1,500
	9,000

Suppose that the analysis above showed that it cost £250 to process a customer's order. This would indicate to sales staff that it may not be worthwhile chasing orders with a low sales value. By eliminating lots of small orders and focusing on those with a larger value, demand for the activities associated with customer order processing should fall, with spending decreasing as a consequence.

4.11 *Problems associated with cost reduction and ABM*

(a) The extent to which activity based approaches can be applied is very dependent on an organisation's ability to identify its main activities and their associated cost drivers.

(b) If a system of 'conventional' responsibility centres has been carefully designed, this may already be a reflection of the key organisational activities. For example, a despatch department might be a cost centre, but despatch might also be a key activity.

(c) In some circumstances, the 'pooling' of activity based costs and the identification of a single cost driver for every cost pool may even hamper effective control if the cost driver is not completely applicable to every cost within that cost pool. For example, suppose the cost of materials handling was allocated to a cost pool for which the cost driver was the number of production runs. Logically, to control the cost of materials handling the number of production runs should be controlled. If the cost is actually driven by the weight of materials being handled, however, it can only be controlled if efforts are made to use lighter materials where possible.

Activity analysis

4.12 The activity based analysis above provides information not available from a traditional cost analysis. Why was £1,500 spent on resolving customer orders, for example. An **activity analysis** usually **surprises managers** who had not realised the amount being spent on certain activities. This leads to **questions** about the **necessity for particular activities** and, if an activity is required, whether it can be carried out more effectively and efficiently.

4.13 Such questions can be answered by classifying activities as value added or non-value added (or as core/primary, support or diversionary/discretionary).

Value-added and non-value-added activities

> **KEY TERMS**
>
> An activity may increase the worth of a product or service to the customer; in this case the customer is willing to pay for that activity and it is considered **value-added.** Some activities, though, simply increase the time spent on a product or service but do not increase its worth to the customer; these activities are **non-value-added.**
>
> (Rayborn, Barfield and Kinney, *Managerial Accounting*)

4.14 As an example, **getting luggage on the proper flight is a value-added activity** for airlines, **dealing with the complaints from customers whose luggage gets lost is not.**

4.15 The **time** spent on **non-value-added activities** creates additional costs that are unnecessary. If such activities were **eliminated, costs** would **decrease without affecting the market value or quality of the product or service.**

4.16 The processing **time** of an organisation is made up of four types.

(a) **Production** or **performance time** is the actual time that it takes to perform the functions necessary to manufacture the product or perform the service.

(b) Performing quality control results in **inspection time.**

(c) Moving products or components from one place to another is **transfer time.**

(d) Storage time and time spent waiting at the production operation for processing are **idle time.**

4.17 **Production time is value added. The other three are not. The time from receipt of an order to completion of a product or performance of a service equals production time plus non-value-added time.**

4.18 JIT would of course eliminate a significant proportion of the idle time occurring from storage and wait processes but it is important to realise that **very few organisations can completely eliminate all quality control functions and all transfer time**. If managers understand the non-value-added nature of these functions, however, they should be able to **minimise** such activities as much as possible.

4.19 Sometimes non-value-added activities arise because of inadequacies in existing processes and so they cannot be eliminated unless these inadequacies are addressed.

(a) The National Health Service (NHS) is a classic example of this. Some heart patients on the NHS wait up to four months for critical heart surgery. During this time they are likely to be severely ill on a number of occasions and have to be taken to hospital where they spend the day receiving treatment that will temporarily relieve the problem. This non-value-added activity is totally unnecessary and is dependent on an inadequate process: that of providing operations when required.

(b) Customer complaints services can be viewed in the same way: eliminate the source of complaints and the need for the department greatly reduces.

(c) Setting up machinery for a new production run is a non-value-added cost. If the number of components per product can be reduced the number of different components made will reduce and therefore set-up time will also reduce.

4.20 One of the **costliest** things an organisation can do is to **invest in equipment and people to make non-value-added activities more efficient**. The objective is to eliminate them altogether or subject them to a major overhaul, not make them more efficient. For example, if a supplier of raw materials makes a commitment to supply high-quality materials, inspection is no longer required, and buying testing equipment and hiring more staff to inspect incoming raw material would waste time and money. **Non-value-added activities are not necessary for an organisation to stay in business.**

Core/primary, support and diversionary/discretionary activities

4.21 This is an alternative classification of activities.

> **KEY TERMS**
>
> A **core** or **primary activity** is one that adds value to a product, for example cutting and drilling materials and assembling them.
>
> A **secondary activity** is one that supports a core activity, but does not add value in itself. For example setting up a machine so that it drills holes of a certain size is a secondary activity.
>
> **Diversionary** or **discretionary activities** do not add value and are symptoms of failure within an organisation. For instance repairing faulty production work is such an activity because the production should not have been faulty in the first place.

4.22 The aim of ABM is to try to eliminate as far as possible the diversionary activities but, as with non-value-added activities, experience has shown that it is usually impossible to eliminate them all, although the time and cost associated with them can be greatly reduced.

Design decisions

4.23 In many organisations today, roughly 80% of a product's costs are committed at the product design stage, well before production begins. By **providing product designers with cost driver information** they can be encouraged to **design low cost products that still meet customer requirements.**

4.24 The identification of appropriate cost drivers and tracing costs to products on the basis of these cost drivers has the potential to **influence behaviour to support the cost management strategies of the organisation.**

4.25 For example, suppose product costs depend on the number and type of components. A product which is designed so that it uses fewer components will be cheaper to produce. A product using standard components will also be cheaper to produce. Management can influence the action of designers through overhead absorption rates if overheads are related to products on the basis of the number of component parts they contain. Hitachi's refrigeration plant uses this method to influence the behaviour of their product designers and ultimately the cost of manufacture.

Cost driver analysis

4.26 To reflect today's more **complex business environment**, recognition must be given to the fact that **costs are created and incurred because their cost drivers occur at different levels. Cost driver analysis investigates, quantifies and explains the relationships between cost drivers and their related costs.**

Classification level	Cause of cost	Types of cost	Necessity of cost
Unit level costs	Production/acquisition of a single unit of product or delivery of single unit of service	Direct materials Direct labour	Once for each unit produced
Batch level costs	A group of things being made, handled or processed	Purchase orders Set-ups Inspection	Once for each batch produced
Product/process level costs	Development, production or acquisition of different items	Equipment maintenance Product development	Supports a product type or a process
Organisational/ facility costs		Building depreciation Organisational advertising	Supports the overall production or service process

(Adapted from Raiborn *et al*)

4.27 Traditionally it has been assumed that if costs did not vary with changes in production at the unit level, they were fixed rather than variable. The analysis above shows this assumption to be false, and that costs vary for reasons other than production volume. To determine an accurate estimate of product or service cost, **costs should be accumulated at each successively higher level of costs.**

4.28 Unit level costs are allocated over number of units produced, batch level costs over the number of units in the batch, product level costs over the number of units produced by the product line. These costs are all related to units of product (merely at different levels) and so can be gathered together at the product level to match with revenue. Organisational level costs are not product related, however, and so should simply be deducted from net revenue.

4.29 Such an approach gives a far greater insight into product profitability.

Continuous improvement

4.30 Continuous improvement **recognises the concept of eliminating non-value-added activities** to reduce lead time, make products or perform services with zero defects, reduce product costs on an ongoing basis and simplify products and processes. It focuses on including employees in the process as they are often the best source of ideas.

Operational control

4.31 '**To control costs, managers must understand where costs are being incurred and for what purpose**. Some of this understanding will come from differentiating between value-added and non-value-added activities. Some will come from the better information generated by more appropriate tracing of overhead costs to products and services. Some will come from viewing fixed costs as long-term variable overheads and recognising that certain activities will cause those costs to change. Understanding costs allows manager to visualise what needs to be done to controls those costs, to implement cost reduction activities, and to plan resource utilisation.

......By better understanding the underlying cost of making a product or performing a service, managers obtain **new insight into product or service profitability**. Such insight could **result in management decisions** about expanding or contracting product variety, raising or reducing prices, and entering or leaving a market. For example, managers may decide to raise selling prices or discontinue production of low-volume speciality output, since that output consumes more resources than does high-volume output. Managers may decide to discontinue manufacturing products that require complex operations. Or, managers may reap the benefits from low-volume or complex production through implementing high-technology processes.'

(Raiborn *et al*, with BPP emphasis)

4.32 Innes and Mitchell (*'Activity Based Costing'*) report (with BPP emphasis) that in some organisations:

'ABCM has also been used in **make-or-buy decisions** and has led to the sub-contracting of certain activities. In another engineering company the ABCM information on purchasing **concentrated** managers' **attention** on problems such as **late deliveries, short deliveries and poor-quality raw materials**. This information enabled this engineering company to identify twenty problem suppliers and take the necessary corrective action, which varied from changing suppliers to working with others to overcome the existing problems.'

Performance evaluation

4.33 ABM encourages and rewards employees for developing new skills, accepting greater responsibilities, and making suggestions for improvements in plant layout, product design, and staff utilisation. Each of these improvements reduces non-value-added time and cost. In addition, by focusing on activities and costs, ABM is better able to provide more appropriate measures of performance than are found in more traditional systems.

4.34 **To monitor the effectiveness and efficiency of activities**, performance measures relating to volume, time, quality and costs are needed.

   (a) Activity **volume** measures provide an indication of the throughput and capacity utilisation of activities. For example reporting the number of times an activity such as setting-up is undertaken focuses attention on the need to investigate ways of reducing the volume of the activity and hence future costs.

   (b) To increase customer satisfaction, organisations must provide a speedy response to customer requests and reduce the time taken to develop and bring a new product to the market. Organisations must therefore focus on the **time** taken to complete an activity or sequence of activities. This time can be reduced by eliminating (as far as is possible) the time spent on non-value-added activities.

   (c) A focus on value chain analysis is a means of enhancing customer satisfaction. The value chain is the linked set of activities from basic raw material acquisition all the way through to the end-use product or service delivered to the customer. By viewing each of the activities in the value chain as a supplier-customer relationship, the opinions of the customers can be used to provide useful feedback on the **quality** of the service provided by the supplying activity. For example the quality of the service provided by the processing of purchase orders activity can be evaluated by users of the activity in terms of the speed of processing orders and the quality of the service provided by the supplier chosen by the purchasing activity. Such qualitative evaluations can be supported by quantitative measures such as percentage of deliveries that are late.

   (d) **Cost** driver rates (such as cost per set-up) can be communicated in a format that is easily understood by all staff and can be used to motivate managers to reduce the cost of performing activities (given that cost driver rate × activity level = cost of activity). Their use as a measure of performance can induce dysfunctional behaviour, however. By splitting production runs and therefore having more set-ups, the cost per set-up can be reduced. Workload will be increased, however, and so in the long run costs could increase.

Other issues

4.35 Benchmarking is covered in Chapter 8.
Business process re-engineering is covered in Chapter 6.
Customer profitability analysis is covered in Chapter 21.
Pricing and product mix decisions using ABC are covered in Chapter 23.

Problems with ABM

4.36 ABM is not a panacea, however.

   (a) The **amount of work** in setting up the system and in data collection must be considered.

   (b) **Organisational and behavioural consequences.** Selected activity cost pools may not correspond to the formal structure of cost responsibilities within the organisation (the purchasing activity may spread across purchasing, production, stores, administrative and finance departments) and so determining 'ownership' of the activity and its costs may be problematic. We have already mentioned the behavioural impact of some performance measures.

Chapter roundup

- The **contingency approach to management accounting** is based on the premise that there is no universally appropriate accounting system applicable to all organisations in all circumstances. Efficient systems depend on awareness of the system designer of the specific environmental factors which influence their creation.

- The **institutional view** is that organisations adopt situations and processes to please outsiders, and these come to take on rule-like status.

- **Isomorphism** is the term used to describe the move towards similarity in organisations.

- **Powell** and **Di Maggio** identified three mechanisms through which **institutional isomorphism** occurs.

  ° Coercive forces
  ° Mimetic forces
  ° Normative forces

- A focus on the **activities** that a business carries out lies behind much modern thinking.

- **Activity based management (ABM)** includes performing activities more efficiently, eliminating the need to perform certain activities that do not add value for customers, improving the design of products and developing better relationships with customers and suppliers. The goal of ABM is to enable customer needs to be satisfied while making fewer demands on organisational resources.

Quick quiz

1   What are the four contingent variables discussed in this chapter?

   A   Environment, technology, size, culture
   B   Environment, resources, size, culture
   C   Processes, resources, size, structure
   D   Processes, technology, control, structure

2   *Fill in the blanks in the sentences below.*

   ………………….. is the term used to describe a move towards similarity.

   ………………….. is 'the emergence of a common structure and approach among organisations in the same field'.

3   *Match the correct description to the three terms below.*

Term		Descriptions	
(a)	Coercive forces	(1)	Mechanisms which encourage imitation
(b)	Mimetic forces	(2)	Pressures exerted by parties upon which an organisation is dependent
(c)	Normative forces	(3)	Forces which expect change to meet certain standards of professionalism

4   Inspection time is value added. *True or false?*

5   *Choose the appropriate term from those highlighted.*

   A **diversionary/ secondary/ core/ primary/ discretionary** activity supports a core activity, but does not add value in itself.

Answers to quick quiz

1   A

2   Isomorphism
    Institutional isomorphism

3   (a)   (2)

    (b)   (1)

    (c)   (3)

4   False

5   Secondary.

Now try the question below from the Exam Question Bank

Number	Level	Marks	Time
3	Exam	20	36 mins

Chapter 4

TRENDS IN MANAGEMENT ACCOUNTING

Topic list	Syllabus reference
1 The changing business environment	1(c)
2 Life cycle costing and target costing	1(c)
3 Backflush accounting	1(c)
4 Environmental management accounting	1(c)
5 Other recently adopted management accounting techniques	1(c)
6 The changing practice of management accounting	1(c)
7 Bringing new techniques to the awareness of management accounting practitioners	1(c)
8 The influence of structure, culture and strategy	1(c)
9 The continuing effectiveness of traditional techniques	1(c), 1(d)

Introduction

This chapter provides you with detail about **trends in management accounting** and about **current techniques and methods used within the management accounting framework.**

Section 1 provides a general introduction to this chapter. **Section 2** looks at topics you have encountered in your studies for Paper 2.4, whereas **Sections 3 and 4** cover topics completely new to you and the subject of recent articles by the examiner.

After looking at a number of other recently introduced management accounting techniques in **Section 5**, we go on to consider a number of associated topics such as the role of the management accountant today, and the way in which management accounting practitioners are made aware of new techniques.

In the last section of the chapter we also consider the **relevance** of traditional management accounting techniques in a rapidly changing businesses environment.

Section 4 – Trends in management accounting techniques and methods

- Discuss the expansion in the scope of management accounting in the last 40 years
- Identify and discuss some recently adopted management accounting techniques
- Explain how new techniques may be evaluated
- Discuss the ways in which management accounting practitioners are made aware of new techniques
- Illustrate how an organisation's structure, culture and strategy will influence the adoption of new methods and techniques
- Assess the continuing effectiveness of traditional techniques within a rapidly changing business environment

BPP PROFESSIONAL EDUCATION

Section 21 – Budgeting and budgetary control III

- Enumerate the strengths and weaknesses of alternative budget models such as activity based

- Identify and appraise current developments in budgeting

Section 24 – Pricing II

- Explain the operation of target pricing in achieving a desired market share

Exam guide

A core syllabus area is 'traditional management accounting activities' and so you could be asked to assess the usefulness of such activities in the modern business environment. Much of what is covered in this chapter should serve as background to questions.

The issues covered in this chapter are useful background to the Oxford Brookes degree Research and Analysis Project Topic 1, which requires you to analyse the efficiency and/or effectiveness of a management accounting technique in an organisational setting.

---

1   THE CHANGING BUSINESS ENVIRONMENT

Changing competitive environment

For manufacturing organisations

1.1   **Before the 1970s, barriers of communication** and **geographical distance** limited the extent to which overseas organisations could compete in domestic markets. Cost increases could often be passed on to customers and so there were **few efforts to maximise efficiency and improve management practices,** or to reduce costs. **During the 1970s,** however, **overseas competitors** gained access to domestic markets by **establishing global networks for acquiring raw materials and distributing high-quality, low-priced goods.** To succeed, organisations had to compete against the best companies in the world.

For service organisations

1.2   **Prior to the 1980s,** many service organisations (such as the utilities, the financial services and airlines industries) were either **government-owned monopolies** or were **protected by a highly-regulated, non-competitive environment. Improvements in quality and efficiency** of operations or levels of profitability were not expected, and costs increases were often covered by increasing service prices. Cost systems to measure costs and profitability of individual services were not deemed necessary.

The competitive environment for service organisations changed radically in the **1980s,** however, following **privatisation** of government-owned monopolies and **deregulation.** The resulting intense competition and increasing product range has led to the **requirement for cost management and management accounting information systems** which allow service organisations to assess the costs and profitability of services, customers and markets.

Changing product life cycles

1.3   Today's **competitive environment,** along with high levels of **technological innovation** and **increasingly discriminating and sophisticated customer demands,** constantly **threaten a product's life cycle.**

1.4 Organisations can no longer rely on years of high demand for products and so, to compete effectively, they need to continually **redesign their products** and to **shorten the time it takes to get them to the market place.**

1.5 In many organisations today, up to **90% of a product's life cycle cost is determined by decisions made early** within the cycle, **at the design stage. Management accounting systems that monitor spending and commitment to spend during the early stages of a product's life cycle** are therefore becoming increasingly important.

Changing customer requirements

1.6 Successful organisations in today's competitive environment make **customer satisfaction** their **priority** and concentrate on the following **key success factors.**

   (a) **Cost efficiency**

   (b) **Quality,** by focusing on total quality management (TQM), which is considered in more detail below.

   (c) **Time** (providing a speedier response to customer requests, ensuring 100% on-time delivery and reducing the time taken to develop and bring new products to market)

   (d) **Innovation** (developing a steady stream of innovative new products and having the flexibility to respond to customer requirements)

1.7 They are also taking on board **new management approaches.**

   (a) **Continuous improvement** (a facet of TQM, being a continuous search to reduce costs, eliminate waste and improve the quality and performance of activities that increase customer satisfaction or value)

Exam focus point

Obviously an organisation will seek to minimise costs and maximise levels of quality, an issue examined in June 2002.

   (b) **Employee empowerment** (providing employees with the information to enable them to make continuous improvements without authorisation from superiors)

   (c) **Total value-chain analysis** (ensuring that all the factors which add value to an organisation's products - the value chain of research and development, design, production, marketing, distribution and customer service - are coordinated within the overall organisational framework)

Total quality management (TQM)

KEY TERMS

Total quality management is the process of applying a zero defects philosophy to the management of all resources and relationships within an organisation as a means of developing and sustaining a culture of continuous improvement which focuses on meeting customers' expectations.

Exam focus point

Knowledge of TQM was required in the December 2003 exam.

1.8 Mark Lee Inman listed 'eight requirements of quality' in an ACCA *Students' Newsletter* article, which could be seen as the **characteristics of total quality management programmes**.

(a) Organisation wide there must be acceptance that the only thing that matters is the customer.

(b) There should be recognition of the all-pervasive nature of the customer-supplier relationship, including internal customers; passing sub-standard material to another division is not satisfactory

(c) Instead of relying on inspection to a predefined level of quality, the cause of the defect in the first place should be prevented.

(d) Each employee or group of employees must be personally responsible for defect-free production or service in their domain.

(e) There should be a move away from 'acceptable' quality levels. Any level of defects must be unacceptable.

(f) All departments should try obsessively to get thing right first time; this applies to misdirected phone calls and typing errors as much as to production.

(g) Quality certification programmes should be introduced.

(h) The cost of poor quality should be emphasised; good quality generates savings.

Changing approaches to manufacturing

1.9 Traditionally, manufacturing industries have fallen into a few broad groups according to the **nature of the production process** and **materials flow**.

1.10 In recent years, however, a new type of manufacturing system known as **group technology** (or **repetitive manufacturing**) has emerged. The system involves a **flexible or cellular arrangement of machines** which **manufacture groups of products having similar manufacturing requirements**. By grouping together facilities required to produce similar products, some of the **benefits** associated with flow production systems (lower throughput times, easier scheduling, reduced set-up times and reduced work in progress) are possible to achieve. Moreover, the increase in **customer demand for product diversity can be satisfied** by such a manufacturing system.

Dedicated cell layout

1.11 The modern development in this sphere is to merge the flexibility of the functional layout with the speed and productivity of the product layout. **Cellular** manufacturing involves a **U-shaped flow** along which are arranged a number of different machines that are used to make products with similar machining requirements.

1.12 The machines are operated by workers who are **multi-skilled** (can operate each machine within the cell rather than being limited to one operation such as 'lathe-operator', 'grinder', or whatever) and are able to perform routine preventive maintenance on the cell machines. The aim is to facilitate **just-in-time** production (see below) and obtain the associated improvements in **quality** and reductions in **costs**.

Just-in-time (JIT) systems

ATTENTION

JIT was one of the topics of an article by the examiner which appeared in the April 2004 edition of *Student Accountant* ('Just-in-time operations and backflush accounting'). Could this signify its appearance in the exam you face?

KEY TERMS

Just-in-time (JIT) is 'A system whose objective is to produce or to procure products or components as they are required by a customer or for use, rather than for stock. A JIT system is a 'pull' system, which responds to demand, in contrast to a 'push' system, in which stocks act as buffers between the different elements of the system, such as purchasing, production and sales.'

Just-in-time production is 'A system which is driven by demand for finished products whereby each component on a production line is produced only when needed for the next stage'.

Just-in-time purchasing is 'A system in which material purchases are contracted so that the receipt and usage of material, to the maximum extent possible, coincide'.

(CIMA *Official Terminology*)

1.13 Although often described as a technique, JIT is more of a **philosophy or approach to management** since it encompasses a **commitment to continuous improvement** and the **search for excellence** in the design and operation of the production management system.

1.14 JIT has the following **essential elements**.

Element	Detail
JIT purchasing	Parts and raw materials should be purchased as near as possible to the time they are needed, using **small frequent deliveries against bulk contracts**. Stock levels are therefore minimised.
Close relationship with suppliers	In a JIT environment, the responsibility for the **quality of goods lies with the supplier**. A **long-term commitment** between supplier and customer should therefore be established. If an organisation has confidence that suppliers will deliver material of 100% quality, on time, so that there will be no rejects, returns and hence no consequent production delays, **usage of materials can be matched with delivery of materials and stocks can be kept at near zero levels**.

Element	Detail
Uniform loading	All parts of the productive process should be operated at a speed which matches the rate at which the final product is demanded by the customer. Production runs will therefore be shorter and there will be smaller stocks of finished goods because output is being matched more closely to demand (and so storage costs will be reduced).
Set-up time reduction	Machinery set-ups are **non-value-added activities** (see below) which should be reduced or even eliminated.
Machine cells	Machines or workers should be **grouped by product or component** instead of by the type of work performed. Products can flow from machine to machine without having to wait for the next stage of processing or returning to stores. **Lead times and work in progress are thus reduced.**
Quality	Production management should seek to **eliminate scrap and defective units** during production, and to avoid the need for reworking of units since this stops the flow of production and leads to late deliveries to customers. Product quality and production quality are important 'drivers' in a JIT system.
Pull system (Kanban)	Products/components are only produced when needed by the next process. Nothing is produced in anticipation of need, to then remain in stock, consuming resources.
Preventative maintenance	Production systems must be reliable and prompt, without unforeseen delays and breakdowns.
Employee involvement	Workers within each machine cell should be trained to operate each machine within that cell and to be able to perform routine preventative maintenance on the cell machines (ie to be **multiskilled and flexible**).

Case example

The following extract from an article in the *Financial Times* illustrates how 'just-in-time' some manufacturing processes can be. The emphasis is BPP's.

'Just-in-time manufacturing is down to a fine art at *Nissan Motor Manufacturing (UK)*. **Stockholding of some components is just ten minutes** - and the holding of all parts bought in Europe is less than a day.

Nissan has moved beyond just-in-time to **synchronous supply** for some components, which means manufacturers deliver these components directly to the production line minutes before they are needed.

These manufacturers do not even receive an order to make a component until the car for which it is intended has started along the final assembly line. Seat manufacturer *Ikeda Hoover*, for example, has about 45 minutes to build seats to specification and deliver them to the assembly line a mile away. It delivers 12 sets of seats every 20 minutes and they are mounted in the right order on an overhead conveyor ready for fitting to the right car.

Nissan has **close relationships with this dozen or so suppliers** and deals exclusively with them in their component areas. It involves them and even their own suppliers in discussions about future needs and other issues. These companies have generally established their own manufacturing units close to the Nissan plant.

Other parts from further afield are collected from manufacturers by *Nissan* several times at fixed times. This is more efficient than having each supplier making individual haulage arrangements.'

Problems associated with JIT

1.15 JIT should not be seen as a panacea for all the endemic problems associated with Western manufacturing. It might not even be appropriate in all circumstances.

(a) It is **not always easy to predict patterns of demand**.

(b) JIT makes the organisation **far more vulnerable to disruptions in the supply chain**.

(c) JIT, originated by Toyota, was designed at a time when all of Toyota's manufacturing was done within a 50 km radius of its headquarters. Wide geographical spread, however, makes this difficult.

Case examples

- 'Just-in-time works well during normal business times. Companies that once kept months of safety stock now get by with days, or even hours of materials ... . But how about when your industry [high-tech] suddenly undergoes a tremendous boom, and demand far exceeds projections for parts? ... Just look at cell phones. The worldwide boom in cellular phone sales wasn't exactly a surprise – sales of these units have been on a fast climb for years. Yet one distributor reports a wait of 18 months to obtain high-frequency transistors for hand held devices.'

('Just in time, or just too late?', Doug Bartholomew, *Industry Week,* August 2000)

- The Kobe earthquake in Japan in 1995 severely disrupted industry in areas unaffected by the actual catastrophe. Plants that had not been hit by the earthquake were still forced to shut down production lines less than 24 hours after the earthquake struck because they held no buffer stocks which they could use to cover the shortfall caused by non delivery by the Kobe area suppliers.

- In October 1991 the workforce at the French state-owned car maker *Renault's* gear-box production plant at Cléon went on strike. The day afterwards a British plant had to cease production. Within two weeks *Renault* was losing 60% of its usual daily output. The weaknesses were due to the following.

  ○ Sourcing components from one plant only

  ○ Heavy dependence on in-house components

  ○ Low inventory

  ○ The fact '...that Japanese-style management techniques depend on stability in labour relations, something in short supply in the French public sector'.

(*Financial Times*, 31 October 1991)

Modern versus traditional stock control systems

1.16 There is no reason for the newer approaches to supersede the old entirely. A restaurant, for example, might find it preferable to use the traditional economic order quantity approach for staple non-perishable food stocks, but adopt JIT for perishable and 'exotic' items. In a hospital a stock-out could, quite literally, be fatal, and JIT would be quite unsuitable.

Costing implications of JIT

1.17 The examiner detailed these in the article mentioned above.

'Just-in-time manufacturing enables purchasing, production, and sales to occur in quick succession with stock being maintained at minimum levels. The absence of stock renders decisions regarding cost-flow assumptions (such as weighted average or first-in, first-out) or stock costing methods (such as absorption or marginal costing) unimportant. This is because all of the manufacturing costs attributable to a period flow directly into cost of goods sold. Job costing is simplified by the rapid conversion of direct materials into finished goods that are then sold immediately.'

Advanced manufacturing technology (AMT)

1.18 Organisations need to be able to compete in today's fast-moving, sophisticated world markets. As noted above, they need to be innovative and flexible and be able to deal with short product life cycles. They need to be able to offer greater product variety whilst maintaining or reducing their costs. They may want to reduce set-up times and inventories and have the greatest possible manufacturing flexibility. AMT helps them to do this.

> **KEY TERM**
>
> **Advanced manufacturing technology (AMT)** encompasses automatic production technology, computer-aided design and manufacturing, flexible manufacturing systems and a wide array of innovative computer equipment.

The limitations of traditional management accounting

1.19 It has been argued that traditional management accounting systems are inadequate for a modern business environment that focuses on marketing, customer service, employee involvement and total quality, and for modern industry using advanced manufacturing technology.

1.20 **Absorption costing**

The traditional methods of costing products have been largely based on absorption costing with direct labour hour recovery rates. As we will see, these methods are inappropriate in the modern environment.

1.21 **Standard costing**

Doubts about the suitability in the modern business environment of both the general philosophy and the detailed operation of standard costing have arisen. We look at this in more detail in Section 8.

1.22 **Short-term financial measures**

Much of the output of traditional management accounting consists of short-term financial performance measures such as costs, variances and so on. Many of these are **produced too long after the event** and are **too narrowly focused**. A much **wider view is now necessary**, together with the realisation that **expenditure cannot continue to be evaluated on purely financial grounds**, because the non-financial benefits can be extremely important (for example better product quality) and not all of the financial benefits are easily quantified (for example shorter set-up times, improved capacity utilisation). Non-financial indicators are considered in Chapter 12.

1.23 **Cost accounting methods**

Traditional cost accounting traces raw materials to various production stages via WIP, to the next stage and finally to finished goods, resulting in literally thousands of transaction entries. With just-in-time systems, production flows through the factory on a continual basis with near-zero inventories and very low batch sizes and so such transaction entries become **needlessly complicated and uninformative**. Cost accounting and recording systems can therefore be **greatly simplified in the modern environment**. **Backflush costing** is one possible approach.

1.24 **Performance measures**

Traditional management accounting performance measures can **produce the wrong type of response.**

Measurement	Response	Consequence of action
Purchase price variance	Buy in greater bulk to reduce unit price	Excess stocks Higher holding costs Quality and reliability of delivery times ignored
Labour efficiency variance	Encourage greater output	Possibly excess stocks of the wrong products
Machine utilisation	Encourage more running time	Possibly excess stocks of the wrong products
Cost of scrap	Rework items to reduce scrap	Production flow held up by re-working
Scrap factor included in standard costs	Supervisor aims to achieve actual scrap = standard scrap	No motivation to get it right first time
Traditional absorption costing	Produce more output to reduce unit costs and/or over recover overhead	Excess stocks, possibly of unwanted products
Cost centre reporting	Management focus is on cost centre activities, not overheads	Lack of attention to activities where cost reduction possibilities might exist

We consider the use of performance measures in Chapters 10 to 15.

1.25 We return to the relevance of traditional management accounting at the end of the chapter.

The solution

1.26 Whether all, or any, of the above criticisms are well founded is, of course, debatable. What is indisputable, however, is that **changes are taking place in management accounting** in order to meet the challenge of modern developments.

2 LIFE CYCLE COSTING AND TARGET COSTING

Life cycle costing

What are life cycle costs?

2.1 Life cycle costs are incurred for products and services **from their design stage through development to market launch, production and sales, and their eventual withdrawal from the market.**

2.2 **Traditional management accounting systems** in general only report costs at the physical production stage of the life cycle and do not accumulate costs over the entire life cycle. They **assess a product's or project's profitability on a periodic basis.** Life cycle costing, on the other hand, considers a product's/project's entire life.

KEY TERM

Life cycle costing tracks and accumulates actual costs and revenues attributable to each product or project over the entire product/project life cycle

2.3 The **total profitability** of any given product/project can therefore be determined.

2.4 **Traditional management accounting systems** usually total **all non-production costs** and record them as a **period expense**. **Using life cycle costing** such costs are **traced to individual products over complete life cycles.**

(a) The total of these costs for each individual product can therefore be reported and compared with revenues generated in the future.

(b) The visibility of such costs is increased.

(c) **Individual product profitability can be more fully understood** by attributing *all* costs to products.

(d) As a consequence, **more accurate feedback information** is available on the organisation's success or failure in developing new products. In today's competitive environment, where the ability to produce new and updated versions of products is paramount to the survival of an organisation, this information is vital.

2.5 It is reported that some organisations operating within an **AMT environment** find that approximately **90% of a product's life cycle cost is determined by decisions made early within the cycle** at the design stage. Life cycle costing is therefore particularly suited to such organisations and products, monitoring spending and commitments to spend during the early stages of a product's life cycle.

2.6 In order to compete effectively in today's competitive market, organisations need to **redesign continually their products** with the result that **product life cycles** have become much **shorter**. The **planning, design and development stages of a product's cycle** are therefore **critical to an organisation's cost management process**. Cost reduction at this stage of a product's life cycle, rather than during the production process, is one of the most important ways of reducing product cost.

Case example

General Motors estimate that 70% of the cost of manufacturing truck transmissions is determined in the design stage. Estimates for other companies and products often exceed 80%.

2.7 **Examples of costs that are determined at the design stage**

- The number of different components
- Whether the components are standard or not
- The ease of changing over tools
- Type of packaging

2.8 Japanese companies developed **target costing** as a response to the problem of **controlling and reducing costs over the product life cycle**.

KEY TERM

Target cost is an estimate of a product cost which is derived by subtracting a desired profit margin from a competitive market price.

'Target cost management has been defined as a system that is effective in managing costs in new-product design and development stages. It has also been viewed as allowing the production cost of a proposed product to be identified so that when sold it generates the desired profit level. ... Target cost management has also been viewed as playing a useful role in enabling an enterprise to set and support the attainment of cost levels to effectively reflect its planned financial performance. ...What appears to be evident is that there are almost as **many conceptions of target costing** as there are companies deploying the approach and there are probably many **companies engaging in various aspects of target cost management without referring to the term**.

Target cost management has been posited to assist in the pursuit of product development time reduction, as well as the quality definition for a new product and cost containment generally. It has therefore been perceived as a managerial tool simultaneously to **address time, quality and cost issues**.'

(A Bhimani and H Okano, 'Targeting excellence: target cost management at Toyota in the UK', *Management Accounting,* June 1995 (with BPP's emphasis))

Case example

'When Toyota developed the Lexus to compete with BMW, Mercedes and Jaguar, it employed two basic concepts: reverse engineering and target costing. In essence, it sought to produce a car with BMW 7-series attributes at a BMW 5-series price. Cost was the dominant design parameter that shaped the development of the Lexus, as it was later with Nissan's Infiniti.

The response from Mercedes Benz, one of the competitors who lost market share through this strategy, was to acknowledge that its cars were over-engineered and too expensive and to change its product-development process to determine target product costs from competitive market prices.

(B Nixon, J Innes and J Rabinowitz, *Management Accounting for Design,* Management Accounting, September 1997)

2.9 Target costing requires managers to change the way they think about the relationship between cost, price and profit.

(a) The **traditional approach** is to **develop a product, determine the expected standard production cost** of that product and **then set a selling price** (probably based on cost) with a resulting profit or loss. Costs are controlled through variance analysis at monthly intervals.

(b) The **target costing approach** is to develop a **product concept** and the primary specifications for performance and design and then to **determine the price customers would be willing to pay** for that concept. The **desired profit margin is deducted from the price leaving a figure that represents total cost.** This is the target cost and the product must be capable of being produced for this amount otherwise the product will not be manufactured. **During the product's life the target cost will constantly be reduced** so that the **price can fall. Continuous cost reduction techniques** must therefore be employed.

The target costing process

2.10 *Step 1.* **Analyse the external environment** to ascertain what customers require and what competitors are producing. Determine the **product concept**, the **price** customers will be willing to pay and thus the **target cost**.

Step 2. **Split the total target cost into broad cost categories** such as development, marketing, manufacturing and so on. **Then split up the manufacturing target cost per unit across the different functional areas of the product. Design the product so that each functional product area can be made within the target cost.** If a functional product area cannot be made within the target cost, so that a **cost gap** exists between the currently achievable cost and the target cost, the targets for the other areas must be reduced, or the product redesigned or scrapped. The product should be developed in an atmosphere of **continuous improvement** using **value engineering techniques** and **close collaboration with suppliers,** to enhance the product (in terms of service, quality, durability and so on) and reduce costs.

> ### KEY TERM
>
> **Value engineering** aims to help design products which meet customer requirements at the lowest cost while assuring the required standards of quality and reliability are maintained.

Step 3. Once it is decided that it is feasible to meet the total target cost, **detailed cost sheets** will be prepared and **processes formalised**.

2.11 It is possible that management may decide to go ahead and manufacture a product whose target cost is well below the currently attainable cost (so that there is a **cost gap**), the currently attainable cost being determined by current technology and processes. If this is the case management will **set benchmarks for improvement** towards the target costs, by specified dates.

2.12 **Options available to reduce costs**

- **Training** staff in more efficient techniques
- Using **cheaper staff**
- Acquiring new, more **efficient technology**
- Cutting out **non-value-added activities**

2.13 Even if the product can be produced within the target cost the story does not end there. **Once the product goes into production target costs will gradually be reduced.** These reductions will be incorporated into the budgeting process. This means that cost savings must be actively sought and made continuously. Value analysis will be used to reduce costs if and when targets are missed.

> ### KEY TERM
>
> **Value analysis** involves examining the factors which affect the cost of a product or service, so as to devise ways of achieving the intended purpose most economically at the required standards of quality and reliability.

The target costing process

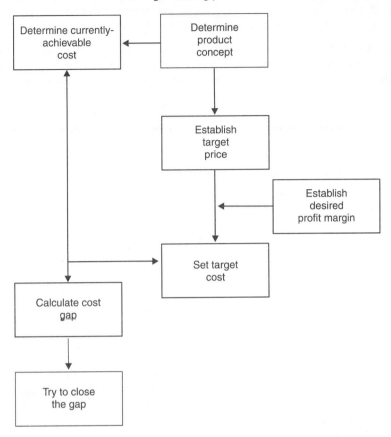

Case example

The following comments appeared in an article in the *Financial Times* in January 1993. (Emphasis is BPP's.)

'Mercedes-Benz, one of the world's most prestigious and tradition-laden carmakers, has taken its time to wake up to the daunting dimensions of the challenges it faces in the **rapidly-changing world car market** of the 1990s.

The company has accepted that radical changes in the world car market mean that Mercedes-Benz will no longer be able to demand premium prices for its products based on an image of effortless superiority and a content of the ultimate in automotive engineering.

Instead of developing the ultimate car and then charging a correspondingly sky-high price as in the past, Mercedes-Benz is taking the dramatic and radical step of moving to 'target pricing'. **It will decide what the customer is willing to pay** in a particular product category – priced against its competitors – it will **add its profit margin** and then the real work will begin to **cost every part and component to bring in the vehicle at the target price**.

The following extracts are from an article which appeared three months later.

'The marketing motto for the Mercedes-Benz compact C-class is that it offers customers more car for their money.

It is the first practical example of the group's new pricing policy. The range embodies a principle new to Mercedes which states that **before any work starts a new product will be priced according to what the market will bear and what the company considers an acceptable profit. Then each component and manufacturing process will be costed to ensure the final product is delivered at the target price**.

Under the old system of building the car, adding up the costs and then fixing a price, the C-class would have been **between 15 per cent and 20 per cent dearer** than the 10-year-old outgoing 190 series, Mr Vöhringer said.

Explaining the practical workings of the new system, he explained that project groups for each component and construction process were instructed without exception to increase productivity by between 15 and 25 per cent. And they had to reach their targets in record time.

One result was that development time on the new models was cut to 40 months, about a third less than usual. But the most important effect, according to Mr Vöhringer, has been to **reduce** the **company's cost disadvantages** *vis-à-vis* **Japanese competitors in this class from 35 per cent to only 15 per cent.**'

Question: standard costing v target costing

Fill in the blank spaces ((a) to (d)) in the table below to show how standard costing and target costing differ.

Stage in product lifecycle	Standard costing approach	Target costing approach
Product concept stage	No action	(a)
Design stage	(b)	Keep costs to a minimum
Production stage	Costs are controlled using variance analysis	(c)
Remainder of life	(d)	Target cost reduced, perhaps monthly

Answer

(a)   Set the selling price and required profit and determine the resulting target cost
(b)   Set standard cost and a resulting standard price
(c)   Constant cost reduction
(d)   Standards usually revised annually

3   BACKFLUSH ACCOUNTING

> **ATTENTION**
>
> Along with JIT, backflush accounting was the topic of an article by the examiner which appeared in the April 2004 edition of the *Student Accountant*.

3.1   Backflush accounting is the name given to the method of keeping cost accounts employed if **backflush costing** is used. The two terms are almost interchangeable.

3.2   **Traditional costing systems** use **sequential tracking** (also known as **synchronous tracking**) to track costs sequentially as products pass from raw materials to work in progress, to finished goods and finally to sales. In other words, material costs are charged to WIP when materials are issued to production, direct labour and overhead costs are charged in a similar way as the cost is incurred or very soon after.

3.3   If a production system such as **JIT** is used, sequentially tracking means that **all entries are made at almost the same moment** and so a different accounting system can be used. In **backflush costing/accounting, costs are calculated and charged when the product is sold, or when it is transferred to the finished goods store.**

KEY TERM

Backflush costing is 'a more simplified costing system for allocating costs between inventories and cost of goods sold...... The purpose of this is to eliminate detailed accounting transactions. Rather than tracking the movement of materials through the production process, a backflush costing system focuses first on the output of the organisation and then works backwards when allocating cost between costs of goods sold and inventories, with no separate accounting for WIP.'

Drury

3.4 The rather unattractive name for the system comes from the fact that **budgeted or standard costs are used to work backwards to 'flush' out manufacturing costs** for the units produced. The application of **standard costs** to finished goods units, or to units sold, is used in order to **calculate cost of goods sold**, thereby **simplifying** the costing system and creating **savings in administrative effort. In a true backflush accounting system, records of materials used and work in progress** are **not required** as material cost can be calculated from either finished goods or goods sold.

3.5 Backflush costing runs **counter to the principle enshrined in SSAP 9**, and the staple of cost accounting for decades, that stock and WIP should be accounted for by calculating cost and net realisable value of 'each item of stock separately'. The substantial **reduction in stocks that is a feature of JIT** means that **stock valuation is less relevant,** however, and therefore the **costing system** can be **simplified** to a considerable extent. In the 1980s, Johnson & Kaplan in fact wrote that **management rarely requires a value to be placed on stock for internal management purposes,** the **value only being required for external reporting.**

3.6 Backflush costing is therefore **appropriate** for organisations trying to keep **stocks to the very minimum.** In such circumstances, the **recording** of every little increase in stock value, as each nut and bolt is added, is simply an expensive and **non-value-added activity** that should be **eliminated**.

3.7 EXAMPLE: WORKING BACKWARDS FROM OUTPUT

To take a **very simplified example**, if backflush costing is used, the management accountant might extract the following information from the monthly accounting transaction records and production records.

Orders completed and despatched in July	196 units
Orders prepared in advance 1 July	3 units
Orders prepared in advance 31 July	2 units
Scrapped items	5 units
Conversion costs in the month	£250,000
Material costs in the month	£475,000

This is enough to place a value on stocks and production as follows.

	Units		£
B/f	(3)	Conversion costs	250,000
Despatched	196	Material costs	475,000
Scrapped	5	Total costs	725,000
C/f	2		
Units produced	200		

Cost per unit is £725,000 divided by 200 units = £3,625

In this case a single process account could be drawn up as follows.

	Dr (£)	Cr (£)
Stock b/fwd (3 × £3,625)	10,875	
Materials	475,000	
Conversion costs	250,000	
To finished goods (196 × £3,625)		710,500
Losses etc written off to P& L (5 × £3,625)		18,125
Stock c/fwd (2 × £3,625)		7,250
	735,875	735,875

3.8 **Arguments of traditional management accountants**

(a) The figure for **losses** here is **inaccurate**. They would say that in reality the faulty goods would have been scrapped when only partially complete and it is wrong to value them at the same cost as a fully finished good unit.

(b) Using this approach, the figure for stocks b/fwd and c/fwd will not tie up with the accounts for last month and next month, because the material and conversion costs may be different.

3.9 **Reply of modern management accountants**

(a) **Losses** represent only about 2% of total cost and are **not material**. In any case putting a value to them is less **important** than **improving the quality of production procedures** (on the basis of **TQM** practices and non-financial production information) to ensure that they do not occur again.

(b) **Finished good stocks represent between 1% and 2% of total cost and are immaterial.** Slight discrepancies in valuation methods of b/fwds and c/fwds will amount to a **fraction** of a percentage, and can be written off in the month as a small **variance**.

(c) Even with computers the **cost of tracing units** every step of the way through production – with 'normal' and 'abnormal' losses, equivalent units and numerous process accounts – **is simply not worth it, in terms of the benefit derived** from the information it provides.

Variants of backflush costing

3.10 (a) **Trigger points determine when the entries are made in the accounting system.** There will be either one or two trigger points that trigger entries in the accounts.

(i) When materials are purchased/received
(ii) When goods are completed or when they are sold

In a **true JIT system** where no stocks are held the **first trigger**, when raw materials are purchased, is **unnecessary**.

(b) **Actual conversion costs are recorded as incurred,** just as in conventional recording systems. **Conversion costs are applied to products at the second trigger point based on a standard cost**. It is assumed that any conversion costs not applied to products are carried forward and disposed of at the period end.

(c) **Direct labour** is included as an **indirect cost in conversion cost with overheads**. (Production is only required when there is demand for it in a JIT system, and so production labour will be paid regardless of the level of activity.)

(d) All **indirect costs** are treated as a **fixed period expense**.

3.11 EXAMPLE: ACCOUNTING ENTRIES AT DIFFERENT TRIGGER POINTS

The transactions for period 8 20X1 for Clive Ltd are as follows.

Purchase of raw materials	£24,990
Conversion costs incurred	£20,220
Finished goods produced (used in methods 2 & 3 only)	4,900 units
Sales	4,850 units

There are no opening stocks of raw materials, WIP or finished goods. The standard cost per unit is made up of £5.10 for materials and £4.20 for conversion costs.

3.12 SOLUTION FOR 1 TRIGGER POINT – when goods are sold (method 1)

This is the simplest method of backflush costing. There is only one **trigger point** and that is **when the entry to the cost of goods sold account is required** when the goods are sold. (This method assumes that units are sold as soon as they are produced.)

			£	£
(a)	DEBIT	Conversion costs control	20,220	
	CREDIT	Expense creditors		20,220
	Being the actual conversion costs incurred			
(b)	DEBIT	Cost of goods sold (4,850 × £9.30)	45,105	
	CREDIT	Creditors (4,850 × £5.10)		24,735
	CREDIT	Conversion costs allocated (4,850 × £4.20)		20,370
	Being the standard cost of goods sold			
(c)	DEBIT	Conversion costs allocated	20,370	
	CREDIT	Cost of goods sold		150
	CREDIT	Conversion costs control		20,220
	Being the under or over allocation of conversion costs			

3.13 SOLUTION FOR 1 TRIGGER POINT – when goods are completed (method 2)

This is very similar to the solution above but in this instance the **trigger** is the completion of a unit and its **movement into finished goods store**. The accounting entries are as follows.

			£	£
(a)	DEBIT	Conversion costs control	20,220	
	CREDIT	Expense creditors		20,220
	Being the actual conversion costs incurred			
(b)	DEBIT	Finished goods stock (4,900 × £9.30)	45,570	
	CREDIT	Creditors (4,900 × £5.10)		24,990
	CREDIT	Conversion costs allocated (4,900 × £4.20)		20,580
	Being the standard cost of goods produced			
(c)	DEBIT	Cost of goods sold (4,850 × £9.30)	45,105	
	CREDIT	Finished goods stock		45,105
	Being the standard cost of goods sold			
(d)	DEBIT	Conversion costs allocated	20,580	
	CREDIT	Cost of goods sold		360
	CREDIT	Conversion costs control		20,220
	Being the under or over allocation of conversion costs			

The end of period finished goods stock balance is £465 (50 × £9.30).

Question: backflush accounting

RM Ltd uses backflush accounting in conjunction with JIT. The system does not include a raw material stock control account. During control period 7, 300 units were produced and sold and conversation costs of £7,000 incurred. The standard unit cost is £55, which includes material of £25.

What is the debit balance on the cost of goods sold account at the end of control period 7?

Answer

	£
Conversion cost allocated to cost of goods sold a/c = 300 × (£55 – 25)	9,000
Conversion cost incurred	7,000
Difference set against cost of goods sold a/c	2,000
Standard charge to cost of goods sold a/c (300 × £55)	16,500
Charge to cost of goods sold a/c	14,500

3.14 SOLUTION FOR 2 TRIGGER POINTS – (method 3)

There are two **trigger points**, the **first** when **materials and components are received** and the **other** at the **point of transfer to finished goods**.

			£	£
(a)	DEBIT	Raw materials	24,990	
	CREDIT	Creditors		24,990
	Being the purchase of raw materials on credit			
(b)	DEBIT	Conversion costs control	20,220	
	CREDIT	Expense creditors		20,220
	Being the actual conversion costs incurred			
(c)	DEBIT	Finished goods stock (4,900 × £9.30)	45,570	
	CREDIT	Raw materials		24,990
	CREDIT	Conversion costs allocated		20,580
	Being the standard cost of goods produced			
(d)	DEBIT	Cost of goods sold (4,850 × £9.30)	45,105	
	CREDIT	Finished goods stock		45,105
	Being the standard cost of goods sold			
(e)	DEBIT	Conversion costs allocated	20,580	
	CREDIT	Cost of goods sold		360
	CREDIT	Conversion costs control		20,220
	Being the under or over allocation of conversion costs			

3.15 Here are the ledger accounts in respect of the above transactions.

RAW MATERIALS

	£			£
Creditors	24,990		Finished goods	24,990

FINISHED GOODS

	£			£
Raw materials	24,990		Cost of goods sold	45,105
Conversion costs	20,580		Balance c/f	465
	45,570			45,570

CONVERSION COSTS

	£		£
Creditors	20,220	Finished goods	20,580
Balance c/f	360		
	20,580		20,580

COST OF GOODS SOLD

	£		£
Finished goods	45,105	Profit and loss account	45,105

3.16 Note that the **WIP account is eliminated** using all methods. In a JIT system the vast majority of manufacturing costs will form part of the cost of sales and will not be deferred in closing stock values. In such a situation the amount of work involved in tracking costs through WIP, cost of sales and finished goods is unlikely to be justified. This considerably **reduces the volume of transactions recorded** in the internal accounting system.

3.17 The successful operation of backflush costing rests upon **predictable levels of efficiency** and **stable material prices and usage**. In other words there should be **insignificant cost variances**.

Possible problems with backflush costing

3.18 (a) **It is only appropriate for JIT operations** where production and sales volumes are approximately equal.

(b) Some people claim that it **should not be used for external reporting** purposes. If, however, **stocks are low** or are practically **unchanged** from one accounting period to the next, operating income and stock valuations derived from backflush accounting will **not be materially different from the results using conventional systems**. Hence, in such circumstances, backflush accounting is acceptable for external financial reporting.

(c) It is **vital** that adequate production controls exist so that **cost control during the production process is maintained**.

Advantages of backflush costing

3.19 (a) It is much **simpler**, as there is no separate accounting for WIP.

(b) Even the **finished goods** account is **unnecessary**, as we demonstrated in the first example above.

(c) The number of **accounting entries should be greatly reduced**, as are the supporting vouchers, documents and so on.

(d) The system should **discourage** managers from **producing simply for stock** since working on material does not add value until the final product is completed or sold.

Question: backflush accounting and behavioural issues

How might backflush accounting, with goods being sold as the one trigger point, be said to manipulate employees to behave in a certain way?

Answer

Employees have to concentrate on making sales because cost of sales is the trigger, and so nothing gets recorded until a sale is made.

Unlike in traditional systems, when management can increase profit by producing for finished goods stock, there is no benefit in producing for stock.

4 ENVIRONMENTAL MANAGEMENT ACCOUNTING

> **KEY TERM**
>
> **Environmental management accounting (EMA)** 'is the generation and analysis of both financial and non-financial information in order to support internal environmental management processes'.   *Shane Johnson (Paper 3.3 examiner)*

4.1 In the January 2004 edition of *Student Accountant*, there was an **article** on environmental management accounting by the **examiner**. We have **reproduced** this article in full at the **back of the text**. We strongly recommend that you read through this article very carefully, as its appearance could suggest the inclusion of the topic in one of the next few sittings of the exams.

4.2 The **main points** made in the article are as follows.

(a) **Major incidents** like the Bhopal chemical leak and the Exxon Valdez oil spill have significantly **raised the profile of environmental issues** over the last 20 years or so.

(b) Poor environmental behaviour can result in **'fines, increased liability to environmental taxes, loss in value of land, destruction of brand values, loss of sales, consumer boycotts, inability to secure finance, loss of insurance cover, contingent liabilities, law suits, and damage to corporate image'**.

(c) Environmental issues need to be **managed before they can be reported** externally, and so changes are needed to management accounting systems.

(d) Management accounting techniques tend to **underestimate** the **cost** of poor environmental behaviour, underestimate the benefits of improvements and can **distort** and **misrepresent** environmental issues, leading managers to make **decisions that are bad** for business and bad for the environment.

(e) Most **conventional accounting systems** are unable to apportion **environmental costs** to products, processes and services and so they are simply **classed as general overheads**. 'Consequently, managers are unaware of these costs, have no information with which to manage them and have no incentive to reduce them.' Environmental management accounting (EMA), on the other hand, attempts to make all relevant, significant costs visible so that they can be considered when making business decisions.

(f) Management accounting techniques which are useful for the identification and management of environmental costs include:

(i) **Input/output analysis** ('records material flows with the idea that 'what comes in must go out – or be stored")

(ii) **Flow cost accounting** (aims to reduce the quantities of materials, which leads to increased ecological efficiency)

(iii) **ABC** (distinguishes between environment-related costs and environment-driven costs)

(iv) **Life cycle costing** (used to advantage by Xerox Limited for its logistic chain)

(g) The major areas for the application of EMA are 'in the assessment of **annual environmental costs/expenditures, product pricing, budgeting, investment appraisal, calculating costs and savings of environmental projects,** or **setting quantified performance targets**'.

(h) Good environmental management can be seen as a **key component of TQM** (objectives such as zero waste).

(i) Although various classifications have been suggested, 'The most significant **problem** of EMA lies in the **absence of a clear definition of environmental costs**. This means that organisations are not monitoring and controlling such costs.'

4.3 Martin Bennett and Peter James ('The green bottom line: management accounting for environmental improvement and business benefit', *Management Accounting*, November 1998) looked at the **ways in which a company's concern for the environment can impact on its performance.**

(a) **Short-term savings** through waste minimisation and energy efficiency schemes can be substantial.

(b) Companies with poor environmental performance may face **increased cost of capital** because investors and lenders demand a higher risk premium.

(c) There are a growing number of **energy and environmental taxes**, such as the UK's landfill tax.

(d) **Pressure group campaigns** can cause damage to reputation and/or additional costs.

(e) Environmental legislation may cause the '**sunsetting**' of products and opportunities for '**sunrise' replacements**.

(f) The cost of processing input which becomes **waste** is equivalent to 5-10% of some organisation's turnover.

(g) The phasing out of CFCs has led to markets for alternative products.

4.4 They went on to suggest six main **ways in which business and environmental benefits can be achieved.**

(a) **Integrating the environment into capital expenditure decisions** (by considering environmental opposition to projects which could affect cash flows, for example)

(b) **Understanding and managing environmental costs.** Environmental costs are often 'hidden' in overheads and environmental and energy costs are often not allocated to the relevant budgets.

(c) **Introducing waste minimisation schemes**

(d) **Understanding and managing life cycle costs.** For many products, the greatest environmental impact occurs upstream (such as mining raw materials) or downstream from production (such as energy to operate equipment). This has led to producers being made responsible for dealing with the disposal of products such as cars, and government and third party measures to influence raw material choices. Organisations therefore need to identify, control and make provision for environmental life cycle costs and work with suppliers and customers to identify environmental cost reduction opportunities.

(e) **Measuring environmental performance.** Business is under increasing pressure to measure all aspects of environmental performance, both for statutory disclosure reasons and due to demands for more environmental data from customers.

(f) **Involving management accountants in a strategic approach to environment-related management accounting and performance evaluation.** A 'green accounting team' incorporating the key functions should analyse the strategic picture and identify opportunities for practical initiatives. It should analyse the short-, medium- and long-term impact of possible changes in the following.

- **Government policies,** such as on transport
- **Legislation and regulation**
- **Supply conditions,** such as fewer landfill sites
- **Market conditions,** such as changing customer views
- **Social attitudes,** such as to factory farming
- **Competitor strategies**

Possible action includes the following.

(i) Designating an **'environmental champion'** within the strategic planning or accounting function to ensure that environmental considerations are fully considered.

(ii) Assessing whether **new data sources** are needed to collect more and better data

(iii) Making **comparisons** between sites/offices to highlight poor performance and generate peer pressure for action

(iv) Developing **checklists** for internal auditors

Such analysis and action should help organisations to better understand present and future environmental costs and benefits.

We return to environmental issues in terms of organisational objectives in Chapter 10.

5 OTHER RECENTLY ADOPTED MANAGEMENT ACCOUNTING TECHNIQUES

Customer profitability analysis

5.1 In certain circumstances a useful approach to performance evaluation may be the analysis of **profitability by customer** or customer group. Profitability can vary widely between different customers because various **overhead costs** are, to some extent, variable and **'customer-driven'**. These overheads include things like discounts and distribution costs.

5.2 Customer profitability analysis relates these variabilities in cost to individual customers or customer groups. Managers can use this information to check whether or not individual customers are actually profitable to sell to, and to assess whether profitability can be improved for any customer by switching effort from one type of overhead activity to another, or by reducing spending on some overhead activities. We look at this topic in more detail in Chapter 21.

Zero based budgeting

5.3 As you will see later in the text, zero based budgeting (ZBB) was developed in the 1970s in an attempt to provide more efficiency and effectiveness in budgeting.

Strategic management accounting

5.4 This is something we looked at in depth in Chapter 1 and which we revisit in Chapter 16.

Theory of constraints

5.5 The theory of constraints (TOC) is an **approach to production management**. Its key financial concept is to turn materials into sales as quickly as possible, thereby maximising the net cash generated from sales. This is achieved by striving for balance in production processes, and so evenness of production flow is also an important aim.

> **KEY TERMS**
>
> **Theory of constraints (TOC)** is an approach to production management which aims to maximise sales revenue less material and variable overhead cost. It focuses on factors such as bottlenecks which act as constraints to this maximisation.
>
> **Bottleneck resource** or **binding constraint** – an activity which has a lower capacity than preceding or subsequent activities, thereby limiting throughput.
>
> *CIMA Official Terminology*

5.6 **One process will inevitably act as a bottleneck** (or limiting factor) and constrain throughput – this is known as the **binding constraint** in TOC terminology. Steps should be taken to remove this by buying more equipment, improving production flow and so on. But ultimately there will always be a binding constraint, unless capacity is far greater than sales demand or all processes are totally in balance, which is unlikely.

5.7 **Output through the binding constraint should never be delayed or held up otherwise sales will be lost**. To avoid this happening a **buffer stock should be built up immediately prior to the bottleneck** or binding constraint. **This is the only stock that the business should hold,** with the exception of possibly a very small amount of finished goods stock and raw materials that are consistent with the JIT approach.

5.8 **Operations prior to the binding constraint should operate at the same speed as the binding constraint**, otherwise work in progress (other than the buffer stock) will be built up. According to TOC, stock costs money in terms of storage space and interest costs, and so **stock is not desirable.**

5.9 **The overall aim of TOC is to maximise throughput contribution (sales revenue – material cost) while keeping conversion cost (all operating costs except material costs) and investment costs (stock, equipment and so on) to the minimum.** A strategy for increasing throughput contribution will only be accepted if conversion and investment costs increase by a lower amount than the increase in contribution.

Throughput accounting

5.10 The concept of throughput accounting has been developed from TOC as an **alternative system of cost and management accounting in a JIT environment.**

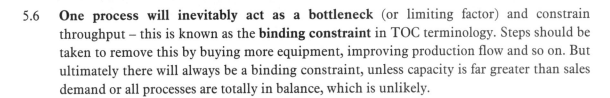

KEY TERM

Throughput accounting (TA) is an approach to accounting which is largely in sympathy with the JIT philosophy. In essence, TA assumes that a manager has a given set of resources available. These comprise existing buildings, capital equipment and labour force. Using these resources, purchased materials and parts must be processed to generate sales revenue. Given this scenario the most appropriate financial objective to set for doing this is the maximisation of throughput (Goldratt and Cox, 1984) which is defined as: sales revenue *less* direct material cost.

(Tanaka, Yoshikawa, Innes and Mitchell, *Contemporary Cost Management*)

5.11   TA for JIT is said to be based on three concepts.

(a)   **Concept 1**

In the short run, **most costs in the factory (with the exception of materials costs)** are fixed (the opposite of ABC, which assumes that all costs are variable). These fixed costs include direct labour. It is useful to group all these costs together and call them **Total Factory Costs (TFC)**

(b)   **Concept 2**

In a JIT environment, all stock is a 'bad thing' and the **ideal inventory level is zero.** Products should not be made unless there is a customer waiting for them. This means **unavoidable idle capacity in some operations must be accepted**, except for the operation that is the bottleneck of the moment.

Work in progress should be **valued at material cost only** until the output is eventually sold, so that no value will be added and no profit earned until the sale takes place. Working on output just to add to work in progress or finished goods stock creates no profit, and so should not be encouraged.

(c)   **Concept 3**

Profitability is determined by the rate at which 'money comes in at the door' (that is, sales are made) and, in a JIT environment, this depends on **how quickly goods can be produced to satisfy customer orders**. Since the goal of a profit-orientated organisation is to make money, stock must be sold for that goal to be achieved.

Question: throughput accounting

How are these concepts a direct contrast to the fundamental principles of conventional cost accounting?

Answer

Conventional cost accounting	Throughput accounting
Stock is an asset.	Stock is not an asset. It is a result of unsynchronised manufacturing and is a barrier to making profit.
Costs can be classified either as direct or indirect.	Such classifications are no longer useful.
Product profitability can be determined by deducting a product cost from selling price.	Profitability is determined by the rate at which money is earned.
Profit can be increased by reducing cost elements.	Profit is a function of material cost, total factory cost and throughput.

Bottleneck resources

5.12 The aim of modern manufacturing approaches is to match production resources with the demand for them. This implies that there are **no constraints, termed bottleneck resources** in TA, within an organisation. The throughput philosophy entails the identification and elimination of these bottleneck resources. Where it cannot be eliminated, and to avoid the build-up of work in progress, **production must be limited to the capacity of the bottleneck resource.** If a rearrangement of existing resources or buying-in resources does not alleviate the bottleneck, investment in new equipment may be necessary. The elimination of one bottleneck is likely to lead to the creation of another at a previously satisfactory location, however. The management of bottlenecks therefore becomes a primary concern of the manager seeking to increase throughput.

5.13 There are other factors which might limit throughput other than a lack of production resources (bottlenecks).

   (a) The existence of an uncompetitive selling price

   (b) The need to deliver on time to particular customers. If one customer's order has to take priority through the production process, orders for other customers will be held up in WIP.

   (c) The lack of product quality and reliability

   (d) The lack of reliable material suppliers

Is it good or bad?

5.14 TA is seen by some as **too short term,** as all costs other than direct material are regarded as fixed. Moreover, it **concentrates on direct material costs** and does nothing for the control of other costs such as overheads. These characteristics make throughput accounting a **good complement for ABC,** however, since ABC focuses on labour and overhead costs.

5.15 TA attempts to maximise throughput whereas traditional systems attempt to maximise profit. By attempting to maximise throughput an organisation could be producing in excess of the profit-maximising output. **Production scheduling** problems inevitably mean that the profit-maximising output is never attained, however, and so a **throughput maximising approach** could well **lead to the profit-maximising output** being achieved.

5.16 TA helps to direct attention to bottlenecks and focus management on the key elements in making profits, inventory reduction and reducing the response time to customer demand.

Financial and non-financial performance measures

5.17 As we will see later in the text, the collection and reporting of **non-financial quantitative and qualitative information** on key success factors has increased in **importance.** Non-financial performance measures tend to focus on quality, reliability, customer satisfaction, supplier performance and so on. A mass of measures now exists.

   (a) Measures may **conflict** so that one may be improved at the expense of another.

   (b) The value of the non-financial measures in achieving overall organisational success in financial terms is not always obvious.

5.18 The need to **link financial and non-financial measures** is therefore of increasing importance. The **balanced scorecard,** covered in Chapter 14, is an attempt to do this.

6 THE CHANGING PRACTICE OF MANAGEMENT ACCOUNTING

6.1 Cost management has two aspects.

(a) Finding out what causes costs to be incurred

(b) Using this knowledge to ensure that **costs are controlled in a way that helps with the achievement of an organisation's objectives**

6.2 To paraphrase Innes and Mitchell (*Overhead Cost*), **if costs are not incurred in order to satisfy customers by delivering appropriate products and services, at a time when they are wanted, at a standard and quality that is expected and at a price which is competitive, then costs are not being properly managed.**

6.3 The impact of an increased emphasis on cost management for the management accountant is discussed in Cooper's article in *Management Accounting* ('The Changing Practice of Management Accounting, March 1996). This may be summarised as follows.

(a) Management accounting is **growing in importance** because new cost management techniques require cost information that is not currently collected.

(b) Accounting information needed on the shop floor will be **collected by the (empowered) members of the workforce** who use the information, rather than by accountants.

(c) Management accountants will have a **supportive and monitoring role** rather than being deeply involved in the day-to-day work of management accounting.

(d) Management accountants will play a **key role** in **developing new information systems** in environments where management accounting has been weak in the past, such as public sector organisations. They will **need to work in partnership with functional specialists,** especially in organisations such as hospitals where an understanding of clinical processes is needed for effective cost management.

(e) **Many cost management techniques** (for example designing products with fewer components) **do not really rely on management accounting at all**.

(f) **IT reduces the need for management accountants** to be involved in the preparation and use of management accounting information, once the system has been designed and implemented.

7 BRINGING NEW TECHNIQUES TO THE AWARENESS OF MANAGEMENT ACCOUNTING PRACTITIONERS

7.1 Many of the recent developments in management accounting techniques were originated by **academic researchers**.

7.2 These academics are often examiners, teachers and textbook writers and so the **professional education system,** via the interaction of academics and future generations of accountants, is one of the most effective vehicles for introducing and establishing new ideas and practices into management accounting.

7.3 The **accounting press,** to which academics increasingly contribute, also brings research to the attention of accounting practitioners, and **consultancy firms** attempt to translate the results of academic research into improvements in management accounting systems – a process that may be difficult for practising management accountants due to day to day work pressures. Of course, this is not to say that it is impossible for practising accountants to develop new techniques as solutions to practical problems they encounter in their work environment.

7.4 **ABC** is probably one of the best known management accounting techniques to have arisen from academic research.

7.5 It was developed and publicised by Kaplan *et al* (via academic journals, a book and in conjunction with consultants) in the 1980s. The component parts of the overall idea of ABC may well have been used individually by practising accountants, but Kaplan developed them into a comprehensive theory for the modern manufacturing and service industries.

8   THE INFLUENCE OF STRUCTURE, CULTURE AND STRATEGY

8.1 The manner in which new methods and techniques are adopted will of course vary from organisation to organisation, from industry sector to industry sector.

8.2 For example, **service organisations** have historically had relatively unsophisticated budgeting and control systems and so they have an advantage over manufacturing organisations in that the introduction of **activity based approaches** is likely to be less disruptive to existing systems and more easily accepted by managers, to whom the whole concept of costing is new.

The influence of structure

8.3 In recent years there has been an emphasis on **flexibility** and **adaptability** in organisational structure, particularly since the pace of change in the technological and competitive environment has put pressure on businesses to innovate, to adopt a market orientation.

8.4 Part of this shift in emphasis has been a trend away from function-based structures towards **task-centred structures,** such as **multidisciplinary project teams,** which draw experience, knowledge and expertise together from different functions to facilitate **flexibility and innovation**. In particular, the concept of the **matrix organisation** has emerged. These involve dual reporting lines, so that an individual reports to a functional manager and an area manager. They therefore divide authority between functional managers and product or project team managers or co-ordinators – thus challenging classical assumptions about 'one man one boss'.

8.5 With interdisciplinary co-operation, mixing of skills and expertise, and increased responsibility of managers, such a structure facilitates the adoption of new methods and techniques.

8.6 More **formal and constrained structures,** such as heavily **centralised** structures, **restrict the flow of ideas** around the organisation. Managers have **insufficient authority** to try out new methods or techniques.

The influence of culture

8.7   Culture can have a significant impact on an organisation's willingness to embrace new methods and techniques.

8.8   For example, **bureaucratic cultures,** in which job descriptions establish definite tasks for each person's job and procedures are established for many work routines, are likely to **constrict the impetus for change**.

8.9   Organisations with cultures in which **predictability and reliability** are valued, in which **formal** ways of behaviour are encouraged, will continue to **use tried and tested methods** and techniques to maintain stability.

8.10   On the other hand, cultures in which **innovation** and **creativity** are highly prized, in which individuals are encouraged to **participate** and to get involved, in which **risk taking** is not frowned upon, will tend to be associated with **organisations using ABC** and other new methods and techniques.

8.11   Undoubtedly the most profound influences on western corporate culture in the 1990s have been ideas borrowed from **Japanese management**. 'Philosophies' such as JIT and TQM have a direct impact on business areas that have long been the preserve of accountants – purchasing and stock control, quality costs, waste and scrap and so on. And the Japanese **teamworking** approach is a radical change from the individualistic culture of the West.

The influence of strategy

8.12   Organisations that hope to compete effectively in today's competitive market need to adopt **strategies** which aim at **satisfying customers**. This requires a focus on **quality**, on **time** and on **innovation**. These key success factors can be most successfully achieved by adopting **TQM and JIT** (and hence throughput accounting).

8.13   Organisations pursuing strategies based on **cost efficiency** could find that use of **activity-based approaches**, **life cycle costing** and **customer profitability analysis** provide useful insights.

Exam focus point

In an exam, if asked how successful the adoption of new methods and techniques are likely to be in a particular organisations, think in terms of structure, culture and strategy. A heavily centralised organisation, where responsibility is vested in a board of ageing directors who have not read a journal or attended a conference in twenty years and who have followed the same strategy since 1960, is unlikely to adopt target costing.

9   THE CONTINUING EFFECTIVENESS OF TRADITIONAL TECHNIQUES

Standard costing in the modern environment

Exam focus point

The relevance of standard costing in the modern environment was examined in December 2003, while the relevance of traditional management accounting control systems was examined in June 2004.

Standard costing and new technology

9.1 Standard costing has traditionally been associated with labour-intensive operations, but it can be applied to capital-intensive production too.

9.2 It is quite possible that with advanced manufacturing technology variable overheads are incurred in relation to machine time rather than labour time, and **standard costs should reflect this** where appropriate.

9.3 With **computer aided design/computer aided manufacture (CADCAM)** systems, the planning of manufacturing requirements can be computerised, so that standard costs can be constructed by computer, saving administrative time and expense while providing far **more accurate standards**.

Standard costing and new philosophy

9.4 It has been argued that traditional variance analysis is unhelpful and **potentially misleading** in the modern organisation, and can make managers focus their attention on the wrong issues, for example **over-producing** and stockpiling finished goods, because higher production volumes mean that overheads are spread over more units. Here are two examples.

(a) **Efficiency variance.** Adverse efficiency variances should be avoided, which means that managers should try to prevent idle time and to keep up production. In a TQM environment using just-in-time manufacturing, action to eliminate idle time could result in the manufacture of unwanted products that must be held in store and might eventually be scrapped. Efficiency variances could focus management attention on the wrong problems.

(b) **Materials price variance.** In a JIT environment, the key issues with materials purchasing are supplier reliability, materials quality, and delivery in small order quantities. Purchasing managers shouldn't be shopping around every month looking for the cheapest price. Many JIT systems depend on long-term contractual links with suppliers, which means that material price variances are not relevant for control purposes.

9.5 The **role of standards and variances in the modern business environment** is viewed as follows by George Brown (examiner of the equivalent paper under the old syllabus).

> 'The rate of change in product type and design due to technological improvement, customer requirements and increased competition has led to rapid change in how businesses operate. The need to respond to customer demands for speedy availability of products, shortening product life cycles and higher quality standards has contributed to a number of changes in the way businesses operate...just-in-time systems...total quality programmes.....greater emphasis on the value chain.....accurate product costing and pricing information......improved speed and flexibility of information availability...'   ('Standard costing – a status check')

9.6 **Standard costing,** on the other hand, is most appropriate in a stable, standardised and repetitive environment and one of the main objectives of standard costing is to ensure that processes conform to standards, that they do not vary, and that variances are eliminated. This may seem **restrictive and inhibiting in the business environment of the twenty first century.** (In fact, in the article referred to above, George Brown attempts to show that concerns about the restrictive and inhibiting nature of standard costing have been raised since it was first used and that efforts have continuously been made (such as planning and operating variances) to redesign standards and variances to maintain their relevance in an environment of change.)

9.7 Other problems with using standard costing in today's environment

(a) Variance analysis concentrates on only a **narrow range of costs**, and does not give sufficient attention to issues such as quality and customer satisfaction.

(b) Standard costing places **too much emphasis on direct labour costs**. Direct labour is only a small proportion of costs in the modern manufacturing environment and so this emphasis is not appropriate.

(c) Many of the variances in a standard costing system focus on the control of **short-term variable costs**. In most modern manufacturing environments, the majority of costs, including direct labour costs, tend to be fixed in the short run.

(d) The use of standard costing relies on the existence of **repetitive operations** and relatively **homogeneous** output. Nowadays many organisations are forced continually to respond to customers' changing requirements, with the result that output and operations are not so repetitive.

(e) Standard costing systems were **developed** when the **business environment** was more **stable** and **less prone to change**. The current business environment is more dynamic and it is not possible to assume stable conditions.

(f) Standard costing systems **assume** that **performance to standard is acceptable**. Today's business environment is more focused on continuous improvement.

(g) Most standard costing systems produce **control statements weekly or monthly**. The modern manager needs much more prompt control information in order to function efficiently in a dynamic business environment.

Standard costing and TQM

9.8 Standard costing concentrates on **quantity** and ignores other factors contributing to effectiveness. In a **total quality environment**, however, quantity is not an issue; quality is. Effectiveness in such an environment therefore centres on high quality output (produced as a result of high quality input and the elimination of non-value adding activities) and the cost of failing to achieve the required level of effectiveness is measured not in variances, but in terms of **internal and external failure costs**, neither of which would be identified by a traditional standard costing analysis.

9.9 Standard costing systems might measure, say, **labour efficiency** in terms of individual tasks and level of **output.** In a total quality environment, labour is more likely to be viewed as a number of **multi-task** teams who are responsible for the completion of a part of the production process. The effectiveness of such a team is more appropriately measured in terms of **re-working** required, **returns** from customers, **defects** identified in subsequent stages of production and so on.

Quality-related costs

9.10 A concern for **good quality saves money**; it is **poor quality that costs money.**

> **KEY TERMS**
>
> **Prevention costs** represent the cost of any action taken to investigate, prevent or reduce defects and failures.
>
> **Appraisal costs** are the costs of assessing quality achieved.
>
> **KEY TERMS (cont'd)**

Internal failure costs are costs arising within the organisation of failure to achieve the quality specified.

External failure costs are costs arising outside the manufacturing organisation of failure to achieve specified quality (after transfer of ownership to the customer).

The **costs of conformance** are those incurred in ensuring that the level of quality required is achieved. Appraisal costs and prevention costs are costs of conformance.

Costs of non-conformance are incurred when the level of quality which should apply is not achieved. Internal and external failure costs are costs of non-conformance.

Quality-related costs	Example
Prevention costs	Quality engineering
	Design/development of quality control/inspection equipment
	Maintenance of quality control/inspection equipment
	Administration of quality control
	Training in quality control
Appraisal costs	Acceptance testing and performance testing
	Inspection of goods inwards
	Inspection costs of in-house processing
Internal failure costs	Failure analysis and re-inspection costs
	Losses from failure of purchased items
	Losses due to lower selling prices for sub-quality goods
	Costs of reviewing product specifications after failures
External failure costs	Administration and costs of customer complaints section
	Product liability costs
	Cost of repairing products returned from customers
	Cost of replacements due to sub-standard products/marketing errors

Can standard costing and TQM co-exist?

9.11 Arguably, there is little point in running both a total quality management programme and a standard costing system simultaneously.

(a) Predetermined standards are at odds with the philosophy of **continual improvement** inherent in a total quality management programme.

(b) Continual improvements are likely to alter methods of working, prices, quantities of inputs and so on, whereas standard costing is most appropriate in a stable, standardised and repetitive environment.

(c) Material standard costs often incorporate a planned level of scrap. This is at odds with the TQM aim of **zero defects** and there is no motivation to 'get it right first time'.

(d) Attainable standards, which make some allowance for wastage and inefficiencies are commonly set. The use of such standards conflicts with the **elimination of waste** which is such a vital ingredient of a TQM programme.

(e) Standard costing control systems make individual managers **responsible** for the variances relating to their part of the organisation's activities. A TQM programme, on the other hand, aims to make **all personnel** aware of, and responsible for, the importance of supplying the customer with a quality product.

Question: TQM and variance analysis

One of the basic tenets of total quality management is 'get it right first time'. Is variance reporting a help or a hindrance in this respect?

Answer

In theory it should not be of any relevance at all, because variances will not occur. In practice an organisation will not get everything right first time and variance reporting may still draw attention to areas for improvement - **if the standard and 'being right' are the same thing.**

The role in modern business of standards and variances

9.12 Two surveys ((Puxty and Lyall (1989) and Drury *et al* (1993)) have confirmed the **continued wide use of standard costing systems**. Drury *et al*, for instance, showed that 76% of the responding organisations operated a standard costing system.

9.13
- **Planning**. Even in a TQM environment, budgets will still need to be quantified. For example, the planned level of prevention and appraisal costs needs to be determined. Standards, such as returns of a particular product should not exceed 1% of deliveries during a budget period, can be set.

- **Control**. Cost and mix changes from plan will still be relevant in many processing situations.

- **Decision making**. Existing standards can be used as the starting point in the construction of a cost for a new product.

- **Performance measurement**. If the product mix is relatively stable, performance measurement may be enhanced by the use of a system of planning and operational variances.

- **Product pricing**. Target costs may be compared with current standards, and the resulting 'cost gap' investigated with a view to reducing it or eliminating it using techniques such as value engineering.

- **Improvement and change**. Variance trends can be monitored over time.

- **Accounting valuations**. Although the operation of a JIT system in conjunction with backflush accounting will reduce the need for standard costs and variance analysis, standards may be used to value residual stocks and the transfers to cost of sales account.

Question: variance analysis and product quality

AB plc has been receiving an increasing number of customer complaints about a general weakness in the quality of its products in recent months. The company believes that its future success is dependent on product quality and it is therefore determined to improve it.

Required

Describe the contribution that variance analysis can make towards the aim of improved product quality.

Answer

Variance analysis can be used to enhance product quality and to keep track of quality control information. This is because variance analysis measures both the planned use of resources and the actual use of resources in order to compare the two.

As variance analysis is generally expressed in terms of purely quantitative measures, such as quantity of raw materials used and price per unit of quantity, issues of quality would appear to be excluded from the reporting process. Quality would appear to be an excuse for spending more time, say, or buying more expensive raw materials.

Variance analysis, as it currently stands, therefore needs to be **adapted** to take account of quality issues.

(i) Variance analysis reports should routinely include **measures such as defect rates**. Although zero defects will be most desirable, such a standard of performance may not be reached at first. However there should be an expected rate of defects: if this is exceeded then management attention is directed to the excess.

(ii) The **absolute number of defects** should be measured *and* **their type**. If caused by certain materials and components this can shed light on, say, a favourable materials price variance which might have been caused by substandard materials being purchased more cheaply. Alternatively, if the defects are caused by shoddy assembly work this can shed light on a favourable labour efficiency variance if quality is being sacrificed for speed.

(iii) It should also be possible to provide **financial measures for the cost of poor quality**. These can include direct costs such as the wages of inspection and quality control staff, the cost of time in rectifying the defects, and the cost of the materials used in rectification.

(iv) Measures could be built into materials price and variance analysis, so that the **materials price variance** as currently reported includes a **factor reflecting the quality of materials purchased**.

Question: the value of standard costing today

Can you think of some ways in which a standard costing system could be adapted so that it is useful in the modern business environment?

Answer

Here are some ideas.

(a) **Non-financial measures** can be included within management control reports. Examples include number of defects, percentage of on-time deliveries, and so on.

(b) Even when output is not standardised, it may be possible to identify a number of **standard components and activities** whose costs may be controlled effectively by the setting of standard costs and identification of variances.

(c) The use of computer power enables standards to be **updated rapidly** and more frequently, so that they remain useful for the purposes of control by comparison.

(d) The use of **ideal standards** and **more demanding performance levels** can combine the benefits of **continuous improvement** and standard costing control.

(e) **Information**, particularly of a non-financial nature, can be **produced more rapidly** with the assistance of **computers**. For example the use of on-line data capture can enable the continuous display of real time information on factors such as hours worked, number of components used and number of defects.

Conventional budgeting in a changing environment

9.14 Surveys suggest that very few senior managers believe that conventional budget, cost centre and variance reporting is a 'very effective' control mechanism. Traditional budgetary control is seen as a **costly and burdensome** routine, reinforcing **bad practice** and **constraining response** in a rapidly changing commercial environment.

9.15 **Reasons for this**

(a) People prefer to be **in control**, and dislike **being** controlled. **Control has become constraint**, suffocating managerial initiative and running completely counter to the empowering philosophy of total quality and continuous improvement.

(b) The process of negotiation and adjustment that follows the initial budget proposals results in individual departmental budgets that **bear little relation to the strategy** that gave rise to the original proposals.

(c) Budgets are often expressed in **financial terms** using established ledger headings, which is convenient for the finance function but of limited use for departmental managers. **Non-financial measures** are the exception rather than the rule.

(d) Managers are inclined to reduce department budgets crudely. The errors that ensue and their correction in other parts of the organisation costs more overall than is saved by the original reduction.

Total Quality Management and budgeting

9.16 Total quality management is an organisational philosophy with two main themes, **get it right first time** and **continuous improvement**.

9.17 Where such a philosophy is adopted this has a number of implications for the use of budgeting and budgetary control.

(a) **Negative feedback** is a clear indication that the operation in question is falling short of the required target, assuming that '**not getting it right**' means failing to meet the budget.

(b) **Positive feedback** indicates that there is further potential for **improvement**: feedforward control action should be taken to encourage this in future periods.

We look at feedback in more detail later in the text.

9.18 The TQM approach has the potential to eliminate many of the unfortunate **behavioural** consequences of traditional budgetary control. It attempts to appeal to everybody's **innate desire to do better** and turns this into a corporate mission. Ideally where such an organisational culture has taken hold, the budgetary control system will be viewed by managers as part of the organisation's overall quality control system.

9.19 The **management accountant** can contribute here by being aware of the general movement within the organisation and taking a contingent approach, redesigning management reports in a **style and language** that is compatible with the philosophy. Far from usurping the role of budgets as the means of controlling performance, the TQM movement may offer budgetary control a new role as a key part of a more radical and broadly-based attempt to **change attitudes** and achieve goal congruence.

Activity based budgeting (ABB)

9.20 Implementing ABC leads to the realisation that the **business as a whole** needs to be **managed** with far more reference to the behaviour of activities and cost drivers identified. For example, traditional budgeting may make managers 'responsible' for activities which are driven by factors beyond their control: the **personnel department** cost of setting up new employee records is driven by the number of new employees required by managers **other than the personnel manager.**

9.21 ABB involves defining the activities that underlie the financial figures in each function and using the **level of activity** to decide how much resource should be **allocated**, how well it is being **managed** and to **explain variances** from budget.

9.22 ABB is therefore based on the following **principles**.

(a) It is activities which drive costs and the aim is to control the causes (drivers) of costs rather than the costs themselves, with the result that in the long term, costs will be better managed and better understood.

(b) Not all activities are value adding and so activities must be examined and split up according to their ability to add value.

(c) Most departmental activities are driven by demands and decisions beyond the immediate control of the manager responsible for the department's budget.

(d) Traditional financial measures of performance are unable to fulfil the objective of continuous improvement. Additional measures which focus on drivers of costs, the quality of activities undertaken, the responsiveness to change and so on are needed.

9.23 EXAMPLE: ABB

A stores department has two main activities, receiving deliveries of raw materials from suppliers into stores and issuing raw materials to production departments. Two major cost drivers, the number of deliveries of raw materials and the number of production runs, have been identified. Although the majority of the costs of the department can be attributed to the activities, there is a small balance, termed 'department running costs', which includes general administration costs, part of the department manager's salary and so on.

Based on activity levels expected in the next control period, the following cost driver volumes have been budgeted.

250 deliveries of raw materials
120 production runs

On the basis of budgeted departmental costs and the cost analysis, the following budget has been drawn up for the next control period.

Cost	Total £'000	Costs attributable to receiving deliveries £'000	Costs attributable to issuing materials £'000	Dept running costs £'000
Salaries – management	25	8	12	5
Salaries – store workers	27	13	12	2
Salaries – administration	15	4	5	6
Consumables	11	3	5	3
Information technology costs	14	5	8	1
Other costs	19	10	6	3
	111	43	48	20
Activity volumes		250	120	
Cost per unit of cost driver		£172	£400	£20,000

Points to note

(a) The apportionment of cost will be subjective to a certain extent. The objective of the exercise is that the resource has to be justified as supporting one or more of the activities. Costs cannot be hidden.

(b) The cost driver rates of £172 and £400 can be used to calculate product costs using ABC.

(c) Identifying activities and their costs helps to focus attention on those activities which add value and those that do not.

(d) The budget has highlighted the cost of the two activities.

9.24 Some writers treat ABB as a complete **philosophy** in itself and attribute to it all the good features of strategic management accounting, zero base budgeting, total quality management, and other ideas. For example, the following claims have been made.

(a) Different **activity levels** will provide a foundation for the 'base' package and incremental packages of **ZBB**.

(b) It will ensure that the organisation's overall **strategy** and any actual or likely changes in that strategy will be taken into account, because it attempts to manage the business as the **sum of its interrelated parts**.

(c) **Critical success factors** will be identified and performance measures devised to monitor progress towards them. (A critical success factor is an activity in which a business **must** perform well if it is to succeed).

(d) Because concentration is focused on the **whole of an activity**, not just its separate parts, there is more likelihood of **getting it right first time**. For example what is the use of being able to **produce** goods in time for their despatch date if the budget provides insufficient resources for the distribution manager who has to **deliver** them?

The future of budgeting

9.25 **Recent research** shows that **80%** of companies are **dissatisfied** with their planning and budgeting processes.

9.26 **Criticisms of traditional budgeting**

- Time consuming and costly
- Major barrier to responsiveness, flexibility and change
- Adds little value given the amount of management time required
- Rarely strategically focused
- Makes people feel undervalued
- Reinforces departmental barriers rather than encouraging knowledge sharing
- Based on unsupported assumptions and guesswork as opposed to sound, well-constructed performance data
- Developed and updated infrequently

9.27 **Ways in which companies are adapting planning and budgeting processes**

- Use of rolling forecasts
- Separation of the forecasting process from the budget to increase speed and accuracy and reduce management time
- Focus on the future rather than past performance
- Use of the balanced scorecard

9.28 Some companies such as the Swedish bank Svenska Handelsbanken (now one of Europe's most successful banks) have abandoned budgeting completely.

Chapter roundup

- Changes to the **competitive environment**, **product life cycles** and **customer requirements** have had a significant impact on the modern business environment.

- In the context of **TQM**, quality means getting it right first time and improving continuously.

- **Cellular manufacturing** aims to facilitate **just-in-time production** and obtain the associated improvements in quality and reductions in costs.

- **JIT** aims for zero inventory and perfect quality and operates by demand-pull. It consists of **JIT purchasing** and **JIT production** and results in lower investment requirements, space savings, greater customer satisfaction and increased flexibility.

- **AMT** helps organisations to be innovative and flexible and to be able to deal with short product life cycles.

- It has been argued that **traditional management accounting systems** are inadequate for a modern business environment that focuses on marketing, customer service, employee involvement and total quality, and for modern industry using AMT.

- **Life cycle costing** assists in the planning and control of a product's life cycle costs by monitoring spending and commitments to spend during a product's life cycle.

- **Target costing** is a pro-active cost control system. The target cost is calculated by deducting the target profit from a predetermined selling price based on customers' views. Techniques such as value analysis are used to change production methods and/or reduce expected costs so that the target cost is met.

- **Backflush accounting** is a method of accounting that can be used with JIT production systems. It saves a considerable amount of time as it avoids the need to make a number of accounting entries that are required by traditional cost accounting systems.

- **Environmental management accounting (EMA)** 'is the generation and analysis of both financial and non-financial information in order to support internal environmental management processes'.

- **Other recently adopted management accounting techniques** include the following.
    - Customer profitability analysis
    - Zero based budgeting
    - Strategic management accounting
    - Throughput accounting
    - Financial and non-financial performance measures

- The increased emphasis on **cost management** has had a significant impact on management accounting.

- Management accounting **practitioners** become aware of new techniques via the professional education system, the accounting press and consultancy firms.

- **Structure**, **culture** and **strategy** impact on the manner in which new methods and techniques are adopted.

- The **role of standards, variances and budgeting** in the modern business environment is open to question.

- Quality-related costs can be divided into **prevention**, **appraisal**, **internal failure** and **external failure costs**.

Quick quiz

1   Complete the table below to show a possible response to each of the traditional performance measures and a consequence of that response.

Measurement	Response	Consequence of action
Purchase price variance		
Labour efficiency variance		
Cost of scrap		
Scrap factor included in standard costs		

2   *Fill in the blanks.*

A target cost is an estimate of a product cost which is derived by subtracting .... from a ....

3   *Choose the appropriate word(s) from those highlighted in the following statements about throughput accounting.*

(a)   In the short run, most costs in the factory (with the exception of **labour/material** costs) are **fixed/variable**.

(b)   In a JIT environment, stock is a **good/bad** thing, and the ideal inventory level is **zero/based on the EOQ model**.

(c)   Unavoidable idle capacity in some operations **can never be accepted/must be accepted**.

(d)   Work in progress is valued at **material cost only/TFC**.

(e)   Profitability is determined at the rate at which **sales are made/goods are produced**.

4   Life cycle costing is particularly useful in an AMT environment, where 10% of a product's life cycle costs might be determined by decisions made early within the cycle at the design stage. *True or false?*

5   *Fill in the missing words.*

(a)   Standard costing concentrates on .... whereas the issue in TQM is ....

(b)   Using standard costing, the cost of failing to achieve the required level of effectiveness is measured in .... ; in TQM, it is measured in terms of ....

(c)   Standard costing systems might measure labour efficiency in terms of .... In a TQM environment, effectiveness is more appropriately measured in terms of ....

6   *Choose the correct words from those highlighted.*

(a)   Backflush accounting is a cost accounting system which focuses on the (1) **input/output** of an organisation and then works (2) **forwards/backwards** to allocate costs between cost of goods sold and stock.

(b)   The point at which a physical activity causes an entry in the accounts of a backflush system is known as the (3) **trigger point/bottleneck**.

Answers to quick quiz

1	Measurement	Response	Consequence of action
	Purchase price variance	Buy in greater bulk to reduce unit price	Excess stocks Higher holding costs Quality and reliability of delivery times ignored
	Labour efficiency variance	Encourage greater output	Possibly excess stocks of the wrong products
	Cost of scrap	Rework items to reduce scrap	Production flow held up by re-working
	Scrap factor included in standard costs	Supervisor aims to achieve actual scrap = standard scrap	No motivation to get it right first time

2   a desired profit margin
      competitive market price

3   (a)   material
             fixed

     (b)   bad
             zero

     (c)   must be accepted

     (d)   material cost only

     (e)   sales are made

4   False. The percentage is usually much higher.

5   (a)   quantity
             quality

     (b)   variances
             internal and external failure costs

     (c)   individual tasks and level of output
             reworking required, returns, defects

6   (1)   output
     (2)   backwards
     (3)   trigger point

Now try the question below from the Exam Question Bank

Number	Level	Marks	Time
4	Exam	20	36 mins

Chapter 5

TECHNOLOGICAL CHANGE AND MANAGEMENT ACCOUNTING

Topic list	Syllabus reference
1 Information needs of manufacturing and service businesses	1(c), 1(d)
2 Instant access to data	1(c), 1(d)
3 Remote input of data	1(c), 1(d)
4 Developing management accounting systems	1(c), 1(d)

Introduction

This chapter describes the **effect** of the **rate of change of technology on management accounting**. We begin by looking at the **changing information requirements** of business by contrasting the information needed by traditional manufacturing organisations with that needed by the service sector today.

In the second and third sections of the chapter we look at how modern IT systems have enabled the **remote input of and instant access to management accounting data**, while the final section looks at **how and why management accounting systems develop**.

Given the general nature of the topics covered in this chapter, you will not be surprised to learn that you encounter many of them again as you work through this text. Qualitative data and service businesses are two such topics.

Study guide

Section 5 – Technological change and management accounting

- Discuss the changing accounting information needs of modern service orientated business compared with the needs of traditional manufacturing industry

- Discuss how modern IT systems provide the opportunity for instant access to management accounting data throughout an organisation

- Discuss how modern IT systems facilitate the remote input of management accounting data in an acceptable format by non-finance specialists

- Explain how modern information systems provide instant access to previously unavailable data that can be used for benchmarking and control purposes

- Discuss the need for businesses to continually refine and develop their management accounting systems if they are to prosper in an increasingly competitive and global market

Exam guide

The Pilot paper demonstrates the potential importance of service businesses, as both of the compulsory questions are set in a service environment – a water supply business and a health centre.

The issues covered in this chapter are useful background to the following Oxford Brookes degree Research and Analysis Projects.

- Topic 2, which requires you to analyse how the application of technology can contribute to an organisation's efficiency and /or effectiveness
- Topic 5, which requires you to identify the effects of globalisation on an industry of your choice

1 INFORMATION NEEDS OF MANUFACTURING AND SERVICE BUSINESSES

Information needs of manufacturing businesses

1.1 All manufacturing businesses follow a simple model.

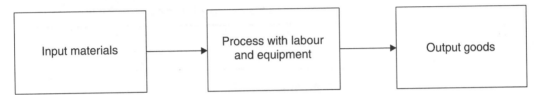

1.2 The information required by even modern manufacturing organisations is still based on the demands of this model.

1.3 A variety of performance indicators are used by manufacturing businesses, but there are some over-riding considerations.

Consideration	Detail
Cost behaviour	Labour is generally a variable cost. Machinery is a fixed cost. Modern technology requires more overheads. (With advanced manufacturing technology, there is a higher proportion of fixed equipment costs compared with variable labour costs.)
Quality	Important in terms of output adherence to production specification
Time	Production bottlenecks; delivery times; deadlines; machine speed
Innovation	Required in products and processes
Valuation	Despite the tendency towards low stock and just in time delivery, many businesses still have to give a value to stock of raw materials or finished goods, as a major element in their profit calculations. Whether complicated tracking systems are needed is a different question.

We look at the first four of these considerations in more detail in the following paragraphs.

1.4 **Cost behaviour information**

Uses	Comment
Planning	Standard costs can be outlined, and actual costs compared with them.
Decision making	Estimates of future costs may be needed to assess the likely profitability of a product.
Control	Total cost information can be monitored, to ensure the best rates for supplies.

1.5 **Quality** information is used to ensure that 'customer satisfaction' is built into the manufacturing system and its outputs.

Uses	Comment
Planning	Ensure that products are well designed and manufactured according to specification.
Decision making	Businesses have a choice as to what level of quality they 'build' into a product. Quality is not perfection, it is 'fitness for use'.
Control	Falling levels of quality are an alarm bell – if products are not manufactured according to their design specification, there will be more rejects, more waste and more dissatisfied customers. This means higher costs and lower profits.

1.6 **Time**

Uses	Comment
Planning	Manufacturing time has to be scheduled to ensure the most efficient use of the system; if production can be smoothed over a period, this ensures effective capacity utilisation. Throughput time is thus important.
Decision making	Time is relevant to decision making, as it indicates a firm's ability to keep its promises to its customers for delivery and so on.
Control	• New product development (from conception to implementation) • Speed of delivery • Bottlenecks • In just-in-time systems, where firms hold little material stocks, time is a measure of a factory's ability to function at all. Stock levels will be measured not in units but in day's supplies • As a measure of efficiency (eg stock turnover, asset turnover)

1.7 **Innovation**

Uses	Comment
Planning	• New product development • Speed to market • New process
Control	This generally refers to the launch and design of new products.

1.8 The **experience curve** can be used in strategic control of costs and is relevant to 'time' and 'innovation'. It suggests that as output increases, the cost per unit of output falls, for these reasons.

(a) **Economies of scale** - in other words an increased volume of production leads to lower unit costs, as the firm approaches full capacity.

(b) A genuine '**learning effect**' as the workforce becomes familiar with the job and learns to carry out the task more efficiently. As a process is repeated, it is likely that costs will reduce due to **efficiency, discounts** and **reduced waste**.

(c) **Technological improvements**.

1.9 This brings us on to **target costing**, already mentioned in Chapter 4.

(a) In the short run, because of development costs and the learning time needed, costs are likely to exceed price.

(b) In the longer term, costs should come down (for example, because of the experience curve) to their target level.

Strategic, tactical and operational information

1.10 The information requirements of manufacturing businesses can also be considered in terms of the three levels we covered in Chapters 1 and 2.

Information type	Examples
Strategic	Future demand estimates
	New product development plans
	Competitor analysis
Tactical	Variance analysis
	Departmental accounts
	Stock turnover
Operational	Production reject rates
	Materials and labour used
	Stock levels

1.11 The information requirements of commercial organisations are influenced by the need to make and monitor profit. Information that contributes to the following measures is important.

- Changeover times
- Number of common parts
- Level of product diversity
- Product and process quality

Service businesses

1.12 Before we delve into the detail, here's the big picture. According to 1997 figures, **32 of the top UK companies were in the service sector**, and 13 of these 32 employed over one million people in total.

1.13 Despite the apparent domination in the service sector as a whole by a few large companies, in reality **most service organisations are very small** (as normal experience would suggest): 98% of all service enterprises, for instance, have a turnover of less than £5 million. So we are talking of a very **large number** of organisations, many of them quite small, but collectively

Part A: Management accounting framework

accounting for a powerful proportion of the workforce: in 1996, the number of **people employed in the service sector** was more than **four times as large** as the numbers employed in **manufacturing**.

Types of service business

1.14 With this in mind, we can identify different types of service.

Type	Comment
Mass service	The delivery of the same, very standardised service to many people, as a transaction, for example cheque processing.
Personalised service	This service is unique to the recipient, such as dentistry: every mouth is different, even though standard procedures are adopted to ensure best practice.

1.15 **Examples of service businesses**

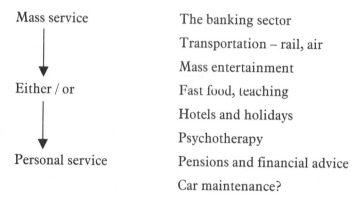

Mass service	The banking sector
	Transportation – rail, air
	Mass entertainment
Either / or	Fast food, teaching
	Hotels and holidays
	Psychotherapy
Personal service	Pensions and financial advice
	Car maintenance?

1.16 Service activities therefore cut across all sectors of the economy. In the UK, **healthcare** is provided by the **public sector** but also by the **private sector** (for-profit). The objectives may differ even though the activities remain the same.

> **KEY TERM**
>
> '**Services** are any activity of benefit that one party can offer to another that is essentially intangible and does not result in the ownership of anything. Its production may or may not be tied to a physical product.'
>
> (P Kotler, *Social Marketing*)

1.17 **Five major characteristics of services that distinguish services from manufacturing**

(a) **Intangibility** refers to the lack of substance which is involved with service delivery. Unlike goods (physical products such as confectionery), there is no substantial material or physical aspects to a service: no taste, feel, visible presence and so on. For example, if you go to the theatre, you cannot take the 'play' with you.

(b) **Inseparability/simultaneity.** Many services are created at the same time as they are consumed. (Think of **dental treatment**.) No service exists until it is actually being experienced/consumed by the person who has bought it.

(c) **Variability/heterogeneity.** Many services face the problem of maintaining **consistency in the standard of output**. It may be hard to attain precise standardisation of the service offered, but customers expect it (such as with fast food).

 88

(d) **Perishability.** Services are innately perishable. The services of a beautician are purchased for a period of time.

(e) **No transfer of ownership.** Services do not result in the transfer of property. The purchase of a service only confers on the customer access to or a right to use a facility.

1.18 Most 'offers' to the public contain a **product** and **service** element.

Quantitative/qualitative information and services

1.19 The **dental practice needs** a mix of **quantitative** and **non-quantitative** information to price its services properly, to optimise capacity utilisation and to monitor performance. Many small service businesses have similar concerns, for example garages or beauty parlours.

(a) They need to control the **total cost** of providing the **service operation**.

(b) They need positive **cash flow** to **finance activities**.

(c) They need **operating information** to identify how costs are incurred and on what services.

1.20 Arguably, small service businesses, whose expenses are mainly overheads, provide a model, in miniature, of the requirements of **activity based costing**, mentioned in Chapter 3.

1.21 Are '**mass services**' any different?

(a) Because mass services, such as cheque clearing, are largely automated, there may be a large **fixed cost base**.

(b) Even if a service is heavily automated, each time the service is performed is a 'moment of truth' for the customer. Ensuring consistency and quality is important but this is true for small service businesses too.

KEY TERMS

Quantitative information is information that can be expressed in numbers. A sub-category of quantitative information is **financial information** (also known as **monetary information**), which is information that can be expressed in terms of money.

Qualitative information is information that cannot be expressed in numbers.

Non-financial information (or **non-monetary information**) is information that is not expressed in terms of money, although this does not mean that it cannot be expressed in terms of money.

Question: monetary and non-monetary information

Identify some possible items of **monetary** and **non-monetary information** for a monthly report for a dentistry practice. (*Hint*. Ask yourself what is the key resource of the practice).

Answer

(a) **Monthly receipts and payments**

    (i)   Receipts include payments from the government for publicly-funded work, fees for private work and so on.

    (ii)   Payments include operating costs such as wages for nursing staff, reception staff, rent, insurance, electricity, telephone expenses, medical equipment, medicine and so on.

PROFESSIONAL EDUCATION

(b) **Capacity utilisation**. In other words, how busy has the practice been? Have all available appointments been booked or were there times when the dentist and his/her staff were kicking their heels? Just by looking at the **appointments diary** you can make comparatives.

(c) **Treatment costs.** This is slightly harder to estimate. Simple treatments such as teeth cleaning, can be performed by the dental hygienist. Other treatments, such as root canal surgery, require the dentist and perhaps a dental nurse in attendance.

The 'cost' of these resources differs, so there may be a standard price list. The **cost driver** is **time**.

The dentist will probably profit more from relatively expensive treatments, such as 'crowns', but these come at a cost.

The **mix** of treatments offered is thus significant, in the total profitability of the practice.

However, this information, while useful to monitor the financial health of the practice, does not give us a sufficiently detailed picture of the operating performance. The key resource is **time,** the dentist's time, and staff time.

For the **long-term health** of the practice, matters such as **customer satisfaction** and **repeat business** must be considered. (Does your dentist remind you to have a check up every six months?)

Question: quantitative v qualitative, financial v non-financial

Categorise the following statements as either financial, qualitative, quantitative or non-financial, whichever *one* of these you think is most appropriate.

(a) I bought 4 bananas.

(b) I bought £1's worth of bananas.

(c) I like bananas.

(d) I can afford 1lb of bananas.

Answer

We stressed that you should put each statement into one category only to make sure that you take in the essential points. For example, statement (a) is actually both quantitative and non-financial, but we would call it 'quantitative' only, because there is no suggestion of money being involved.

If you are uneasy about the idea that the statement 'I like bananas' *cannot* be expressed in monetary terms you are ready to read on.

1.22 Colin Drury (*Management and Cost Accounting*) describes **qualitative factors** as those 'that can be expressed in monetary terms only with much difficulty or imprecision'. Thus the information 'German people are very fond of bananas' could be expressed as 'The value of the German banana market is £x million pa', but the value of x is very questionable.

1.23 EXAMPLE: QUALITATIVE INFORMATION

As a more elaborate example, consider a firm which is thinking of sacking many of its customer service staff and replacing them by automated telephone answering systems. Now consider how difficult it would be to obtain the following information in order to appraise a decision whether or not to replace staff with an untested system.

(a) The cost of **being sure** that the new system would do the job as well as people can

(b) The cost of **loss of morale** amongst other workers if large numbers are made redundant

(c) The cost of **compensating** the redundant staff for the psychological and financial impact of the decision on themselves and their families

(d) The cost of **relocating** people

(e) The cost of **retraining** staff made redundant to improve their job prospects

(f)   The cost to the community in **social and financial terms** of unemployment or relocation

1.24   These are not just political points. The company's treatment of its staff may have a profound impact upon its ability to **recruit** skilled employees in the future and on the way the company is **perceived** by potential **customers**. Whether the costs can be established or not, the questions need to be considered.

1.25   **Service industries,** perhaps more than manufacturing firms, **rely on their staff**. Front-line staff are those who convey the 'service' – and the experience of the brand – to the consumer. They convey the 'moment of truth' with the customer.

Case example

In the late 1990s, BA went through a cost-cutting exercise, prompting a strike by airline service staff, leading to loss of business and damage to the brand.

1.26   Management **information** therefore has to include **intangible factors** such as how customers feel about the service, whether they would use it again, and so on.

1.27   There are some demonstrable relationships between **staff turnover** and **positive customer experiences**. High staff turnover not only means higher recruitment and training costs but it may also have an adverse impact on the firm's ability to **retain** customers (which is cheaper than finding new ones).

1.28   For service businesses, **management accounting information** should **incorporate** the **key drivers of service costs**.

- Repeat business
- Churn rate (for subscriptions)★
- Customer satisfaction surveys, complaints
- Opportunity costs of not providing a service
- Avoidable / unavoidable costs

★ For any given period of time, the number of participants who discontinue their use of a service divided by the average number of total participants is the churn rate. Churn rate provides insight into the growth or decline of the subscriber base as well as the average length of participation in the service.

Case example

Banks

UK clearing banks and building societies typically have high fixed costs of running a network of branches. At the same time, they are trying to promote internet and other services, as they are competing with internet-only banks, such as Egg.

The traditional banks have responded in a number of ways

- Set up their own internet operations, which offer higher rates of interest for savers
- Closing down branches, at a cost of adverse publicity at times

However, there have been some opposing trends

- NatWest, has advertised that it has put a moratorium on closure programmes
- Most of the internet banks are not making money; some see the benefit of opening branches

The key issue is productivity. The expensive branch networks are useful for selling other services.

Strategic, tactical and operational information

1.29 Just as we did for manufacturing businesses, we can consider the strategic, tactical and operational information requirements of service businesses.

Information type	Examples
Strategic	Forecast sales growth and market share
	Profitability, capital structure
Tactical	Resource utilisation such as average staff time charged out, number of customers per hairdresser, number of staff per account
	Customer satisfaction rating
Operational	Staff timesheets
	Customer waiting time
	Individual customer feedback

1.30 Organisations have become **more customer and results orientated** over the last decade. As a consequence, **the differences between service organisations' and other organisations' information requirements has decreased.** Businesses have realised that most of their activities can be measured, and many can be measured in similar ways regardless of the business sector.

2   INSTANT ACCESS TO DATA

Via distribution of data

2.1 Developments in IT have facilitated the distribution of data, making it instantly available to those who require it. Such developments are known generally as office automation systems.

- Word processing
- Electronic schedules
- Desktop databases (see below)
- Web publishing
- Voice mail
- E-mail

Via sharing of data

2.2 There have also been significant developments in the ways in which data can be shared.

Groupware

2.3 Groupware is a term used to describe **software** that provides **functions that can be used by collaborative work groups.**

2.4 Typically, groups using groupware are small project-oriented teams that have important tasks and tight deadlines.

2.5 **Features** might include the following.

(a) A **scheduler** allowing users to keep track of their schedule and plan meetings with others

(b) An **address book**

(c) '**To do**' lists

(d) A **journal,** used to record interactions with important contacts, items (such as e-mail messages) and files that are significant to the user, and activities of all types and track them all without having to remember where each one was saved

(e) A **jotter** for jotting down notes as quick reminders of questions, ideas, and so on

(f) File sharing and distribution utilities

2.6 There are clearly advantages in having information such as this available from the desktop at the touch of a button, rather than relying on scraps of paper, address books, and corporate telephone directories. It is when groupware is used to **share information** with colleagues that it comes into its own. Here are some of the features that may be found.

(a) **Messaging,** comprising an **e-mail** in-box which is used to send and receive messages from the office/home/on the road and **routing** facilities, enabling users to send a message to a single person, send it sequentially to a number of people (who may add to it or comment on it before passing it on), or sending it to everyone at once.

(b) Access to an **information database,** and customisable '**views**' of the information held on it, which can be used to standardise the way information is viewed in a workgroup.

(c) **Group scheduling,** to keep track of colleagues' itineraries.

(d) **Public folders**. These collect, organise, and share files with others on a team or across the organisation.

(e) **Hyperlinks** in mail messages. The recipient can click the hyperlink to go directly to a Web page or file server.

Intranets

> **KEY TERM**
>
> An **intranet** is an internal network used to share information. Intranets utilise Internet technology. A firewall surrounding an intranet fends off unauthorised access.

2.7 The idea behind an 'intranet' is that companies set up their own **mini version of the Internet.** Intranets use a combination of the organisation's own networked computers and Internet technology. Each employee has a browser, used to access a server computer that holds corporate information on a wide variety of topics, and in some cases also offers access to the Internet.

2.8 Potential applications include company newspapers, induction material, online procedure and policy manuals, employee web pages where individuals post details of their activities and progress, and **internal databases** of the corporate information store.

2.9 The **benefits** of intranets are diverse.

(a) Savings accrue from the **elimination of storage**, **printing** and **distribution** of documents that can be made available to employees on-line.

(b) Documents on-line are often **more widely used** than those that are kept filed away, especially if the document is bulky (eg manuals) and needs to be searched. This means that there are **improvements in productivity** and **efficiency**.

(c) It is much **easier to update** information in electronic form.

(d) Wider access to corporate information should open the way to **more flexible working patterns**, as material available on-line may be accessed from remote locations.

2.10 **Remote access** to intranets can be available **quickly** and **easily**. This means that people working at different parts of the organisation or away from the office can access data when they need it. Developments in IT allow information from a data warehouse (see below) to be displayed and Excel has facilities to post spreadsheets straight to the intranet and for users to drill down to the detail from a summary level.

Extranets

> **KEY TERM**
>
> An **extranet** is an intranet that is accessible to authorised outsiders.

2.11 Whereas an intranet resides behind a firewall and is accessible only to people who are members of the same company or organisation, an extranet provides various levels of accessibility to outsiders.

2.12 Only those outsiders with a valid username and password can access an extranet, with varying levels of access rights enabling control over what people can view. Extranets are becoming a very popular means for **business partners to exchange information**.

Databases

2.13 A **typical accounting application package** processes only one sort of data. A payroll file processes only payroll data and a stock file only stock data. An organisation might end up with separate files and processing subsystems for each area of the business. However, in many cases the underlying data used by each application might be the same. A major consequence is that data items are duplicated in a number of files (**data redundancy**). They are input more than once (leading to **errors and inconsistencies**) and held in several files (**wasting space**). For example, data relating to the hours which an hourly-paid employee has worked on a particular job is relevant both to the payroll system, as the employee's wages will be based on the hours worked, and to the job costing system, as the cost of the employee's time is part of the cost of the job.

2.14 The **problem of data redundancy is overcome**, partly at least, by an **integrated system**. An integrated system is a system where **one set of data is used for more than one application**. In a cost accounting context, it might be possible to integrate parts of the sales ledger, purchase ledger, stock control systems and nominal ledger systems, so that the data input to the sales ledger updates the nominal stock ledger automatically. The diagram below might make this more clear. It deals with stock control, sales order and purchases applications.

(a) **Application-specific systems**

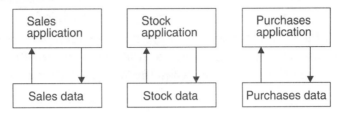

(b) **Integrated systems**

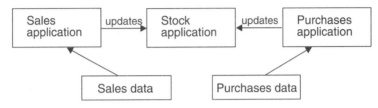

(c) **Database**

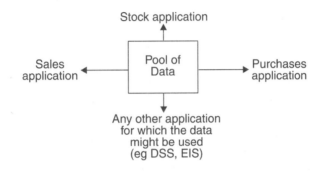

2.15 The integrated systems approach, where different applications update each other, is a half way house between a system based on separate application-specific files and a database approach.

> **KEY TERM**
>
> Broadly speaking, a **database** is a file of data organised in such a way that it can be used by many applications.

2.16 Using the example of hours worked given above, the following situations are possible.

(a) The employee's hours are **input twice**, once to the payroll application, once to the job costing system, in a non-integrated system of **application-specific files**.

(b) In an **integrated system**, the data would have been **input once**, to the payroll application. The payroll application would have been used to update the job costing application.

(c) In a **database system** it would only be **input once** and would be **immediately available to both systems**.

2.17 A database provides a **comprehensive file of data for a number of different users. Each user will have access to the same data,** and so different departments **cannot keep their own data files**, containing duplicate information but where the information on one file disagrees with the corresponding information on another department's file.

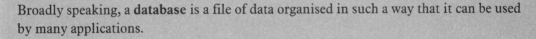

Database management systems

2.18 The database management system (DBMS) is a complex **software** system **which organises the storage of data in the database in the most appropriate way** to facilitate its storage, retrieval and use in different applications. It also provides the **link between** the **user and the data**. How a DBMS works is shown in the following diagram.

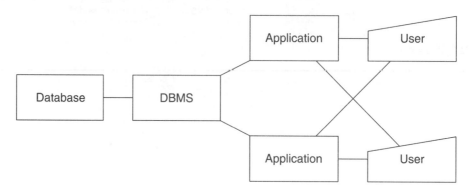

Data warehousing

2.19 A **data warehouse** contains **data from a range of internal** (eg sales order processing system, nominal ledger) **and external sources**. One reason for including individual transaction data in a data warehouse is that if necessary the user can drill-down to access transaction-level detail. Data is increasingly obtained from newer channels such as customer care systems, outside agencies or websites.

2.20 The warehouse provides a coherent **set of information** to be **used across the organisation** for management **analysis** and **decision making**. The reporting and query tools available within the warehouse should facilitate management reporting and analysis.

2.21 The reporting and query tools used within the warehouse need to be flexible enough to allow multidimensional data analysis, also known as on-line analytical processing (**OLAP**). Each aspect of information (eg product, region, price, budgeted sales, actual sales, time period and so on) represents a different dimension. OLAP enables data to be viewed from each dimension, allowing each aspect to be viewed in relation to the other aspects. So, for example, information about a particular product sold in a particular region during a particular period would be available on-line and instantly.

2.22 Organisations may build a single central data warehouse to serve the entire organisation or may create a series of smaller **data marts**. A data mart holds a selection of the organisation's data for a specific purpose.

2.23 A data mart can be constructed more quickly and cheaply than a data warehouse. However, if too many individual data marts are built, organisations may find it is more efficient to have a single data warehouse serving all areas.

2.24 **Advantages of setting up a data warehouse system**

   (a) Decision makers can access data without affecting the use of operational systems.

   (b) Having a wide range of data available to be queried easily encourages the taking of a wide perspective on organisational activities.

   (c) Data warehouses have proved successful in a number of areas.

      (i) Quantifying the effect of marketing initiatives

(ii)   Improving knowledge of customers

(iii)   Identifying and understanding an enterprise's most profitable revenue streams

(d)   Information can be made available to business partners. For example, if customer sales order information is in the data warehouse, it could be made available to customers and even suppliers. Internal information on products and services could also be provided.

2.25   The components of a data warehouse are shown in the following diagram.

Components of a data warehouse

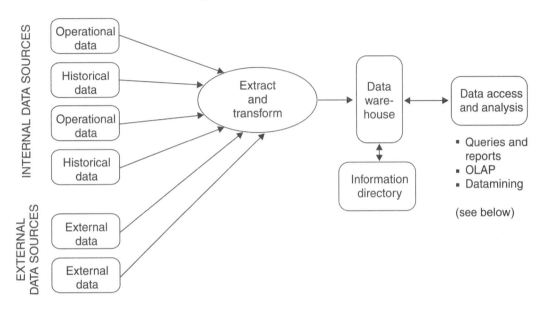

Datamining

KEY TERM

Datamining software looks for hidden patterns and relationships in large pools of data.

2.26   True datamining software discovers **previously unknown relationships**. Datamining provides insights that can not be obtained through OLAP. The hidden patterns and relationships the software identifies can be used to guide decision making and to **predict future behaviour**.

Case examples: Datamining

(1)   The American retailer Wal-Mart discovered an unexpected relationship between the sale of **nappies** and **beer!** Wal-Mart found that both tended to sell at the same time, just after working hours, and concluded that men with small children stopped off to buy nappies on their way home, and bought beer at the same time. Logically therefore, if the two items were put in the same shopping aisle, sales of both should increase. Wal-Mart tried this and it worked.

(2)   Some credit card companies have used datamining to predict which customers are likely to switch to a competitor in the next few months. Based on the datamining results, the bank can take action to retain these customers.

BPP
PROFESSIONAL EDUCATION

Case example

Data mining software

The following is extracted from marketing material for a data mining product called the *NeoVista Decision Series*. (Emphases provided by BPP).

Understand The Patterns In Your Business and Discover The Value In Your Data

Within your **corporate database** resides extremely **valuable information** - information that reflects how your **business processes operate** and how your **customers behave**. Every transaction your organisation makes is captured for accounting purposes, and with it, a wealth of potential knowledge.

When properly analysed, organised and presented, this information can be of enormous value. **Conventional 'drill down' database query techniques** may reveal some of these details, but much of the valuable knowledge content will remain hidden, simply because the **trends and relationships are not obvious to even the expert observer**.

The NeoVista Decision Series is a suite of knowledge discovery software specifically designed to address this challenge. Analysing data without any preconceived notion of the patterns it contains, the Decision Series seeks out relationships and trends, and presents them in easy to understand form, enabling better business decisions. The Decision Series is being used today by **leading corporations to discover the hidden value in their data**, providing them with major competitive advantages and organisational benefits.

Business Solutions

A Large Multi-National **Retailer** uses the Decision Series to refine inventory stocking levels, by store and by item, to dramatically reduce out-of-stock or **overstocking situations and thereby improve revenues and reduce forced markdowns**.

A **Health Maintenance Group** uses the Decision Series to predict which of its members are most at risk from specific major illnesses. This presents opportunities for timely medical intervention and preventative treatment to promote the patient's well being and reduce the healthcare provider's costs.

An **International Retail Sales Organisation** uses the Decision Series to optimise store and department layouts, resulting in more accurate targeting of products to maximise sales within the scope of available resources.

NeoVista has contributed to improved business and service operations in these companies by exploring their existing data using the Decision Series' advanced knowledge discovery techniques. NeoVista's unique software can be applied to a wide range of business problems, allowing you to:

Determine the relationships that lie at the heart of your business.

Make **reliable estimates of future behaviour** based on sophisticated analyses of past events.

Make **business decisions with a higher degree of understanding and confidence**.

Let Your Data Enhance Your Business Decisions

Data mining is renowned for exposing important facts and anomalies within data warehouses. The NeoVista Decision Series' knowledge discovery methodology has the proven ability to expose the patterns that are not merely interesting, but which are critical to your business. These patterns provide you with an advantage through insight and knowledge that your competition may never discover.

Reports

2.27 To make use of data, a suitable reporting framework is needed. **Enterprise resource planning** packages aim to integrate all of a company's applications to give a **single point of access**. A problem is that accessing source data is difficult if it is held in different formats and systems.

Case example

Time and time again finance directors say that their key IT issue is lack of reporting capabilities in the systems they are using. Reporting problems tend to fall into three categories.

First, the **inability to access the source data**. This is either because it is in a format that cannot be accessed by PC technology or it is held in so many places that its structure is incomprehensible to a member of the finance team.

Second, the **tools to make the enquiries** or produce the reports are often **difficult to use** and do not produce the reports in a 'user friendly' format with 'drill down' capabilities.

Third, there is the issue of **consistency of information** across systems. In order to get an overall picture of your organisation's performance you will usually need to access data from different operation applications. All too often the data is not the same across these systems.

The argument for replacing what you have is well rehearsed. New systems promise the latest technology for reporting and enquiries. **Enterprise Resource Planning (ERP)** packages promise to integrate your different applications smoothly and give you a single point of access to all data. **Customer Relationship Management (CRM)** software has been added to this recipe to give this approach a better chance of happening.

There are a myriad of reporting tools costing from a few pounds to hundreds of thousands of pounds. One that is regularly overlooked is the **spreadsheet**. Excel is the product most commonly used by accountants. With the advent of Microsoft Office 2000 there is a bewildering array of features to present information on your desktop or paper. **Pivot tables** are starting to be used more widely for multi-dimensional analysis and can be combined with the increasingly powerful **graphical capabilities** of Excel. Spreadsheets are much underrated and it is surprising how many organisations go out and buy expensive new knowledge-management tools when they already have a product on their computer that will deliver all the reporting/enquiry performance they require.

So, see how far your spreadsheet will take you and see if you can avoid the cost of another new IT tool.

Adapted from an article by John Tate, *Management Accounting,* April 2000

3 REMOTE INPUT OF DATA

3.1 It is no longer the case that data input requires someone to sit at a desk and to tap away at a keyboard. There is a wide range of data capture techniques, a number of which allow staff to input data into the organisation's system whether or not they are in the office.

(a) Sales staff can communicate sales orders directly to head office using laptop computers.

(b) Supermarkets can use bar coding and Electronic Point of Sale (EPOS) devices to capture stock level information on the supermarket floor.

4 DEVELOPING MANAGEMENT ACCOUNTING SYSTEMS

4.1 Most information is provided by an information system, or management information system (MIS).

KEY TERM

Management information system is 'a system to convert data from internal and external sources into information and to communicate that information, in an appropriate form, to managers at all levels in all functions to enable them to make timely and effective decisions for planning, directing and controlling the activities for which they are responsible'.

Lucey

A management information system is therefore a system of disseminating information which will enable managers to do their job.

4.2 Management information is by no means confined to accounting information, but until relatively recently accounting information systems have been the most formally-constructed and well-developed part of the overall information system of a business enterprise. This is still the case in all but the most advanced organisations.

4.3 Most management information systems are not designed, but **grow up informally**, with each manager making sure that he or she gets all the information considered necessary to do the job. Much accounting information, for example, is easily obtained, and managers can often get along with frequent face-to-face contact and co-operation with each other. Such an informal system works best in small organisations.

4.4 However, **some** information systems are **specially designed**, often because the introduction of computers has forced management to consider its information needs in detail. This is especially the case in large companies.

4.5 Management should try to **develop/implement** a management information system for their enterprise **with care**. If they allow the MIS to develop without any formal planning, it will almost certainly be inefficient because data will be obtained and processed in a random and disorganised way and the communication of information will also be random and hit-and-miss.

   (a) Some managers will keep data in their heads and will not commit information to paper. Stand-ins/successors will not know as much as they could and should because no information has been recorded to help them.

   (b) The organisation will not collect and process all the information that it should.

   (c) Information may be available but not disseminated to the appropriate managers.

   (d) Information is communicated late because the need to communicate it earlier is not understood and appreciated by the data processors.

4.6 The **consequences of a poor MIS** might be dissatisfaction amongst employees who believe they should be told more, a lack of understanding about what the targets for achievement are and a lack of information about how well the work is being done.

4.7 Whether a management information system is formally or informally constructed, it should therefore have **certain essential characteristics**.

   (a) The **functions of individuals and their areas of responsibility** in achieving company objectives should be **defined**.

   (b) **Areas of control** within the company (eg cost centres, investment centres) should also be clearly **defined**.

   (c) Information required for an area of control should flow to the manager who is responsible for it. (**Management structure of the organisation should therefore be considered**.)

4.8 Three particular types of management information system deserve special mention.

Type of MIS	Detail
Decision support systems (DSS)	Used by management **to help make decisions on poorly defined problems** (with **high levels of uncertainty**). They provide access to information with a wide range of information gathering and analytical tools. Decision support systems allow the manager to scan the environment, consider a number of alternatives and evaluate them under a variety of potential conditions. There is a major emphasis upon flexibility and user-friendliness.
Executive information systems (EIS)	Give executives a straightforward **means of access to key internal and external data**. They provide **summary-level data,** captured from the organisation's main systems (which might involve integrating the executive's desk top PC with the organisation's mainframe), **data manipulation facilities** (such as comparison with budget or prior year data and trend analysis) and **user-friendly presentation** of data.
Expert systems	Draw on a **computerised knowledge base** (such as details of the workings of tax legislation) and can give **factual answers to specific queries,** as well as **indicating** to the user **what a decision ought to be in a particular situation.**

Question: types of management information system

Read the following extracts.

(a) 'Direct Line's speed of response and cost advantage derive from its policy of only accepting low risk business and the use of sophisticated computer systems which allow telesales staff to key in essential details and respond to applications for insurance instantly rather than having to spend days waiting for a decision from an underwriter.'
(Financial Times, November 1992)

(b) 'Know-How has set out to formulate and make accessible a wealth of internal information. The map references to such information previously existed only in the heads of experienced solicitors. Now, documents are analysed before data entry by experts who predict how they are likely to be of use in the future and encapsulate carefully-coded keywords in the text.

Typically, the information on the system is used to shed light on new situations and interpret them in the light of previous experience.'
(Financial Times, February 1993: article on Linklater & Paines, solicitors)

(c) 'Instant access to summary information, the potential for highlighting exceptions or variances with budget and the ease with which executives can find the reasons for a variance, in terms of an individual salesman's performance, have thrown up major implications for entire organisations'.
(Financial Times, October 1992)

Required

Decide which of these extracts describes a decision support system, which an executive information system and which an expert system.

Answer

The point of exercises like this one is to bring some real life to the factual information in the main body of the text, so be sure to read the extracts. The answers are (b), (c), (a) respectively.

Setting up a management accounting system

4.9 Taking a broad view, the following factors should be considered when setting up a management accounting system (which is just one part of an overall MIS).

(a) The **output required**. This is just another way of saying that the management accountant must **identify the information needs of managers**. If a particular manager finds pie-charts most useful the system should be able to produce them. If another manager needs to know what time of day machinery failures occur, this information should be available. Levels of detail and accuracy of output and methods of processing must be determined in each case.

(b) **When the output is required**. If information is needed within the hour the system should be capable of producing it at this speed. If it is only ever needed once a year, at the year end, the system should be designed to produce it **on time**, no matter how long it takes to produce.

(c) The **sources of input information**. It is too easy to state that the outputs required should dictate the inputs made. The production manager may require a report detailing the precise operations of his machines, second by second. However, the management accounting system could only acquire this information if suitable production technology had been installed.

The need for management accounting systems to develop

4.10 In the Study Guide, the ACCA states that management accounting systems need to be defined and developed 'in an increasingly competitive and global environment'.

4.11 **Environmental analysis** is covered in detail in compulsory Paper 3.5 *Strategic Business Planning and Development*.

4.12 We shall now describe some pointers for issues of **competition** and **globalisation**. The key development is the use of management accounting systems for strategic decision making.

(a) **Competition**

Impact	Management accounting impact
• More competitors	Better competitor intelligence
	Model competitor cost structures
• More competing products	Identify which features add most value; model impact on cost
• Faster response	Management accounting information has to be produced speedily and be up-to-date for decision making

(b) **Globalisation**

Impact	Management accounting impact
• Increases competition	• Similar impact to (a)
	• Attention to **behavioural** impact on management accounting systems in different markets
• Access to overseas capital	• The cost of operating in different local markets
	• Aggregating information
• Overseas activities	• Repaid for exchange differences

4.13 We consider management accounting systems in more depth in Part B.

Exam focus point

Note that the topics covered in this chapter have yet to be examined in their own right.

Chapter roundup

- Unlike manufacturing companies, services are characterised by **intangibility, inseparability, variability, perishability** and no **transfer of ownership.**

- **Mass services** are standard services provided to large numbers of people, and are often automated. **Personal services** vary on the circumstances of the service delivery, and are generally one-to-one.

- Given that the expenses of small service businesses tend to be overheads, **ABC** is of particular relevance.

- **Service businesses need the same aggregate information** as manufacturing firms, but also need performance data as to their cost and volume drivers. Operational information is likely to be more qualitative.

- **Access to data** has been facilitated by **groupware**, **intranets, extranets, databases, data warehousing** and **data mining.**

- Developments in IT have also enabled the **remote input of data**.

- Developments in IT have revolutionised the **potential for management accounting data**, increasing the volume and variety of **potential reports. Data mining** is able to identify relationships between different transactions.

- **Globalisation** and **competition** require an external, forward-looking focus, with greater facilities for modelling.

Quick quiz

1   Which of the following are the five major characteristics of services that distinguish services from manufacturing?

    (a)   Intangibility
    (b)   Perishability
    (c)   Inseparability
    (d)   No transfer of ownership
    (e)   Heterogeneity
    (f)   Variability
    (g)   Simultaneity

2   The only difference between an intranet and an extranet is that an extranet was designed by someone external to the organisation. *True or false?*

3   *Match the terms to their diagrams.*

    Terms

    Application-specific system

    Database

    Integrated system

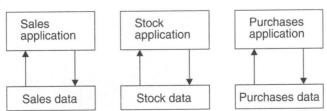

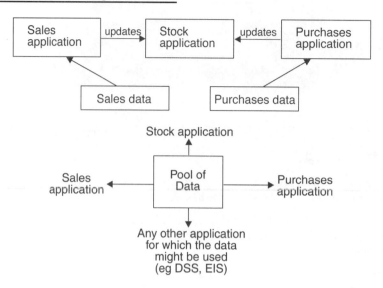

4   *Choose the correct word from those highlighted.*

A data **mart/shop/warehouse/factory** contains data from a range of internal and external sources.

5   *Fill in the blank.*

.... software looks for hidden patterns and relationships in large pools of data.

Answers to quick quiz

1   This was a bit of a trick question as there are no 'odd ones out'. Inseparability and simultaneity mean the same thing, as do variability and heterogeneity.

2   False. An extranet is an intranet that is accessible to authorised outsiders.

3   The first diagram shows an application specific system, the second an integrated system. The third diagram shows a database.

4   Both data warehouse and datamart would be acceptable. A datamart holds a selection of the organisation's data for a specific purpose whereas a data warehouse services the entire organisation.

5   Data mining

Now try the question below from the Exam Question Bank

Number	Level	Marks	Time
5	Exam	20	36 mins

Chapter 6

CHANGES IN BUSINESS STRUCTURE AND MANAGEMENT ACCOUNTING

Topic list	Syllabus reference
1 Organisation structure	1(d)
2 Teamwork and empowerment	1(d)
3 Business integration	1(d)
4 Business process re-engineering	1(d)

Introduction

This chapter discusses some of the recent **changes in business structures** and how these will **impact on management accounting**.

These first five chapters should provide you with an understanding of the **management accounting framework** within which management accounting systems (Part B of the Text) must be used and performance measures (Part C), planning and control (Part D) and decision making (Part E) carried out.

Study guide

Section 6 – Changes in business structure and management accounting

- Identify the particular information needs of organisations adopting a team/project focus

- Discuss the concept of business integration and the linkage between people, operations, strategy and technology

- Explain the influence of Business Process Re-engineering on systems development

- Identify and discuss the required changes in management accounting systems as a consequence of empowering staff to manage sectors of a business

Exam guide

Section A of the Pilot paper features different types of organisation, and question 5 asks you to discuss, in principle, how you would design an effective management system, making references to organisation types. This suggests that organisational issues both provide **context to questions** and can be the **specific subject** of a question.

1 ORGANISATION STRUCTURE

The design of organisations

1.1 Organisational design or structure implies a framework or mechanism with a number of purposes.

(a) **Link individuals** in an established network of relationships so that authority, responsibility and communications can be controlled

(b) **Group together** (in any appropriate way) the **tasks** required to fulfil the objectives of the organisation, and allocate them to suitable individuals or groups

(c) Give each individual or group the **authority** required to perform the allocated functions, while **controlling behaviour and resources** in the interests of the organisation as a whole

(d) **Co-ordinate** the objectives and activities of separate units, so that overall aims are achieved without gaps or overlaps in the flow of work required

(e) **Facilitate the flow** of work, information and other resources required, through planning, control and other systems

Ways to structure an organisation

1.2 Organisations are typically split into departments or divisions. There are six **basic approaches to departmentation and divisionalisation.**

Approach	Detail
Function	This is departmentation by type of work done (eg finance department, marketing department, production function). <ul><li>Expertise is concentrated, enabling effective division of labour</li><li>Problems include poor communication between functional specialists</li></ul>
Geographic area	Reporting relationships are organised by geography. In each area functional specialists report to an area boss, who ensures co-ordination. <ul><li>This enables greater flexibility at local level, and allows experimentation</li><li>Some managerial work is duplicated</li></ul>
Product/ brand	A divisional manager for each product is responsible for marketing and production. Some divisions are effectively run as independent businesses, in which case the division's finance specialists will report to the division's head. <ul><li>Individual product profitability can be easily identified</li><li>There is increased managerial complexity, and problems of resource allocation</li></ul>
Customer/ market segment	Reporting relationships are structured by type of customer
Hybrid designs	In practice, organisations may draw on a number of these approaches. Product/brand departmentation for marketing and production, say, might be combined with a centralised R&D function. This is because some activities are better organised on a functional basis (for reasons of economies of scale) whereas others are more suited, say, to product/brand departmentation (eg marketing).
Matrix designs	These involve dual reporting lines (eg an individual will report to a functional boss and an area boss).

Influences on organisation design

1.3 Many factors influence the structural design of the organisation.

Factor	Detail
Size	As an organisation gets larger, its structure gets more complex: specialisation and subdivision are required. The process of controlling and co-ordinating performance, and communication between individuals, also grows more difficult as the 'top' of the organisation gets further from the 'bottom', with more intervening levels. The more members there are, the more potential there is for interpersonal relationships and the development of the informal organisation.
Task (the nature of its work)	Structure is shaped by the division of work into functions and individual tasks, and how these tasks relate to each other. Depending on the nature of the work, this can be done in a number of ways. The complexity and importance of tasks will affect the amount of supervision required, and so the ratio of supervisors to workers. The nature of the market will dictate the way in which tasks are grouped together: into functions, or sales territories, or types of customer.
Staff	The skills and abilities of staff will determine how the work is structured and the degree of autonomy or supervision required. Staff aspirations and expectations may also influence job design, and the amount of delegation in the organisation, in order to provide job satisfaction.
Legal, commercial, technical and social environment	Examples include: economic recession necessitating staff streamlining especially at middle management level, market pressures in the financial services sector encouraging a greater concentration of staff in specialised areas and at the bank/customer interface, technology reducing staff requirements but increasing specialisation.
Age	The time it has had to develop and grow, or decline, whether it is very set in its ways and traditional, or experimenting with new ways of doing things and making decisions.
Culture and management style	How willing management is to delegate authority at all levels, how skilled they are in organisation and communication (for example in handling a wider span of control), whether teamwork is favoured, or large, impersonal structures are accepted by the staff.

Question: influences on organisation design

Consider how each of the factors listed in Paragraph 1.3 might affect the structural design of a service organisation (for example, a bank) and a manufacturing organisation (for example, a cement manufacturer).

Answer

Just taking elements of the first two factors as an example, a small bank may have just one office located in the area where it does its business - probably the City of London - and employ fairly specialised autonomous staff. A large bank may need a network of branches and regional offices as well as a central HQ and would employ a larger proportion of relatively unskilled workers, with greater supervision. Remember that the new 'Internet' banks or banks such as first direct are structured around call centres.

A cement manufacturer would need to have its production facilities located on top of the natural resources used. Larger organisations might have administrative offices and distribution depots elsewhere. The distinction between 'productive' workers and administrative workers would be much more marked than in a bank, and these differences would be accentuated the larger the organisation was.

2   TEAMWORK AND EMPOWERMENT

2.1   Read the case example below about a new 'type' of organisation. Consider, particularly, the management accounting information needed for overall control.

Case example

Catalyst Technology Solutions

CTS provide disaster-recovery services for businesses. If a client is hit by fire or flood, or a computer malfunction, they can reload their companies' data onto the Catalyst system and continue to operate as if the crisis had never happened.

The Woking office stands empty, so if a client's premises have been destroyed, they can move in their whole operation. Catalyst's hi-tech house-bound employees do not have much in common with the traditional image of homeworkers - its networked workforce is only possible because of new technology. 'I know no other business that looks like this,' Mr Hixon says. 'Our competitors find it impossible to copy us because they are stuck in a culture which involves people sitting in offices with a manager in a glass-fronted office watching them and shouting when he wants attention.'

The modern equivalent of electrically-driven steam machinery is the outdated hierarchical structures most companies still rely on. Most have a command and control culture designed for a pre-IT age where information and instructions are handed from top layer of management down through the hierarchy. At Catalyst, information is disseminated throughout the company so everybody has access to all the documents relevant to the projects they are working on. Employees working without a manager peering over their shoulder involves a high degree of trust.

Businesses such as Catalyst could be ushering in the productivity revolution in the UK as companies start to base their structure around the potential of information technology.

Mr Hixon has further plans for revolutionising Catalyst. A new telephone system will soon automatically route calls to workers' home numbers or another location, and divert them to a secretary if the call is unanswered.

Teams

> **KEY TERM**
>
> A **team** is a 'small number of people with complementary skills who are committed to a common purpose, performance goals and approach for which they hold themselves basically accountable'.

2.2   Although many people enjoy working in teams, their popularity in the work place arises because of their effectiveness in fulfilling the organisation's work.

2.3   **Aspects of teams**

(a)   **Work organisation.** Teams combine the skills of different individuals and avoid complex communication between different business functions.

(b) **Control.** Fear of letting down the team can be a powerful motivator, hence teams can be used to control the performance and behaviour of individuals. Teams can also be used to resolve conflict.

(c) **Knowledge generation.** Teams can generate ideas.

(d) **Decision making.** Teams can be set up to investigate new developments and decisions can be evaluated from more than one viewpoint.

2.4 The basic work units of organisations have traditionally been specialised functional departments. In more **recent** times, organisations are adopting **small, flexible teams**. Teamworking allows **work** to be **shared** among a number of individuals, so it gets done **faster** without people losing sight of their whole tasks or having to co-ordinate their efforts through lengthy channels of communication.

2.5 A team may be called together **temporarily**, to achieve specific task objectives (**project team**), or may be **more or less permanent**, with responsibilities for a particular product, product group or stage of the production process (a **product or process team**). There are two basic approaches to the organisation of team work: multi-skilled teams and multi-disciplinary teams.

Multi-disciplinary teams

2.6 Multi-disciplinary teams bring together individuals with **different skills** and specialisms, so that their skills, experience and knowledge can be **pooled or exchanged**. Teamworking of this kind encourages freer and faster communication between disciplines in the organisation.

(a) Teamworking increases workers' **awareness of their overall objectives** and targets.

(b) Teamworking **aids co-ordination**.

(c) Teamworking **helps to generate solutions to problems**, and suggestions for improvements, since a multi-disciplinary team has access to more 'pieces of the jigsaw'.

Multi-skilled teams

2.7 A team may simply bring together a number of individuals who have **several skills** and can perform any of the group's tasks. These tasks can then be shared out in a more flexible way between group members, according to who is available and best placed to do a given job at the time it is required.

Case example

(Adapted from *People Management* October 1997)

The annual staff survey at *Nationwide Building Society* usually places its **customer service teams** for mortgages and insurance at mid-table in terms of employee satisfaction. This year the teams are at the top. At the same time their **productivity** has increased by half, sickness absence has fallen by 75 percent and overtime is down to zero.

In the early 1990s Nationwide began to abandon traditional management hierarchies in the non-retail part of its business. In customer service, they were looking for an approach that would further develop multi-skilling while supporting a **flatter structure**. **Self-managed teamworking** seemed the obvious answer, as it also addressed issues such as morale and job satisfaction.

They work on the premise that the people who know how best to carry out and improve their own work are the teams themselves. Members have **shared authority** and responsibility to plan, implement and control how their targets are achieved.

In 1995 the Nationwide began a project in the Northampton administrative centre, revolutionising the basis under which the 12 teams in the mortgage and insurance customer service department operated. They increased the level of training and worked on their decision-making, conflict management and team-building skills. Each team had between nine and 18 members, including a leader, but he or she had a coaching, rather than directing, role.

When work comes in, the **team decides** who is the most appropriate person to take it on, depending on skills and existing workloads. While teams are encouraged to share resources with each other when necessary, there is also a competitive element. But this is never allowed to detract from the **performance of the department** - you are only as good as your worst-performing team.

The **results** of each team are charted, allowing comparative league tables to be created. Initially, one team finished consistently at the foot of the **productivity table**. Its members consulted colleagues in the more successful teams and altered their **work processes** accordingly.

Members compared their sickness and overtime figures with those of other teams, and then took responsibility for **controlling** these elements. Often this was done using a sense of ownership and pride which, could with peer pressure, reduce the need for managerial intervention.

There are several aspects of implementation to be addressed if self-managed teams are to be successful.

- First, there must be clear business reasons for the move.

- There also needs to be recognition by all involved parties that self-managed teams are not a quick fix.

- Another primary issue is that of 'buy-in' and gaining commitment at all levels, while communicating effectively.

- Another important prerequisite is to **assess the organisation's existing systems** and procedures within which the new teams may have to work.

Delayering and empowerment

2.8 In recent years, many large organisations have recognised that a large number of management layers led to communication problems, overlapping responsibilities and problems with planning and control. As companies sought ways to **cut costs**, they realised that **developments in technology meant** the **information processing traditionally done by middle managers could be done by computer** just as effectively.

2.9 Middle managers thus tended to have too little to do while those lower down the hierarchy were getting frustrated. The trend for some time has therefore been one of **delayering, downsizing** and **empowerment**. All of these reduce the need for managerial intervention.

> ### KEY TERMS
>
> **Delayering** is removing layers of middle management.
>
> **Empowerment** is the delegation of certain aspects of business decisions to those lower down in the hierarchy or in 'front line' positions.

2.10 For example, customer service staff may have the discretion to issue on the spot refunds or discounts. Key operational decisions can be made without reference to higher authority, providing that certain limits are adhered to.

2.11 **Team working, empowerment** and **delayering** have had a significant **impact** on **how information is processed** in an organisation.

Management accounting implications of team working and empowerment

2.12 One merit of the **'old-style'** organisational **hierarchy** was that **structure** and **information processing requirements** were **clear**.

(a) In a functional organisation, all the data relating to a particular function would be gathered together, passed up and only aggregated at the highest level. Feedback would come later after the data had been aggregated.

(b) While functional costs could be collected, this could make it more difficult for the overall profitability, say, of different activities of the business to be assessed.

(c) Feedback would be given in terms of **instructions** from the supervisor.

2.13 In a **team-based** organisation with fewer hierarchical layers, there may be more **confusion** as to the nature of the organisation. Look at the *Nationwide* case example earlier in this chapter.

(a) If teams are empowered, they will need **targeted information** to make decisions.

(b) Each team has to have **feedback** as to how it is **performing in relation** to other teams and in relation to performance measures for the company as a whole.

(c) Those supporting the teams and regulating the performance of the organisation to satisfy its stakeholders will also need information for decision making to enable them to take **resource allocation decisions**.

2.14 **Characteristics of the information needs of a team-based or empowered organisation**

Issue	Comment
Mixture of financial and non-financial information	Teams carry out activities but may not know the financial implications of these activities.
Transparency and immediacy	If team-based working is to encourage flexibility, the team needs to have information quickly.
Common data definitions	To enable comparison between teams, it must be clear what is being measured.
Relevance	Information provided must be relevant to the needs of the team, so that it is used.
Aggregation	It should still be possible to obtain a broad overview of how the organisation is doing, identifying revenue streams and cash flows.
Responsibility centres	There may have to be a budget for each team, as determined by the activities with which it is involved.

3 BUSINESS INTEGRATION

3.1 There is one easy definition of business integration, although the ACCA's Study Guide mentions the **linkage** between four particular aspects.

- **People**
- **Operations**
- **Strategy**
- **Technology**

> ### KEY TERM
>
> **Integration** means that all aspects of the business must be aligned to secure the most efficient use of the organisation's resources so that it can achieve its objectives effectively.

McKinsey 7S model

3.2 The McKinsey 7S model describes the **links** between the **organisation's behaviour** and the **behaviour of individuals** within it.

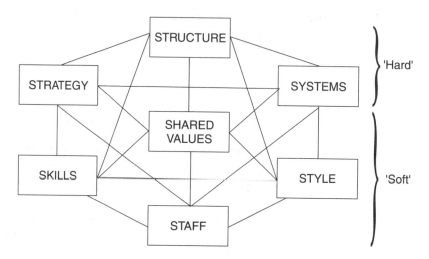

3.3 **Hard elements of business behaviour**

(a) **Structure**. The organisation structure refers to the formal division of tasks in the organisation and the hierarchy of authority from the most senior to junior.

(b) **Strategy**. How the organisation plans to outperform its competitors, if it is a business, or how it intends to achieve its objectives. This is linked to shared values.

(c) **Systems**. These include the technical systems of accounting, personnel, management information and so forth. These are linked to the skills of the staff.

These 'hard' elements are easily quantified and defined, and deal with facts and rules.

3.4 **Soft elements are equally important.**

(a) **Style** refers to the **corporate culture** which is the shared assumptions, ways of working, attitudes and beliefs.

(b) **Shared values** are the guiding beliefs of people in the organisation as to why it exists. (For example, people in a hospital seek to save lives.)

(c) **Staff** are the people in the organisation.

(d) **Skills** refer to those things that the organisation does well. For example, BT is good at providing a telephone service, but even if the phone network is eventually used as a transmission medium for TV or films, BT is unlikely to make those programmes itself.

3.5 **All elements,** both hard and soft, **must pull in the same direction for the organisation to be effective.**

The value chain

3.6 A more **sophisticated** model of business integration is the value chain. It offers a bird's eye view of the firm, of what it does and the **way in which its business activities are organised.**

3.7 Before we go any further it is important that you realise that **business activities** are **not the same as business functions**.

   (a) **Functions** are the **familiar departments** of a business (production, finance and so on) and **reflect** the **formal organisation structure** and the distribution of labour.

   (b) **Activities** are **what actually goes on,** and the **work that is done**. A single activity can be performed by a number of functions in sequence. Activities are the means by which a firm **creates value** in its products. (They are sometimes referred to as **value activities**.) Activities **incur** costs, and, in combination with other activities, provide a product or service which **earns revenue**.

3.8 For example, most organisations need to secure resources from the environment. This activity can be called procurement. Procurement will involve more departments than purchasing, however; accounts will certainly be involved and possibly production and quality assurance.

3.9 The ultimate **value** a firm **creates** is measured by the **amount customers are willing to pay** for its products or services **above the cost of carrying out value activities**. A firm is profitable if the realised value to customers exceeds the collective cost of performing the activities.

3.10 According to Porter, the **value activities** of any firm can be divided into **nine types** and then analysed into a **value chain**. This is a **model of activities** (which **procure inputs, process them** and **add value** to them in some way, to **generate outputs** for customers) and the **relationships between them**.

KEY TERM

The **value chain** is 'The sequence of business activities by which, from the perspective of the end user, value is added to the products or services produced by an organisation'.

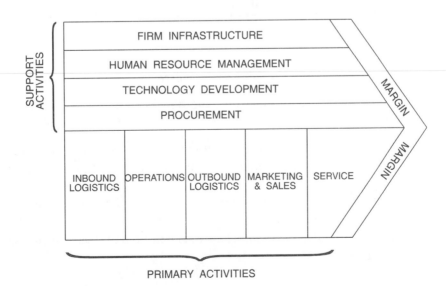

Activities

3.11 **Primary activities** are directly related to production, sales, marketing, delivery and service.

Activity	Comment
Inbound logistics	Receiving, handling and storing inputs to the production system: warehousing, transport, stock control and so on.
Operations	Convert resource inputs into a final product. Resource inputs are not only materials. People are a resource especially in service industries. Note that this is not just applicable to manufacturing firms, hence the careful choice of name. Service companies also have operations.
Outbound logistics	Delivering the product to customers; this may include storage, testing, bulk transport, packaging, delivery and so on.
Marketing and sales	Informing customers about the product, persuading them to buy it, and enabling them to do so: advertising, promotion and so on.
After sales service	Installing products, repairing them, upgrading them, providing spare parts and so forth.

3.12 **Support activities** provide purchased inputs, human resources, technology and infrastructural functions to support the primary activities. The first three tend to provide specific elements of support to the primary activities.

Activity	Comment
Procurement	Acquire the resource inputs to the primary activities (eg purchase of materials, subcomponents equipment).
Technology development	Product design, improving processes and/or resource utilisation.
Human resource management	Recruiting, training, developing and rewarding people.
Firm infrastructure	General management, planning, finance, quality control, public and legal affairs: these activities normally support the chain as a whole rather than individual activities. They are crucially important to an organisation's strategic capability in all primary activities.

Linkages

3.13 **Linkages** connect the activities of the value chain, wherever they take place.

(a) **Activities in the value chain affect one another**. For example, more costly product design or better quality production might reduce the need for after-sales service.

(b) **Linkages require co-ordination**. For example, Just In Time requires smooth functioning of operations, outbound logistics and service activities such as installation.

3.14 Because activities can be spread across departments, rather than corresponding to neat, organisation chart boundaries, managing them for best effect can be extremely difficult. Cost control can be a particular problem. The dispersion of activities also complicates the management of linkages.

114

Value system

3.15   **Activities** and **linkages that add value do not stop** at the organisation's **boundaries**. For example, when a restaurant serves a meal, the quality of the ingredients - although they are chosen by the cook - is determined by the grower. The grower has added value, and the grower's success in growing produce of good quality is as important to the customer's ultimate satisfaction as the skills of the chef. A **firm's value chain** is **connected** to what Porter calls a **value system**.

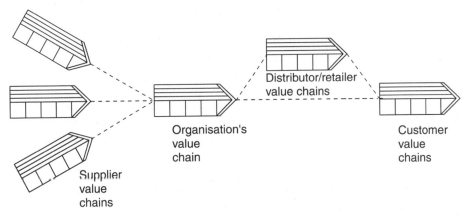

3.16   **How an organisation can use the value chain to secure competitive advantage**

- Invent new or better ways to do activities
- Combine activities in new or better ways
- Manage the linkages in its own value chain
- Manage the linkages in the value system

Linkage between people, operations, strategy and technology

3.17   Having looked at two models of business integration, we will now consider some of the linkages in the four elements the ACCA have identified.

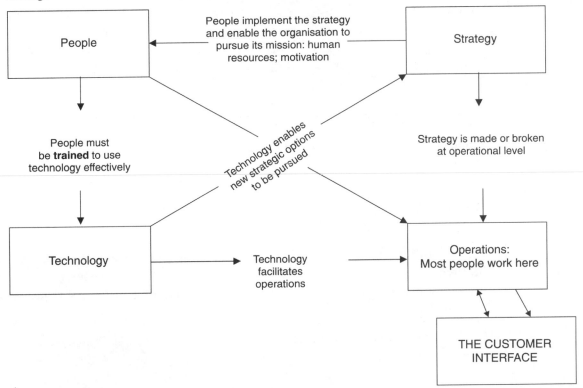

BPP PROFESSIONAL EDUCATION

3.18 Here are some of the issues that impact on the linkages.

Element	Issues
People	• Quantity • Skills level • Motivation • Deployment
Strategy	• Direction • Implication for resources
Technology	• Equipment • Work organisation • Information
Operations	• Procedures • Empowerment • Customer relations • Quality

4 BUSINESS PROCESS RE-ENGINEERING

4.1 Business process re-engineering involves focusing attention **inwards** to consider how business **processes** can be **redesigned** or re-engineered to **improve efficiency**. It *can* lead to fundamental changes in the way an organisation functions. In particular, it has been realised that processes which were developed in a paper-intensive processing environment may not be suitable for an environment that is underpinned by IT.

4.2 The main writing on the subject is Hammer and Champy's *Reengineering the Corporation* (1993), from which the following definition is taken.

> ### KEY TERM
>
> **Business Process Re-engineering (BPR)** is the fundamental rethinking and radical redesign of business processes to achieve dramatic improvements in critical contemporary measures of performance, such as cost, quality, service and speed.

4.3 The key words here are **fundamental, radical, dramatic** and **process**.

(a) **Fundamental** and **radical** indicate that BPR is somewhat akin to zero base budgeting: it starts by asking basic questions such as 'why do we do what we do', without making any assumptions or looking back to what has always been done in the past.

(b) **Dramatic** means that BPR should achieve 'quantum leaps in performance', not just marginal, incremental improvements.

(c) **Process**. BPR recognises that there is a need to change functional hierarchies: 'existing hierarchies have evolved into functional departments that encourage functional excellence but which do not work well together in meeting customers' requirements' (Rupert Booth, *Management Accounting*, 1994).

KEY TERM

A **process** is a collection of activities that takes one or more kinds of input and creates an output.

4.4   For example, order fulfilment is a process that takes an order as its input and results in the delivery of the ordered goods. Part of this process is the manufacture of the goods, but under **BPR** the **aim** of **manufacturing** is **not merely to make** the goods. Manufacturing should aim to **deliver the goods that were ordered,** and any aspect of the manufacturing process that hinders this aim should be re-engineered. The first question to ask might be 'Do they need to be manufactured at all?'

4.5   A **re-engineered process** has certain **characteristics**.

- Often several jobs are **combined** into one.
- Workers often **make decisions.**
- The **steps** in the process are performed in **a logical order.**
- **Work** is performed where it **makes most sense.**
- Checks and controls may be reduced, and **quality 'built-in'.**
- One manager provides a **single point of contact.**
- The advantages of **centralised and decentralised** operations are combined.

Case example

Based on a problem at a *major car manufacturer*.

A company employs 25 staff to perform the standard accounting task of matching goods received notes with orders and then with invoices. About 80% of their time is spent trying to find out why 20% of the set of three documents do not agree.

One way of improving the situation would have been to computerise the existing process to facilitate matching. This would have helped, but BPR went further: why accept any incorrect orders at all? What if all the orders are entered onto a computerised database? When goods arrive at the goods inwards department they either agree to goods that have been ordered or they don't. It's as simple as that. Goods that agree to an order are accepted and paid for. Goods that are not agreed are sent back to the supplier. There are no files of unmatched items and time is not wasted trying to sort out these files.

Principles of BPR

4.6   **Seven principles for BPR** (Hammer)

(a) Processes should be designed to achieve a desired **outcome rather than** focusing on existing **tasks.**

(b) **Personnel who use** the **output** from a process should **perform the process.** For example, a company could set up a database of approved suppliers; this would allow personnel who actually require supplies to order them themselves, perhaps using on-line technology, thereby eliminating the need for a separate purchasing function.

(c) **Information processing** should be **included in the work which produces the information.** This eliminates the differentiation between information gathering and information processing.

(d) **Geographically dispersed resources** should be **treated** as if they are **centralised.** This allows the benefits of centralisation to be obtained, for example, economies of scale

BPP
PROFESSIONAL EDUCATION

through central negotiation of supply contracts, without losing the benefits of decentralisation, such as flexibility and responsiveness.

(e) **Parallel activities** should be **linked rather than integrated.** This would involve, for example, co-ordination between teams working on different aspects of a single process.

(f) 'Doers' should be allowed to be **self-managing.** The traditional **distinction** between **workers** and **managers** can be **abolished**: decision aids such as expert systems can be provided where they are required.

(g) **Information** should be **captured once** at **source.** Electronic distribution of information makes this possible.

Business processes and the technological interdependence between departments

4.7 The value chain describes a series of activities from input of raw materials to output of finished goods/services for the customers. These activities may be organised into departments even though the actual process of adding value may cross departmental boundaries.

4.8 The **links between different departments of a business can vary,** however, and hence the **need to manage the relationships between them. Interdependence** is the extent to which **different departments depend on each** other to accomplish their tasks. It is possible to identify three types of interdependence.

- **Pooled**
- **Sequential**
- **Reciprocal**

Pooled interdependence

4.9 In pooled interdependence, each department/section works **independently** of the others, subject to achieving the overall goals of the organisation. Let us take the example of a clearing bank.

(a) **Horizontal communication.** The branches of major building societies and clearing banks in the UK rarely have to communicate with each other and so the need for co-ordination with each other is low, providing the technology is adhered to. **The firm as a whole co-ordinates by standardising work processes.**

(b) They serve different geographical areas and have their own customers. They are dispersed.

(c) Each branch is selling the same standard services and shares financial resources.

Pooled interdependence

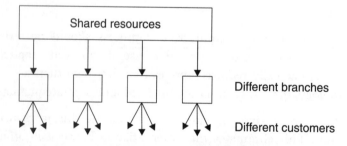

4.10 A **mediating technology,** embodying **standardised rules and approaches,** is used to connect the organisation's resources, its branches and customers. An example would be standard credit **scoring programmes to ensure that credit applications are treated on the**

same basis in different branches. This effectively supports empowered teams at operational level.

Sequential interdependence

4.11 A **sequence** is a **linked** chain of activities with a **start** and **end** point. An example is an assembly line: raw materials are taken, moulded to the right sizes and shapes and are assembled into a product. The **outputs** of each stage sequence must be precisely tailored to the **inputs** of the next - standardisation of outputs, might be one form of co-ordination used. The first activity must be performed correctly before the second can be tackled. **Long-linked technology** is the term used to describe the dependence of one stage of the production process on preceding stages. **Management effort is required to ensure that the transfer of resources between departments is smooth.** They thus need information about the process as a whole.

Sequential interdependence

Reciprocal interdependence

4.12 Reciprocal interdependence exists when a **number of departments acquire inputs from and offer outputs to each other**. In other words, while resources have to be transferred, there is **no preset sequence**. The output of one department might be sent to another for processing, and then returned to the original department.

4.13 **Intensive technologies** are used to provide a variety of products/services to a 'customer'. The 'customer' might be shifted between a variety of departments, which must communicate with each other. A hospital is a good example: a patient may see a number of specialists.

Reciprocal interdependence

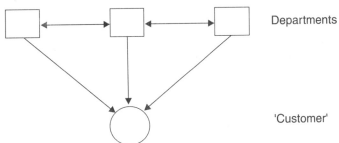

BPR and organisation structure and systems

4.14 You should now have some idea as to the complexities of business processes overlapping different departments. **Some organisations have redesigned their structures on the lines of business processes,** adopting BPR to **avoid** all the co-ordination problems caused by reciprocal interdependence.

4.15 **Key characteristics of organisations which have adopted BPR**

(a) **Work units change from functional departments to process teams**, which **replace the old functional structure**.

(i)   For example, within a functional framework, a sales order may be handled by many different people, in different departments or business functions. (One person takes the order in the department, and one person delivers).

(ii)   In process teams, the people are grouped together. A case team might combine to do all the work on a process and this applies not only to one-off projects but to recurring work.

Multi-skilling also means that one individual does many of the tasks in a process.

(b)   **Jobs change.** People do more, as team members are responsible for results. This ties in with **job enlargement** and **job enrichment**.

(c)   **People's roles change.** They are empowered to make decisions relevant to the process.

(d)   **Performance measures concentrate on results** rather than activities. Process teams create 'value' which is measurable.

(e)   Organisation structures change from **hierarchical** to **flat** (ie delayered).

(i)   When a process becomes the work of a **whole team**, managing the process is the **team's responsibility**. Interdepartmental issues become matters the team resolves itself, rather than matters requiring managerial intervention.

(ii)   Companies require less managerial input. **Managers have less to do**, there are fewer of them and so fewer layers.

(iii)   Organisation structure determines lines of communication, and in many organisations is a weighty issue. This is not the case in process organisations, as **lines of communication 'naturally' develop around business processes**.

Implications of BPR for accounting systems

4.16

Issue	Implication
Performance measurement	Performance measures must be built around processes not departments: this may affect the design of responsibility centres.
Reporting	There is a need to identify where value is being added.
Activity	ABC might be used to model the business processes.
Structure	The complexity of the reporting system will depend on the organisational structure. Arguably the reports should be designed round the process teams, if there are independent process teams.
Variances	New variances may have to be developed.

Exam focus point

An answer to question 5 of the December 2001 exam should have included many of the issues covered in Chapters 3, 4 and 5. The question focused on the **required amendments** to the **MIS** to **meet changes in the business environment** (in terms of structure, lines of reporting, resourcing, employment, stock control and production). As the examiner stated in his comments on the exam, 'The six changes were not esoteric flights of fancy but common business events that the candidates would have either experienced or should have had an awareness – none of the listed events should have taken a final examination student by surprise'.

Chapter roundup

- Organisation structure describes the deployment of human resources in an organisation, and the chain of command, and a structure of accountability.

- Typically, information flows follow organisation structure.

- Organisation structure is a way of securing long-term services by avoiding some 'transactions' costs.

- Traditional hierarchies are giving way to organisations with **empowered teams.** These teams have considerable decision making power within defined parameters.

- To monitor performance, an information system should provide relevant, targeted information, but this should also be aggregated so that performance can be monitored at corporate level. In such an environment, transparency of information is of value.

- Although it is easy to look at a business as a grouping of specialised **departments**, in practice, **value is added** by **activities and processes** which may span a number of departments. These need to be **linked** effectively to create value.

- **Business process re-engineering** involves focusing attention inwards to consider how business processes can be redesigned or reengineered to improve efficiency.

Quick quiz

1   *Complete the following table.*

How organisations can be structured	Description
By	By type of work done
By	
By	
By	
.... designs	Using a number of approaches
.... designs	Involve dual reporting lines

2   *Fill in the blanks in the following statement.*

Factors which influence the structural design of an organisation include ...., ..., ..., ..., ... and ....

3   *Match the type of team to the correct description.*

Types of team
Multi-disciplinary
Multi-skilled

Descriptions
(a) Individuals have different skills and specialisms which can be pooled.
(b) Individuals have several skills and can perform any of the group's tasks.

4   *Complete the following diagram of the value chain.*

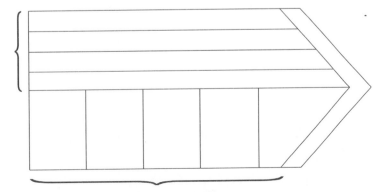

5   The introduction of BPR causes organisation structures to change from flat to hierarchical. *True or false?*

Answers to quick quiz

1

How organisations can be structured	Description
By **function**	By type of work done
By **geographic area**	
By **product/brand**	
By **customer/market segment**	
Hybrid designs	Using a number of approaches
Matrix designs	Involve dual reporting lines

2   Size   Legal, commercial, technical and social environment
     Task   Age
     Staff   Culture and management style

3   Multi-disciplinary (a)
     Multi-skilled   (b)

4

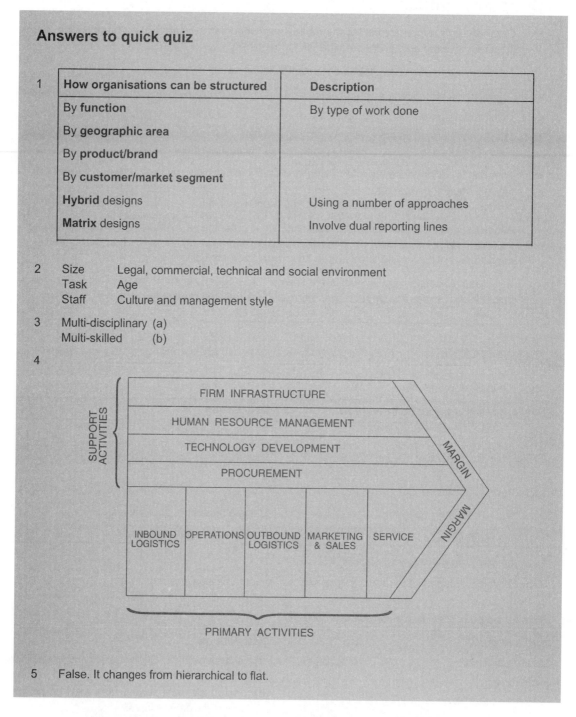

5   False. It changes from hierarchical to flat.

Now try the question below from the Exam Question Bank

Number	Level	Marks	Time
6	Exam	20	36 mins

Part B
Design of management accounting systems

Chapter 7

SYSTEM DESIGN AND SYSTEM OBJECTIVES

Topic list	Syllabus reference
1 Information and management structure	2(a)
2 Objectives of management accounting and management accounting information	2(a)
3 Attributes and principles of management accounting information	2(a)
4 Management accounting information within the management information system	2(a)
5 Open and closed systems	2(a)
6 Contingent factors	2(a)
7 Human behaviour and management accounting	2(a)
8 Information and responsibility accounting	2(a)

Introduction

This chapter provides an **introduction** to the part of the text that covers the design of management accounting systems and looks at **management accounting information**, at the type of information that is required and how it used within the organisation.

Remember that we looked at strategic planning, management control and operational control information in Chapters 1 and 2.

Study guide

Section 7 – System design and system objectives

- Describe, with reference to management accounting, ways in which the information requirements of a management structure are affected by the features of the structure

- Evaluate the objectives of management accounting and management accounting information

- List and explain the attributes and principles of management accounting information

- Explain the integration of management accounting information within an overall information system

- Define and discuss the merits of, and potential problems with, open and closed systems

- Suggest the ways in which contingent (internal and external) factors influence management accounting and its use

- Illustrate how anticipated human behaviour will influence the design of a management accounting system

- Explain and discuss the impact of responsibility accounting on information requirements

BPP
PROFESSIONAL EDUCATION

Exam guide

The uses of management information is one of the core areas of the syllabus. You could face a question specifically on the topics in this chapter or you may need to use them as a framework for a wider question.

The issues covered in this chapter are useful background to the Oxford Brookes degree Research and Analysis Project Topic 9, which requires you to examine how to plan, develop and implement an appropriate information system in an organisation.

---

1 INFORMATION AND MANAGEMENT STRUCTURE

1.1 Management structure varies considerably between different types of entity.

    (a) Company A might be structured on a **divisional** basis as follows.

        (i) A **holding company** board of directors

        (ii) **Subsidiary companies**, each with its own board of directors. Each subsidiary might be a division of the company, such as:

            (1) Hotels division
            (2) Betting shops and casinos division
            (3) Entertainments products division
            (4) Property developments division

    (b) In contrast, Company B might be organised on a **functional** basis as follows.

        (i) Manufacturing
        (ii) Sales and marketing
        (iii) Administration

    Within the sales function, there might be an organisation structure based on sales regions and sales areas within each region. Within the manufacturing function, there might be two or more factories, with separate departments within each factory and separate sections within each department.

Information requirements

1.2 Consider the position of a divisional manager of the entertainments products division of company A as compared with that of a functional manager of company B. Do you think that their information requirements are the same? If you **apply the principles of responsibility accounting** it will be clear that they are not.

    (a) The divisional manager needs to be fully informed about all aspects of his division's activities because he or she is responsible for selling strategy, manufacturing strategy, investment policy and so on.

    (b) The functional manager is only responsible for a part of his organisation's activities and so detailed information need only be supplied to him if it concerns his own function. He or she needs to be aware of how other functions are performing only insofar as his own function's activities need to be co-ordinated with those of other activities.

1.3 As a provider of information the management accountant therefore needs to realise that each manager should be **given information according to what his or her responsibilities are,** and this is dictated by the management structure.

2 OBJECTIVES OF MANAGEMENT ACCOUNTING AND MANAGEMENT ACCOUNTING INFORMATION

The objectives of management accounting

2.1 As its name implies, management accounting involves the **provision of information for managers to use**. This is the main distinction between management accounting and financial and cost accounting.

(a) Financial accounting systems provide information to shareholders and to other interested parties. Cost accounting systems aim primarily to accumulate costs for stock valuation to meet the requirements of external reporting to shareholders.

(b) Management accounting systems provide information specifically for the use of managers within the organisation.

2.2 Managers need information that financial accounting systems and cost accounting systems on their own do not provide.

(a) They need more **detailed** information, to help them to run the business.

(b) They also need **forward-looking** information, for planning.

(c) They will want data to be **analysed differently**, to suit their specific requirements for information.

The objectives of management accounting information

2.3 Management accounting information is used by managers for a variety of purposes.

(a) **To measure profits and put a value to stocks**.

Management accounting systems can be used to analyse the profitability of the business as a whole, and of the individual divisions, departments or products within the business.

Putting a value to closing stocks is an element in the measurement of profits in a period (as well as for balance sheet valuation purposes) and costing systems are used to derive stock values.

(b) **To plan for the future**. Managers have to plan and they need information to do this, much of it management accounting information.

(c) **To control the business**. Controlling the resources of the business, for example in order to achieve satisfactory profits, is a major function of management. Managers need to know the following.

(i) What they want the business to achieve (targets or standards)
(ii) What the business is actually achieving

By comparing the actual achievements with targeted performance, management can decide whether control action is needed.

Much control information is of an accounting nature because costs, revenues, profits and asset values are major factors in how well or how badly a business performs.

(d) **To make decisions**. As we have seen, managers are faced with several types of decision.

(i) Strategic decisions (which relate to the longer term objectives of a business) require information which tends to relate to the organisation as a whole, is in summary form and is derived from both internal and external sources.

(ii) Tactical and operational decisions (which relate to the short or medium term and to a department, product or division rather than the organisation as a whole) require information which is more detailed and more restricted in its sources.

3 ATTRIBUTES AND PRINCIPLES OF MANAGEMENT ACCOUNTING INFORMATION

It should be good information

3.1 Management accounting information should possess the attributes and principles of **good information**.

- It should be **relevant** for its purpose.
- It should be **complete** for its purpose.
- It should be sufficiently **accurate** for its purpose.
- It should be **clear** to the manager using it.
- The manager using it should have **confidence** in it.
- It should be **communicated** to the appropriate manager.
- It should not be excessive, its **volume** should be **manageable**.
- It should be **timely** (in other words communicated at the most appropriate time).
- It should be communicated by an appropriate **channel of communication**.
- It should be provided at a **cost which is less than the value of the benefits** it provides.

Let us have a look at those qualities in a bit more detail.

3.2 Relevance

Information must be relevant to the purpose for which a manager wants to use it. In practice, far too many reports **fail to 'keep to the point'** and contain **purposeless, irritating paragraphs** which only serve to annoy the managers reading them. The consequences of irrelevant information are that managers might be confused by the information and might waste time.

3.3 Completeness

A manager should have all the information he needs to do his job properly. **If he does not have a complete picture of the situation, he might well make bad decisions.** Suppose that the debt collection section of a company is informed that a customer owes £10,000 and the debt is now 4 months overdue. A strongly-worded letter is sent to the customer demanding immediate payment. If an important piece of information had been kept from the debt collection section, for example that the customer had negotiated special credit terms of 6 months, sending a demand for payment is not a correct course of action.

3.4 Accuracy

Using incorrect information could have serious and damaging consequences. However, information should only be **accurate enough for its purpose** and there is no need to go into unnecessary detail for pointless accuracy.

(a) Some tasks of supervisors and clerical staff might need information that is accurate to the nearest penny, second or kilogram. For example, a cashier will do a bank reconciliation to the exact penny and purchase ledger staff will pay creditors exactly what they are owed. Much financial accounting information for day-to-day transactions must indicate amounts to the exact penny.

(b) Middle managers might be satisfied with revenues and costs rounded to the nearest £100 or £1,000, since greater detail would serve no purpose. For example, in budgeting, revenue and cost figures are often rounded to the nearest £1,000. Trying to be more exact would not improve the quality of the information.

(c) Senior managers in a medium-sized to large organisation might be satisfied with figures to the nearest ten thousand pounds, or even hundred thousand or million pounds. Estimates to the nearest pound at this level of decision making would be inappropriate and unnecessary.

3.5 Clarity

If the manager does not understand information properly he cannot use it properly. Lack of clarity is one of the causes of a breakdown in communication, which is referred to in information system theory as 'noise'. It is therefore important to choose the most appropriate presentation medium or channel of communication.

3.6 Confidence

Information must be **trusted by the managers who are expected to use it.** However not all information is certain. An important issue is therefore how to take account of uncertainty and incorporate it into the information, in order to make the information realistic. Strategic information, such as long-term planning information, is uncertain because of the time span involved. However, if the assumptions underlying the information are clearly stated, this should improve the level of confidence the user will have in the information.

3.7 Communication

Within any organisation, **individuals are given the authority to do certain tasks, and they must be given the information they need to do them.** An office manager might be made responsible for controlling expenditures in his office, and given a budget expenditure limit for the year. As the year progresses, he might try to keep expenditure in check but unless he is told throughout the year what is his current total expenditure to date, he will find it difficult to judge whether he is keeping within budget or not.

Information that is needed **might be communicated to the wrong person**. It might be communicated to a person who does not have the authority to act on it, or who is not responsible for the matter and so does not need it.

3.8 Volume

There are physical and mental limitations to what a person can read, absorb and understand properly before taking action. An enormous mountain of information, even if it is all relevant, cannot be handled. Reports to management must therefore be **clear and concise**. In many systems, control action works on the **'exception' principle** (attention is focused on those items where performance differs significantly from standard or budget). This is especially true of information for management control.

3.9 Timing

Information which is **not available until after a decision is made** will be useful only for comparisons and longer-term control, and **may serve no purpose** even then.

Information prepared **too frequently** wastes resources. If, for example, a decision is taken at a monthly meeting about a certain aspect of a company's operations, information to make the decision is only required once a month, and weekly reports would be a time-consuming waste of effort.

The **frequency** with which information is provided should **depend on the needs of the managers for whom it is provided.**

3.10 Channel of communication

There are **occasions when using one particular method of communication will be better than others.** For example, job vacancies should be announced in a medium where they will be brought to the attention of the people most likely to be interested. The channel of communication might be the company's in-house journal, a national or local newspaper, a professional magazine, a job centre or school careers office. Some internal memoranda may be better sent by 'electronic mail'. Some information is best communicated informally by telephone or word-of-mouth, whereas other information ought to be formally communicated in writing or figures.

3.11 Cost

The **benefits obtainable from the information must exceed the costs of acquiring it.** Whenever management is trying to decide whether or not to produce information for a particular purpose (for example whether to computerise an operation), a cost/benefit study ought to be made. For information to have value, it must lead to a decision to take action which results in reducing costs, eliminating losses, increasing sales, better utilisation of resources and so on.

Question: good information

(a) How could an answer to an exam question display each of the qualities of good information?

(b) Your financial director has just asked you to find out for him the current value of your organisation's stock as part of his preparation for a meeting this afternoon. Describe the features of a report that you could prepare that would respond to this request in the **worst possible way.**

Answer

(a) Work through Paragraphs 3.2 to 3.11 with an exam solution in mind. For example an answer is not 'cost effective' if it contains reams of writing in response to a part worth only 2 marks.

(b) The **best possible** report would be a single top sheet showing the total figure: 'Total value of stocks as at (today's date): £3.1m', say. This might be backed up by a slightly more detailed analysis of raw material, WIP and finished goods, or according to product types, but only rounded totals need be given.

(b) The **worst possible** answer would be as far removed from this as possible. Work through each of the items in Paragraphs 3.2 to 3.11, thinking of ways that a report could fail to deliver the information required. For example, closing down production and calling in a team of management consultants to conduct a stock take would be a highly cost-ineffective response.

Other attributes of management accounting information

It may be quantitative or qualitative

3.12 Traditionally for cost and management accounting, and still for the purposes of financial accounting and tax, the main type of information used by accountants is **monetary information.** Indeed, a fundamental accounting concept is that 'accounts' only deal with items to which a monetary value can be ascribed. Money has been seen as an **objective measure** which is understood by all managers, whatever their function in the business.

3.13 So long as **profit maximisation** remains the primary **objective** of most businesses, **monetary information** will continue to be of great **importance**. However, it is becoming increasingly clear that money has occupied its position as the **lingua franca** of managers because it is the only form in which information has to be, and therefore is, available in a sufficiently accessible form. Thanks to **information technology** this is no longer the case. The information used by management accountants will increasingly be **information of all types, drawn from all available sources**.

3.14 However, what we call '**financial information**' has always been capable of being **broken down into a monetary price** on the one hand, and a **non-monetary component** on the other. 'Wages' represents the price of the number of hours worked by a certain number of people. 'Materials costs' are the price of so many kilograms or litres or units of physical substances. The non-monetary component is likely to be more meaningful to many managers.

3.15 **Non-financial information** may also be expressed in terms of **percentages** and **ratios**. For example, details of the number of products returned relative to the number sold gives an indication of product quality. Labour turnover may give an indication of (amongst many other things) whether the remuneration offered is set at a realistic level.

3.16 Information need not be quantitative at all to be of interest to management. 'Closing down the factory will have a major adverse social impact in the area and will damage the organisation's reputation' is a highly significant factor to be taken into account when the decision is made about the future of the factory.

It should be free from bias

3.17 **Bias** may creep into management accounting information in ways such as the following.

(a) A variance report may highlight a manager's failure to achieve a budget target without recognising that, say, the adverse variance against the budget is only half as large this month as it was last month. **Comparative information** should be presented as well if the information is to be interpreted fairly.

(b) A manager in a large company will compare information about the price of supplies on the open market with the price that will be charged to her for the supplies if she buys them from another division or subsidiary of her company. If she finds that the goods produced by the competitor company are cheaper she will buy them from outside, but for a variety of reasons this may not be in the best interests of the company as a whole. The internal price needs to be '**neutral**' so that it leads the manager to take the decision that is in the **best interests of both her own division and of the company as a whole**.

It is generally forward looking

3.18 Unlike financial accounting, for example, management accounting is only concerned with **information relating to the past if it is a useful guide to what will happen in the future**. Details of the labour requirements for a particular production process this year may be relevant to planning and controlling the activity of labour engaged in that process next year, but only if no changes to the process are envisaged.

Simon's attributes of accounting information

3.19 We mentioned this briefly in Chapter 3.

(a) It should be useful for **scorekeeping**. This is basically an exercise in keeping track of financial data so as to enable management to see how well the organisation is doing overall.

(b) It should be **attention directing**. Management accounting should provide reports on key areas of organisational performance and highlight important issues and problems upon which management should focus.

(c) It should be useful for **problem solving**. This aspect of management accounting information is generally associated with the analysis of one-off problems and decisions. The information should provide a means of evaluating alternative responses to such situations.

3.20 Typically all three attributes will be included in an item of management accounting information but the balance between the three will depend on given circumstances.

4 MANAGEMENT ACCOUNTING INFORMATION WITHIN THE MANAGEMENT INFORMATION SYSTEM

Management accounting information within the management information system

4.1 The management accountant's traditional role in an organisation is to provide information to help with planning and control decisions by other managers throughout the organisation.

Management accounting can **provide a basis for much control reporting** by doing the following.

Step 1. Recording actual results

Step 2. Analysing actual results and comparing them with the target, plan or budget

Step 3. Reporting actual results and the comparisons with plan to the managers who are responsible for whatever control action might be necessary

4.2 Management accountants are **not the only people** in an organisation **who provide control information.**

(a) Salespeople or market researchers will provide control information about customers and sales demand.

(b) Quality controllers will provide control information about product quality.

(c) Maintenance staff will provide information about the amount of maintenance and repair work, and reasons for breakdowns.

(d) Research and development staff will provide control information about the progress of product development projects.

4.3 Such information tends to be **highly user-specific and localised** whereas **management accounting systems** provide feedback on **every aspect** of an organisation's operations using the **common denominator, money.**

4.4 The diagram below shows the **division of responsibilities in a typical system.**

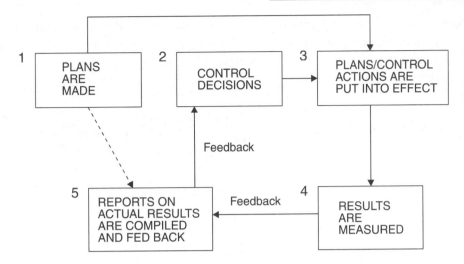

Activities 1, 2, 3 and some of 4 will be done by line managers and their subordinates.

Activity 5 and some of 4 will be done by the management accountant, whose main role is to **provide feedback**. In budgeting, the management accountant, in the role of budget controller, may be required to co-ordinate and consolidate the plans of the various departments into a single master budget. The comparison of actual results with plan is a task that is begun by the management accountant (activity 5) but completed by the line manager (activity 2).

The future

4.5 For as long as budgetary control **based on money** remains central to the co-ordination and control of organisations, management accounting information will retain its **central place** within the overall management information system. Financial information will always be extremely important because commercial organisations aim to make profits and even non-profit-making organisations or public sector bodies must break even financially or keep spending within budgeted limits.

4.6 The **role of the management accountant** and the **type of information** he is expected to provide is **changing. Developments in information technology** mean that almost instantaneous feedback can in theory be obtained at the touch of a button. The impact on the traditional management accounting function could be profound.

5   OPEN AND CLOSED SYSTEMS

5.1 The word **system** is impossible to define satisfactorily (the tax 'system', the respiratory 'system', the class 'system'). Basically it means **something that connects things up.**

> **KEY TERM**
>
> A **closed system** is isolated and shut off from the environment, is unaffected by the environment and cannot influence the environment.

5.2 Closed systems are seldom, if ever, found in naturally occurring situations. A typical example of a closed system would be a chemical reaction that takes place under controlled conditions within a laboratory. Closed systems can be created to **eliminate external factors** and then used to **investigate the relationship between known variables** in an experiment.

133

5.3 All social systems have some interaction with the environment and so cannot be closed systems. A commercial organisation, for example, could not operate as a closed system as it would be unable to react to the external environment and so would not be commercially or economically viable.

> ### KEY TERM
>
> An **open system** is connected to and interacts with the environment and is influenced by it.

5.4 An open system **accepts inputs from its surroundings, processes the inputs in some manner and then produces an output.** The **input parameters** can be **foreseen** or be **unpredictable.** Similarly, **outputs** can either be **predicted** or **unforeseen.** For example, consider a metal smelting works. Predictable inputs would include items like the raw materials and coal while the predictable outputs would be ash, smoke and the smelted metal. If the raw material to be smelted became contaminated in some way, it is likely that an undesirable product would be produced. These are examples of unforeseen inputs and outputs.

5.5 All social systems, including **business organisations,** are **open systems**. For example, a business is a system where management decisions are influenced by or have an influence on suppliers, customers, competitors, the government and society as a whole. Employees are obviously influenced by what they do in their job, but as members of society at large they are also part of the external environment, just as their views and opinions expressed within the business are often a reflection of their opinions as members of society at large.

6 CONTINGENT FACTORS

> ### KEY TERM
>
> A **contingent factor** is a factor that may or may not apply, depending upon the specific circumstances. The three main contingent factors are technology, organisation structure and the environment.

6.1 As we saw in Chapter 3, studies of the contingency approach to management accounting typically look at the way in which the contingent factors affect the design of management accounting systems and hence the way in which management accounting information is used.

Factor	Explanation
Technology	Obviously a **computerised accounting system** is differently designed to a manual one. Also, the nature of the **production process** determines the level of detail and accuracy that can be achieved. We have already seen the profound impact that **advanced manufacturing technology** is having on management accounting.

Factor	Explanation
Organisation structure	Essentially this is the 'social' factor, the different **relationships** that can exist between the various **parts** of an organisation and the **people** within them, the relative size of those parts and the degree of interdependence. **Responsibility accounting** systems are a good example.
The environment	Factors include the **competitive** environment in which the organisation operates and the degree of **uncertainty** that exists. For example, where there is intense competition on **price**, the accounting system needs to control **costs** very closely; where competition is based on **product differentiation**, information about product **quality** is vital. An organisation that is continually launching **new products** needs more sophisticated **forecasting** capability from its system than one that is well-established in a **stable, predictable** market.

7 HUMAN BEHAVIOUR AND MANAGEMENT ACCOUNTING

7.1 Managers have an impact upon information, whether they intend to or not, simply because they are people.

(a) As people, they have **personal needs and motivations** which are quite **separate from the objectives of the organisation** but which cannot fail to influence the workings of it.

(b) People are the receivers of information, but because they are people they do **not all necessarily respond in the same way to the same information**.

(c) People are also the senders of information, but because they are people they do **not necessarily send** the **information they ought to send**.

7.2 Management accounting **systems** have to **develop ways of overcoming the problems of human behaviour** – by allocating responsibility, encouraging participation in decision making, devising ways of measuring and rewarding behaviour that contribute to organisational objectives and so on. Much has been written on the subject, and we shall return to it in later parts of the text.

8 INFORMATION AND RESPONSIBILITY ACCOUNTING

KEY TERMS

Responsibility accounting is a system of accounting that segregates revenues and costs into areas of personal responsibility in order to monitor and assess the performance of each part of an organisation.

A responsibility centre is any part of an organisation which is headed by a manager who has direct responsibility for its performance.

8.1 If a manager is to bear responsibility for the performance of his area of the business he will need information about its performance. In essence, a manager needs to know three things.

Requirements	Examples of information
What are his resources?	Finance, stocks of raw materials, spare machine capacity, labour availability, the balance of expenditure remaining for a certain budget, target date for completion of a job.
At what rate are his resources being consumed?	How fast is his labour force working, how quickly are his raw materials being used up, how quickly are other expenses being incurred, how quickly is available finance being consumed?
How well are the resources being used?	How well are his objectives being met?

8.2 This is the content of the information provided, but decisions must also be made as to the **level of detail** that is provided and the frequency with which information is provided. Moreover the **cost** of providing information must be **weighed against the benefit** derived from it.

8.3 In a traditional system managers are given monthly reports, but there is no logical reason for this except that it ties in with financial reporting cycles and may be administratively convenient. With **modern systems**, however, there is a danger of **information overload**, since information technology allows the information required to be made available much more frequently.

8.4 The **task of the management accountant**, therefore, is to learn from the managers of responsibility centres **what information** they need, in **what form** and at **what intervals**, and then to design a system that enables this to be provided.

8.5 It is to this end that responsibility centres are usually divided into **different categories** (cost centres, revenue centres, profit centres and investment centres).

Exam focus point

The two compulsory questions in Section A will have a significant computational element. One or two of the questions in Section B will be purely discursive.

Chapter roundup

- Each manager needs to be given information according to what his or her **responsibilities** are.

- Management accounting information is used by managers for a **variety of purposes.**

- Management accounting information should posses the attributes and principles of **good information**. It may be **quantitative** or **qualitative**, it should be **free from bias** and it is generally **forward looking. Simon** specified three **attributes** of accounting information.

- The **role of the management accountant** and **the type of information** he is expected to provide is **changing.**

- Systems can be **open** or **closed.**

- A **contingent factor** is a factor that may or may not apply, depending upon specific circumstances.

- Management accounting systems have to develop ways of overcoming the problems of **human behaviour.**

- The management accountant has to learn from managers of **responsibility centres** what information they need, in what form and at what intervals, and then has to design a system that enables this information to be provided.

Quick quiz

1   *Complete the nine qualities of good information listed below.*

- It should be .... for its purpose.
- It should be .... for its purpose.
- It should be sufficiently .... for its purpose.
- It should be .... to the manager using it.
- The manager using it should have .... in it.
- It should be .... to the appropriate manager.
- It should not be excessive, its .... should be ....
- It should be .... (in other words communicated at the most appropriate time).
- It should be communicated by an appropriate ....
- It should be provided at a .... it provides.

2   *Fill in the blanks in the definitions below.*

Quantitative information is information that can be expressed in numbers. A sub-category of quantitative information is ....(also known as ....), which is information that can be expressed in terms of money.

.... is information that cannot be expressed in numbers.

.... (or ....) is information that is not expressed in terms of money.

3   What are Simon's attributes of accounting information?

A   Scorekeeping, forward looking, problem solving
B   Forward looking, quantitative, neutral
C   Scorekeeping, attention directing, problem solving
D   Attention directing, neutral, comparative

4   Open systems are seldom, if ever, found in naturally occurring situations. *True/False?*

5   What are the three main contingent factors?

A   Technology, structure, environment
B   Size, technology, environment
C   Structure, strategy, culture
D   Culture, systems, size

6   Which of the four general objectives of management accounting information is missing from the list below?

- To measure profits and put a value to stocks
- To control the business
- To make decisions

Answers to quick quiz

1   Have a look at Paragraph 3.1 if you had trouble.

2   Quantitative information is information that can be expressed in numbers. A sub-category of quantitative information is **financial information** (also known as **monetary information)**, which is information that can be expressed in terms of money.

Qualitative information is information that cannot be expressed in numbers.

Non-financial information (or **non-monetary information**) is information that is not expressed in terms of money.

3   C

4   False. It is closed systems that are seldom found.

5   A

6   To plan for the future

Now try the question below from the Exam Question Bank

Number	Level	Marks	Time
25	Exam	20	36 mins

Question 25 is a pilot paper question and has been fully analysed to provide you with guidance on how to approach Paper 3.3 questions.

Chapter 8

INTERNAL AND EXTERNAL SOURCES OF INFORMATION

Topic list	Syllabus reference
1 Internal sources of management accounting information	2(b)
2 Internally-sourced information for control purposes	2(b)
3 Costs of internally-sourced information	2(b)
4 Controls over generating and distributing internal information	2(b)
5 Capacity and development potential of a system	2(b)
6 Security	2(b)
7 External sources of information	2(b)
8 Costs, benefits and limitations of external information	2(b)
9 External information and the management accounting system	2(b)

Introduction

In this chapter we discuss the internal and external sources of information. **External information** is vital for strategic planning and performance feedback, but it is rarely directly input into a management accounting system. That is the role of **internal information**. Strategic management accounting has to be externally orientated and future orientated, however, and so external information needs to be taken into account.

Study guide

Section 8 – Internal sources of information

- Identify the principal internal sources of management accounting information

- Illustrate how these principal sources of information might be used for control purposes

- Identify the direct data capture and process costs of internally generated management accounting information

- Identify the indirect costs of producing internal information

- Explain the principal controls required in generating and distributing internal information

- Discuss the factors that need to be considered when determining the capacity and development potential of a system

- Explain the procedures that may be necessary to ensure security of highly confidential information that is not for external consumption

Section 9 – External sources of information

- Identify common external sources of information

- Identify the costs associated with these external sources

BPP
PROFESSIONAL EDUCATION

- Discuss the limitations of using externally generated information

- Identify the categories of external information that are likely to be a useful addition to an organisation's management accounting system

- Illustrate how the information might be used in planning and control activities

Exam guide

The Study Guide lets you off fairly lightly here.

In short it appears, at this Level 3 paper, that you have to list, apply some common sense and use your imagination to see how the information can be employed. Consequently, you are unlikely to find a whole exam question on these topics.

1 INTERNAL SOURCES OF MANAGEMENT ACCOUNTING INFORMATION

1.1 **Capturing** data/information from inside the organisation involves the following.

(a) A **system for collecting or measuring transactions data** – for example sales, purchases, stock turnover and so on – which sets out procedures for **what** data is collected, **how frequently, by whom** and by **what methods,** and how it is **processed, and filed** or **communicated.**

(b) **Informal communication** of information between managers and staff (for example, by word-of-mouth or at meetings).

(c) **Communication between managers.**

Sources of monetary and non-monetary information

The financial accounting records

1.2 You are by now very familiar with the idea of a system of sales ledgers and purchase ledgers, general ledgers, cash books and so on. These records provide a **history of an organisation's monetary transactions**.

1.3 Some of this information is of great value outside the accounts department - most obviously, for example, sales information for the marketing function. Other information, like cheque numbers, is of purely administrative value within the accounts department.

1.4 You will also be aware that to maintain the integrity of its financial accounting records, an organisation of any size will have systems for and **controls over transactions**. These also give rise to valuable information.

1.5 A stock control system is the classic example: besides actually recording the monetary value of purchases and stock in hand for external financial reporting purposes, the system will include purchase orders, goods received notes, goods returned notes and so on, and these can be analysed to provide management information about **speed** of delivery, say, or the **quality** of supplies.

Other internal sources

1.6 Much information that is not strictly part of the financial accounting records nevertheless is closely tied in to the accounting system.

(a) Information about personnel will be linked to the **payroll** system. Additional information may be obtained from this source if, say, a project is being costed and it is necessary to ascertain the availability and rate of pay of different levels of staff.

(b) Much information will be produced by a **production** department about machine capacity, movement of materials and work in progress, set up times, maintenance requirements and so on.

(c) Many service businesses - notably accountants and solicitors - need to keep detailed records of the **time** spent on various activities, both to justify fees to clients and to assess the efficiency of operations.

1.7 **Staff** themselves are one of the primary sources of internal information. Information may be obtained either **informally** in the course of day-to-day business or **formally** through **meetings, interviews** or **questionnaires**.

Question: sources of information

Think of at least one piece of non-monetary information that a management accountant might obtain from the following sources in order to make a decision about a new product.

(a) Marketing manager
(b) Vehicle fleet supervisor
(c) Premises manager

(d) Public relations officer
(e) Head of research

---

2 INTERNALLY-SOURCED INFORMATION FOR CONTROL PURPOSES

2.1 **Control** is dependant on the **receipt and processing of information**, both to plan in the first place and to compare actual results against the plan, so as to judge what control measures are needed.

2.2 **Plans** will be based on an **awareness of the environment** (from externally-sourced information) and on the **current performance of the organisation** (based on internal information such as, for example, sales volumes, costs and so on).

2.3 **Control** is achieved through **feedback** – information about actual results produced from within the organisation (that is internal information) such as variance control reports for the purpose of helping management with control decisions.

2.4 We will be looking at control in far greater detail later in the text.

3 COSTS OF INTERNALLY-SOURCED INFORMATION

3.1 The costs to an organisation of the collection, processing and production of internal information can be divided into three types.

Cost	Examples
Direct data capture	• Use of bar coding and scanners (for example, in retailing and manufacturing)
	• Employee time spent filling in timesheets
	• Secretary time spent taking minutes at a meeting

Cost	Examples
Processing	• Payroll department time spent processing and analysing personnel costs
	• Time for personnel to input data (for example, in relation to production) on to the MIS
Inefficient use of information	• Information collected but not needed
	• Information stored long after it is needed
	• Information disseminated more widely than necessary
	• Collection of the same information by more than one method
	• Duplication of information

4 CONTROLS OVER GENERATING AND DISTRIBUTING INTERNAL INFORMATION

4.1 Controls over generating internal information in routine reports

(a) Carry out a **cost/benefit analysis.** How **easy** is the report to prepare **compared** with the **usefulness** of the decisions that can be taken as a result of its production? The cost of preparing the report will in part be determined by **who** is preparing it. The cost can be reduced if its preparation can be **delegated** by a director to a junior member of staff.

(b) A **trial** preparation process should be carried out and a **prototype** prepared. Users should be asked to confirm that their requirements will be met.

(c) A **consistent** format and consistent definitions should be used to ensure that reporting is **accurate** and the chance of misinterpretation is minimised. Standard **house styles** will ensure that time is not wasted by managers, staff and report writers on designing alternative layouts.

(d) The **originator** of the report should be clearly identified so that users' queries can be dealt with quickly.

(e) The report should set out clearly **limits to the action** that users **can take as a result** of the information in the report. This will ensure that the organisation's system of responsibilities is maintained.

(f) The **usefulness** of the report should be **assessed** on a periodic basis to ensure that its production is necessary.

4.2 Controls over generating internal information in ad-hoc reports (such as for onc-off decisions)

(a) Carry out a **cost/benefit** analysis as above.
(b) Ensure that the required information **does not already exist** in another format.
(c) Brief the report writer so that the **relevant information only** is provided.
(d) Ensure that the **originator** is clearly identified.
(e) Ensure that report writers have access to the **most up-to-date information.**

4.3 Controls over distributing internal information

(a) **Procedures manual** (for standard reports)

    (i) Indicates what standard reports should be issued and when (for example, budgetary control report for department X on a monthly basis)

    (ii) Sets out the format of standard reports

(iii)   Makes clear who should receive particular standard reports

(iv)   Indicates whether reports should be shredded (if confidential) or just binned

(v)   Makes clear what information should be regarded as highly confidential

(b)   **Other controls**

(i)   **Payroll and personnel information** should be kept in a **locked** cabinet or be protected by **password** access on a computer system.

(ii)   All employees should be **contractually required not to divulge confidential information.**

(iii)   The internal mail system should make use of '**private and confidential**' **stamps**.

(iv)   An appropriate **e-mail policy** should be set up.

(1)   E-mail is best suited to short messages rather than detailed operational problems.

(2)   E-mail provides a relatively permanent means of communication, which may be undesirable for confidential/'off-the-record' exchanges.

(3)   Staff may suffer from information overload.

(4)   It is uncomfortable to read more than a full screen of information. Longer messages will either not be read properly or will be printed out (in which case they may just as well have been circulated in hard copy form).

4.4   If information is held on a server

- Controls over viruses and hacking
- Clearly understood policy on the use of e-mails and corporate IT
- Password system to restrict access to particular files

5   CAPACITY AND DEVELOPMENT POTENTIAL OF A SYSTEM

5.1   A number of factors must be considered when determining the capacity and development potential of a system.

(a)   **The organisation's long-term plans**. If an organisation is expecting to grow and expand, its information system must have the capacity to be able to deal effectively with that growth and expansion. For example, does it intend introducing computerised point of sale terminals at cash desks?

(b)   **The pace of change in technology**. Does the organisation want to move into e-commerce? Does it intend to invest heavily in advanced manufacturing technology?

(c)   **Cost**. The value of any benefits from an expansion in capacity or a development in the system must be greater than the associated cost.

(d)   **A source of competitive advantage**. For example, many organisations now offer an on-line shopping service.

(e)   **Management information required**. An organisation may wish to consider the use of a particular type of management information system, such as a decision support system or an expert system, to enhance the flexibility and depth of the information available to the organisation. The desire to implement a particular management accounting technique, such as activity based costing, may require developments to the system.

(f)   **Stakeholders**. System capacity and development may be influenced by various stakeholder groups. For example, an electronic data interchange (EDI) system allows communication between the organisation, its **suppliers** and its **customers.** **Government regulations** may require particular features in an information system so as to allow certain reporting.

(g) **Marketing.** How does the organisation identify markets? Does it need to expand its system to allow it to use database systems to analyse the market place?

5.2 In today's competitive environment, where the pace of change in information systems and technology is rapid, organisations must be flexible enough to adapt to change quickly and must plan for expansion, growth and innovation within information systems.

6 SECURITY

6.1 **Disaffected employees** have potential to do deliberate damage to valuable corporate data or systems, especially if the information system is networked, because they may have access to parts of the system that they are not really authorised to use.

6.2 If the organisation is linked to an external network, **people outside** the company (hackers) may also be able to get into the company's internal network, either to steal data or to damage the system.

Case example

A third of the UK's largest companies and public sector organisations were victims of hacking during 2000/2001. Hackers raided bank accounts, stole information, graffitied sites, crashed networks and blanked computer chips. Many of the victims were well known firms such as Lloyds of London, HSBC and Abbey National, and the security of the government's internet service is said to be a shambles.

6.3 Various **procedures** are therefore necessary to **ensure the security of highly confidential information that is not for external consumption.**

Passwords

6.4 Passwords are a set of characters allocated to a person, terminal or facility which have to be keyed into the system before further access is permitted.

6.5 In order to access a system the user needs first to enter a string of characters. If what is entered matches a password issued to an authorised user or valid for that particular terminal the system permits access. Otherwise the system **shuts down** and may **record the attempted unauthorised access.**

6.6 Keeping track of these attempts can alert managers to repeated efforts to break into the system; in these cases the culprits might be caught, particularly if there is an apparent pattern to their efforts.

6.7 The restriction of access to a system with passwords is **effective** and **widely used** but the **widespread and growing use of PCs and networks** is making **physical isolation virtually impossible.** The wider use of information systems requires that access to the system becomes equally widespread and easy. **Requirements for system security must be balanced by the operational requirements for access:** rigidly enforced isolation of the system may significantly reduce the value of the system.

Logical access systems

6.8 Whereas **physical access control (doors, locks and so on)** is concerned with the prevention of unauthorised persons **gaining access to the hardware, logical access control** is concerned with **preventing those who already have access to a terminal or a computer from gaining access to data or software.**

6.9 In a logical access system, data and software, or individual computer systems, will be **classified according to the sensitivity and confidentiality of data.**

(a) Thus payroll data or details of the draft corporate budget for the coming year may be perceived as highly sensitive and made available to identified individuals only.

(b) Other financial information may be made available to certain groups of staff only, for example members of the finance function or a certain grade of management.

(c) Other data may be unrestricted.

6.10 A logical access system performs three operations when access is requested.

- Identification of the user
- Authentication of user identity
- Check on user authority

Database controls

6.11 Databases present a particular problem for computer security. In theory, the database can be **accessed by large numbers of people,** and so the possibility of **alteration, unauthorised disclosure or fraud is so much greater than with application-specific files.**

6.12 It is possible to construct **complicated password systems,** and the system can be **programmed** to give a limited view of its contents to particular users or restrict the disclosure of certain types of information to particular times of day. It is possible to build a set of **privileges** into the system, so allowing authorised users with a particular password to access more information.

6.13 There are problems ensuring that individuals do not circumvent the database by means of **inference,** however. If you ask enough questions, you should be able to infer from the replies the information you are really seeking.

6.14 For example, the database forbids you to ask if John is employee Category A. However, if you know there are only three employee categories, A, B, and C, and there is no prohibition on asking about categories B and C, you can work out the members of category A by process of elimination (ie neither B, or C, therefore A).

6.15 So-called 'inference controls' exist to make this difficult by **limiting the number of queries, or by controlling the overlap between questions.**

Firewalls

6.16 Systems can have firewalls to **prevent unauthorised access into company systems.** Firewalls can be implemented in both **hardware and software,** or a combination of both. Firewalls are frequently used to **prevent unauthorised Internet users from accessing private networks connected to the Internet, especially Intranets.** All messages entering or leaving the Intranet pass through the firewall, which examines each message and blocks those that do not meet specified security criteria.

Encryption

6.17 Information transmitted from one part of an organisation to another may be intercepted. Data can be encrypted (**scrambled**) in an attempt to make it **unintelligible to eavesdroppers**.

Other safety measures

6.18 **Authentication** is a technique for making sure that a message has come from an authorised sender.

6.19 **Dial back security** operates by requiring the person wanting access to the network to dial into it and identify themselves first. The system then dials the person back on their authorised number before allowing them access.

6.20 All attempted violations of security should be automatically **logged** and the log checked regularly. In a multi-user system, the terminal attempting the violation may be automatically disconnected.

Personal data

6.21 In recent years there has been a growing popular fear that **information about individuals which is stored on computer files** and processed by computer can be **misused**.

6.22 In particular, it is felt that an individual could easily be **harmed** by the existence of computerised data about himself which was **inaccurate** or **misleading** and which could be **transferred** to unauthorised third parties at high speed and little cost.

6.23 As a result most countries have introduced **legislation** designed to protect the individual. In the UK the current legislation is the Data Protection Act 1998.

Personnel security planning

6.24 Certain employees will always be placed in a position of trust, for example senior systems analysts, the database administrator and the computer security officer. With the growth of networks, almost all employees may be in a position to do damage to a computer system. A recent report claims that 80% of hacking is done by employees.

6.25 Although most employees are honest and well-intentioned, it may be relatively easy for individuals to **compromise the security** of an organisation if they wish to do so. The following types of measure are therefore necessary.

- Careful recruitment
- Job rotation
- Supervision and observation by a superior
- Review of computer usage (for example via systems logs)
- Enforced vacations

6.26 The key is that **security should depend on the minimum possible number of personnel;** although this is a weakness, it is also a strength.

7   EXTERNAL SOURCES OF INFORMATION

7.1   Capturing information from outside the organisation might be carried out formally and entrusted to particular individuals, or might be 'informal'.

7.2   **Examples of formal collection of data from outside sources**

(a)   A company's **tax specialists** will be expected to gather information about changes in tax law and how this will affect the company.

(b)   Obtaining information about any new legislation on health and safety at work, or employment regulations, must be the responsibility of a particular person - for example the company's **legal expert** or **company secretary** - who must then pass on the information to other managers affected by it.

(c)   Research and development (R & D) work often relies on information about other R & D work being done by another company or by government institutions. An **R & D official** might be made responsible for finding out about R & D work outside the company.

(d)   **Marketing managers** need to know about the opinions and buying attitudes of potential customers. To obtain this information, they might carry out market research exercises.

7.3   **Informal** gathering of information from the environment **goes on all the time, consciously or unconsciously,** because the employees of an organisation learn **what is going on in the world around** them - perhaps from newspapers, television reports, meetings with business associates or the trade press.

7.4   Organisations hold external information such as invoices, letters, advertisements and so on **received from customers and suppliers**. But there are many occasions when an active search outside the organisation is necessary.

Specific external sources

7.5   **Directories**. Examples (of business directories) include the following (although there are many others).

- Kompass Register (Kompass)
- Who owns Whom (Dun and Bradstreet)
- Key British Enterprises (Dun and Bradstreet)

7.6   **Associations**. There are associations in almost every field of business and leisure activity. All these bodies collect and publish data for their members which can be of great interest to other users. Examples of such bodies include the Road Haulage Association (RHA), the British Association of Ski Instructors and the ACCA!

7.7   **Government agencies.** The government is a major source of economic information and information about industry and population trends. Examples of UK government publications are as follows.

(a)   **National Statistics,** divided into 13 separate themes such as economy, health, labour market etc.

(b)   The **Digest of UK Energy Statistics** (published annually)

(c)   **Housing and Construction Statistics** (published quarterly)

(d) **Financial Statistics** (monthly)

(e) **Economic Trends** (monthly)

(f) **Census of Population**. The Office for National Statistics publishes continuous datasets including the **National Food Survey**, the **Household Survey** and the **Family Expenditure Survey**

(g) **Department of Employment Gazette** (monthly) gives details of employment in the UK

(h) **British Business**, published weekly by the Department of Trade and Industry, gives data on industrial and commercial trends at home and overseas

(i) **Business Monitor** (published by the Business Statistics Office), gives detailed information about various industries

(j) **Social Trends** (annually)

Official statistics are also published by other government bodies such as the European Union, the United Nations and local authorities.

7.8 **Other published sources.** This group includes all other publications, including some **digests** and **pocket books** and **periodicals** (often available in the public libraries).

7.9 **Syndicated services.** The sources of secondary data we have looked at so far have generally been **free** because they are **in the public domain**. Inexpensiveness is an advantage which can be offset by the fact that the information is **unspecific** and needs **considerable analysis** before being useable. A middle step between adapting secondary data and commissioning primary research is the **purchase of data collected by market research companies** or business publishing houses. The data tend to be expensive but less costly than primary research.

7.10 **Consumer panels.** A form of continuous research which result in secondary data often bought in by marketers is that generated by **consumer panels**. These constitute a representative sample of individuals and households whose buying activity in a defined area is monitored either continuously (every day, with results aggregated) or at regular intervals, **over a period of time**. There are panels set up to monitor purchases of groceries, consumer durables, cars, baby products and many others.

Information from customers

7.11 Customers can provide useful information.

(a) Firms send out satisfaction questionnaires and market research.
(b) Customer comments and complaints sent voluntarily can suggest improvements.

Information from suppliers

7.12 Supplier information comes in several categories.

Information	Comment
'Bid' information	A supplier pitching for a product will detail products, services and prices. This is before a deal is done.
Operational information	If a firm has placed a particular job or contract with a supplier, the supplier may provide details of the stages in the manufacturing process, eg the delivery time.

Information	Comment
Pricing information	Component prices vary from industry to industry; some are volatile.
Technology	Technological developments in the supplier's industry can affect the type of input components, their cost and their availability.

The Internet

> **KEY TERM**
>
> The **Internet** is a global network connecting millions of computers.

7.13 The Internet offers efficient, fast and cost effective **email**, and massive information **search and retrieval facilities**. There is a great deal of financial information available and users can also **access publications** and news releases issued by the Treasury and other Government departments.

7.14 Besides its usefulness for **tapping into worldwide information resources,** businesses are also using it to **provide information about their own products and services** and to conduct **research** into their competitors' activities.

7.15 The Internet offers a **speedy** and **impersonal** way of getting to know the basics (or even the details) of the services that a company provides. For businesses the advantage is that it is much **cheaper** to provide the information in electronic form.

7.16 The Internet is commonly used to **access information about suppliers**.

  (a) A firm can visit a supplier's website for details of products and services.

  (b) The user can search a number of websites through a browser. Note that the Internet may not contain every supplier; arguably it should not be relied upon as the sole source.

  (c) A number of business-to-business sites have been opened. Participating members offer their services, and can offer quotes. A lot of the communication search problem is avoided.

Case example

Dotgain.co.uk is a website for printers and publishers. A publisher who wants to have a book printed requests a quote by entering details of jobs and timescales on the site. Any printers who are interested in supplying a quote can contact the book publisher directly via e-mail.

Other sites, such as *paperx.com* offer up to date market information, standard indices on paper prices as well as providing a quotation service in several languages.

Moreover, paperx.com is supporting the creation of PapiNet.xml, a standard language in which suppliers and customers can exchange information about paper.

Significance

  • Printers have a wider opportunity to source paper from suppliers all over the world.

  • The lead-time between finding information and obtaining a quote is much reduced, leading to quicker decision making.

- Customers (publishers) can have a better idea of conditions and trends in the market.
- This information is now much cheaper to obtain.

Database information

7.17 A **management information system** or **database** should provide managers with a **useful flow** of **relevant information** which is **easy to use** and **easy to access**. Information is an important corporate resource. Managed and used effectively it can provide considerable competitive advantage and so it is a worthwhile investment.

7.18 It is now possible to access large volumes of generally available information through databases held by public bodies and businesses.

(a) Some **newspapers** offer computerised access to old editions, with search facilities looking for information on particular companies or issues. FTPROFILE, for example, provides on-line business information.

(b) **Public databases** are also available for inspection.

Dun and Bradstreet provide general business information. **AC Nielsen** operate on-line information regarding products and market share.

7.19 Developments in information technology allow businesses to have access to the databases of **external organisations**. Reuters, for example, provides an on-line information system about money market interest rates and foreign exchange rates to firms involved in money market and foreign exchange dealings, and to the treasury departments of a large number of companies. The growing adoption of technology at **point of sale** provides a potentially invaluable source of data to both retailer and manufacturer.

Case example

CACI is a company which provides market analysis, information systems and other data products to clients. It advertises itself as 'the winning combination of marketing and technology".

As an illustration of the information available to the marketing manager through today's technology, here is an overview of some of their products.

Paycheck	This provides income data for all 1.6 million individual post codes across the UK. This enables companies to see how mean income distribution varies from area to area.
People UK	This is a mix of geodemographics, life stage and lifestyle data. It is person rather than household specific and is designed for those companies requiring highly targeted campaigns.
InSite	This is a geographic information system (GIS). It is designed to assist with local market planning, customers and product segmentation, direct marketing and service distribution.
Acorn	This stands for A Classification of Residential Neighbourhoods, and has been used to profile residential neighbourhoods by post code since 1976. ACORN classifies people in any trading area or on any customer database into 54 types.
Lifestyles UK	This database offers over 300 lifestyle selections on 44 million consumers in the UK. It helps with cross selling and customer retention strategies.
Monica	This can help a company to identify the age of people on its database by giving the likely age profile of their first names. It uses a combination of census data and real birth registrations.

On-line databases

7.20 Most external databases are on-line databases, which are very large computer files of information, supplied by **database providers** and managed by 'host' companies whose business revenue is generated through charges made to **users**. Access to such databases is open to anyone prepared to pay, and who is equipped with a PC plus a modem (to provide a phone link to the database) and communication software. These days there are an increasing number of companies offering free internet access. Most databases can be accessed around the clock.

> **Exam focus point**
>
> Part of a December 2002 question (for five marks) required candidates to identify relevant sources of external information to enable a motor component manufacturer to improve its awareness of the external environment.

8 COSTS, BENEFITS AND LIMITATIONS OF EXTERNAL INFORMATION

Costs

8.1 Identifying the costs of obtaining external data is not difficult. Effectively there are five types of cost.

Cost	Examples
Direct search costs	• Cost of a marketing research survey (these can be considerable)
	• Subscriptions to online databases
	• Subscriptions to magazines, services
	• Download fees
Indirect access costs	• Management and employee time spent finding useful information
	• Wasted management and employee time on unsuccessful searches for information
	• Time theft – using office equipment and facilities for private internet activity during working hours
	• Spurious accuracy / redundancy
	• Wasted management and employee time on excessive searching
	• Wasted time on trying to find spurious accuracy
Management costs	• Recording, processing and dissemination of external information
	• Wasted time due to information overload
	• Wasted time on excessive processing
Infrastructure costs	• Installation and maintenance of computer networks, servers, landlines etc to facilitate internet searching and internal electronic communication

Cost	Examples
Time-theft	• Wasted time caused by abuse of Internet and e-mail access facilities
	• Lost time
	• Cost of monitoring and disciplinary procedures
	• Information overload

8.2 Effect of the Internet

As can be seen from the earlier case example, the **Internet** can significantly reduce search time and search cost. More information can be had for less money.

Benefits and limitations of external data

8.3 The benefits can be quantified in the following terms.

(a) The quality of **decisions** that the data has influenced

(b) **Risk / uncertainties** avoided by having the data

(c) The organisation's ability to **respond** appropriately to the environment or to **improve** its performance

8.4 One of the principal **limitations** of external data is that its **quality** cannot be guaranteed. Its **quality** will depend on the following characteristics.

(a) The **producers** of the data. (They may have an axe to grind; trade associations may not include data which runs counter to the interests of its members.)

(b) The **reason for the data** being collected in the first place

(c) The **collection method**. (Random samples with a poor response rate are particularly questionable.)

(d) The **age** of the data. (Government statistics and information based on them are often relatively dated, though information technology has speeded up the process.)

(e) **How parameters were defined**. (For instance, the definition of family used by some researchers could well be very different to that used by others.)

8.5 Using poor quality external data can have disastrous consequences: projects may proceed on the basis of overstated demand levels; opportunities may not be grasped because data is out of date and does not show the true state of the market.

8.6 **Advantages arising from the use of secondary (as opposed to primary) data**

(a) The data may solve the problem without the need for any primary research: **time and money is thereby saved**.

(b) **Cost savings** can be substantial because secondary data sources are a great deal **cheaper** than those for primary research.

(c) **Secondary data**, while not necessarily fulfilling all the needs of the business, can be of great use.

(i) **Setting the parameters**, defining a hypothesis, highlighting variables, in other words, helping to focus on the central problem.

152

(ii) **Providing guidance,** by showing past methods of research and so on, for primary data collection.

(iii) **Helping to assimilate the primary research** with past research, highlighting trends and the like.

(iv) **Defining sampling parameters** (target populations, variables and so on).

8.7 **Disadvantages to the use of secondary data**

(a) **Relevance.** The data may not be relevant to the research objectives in terms of the data content itself, classifications used or units of measurement.

(b) **Cost.** Although secondary data is usually cheaper than primary data, some specialist reports can cost large amounts of money. A cost-benefit analysis will determine whether such secondary data should be used or whether primary research would be more economical.

(c) **Availability.** Secondary data may not exist in the specific product or market area.

(d) **Bias.** The secondary data may be biased, depending on who originally carried it out and for what purpose. Attempts should be made to obtain the most original source of the data, to assess it for such bias.

(e) **Accuracy.** The accuracy of the data should be questioned.

8.8 The golden rule when using secondary data is **use only meaningful data.** It is obviously sensible to begin with internal sources and a firm with a good management information system should be able to provide a great deal of data. External information should be consulted in order of ease and speed of access: directories, catalogues and indexes before books, abstracts and periodicals (Stoll and Stewart, 1984).

9 EXTERNAL INFORMATION AND THE MANAGEMENT ACCOUNTING SYSTEM

9.1 **External information** is useful to **management accounting systems** insofar as it contributes to **planning, decision making** and **control.** Here are **examples.**

Management function	Type of information	Accounting document/process
Planning	• Demand estimates • Market research	• Sales budget
Decision making	• Demand estimates • Market research • Competitor research	• Breakeven analysis • Production costs of providing product features • Competitor costs
Control	• Demand estimates • Price variances	• Sales variance reports • Benchmarking for variances (see below)

9.2 As we mentioned earlier, however, the **value of external information for planning, control and decision making** will very much **depend** on the **quality of the information,** which is very **difficult to assess and/or guarantee.**

Question: externally- and internally-sourced information

Cast your mind back to Chapters 1 and 2. Does strategic planning, control and decision making use mostly externally- or internally-sourced information?

Answer

Planning, control and decision making at strategic level uses mostly externally-sourced information. Operational planning, control and decision making uses mostly internally-sourced information. Management control activities use a mixture of both.

9.3   Clearly, **some external information**, such as 'technological' or 'political' developments, **does not feed into the management accounting system**, even though it can be in a broader category of management information.

9.4   External information of a **quantitative** nature is **easier to feed into the management accounting system**. For example, forecasts of revenues, costs and profits derived from market research and targets based on competitors' performance (the information having been sourced from the Internet) are easier to incorporate than qualitative information.

Exam focus point

Paper 3.3 is less 'numbers orientated' than its equivalent paper under the old syllabus and so it is important to bear in mind the following comment by the examiner.

'Candidates who chose to answer discursive questions in preference to those with computational elements should not regard them as an easy option that provides them with the opportunity to write down all they know in the time available – they need to be disciplined in their approach and answer the question posed'.

Benchmarking

Exam focus point

Benchmarking was the topic of a December 2003 question.

9.5   Traditionally, control involves the comparison of actual results with an internal standard or target. The practice of **setting targets using external information** is known as benchmarking.

KEY TERM

Benchmarking. 'The establishment, through data gathering, of targets and comparators, through whose use relative levels of performance (and particularly areas of underperformance) can be identified. By the adoption of identified best practices it is hoped that performance will improve. Types of benchmarking include the following.

- **Internal benchmarking**. A method of comparing one operating unit or function with another within the same industry.

- **Functional benchmarking**. Internal functions are compared with those of the best external practitioners of those functions, regardless of the industry they are in (also known as operational benchmarking or generic benchmarking).

- **Competitive benchmarking**. Information is gathered about direct competitors, through techniques such as reverse engineering.★

- **Strategic benchmarking**. A type of competitive benchmarking aimed at strategic action and organisational change.

★ Reverse engineering is the process of buying a competitor's product and dismantling it, in order to understand its content and configuration.

9.6 As you will see from the list of the types of benchmarking, a benchmarking exercise **doesn't necessarily have to involve the comparison of operations with those of a competitor**. In fact, it might be difficult to persuade a direct competitor to part with any information which is useful for comparison purposes. Functional benchmarking, for example, does not always involve direct competitors. A railway company could be identified as the 'best' in terms of on-board catering, and an airline company that operates on different routes would seek opportunities to improve by sharing information and comparing their own catering operations with those of the railway company.

9.7 Benchmarking can be divided into stages.

Step 1. **Set objectives** and determine the areas to benchmark

Step 2. Establish **key performance measures**

Step 3. **Select organisations** to study

Step 4. **Measure** own and others' performance

Step 5. **Compare** performances

Step 6. Design and implement **improvement programme**

Step 7. **Monitor** improvements

9.8 **Financial information** about competitors is **easier** to acquire than non-financial information. Information about **products** can be obtained from **reverse engineering**, **product literature**, **media comment** and **trade associations**. Information about **processes** (how an organisation deals with customers or suppliers) is more **difficult** to find.

9.9 Such information can be obtained from **group companies** or possibly **non-competing organisations** in the same industry (such as the train and airline companies mentioned above).

9.10 There are three levels of benchmarking.

Level of benchmarking	Through	Examples of measures
Resources	Resource audit	Quantity of resources • Revenue/employee • Capital intensity Quality of resources • Qualifications of employees • Age of machinery • Uniqueness (eg patents)
Competences in separate activities	Analysing activities	Sales calls per salesperson Output per employee Materials wastage
Competences in linked activities	Analysing overall performances	Market share Profitability Productivity

9.11 When selecting an appropriate benchmark basis, companies should ask themselves the following questions.

(a) Is it possible and easy to obtain **reliable competitor** information?

(b) Is there any wide **discrepancy** between different **internal divisions**?

(c) Can **similar processes** be identified in **non-competing environments** and are these non-competing companies willing to co-operate?

(d) Is best practice operating in a similar environmental setting?

(e) Is there time to complete the study?

(f) It is possible to benchmark companies with similar objectives and strategies

9.12 **Why use benchmarking?**

(a) **Position audit.** Benchmarking can assess a firm's existing position, and provide a basis for establishing standards of performance.

(b) The sharing of information can be a **spur to innovation**.

(c) Its flexibility means that it can be used in both the **public and private sectors** and by people at different levels of responsibility.

(d) **Cross comparisons** (as opposed to comparisons with similar organisations) are more likely to expose radically different ways of doing things.

(e) It is an effective method of **implementing change**, people being involved in identifying and seeking out different ways of doing things in their own areas.

(f) It identifies the **processes** to improve.

(g) It helps with **cost reduction**.

(h) It improves the **effectiveness** of operations.

(i) It delivers **services** to a defined standard.

(j) It provides a focus on **planning**.

(k) It can provide early warning of **competitive disadvantage**.

(l) It should lead to a greater incidence of **team working** and **cross-functional learning**.

9.13 Disadvantages

(a) It implies there is **one best way** of doing business - arguably this boils down to the difference between efficiency and effectiveness. A process can be efficient but its output may not be useful. Other measures (such as amending the value chain) may be a better way of securing competitive advantage.

(b) The benchmark may be **yesterday's solution to tomorrow's problem**. For example, a cross-channel ferry company might benchmark its activities (eg speed of turnround at Dover and Calais, cleanliness on ship) against another ferry company, whereas the real competitor is the Channel Tunnel.

(c) It is a **catching-up exercise** rather than the development of anything distinctive. After the benchmarking exercise, the competitor might improve performance in a different way.

(d) It depends on **accurate** information about comparator companies.

(e) It can be difficult to decide **which activities to benchmark**.

Case example

Below are extracts from a report on benchmarking in *The Times* in 2003.

British police are to be compared with overseas forces under Home Office plans. Within three years, 43 forces including the Metropolitan Police will be measured on international league tables covering murder rates, burglaries, street crime and arrests.

Scotland Yard's operations will also be tested against the crime-solving records of a group of 'world cities', including Tokyo, Sydney, Paris, Frankfurt and New York.

The [Home Office standards] unit has already created a series of measurements for groups of similar forces and chief constables can now check their officers' performance against regional and national figures each month.

Dr Bond [head of the unit] told MPs: 'We are working up some benchmarking data internationally. The wider question once you have looked at UK police performance is, "How does that compare internationally?" We don't know at the moment.'

He said that international comparisons could include the number of crimes in different categories, detection rates and underlying patterns of crime. The comparisons would also take into account the infrastructure of countries and cities such as transport systems.

Dr Bond said that officers in a small country station can already check national databanks for the record of a comparable station on the other side of the country and look at new ideas for improving crime reduction.

The international comparison will include a similar databank where British police can look at the work of other forces and learn new techniques.

External comparisons: make or buy

9.14 Another instance in which a firm may compare its own performance with another firm's performance is the **familiar 'make or buy' problem**. You may not be used to seeing this as a **performance measurement issue**. Try the question below.

Question: make or buy

A firm is considering contracting out production of three components because specialist companies have offered to supply them at a price which is lower than the direct cost the firm currently achieves in-house. The firm will continue to produce all other components itself, however, since none of the offers made by external suppliers for these components are as low as the direct costs currently achieved in-house.

    (a)   What further cost comparisons should be made to aid the decision?

    (b)   What other information ought to be obtained?

Answer

(a)   **Before and after comparisons** should be made in areas such as the following.

- Some costs of the contracted-out components, such as design, may still not be avoided.

- The costs of the remaining internally-produced components may rise because overheads will be spread over a smaller number of items. This may make external offers to produce other components more viable in comparison.

- The costs of procurement of components and materials will change.

- The costs of production planning will change.

(b)   **Other information** that should be obtained includes the following.

- Are the quotations from the external suppliers genuine? Perhaps they are just quoting low prices to gain the initial business. The internal cost is one that the firm knows is genuine.

- Even if the initial price is genuine, will it remain the same for as long as the components are needed? Could the firm keep down its own internal costs over the longer term?

- Are delivery and quality assured? The firm controls these aspects at present and premiums may be payable to be certain of future supplies.

These are all fairly obvious points but it may not have occurred to you before that such considerations are relevant to performance measurement.

Chapter roundup

- **Internal** sources of **information** include the financial accounting records and other systems closely tied to the accounting system.

- Much control is achieved through the **feedback** of internal information.

- Be aware of the **cost** of inefficient use of information.

- **Controls** need to be in place over the generation of internal information in routine and ad-hoc reports.

- A **procedures manual** sets out controls over distributing internal information.

- A number of procedures can be used to ensure the **security of highly confidential information that is not for external consumption.**

  ○ Passwords
  ○ Logical access systems
  ○ Database controls
  ○ Firewalls
  ○ Personnel security planning

- In today's competitive environment, where the pace of change in information systems and technology is rapid, organisations must be flexible enough to adapt to change quickly and must **plan for expansion, growth and innovation** within information systems.

- **External information** tends to be more relevant to strategic and tactical decisions than to operational decisions. (Benchmarking is an exception.)

- There are many sources of external information.

- **Secondary data**, such as government statistics or data provided by on-line databases, is not collected by or for the user.

- **Primary data** – more expensive than secondary data – is more tailored to the user's exact needs. Market research is an example.

- There are specific **costs** to obtaining data, but also to maintaining the infrastructure supporting data collection and distribution.

- The **value** of external data is its contribution to planning, decision making and control.

- **Benchmarking** schemes enable precise comparisons to be drawn between firms. The use to which benchmarking information is put is the key to its value. Benchmarking is best for firms which have to 'catch up' rather than innovate.

- The **Internet** increases the richness of external data and reduces the cost of searching for it.

Quick quiz

1   Reports, memos and records of meetings are examples of formal information. *True or false?*

2   *Choose the correct words from those highlighted.*

   Logical/physical access control is concerned with preventing those who **do not have access/already have access** to a terminal or computer from gaining access to **hardware/data or software.**

3   Five measures to control the ability of individuals to compromise the security of an organisation were listed in the chapter. What are they?

   1 ....
   2 ....
   3 ....
   4 ....
   5 ....

4   'Published data is always reliable.' *True or false?*

Part B: Design of management accounting systems

5   *Provide an example for each of the following costs of obtaining external information.*

Direct search costs   ....

Indirect access costs   ....

Management costs   ....

Infrastructure costs   ....

Time-theft   ....

6   What are the four types of benchmarking?

A   Internal, functional, competitive, external
B   Internal, divisional, competitive, external
C   Divisional, external, comparative, empowered
D   Internal, functional, strategic, competitive

Answers to quick quiz

1   True

2   logical
     already have access
     data or software

3   • Careful recruitment
     • Job rotation
     • Supervision and observation by a superior
     • Review of computer usage (for example via systems logs)
     • Enforced vacations

4   False. 'Reliability' of data for a decision is determined by its age, the sample and data definitions. By 'published' data, include the Internet – a source of falsehoods as well as information.

5   See Paragraph 8.1.

6   D

Now try the question below from the Exam Question Bank

Number	Level	Marks	Time
7	Exam	20	36 mins

Chapter 9

RECORDING, PROCESSING AND REPORTING INFORMATION

Topic list	Syllabus reference
1 Information processing cycle	2(c)
2 Information collection and analysis	2(c)
3 Collecting, recording and processing information	2(c)
4 Reporting information	2(c), 2(d)

Introduction

Having looked at how to source information in Chapter 8, we are now going to see how to **collect, record, process, analyse** and **disseminate** it.

This chapter completes our look at the management accounting systems within which performance measurement (Chapters 10 to 15), planning and control (Chapters 16 to 19) and decision making (Chapters 20 to 21) must be carried out.

Study guide

Section 10 – Recording and processing information

- Identify the stages in the information processing cycle in the context of accounting information

- Identify how the collection and analysis of information is influenced by management accounting principles and techniques used by an organisation

- Describe the systems involved in the collection and recording of monetary and non-monetary information

- Illustrate how the type of business entity will influence the recording and processing methods

- Explain how IT developments may influence recording and processing systems

- Discuss the difficulties associated with recording and processing data of a qualitative nature

Exam guide

You could get a 'theoretical' question on the topics covered in this chapter or you might need to apply the principles we look at to a particular scenario, such as how to disseminate certain decision-making information.

The issues covered in this chapter are useful background to the following Oxford Brookes degree Research and Analysis Projects.

- Topic 2, which requires you to analyse how the application of technology can contribute to an organisation's efficiency and /or effectiveness

- Topic 9, which requires you to examine how to plan, develop and implement an appropriate information system in an organisation

1 INFORMATION PROCESSING CYCLE

1.1 The processing of accounting information is a recurrent series of operations with the following stages.

(a) Input

(b) Processing

    (i) Sorting, classifying, analysing, calculating and so on
    (ii) Storage in readily retrievable form

(c) Output

1.2 Here, for example, is a diagrammatic representation of the consolidation stage of the budgeting process.

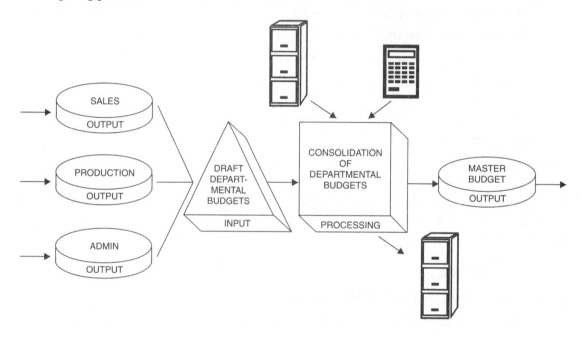

1.3 Here are some other examples.

Input	Process	Output
Data from the payroll system	Comparison with standard/budget data	Variance analysis reports
Data from the stock control system	Matching with production levels	Product costing statements
Data about activity levels	Multiplication by cost driver rates	ABC costs

1.4 Note how an organisation's **information system runs in parallel with, and shadows,** its **production system**.

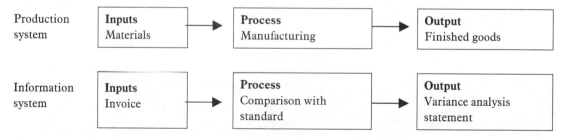

2 INFORMATION COLLECTION AND ANALYSIS

2.1 An organisation's **needs for information** are **influenced profoundly by the uses** to which it wants to put the information.

For example, you should remember that a great many organisations accumulate cost information for their products using absorption costing, whereby a proportion of all overheads is allocated to and 'absorbed' into the cost of individual units using various pre-determined absorption rates. Other businesses use marginal costing, whereby units of product are costed at variable cost only. Clearly if an organisation wants to **change from marginal costing to absorption costing** it may find that it cannot do so until it has **re-analysed or collected afresh information** about, say, machine hours, or about number of employees by function, or about whatever else is to be used as the absorption base.

2.2 This problem is more acute for organisations wishing to adopt **modern techniques** like just-in-time production or activity based costing, whose **information needs are quite different** from those of traditional methods.

2.3 The same applies to *ad hoc* **decision-making situations:** if an organisation wants to use learning curve theory it cannot do so without first understanding what information will be needed and then devising a means of collecting it.

3 COLLECTING, RECORDING AND PROCESSING INFORMATION

Collecting information

3.1 This is an issue we covered in some depth in Chapter 8.

3.2 An organisation collects a great deal of information in the course of its business.

3.3 In the first place there is the information that it **sends out to and receives from others.**

- Orders for materials
- Payments in the form of cheques
- Delivery notes
- Invoices and statements
- Brochures
- Price lists and promotional material.

All of these are initiated by and give rise to other information communicated by telephone or by letter, say.

3.4 Then there is the **formal information that passes to and fro within the organisation.**

- Memos and internal reports

- Notices on the notice board

- Records of meetings

- Information associated with internal systems such as job cards, stock requisitions, time sheets and so on

3.5 An organisation will also take advantage of, and indeed rely on, **informal communication.**

- Between mangers and subordinates
- Between subordinates and their colleagues
- With third parties

This may be by word of mouth, at meetings, by telephone or by some other means.

3.6 Obtaining information from **external sources** might be formally delegated to particular individuals, such as a market research manager; it might also be 'informal'. **Informal gathering of information from outside sources** goes on all the time, consciously or unconsciously, because the employees of an organisation learn what is going on in the world around them – from newspapers, television, experience or other people.

Recording information

3.7 It is **impossible to be prescriptive about the way such information should be recorded**.

(a) A concertina file, a cash book and the proprietor's memory may be adequate for a very small business.

(b) Large companies will need huge computerised databases.

A general rule states the obvious – any **information that is needed should be recorded and stored in such a way that it can be readily retrieved**.

Question: processing accounting information

Consider the following extracts from Tom Peters' book *Liberation Management* (1992).

'Organisations are pure information processing machines – nothing less, nothing more: organisational structures, including hierarchies, capture, massage and channel information – period.'

'Like it or not, the farmer gets no more than a penny or two from the 50 cents or so that a can of tomato soup brings the retailer. Only a little of the rest is absorbed by processing and canning. Distribution, logistics, advertising, wholesaling, and retailing claim the big bucks. That is, information processing – creating connections between the product (the tomato with a little water and a few chemical additives) and the consumer.'

To what extent do you think that the processing of accounting information can be described as 'creating connections between the product and the consumer'?

Answer

Think about who initiates information that passes through the organisation and who is the ultimate recipient of it. Who, for example, is the ultimate recipient of information provided to decide on the price of a product?

Types of business entity and recording and processing methods

3.8 Different types of business will require different recording and processing methods.

(a) A factory which runs a **single continuous production line** may have relatively **simple, structured information requirements** and hence will **not** require **sophisticated recording and processing methods**. The **information cycle** and hence **management accounting reporting** may only be required on a **monthly** or **quarterly** basis.

(b) A **modern 'world class' manufacturer** is likely to operate in an environment in which **product life cycles** are very **short** and a high level of **flexibility** is required to satisfy sophisticated customer requirements. A **large range** of customised products will be produced. **Information requirements** are thus **less structured**, *ad-hoc* **reports** will be required and the **information cycle** will need to be very **short**. Significant **investment** in **IT** will be required to provide the necessary information.

(c) Organisations that need **accurate** and **up to date** information on, say, stock levels, need to use some form of **on-line real time** approach. Large retail stores, for example, use **electronic point of sales** (EPOS) devices, which include **bar code** readers, providing immediate sales and stock level information.

(d) If **accuracy** and **processing volume** is important, as in the banking sector, **magnetic ink character recognition (MICR)** can be used to process thousands of cheques and deposit slips quickly and accurately.

(e) Other organisations might record and process information periodically rather than in real time. **Batch processing,** for example, might be used by a small bookshop to update its stock records at the end of a day.

(f) Smaller organisations might rely on **manual** recording and processing methods, although advances in information technology mean that computerised methods are at everyone's disposal.

> **IMPORTANT POINT**
>
> In general the methods used for recording and processing information should suit the **volume** of data, the level of **accuracy** required and the **speed** with which the information is required.

Developments in IT and recording and processing systems

3.9 The management accounting information system might be **connected to and be able to receive data from other information systems** within the firm such as the purchasing system, the production planning and scheduling system and the firm's overall financial system. These various systems may be found on mainframe computers or networked personal computers, and may be geographically close or distant. Nowadays, **modems** and **commercial telecommunications systems** allow distant computers to **communicate** with each other and to send and receive information. This information can then be **downloaded** on to personal computers (PCs) using compatible software.

PCs

3.10 The advent of cheap and powerful PCs has transformed the role of management information systems. **High volumes** of data can be sourced from outside the organisation (using **electronic data interchange**) or from within it (from the computers running the automated production process for example). Such data can be stored, retrieved and processed into information and reported in a timely and ultimately cost-effective manner.

Spreadsheet packages

3.11 The availability of spreadsheet packages means that managers are able to **download data** from a **database** and **manipulate** it as they like. The speed, ease of use and capacity of PCs is such that, when combined with the power of the spreadsheet, most of the business **analysis** problems that a manager might wish to tackle can be dealt with. This means that managers can carry out their **own investigations and analyses** as and when they wish. In the recent past, it was necessary to design and develop purpose-built information processing and reporting systems that were inflexible, took months or years to become available and were extremely expensive.

Database packages

3.12 Networked PCs containing spreadsheet software which are connected to databases enable managers to **access and manipulate data** far more effectively and at a **fraction of the cost** of previous generations of management information systems. Both standard and *ad-hoc* **reporting is facilitated** and any number of managers can make use of the data, thereby **reducing duplication** of effort and speeding up the control and decision-making process.

Software packages

3.13 **Modern** management accounting **techniques** (such as ABC) and modern **production methods** (such as JIT) require management information systems that can access **large amounts of data** and report **accurate detailed information frequently**. In the past, the excessive cost and time to carry out the necessary tasks manually meant this sort of information simply could not be provided. Advances in the **power of PCs** and the **sophistication of software packages** mean that MIS are a necessary part of the organisational framework in the modern business environment.

E-mail systems

3.14 These allow information to be transmitted **quickly** throughout an organisation and **around the world**, considerably improving an organisation's efficiency and effectiveness, its response to problems and its decision-making process.

Computer Telephony Integration (CTI)

3.15 CTI systems **gather information** about callers such as their telephone number and customer account number or demographic information (age, income, interests and so on). This is stored on a customer **database** and can be **called up and sent to the screen** of the person dealing with the call, perhaps before the call has even been put through.

Order forms with key details entered already can be displayed on screen automatically.

Recording and processing qualitative data

3.16 We looked at qualitative information in Chapters 5 and 7 and we will return to it again later in the text.

3.17 Given that qualitative data is **subjective and judgmental**, its recording is likely to be problematic. The number of sales made is easy to record; the reasons why sales are lost is not.

3.18 To overcome this problem **quantitative surrogates** are often used for important qualitative information, but this often distorts the message being conveyed.

4 REPORTING INFORMATION

Dissemination

4.1 Once information has been produced by an information processing system it must be passed on to those users who require it. This dissemination of information can take place via a variety of reports.

Format of report	Detail
Scheduled reports	Produced at fixed time intervals (such as monthly for the payroll report) in a standard format (such as the sales statistics by region, with comparative figures) to provide a basic element of feedback to the organisation's control system.
Exception reports	As part of a system of reporting by exception, they highlight situations where standards set have not been attained or have been exceeded, and where the variations are larger than could be expected by a normal fluctuation. Management attention is thus directed towards situations where the system behaviour is unusual.
Demand reports	Produced as requested. The content may be different to what is normally produced. Alternatively, a manager may require, at an unusual time, information that would normally be provided every month as a matter of routine.
Planning (predictive) reports	Deal in future events, and how the organisation will respond to them. They might simply consist of an annual forecast for the next few months, in comparison with budget or previous years, or be prepared by the computer system using a statistical program.

Management style and information

4.2 The style of the management of an organisation will affect the way in which information is used within that organisation.

4.3 Organisations differ in the style of management they adopt, as of course do individual managers. One method of distinguishing between management styles is to describe them as follows.

(a) **Hierarchical styles**. Levels of managers are ranked one above the other, and management is conducted accordingly.

(b) **Democratic styles**. At its most extreme, all managers are equal.

4.4 The **information requirements** will differ for either style. Consider how plans will be made and how information enabling implementation will be disseminated.

(a) In the **hierarchical** organisation the plans will come from the top and will be communicated through several layers of management. The risk of **noise** and **distortion** is high, so that the MD's idea for a new product may look very different by the time it has passed down to the supervisor who has to oversee its manufacture. **Information passes up the organisation as well as down**, and there is the same risk: C wants to impress his manager, B, who wants to impress his manager, A, and so information about actual performance is likely to be amended to suit the perceived preferences of each successive level.

(b) In the **democratic** organisation **those responsible for implementing the plan also have a say in its formulation**. At the **extreme**, all **managers have the same information needs** because all are equally involved in all aspects of the organisation's activities.

4.5 Either style presents **problems** for the provider of information. In the **hierarchical** organisation the problem is to **prevent human bias and procrastination**. In the democratic organisation the problem is one of **volume and politics**: how much common information needs to be provided to maintain the democracy and do people withhold information to gain power or protect their own position?

Information needs in different contexts

4.6 We have indicated that *all* information is potentially relevant to the work of a management accountant, but this does not mean that all information has to be taken into account in every situation.

4.7 As we have said already, unlike financial accounting **management accounting** is only concerned with **information relating to the past if it is a useful guide to what will happen in the future.** Details of the labour requirements for a particular production process this year may be relevant to planning and controlling the activity of labour engaged in that process next year, but only if no changes to the process are envisaged. If the management accountant is providing information to help with the decision to automate the process, the relevant sources of information regarding future labour requirements might be the supplier of the new equipment, his advertisement in a trade magazine, other users, calculations prepared by the production department, details of existing machine operating skills and training requirements from the personnel department, and so on.

4.8 In a later chapter we shall give detailed consideration to the question of relevant information, focusing on the question of which costs are relevant to a particular decision.

Influence of trend, materiality and controllability issues

Trend

4.9 A trend is the **way in which something moves over time**. Present information should **not be considered in isolation** from the past trend and the likely future trend. For example, three lost customers in a month may be just a blip, or may seem so, but if it is the sixth month in which three customers have been lost something is going wrong.

Materiality

4.10 The financial accounting principle of materiality can also be applied to management accounting in the sense that it is equally **fruitless to expend resources obtaining information that will not affect the overall view that is taken of a matter.** Investment appraisal provides a good example. If a project is reckoned to be likely to make a large loss overall, it is not material whether that loss is calculated to be £2.4m or £2.5m. The project will not go ahead in any case.

4.11 On the other hand a difference that may seem immaterial in one context may not be in another. A gram of raw material may cost £0.003p and another supplier may offer it at £0.0029p per gram. If a business only uses 100g per month, this is not very significant. If it uses 10,000 kilograms per month, it makes quite a lot of difference!

4.12 On the whole it is characteristic of **management accountants to work to a higher degree of accuracy and in a greater level of detail than financial accountants.**

Controllability

4.13 Controllability influences information requirements in the sense that a **business needs to be able to distinguish between matters that it can take action to change and those that are unavoidable.** Again, there is no point in expending resources on the latter, except to identify them.

4.14 Controllability of events **within an organisation** is particularly relevant to the operation of a **responsibility accounting system.** Managers should not be made responsible for matters that are controlled by somebody else in the organisation. The information individual managers require is information about their own areas of responsibility.

Exam focus point

Questions on this chapter's topics will be discursive. At least one of the questions in Section B will be purely discursive. Part of a December 2002 Section B question required candidates to suggest how an external environment information system could be introduced into a company. The issues covered in this chapter and Chapter 7 (responsibility accounting, attributes and principles of information, dissemination) are relevant.

Chapter roundup

- An organisation's information system runs in parallel with, and shadows, its production system.

- An organisation's **needs** for information are profoundly **influenced by the uses** to which it wants to put the information.

- An organisation collects both **formal and informal information** by both **formal and informal communication channels**.

- The **type of business entity** will influence the recording and processing methods adopted.

- The advent of cheap and powerful **PCs** has transformed the role of management information systems.

- **Management style**, and **trend, materiality and controllability** impact on the way in which information is reported.

Quick quiz

1   What are the main stages of information processing?

    A   Input, processing, output
    B   Input, sorting, storage
    C   Collecting, sorting, storage
    D   Collecting, analysing, output

2   A notice on a notice board provides formal information. *True or false?*

3   What is MICR?

    A   Maintenance in computer realities
    B   Mainframe interface computer recognition
    C   Magnetic interface computer result
    D   Magnetic ink character recognition

4   *Fill in the blanks in the following statements about management style.*

    (a)   In the .... organisation, noise and distortion is high.

    (b)   In the .... organisation, at the extreme, all management have the same information needs.

Answers to quick quiz

1   A
2   True
3   D
4   (a)   hierarchical
     (b)   democratic

Now try the question below from the Exam Question Bank

Number	Level	Marks	Time
8	Exam	20	36 mins

Part C
Performance measurement

Chapter 10

THE PERFORMANCE HIERARCHY

Topic list	Syllabus reference
1 Mission statements and vision	3(a)
2 Goals and objectives: an introduction	3(a)
3 Corporate objectives	3(a)
4 Subsidiary or secondary objectives	3(a)
5 Social and ethical obligations	3(a)
6 The short term and long term	3(a)
7 The planning gap and strategies to fill it	3(a)
8 Factors to consider when assessing performance	3(c)
9 Comparing performance in different countries	3(c)
10 Operational performance	3(a)
11 Planning and control at different levels in the performance hierarchy	3(a)

Introduction

Although Paper 3.3 covers performance management, the planning activities covered in this chapter are an important aspect of performance management, as **plans express targets and standards against which actual performance is assessed.** They therefore provide a useful **introduction** to this part of the text on performance measurement.

Note that **mission** and **ethical obligations** are covered here: they are hard to measure quantitatively but managers tend to have a good idea as to what is good and bad practice.

Study guide

Section 11 – Performance hierarchy

- Discuss the purpose of a mission statement and the pursuit of a vision

- Discuss the structure and content of a mission statement

- Explain how high level corporate objectives are developed

- Identify strategic objectives and how they may be incorporated into the corporate plan

- Explain how strategic objectives are cascaded down the organisation via the formulation of subsidiary objectives

- Identify any relevant social and ethical obligations that should be considered in the pursuit of corporate objectives

- Discuss the concept of the 'planning gap' and alternative strategies to 'fill the gap'

- Identify the characteristics of operational performance

- Contrast the relative significance of planning as against controlling activities at different levels in the performance hierarchy

---

Section 14 – Performance measurement for non-profit seeking organisations

- Discuss the potential for diversity in objectives depending on organisation type

Section 15 – Performance - a broad perspective

- Comment on the need to consider the environment in which an organisation is operating when assessing its performance

Exam guide

The topics covered here are common to other papers at this level, namely 3.4 *Business Information Management* and 3.5 *Strategic Business Planning and Development*. In the exam for **this paper**, you should **focus** on the implication of mission and objectives for **performance management**. In other words, this is **not**, emphatically, a **paper about strategy** as such.

---

1 MISSION STATEMENTS AND VISION

1.1   Underlying the behaviour and management processes of most organisations are one or two **guiding ideas**, which **influence the organisation's activities**. Management writers typically analyse these into two categories: vision and mission.

> **IMPORTANT POINT**
>
> **Mission:** What is the business for?
>
> **Vision:**   Where is the business going?

Case example

Beyond petroleum

Vision

In the early 1990s, BP articulated its 'vision' as follows:

'With our bold, innovative strategic agenda, BP will be the world's most successful oil company in the 1990's and beyond.'

Now in 2000, BP has effectively rebranded itself, with an advertising campaign with the strapline 'beyond petroleum'. Although petrol is the world's principal source of global warming, BP is trying to promote an 'environmentally conscious' message, by repositioning itself as an energy company and investing more in alternative or renewable sources of energy such as solar power.

Arguably, the 'vision' has changed. From the stated desire to be the world's most successful oil company, BP has moved to a state 'beyond' petroleum.

But what about **mission**? Mission describes the **purpose** of the company, in other words why it exists at all. Many organisations interpret their mission in terms of stakeholders, typically the owners or shareholders and customers.

BP once described itself as follows:

'BP is a family of businesses principally in oil and gas exploration and production, refining and marketing, chemicals and nutrition. In everything we do we are committed to **creating wealth**, always with integrity, to reward the stakeholders in BP – our shareholders, our employees, our customers and suppliers and the community.'

(BPP emphasis)

1.2   A **vision** for the future has three aspects.

- What the business *is* now
- What it *could* be in an ideal world
- What the ideal world would be like

1.3 A **vision** gives a **general sense of direction** to the company. A vision, it is hoped, enables **flexibility** to exist in the context of a **guiding idea**.

Mission

> **KEY TERM**
>
> **Mission** 'describes the organisation's basic function in society, in terms of the products and services it produces for its clients'. (Mintzberg)

Case example

The Co-op

The Co-operative movement is a good example of the role of mission. It's mission is not simply profit. Being owned by suppliers/customers rather than external shareholders, it has always, since its foundation, had a wider social concern.

The Co-op has been criticised by some analysts on the grounds that it is insufficiently profitable, certainly in comparison with supermarket chains such as Tesco. The Co-op has explicit **social** objectives, however. In some cases it will retain stores which, although too small to be as profitable as a large supermarket, provide an important social function in the communities which host them.

Of course, the Co-op's performance as a retailer can be improved, but judging it on the conventional basis of profitability ignores its social objectives.

1.4 An expanded definition of mission includes four elements.

Elements of mission	Detail
Purpose	Why does the company exist? • To create wealth for shareholders? • To satisfy the needs of all stakeholders (including employees, society at large, for example)?
Strategy	Mission provides the commercial logic for the company, and so defines the following. • Nature of its business • Products/services it offers; competitive position • The competences and competitive advantages by which it hopes to prosper, and its way of competing
Policies and standards of behaviour	The mission needs to be converted into everyday performance. For example, a firm whose mission covers excellent customer service must deal with simple matters such as politeness to customers, speed at which phone calls are answered and so forth.
Values and culture	Values are the basic, perhaps unstated, beliefs of the people who work in the organisation

175

Mission statements

Exam focus point

Mission statements were examined in December 2002.

1.5 Although many organisations do not have a clearly defined mission, they are becoming increasingly common, especially in larger organisations, and are usually set out in the form of a mission statement. This **written declaration of an organisation's central mission** is a useful concept that can:

(a) Provide a ready reference point against which to make decisions

(b) Help guard against there being different (and possibly misleading) interpretations of the organisation's stated purpose

(c) Help to present a clear image of the organisation for the benefit of customers and the general public

1.6 Most mission statements will address some of the following aspects.

(a) The **identity** of the persons for whom the organisation exists (such as shareholders, customers and employees)

(b) The **nature of the firm's business** (such as the products it makes or the services it provides, and the markets it produces for)

(c) Ways of **competing** (such as reliance on quality, innovation, technology and low prices; commitment to customer care; policy on acquisition versus organic growth; and geographical spread of its operations)

(d) **Principles of business** (such as commitment to suppliers and staff; social policy, for example, on non-discrimination or environmental issues)

(e) **Commitment to customers**

1.7 A number of questions need to be considered when a mission statement is being formulated.

- Who is to be served and satisfied?
- What need is to be satisfied?
- How will this be achieved?

Case example

The *Financial Times* reported the result of research by the Digital Equipment Corporation into a sample of 429 company executives.

- 80% of the sample have a formal mission statement.
- 80% believed mission contributes to profitability.
- 75% believe they have a responsibility to implement the mission statement.

1.8 Mission statements might be reproduced in a number of places (at the front of an organisation's annual report, on publicity material, in the chairman's office, in communal work areas and so on) as they are used to communicate with those inside and outside the organisation.

1.9 There is no standard format, but they should possess certain characteristics.

- **Brevity** - easy to understand and remember
- **Flexibility** - to accommodate change
- **Distinctiveness** - to make the firm stand out
- **Open-ended** – not stated in quantifiable terms

They tend to **avoid commercial terms** (such as profit) and **do not refer to time frames** (some being carved in stone or etched on a plaque!).

1.10 A mission does not have to be internally orientated. Some of the most effective focus outwards – on customers and/or competitors. Most mission statements tend to place an **emphasis on serving the customer.**

Case examples

(a) Here is the ACCA's mission statement.

'ACCA's mission is to provide quality professional opportunities to people of ability and application, to be a leader in the development of the global accountancy profession, to promote the highest ethical and governance standards, to work in the public interest, and to be a leader in the knowledge-based profession of the 21st century.'

(b) **Private sector organisations** (such as Tesco, ICI and Kodak) traditionally seek to make a profit, but increasingly companies try to project other images too, such as being environmentally friendly, being a good employer, or being a provider of friendly service. Here's one such example.

'The purpose of Motorola is to honourably service the needs of the community by providing products and services of superior quality at a fair price to our customers.'

Public sector organisations (such as local councils, colleges and hospitals) provide services and increasingly seek to project quality, value for money, green issues, concern for staff (equal opportunities) and so on as missions. This is illustrated by the following examples.

'The college recognises that its purpose through partnership with the community, including employers and organisations, is to provide easily accessible, structured learning opportunities to enable people to maximise their creative employment potential.'

(Coalville Technical College, Leicestershire)

'We at the Leicester Royal Infirmary will work together to become the best hospital in the country, with an outstanding local and national reputation for out treatment, research and teaching.

We will give to each patient the same care and consideration we would give to our family.'

(Leicester Royal Infirmary)

Voluntary and community sector organisations cover a wide range of organisations including charities, trades unions, pressure groups and religious organisations. They usually exist either to serve a particular need or for the benefit of their membership. Such organisations do need to raise funds but they will rarely be dedicated to the pursuit of profit. Their mission statements are likely to reflect the particular interests they serve (and perhaps the values of their organisation). Here are some examples.

'To achieve the conservation of nature and ecological processes by:

- Preserving genetic species and ecosystem diversity

- Ensuring that the use of renewable natural resources is sustainable both now and in the longer term, for the benefit of all life on earth

- Promoting actions to reduce, to a minimum, pollution and the wasteful exploitation and consumption of resources and energy.'

(The World Wide Fund for Nature)

'The preservation of life from shipwreck'

(Royal National Lifeboat Institution)

(c)   The following statements were taken from annual reports of the organisations concerned. Are they mission statements? If so, are they any good?

    (i)   Before its succession of mergers, **Glaxo** described itself as 'an integrated research-based group of companies whose corporate purpose is to create, discover, develop, manufacture and market throughout the world, safe, effective medicines of the highest quality which will bring benefit to patients through improved longevity and quality of life, and to society through economic value.'

    (ii)   **The British Film Institute** claimed 'The BFI is the UK national agency with responsibility for encouraging and conserving the arts of film and television. Our aim is to ensure that the many audiences in the UK are offered access to the widest possible choice of cinema and television, so that their enjoyment is enhanced through a deeper understanding of the history and potential of these vital and popular art forms.'

Mission and planning

1.11   Although the mission statement might be seen as a set of abstract principles, it can play an important **role in the planning process**.

    (a)   **Inspires planning**. Plans should develop activities and programmes consistent with the organisation's mission.

    (b)   **Screening**. Mission also acts as a yardstick by which plans are judged.

    (c)   Mission also affects the **implementation** of a planned strategy, in the culture and business practices of the firm.

> **IMPORTANT POINT**
>
> **Factors to incorporate in a mission statement**
>
> - The business areas in which the organisation will operate
> - The organisation's reason for existence
> - The stakeholder groups served by the organisation

2   GOALS AND OBJECTIVES: AN INTRODUCTION

> **IMPORTANT POINT**
>
> There is much confusion over the terms 'goals' and 'objectives'. Some writers use the terms interchangeably while others refer to them as two different concepts, unfortunately with no consistency as to which term refers to which concept.
>
> Here we will use the following definitions/distinctions.
>
> - (Shorter-term) **objectives** are the means by which (longer-term) **goals** can ultimately be achieved.
>
> - **Goals** are based on an individual's value system whereas **objectives** are based on practical needs.
>
> - **Goals** are therefore more subjective than **objectives**.

2.1   In particular, **operational goals** can be **expressed as quantified (SMART) objectives**: **S**pecific, **M**easurable, **A**ttainable, **R**esults-orientated, **T**ime-bounded

- Mission: deliver a quality service

- Goal: enhance manufacturing quality

- Objectives: over the next twelve months, reduce the number of defects to 1 part per million

2.2 **Non-operational goals** or **aims** cannot be expressed as objectives.

(a) A university's goal might be to '**seek truth**'. This cannot really be expressed as a quantified objective. To 'increase truth by 5% this year' does not make a great deal of sense.

(b) **Customer satisfaction** is a goal, but satisfying customers and ensuring that they remain satisfied is a continuous process that does not stop when one target has been reached.

2.3 In practice, most organisations set themselves quantified objectives in order to enact the corporate mission.

2.4 **Features of goals and objectives in organisations**

(a) **Goal congruence.** Goals should be consistent with each other.

(i) **Across all departments.** There should be **horizontal** consistency. In other words, the goals set for different parts of the organisation should be consistent with each other.

(ii) **At all levels.** Objectives should be consistent **vertically**, in other words at all levels in the organisation.

(iii) **Over time.** Objectives should be consistent with each other over time.

(b) An objective should **identify the beneficiaries** as well as the nature and size of the benefit.

2.5 **Types of goal and how they are developed**

Goal	Comment
Ideological goals	These goals focus on the organisation's mission. They are shared sets of beliefs and values.
Formal goals	Such goals are imposed by a dominant individual or group such as shareholders. People work to attain these goals as a route to their personal goals.
Shared personal goals	Individuals reach a consensus about what they want out of an organisation (eg a group of academics who decide they want to pursue research).
System goals	Derive from the organisation's existence as an organisation, independent of mission.

2.6 Organisations set goals in a number of different ways.

Method	Comment
Top-down	Goals and objectives are structured from 'top to bottom', a cascading process down the hierarchy, with goals becoming more specific the 'lower' down the hierarchy.
Bottom-up	People in individual departments set their own goals, which eventually shape the overall goals of the organisation.
By precedent	Some goals are set simply because they have been set before (eg last year's sales targets plus 5%)
By 'diktat'	A few key individuals dictate what goals should be.
By consensus	Goals and objectives are achieved by a process of discussion amongst managers – reputedly, Japanese companies employ this approach.

2.7 The **setting** of **objectives** is very much a **political process**: objectives are formulated following **bargaining** by the various interested parties.

- Shareholders want profits.
- Employees want salaries and good working conditions.
- Managers want power.
- Customers demand quality products and services.

These **conflicting** requirements make it **difficult** to **maximise** the **objectives** of any **one particular group**. The objectives have to **change over time**, too, to reflect the changing membership of the groups.

3 CORPORATE OBJECTIVES

3.1 Corporate objectives are set as part of the corporate planning process, which is discussed in more detail in Chapter 16. Basically, the **corporate planning process** is concerned with the **selection** of **strategies** which will **achieve** the **corporate objectives** of the organisation.

3.2 **Corporate objectives** concern the **firm as a whole,** and should relate to the **key factors for business success.**

- Profitability
- Market share
- Growth
- Cash flow
- Return on capital employed
- Risk
- Customer satisfaction
- Quality
- Industrial relations
- Added value
- Earnings per share

3.3 Similar objectives can be developed for each **strategic business unit (SBU).** (An SBU is a part of the company that for all intents and purposes has its own distinct products, markets and assets.)

3.4 **Unit objectives,** on the other hand, **are specific to individual units of an organisation.**

Types	Examples
Commercial	• Increase the number of customers by x% (an objective of a sales department)
	• Reduce the number of rejects by 50% (an objective of a production department)
	• Produce monthly reports more quickly, within 5 working days of the end of each month (an objective of the management accounting department)
Public sector	• Introduce x% more places at nursery schools (an objective of a borough education department)
	• Respond more quickly to calls (an objective of a local police station, fire department or hospital ambulance service)
General	• Resources (eg cheaper raw materials, lower borrowing costs, 'top-quality college graduates')
	• Market (eg market share, market standing)
	• Employee development (eg training, promotion, safety)
	• Innovation in products or processes
	• Productivity (the amount of output from resource inputs)
	• Technology

Primary and secondary objectives

3.5 An organisation has many objectives: even a mission may have multiple parts. It has been argued that there is a **limit** to the **number of objectives** that a manager can **pursue effectively**. Too many and the manager cannot give adequate attention to each and/or the focus may inadvertently be placed on minor ones. Some objectives are more important than others. It has therefore been suggested that there should be one **primary corporate objective** (restricted by certain constraints on corporate activity) and other **secondary objectives**. These are **strategic objectives** which should **combine to ensure the achievement of the primary corporate objective**.

(a) For example, if a company sets itself a **primary objective** of **growth in profits**, it will then have to develop strategies by which this primary objective can be achieved.

(b) **Secondary objectives** might then be concerned with sales growth, continual technological innovation, customer service, product quality, efficient resource management (eg labour productivity) or reducing the company's reliance on debt capital.

Diversity in objectives

3.6 In general terms, all organisations have objectives which necessitate the conversion of inputs into outputs, but objectives vary depending on organisation type.

Question: objectives

What objectives might a bank have? How about a building society?

Answer

The prime corporate objective of a **bank** will be financial (growth in profits). Banks are also expected to uphold a high standard of ethical behaviour towards customers.

The principal objective of a **building society** is raising funds for making advances secured upon land and buildings for residential use.

Other objectives

- Protection of the investments of shareholders/depositors/members

- Promoting and securing financial stability

- Competing successfully with banks, insurance companies, estate agents and other building societies

4 SUBSIDIARY OR SECONDARY OBJECTIVES

4.1 Whatever primary objective or objectives are set, **subsidiary objectives** will then be **developed beneath** them.

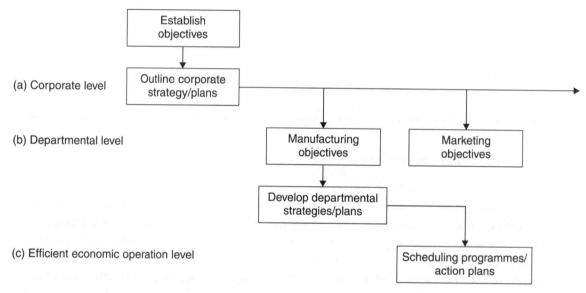

4.2 The overall objectives of the organisation will indicate different requirements for different functions.

Types of subsidiary objective

4.3 **Financial**

We will be considering these in the next chapter.

4.4 **Technological**

- A commitment to product design and production methods using current and new technology

- A commitment to improve current products through research and development work

- A commitment to a particular level of quality

4.5   **Product-market goals**

Objectives for products and markets	Comment
Market leadership	Whether the organisation wants to be the market leader, or number two in the market etc
Coverage	Whether the product range needs to be expanded
Positioning	Whether there should be an objective to shift position in the market - eg from producing low-cost for the mass market to higher-cost specialist products
Expansion	Whether there should be a broad objective of 'modernising' the product range or extending the organisation's markets

Product market objectives are **key**, as the organisation satisfies its shareholders by operating in product market areas. Most major product market objectives are **set at corporate level**.

4.6   **Other objectives**

(a)   Objectives for the **organisation structure** are particularly important for growing organisations.

(b)   **Productivity objectives.** When an organisation is keenly aware of a poor profit record, cost reduction will be a primary consideration. Productivity objectives are often quantified as targets to reduce unit costs **and increase output per employee** by a certain percentage each year.

(c)   **Expansion or consolidation** objectives are concerned with the question of whether there is a need to expand, or whether there is a need to consolidate for a while.

Ranking objectives and trade-offs

4.7   Where there are multiple objectives a **problem of ranking** can arise.

(a)   **There is never enough time or resources** to achieve all of the desired objectives.

(b)   **There are degrees of accomplishment.** For example, if there is an objective to achieve a 10% annual growth in earnings per share, an achievement of 9% could be described as a near-success. When it comes to ranking objectives, a target ROI of, say, 25% might be given greater priority than an EPS growth of 10%.

4.8   When there are **several key objectives, some** might be **achieved only at the expense of others.** For example, attempts to achieve a good cash flow or good product quality, or to improve market share, might call for some sacrifice of short-term profits.

4.9   For example, there might be a choice between the following two options.

Option A   15% sales growth, 10% profit growth, a £2 million negative cash flow and reduced product quality and customer satisfaction

Option B   8% sales growth, 5% profit growth, a £500,000 surplus cash flow, and maintenance of high product quality/customer satisfaction

If the firm chose option B in preference to option A, it would be trading off sales growth and profit growth for better cash flow, product quality and customer satisfaction. It may feel that the long-term effect of reduced quality would negate the benefits under Option A.

4.10 One of the tasks of strategic management is to ensure **goal congruence**. Some objectives may not be in line with each other, and different stakeholders have different sets of priorities.

Departmental plans and objectives

4.11 Implementation involves three tasks.

(a) **Document the responsibilities** of divisions, departments and individual managers.

(b) **Prepare responsibility charts** for managers at divisional, departmental and subordinate levels.

(c) **Prepare activity schedules** for managers at divisional, departmental and subordinate levels.

Responsibility charts

4.12 Responsibility charts can be drawn up for management at all levels in the organisation, including the board of directors. They show the **control points** that indicate what needs to be achieved and how to recognise when things are going wrong. For each manager, a responsibility chart will have **four main elements**.

- The manager's major **objective**
- The manager's general **programme for achieving** that objective
- **Sub-objectives**
- Critical **assumptions** underlying the objectives and the programme

4.13 EXAMPLE: RESPONSIBILITY CHARTS FOR MARKETING DIRECTOR

(a) **Major objective and general programme:** to achieve a targeted level of sales, by means of selling existing well-established products, by breaking into some new markets and by a new product launch

(b) **Sub-objectives:** details of the timing of the product launch; details and timing of promotions, advertising campaigns and so on

(c) **Critical assumptions:** market share, market size and conditions, competitors' activity and so on.

Activity schedules

4.14 **Successful implementation** of corporate plans also means **getting activities started** and **completed on time**. Every manager should have an **activity schedule** in addition to his responsibility chart, which identifies what **activities he must carry out and the start up and completion dates** for each activity. The principles of **network analysis** can usefully be applied here. Critical activities and float times can be identified.

4.15 Critical dates might include equipment installation dates and product launch dates. In some markets, the launch date for a new product or new model can be extremely important, with an aim to gain maximum exposure for the product at a major trade fair or exhibition. New car models must be ready for a major motor show, for example. If there is a delay in product launch there might be a substantial loss of orders which the trade fair could have generated.

4.16 Consequently, **to ensure co-ordination**, the various **functional objectives** must be **interlocked**.

  (a) **Vertically** from top to bottom of the business.

  (b) **Horizontally**, for example, the objectives of the production function must be linked with those of sales, warehousing, purchasing, R&D and so on.

  (c) **Over time**. Short-term objectives can be regarded as intermediate milestones on the road towards long-term objectives.

IMPORTANT POINT

Hierarchy of objectives

The hierarchy of objectives which emerges is this.

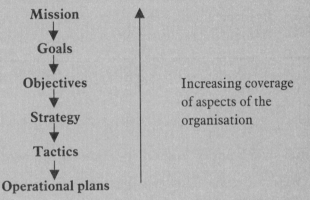

Objectives are normally established within this hierarchical structure. Each level of the hierarchy derives its objectives from the level above, so that all ultimately are founded in the organisation's mission. Objectives therefore cascade down the hierarchy so that, for example, strategies are established to achieve objectives and they, in turn, provide targets for the purposes of tactical planning.

Case example

Cash burn and 'new' economy

The operating and stock market performance of a variety of internet companies has been very volatile in recent years.

A number of different valuation models were adopted, and investors (and stock brokers) abandoned 'boring' performance indicators such as profitability.

  • Market share bought at whatever expense; number of subscribers. In January 2001, amazon.com announced it was to lay off staff in a bid to return to operating profitability.

  • 'Cash burn' – effectively, the rate of cash outflows. Obviously a lower burn rate was 'healthier' as it offered more time for cash inflows to start.

---

5 SOCIAL AND ETHICAL OBLIGATIONS

5.1 **Public opinion** and attitudes, and **legal and political pressures**, mean that organisations can **no longer concentrate solely on financial corporate objectives**. Environmental and social obligations now play a part in shaping an organisation's objectives.

Stakeholder approach

5.2 An organisation's stakeholders have a significant impact on its social and ethical obligations.

> **KEY TERM**
>
> **Stakeholders** are 'groups or individuals having a legitimate interest in the activities of an organisation, generally comprising customers, employees, the community, shareholders, suppliers and lenders'.
>
> (CIMA *Official Terminology*)

5.3 There are three broad types of stakeholder in an organisation, as follows.

- **Internal** stakeholders (employees, management)
- **Connected** stakeholders (shareholders, customers, suppliers, financiers)
- **External** stakeholders (the community, government, pressure groups)

5.4 The stakeholder approach suggests that **corporate objectives** are, or should be, **shaped** and **influenced** by **those** who have **sufficient involvement or interest** in the organisation's operational activities.

Internal stakeholders: employees and management

5.5 Because employees and management are so **intimately connected** with the company, their objectives are likely to have a **strong influence** on how it is run. They are interested in the following issues.

(a) The **organisation's continuation and growth**. Management and employees have a special interest in the organisation's continued existence.

(b) Managers and employees have **individual interests** and goals which can be harnessed to the goals of the organisation.

- Jobs/careers
- Money
- Promotion
- Benefits
- Satisfaction

For managers and employees, an organisation's social obligations will include the provision of safe working conditions and anti-discrimination policies.

Connected stakeholders

5.6 **Increasing shareholder value** should assume a **core role** in the strategic management of a business. If **management performance** is **measured and rewarded by reference to changes in shareholder value** then shareholders will be happy, because managers are likely to **encourage long-term share price growth**.

Connected stakeholder	Interests to defend
Shareholders (corporate strategy)	• Increase in shareholder wealth, measured by profitability, P/E ratios, market capitalisation, dividends and yield • Risk
Bankers (cash flows)	• Security of loan • Adherence to loan agreements
Suppliers (purchase strategy)	• Profitable sales • Payment for goods • Long-term relationship
Customers (product market strategy)	• Goods as promised • Future benefits

5.7 Even though **shareholders** are deemed to be interested in return on investment and/or capital appreciation, many want to **invest** in **ethically-sound** organisations.

Case example

A survey of FTSE 100 companies conducted by the *Financial Times* asked what part leading shareholders play in the running of companies and what top directors think of their investors.

Almost half of those surveyed felt that their main shareholders 'rarely or never' offered any useful comments about their business. 69% of respondents however felt that their major investors understood their business well or very well. 89% did not feel hampered by shareholders in taking the correct long term strategy.

Almost all directors felt their biggest shareholders were in it for the long term. This latter point probably reflects the fact that the top ten fund managers own 36 per cent of the FTSE 100 – few fund managers can afford to move out of a FTSE 100 company altogether and therefore remain long term shareholders whether the investment is liked or not.

There is a perceived trend towards greater involvement and communication. To quote one director: 'Investors are much more sensitive to their responsibilities than in the past because they are looked on as the guardians of the corporate conscience.'

External stakeholders

5.8 External stakeholder groups - the government, local authorities, pressure groups, the community at large, professional bodies - are likely to have quite diverse objectives.

External stakeholder	Interests to defend
Government	• Jobs, training, tax
Interest/pressure groups / charities / 'civil society'	• Pollution • Rights • Other

5.9 It is external stakeholders in particular who **induce social and ethical obligations**.

Social responsibility

5.10 Why should organisations play an active social role in the society within which they function?

(a) **'The public' is a stakeholder in the business.** A business only succeeds because it is part of a wider society. Giving to charity is one way of **enhancing the reputation** of the business.

(b) **Charitable donations** and artistic **sponsorship** are a useful medium of **public relations** and can reflect well on the business.

(c) Involving managers and staff in **community activities** is good **work experience**.

(d) It helps create a **value culture** in the organisation and a sense of mission, which is good for motivation.

(e) In the long term, upholding the community's values, responding constructively to criticism, contributing towards community well-being might be good for business, as it **promotes the wider environment** in which businesses flourish.

(f) There is increasing **political pressure** on businesses to be socially responsible. Such activities help 'buy off' environmentalists.

Case example

The 2000 Davos ('World Economic Conference') summit, a conference for senior politicians and business people, discussed **globalisation.** Increasing numbers of pressure groups are focusing on globalisation as a source of increasing pollution and inequality. Winning the **propaganda battle** is an important issue for business.

Case example

Arriva plc

Arriva plc operates bus services in the UK and Europe. It has a turnover of £1.5bn and 30,000 employees. Here is an extract from its 1999 accounts.

A community focus

Through its various businesses ARRIVA has a strong presence in the communities it serves in the UK and mainland Europe. In many of those communities the services provided by ARRIVA are an integral part of daily life.

The Company's objective is to make the ARRIVA brand universally recognised as a consistent deliverer of high quality passenger transport and also, in the UK, to deliver responsive, high quality motor services. It also seeks to make a positive contribution to the quality of life within local communities by supporting charitable and non-profit making organisations.

ARRIVA is a member of Business in the Community, an organisation established to help business contribute to the social and economic regeneration of local communities by sharing their skills, expertise, influence and time.

In the North-East of England, a number of employees have joined Business in the Community's 'Roots and Wings' mentoring programme. Following training, each employee is available to offer help, advice and support for pupils at a local school – Sandhill View School in Sunderland. This contribution will assist the youngsters in making the transition from the classroom to the world of work as smooth as possible. Currently a pilot project within the Company, it is hoped to expand the programme to other regions served by ARRIVA.

The mentoring programme is one of a number of examples where ARRIVA employees play an important role in supporting their local communities in the UK, Denmark, The Netherlands, Spain and Sweden.

As well as working with local communities and organisations ARRIVA works at a national level to seek improvements locally. Blindness is one of the most common forms of disability. For many blind and partially sighted people, public transport is an essential element in maintaining independence.

In 1999, ARRIVA helped the Royal National institute for the Blind (RNIB) to launch a transport campaign. Called 'Rights of Way', it seeks to address the problems that blind and partially sighted people face when they use buses and trains.

Over the next two years ARRIVA will be working with the RNIB to identify improvements in the way we operate our services to meet the needs of the people represented by the RNIB and other disabled customers.

5.11 There are **three contrasting views** about a corporation's responsibilities.

(a) If the company **creates** a social problem, it must **fix** it (eg Exxon (see below)).

(b) The multinational corporation has the resources to fight poverty, illiteracy, malnutrition, illness and so on. This approach **disregards who** actually **creates** the problem.

Case example

Such an approach dates back to Henry Ford, who said 'I do not believe that we should make such an awful profit on our cars. A reasonable profit is right, but not too much. So it has been my policy to force the price of the car down as fast as production would permit, and give the benefits to the users and the labourers, with surprisingly enormous benefits to ourselves.'

(c) Companies **already discharge their social responsibility**, simply by increasing their profits and thereby contributing more in taxes. If a company was expected to divert more resources to solve society's problems, this would represent a double tax.

The social audit

5.12 Social audits involve five key elements.

- Recognising a firm's rationale for engaging in socially responsible activity
- Identification of programmes which are congruent with the mission of the company
- Determination of objectives and priorities related to this programme
- Specification of the nature and range of resources required
- Evaluation of company involvement in such programmes past, present and future

5.13 Whether or not a social audit is used depends on the degree to which social responsibility is part of the **corporate philosophy**.

Case example

In the USA, social audits on environmental issues have increased since the Exxon Valdez catastrophe in which millions of gallons of crude oil were released into Alaskan waters.

Summary

5.14 A useful summary of the current situation of corporate social responsibility reporting was included in 'How to be good' by Cathy Hayward (*Financial Management*, October 2002).

- Tony Blair challenged 350 of the UK's top businesses to publish environmental reeports by the end of 2001. Fewer than a quarter of these did so.

- This summer more than 30 investment institutions wrote to the world's 500 largest companies calling on them to reveal how they are tackling environmental and ethical issues.

- In June, Linda Perham MP tabled a private member's bill that would introduce mandatory environmental reports and establish a new regulatory body for corporate environmental and social standards. An early-day motion supporting its principles has been signed by 150 MPs.

- The European Commission white paper on CSR rejected mandatory social and environmental reporting. It plans to increase awareness of the business case for CSR through a multi-stakeholder forum of 40 representatives from business, trades unions, consumer groups and non-governmental organisations.

- The Institute of Social and Ethical AccountAbility is developing AA1000S, the world's first assurance standard for social and sustainability reporting.

- A Mori poll has found that [92 per cent of the British public believe that multinational companies should meet the highest human health, animal welfare and environmental standards wherever they are operating, and] that almost 90 per cent of British people believe the government should protect the environment, employment conditions and health even when this conflicts with the interests of multinationals.

- A survey by the National Union of Students has shown that more than 75 per cent of student jobseekers would not work for an "ethically unsound" employer.'

Ethics and ethical conduct

5.15 Whereas **social responsibility** deals with the organisation's **general stance towards society,** and affects the **activities** the organisation **chooses** to do, **ethics** relates far more to **how** an organisation **conducts** individual transactions.

5.16 Organisations are coming under increasing pressure from a number of **sources** to behave more ethically.

- Government
- UK and European legislation
- Treaty obligations (such as the Rio Summit)
- Consumers
- Employers
- Pressure groups

5.17 These sources of pressure expect an **ethical attitude towards** the following.

- Stakeholders
- Animals
- Green issues (such as pollution and the need for re-cycling)
- The disadvantaged
- Dealings with unethical companies or countries

5.18 A clear example of unethical conduct is **bribery.**

(a) In some countries, government officials routinely demand bribes, to supplement their meagre incomes. For example customs officials demand 'commission' before releasing documentation enabling goods to move from the warehouse.

(b) More serious bribes occur when companies bid for large public sector contracts, and pay substantial amounts to politicians and key decision makers.

5.19 The boundary between dubious ethics and criminality has shifted over the years, particularly with increased standards of corporate governance. **Insider dealing,** whereby individuals benefit from unpublished information which may affect the share price, used to be normal practice (a perk of working in stock broking); now it is a crime.

5.20 Reidenbach and Robin usefully distinguish between **five different attitudes to corporate ethics**. The following is an adapted version of a report in the *Financial Times*.

(a) **Amoral organisations**

Such organisations are prepared to **condone any actions that contribute to the corporate aims** (generally the owner's short-term greed). Getting away with it is the only criterion for success. Getting caught will be seen as bad luck. In a nutshell, there is **no set of values other than greed**. Obviously, this company gets away without a written code.

(b) **Legalistic organisations**

Such organisations **obey the letter of the law but not necessarily the spirit of it,** if that conflicts with economic performance. Ethical matters will be ignored until they become a problem. Frequent problems would lead to a formal code of ethics that says, in effect, 'Don't do anything to harm the organisation'.

(c) **Responsive companies**

These organisations take the view - perhaps cynically, perhaps not - that there is **something to be gained from ethical behaviour.** It might be recognised, for example, that an enlightened attitude towards staff welfare enabled the company to attract and retain higher calibre staff. If such a company has a formal code of ethics it will be one that reflects concern for all stakeholders in the business.

(d) **Emerging ethical (or 'ethically engaged') organisations**

They take an **active** (rather than a reactive) **interest in ethical issues**.

'Ethical values in such companies are part of the culture. Codes of ethics are action documents, and contain statements reflecting core values. A range of ethical support measures are normally in place, such as ethical review committees; hotlines; ethical audits; and ethics counsellors or ombudsmen.

Problem solving is approached with an awareness of the ethical consequence of an action as well as its potential profitability, and pains are taken to uphold corporate values.'

(e) **Ethical organisations**

These organisations have a **'total ethical profile'**: a philosophy that informs everything that the company does and a commitment on the part of everyone to carefully selected core values.

Case example

The Co-operative Bank, which has a strong record of ethical reporting, publishes a partnership report. This is an independently-audited ethical and ecological health check that considers how the bank is meeting its obligations to customers, employees and their families, shareholders, suppliers, local communities, national and international society and past and future generations.

According to an article in *Financial Management* ('How to be good,' Cathy Hayward, October 2002), the ethical and ecological positioning of the Co-operative bank contributed more than £20 million, or 20 per cent, of its profits in 2001. Almost a third of its current account customers (the bank's key market) were with the bank primarily because of its ethical policies, according to a survey.

Corporate codes and corporate culture

Case example

British Airways got caught in 1993 waging a 'dirty tricks' campaign against its competitor **Virgin Atlantic**. British Airways maintained that the offending actions (essentially, the poaching of Virgin's customers) were those of a small group of employees who overstepped the bounds of 'proper' behaviour in their eagerness to foster the interests of their employer.

An alternative view digs a little deeper. Some observers believed that the real villain of the piece was **British Airways' abrasive corporate culture**, inspired by the then chairman of BA, Lord King.

One of BA's responses to its defeat in the courts against Virgin and the bad publicity arising from the case was to **introduce a code of ethics**.

5.21 Many commentators would argue that the introduction of a **code of ethics** is **inadequate** on its own. To be effective a code needs to be **accompanied** by **positive attempts to foster guiding values, aspirations and patterns of thinking that support ethically sound behaviour** - in short a **change of culture**.

5.22 Increasingly organisations are responding to this challenge by devising **ethics training programmes** for the entire workforce, instituting comprehensive **procedures for reporting and investigating ethical concerns** within the company, or even setting up an **ethics office** or department to supervise the new measures. About half of all major companies now have a formal code of some kind.

5.23 Lynne Paine (*Harvard Business Review*, March – April 1994) suggests that ethical decisions are becoming more important as, in the US at least, penalties for companies which break the law are becoming tougher. Paine describes two approaches to the management of ethics in organisations.

(a) A **compliance-based** approach is primarily designed to ensure that the company and its personnel act within the letter of the law. Mere compliance is not an adequate means for addressing the full range of ethical issues that arise every day. This is especially the case in the UK, where voluntary codes of conduct and self-regulating institutes are perhaps more prevalent than in the US.

(b) An **integrity-based approach** combines a concern for the law with an emphasis on managerial responsibility for ethical behaviour. When integrated into the day-to-day operations of an organisation, such strategies can help prevent damaging ethical lapses.

5.24 It would seem to follow that the imposition of social and ethical responsibilities on management should come from within the organisation itself, and that the organisation should issue its own code of conduct for its employees.

Code of conduct

5.25 A **corporate code** typically contains a **series of statements setting out the company's values and explaining how it sees its responsibilities towards stakeholders**.

Question: employees and ethics

How can an organisation influence employee behaviour towards ethical issues?

Answer

Here are some suggestions.

- Recruitment and selection policies and procedures
- Induction and training
- Objectives and reward schemes
- Ethical codes
- Threat of ethical audit

The impact of a corporate code

5.26 A code of conduct can set out the company's expectations, and in principle a code may address many of the problems that the organisations may experience. However, **merely issuing a code is not enough**.

(a) The **commitment of senior management** to the code needs to be real, and it needs to be very clearly communicated to all staff. Staff need to be persuaded that expectations really have changed.

(b) Measures need to be taken to **discourage previous behaviours** that conflict with the code.

(c) **Staff need to understand** that it is in the **organisation's best interests** to change behaviour, and become committed to the same ideals.

(d) Some employees – including very able ones - may find it very difficult to buy into a code that they **perceive may limit their own earnings** and/or restrict their freedom to do their job.

(e) In addition to a general statement of ethical conduct, **more detailed statements** (codes of practice) will be needed to set out formal procedures that must be followed.

Case example

Here is an example of United Biscuits plc's code of conduct.

'These "guiding principles", taken in conjunction with our budget and strategic objectives, are important as a description of the way in which we operate.

United Biscuits' business ethics are not negotiable - a well-founded reputation for scrupulous dealing is itself a priceless company asset and the most important single factor in our success is faithful adherence to our beliefs. While our tactical plans and many other elements constantly change, our basic philosophy does not. To meet the challenges of a changing world, we are prepared to change everything about ourselves except our values.

Some employees might have the mistaken idea that we do not care how results are obtained, as long as we get results. This would be wrong: we do care how we get results. We expect compliance with our standard of integrity throughout the company, and we will support an employee who passes up an opportunity or advantage that can only be secured at the sacrifice of a principle.

While it is the responsibility of top management to keep a company honest and honourable, perpetuating ethical values is not a function only of the chief executive or a handful of senior managers. Every employee is expected to take on the responsibility of always behaving ethically whatever the circumstances. Beliefs and values must always come before policies, practices and goals; the latter must be altered if they violate fundamental beliefs.'

6   THE SHORT TERM AND LONG TERM

Long-term and short-term objectives

6.1   **Objectives may be long term and short term.**

(a) For example, a company's **primary objective** might be to increase its earnings per share from 30p to 50p in the next **five years**. A number of **strategies** for achieving the objective might then be selected.

- Increasing profitability in the next twelve months by cutting expenditure
- Increasing export sales over the next three years
- Developing a successful new product for the domestic market within five years

(b) **Secondary objectives** might then be re-assessed to include the following.

    (i) The objective of improving manpower productivity by 10% within twelve months.

    (ii) Improving customer service in export markets with the objective of doubling the number of overseas sales outlets in selected countries within the next three years.

    (iii) Investing more in product-market research and development, with the objective of bringing at least three new products to the market within five years.

6.2 Targets cannot be set without an awareness of what is realistic. Quantified targets for achieving the primary objective, and targets for secondary objectives, must therefore emerge from a realistic 'position audit'.

Trade-offs between short-term and long-term objectives

6.3 Just as there may have to be a trade-off between different objectives, so too might there be a need to make trade offs between short-term objectives and long-term objectives. This is referred to as **S/L trade-off**.

KEY TERM

The **S/L trade-off** refers to the balance of organisational activities aiming to achieve long term and short-term objectives when they are in conflict or where resources are scarce.

6.4 **Decisions which involve the sacrifice of longer term objectives.**

(a) Postponing or abandoning capital expenditure projects, which would eventually contribute to growth and profits, in order to protect short term cash flow and profits.

(b) Cutting R&D expenditure to save operating costs, and so reducing the prospects for future product development.

(c) Reducing quality control, to save operating costs (but also adversely affecting reputation and goodwill).

(d) Reducing the level of customer service, to save operating costs (but sacrificing goodwill).

(e) Cutting training costs or recruitment (so the company might be faced with skills shortages).

6.5 Steps that could be taken to control S/L trade-offs, so that the 'ideal' decisions are taken, include the following.

(a) **Making short-term targets realistic.** If budget targets are unrealistically tough, a manager will be forced to make S/L trade-offs.

(b) **Providing sufficient management information** to allow managers to see what trade-offs they are making. Managers must be kept aware of long-term aims as well as shorter-term (budget) targets.

(c) **Evaluating managers' performance** in terms of contribution to long-term as well as short-term objectives.

7 THE PLANNING GAP AND STRATEGIES TO FILL IT

7.1 Strategic planners need to consider the extent to which new strategies are needed to enable the organisation to achieve its objectives. One technique whereby this can be done is **gap analysis**.

> **KEY TERM**
>
> **Gap analysis** is 'A comparison between an entity's ultimate objective (most commonly expressed in terms of demand, but may be reported in terms of profit, ROCE etc) and the expected performance of projects both planned and underway.'
>
> CIMA *Official Terminology*

> **IMPORTANT POINT**
>
> The planning gap is not the gap between the current position of the organisation and the forecast desired position.
>
> Rather, it's the gap between the forecast position from continuing with current activities, and the forecast of the desired position.

7.2 **Purpose of gap analysis**

(a) Determine the organisation's targets for achievement over the planning period

(b) Establish what the organisation would be expected to achieve if it 'did nothing' (did not develop any new strategies, but simply carried on in the current way with the same products and selling to the same markets)

This **difference is the 'gap'. New strategies** will then have to be developed which will **close this gap,** so that the organisation can expect to achieve its targets over the planning period.

7.3 A **forecast based on doing nothing** will probably provide an unrealistic estimate of future performance, but it is **useful**.

(a) The forecast is used to determine the requirement for new strategies and so it must exclude such strategies.

(b) Including the impact of strategies of which the organisation has little or no experience will produce an even more inaccurate forecast.

(c) It reduces the complexity involved in the forecasting exercise.

(d) It provides an assessment of what could be achieved without taking on new risk.

7.4 Forecasts must cover a period far enough into the future to reveal any significant gap. **How far ahead** an organisation needs to plan, however, will depend on the **lead time for corrective action to take effect,** which in turn depends on the **nature of the organisation's business** and the **type of action required**.

The profit gap

7.5 As an example, the profit gap is the **difference between the target profits and the profit objectives as forecast**.

(a) First of all the firm can estimate the effects on the gap of any projects or strategies in the pipeline. Some of the gap might be filled by a new project.

(b) Then, if a gap remains, new strategies have to be considered to close the gap.

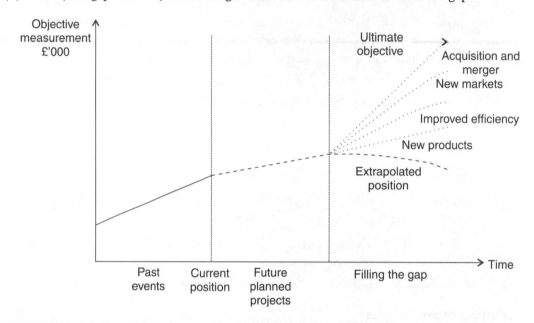

Exam focus point

Knowledge of gap analysis and the ability to draw a diagram similar to that above was required in the June 2003 exam.

7.6 **Possible problems**

(a) The financial propositions may be susceptible to **inflation** - there is no easy way of dealing with this problem.

(b) More serious, however, is **risk**: remember that in many cases a higher return can equate to a higher risk. In seeking to develop strategies to give a higher return, the firm may, unwittingly, be raising its risk profile.

(c) The organisation has **insufficient resources** to enable it to carry out the necessary strategies.

7.7 **Activities to bridge the gap between targets and expectations**

(a) Sometimes the gap can be 'filled' by **incremental improvements** to current activities. For example, **cost reduction** can go a long way to raising profits.

(b) At other times, more **radical changes** to the product market mix are called for and a **combination** of the following will be pursued.

(i) **Market penetration**: raise revenue by selling more of the same product to the existing market

(ii) **Market development**: increase the scope of operations by selling the current product in new markets (eg overseas)

(iii) **Product development**: develop new products to sell to existing markets

(iv) **Diversification** – go into a new line of business completely (new products)

(c) Profitability can be enhanced at times by **withdrawing** from a business.

(d) Such strategies can be achieved by **internally generated (organic) growth** or by **acquisition**.

Case example

Pearson: 'a web of increasingly connected media businesses'

In 1997, Pearson set itself a target of 'achieving double-digit growth in adjusted earnings per share'. In 1999, adjusted EPS were up 15%. There were three reasons for this performance.

(a) Withdrawal from some business areas (Pearson having been involved in businesses as diverse as newspapers and crockery)

(b) Exploitation of its existing intellectual property (eg books, Penguin, the Financial Times) and, in Internet activities, by developing its brands

(c) Focus on growth by acquisitions (eg the publisher Simon & Schuster in 1998)

Interestingly Pearson sets itself substantial targets for social responsibilities in terms of sustainable resources. Furthermore the 1999 personnel committee report stated that 'Pearson wants to be the best company to work for in the world'.

---

8 FACTORS TO CONSIDER WHEN ASSESSING PERFORMANCE

Exam focus point

Questions in both December 2002 and June 2003 required candidates to consider these factors.

Economic environment

8.1 Gross domestic product

- Has it grown or fallen?
- How has demand for goods/services been affected by the growth/fall?

8.2 Local economic trends

- Are local businesses rationalising or expanding?
- Are office/factory rents increasing/falling?
- In what direction are house prices moving?
- Are labour rates on the increase?

8.3 Inflation

(a) Is a high rate making it difficult to plan, owing to the uncertainty of future financial returns? Inflation and expectations of it help to explain short termism.

(b) Is the rate depressing consumer demand?

(c) Is the rate encouraging investment in domestic industries?

(d) Is a high rate leading employees to demand higher money wages to compensate for a fall in the value of their wages?

8.4 **Interest rates**

- How do these affect consumer confidence and liquidity, and hence demand?
- Is the cost of borrowing increasing, thereby reducing profitability?

8.5 **Exchange rates**

- What impact do these have on the cost of overseas imports?
- Are prices that can be charged to overseas customers affected?

8.6 **Government fiscal policy**

(a) Are consumers increasing/decreasing the amount they spend due to tax and government spending decisions?

(b) How is the government's corporation tax policy affecting the organisation?

(c) Is VAT affecting demand?

8.7 **Government spending**

Is the organisation a supplier to the government (such as a construction firm) and hence affected by the level of spending?

8.8 **Business cycle**

- Is the economy booming or in recession?
- Does the organisation follow the business cycle or is it in a counter-cyclical industry?
- What is the forecast state of the economy?

8.9 **International factors**

How do the characteristics of overseas markets affect demand/supply?

Legal factors

8.10 (a) **Employment law.** What is the impact of Social Charter provisions? Minimum wage? Anti-discriminatory legislation?

(b) **Marketing and sales.** How do laws to protect consumers (such as on refunds and replacements) affect the organisation?

(c) **Environment.** Is the organisation affected by laws on pollution control and waste disposal?

(d) **Regulators.** Is the organisation in an industry subject to regulators (such as electricity, gas and water) who have influence over market access, competition and pricing policy?

Political factors

8.11 (a) Is the government policy to encourage firms to increase/cut capacity? Are incentives being offered to locate in a particular area?

(b) Is the organisation affected by government plans for divestment/rationalisation?

(c) Is government policy discouraging entry into an industry, by restricting investment or competition or by making it harder, by use of quotas and tariffs, for overseas firms to compete in the domestic market?

(d) Is government policy affecting competition?

(i)   A government's purchasing decisions will have a strong influence on the strength of one firm relative to another in the market (such as armaments).

(ii)   Regulations and controls in the industry will affect the growth and profits in the industry (such as minimum product quality standards).

(iii)   Governments and supra-national institutions such as the EU might impose policies which keep an industry fragmented, and prevent the concentration of too much market share in the hands of one or two producers.

(e)   Does government regulate new products (such as pharmaceuticals)?

EU

8.12   What is the effect of the EU?

- Product standards
- Environmental protection
- Monetary policy
- Research and development
- Regional policy
- Labour costs

Cultural factors

> **KEY TERM**
>
> Charles Handy sums up **culture** as 'that's the way we do things round here'. It is the sum total of the beliefs, knowledge, attitudes of mind and customs to which people are exposed.

8.13   There are many **factors which influence an organisation's culture**.

Influencing factor	Detail
Economic conditions and strategy	In prosperous times organisations will either be complacent or adventurous, full of new ideas and initiatives. In recession they may be depressed, or challenged. The struggle against a main competitor may take on 'heroic' dimensions.
The nature of the business and its tasks	The types of technology used in different forms of business create the pace and priorities associated with different forms of work. Task also influences work environment to an extent.
Leadership style	The approach used in exercising authority will determine the extent to which subordinates feel alienated and uninterested or involved and important. Leaders are also the creators and 'sellers' of organisational culture: it is up to them to put across the vision.
Policies and practices	The level of trust and understanding which exists between members of an organisation can often be seen in the way policies and objectives are achieved, for example the extent to which they are imposed by tight written rules and procedures or implied through custom and understanding.

Influencing factor	Detail
Structure	The way in which work is organised, authority exercised and people rewarded will reflect an emphasis on freedom or formal control, flexibility or rigidity.
Characteristics of the work force	Organisation culture will be affected by the demographic nature of the workforce, for example its typical manual/clerical division, age, sex and personality.

The value of culture

8.14 **'Positive' organisational culture** may therefore be important in its **influence** on the following.

(a) The **motivation and satisfaction of employees** (and possibly therefore their performance) by encouraging commitment to the organisation's values and objectives, making employees feel valued and trusted, fostering satisfying team relationships, and using 'guiding values' instead of rules and controls.

(b) The **adaptability of the organisation**, by encouraging innovation, risk-taking, customer care, willingness to embrace new methods and technologies etc.

(c) The **image of the organisation**. The cultural attributes of an organisation (attractive or unattractive) will affect its appeal to potential employees and customers.

Cultural problems

8.15 The symptoms of a negative, unhealthy or failing culture (and possibly organisation as a whole) might be as follows.

(a) **No 'visionary' element:** no articulated beliefs or values widely shared, nor any sense of the future.

(b) **No sense of unity** - because no central driving force. Hostility and lack of co-ordination may be evident.

(c) **No shared norms of dress, habits or ways of addressing others.** Sub-cultures may compete with each other for cultural 'superiority'.

(d) **Political conflict and rivalry**, as individuals and groups vie for power and resources and their own interests.

(e) **Focus on the internal workings of the organisation** rather than opportunities and changes in the environment. In particular, disinterest in the customer.

(f) **Preoccupation with the short term.**

(g) **Low employee morale**, expressed in low productivity, high absenteeism and labour turnover, 'grumbling'.

(h) **Abdication by management of the responsibility** for doing anything about the above - perhaps because of apathy or hopelessness.

(i) **No innovation or welcoming of change:** change is a threat and a problem.

(j) **Rigorous control and disciplinary systems** have to be applied, because nothing else brings employees into line with the aims of the business.

(k) **Lacklustre marketing,** company literature and so on.

Changing a culture

8.16 It may be possible to 'turn round' a negative culture, or to change the culture into a new direction.

(a) The **beliefs expressed by managers and staff** can be used to 'condition' people, to sell a new culture to the organisation by promoting a new sense of corporate mission, or a new image. **Slogans, mottos** ('we're getting there'), **myths** and so on can be used to energise people and to promote particular values which the organisation wishes to instil in its members.

(b) **Leadership** provides an impetus for cultural change: attitudes to trust, control, formality or informality, participation, innovation and so on will have to come from the top - especially where changes in structure, authority relationships or work methods are also involved. The first step in deliberate cultural change will need to be a '**vision**' and a **sense of** '**mission**' on the part of a powerful individual or group in the organisation.

(c) The **reward system** can be used to encourage and reinforce new attitudes and behaviour, while those who do not commit themselves to the change miss out or are punished, or pressured to 'buy in or get out'.

(d) The **recruitment and selection policies** should reflect the qualities desired of employees in the new culture. To an extent these qualities may also be encouraged through induction and training.

(e) Visible **emblems** of the culture - for example design of the work place and public areas, dress code, status symbols - can be used to reflect the new 'style'.

Management accounting and organisational culture

8.17 The relevance of organisational culture to management accounting can be explained in simple terms. The business of management accounting is to provide managers with information to help them run the business. **If the management accountant is not sensitive to the culture of his organisation he will not understand how it is run and will not know what sort of information to provide.**

Question: management accounting and organisational culture

Robert Waterman (of Peters and Waterman fame) has published a book entitled *The Frontiers of Excellence* (1994), which argues that leading companies today, and those that have been successful over long periods, do not put the shareholders first. Instead they concentrate on 'putting people first', the people in question being employees and customers.

How could a management accounting system foster such a culture, or undermine it?

Answer

A system to **foster** the 'people' culture would collect and analyse data about employee performance and customer reaction, provide the basis for rewards for what is good in these terms, and supply information that indicates to people how they could do better. The culture would be **undermined** by a system that concentrates solely on reporting in figures and language aimed at the stock market.

8.18 Undoubtedly the most **profound influences** on Western corporate cultures in the 1990s have been ideas borrowed from **Japanese management**. 'Philosophies' such as **Just-in-Time** and **Total Quality Management** have a direct impact on business areas that have long been the preserve of accountants - purchasing and stock control, quality costs, waste and scrap and so on. The Japanese **teamworking** approach is a radical change from the individualistic culture of the West, and this has further implications for performance measurement and reporting.

8.19 In **some organisations**, however, **management accounting and organisational culture may have little relevance to one another**.

> '... in a company which is **dominated by engineering or marketing concerns, accounting controls may form a ritualistic function**. The accountants may be content to prepare cost-based performance reports and all managers may take part in budgeting meetings. However, everybody may know that effective control and performance is related to new product design and successful product launches. Alternatively such apparent conflicts could be a cause of stress and disruption, creating an even wider rift between functional cultures and engendering frustration among accountants regarding their 'rightful place' in the organisation.'
>
> Kim Langfield-Smith, 'Organisational culture and control', in Berry Broadbent and Otley, ed. *Management Control* (1995)

9 COMPARING PERFORMANCE ACROSS DIFFERENT COUNTRIES

Exam focus point

This issue was examined in December 2002 in terms of managerial performance.

9.1 Multinational organisations in particular, with divisions in a number of countries, will need to compare the performance of their overseas divisions. And today's global economy means that organisations in general may wish to benchmark performance with organisations based in different countries.

9.2 In addition to the obvious exchange rate fluctuations which must be taken into account when interpreting performance across different countries, there are a number of other factors which should be considered.

Factor	Details
Local environmental conditions	Some organisations/divisions may be operating under more difficult conditions than others and the interpretation of results must take full account of such differences.
Local legislation	The legislation affecting some organisations/divisions may be more restrictive than for others. For example strict pollution control legislation may increase the costs of some organisations/ divisions compared with others.
The availability of resources	Some organisations/divisions may have easier access to resources such as labour and materials and differences in the relative quality of the resources may affect organisations'/ divisions' comparative profitability.
The nature and extent of local competition	Some organisations/divisions may be operating in countries where they are subject to intensive competition. This may affect their performance compared with an organisation/division which does not experience widespread competition.
Taxation, interest rates and inflation	Tax rates may vary between countries and differences in inflation and interest rates will also influence the financial performance of organisations/divisions.

Factor	Details
Local management	The different levels of expertise of management teams in various countries will affect other organisations'/divisions' actual and potential financial performance.
Government support	Any grants or other support which organisations/divisions may be receiving from local government should be taken into account when judging financial performance.

Multinational performance analysis

9.3 The distances involved, the diversity of conditions and personnel and the sheer scale of the operations make appraisal of multinational organisations a difficult and complex task. Those appraising performance in multinational companies therefore face the following **problems**.

- **Differences in accounting statements, standards and policies**

- **Distance** and possible **remoteness of divisions from head office**, causing delays and problems of information dissemination and management motivation

- **Currency exchange rate fluctuations**

- **Different inflation rates**

- **Differing taxation and law**

- **Transfer pricing difficulties**

- **Delivery problems**

- **Local trade policies**

- **Government policies and restrictions**

- **Variation in management and worker skills**

10 OPERATIONAL PERFORMANCE

10.1 The Study Guide requires you to '**identify the characteristics of operational performance**'.

10.2 Operations are the day to day activities that are carried out in order to achieve specific targets and objectives. Here are some examples.

Sector	Operations carried out by ...
Fast-food	Staff employed at a McDonald's checkout
Bank	Dealer on the forex markets
Law	Solicitor finalising the details of a contract for a client
Call centre	People hosting the switch board
Media	TV camera-person, or presenter
	Website construction
Manufacturing	Assembly line worker
Construction	Building site operations

10.3   These examples show that operations are directly focused on **activities which immediately add value to the customer**.

10.4   Unlike strategy, which involves taking decisions, operations have the following **characteristics**.

- **Customer-facing,** in service industries
- **Specialised,** as the tasks are closely defined
- **More likely to be routine,** but this is not true of all 'operations'
- **Limited in scope**
- Characterised by **short time horizons**
- **Easier to automate** than some management tasks

10.5   **The significance of operations**

(a)   Many operational activities require **expert or specialised skills** – such as surgery.

(b)   Operations can be areas of **significant risk** for a company and its customers.

Case example

Railtrack's management of its operations have been criticised in the UK media, as a result of poor review and maintenance of rails. This is widely believed to be the cause of the Hatfield rail crash, which led to four deaths. (Needless to say, this has had a significant business impact on Railtrack and the companies paying to run trains on the network.)

(c)   Operations are **'moments of truth'** between the firm and its customers. A company's reputation can be made or broken by the quality of its goods and services, which are determined by operational quality and consistency.

(d)   The **operational infrastructure** comprises the most **significant element of cost** for most businesses.

(e)   The most **well-designed strategy** can be **destroyed by poor implementation** at operational level.

(f)   Operations and the deployment of operational activities are a key determinant of **organisation structure**.

Exam focus point

In the first sitting of Paper 3.3 (December 2001), candidates had to comment on the operational performance of both a profit-seeking and a non-profit seeking organisation. Given the data provided in the scenario to the question, the analysis had to concentrate on utilisation of facilities.

11   PLANNING AND CONTROL AT DIFFERENT LEVELS IN THE PERFORMANCE HIERARCHY

Planning

11.1   Although it implies a 'top down' approach to management, we could describe **a cascade of goals, objectives and plans** down through the layers of the organisation. The **plans** made at the **higher levels** of the performance hierarchy provide a **framework** within which the plans at the lower levels must be achieved. The **plans** at the **lower levels** are the **means** by which the plans at the higher levels are achieved.

11.2 It could therefore be argued that without the plans allied directly to the vision and corporate objective the operational-level and departmental plans have little meaning. **Planning** could therefore be deemed as **more significant** at the **higher levels** of the performance hierarchy than the lower levels.

11.3 This is not to say that planning at an operational level is not important. It is just that the two types of planning are different.

Level	Detail
Corporate plans	• Focused on overall performance • Environmental influence • Set plans and targets for units and departments • Sometimes qualitative (eg a programme to change the culture of the organisation) • Aggregate
Operational plans	• Based on objectives about 'what' to achieve • Specific (eg acceptable number of 'rings' before a phone is answered) • Little immediate environmental influence • Likely to be quantitative • Detailed specifications • Based on 'how' something is achieved • Short time horizons

Control

11.4 Consider how the activities of **planning** and **control** are **inter-related**.

(a) **Plans** set the targets.

(b) **Control** involves two main processes.

   (i) **Measure** actual results against the plan.

   (ii) **Take action** to adjust actual performance to achieve the plan or to change the plan altogether

Control is therefore **impossible without planning.**

11.5 The essence of control is the **measurement of results** and **comparing** them with the original **plan**. Any deviation from plan indicates that **control action** is required to make the results conform more closely with plan.

> **KEY TERM**
>
> **Feedback** occurs when the results (outputs) of a system are used to control it, by adjusting the input or behaviour of the system.

11.6 A business organisation uses feedback for control.

(a) **Negative feedback** indicates that results or activities must be brought back on course, as they are deviating from the plan.

(b) **Positive feedback** results in control action continuing the current course. You would normally assume that positive feedback means that results are going according to plan and that no corrective action is necessary: but it is best to be sure that the control system itself is not picking up the wrong information.

(c) **Feedforward control** is control based on **forecast** results: in other words if the forecast is bad, control action is taken well in advance of actual results.

We will look at these concepts in the context of budgetary control in a later chapter.

11.7 Looking at the diagram below, you can see lines called 'single loop' and 'double loop' feedback.

(a) **Single loop feedback** is control, like a thermostat, which regulates the output of a system. For example, if sales targets are not reached, control action will be taken to ensure that targets will be reached soon. The plan or target itself is not changed, even though the resources needed to achieve it might have to be reviewed.

(b) **Double loop feedback** is of a different order. It is information used to **change the plan itself**. For example, if sales targets are not reached, the company may need to change the plan.

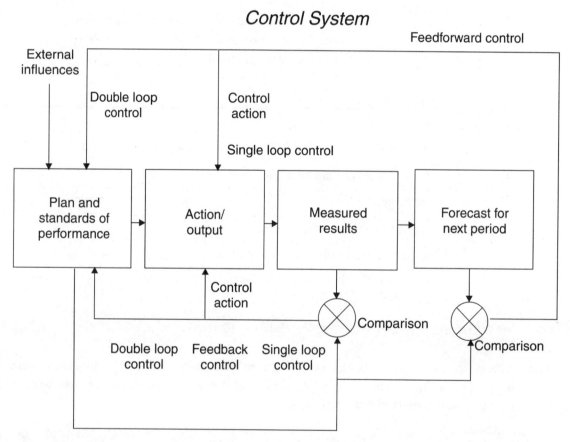

Control System

11.8 You might think that control can only occur at the lower-levels of the performance hierarchy, as that is the type of control you have encountered in your studies to date (standard costing, budgetary control).

11.9 **Features of control at lower-levels of the performance hierarchy**

- Exercised externally by management or, in the case of empowered teams, by the staff themselves

- Immediate or rapid feedback

- Single loop feedback (ie little authority to change plans or targets)

11.10 **Control** does occur at the **higher-levels of the hierarchy**, however, and has the following **characteristics.**

- Exercised by external stakeholders (eg shareholders)
- Exercised by the market
- Double loop feedback (ie relatively free to change targets)
- Often feedforward elements

Summary

11.11 The best way to envisage the differences is by **two case examples**.

Case examples

(a) **Call centres**

Staff manning call centres, employing an increasing number of people in the UK, are subject to precise controls and targets.

- The longest time a phone should ring before it is answered
- Speed of dealing with the caller's query
- Rehearsal of a 'script', or use of precise responses or prompts from software

Staff who take too long dealing with queries may be counselled or dismissed.

The targets are precisely and exactly linked to the service provided and provide rapid feedback. **Control and planning** is exercised **over the process of delivery**.

(b) **Senior management**

Senior management initiate the planning process, but their time is planned to a far less rigid degree than people at operational level.

For example, the Chief Executive of Railtrack is responsible to shareholders but, given the nature of the industry and its reliance on government subsidies, must also be accountable to other stakeholders. The market is mainly concerned with results. Controls over corporate governance – over how the company is run – are mainly to do with ensuring the transparency and integrity of the governance process.

11.12 We will be considering strategic planning and control in more detail in Chapter 16. Budgetary planning and control (control at the lower levels of the hierarchy) is covered in Chapters 17 to 19.

Chapter roundup

- **Vision** is orientated towards the future, to give a sense of direction to the organisation.

- **Mission** describes an organisation's basic purpose, what it is trying to accomplish.

- A **mission statement** should be brief, flexible and distinctive, and is likely to place an emphasis on serving the customer.

- **Goals** and **objectives** are set out to give flesh to the mission in any particular period.

- Goals can be set in many different ways: top down; bottom up; imposed; consensus; precedent.

- Goals and objectives for the organisation as a whole concentrate on overall measures of performance, often set in financial terms.

- **Primary corporate objectives** are supported by **secondary objectives**, for example for product development or market share. In practice there may be a trade off between different objectives.

- Goals and objectives are often set with **stakeholders** in mind. For a business, adding value for shareholders is a prime corporate objective, but other stakeholders need to be satisfied. There is no agreement as to the extent of the **social** or **ethical** responsibilities of a business.

- The **S/L trade-off** refers to the balance of organisational activities aiming to achieve long-term and short-term objectives when they conflict or where resources are scarce.

- Forecasts based on current performance may reveal a **gap** between the firm's objectives and the likely outcomes. New strategies (eg market penetration, market development, product development, diversification, withdrawal) are developed to fill the gap.

- A wide variety of **economic, political, cultural and legal factors** need to be taken into consideration when assessing performance.

- When **interpreting performance across different countries**, a number of factors should be considered.

  - Exchange rate fluctuations
  - Local environmental conditions
  - Local legislation
  - Availability of resources

  - Nature and extent of local competition
  - Taxation, interest rates, inflation
  - Local management
  - Government support

- **Operations** can make or break strategies. They are directly focused on value-adding activities.

- **Planning** and **control** occurs at all levels of the performance hierarchy to different degrees.

Quick quiz

1   'In ten years' time, all our activities will be web-enabled.' This is a:

    A   Vision
    B   Mission
    C   Goal
    D   Objective

2   *Fill in the blanks.*

Four constituents of mission might be ...., ..., ... and ....

3   *Place the following terms in the diagram below to show the hierarchy of objectives.*

Terms

Strategy

Objectives

Mission

Operational plans

Tactics

Goals

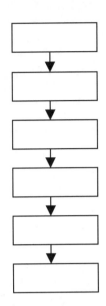

4   *Choose the appropriate words from those highlighted.*

'Increase the number of customers by 8%' is an example of a **corporate/unit/primary** objective, whereas 'increase profits by 5%' is a **unit/primary/secondary** objective.

5   *Match the descriptions to the types of organisation.*

Types of organisation	Descriptions	
Amoral	(a)	Obey the letter but not necessarily the spirit of the law
Legalistic	(b)	Take an active interest in ethical issues
Responsive	(c)	Condone any actions that contribute to corporate aims
Ethically engaged	(d)	Have a 'total ethical profile'
Ethical	(e)	Believe there is something to be gained from ethical behaviour

6   *Insert the following strategies into the four quadrants of the diagram.*

Market penetration
Market development
Product development
Diversification

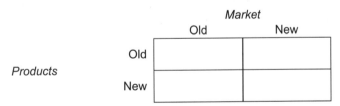

7   Which of the following is not a characteristic of operations?

A   Specialised
B   Long time horizons
C   Easy to automate
D   Routine

Answers to quick quiz

1   Vision, as the statement is future orientated. We do not know what the organisation actually does so it cannot be a mission.

2   Purpose; strategy; policies and standards; values and culture.

3

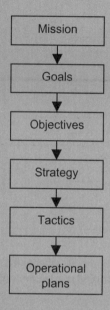

| Mission |
| Goals |
| Objectives |
| Strategy |
| Tactics |
| Operational plans |

4   Unit
    Primary

5   Amoral   (c)
    Legalistic   (a)
    Responsive   (e)
    Ethically engaged   (b)
    Ethical   (d)

6

		Market	
		Old	New
Products	Old	Market penetration	Market development
	New	Product development	Diversification

7   B

Now try the question below from the Exam Question Bank

Number	Level	Marks	Time
9	Exam	20	36 mins

Chapter 11

FINANCIAL PERFORMANCE IN THE PRIVATE SECTOR

Topic list	Syllabus reference
1 The private sector: shareholder benefits	3(b), 3(c)
2 Survival and growth	3(b), 3(c)
3 Profitability	3(b), 3(c)
4 Gearing	3(b), 3(c)
5 Liquidity	3(b), 3(c)
6 Short-run and long-run financial performance	3(b), 3(c)
7 Profits and share value	3(b), 3(c)
8 Comparisons of accounting figures	3(b), 3(c)

Introduction

The examiner is interested in **comparing the public and private sectors** and in this chapter we look at the principal measures used by the private sector to assess performance.

Whereas the public sector tend to use non-financial indicators (see Chapters 12 and 13), the profit-making private sector tend to favour **financial performance measures**. There are four main groups of such measures.

- Those covering growth
- Those covering profitability
- Those covering gearing
- Those covering liquidity

We will be looking at measures in these four areas as we work through this chapter.

Study guide

Session 12 – Financial performance in the private sector

- Explain why the primary objective of financial performance should be concerned with the benefits of the shareholders
- Discuss the crucial objectives of survival and business growth
- Discuss the appropriateness of differing measures of profitability
- Explain why indicators of liquidity and gearing need to be considered alongside profitability
- Compare and contrast short and long run financial performance and the resulting management issues
- Contrast the traditional relationship between profits and share value with the long term profit expectations of the stock market and recent financial performance of new technology/ communication companies

BPP
PROFESSIONAL EDUCATION

1 THE PRIVATE SECTOR: SHAREHOLDER BENEFITS

1.1 Carefully read the case example below.

Case example

The **statement of prospects** below is adapted from the published accounts of a UK printing company, listed on the Stock Exchange (ie a plc) with turnover in 2000 of £110m, operating profits of £16m, and post-tax profit of £10m.

You may be interested in the order of priorities. The emphases have been added by BPP, as have paragraph numbers.

Wyndeham Press plc

Group Strategy

1   Our strategy is to build on our position as one of the leading printers of magazines, brochures etc. offering a complete service for the customer from pre-press and printing to finishing and despatch. We remain focused on making acquisitions to assist in achieving our goal as well as developing our existing businesses.

Capital investment – investment criteria and budgeted expenditure

2   As referred to in the Chairman's and the Chief Executive's review, the last year has been a period of considerable investment for your company. We purchased new presses, finishing equipment and pre-press equipment, at a total cost of £14.1m. We plan to invest a further £14m this year on upgrading existing equipment and expanding capacity by installing additional machines.

Funding structure

See section 4

3   Our closing level of debt is £26.7m of which £23.2m is at fixed rates ranging from 5.9% to 8.1%. The balance is at 1% over base rate and this averaged 6.4% during the period. Given the high level of **operating gearing** within a printing business, we believe our **optimal level of debt/equity** is between 50% - 70%.

4   **Interest cover** has reduced from 14 times to 10.3 times, which is still a very healthy level, and **gearing increased to 56%.** Both ratios are well within our **targets** of a minimum of 8 times interest cover and a maximum of 70% gearing. The **covenants under our debt facilities** require a gearing of less than 85% and debt of less than twice **EBITDA** (earnings before interest, tax, depreciation and amortisation).

See section 3

5   The Group has a progressive dividend policy. **Dividend growth** will follow **earnings growth** and we will maintain **dividend cover at our target of 3 times.** We believe this level of cover should generate sufficient **retained capital** to support the **equity component** of our investment programme.

Key performance indicators and benchmarking of performance

See section 3

6   We benchmark our performance against a peer group of comparable businesses (A, B, C, D). We aim for **top quartile performance** compared to this group in the following categories: **operating profit** as a percentage of sales, **return on capital employed, profit per employee, proportion of repeat business.** We believe we currently rank in the top quartile of the printing sector on all these criteria.

See section 6

7   The group achieved a **return on capital** employed of 29%. In the **long-term, our objective** is a steady rise in return on capital employed as a result of acquisitions, capital expenditure programmes and improvements in efficiency and machine utilisation.

Risks and sensitivities

8   The commercial risks we face in the coming year are:

- If sterling continues to increase in value, overseas companies will become even more competitive on the non-magazine work.

- Whilst we expect a very modest growth in the economy, if economic activity contracts there will be a resultant decline in demand for our services.

Trading prospects

9   Our prospects for the current year are dependent on prices achieved and volume of work. We believe that volume of work will move ahead this year arising from the increased capacity generated by the installation of new plant.

10   We remain confident about the prospects for our business.

Why are shareholders important?

1.2   In the case example above, the 'statement of prospects' is expressed almost exclusively in financial terms, with the exception of paragraph 1. The 'prospects' are not the prospects of the business but the prospects for the **shareholders** who have invested in the company.

1.3   As we saw in the previous chapters, organisations are likely to have a number of goals, objectives and targets which, despite managerial effort to attain goal congruence, are at times likely to conflict. This is often due to the difficulty in satisfying the differing objectives of the organisation's various stakeholder groups.

1.4   But profit-making organisations tend to focus on financial performance in general and on the interests of shareholders in particular.

1.5   The traditional argument for this is that shareholders are the legal owners, the company belongs to them and so their interests are paramount.

Question: long-term owner value

Go back to the case example above. Identify ways in which maximising long-term owner value is Wyndeham Press plc's objective.

Answer

(a)   Group strategy, to serve customers is undertaken with profit in mind

(b)   Capital investment – generate future profits by raising productivity

(c)   Funding structure – there is generally an optimum mix of debt and equity capital. The firm monitors this to raise capital and funds at the cheapest cost – in the shareholders interests'

(d)   Benchmarking of performance. Although these are accounting measures, they do contribute to the long-term performance on the company. Raising return on capital employed means rewarding shareholders more each year for their investment

1.6 **Significance of long-term owner focus**

(a) As maximising shareholder wealth is a **long-term** goal for a business, inevitably managers must decide between **what funds** they want to **disburse now** and **what funds** need to be **maintained** in the business to ensure the prospects of long-term profitability.

(b) Shareholders **own the business,** and so the directors of the company have a **duty** to safeguard their interests.

(c) What the shareholders require as a **return** is used to judge the **validity of investment projects**.

(d) Shareholders assess the **quality of management** by how well the **business performs financially**.

(e) Shareholders are the principal **source of capital investment** in a business. They provide funds on share issues or permit managers to retain profits for investment.

1.7 **What are shareholders interested in?**

• Current earnings

• Future earnings

• Dividend policy

• The relative risk of the investments compared to other investments and the return available

1.8 **Difficulties of incorporating shareholder concerns in performance measurement for managers**

(a) **Accounting.** Shareholders are interested in **future returns** whereas accounts generally provide **historic information**. Accounting measures such as ROCE do not measure shareholder wealth.

(b) **Shareholders** have a different assessment of risk to managers. Managers, typically, worry about their careers, which concern shareholders not at all. Shareholders are concerned about the security of the investment and the likelihood of making a return.

(c) At **operating** level, it is not easy to identify exactly how well a business is doing in relation to other businesses.

(d) Any other yardstick than shareholders' objectives effectively means that managers may run an organisation in their **own** interests.

Why should managers bother to know who their shareholders are?

1.9 A company's senior management should remain aware of who its major shareholders are, and it will often help to retain shareholders' support if the chairman or the managing director meets occasionally with the major shareholders, to exchange views.

(a) The company's management might learn about **shareholders' preferences** for either high **dividends** or high **retained earnings** for profit growth and capital gain.

(b) For public companies, changes in shareholdings might help to explain recent share price movements.

(c) The company's management should be able to learn about **shareholders' attitudes to both risk and gearing**. If a company is planning a new investment, its management might have to consider the relative merits of seeking equity finance or debt finance, and shareholders' attitudes would be worth knowing about before the decision is taken.

(d) Management might need to know its shareholders in the event of an unwelcome takeover bid from another company, to identify key shareholders whose views on the takeover bid might be crucial to the final outcome.

Aligning shareholder and managerial goals

1.10 One way of rewarding managers is **share options.**

(a) This is regarded as a **good thing** as it means that managers have a direct financial interest in increasing owner wealth, ensuring goal congruence.

(b) **Drawbacks** are more subtle.

(i) Managers are rewarded for **past** performance, and the rewards are often **immediate.** They may be incentivised to take **short-term measures**, and ignore the long term.

(ii) There may be a **general** rise in share prices which is not performance related.

Internet businesses

1.11 Between 1995 and 1999, **investors** in **Internet companies** offered **managers** share options, in return for a lower salary and long hours. The share options, potentially, could have made the managers into millionaires. For several years, managers worked long hours for reward that correlated neatly with the rewards offered to shareholders.

1.12 In 2000, the market lost confidence in Internet companies. Hired managers saw a potential $20m reward fall to $2m, and in many cases have left. Founders of the business have stayed on. (*Financial Times* 6/2/01).

1.13 **Conclusions from this episode**

(a) It may be unrealistic to expect managers to take the same risks with their rewards as investors, who are able to spread risks.

(b) Many managers may leave internet companies for more secure environments elsewhere.

(c) Investors may have to return to offering higher salaries.

2 SURVIVAL AND GROWTH

2.1 Successful businesses might report expanding sales volumes, manufacture prestigious brands, receive awards and recognition and be a good company to work for. These may be desirable achievements and objectives, but they are not enough to guarantee the survival and growth of an organisation.

2.2 The clearest **measure of success** for a business is **continued existence and expansion**. It is widely accepted that **growth requires profits** and that **growth produces profits**; growth without profits can mean a company is taken over or goes into liquidation, that it does not survive. So whatever else it aims to do, a business must **make profits** and **make them in perpetuity.**

2.3 Despite the overriding importance of profits, **growth** can be **measured in a number of ways.**

215

Area of growth	Comment
Revenue	In the long term, growth in revenue is only really valuable to investors if it means growth in profits.
Profitability	There are many measures of this (see next section). Growing profitability is more useful if it is related to the level of investment.
Return of investment	A growing return on investment suggests that capital is being used more productively.
Market share	Growth in market share is generally regarded as a good thing, as it can generate economies of scale.
Number of employees	Shareholders are interested in productivity and profit per employee. An increasing head count is a measure of success if people are needed to deliver a service but people need to be employed productively.
Number of products	Growth in the number of products is only useful if the products are profitable.
Cash flow	This is one of the most important measures of growth as it ultimately determines how much a business has to invest.

2.4 Most of the time, **growth** is a sign of **success, provided it is profitable**. This is why it is crucial. At other times, growth can be achieved in many different ways. Look at the case example below, noting the strategies and performance measures (in the last two paragraphs especially).

Case example

From the *Financial Times,* 6 February 2001 (BPP emphasis)

British Airways' recovery appears to be on track, as Rod Eddington, chief executive since May, accelerates the strategy put in place by his predecessor Robert Ayling, ousted in a boardroom coup a year ago. The airline more than doubled operating profits in the nine months to December 31 to £441m (£209m), slightly ahead of expectations.

Mr Eddington said the **strategy of cutting capacity**, switching to **smaller aircraft** and concentrating on **premium traffic** had left it well prepared for any slowdown in the US and the world economy.

Along with the **elimination of unprofitable routes** and the **rationalisation of the lossmaking short haul operations** in Europe, he said the strategy would 'continue to raise margins over the next few years'.

In the third quarter, it recovered from a pre-tax loss of £60m and an operating loss of £2m last time to a pre-tax profit of £65m and an operating surplus of £80m. Pre-tax profits in the first nine months, inflated a year ago by gains from disposals, rose 19 per cent to £215m. Analysts forecast operating profits for the year to March 31 of £377m, up from £84m a year ago.

BA's share price, which has risen sharply from a low in late October of 265p to a 12-month high last Friday of 457½p, fell 8 per cent to 421p yesterday as investors took profits.

After falling into its first loss last year since privatisation 14 years ago, the group's performance has improved strongly with earnings per share of 5.4p in the third quarter, up from losses of 6.6p a year ago. Turnover in the third quarter rose 4.4 per cent to £2.3bn and 4.7 per cent for the nine months to £7.16bn.

Mr Eddington said the results showed the group could 'continue to improve profitability by focusing on core activities and the right network'.

Capacity, which has been cut by about 3.5 per cent this year, would be reduced by a further 9 per cent in the year to March 2002. The investment in product improvements – including the introduction a year ago of flat beds in long haul business class – is paying off, with improving **yields** and increased **market share of premium** passengers. **Passenger yields**, or **average fare level**, were 8.3 per cent higher year-on-year in the third quarter, and the improved profits were achieved despite a 46 per cent rise in fuel costs in the three months.

3 PROFITABILITY

Exam focus point

A 20-mark question in the December 2001 exam required candidates to report on the financial performance of a company from the perspective of a parent company. This required very few calculations but rather commentary on data provided in the scenario.

KEY TERMS

The following are explicitly mentioned in the ACCA's published Study Guide for this paper.

- **ROCE** **Return on capital employed**
- **EPS** **Earnings per share**
- **ROI** **Return on investment**
- **Sales margin** Sales revenue less cost of sales
- **EBITDA** **Earnings before Interest, Tax, Depreciation and Amortisation**
- **Residual Income** A means of measuring the performance of different divisions by charging them an imputed interest charge on the investment in the division
- **NPV** **Net present value**; generally applied to projects but DCF techniques can be applied to evaluate strategic performance
- **IRR** **Internal rate of return**

Case example

Pearson, the education and publishing group, listed the following as 'financial highlights' in its 1999 annual accounts.

- Sales
- Operating profit (before goodwill, exceptional and non-operating items)
- Adjusted earnings per share before internet enterprises
- EBITDA
- Adjusted earnings per share after Internet enterprises
- Dividend per share

It is interesting that Pearson chose to identify adjusted EPS before internet enterprises and after. Internet enterprises have typically high start-up costs. Pearson actively targets sales growth, EBITDA and adjusted earnings per share.

3.1 You need to be able to discuss the **appropriateness** of the measures of 'profitability' specifically identified in the ACCA Study Guide.

3.2 **As a general principle, these measures of performance are only meaningful if they are used for comparison.**

- Over time (equivalent time periods)
- With other measures of performance
- With other companies
- With other industries

Profitability

3.3 A company ought of course to be profitable, and there are obvious checks on **profitability**.

(a) Whether the company has made a profit or a loss on its ordinary activities
(b) By how much this year's profit or loss is bigger or smaller than last year's profit or loss

It is probably better to consider separately the profits or losses on exceptional items if there are any. Such gains or losses should not be expected to occur again, unlike profits or losses on normal trading.

Question: profitability

A company has the following summarised profit and loss accounts for two consecutive years.

	Year 1 £	Year 2 £
Turnover	70,000	100,000
Less cost of sales	42,000	55,000
Gross profit	28,000	45,000
Less expenses	21,000	35,000
Net profit	7,000	10,000

Although the net profit margin is the same for both years at 10%, the gross profit margin is not.

Year 1 $\frac{28,000}{70,000} = 40\%$

Year 2 $\frac{45,000}{100,000} = 45\%$

Is this good or bad for the business?

Answer

An increased profit margin must be good because this indicates a wider gap between selling price and cost of sales. Given that the net profit ratio has stayed the same in the second year, however, expenses must be rising. In year 1 expenses were 30% of turnover, whereas in year 2 they were 35% of turnover. This indicates that administration, selling and distribution expenses or interest costs require tight control.

Percentage analysis of profit between year 1 and year 2

	Year 1 %	Year 2 %
Cost of sales as a % of sales	60	55
Gross profit as a % of sales	40	45
	100	100
Expenses as a % of sales	30	35
Net profit as a % of sales	10	10
Gross profit as a % of sales	40	45

3.4 **Profit on ordinary activities before taxation** is generally thought to be a **better** figure to use than profit after taxation, because there might be unusual variations in the tax charge from year to year which would not affect the underlying profitability of the company's operations.

3.5 Another profit figure that should be calculated is **PBIT: profit before interest and tax**.

(a) This is the amount of profit which the company earned **before having to pay interest to the providers of loan capital**. By providers of loan capital, we usually mean longer-term loan capital, such as debentures and medium-term bank loans, which will be shown in the balance sheet as 'Creditors: amounts falling due after more than one year.' This figure is of particular importance to bankers and lenders.

(b) **How is profit before interest and tax calculated?**

   The profit on ordinary activities before taxation
   plus   **Interest charges on long-term loan capital**

(c) To calculate PBIT, in theory, all we have to do is to look at the interest payments in the relevant note to the accounts. Do not take the net interest figure in the profit and loss account itself, because this represents interest payments less interest received, and PBIT is profit including interest received but before interest payments.

Exam focus point

Part of the 40-mark compulsory question in the June 2002 exam was concerned with calculation of profits, financial consequences and financial impacts for a national motor vehicle breakdown recovery service. Rather than extracts from financial statements, both financial and non-financial management information was provided.

Sales margin

3.6 Sales margin is **turnover less cost of sales**. Look at the following examples.

(a) **Wyndeham Press plc, a printer**

		2000
		£'000
Turnover		89,844
Cost of sales		(60,769)
Gross profit		29,075
Distribution expenses		(1,523)
Administrative expenses		(13,300)
Goodwill amortisation		(212)
Operating profit	(15.6%)	14,040
(Interest etc)		

Cost of sales comprises **direct material** cost, such as paper, and **direct labour**. Distribution and administrative expenses include depreciation. **Sales margin = 32%**.

Sales margin at least shows the contribution that is being made, especially when direct variable costs are very significant.

(b) **Arriva plc, a bus company**

		1999
		£'m
Turnover		1,534.3
Cost of sales		1,282.6
Gross profit		251.7
Net operating expenses		133.8
Operating profit	(7.6%)	117.9
(Interest etc)		

Sales margin = 16%. Clearly a higher percentage of costs are operating costs.

(c) **Lessons to be learnt**

(i) Sales margin as a measure is **not really any use in comparing different industries.**

(ii) Sales margin is **influenced** by the level of **fixed costs.**

(iii) **Trends** in sales margin are of interest. A falling sales margin suggests an organisation has not been able to pass on input price rises to customers.

(iv) **Comparisons** with similar companies are of interest. If an organisation has a lower sales margin than a similar business, this suggests problems in controlling input costs.

In short, the value of sales margin as a measure of performance depends on the cost structure of the industry and the uses to which it is put.

EBITDA: Earnings before interest, tax, depreciation and amortisation

Question: EBITDA

Here is an extract from *Pearson* plc's results for 1999 (with BPP emphasis).

'In addition to the performance measures which form the basis for bonus awards, we focus on a **variety of indicators** to chart our course and, **when necessary, correct it. EBITDA** ... is a close proxy for cash flow and is increasingly used as a basis for valuing media companies such as Pearson.'

Why do you think EBITDA is 'increasingly used as a basis for valuing media companies such as Pearson'?

Answer

Pearson's 1999 sales were £3,332m.

Here is an extract from the company's 31/12/99 balance sheet.

Fixed assets	£m
Intangible	2,457
Tangible	405
Investments in associates	234
Investments: other	99
	3,195

In other words, 76% of Pearson's **fixed assets are intangible** and amount to **goodwill.**

3.7 To see what EBITDA actually does, it is worth identifying **what it omits.**

Item	Comment
Earnings	In practice this equals **profit after tax** for the financial year with some **adjustments,** as you should be aware from your financial accounting studies.
Interest	Essentially this is a **financing cost.** Pearson's balance sheet at 31/12/99 showed net assets of £1.327m. Creditors due over one year were £2.308m, most of which were bonds and commercial paper.
Tax	The government's take is not relevant to the operating performance of the business.
Depreciation and amortisation	This is the P & L charge for **tangible** and **intangible** assets. Depreciation generally represents the writing off of expenditure incurred several years ago, not in itself relevant to performance in any particular financial year.

3.8 **Advantages of EBITDA**

(a) It is a good proxy for **cash flow from operations**, and therefore is a measure of underlying performance. It can be seen as the proportion of operating profits converted to cash.

(b) Tax and interest – while important – are effectively distributions to the government (tax) and a finance charge (interest). They are not relevant to the underlying success of this particular business.

(c) EBITDA is easy to calculate and understand.

(d) EBITDA can be used to assess the performance of a manager who has no control over acquisition and financing policy as it excludes costs associated with assets (depreciation) and debt (interest).

Question: the relevance of interest

When might interest be relevant in a significant way to the **operating** performance of the business?

Answer

- It depends. Short term bank interest can be a significant operating expense.
- Also, a bank itself earns money from an interest margin so interest is at the heart of what it does.

Earnings per share (EPS)

3.9 EPS is a convenient measure as it shows how well the shareholder is doing.

Case example

Pearson's explicit targets

Sales growth	-	reflects growth of business and market share
EBITDA	-	reflects how sales growth impacts on total operating performance
EPS	-	takes all other charges into account to see what is left for shareholders

An extract from Pearson's 1999 accounts

'Adjusted EPS increased by 27% to 53.3p per share, excluding our new internet enterprises… our third successive year of double digit growth. This result was helped by a lower tax rate but reflects real earnings progress.'

3.10 EPS is widely used as a **measure of a company's performance**, especially in **comparing** results over a period **of several years**. A company must be able to sustain its earnings in order to pay dividends and re-invest in the business so as to achieve future growth. Investors also look for **growth in the EPS** from one year to the next.

3.11 EPS is defined (in Financial Reporting Standard 3) as the **profit in pence attributable to each equity (ordinary) share**. This is calculated as follows.

$$\frac{\text{Profit of the period after tax, minority interests and extraordinary items, and after deducting preference dividends}}{\text{Number of equity shares in issue and ranking for dividend}}$$

Extraordinary items are unusual, non-repeating items that affect profit but have effectively been outlawed by FRS 3.

Question: EPS

Walter Wall Carpets plc made profits before tax in 20X8 of £9,320,000. Tax amounted to £2,800,000.

The company's share capital is as follows.

	£
Ordinary share (10,000,000 shares of £1)	10,000,000
8% preference shares	2,000,000
	12,000,000

Required

Calculate the EPS for 20X8.

Answer

	£
Profits before tax	9,320,000
Less tax	2,800,000
Profits after tax	6,520,000
Less preference dividend (8% of £2,000,000)	160,000
Earnings	6,360,000
Number of ordinary shares	10,000,000
EPS	63.6p

3.12 **EPS on its own does not really tell us anything**. It must be seen **in context**.

(a) EPS is used for comparing the results of a company **over time**. Is its EPS growing? What is the rate of growth? Is the rate of growth increasing or decreasing?

(b) Is there likely to be a significant **dilution of EPS** in the future, perhaps due to the exercise of share options or warrants, or the conversion of convertible loan stock into equity?

(c) EPS should not be used blindly to compare the earnings of one company with another. For example, if A plc has an EPS of 12p for its 10,000,000 10p shares and B plc has an EPS of 24p for its 50,000,000 25p shares, we must take account of the numbers of shares. When **earnings are used to compare one company's shares with another**, this is done **using the P/E ratio or perhaps the earnings yield**.

(d) If EPS is to be a reliable basis for comparing results, it **must be calculated consistently**. The EPS of one company must be directly comparable with the EPS of others, and the EPS of a company in one year must be directly comparable with its published EPS figures for previous years. Changes in the share capital of a company during the course of a year cause problems of comparability.

3.13 Note that EPS is a figure based on past data, and it is easily manipulated by changes in accounting policies and by mergers or acquisitions. **The use of the measure in calculating management bonuses makes it particularly liable to manipulation.** The attention given to EPS as a performance measure by City analysts is arguably disproportionate to its true worth. Investors should be more concerned with **future earnings**, but of course estimates of these are more difficult to reach than the readily available figure.

3.14 A **fully diluted EPS** (FDEPS) can be measured where the company has issued securities that might be converted into ordinary shares at some future date, such as convertible loan stock, share warrants or share options. The FDEPS gives investors an appreciation of by how much EPS might be affected if and when the options, warrants or conversion rights are exercised.

Profitability and return: the return on capital employed (ROCE)

3.15 It is impossible to assess profits or profit growth properly without relating them to the amount of funds (the capital) employed in making the profits. An important profitability ratio is therefore **return on capital employed (ROCE)**, which states the profit as a **percentage of the amount of capital employed**.

3.16 **Profit** is usually taken as **PBIT**, and **capital employed** is **shareholders' capital plus 'creditors: amount falling due after more than one year' plus long-term provisions for liabilities and charges.** This is the same as **total assets less current liabilities.** The underlying principle is that we must compare like with like, and so if capital means share capital and reserves plus long-term liabilities and debt capital, profit must mean the profit earned by all this capital together. This is PBIT, since interest is the return for loan capital.

> **KEY TERM**
>
> **Return on capital employed (ROCE)** indicates the productivity of capital employed. It is calculated as:
>
> $$\frac{\text{Profit before interest and tax} \times 100}{\text{Average capital employed}}$$

3.17 The denominator is normally calculated as the average of the capital employed at the beginning and end of the year. Problems of seasonality, new capital introduced or other factors may necessitate taking the average of a number of periods within the year.

Evaluating the ROCE

3.18 What does a company's ROCE tell us? What should we be looking for? There are three **comparisons** that can be made.

(a) The change in ROCE from **one year to the next**

(b) The ROCE being earned by **other companies,** if this information is available

(c) A comparison of the ROCE with **current market borrowing rates**

    (i) What would be the cost of extra borrowing to the company if it needed more loans, and is it earning an ROCE that suggests it could make high enough profits to make such borrowing worthwhile?

    (ii) Is the company making an ROCE which suggests that it is making profitable use of its current borrowing?

Analysing profitability and return in more detail: the secondary ratios

3.19 We may analyse the ROCE, to find out why it is high or low, or better or worse than last year. There are two factors that contribute towards a return on capital employed, both related to turnover.

(a) **Profit margin.** A company might make a high or a low profit margin on its sales. For example, a company that makes a profit of 25p per £1 of sales is making a bigger return on its turnover than another company making a profit of only 10p per £1 of sales.

(b) **Asset turnover**. Asset turnover is a measure of how well the assets of a business are being used to generate sales. For example, if two companies each have capital employed of £100,000, and company A makes sales of £400,000 a year whereas company B makes sales of only £200,000 a year, company A is making a higher turnover from the same amount of assets and this will help company A to make a higher return on capital employed than company B. Asset turnover is expressed as 'x times' so that assets generate x times their value in annual turnover. Here, company A's asset turnover is 4 times and company B's is 2 times.

3.20 Profit margin and asset turnover together explain the ROCE, and if the ROCE is the primary profitability ratio, these other two are the secondary ratios. The relationship between the three ratios is as follows.

Profit margin × asset turnover = ROCE

$$\frac{\text{PBIT}}{\text{Sales}} \times \frac{\text{Sales}}{\text{Capital employed}} = \frac{\text{PBIT}}{\text{Capital employed}}$$

3.21 It is also worth commenting on the **change in turnover** from one year to the next. Strong sales growth will usually indicate volume growth as well as turnover increases due to price rises, and volume growth is one sign of a prosperous company.

Return on investment (ROI)

KEY TERM

Return on investment (ROI) is a form of ROCE and is calculated as:

$$\frac{\text{Profit before interest and tax} \times 100}{\text{Operations management capital employed}}$$

3.22 The ROI compares income with the operational assets used to generate that income. Profit is taken before tax and interest because tax is an appropriation of profit made from the use of the investment, and the introduction of interest charges introduces the effect of financing decisions into an appraisal of operating performance.

3.23 ROI is normally used to apply to investment centres or profit centres. These normally reflect the existing organisation structure of the business.

3.24 **Main reasons for the widespread use of ROI**

(a) **Financial reporting**. It ties in directly with the accounting process, and is identifiable from the profit and loss account and balance sheet, the firm's most important communications media with investors.

(b) **Aggregation**. ROI is a very convenient method of measuring the performance for a division or company as an entire unit.

Other advantages include its ability to permit comparisons to be drawn between investment centres that differ in their absolute size.

Measurement problems: fixed assets

3.25 (a) It is probably most common to use **return on net assets**.

(i) If an investment centre maintains the **same annual profit,** and keeps the **same assets** without a policy of regular fixed asset replacement, its **ROI** will **increase year by year as the assets get older.** This can give a false impression of improving 'real' performance over time.

(ii) It is **not easy** to **compare fairly** the performance of one investment centre with another. Fixed assets may be of different ages or may be depreciated in different ways.

(iii) **Inflation and technological change** alter the cost of fixed assets. If one investment centre has fixed assets bought ten years ago with a gross cost of £1 million, and another investment centre, in the same area of business operations, has fixed assets bought very recently for £1 million, the quantity and technological character of the fixed assets of the two investment centres are likely to be very different.

(iv) Measuring ROI as return on **gross assets ignores the age factor.** Older fixed assets usually cost more to repair and maintain. An investment centre with old assets may therefore have its profitability reduced by repair costs.

(b) **Measurement problems: what are 'assets' anyway?**

Prudence and other accounting principles require that items such as research and development should only be carried forward as an investment in special circumstances. Many 'costs' do have the effect of enhancing the long-term revenue-earning capacity of the business. A good example is **brands:** many firms have capitalised brands for this reason. For **decision-making** and **control** purposes, the expenditure on brands might be better treated as an investment.

The target return for a group of companies

3.26 If a group of companies sets a **target return** for the group as a whole, or if a company sets a target return for each SBU, it might be company policy that no investment project should go ahead in any subsidiary or investment centre unless the project promises to earn at least the target return. Here is an example.

(a) There should be no new investment by any subsidiary in the group unless it is expected to earn at least a 15% return.

(b) Similarly, no fixed asset should be disposed of if the asset is currently earning a return in excess of 15% of its disposal value.

(c) Investments which promise a return of 15% or more ought to be undertaken.

3.27 **Problems with such a policy**

(a) **Investments** are **appraised by DCF** whereas **actual performance** will probably be **measured on the basis of ROI.**

(b) The **target return** makes **no allowance** for the different **risk** of each investment centre.

(c) In a **conglomerate,** an **identical target return** may be **unsuitable** to many businesses in a group.

3.28 Since **managers** will be judged on the basis of the ROI that their centre earns each year, they are likely to be **motivated** into taking those decisions which **increase** their centre's **short-term ROI.**

(a) An investment might be desirable from the group's point of view, but would not be in the individual investment centre's 'best interest' to undertake. Thus there is a lack of **goal congruence**.

(b) In the short term, a desire to increase ROI might lead to projects being taken on without **due regard to their risk**.

(c) Any decisions which **benefit** the company in the **long term** but which **reduce** the ROI in the immediate **short term** would **reflect badly** on the manager's reported performance.

Divisional performance: residual income (RI)

3.29 An alternative way of measuring the performance of an investment centre, instead of using ROI, is residual income (RI).

> ### KEY TERM
>
> **Residual income** is a measure of the centre's profits after deducting a notional or imputed interest cost.

3.30 Its use highlights the finance charge associated with funding.

3.31 The **imputed cost of capital** might be the organisation's **cost of borrowing** or its **weighted average cost of capital**. Alternatively, the cost of capital can be adjusted to allow for the risk characteristics of each investment centre, with a higher imputed interest rate being applied to higher **risk** centres.

The advantages and weaknesses of RI compared with ROI

3.32 **Advantages of using RI**

(a) Residual income **increases in the following circumstances.**

- Investments earning above the cost of capital are undertaken
- Investments earning below the cost of capital are eliminated

(b) Residual income is more **flexible** since a different cost of capital can be applied to investments with different risk characteristics.

3.33 There are two principal weaknesses of RI. The first is that it **does not facilitate comparisons** between investment centres nor does it relate the size of a centre's income to the size of the investment, other than indirectly through the interest charge. The second is that it can be **difficult to decide on an appropriate and accurate measure of the capital employed** upon which to base the imputed interest charge (see comments on ROI).

> ### Exam focus point
>
> Very straightforward RI and ROI calculations were needed in the June 2003 exam. RI and ROI were also examined in June 2004.

Cash flows: NPV and IRR

3.34 The Study Guide mentions NPV and IRR as measures of 'profitability' to be considered in this context.

The advantages and weaknesses of NPV compared with ROI and RI

3.35 **Advantages**

   (a) Cash flows are less subject to manipulation and subjective decisions than accounting profits.
   (b) It considers the opportunity cost of not holding money.
   (c) Risk can be allowed for by adjusting the cost of capital.
   (d) Shareholders are interested in cash flows (both in the short term and long term).

3.36 **Disadvantages**

   The disadvantages of the NPV approach are centred on the assumptions underlying the values of critical variables within the model. For example:

   - The duration of the cash flows
   - The timing of the cash flows
   - The appropriate cost of capital

3.37 NPV and IRR are typically used to evaluate capital investment or other discrete items of expenditure, or to compare investment projects. We look at them in detail in Chapter 26.

3.38 Control and performance measures at a strategic level do need to pay some attention to wealth. Shareholders are interested in cash flow as the safest indicator of business success. According to one model of share valuations, the market value of the shares is based on the expected future dividend.

Cash flows and NPVs for strategic control: shareholder wealth

3.39 **Control** at a **strategic level** should be **based** on measurements of **cash flows** (actual cash flows for the period just ended and revised forecasts of future cash flows). Since the objective of a company might be to maximise the wealth of its shareholders, a control technique based on the measurement of cash flows and their NPV could be a very useful technique to apply. A numerical example might help to illustrate this point.

3.40 Suppose that ABC Ltd agrees to a **strategic plan from 1 January 20X1** as follows.

Year	20X1	20X2	20X3	20X4	20X5	Total
Planned net cash inflow (£'000)	200	300	300	400	500	1,700
NPV at cost of capital 15%	174	227	197	229	249	1,076

3.41 Now suppose that ABC Ltd **reviews** its position **one year later**.

   (a) It can measure its actual total cash flow in 20X1 - roughly speaking, this will be the funds generated from operations minus tax paid and minus expenditure on fixed assets and plus/minus changes in working capital.

   (b) It can revise its forecast for the next few years.

   We will assume that there has been **no change in the cost of capital**. Control information at the end of 20X1 might be as follows.

Year	20X1 (actual)	20X2 (forecast)	20X3	20X4	20X5	Total
Net cash inflow (£'000)	180	260	280	400	540	1,660
NPV at cost of capital 15%	180	226	212	263	309	1,190

3.42 A **control summary** comparing the situation at the start of 20X1 and the situation one year later would now be as follows.

	£'000
Expected NPV as at 1.1.20X1	1,076
Uplift by cost of capital 15%	161
	1,237
Expected NPV as at 1.1.20X2	1,190
Variance	47 (A)

The control information shows that by the end of 20X1, ABC Ltd **shows signs of not achieving the strategic targets** it set itself at the start of 20X1. This is partly because actual cash flows in 20X1 fell short of target by (200-180) £20,000, but also because the revised forecast for the future is not as good now either. In total, the company has a lower NPV by £47,000.

3.43 The **reasons for the failure** to achieve target should be investigated. Here are some possibilities.

(a) A higher-than-expected pay award to employees, which will have repercussions for the future as well as in 20X1

(b) An increase in the rate of tax on profits

(c) A serious delay in the implementation of some major new projects

(d) The slower-than-expected growth of an important new market

Reconciling successive NPVs: summary of the technique

3.44 **Strategic progress** can be **measured** by **reconciling successive net present values and the intervening cash flows.** The arithmetic is straightforward and can be summed up as follows.

Step 1. The previous NPV is uplifted by the cost of capital applicable to the current period.

Step 2. From this uplifted figure is deducted the actual cash flow in the period.

Step 3. The result is the 'benchmark NPV' indicating what the new NPV needs to be if long-term health has been maintained.

Step 4. Comparison of the new NPV with the benchmark produces a variance which can be analysed by cause and by time frame.

3.45 Attempt your own solution to the following question.

Question: strategic progress

XYZ Ltd prepared the following strategic budget for a five-year period 20X3 - 20X7.

Year	Forecast cash flow £'000	Discount factor 18%	NPV £'000
20X3	360	0.847	305
20X4	400	0.718	287
20X5	440	0.609	268
20X6	500	0.516	258
20X7	600	0.437	262
			1,380

Actual cash flows in 20X3 were £400,000 and revised forecasts for the next five years are, in £'000: 20X4 - 420; 20X5 - 450; 20X6 - 480; 20X7 - 540; 20X8 - 560. As from 20X4, the cost of capital has been increased to 20%.

Required

Assess the strategic progress of XYZ Ltd.

Answer

We must compare the *same* period of time and so the new forecast for 20X8 should be ignored. Since 20X3 cash flows are 'actual' a discount factor of 1 is applied.

Year	Forecast cash flow £'000	Discount factor 20%	NPV £'000
20X3	400 (actual)	1.0	400
20X4	420	0.833	350
20X5	450	0.694	312
20X6	480	0.579	278
20X7	540	0.482	260
			1,600

Summary	£'000
Expected NPV as at beginning of 20X3	1,380
Uplift by cost of capital for 20X3 (18%)	248
'Benchmark' NPV	1,628
Expected NPV as per revised forecast, end of 20X3	1,600
Variance	28 (A)

The NPV has fallen by £28,000, in spite of the better-than-expected cash flow in 20X3, and the improved cash flow forecasts for 20X4 and 20X5. The increase in the cost of capital is clearly a major cause of the fall in NPV. (*Note.* The variance caused by the increase from 18% to 20% could be quantified, by re-evaluating the future cash flows in the revised forecast at 18%, but this calculation is not shown here.)

Internal rate of return

3.46 IRR is another way of reviewing investments. The IRR of a project can be compared to the cost of capital. It should be possible in theory to assess an IRR for a company, but other models or measures may be simpler.

Exam focus point

The distinctive features of RI, ROI and NPV, as well as their strengths and weaknesses, had to be explained in compulsory question 2 of the June 2003 exam.

4 GEARING

Capital structure

4.1 The assets of a business must be financed somehow, and when a business is growing, the additional assets must be financed by additional capital. **Capital structure** refers to the **way in which an organisation** is **financed**, by a combination of long-term capital (ordinary shares and reserves, preference shares, debentures, bank loans, convertible loan stock and so on) and short-term liabilities, such as a bank overdraft and trade creditors.

Debts and financial risk

4.2 There are two main **reasons why companies should keep their debt burden under control**.

(a) When a company is heavily in debt, and seems to be getting even more heavily into debt, banks and other would-be lenders are very soon likely to refuse further borrowing and the company might well find itself in trouble.

(b) When a company is earning only a modest profit before interest and tax, and has a heavy debt burden, there will be very little profit left over for shareholders after the interest charges have been paid. And so if interest rates were to go up or the company were to borrow even more, it might soon be incurring interest charges in excess of PBIT. This might eventually lead to the liquidation of the company.

4.3 A high level of debt creates financial risk. **Financial risk** can be seen from different points of view.

(a) **The company** as a whole. If a company builds up debts that it cannot pay when they fall due, it will be forced into liquidation.

(b) **Creditors**. If a company cannot pay its debts, the company will go into liquidation owing creditors money that they are unlikely to recover in full.

(c) **Ordinary shareholders**. A company will not make any distributable profits unless it is able to earn enough profit before interest and tax to pay all its interest charges, and then tax. The lower the profits or the higher the interest-bearing debts, the less there will be, if there is anything at all, for shareholders.

When a company has preference shares in its capital structure, ordinary shareholders will not get anything until the preference dividend has been paid.

The appraisal of capital structures

4.4 One way in which the financial risk of a company's capital structure can be measured is by a **gearing ratio**. A gearing ratio should not be given without stating how it has been defined.

Gearing ratios

> **KEY TERM**
>
> **Financial leverage/gearing** is the use of debt finance to increase the return on equity by using borrowed funds in such a way that the return generated is greater than the cost of servicing the debt. If the return on borrowed funds is less than the cost of servicing the debt, the effect of gearing is to reduce the return on equity.

4.5 Gearing measures the **relationships between shareholders' capital plus reserves, and either prior charge capital or borrowings or both**.

> **KEY TERM**
>
> **Prior charge capital** is capital which has a right to the receipt of interest or preference dividends before any claim is made by ordinary shareholders on distributable earnings. On winding up, the claims of holders of prior charge capital rank before those of ordinary shareholders.

4.6 **Prior charge capital**

(a) Any preference share capital

(b) Interest-bearing long-term capital

(c) Interest-bearing short-term debt capital with less than 12 months to maturity, including any bank overdraft

However, (c) might be excluded.

4.7 Here are some commonly used measures of financial gearing, which are **based** on the **balance sheet values (book values)** of the **fixed interest and equity capital**.

$$\frac{\text{Prior charge capital}}{\text{Equity capital (including reserves)}}$$

$$\frac{\text{Prior charge capital}}{\text{Total capital employed}}$$

4.8 With the **first definition** above, a company is **low geared** if the **gearing ratio** is **less than 100%**, highly geared if the ratio is over 100% and neutrally geared if it is exactly 100%.

Question: financial gearing ratio

From the following balance sheet, compute the company's financial gearing ratio.

	£'000	£'000	£'000
Fixed assets			12,400
Current assets		1,000	
Creditors: amounts falling due within one year			
Loans	120		
Bank overdraft	260		
Trade creditors	430		
Bills of exchange	70		
		880	
Net current assets			120
Total assets less current liabilities			12,520
Creditors: amounts falling due after more than one year			
Debentures		4,700	
Bank loans		500	
			(5,200)
Provisions for liabilities and charges: deferred taxation			(300)
Deferred income			(250)
			6,770

	£'000	£'000	£'000
Capital and reserves			£'000
Called up share capital			
Ordinary shares			1,500
Preference shares			500
			2,000
Share premium account			760
Revaluation reserve			1,200
Profit and loss account			2,810
			6,770

Answer

	£'000
Prior charge capital	
Preference shares	500
Debentures	4,700
Long-term bank loans	500
Prior charge capital, ignoring short-term debt	5,700
Short-term loans	120
Overdraft	260
Prior charge capital, including short-term interest bearing debt	6,080

Either figure, £6,080,000 or £5,700,000, could be used. If gearing is calculated with capital employed in the denominator, and capital employed is net fixed assets plus **net** current assets, it would seem more reasonable to exclude short-term interest bearing debt from prior charge capital. This is because short-term debt is set off against current assets in arriving at the figure for net current assets.

Equity = 1,500 + 760 + 1,200 + 2,810 = £6,270,000

The gearing ratio can be calculated in one of the following ways.

(a) $\dfrac{\text{Prior charge capital}}{\text{Equity}} \times 100\% = \dfrac{6,080}{6,270} \times 100\% = 97\%$

(b) $\dfrac{\text{Prior charge capital}}{\text{Total capital employed}} \times 100\% = \dfrac{5,700}{12,520} \times 100\% = 45.5\%$

4.9 There is **no absolute limit** to what a **gearing ratio** ought to be. Many companies are highly geared, but if a highly geared company is increasing its gearing, it is likely to have difficulty in the future when it wants to borrow even more, unless it can also boost its shareholders' capital, either with retained profits or with a new share issue.

The effect of gearing on earnings

4.10 The level of gearing has a considerable effect on the earnings attributable to the ordinary shareholders. A **highly geared** company must **earn enough profits to cover its interest charges before anything is available for equity**. On the other hand, if borrowed funds are invested in projects which provide returns in excess of the cost of debt capital, then shareholders will enjoy increased returns on their equity.

4.11 **Gearing**, however, also **increases the probability of financial failure** occurring through a company's inability to meet interest payments in poor trading circumstances.

4.12 EXAMPLE: GEARING

Suppose that two companies are identical in every respect except for their gearing. Both have assets of £20,000 and both make the same operating profits (profit before interest and tax: PBIT). The only difference between the two companies is that Nonlever Ltd is all-equity financed and Lever Ltd is partly financed by debt capital, as follows.

	Nonlever Ltd	Lever Ltd
	£	£
Assets	20,000	20,000
10% Loan stock	0	(10,000)
	20,000	10,000
Ordinary shares of £1	20,000	10,000

Because Lever Ltd has £10,000 of 10% loan stock it must make a profit before interest of at least £1,000 in order to pay the interest charges. Nonlever Ltd, on the other hand, does not have any minimum PBIT requirement because it has no debt capital. A company, which is lower geared, is considered less risky than a higher geared company because of the greater likelihood that its PBIT will be high enough to cover interest charges and make a profit for equity shareholders.

Operating gearing

4.13 Financial risk, as we have seen, can be measured by financial gearing. **Business risk** refers to the **risk of making only low profits**, or even losses, **due to the nature of the business** that the company is involved in. One way of measuring business risk is by calculating a company's **operating gearing** or **'operational gearing'**.

> ### KEY TERM
>
> $$\text{Operating gearing or leverage} = \frac{\text{Contribution}}{\text{Profit before interest and tax (PBIT)}}$$

4.14 **If contribution is high but PBIT is low**, fixed costs will be high, and only just covered by contribution. **Business risk**, as measured by operating gearing, will be **high**. If contribution is not much bigger than PBIT, fixed costs will be low, and fairly easily covered. Business risk, as measured by operating gearing, will be low.

> ### Exam focus point
>
> Compulsory question 2 in the December 2002 exam required an assessment of total corporate financial performance of an organisation and of the contribution made by its two divisions. The assessment should have covered the topics included in Sections 3 and 4 of this chapter.

5 LIQUIDITY

5.1 Profitability is of course an important aspect of a company's performance, and debt or gearing is another. Neither, however, addresses directly the key issue of liquidity. A company needs liquid assets so that it can meet its debts when they fall due.

> ### KEY TERM
>
> **Liquidity** is the amount of cash a company can obtain quickly to settle its debts (and possibly to meet other unforeseen demands for cash payments too).

5.2 **Liquid funds**

(a) Cash

(b) Short-term investments for which there is a ready market, such as investments in shares of other companies (NB **not** subsidiaries or associates)

(c) Fixed-term deposits with a bank or building society, for example six month deposits with a bank

(d) Trade debtors

(e) Bills of exchange receivable

5.3 **Some assets are more liquid than others.** Stocks of goods are fairly liquid in some businesses. Stocks of finished production goods might be sold quickly, and a supermarket will hold consumer goods for resale that could well be sold for cash very soon. Raw materials and components in a manufacturing company have to be used to make a finished product before they can be sold to realise cash, and so they are less liquid than finished goods. Just how liquid they are depends on the speed of stock turnover and the length of the production cycle.

5.4 **Fixed assets are not liquid assets.** A company can sell off fixed assets, but unless they are no longer needed, or are worn out and about to be replaced, they are necessary to continue the company's operations. Selling fixed assets is certainly not a solution to a company's cash needs, and so although there may be an occasional fixed asset item which is about to be sold off, probably because it is going to be replaced, it is safe to disregard fixed assets when measuring a company's liquidity.

5.5 In summary, **liquid assets are current asset items that will or could soon be converted into cash, and cash** itself. Two common definitions of liquid assets are **all current assets** or **all current assets with the exception of stocks.**

5.6 **The main source of liquid assets for a trading company is sales.** A company can obtain cash from sources other than sales, such as the issue of shares for cash, a new loan or the sale of fixed assets. But a company cannot rely on these at all times, and in general, obtaining liquid funds depends on making sales and profits.

Why does profit not provide an indication of liquidity?

5.7 If a company makes profits, it should earn money, and if it earns money, it might seem that it should receive more cash than it pays out. In fact, **profits are not always a good guide to liquidity.** Two examples will show why this is so.

(a) Suppose that company X makes all its sales for cash, and pays all its running costs in cash without taking any credit. Its profit for the year just ended was as follows.

	£	£
Sales		400,000
Less costs: running costs	200,000	
Depreciation	50,000	
		250,000
Profit		150,000
Less dividends (all paid)		80,000
Retained profits		70,000

During the year, the company purchased a fixed asset for £180,000 and paid for it in full.

Depreciation is not a cash outlay, and so the company's 'cash profits' less dividends were sales less running costs less dividends = £120,000. However, the fixed asset purchase required £180,000, and so the company's cash position worsened in the year by £60,000, in spite of the profit.

(b) Suppose that company Y buys three items for cash, each costing £5,000, and resells them for £7,000 each. The buyers of the units take credit, and by the end of the company's accounting year, they were all still debtors.

    (i)   The profit on the transactions is £2,000 per unit and £6,000 in total.

    (ii)   The company has paid £15,000 to buy the goods, but so far it has received no cash back from selling them, and so its cash position is so far £15,000 worse off from the transactions.

    (iii)   The effect so far of the transactions is:

Reduction in cash	£15,000
Increase in debtors	£21,000
Increase in profit	£6,000

The increase in assets is £6,000 in total, to match the £6,000 increase in profit, but the increase in assets is the net change in cash (reduced balance) and debtors (increased balance).

5.8 Both of these examples show ways in which a **company can be profitable but** at the same time **get into cash flow problems**. If an analysis of a company's published accounts is to give us some idea of the company's liquidity, profitability ratios are not going to be appropriate for doing this. Instead, we look at liquidity ratios and working capital turnover ratios.

Liquidity ratios

Current ratio

5.9 The standard test of liquidity is the current ratio. It can be obtained from the balance sheet, and is:

Current assets
————————————
Current liabilities

A company should have enough current assets that give a promise of 'cash to come' to meet its commitments to pay its current liabilities. Obviously, a **ratio in excess of 1 should be expected**. Otherwise, there would be the prospect that the company might be unable to pay its debts on time. In practice, a ratio comfortably in excess of 1 should be expected, but what is 'comfortable' varies between different types of businesses.

5.10 **Companies are not able to convert all their current assets into cash very quickly.** In particular, some manufacturing companies might hold large quantities of raw material stocks, which must be used in production to create finished goods. Finished goods might be warehoused for a long time, or sold on lengthy credit. In such businesses, where stock turnover is slow, most stocks are not very liquid assets, because the cash cycle is so long. For these reasons, we calculate an additional liquidity ratio, known as the quick ratio or acid test ratio.

Quick ratio

5.11 The quick ratio, or **acid test ratio**, is:

Current assets less stocks
  Current liabilities

This ratio should ideally be **at least 1** for companies with a **slow stock turnover**. For companies with a **fast stock turnover**, a quick ratio can be **less than 1** without suggesting that the company is in cash flow difficulties.

5.12 Do not forget the other side of the coin. The current ratio and the quick ratio can be bigger than they should be. A company that has large volumes of stocks and debtors might be over-investing in working capital, and so tying up more funds in the business than it needs to. This would suggest poor management of debtors or stocks by the company.

Turnover periods

5.13 We can calculate **turnover periods** for stock, debtors and creditors (the question below revises these calculations). If we add together the stock days and the debtor days, this should give us an indication of how soon stock is convertible into cash. Both debtor days and stock days therefore give us a further indication of the company's liquidity.

Question: liquidity and working capital ratios

Calculate liquidity and working capital ratios from the accounts of a manufacturer of products for the construction industry, and comment on the ratios.

	20X8	20X7
	£m	£m
Turnover	2,065.0	1,788.7
Cost of sales	1,478.6	1,304.0
Gross profit	586.4	484.7
Current assets		
Stocks	119.0	109.0
Debtors (note 1)	400.9	347.4
Short-term investments	4.2	18.8
Cash at bank and in hand	48.2	48.0
	572.3	523.2
Creditors: amounts falling due within one year		
Loans and overdrafts	49.1	35.3
Corporation taxes	62.0	46.7
Dividend	19.2	14.3
Creditors (note 2)	370.7	324.0
	501.0	420.3

	20X8	20X7
	£m	£m
Net current assets		
	71.3	102.9

Notes

		20X8	20X7
		£m	£m
1	Trade debtors	329.8	285.4
2	Trade creditors	236.2	210.8

Answer

	20X8		20X7	
Current ratio	$\frac{572.3}{501.0}$	= 1.14	$\frac{523.2}{420.3}$	= 1.24
Quick ratio	$\frac{453.3}{501.0}$	= 0.90	$\frac{414.2}{420.3}$	= 0.99
Debtors' payment period	$\frac{329.8}{2,065.0} \times 365$	= 58 days	$\frac{285.4}{1,788.7} \times 365$	= 58 days
Stock turnover period	$\frac{119.0}{1,478.6} \times 365$	= 29 days	$\frac{109.0}{1,304.0} \times 365$	= 31 days
Creditors' turnover period	$\frac{236.2}{1,478.6} \times 365$	= 58 days	$\frac{210.8}{1,304.0} \times 365$	= 59 days

As a manufacturing group serving the construction industry, the company would be expected to have a comparatively lengthy debtors' turnover period, because of the relatively poor cash flow in the construction industry. It is clear that the company compensates for this by ensuring that they do not pay for raw materials and other costs before they have sold their stocks of finished goods (hence the similarity of debtors' and creditors' turnover periods).

The company's current ratio is a little lower than average but its quick ratio is better than average and very little less than the current ratio. This suggests that stock levels are strictly controlled, which is reinforced by the low stock turnover period. It would seem that working capital is tightly managed, to avoid the poor liquidity which could be caused by a high debtors' turnover period and comparatively high creditors.

Creditors' turnover is ideally calculated by the formula:

$$\frac{\text{Average stock}}{\text{Purchases}} \times 365$$

However, it is rare to find purchases disclosed in published accounts and so cost of sales serves as an approximation. The creditors' turnover ratio often helps to assess a company's liquidity; an increase in creditor days is often a sign of lack of long-term finance or poor management of current assets, resulting in the use of extended credit from suppliers, increased bank overdraft and so on.

Exam focus point

Don't worry if, in the exam, a financial performance analysis that you prepare does not include a huge range of measures. In the December 2001 exam, for example, candidates were asked to carry out such an analysis but were unable to do this in detail because of inadequate data in the question. The next part of the question asked them to comment on the validity of their appraisal: this gave them the opportunity to highlight the additional data they required.

6   SHORT- AND LONG-RUN FINANCIAL PERFORMANCE

6.1   In the previous chapter we saw how organisations often have to make a trade-off between short-term and long-term objectives which can, of course, be focused on financial performance. Advertising expenditure may be cut to increase short-term profit, but this is likely to be at the expense of long-term financial results.

Case example

In April 2001, the *Financial Times* reported on how efforts to cut costs to boost short-term profits at Marks & Spencer had long-term implications.

To fulfil expectations during the 1990s, staff numbers were limited or reduced, store enhancements were restricted, and relationships with suppliers squeezed. As a result, earnings matched market expectations for a while but eventually 'customers started to notice that value for money was not quite as good as it could have been. That you had to wait to get the attention of a sales assistant. That the shops were dowdy and so was some of the merchandise. These impressions accumulated. Gradually the positive Marks & Spencer anecdotes were replaced by negative ones. Suddenly the company's reputation fell off a cliff. And so did its profits.'

Using ROI

6.2   Suppose that an investment in a fixed asset would cost £100,000 and make a profit of £11,000 p.a. after depreciation. The asset would be depreciated by £25,000 pa for four years. It is group policy that investments must show a minimum return of 15%. The DCF net present value of this investment would just about be positive, and so the investment ought to be approved if group policy is adhered to.

Year	Cash flow (profit before dep'n)	Discount factor	Present value
	£	15%	£
0	(100,000)	1.000	(100,000)
1	36,000	0.870	31,320
2	36,000	0.756	27,216
3	36,000	0.658	23,688
4	36,000	0.572	20,592
		NPV	2,816

6.3   If the investment is measured year by year according to the accounting ROI it has earned, its return is less than 15% in year 1, but more than 15% in years 2, 3 and 4.

Year	Profit	Net book value of equipment (mid-year value)	ROI
	£	£	
1	11,000	87,500	12.6%
2	11,000	62,500	17.6%
3	11,000	37,500	29.3%
4	11,000	12,500	88.0%

6.4   In view of the low accounting ROI in year 1, should the investment be undertaken or not?

(a)   Strictly speaking, **investment decisions should be based on DCF yield**, and should not be guided by short-term accounting ROI.

(b)   Even if accounting ROI is used as a guideline for investment decisions, ROI should be looked at **over the full life** of the investment, not just in the short term. In the short term (in the first year or so of a project's life) the accounting ROI is likely to be low because the net book value of the asset will still be high.

Question: DCF

Why are DCF techniques not commonly used?

Answer

Because they are perceived as being difficult to calculate and understand and because it is difficult in practice to establish an accurate cost of capital.

DCF v ROI

6.5 In spite of the superiority of DCF yield over accounting ROI as a means of evaluating investments, and in spite of the wisdom of taking a longer-term view rather than a short-term view with investments, it is nevertheless an uncomfortable fact that the consideration of short-run accounting **ROI does often influence investment decisions.**

6.6 In our example, it is conceivable that the group's management might disapprove of the project because of its low accounting ROI in year 1. This approach is short-sighted, but it nevertheless can make some sense to a company or group of companies which has to show a satisfactory profit and ROI in its **published accounts** each year, to keep its **shareholders** satisfied with performance.

6.7 A similar mis-guided decision would occur where a divisional manager is worried about the low ROI of his division, and decides to reduce his investment by **scrapping some machinery** which is not currently in use. The reduction in both depreciation charges and assets would immediately improve the ROI. When the machinery is eventually required the manager would then be obliged to buy new equipment. Such a situation may seem bizarre, but it does occur in real life.

6.8 ROI should not be used to guide management decisions but there is a difficult motivational problem. If **management performance** is measured in terms of ROI, any decisions which benefit the company in the long term but which reduce the ROI in the immediate short term would reflect badly on the manager's reported performance. In other words, good investment decisions would make a manager's performance seem worse than if the wrong investment decision were taken instead.

7 PROFITS AND SHARE VALUE

7.1 **Shareholders value shares** on the **basis not of past performance** but of expectations of **future performance.**

Note that **past performance** is useful, however, in that it gives **information** about the quality of the management team, and the business's **success** at devising and executing strategies to maximise shareholders wealth, to date.

7.2 **Shareholders** may have a **view** towards a **particular industry** sector as well as an **individual business.** No matter how well a business is run, it may operate in an unattractive or mature industry sector.

Case example

From the *Guardian* 24/01/01.

Transense Technologies designs sensors for monitoring tyre pressure on cars. It has 10 employees, turnover of £80,000 and a market capitalisation of £269.1m. TT Group [another company] designs and builds headlamp levelling sensors for cars. It has created a variety of innovative electronic systems for cars, mobiles phones and high speed trains. It has 11,500 employees, a turnover of £612m – but a market capitalisation of £240m.

Another example of stock market madness? A triumph of hope-based businesses over the tried and trusted companies with a long track record of profitability?

Or is it evidence of another trend within British industry? The phenomenon of a two speed economy divided between 'new' companies involved in IT, electronics and optical engineering and the 'old' metal bashers of car making, textiles and transport, is well established...

> But the Transense and TT examples, and there are many others, indicate there is also a two speed trend within what the market considers 'old' manufacturing.
>
> This infuriates John Newman, the chief executive of TT Group, who is convinced that he is part of the new economy. 'We are in advanced technology such as electrical components for computers and connectors for high speed trains,' he insists.
>
> Many argue that companies such as Transense are superior to TT Group because they have potentially 'killer applications' that give them a lead on the rest of the market.
>
> One senior engineering analyst said: 'It does not matter how many employees a company has; if they are heavily exposed to the commodity side of the business in a deflationary world, they are not going to attract stock market interest. Those with little intellectual property or proprietary rights are going to be subject to increasing margin pressure.'

7.3 Investors may have a genuinely different view of the prospects of a sector than mangers, so even well-run companies in an industry may feel starved of capital at an appropriate rate. This is because they are always compared with other companies.

7.4 The **management issues** are contradictory.

    (a) Managers have a **personal interest** in the long-term survival of the business.

    (b) Shareholders want a long-term increase in their wealth from investment in a business or other companies in the sector.

7.5 **Short-termism** often occurs, however.

    (a) Managers' performance is measured on short-term results (for example quarterly reporting in the US).

    (b) Even investors are under pressure to maximise the growth in value of their portfolios in a particular period.

The price/earnings (P/E) ratio: profits and share value

7.6 The P/E ratio is the most important yardstick for assessing the relative worth of a share. It is:

$$\frac{\text{Market price in pence}}{\text{EPS in pence}}$$

which is the same as:

$$\frac{\text{Total market value of equity}}{\text{Total earnings}}$$

7.7 The **value** of the P/E ratio reflects the **market's appraisal** of the **shares' future prospects**. In other words, if one company has a higher P/E ratio than another it is because investors either expect its earnings to increase faster than the other's or consider that it is a less risky company or in a more 'secure' industry. The P/E ratio is, simply, a **measure of** the **relationship between the market value of a company's shares and the earnings from those shares**.

7.8 EXAMPLE: PRICE EARNINGS RATIO

A company has recently declared a dividend of 12p per share. The share price is £3.72 cum div and earnings for the most recent year were 30p per share. Calculate the P/E ratio.

7.9 SOLUTION

$$\text{P/E ratio} = \frac{\text{MV ex div}}{\text{EPS}} = \frac{£3.60}{30\text{p}} = 12$$

Changes in EPS: the P/E ratio and the share price

7.10 The dividend valuation model or fundamental theory of share values is the theory that share prices are related to expected future dividends on the shares.

7.11 A common sense approach to assessing what share prices ought to be, which is often used in practice, is a P/E ratio approach.

  (a) The relationship between the EPS and the share price is measured by the P/E ratio

  (b) There is no reason to suppose, in normal circumstances, that the P/E ratio will vary much over time

  (c) So, if the EPS goes up or down, the share price should be expected to move up or down too, and the new share price will be the new EPS multiplied by the constant P/E ratio

7.12 For example, if a company had an EPS last year of 30p and a share price of £3.60, its P/E ratio would have been 12. If the current year's EPS is 33p, we might expect that the P/E ratio would remain the same, 12, and so the share price ought to go up to $12 \times 33\text{p} = £3.96$.

Internet companies

7.13 In 1999/2000 share prices in the US and Europe rose to unprecedented heights. The drivers for this were the rise of **technology stocks**, particularly those relating to **internet companies.**

7.14 **Causes**

  (a) The internet appeared to offer unrivalled opportunities for growth. Everybody wanted to jump on the bandwagon.

  (b) There were influential proponents of the 'new economy' who felt that some economic laws had been re-written.

  (c) Internet firms offered **increasing returns to scale** thanks to **network effects**. In other words, the more people using the Internet, the more useful it becomes for others to use.

  (d) However, despite exciting websites, and huge marketing expenditure, internet companies (such as Boo.com) were made or broken on issues of logistics and distribution.

7.15 Many internet firms used up large amounts of cash before attaining any profits, and so have collapsed.

  (a) B2C (**business-to-consumer companies**) such as Boo.com have lost money. Other retailing sites have kept going, however. Even so, amazon.com has laid off staff. The most successful Internet retailer in the UK is 'old economy' Tesco.

  (b) B2B (**business-to-business internet companies**) have had more success, if they offer something of value.

In fact, a recent study of tech companies by Merrill Lynch reported that their earnings were overstated by an average of 25% compared with what they would be if determined on the basis of generally accepted accounting principles.

7.16 Despite the heady days of 2000, it is a fallacy that Internet companies can avoid the need for profit and positive cash inflows.

> 'From peak to trough, Amazon.com's market value sank by $35 billion as Jeff Bezos (*Time* magazine's "person of the year" in 1999) claimed that his company was profitable on a "proforma basis". But let's get real: its proforma profits were found by ignoring interest payments on nearly $2 billion of debt. That's like saying my holiday home doesn't cost me anything – as long as I ignore the mortgage payments.'

(Ted Stone, 'Trade Secrets', CIMA *Insider*, June 2002)

Exam focus point

One of the key themes of Paper 3.3 exam questions is additional information or data required to provide a more complete assessment of performance. In question 2 of the December 2002 exam, for example, candidates were provided with a range of financial data but nothing on 'qualitative' issues, on competitors or markets, or on long-term plans, all of which are necessary to provide a full review of financial performance.

8 COMPARISONS OF ACCOUNTING FIGURES

8.1 Useful information is obtained from ratio analysis largely by means of comparisons. As we have seen, comparisons that might be made are between the company's results and the results of:

(a) The most recent year and its results in previous years
(b) Other companies in the same industry
(c) Other companies in other industries

Results of the same company over successive accounting periods

8.2 Although a company might present useful information in its five-year or ten-year summary, it is quite likely that the only detailed comparison you will be able to make is between the current year's and the previous year's results. The comparison should give you some idea of whether the company's situation has improved, worsened or stayed much the same between one year and the next.

8.3 Useful comparisons over time

(a) Percentage growth in profit (before and after tax) and percentage growth in turnover

(b) Increases or decreases in the debt ratio and the gearing ratio

(c) Changes in the current ratio, the stock turnover period and the debtors' payment period

(d) Increases in the EPS, the dividend per share, and the market price

8.4 The principal advantage of making comparisons over time is that they give some indication of progress: are things getting better or worse? However, there are some weaknesses in such comparisons.

(a) The effect of **inflation** should not be forgotten.

(b) The progress a company has made needs to be set **in** the **context** of what other companies have done, and whether there have been any special environmental or economic influences on the company's performance.

Putting a company's results into context

8.5 The financial and accounting ratios of one company should be looked at in the context of **what other companies have been achieving,** and also any **special influences** on the industry or the economy as a whole. Here are two examples.

(a) If a company achieves a 10% increase in profits, this performance taken in isolation might seem commendable, but if it is then compared with the results of rival companies, which might have been achieving profit growth of 30% the performance might in comparison seem very disappointing.

(b) An improvement in ROCE and profits might be attributable to a temporary economic boom, and an increase in profits after tax might be attributable to a cut in the rate of corporation tax. When improved results are attributable to factors outside the control of the company's management, such as changes in the economic climate and tax rates other companies might be expected to benefit in the same way.

Comparisons between different companies in the same industry

8.6 Making comparisons between the results of different companies in the same industry is a way of assessing which companies are outperforming others.

(a) Even if **two companies are in the same broad industry (for example, retailing) they might not be direct competitors**. For example, in the UK, the Kingfisher group (including Woolworths/B&Q/Comet) does not compete directly with the Burton/Debenhams group. Even so, they might still be expected to show broadly **similar performance**, in terms of growth, because a boom or a depression in retail markets will affect all retailers. The results of two such companies can be compared, and the company with the better growth and accounting ratios might be considered more successful than the other.

(b) If two companies **are direct competitors**, a comparison between them would be **particularly interesting**. Which has achieved the better ROCE, sales growth, or profit growth? Does one have a better debt or gearing position, a better liquidity position or better working capital ratios? How do their P/E ratios, dividend cover and dividend yields compare? And so on.

8.7 Comparisons between companies in the same industry can help investors to rank them in order of desirability as investments, and to judge relative share prices or future prospects. It is important, however, to make comparisons with caution: a large company and a small company in the same industry might be expected to show different results, not just in terms of size, but in terms of:

(a) Percentage rates of growth in sales and profits

(b) Percentages of profits re-invested (Dividend cover will be higher in a company that needs to retain profits to finance investment and growth.)

(c) Fixed assets (Large companies are more likely to have freehold property in their balance sheet than small companies.)

Exam focus point

As we mentioned in the Exam Guide at the beginning of this chapter, the first sitting of Paper 3.3 required candidates to compare two organisations in the same industry (leisure centres), but one was profit seeking and one was non-profit seeking. The numerical analysis required was not particularly arduous or high level or in-depth (profit margin, profits as a % of NBV of buildings and so on) but sensible commentary on the figures calculated was required. Of the 12 marks available for the financial comparison, five were allocated for commentary.

Comparisons between companies in different industries

8.8 Useful information can also be obtained by comparing the financial and accounting ratios of companies in different industries. An investor ought to be aware of how companies in one industrial sector are performing in comparison with companies in other sectors. For example, it is important to know:

(a) Whether sales growth and profit growth is higher in some industries than in others (For example, how does growth in the financial services industry compare with growth in heavy engineering, electronics or leisure?)

(b) How the return on capital employed and return on shareholder capital compare between different industries

(c) How the P/E ratios and dividend yields vary between industries (For example, if a publishing company has a P/E ratio of, say, 20, which is average for its industry, whereas an electronics company has a P/E ratio of, say, 14, do the better growth performance and prospects of the publishing company justify its higher P/E ratio?)

Chapter roundup

- The overriding **purpose** of a business is to **increase long-term owner wealth**.

- Achieving objectives of **survival** and **growth** ultimately depends on making profits.

- **Measures relating to profit** include sales margin, EBITDA and EPS. More sophisticated measures (ROCE, ROI) take the size of investment into account.

- As well as profitability, **liquidity** and **gearing** are key measures of performance.

- **Gearing ratios** measure the financial risk of a company's capital structure. Business risk can be measured by calculating a company's **operational gearing.**

- A company can be profitable but at the same time get into cash flow problems. Liquidity ratios (**current** and **quick**) and **working capital turnover ratios** give some idea of a company's liquidity.

- **Short-termism** is often due to the fact that managers' performance is measured on short-term results.

- The value of the **P/E ratio** reflects the market's appraisal of the shares' future prospects.

- **Comparisons** might be made between a company's results and the results of the most recent year/previous years, other companies in the same industry and other companies in other industries.

Quick quiz

1   *Fill in the blank.*

    Survival and growth are most likely to be achieved if a business can ....

2   What is EBITDA?

    A   Earnings before interest, tax, debt and amortisation
    B   Earnings before inter-company transactions, tax, debt and amortisation
    C   Extraordinary income before interest, tax, depreciation and annual charges
    D   Earnings before interest, tax, depreciation and amortisation

3   *Fill in the blanks.*

    Profit of the period after ...., ... and

    EPS = ..., and after deducting ....

    Number of .... in issue and ranking for dividend

4   *Choose the correct terms from those highlighted.*

    ROCE = **profit margin/EBITDA/EPS** ×/÷ **ROI/RI/asset turnover**

5   *Choose the correct words from those highlighted.*

    ROI based on profits as a % of net assets employed will (a) **increase/decrease** as an asset gets older and its book value (b) **increases/reduces**. This could therefore create an (c) **incentive/disincentive** to investment centre managers to reinvest in new or replacement assets.

6   An investment centre with capital employed of £570,000 is budgeted to earn a profit of £119,700 next year. A proposed fixed asset investment of £50,000, not included in the budget at present, will earn a profit next year of £8,500 after depreciation. The company's cost of capital is 15%. What is the budgeted ROI and residual income for next year, both with and without the investment?

	ROI	Residual income
Without investment	....	....
With investment	....	....

7   'The use of residual income in performance measurement will avoid dysfunctional decision making because it will always lead to the correct decision concerning capital investments.' *True or false?*

8   *Choose the correct words from those highlighted.*

    In general, a current ratio **in excess of 1/less than 1/approximately zero** should be expected.

9   What measure is used to assess the relationship between the market value of a company's shares and the earnings from those shares?

    A   EBITDA
    B   P/E ratio
    C   EPS
    D   Share price

Answers to quick quiz

1   earn profits in perpetuity

2   D

3
$$EPS = \frac{\text{Profit of the period after tax, minority interests and extraordinary items,}}{\text{Number of equity shares in issue and ranking for dividend}}$$
and after deducting preference dividends

4   ROCE = profit margin × asset turnover

5   (a)   increase
    (b)   reduces
    (c)   disincentive

6

	ROI	Residual income
Without investment	21.0%	£34,200
With investment	20.7%	£35,200

7   False

8   in excess of 1

9   B

Now try the question below from the Exam Question Bank

Number	Level	Marks	Time
26	Exam	40	72 mins

Question 26 is a pilot paper question and has been fully analysed to help you to get to grips with the long compulsory Section A question in the Paper 3.3 exam.

Chapter 12

NON-FINANCIAL PERFORMANCE INDICATORS

Topic list	Syllabus reference
1 NFPIs and financial performance indicators	3(b)
2 Growing emphasis on NFPIs	3(b)
3 The value of NFPIs	3(b)
4 NFPIs in relation to employees	3(b)
5 NFPIs in relation to product/service quality	3(b)
6 Qualitative issues	3(b)

Introduction

Having examined in depth the use of financial performance indicators in the previous chapter, we are now going to look at **non-financial performance indicators** and at the reasons for their **increasing** use.

Study guide

Section 13 – Non-financial performance indicators for business

- Discuss the interaction of NFPIs with financial performance indicators
- Discuss the implications of the growing emphasis on NFPIs
- Identify and comment on the significance of NFPIs in relation to employees
- Identify and comment on the significance of NFPIs in relation to product/service quality
- Discuss the difficulties in interpreting data on qualitative issues
- Discuss the significance of brand awareness and company profile

Exam guide

The examiner has stressed the importance of NFPIs and so expect questions asking you to identify and derive them to appear on a regular basis. 'The appropriateness of financial and non-financial indicators' has been specifically highlighted by the examiner as a potential issue for inclusion in the compulsory questions of the exam.

The issues covered in this chapter are useful background to the Oxford Brookes degree Research and Analysis Project Topic 1, which requires you to analyse the efficiency and/or effectiveness of a management accounting technique in an organisational setting.

1   NFPIS AND FINANCIAL PERFORMANCE INDICATORS

Disadvantages of financial performance indicators

Concentration on too few variables

1.1   If performance measurement systems focus entirely on those items which can be expressed in monetary terms, managers will **concentrate on only those variables** and **ignore** other important variables that cannot be expressed in monetary terms.

1.2   For example, pressure from senior management to **cut costs and raise productivity** will produce **short-term benefits** in cost control but, in the **long term,** managerial performance and motivation is likely to be affected, labour turnover will increase and product quality will fall.

1.3   Reductions in cost can easily be measured and recorded in performance reports, employee morale cannot. **Performance reports** should therefore **include** not only costs and revenues but **other important variables,** to give an indication of expected future results from present activity.

Lack of information on quality

1.4   Traditional responsibility accounting systems also fail to provide **information on the quality or importance of operations**. Drury provides the following example.

> 'Consider a situation where a purchasing department regularly achieved the budget for all expense items. The responsibility performance reporting system therefore suggests that the department was well managed. However, the department provided a poor service to the production departments. Low-cost suppliers were selected who provided poor quality materials and frequently failed to meet delivery dates. This caused much wasted effort in chasing up orders and prejudiced the company's ability to deliver to its customers on time.'

Measuring success, not ensuring success

1.5   **Financial performance indicators** have been said to simply **measure success**. What organisations also require, however, are performance **indicators that ensure success**. Such indicators, **linked** to an organisation's **critical success factors** such as quality and flexibility, will be **non financial** in nature.

2   GROWING EMPHASIS ON NFPIs

2.1   Changes in cost structures and the manufacturing and competitive environments have led to a shift from treating financial figures as the foundation of performance measurement to treating them as one of a range of measures.

Changes in cost structures

2.2   Modern technology requires massive investment and product life cycles have got shorter. A greater proportion of costs are sunk and a large proportion of costs are planned, engineered or designed into a product/service before production/delivery. **At the time the product/service is produced/delivered, it is therefore too late to control costs.**

Changes in competitive environment

2.3 **Financial measures do not convey the full picture** of a company's performance, especially in a **modern business environment**.

> 'In today's worldwide competitive environment companies are competing in terms of product quality, delivery, reliability, after-sales service and customer satisfaction. None of these variables is directly measured by the traditional responsibility accounting system, despite the fact that they represent the major goals of world-class manufacturing companies.'

Changes in manufacturing environment

2.4 New manufacturing techniques and technologies focus on minimising throughput times, stock levels and set-up times. But managers can reduce the costs for which they are responsible by increasing stock levels through maximising output. If a performance measurement system **focuses principally on costs**, managers may **concentrate on cost reduction and ignore other important strategic manufacturing goals**.

Introducing NFPIs

2.5 Many companies are therefore discovering the usefulness of quantitative and qualitative **non-financial performance indicators (NFPIs)**.

KEY TERM

Non-financial performance measures are 'measures of performance based on non-financial information which may originate in and be used by operating departments to monitor and control their activities without any accounting input.

Non-financial performance measures may give a more timely indication of the levels of performance achieved than do financial ratios, and may be less susceptible to distortion by factors such as uncontrollable variations in the effect of market forces on operations.

Examples of non-financial performance measures:

Area assessed	Performance measure
Service quality	Number of complaints
	Proportions of repeat bookings
	Customer waiting time
	On-time deliveries
Production performance	Set-up times
	Number of suppliers
	Days' inventory in hand
	Output per employee
	Material yield percentage
	Schedule adherence
	Proportion of output requiring rework
	Manufacturing lead times

KEY TERM (cont'd)	
Marketing effectiveness	Trend in market share
	Sales volume growth
	Customer visits per salesperson
	Client contact hours per salesperson
	Sales volume forecast v actual
	Number of customers
	Customer survey response information
Personnel	Number of complaints received
	Staff turnover
	Days lost through absenteeism
	Days lost through accidents/sickness
	Training time per employee.'

(CIMA Official Terminology)

3 THE VALUE OF NFPIs

3.1 Unlike traditional variance reports, NFPIs can be provided quickly for managers, per shift, **daily** or even **hourly** as required. They are likely to be easy to calculate, and easier for non-financial managers to understand and therefore to use effectively.

3.2 The beauty of non-financial indicators is that **anything can be compared** if it is **meaningful** to do so. The measures should be **tailored** to the circumstances so that, for example, number of coffee breaks per 20 pages of Study Text might indicate to you how hard you are studying!

3.3 Many suitable measures combine elements from the chart shown below. The chart is not intended to be prescriptive or exhaustive.

Errors/failure	Time	Quantity	People
Defects	Second	Range of products	Employees
Equipment failures	Minute	Parts/components	Employee skills
Warranty claims	Hour	Units produced	Customers
Complaints	Shift	Units sold	Competitors
Returns	Cycle	Services performed	Suppliers
Stockouts	Day	kg/litres/metres	
Lateness/waiting	Month	m^2/m^3	
Misinformation	Year	Documents	
Miscalculation		Deliveries	
Absenteeism		Enquiries	

3.4 Traditional measures derived from these lists like 'kg (of material) per unit produced' or 'units produced per hour' are fairly obvious, but what may at first seem a fairly **unlikely combination** may also be very revealing. 'Absenteeism per customer', for example, may be of no significance at all or it may reveal that a particularly difficult customer is being avoided, and hence that some action is needed.

3.5 There is clearly a need for the information provider to work more closely with the managers who will be using the information to make sure that their needs are properly understood. The measures used are likely to be **developed and refined over time**. It may be that some will serve the purpose of drawing attention to areas in need of improvement but will be of no further relevance once remedial action has been taken. A flexible, responsive approach is essential.

Question: NFPIs

Using the above chart make up five non-financial indicators and explain how each might be useful.

Answer

Here are five indicators, showing you how to use the chart, but there are many other possibilities.

(a) Services performed late v total services performed
(b) Total units sold v total units sold by competitors (indicating market share)
(c) Warranty claims per month
(d) Documents processed per employee
(e) Equipment failures per 1,000 units produced

Don't forget to explain how the ones that you chose might be useful.

NFPIs and financial measures

3.6 Arguably, NFPIs are less likely to be **manipulated** than traditional profit-related measures and they should, therefore, offer a means of counteracting short-termism, since short-term profit at any (non-monetary) expense is rarely an advisable goal. The ultimate goal of commercial organisations in the long run is likely to remain the maximisation of **profit**, however, and so the financial aspect cannot be ignored.

3.7 There is a danger that too many such measures could be reported, leading to **information overload** for managers, providing information that is not truly useful, or that sends conflicting signals. A further danger of NFPIs is that they might lead managers to pursue detailed **operational goals** and become blind to the **overall strategy** in which those goals are set.

3.8 A **combination** of financial and non-financial indicators is therefore likely to be most successful.

The balanced scorecard

3.9 The need to **link financial and non-financial measures** of performance and to identify the **key performance measures** provided the impetus for the development of the balanced scorecard, which we look at in Chapter 14.

4 NFPIS IN RELATION TO EMPLOYEES

4.1 One of the many criticisms of **traditional accounting performance measurement systems** is that they **do not measure the skills, morale and training of the workforce**, which can be as **valuable to an organisation as its tangible assets**. For example if employees have not been trained in the manufacturing practices required to achieve the objectives of the new manufacturing environment, an organisation is unlikely to be successful.

4.2 Employee attitudes and morale can be measured by **surveying** employees. Education and skills levels, promotion and training, absenteeism and labour turnover for the employees for which each manager is responsible can also be monitored.

4.3 The **weighting** attached to employee-orientated NFPIs when assessing managerial performance should be high. High profitability or tight cost control should not be accompanied by 100% labour turnover.

5 NFPIs IN RELATION TO PRODUCT/SERVICE QUALITY

Performance measurement in a TQM environment

5.1 As you know from Chapter 4, Total Quality Management is a highly significant trend in modern business thinking.

5.2 Because **TQM embraces every activity** of a business, performance measures cannot be confined to the production process but must also cover the work of sales and distribution departments and administration departments, the efforts of external suppliers, and the reaction of external customers.

In many cases the measures used will be non-financial ones. They may be divided into three types.

Measuring the quality of incoming supplies

5.3 The quality of output depends on the quality of input materials, and so **quality control** should include procedures for acceptance and inspection of goods inwards and measurement of rejects.

   (a) **Inspection** will normally be based on statistical sampling techniques and the concept of an acceptance quality level (AQL).

   (b) Another approach that can be used is to give each **supplier a 'rating'** for the quality of the goods they tend to supply, and give preference with purchase orders to well-rated suppliers.

   (c) Where a **quality assurance scheme** is in place, the supplier guarantees the quality of goods supplied. This places the onus on the supplier to carry out the necessary quality checks, or face cancellation of the contract.

Monitoring work done as it proceeds

5.4 This will take place at various key stages in the production process. Inspection, based on random sampling and other statistical techniques, will provide a continual check that the production process is under control. The aim of inspection is not really to sort out the bad products from the good ones after the work has been done. The aim is to **satisfy management that quality control in production is being maintained.**

5.5 'In-process' controls include statistical process controls and random sampling, and measures such as the amount of scrap and reworking in relation to good production. Measurements can be made by product, by worker or work team, by machine or machine type, by department, or whatever is appropriate.

Measuring customer satisfaction

5.6 Some sub-standard items will inevitably be produced. In-process checks will identify some bad output, but other items will reach the customer who is the ultimate judge of quality. '**Complaints**' may be monitored in the form of letters of complaint, returned goods, penalty discounts, claims under guarantee, or requests for visits by service engineers.

5.7 Some companies adopt a more pro-active approach to monitoring customer satisfaction by surveying their customers on a regular basis. They use the feedback to obtain an index of customer satisfaction which is used to identify quality problems before they affect profits.

Quality of service

Exam focus point

Candidates had to suggest performance measures to assess service quality in the December 2002 exam, while performance measurement criteria that could be used to assess service quality in a hotel (such as those in the table in Paragraph 5.9) were required in the December 2003 exam.

5.8 Service quality is measured principally by **qualitative measures**, as you might expect, although some quantitative measures are used by some businesses.

(a) If it were able to obtain the information, a retailer might use number of lost customers in a period as an indicator of service quality.

(b) Lawyers use the proportion of time spent with clients.

5.9 Fitzgerald *et al* identify 12 factors pertaining to service quality and the following table shows the measures used and the means of obtaining the information by British Airports Authority, a mass transport service.

Service quality factors	Measures	Mechanisms
Access	Walking distances	Customer survey and internal operational data
	Ease of finding way around	Customer survey
Aesthetics/appearance	Staff appearance	Customer survey
	Airport's appearance	Customer survey
	Quantity, quality, appearance of food	Management inspection
Availability	Equipment availability	Internal fault monitoring system and customer survey
		Customer survey and internal operational data
Cleanliness/tidiness	Cleanliness of environment and equipment	Customer survey and management inspection
Comfort	Crowdedness of airport	Customer survey and management inspection
Communication	Information clarity	Customer survey
	Clarity of labelling and pricing	Management inspection
Courtesy	Courtesy of staff	Customer survey and

Service quality factors	Measures	Mechanisms
		management inspection
Friendliness	Staff attitude and helpfulness	Customer survey and management inspection
Reliability	Number of equipment faults	Internal fault monitoring systems
Responsiveness	Staff responsiveness	Customer survey
Security	Efficiency of security checks	Customer survey
	Number of urgent safety reports	Internal operational data

Question: measuring quality

What do you conclude are the two main means of measuring service quality at BAA?

Measures of customer satisfaction

5.10 You have probably filled in **questionnaires** in fast food restaurants or on aeroplanes without realising that you were completing a customer attitude survey for input to the organisation's management information system.

Case example

Horngren cites the 'Customer Satisfaction Target' used by Holiday Inns, where information is measured by evaluating scores (A-F) on guest inspection cards and imposing a limit of 0.457 guest complaint letters per 1,000 room-nights sold.

5.11 **Other possible measures of customer satisfaction**

(a) Market research information on customer preferences and customer satisfaction with specific product features

(b) Number of defective units supplied to customers as a percentage of total units supplied

(c) Number of customer complaints as a percentage of total sales volume

(d) Percentage of products which fail early or excessively

(e) On-time delivery rate

(f) Average time to deal with customer queries

(g) New customer accounts opened

(h) Repeat business from existing customers

Exam focus point

Seven marks were available in the December 2001 exam for identifying a range of appropriate NFPIs, while five were available in the December 2002 exam.

BPP
PROFESSIONAL EDUCATION

6 QUALITATIVE ISSUES

6.1 There will often be no conclusion that you as the management accountant can draw from qualitative information. Your job is to **be aware of its existence** and report it under the heading of 'other matters to be considered'. In practice of course, many decisions are finally swayed by the strength of the qualitative arguments rather than the cold facts presented in the quantitative analysis, and rightly so.

Exam focus point

As a general guideline, if you are asked to comment on qualitative issues, you should consider matters such as the following.

(a) The impact on or of human behaviour. What will be the reaction on the factory floor? How will managers feel? Will customers be attracted or deterred? Can suppliers be trusted?

(b) The impact on or of the environment ('surroundings'). Is the country in a recession? Is government or legislation influential? Are there 'green' issues to be considered? What is the social impact? What action will competing companies take? Is changing technology a help or a hindrance?

(c) The impact on or of ethics. Is the action in the public interest? Are we acting professionally? Are there conflicts of interest to be considered? Will fair dealing help to win business? Are we treating staff properly?

Branding

6.2 Brand identity conveys a lot of information very quickly and concisely. This helps customers to identify the goods or services and thus helps to **create customer loyalty** to the brand. It is therefore a means of increasing or maintaining sales.

6.3 Where a brand image promotes an idea of **quality,** a customer will be disappointed if his experience of a product fails to live up to his expectations. Quality control is therefore of utmost importance. It is essentially a problem for **service industries** such as hotels, airlines and retail stores, where there is **less possibility** than in the manufacturing sector of **detecting and rejecting the work of an operator before it reaches the customer.** Bad behaviour by an employee in a face-to-face encounter with a customer will **reflect on** the **entire company** and possibly deter the customer from using any of the company's services again.

6.4 **Brand awareness** is an **indicator of a product's/organisation's place in the market. Recall tests** can be used to assess the public's brand awareness.

Company profile

6.5 Company profile is **how an organisation is perceived by a range of stakeholders.** For example, stakeholders may have a negative attitude towards an organisation, perhaps as a result of an ethical issue or a crisis that has struck the organisation and the associated media comment. **Market research** can determine company profile and **marketing campaigns** can improve it if necessary.

Chapter roundup

- **Concentration on financial indicators** means that important goals and factors may be ignored.

- Changes in cost structures, the competitive environment and the manufacturing environment have lead to an **increased use of NFPIs.**

- NFPIs do have advantages over financial indicators but a **combination** of both types of indicator is likely to be most successful.

- NFPIs can usefully be applied to **employees** and product/service **quality**.

- **Qualitative factors** are 'those that can be expressed in monetary terms only with much difficulty or imprecision'.

Quick quiz

1   *Fill in the blanks.*

NFPIs are less likely to be .... than traditional profit-related measures and they should therefore offer a means of counteracting ....

2   A danger of financial performance measures is that they might lead managers to pursue detailed operational goals and become blind to the overall strategy in which those goals are set. *True or false?*

3   Which of the following are not among the service quality factors identified by Fitzgerald *et al*?

A   Comfort, friendliness, security
B   Clarity, cleanliness, reliability
C   Aesthetics, appearance, courtesy
D   Availability, communication, access

Answers to quick quiz

1   manipulated
     short termism

2   False. This is a danger with NFPIs.

3   B   Clarity is not one of the factors.

Now try the question below from the Exam Question Bank

Number	Level	Marks	Time
10	Exam	20	36 mins

Chapter 13

PERFORMANCE MEASUREMENT FOR NON-PROFIT SEEKING ORGANISATIONS

Topic list	Syllabus reference
1 Non-profit seeking organisations	3(b)
2 Achieving objectives in the public sector	3(b)
3 Performance measurement in non-profit seeking organisations	3(b)
4 Value for money	3(b)
5 Politics, performance measurement and undesirable service outcomes	3(b)
6 Government regulation	3(c)

Introduction

This chapter provides a **contrast to Chapter 11** and focuses on performance measurement in non-profit seeking organisations.

Study guide

Section 14 – Performance measurement for non-profit seeking organisations

- Comment on the need to achieve objectives with limited funds that may not be controllable

- Identify and explain ways in which performance may be judged in non-profit seeking organisations

- Comment on the difficulty in measuring outputs when performance is not judged in terms of money or an easily quantifiable objective

- Explain how the combination of politics and the desire to measure public sector performance may result in undesirable service outcomes

- Comment on 'value for money' service as a not-for-profit sector goal

Section 16 – Performance – a broad perspective

- Consider the impact of governmental regulation on the performance measurement techniques used and the performance levels achieved

Exam guide

The examiner's interest in the contrast between the private and public sectors means that this chapter's topics could well appear quite frequently in exam questions. Question 1 of the Pilot paper provides an example of the type of question you could face.

The issues covered in this chapter are useful background to the Oxford Brookes degree Research and Analysis Project Topic 1, which requires you to analyse the efficiency and/or effectiveness of a management accounting technique in an organisational setting.

BPP
PROFESSIONAL EDUCATION

1 NON-PROFIT SEEKING ORGANISATIONS

1.1 Although most people would 'know one if they saw it', there is a surprising problem in clearly defining what counts as a non-profit seeking organisation.

1.2 Bois has suggested that non-profit seeking organisations are defined by recognising that their first objective is to be involved in **non-loss operations** in order to cover their costs and that profits are only made as a means to an end (such as providing a service, or accomplishing some socially or morally worthy objective).

> ### KEY TERM
>
> A **non-profit seeking organisation** is '... an organisation whose attainment of its prime goal is not assessed by economic measures. However, in pursuit of that goal it may undertake profit-making activities.' *(Bois)*
>
> This may involve a number of different kinds of organisation with, for example, differing legal status – charities, statutory bodies offering public transport or the provision of services such as leisure, health or public utilities such as water or road maintenance.

Case example

Oxfam operates more shops than any commercial organisation in Britain, and these operate at a profit. The Royal Society for the Protection of Birds operates a mail order trading company which provides a 25% return on capital, operating very profitably and effectively.

Objectives

1.3 A major problem with many non-profit seeking organisations, particularly government bodies, is that it is extremely **difficult to define their objectives** at all. In addition they tend to have **multiple objectives,** so that even if they could all be clearly identified it is impossible to say which is the overriding objective.

Question: objectives

What objectives might the following non-profit seeking organisations have?

(a)   An army
(b)   A local council
(c)   A charity
(d)   A political party
(e)   A college

Answer

Here are some suggestions

(a)   To defend a country
(b)   To provide services for local people (such as the elderly)
(c)   To help others/protect the environment
(d)   To gain power/enact legislation
(e)   To provide education

1.4 More general objectives for non-profit seeking organisations

- Surplus maximisation (equivalent to profit maximisation)
- Revenue maximisation (as for a commercial business)
- Usage maximisation (as in leisure centre swimming pool usage)
- Usage targeting (matching the capacity available, as in the NHS)
- Full/partial cost recovery (minimising subsidy)
- Budget maximisation (maximising what is offered)
- Producer satisfaction maximisation (satisfying the wants of staff and volunteers)
- Client satisfaction maximisation (the police generating the support of the public)

1.5 It is difficult to judge whether **non-quantitative objectives** have been met. For example, assessing whether a charity has improved the situation of those benefiting from its activities is difficult to research. Statistics related to product mix, financial resources, size of budgets, number of employees, number of volunteers, number of customers serviced and number and location of facilities are all useful for this task.

1.6 The primary objectives of commercial manufacturing and service organisations are likely to be fairly similar and centre on satisfying shareholders. The **range of objectives** of non-profit seeking organisations is as **wide as the range of non-profit seeking organisations**.

Exam focus point

In an exam, if faced with a question on the public sector, remember that you are likely to have had extensive contact with a variety of public sector organisations and have seen something of how they work. Your greatest contact is likely to have been with the public education system, but you will probably have had contact with some local government authorities which provide a wide variety of services from street cleaning, to leisure facilities, to fire services. You may also have had contact with the health service.

Think now about your experiences and use them in the exam.

2 ACHIEVING OBJECTIVES IN THE PUBLIC SECTOR

The link between funding and achieving objectives

2.1 In the private sector, revenues and ultimately profits depend on customers being attracted and returning. In the **public sector**, however, **funding** tends to come direct from the government, **not from those using the public service** (pupils, patients and so on). Obtaining funds, or additional funds, can be a complex political process: there is **not necessarily a link between providing more service and obtaining more funds.** There are limits on the levels of taxation and government borrowing that are possible in a global economy.

2.2 In fact, in much of the public sector, there is no link between success at achieving objectives and funding received. In some instances **poor performance against non-financial objectives leads to higher levels of funding.** An ineffective or inefficient police force will not be closed down, but is likely to justify and obtain additional funding. (In the December 2001 exam, a non-profit seeking organisation received an annual subsidy equal to its financial deficit for the year.)

2.3 The **level of service provided**, which effectively **determines the funding** that an organisation receives, is a **political** decision.

(a) The public sector has to provide services, whether or not they are efficient or economic.

(b) Services have to be provided to all customers. For instance, hospitals cannot turn away emergencies.

(c) Levels of local provision are often determined centrally by experts and formulae.

(d) Local decision making by, say, nominated members of local authorities, can lead to different services being offered in different parts of the country.

(e) Public sector units compete against each other for limited funds.

2.4 Public sector organisations therefore have to provide the **best service possible with the allocated funding**.

Planning

2.5 Planning in the public sector is inhibited by the political system. Governments change, government ministers change more frequently. New ministers wish to 'leave a mark', do something which produces change. **Changes in priorities and/or changes in funding formulae** can be **imposed with little or no notice**.

2.6 **Expenditure increases have to be balanced by appropriate expenditure cuts**. If a hard winter means that more money has to be spent on clearing roads of snow, something, quite possibly road maintenance and resurfacing, will have to be cut. This is because the **budget authorisation** is all important. Once it is taken, **clear authority** has been given to act within its **limits** and in the **way specified** by the detail of the budget. **Very little flexibility** is allowed in moving funds from one budget area to another.

2.7 Public sector organisations have **limited control** over both the **level of funding** they receive and, to an extent, the **objectives they can achieve**.

3   PERFORMANCE MEASUREMENT IN NON-PROFIT SEEKING

ORGANISATIONS

3.1 Commercial organisations generally have market competition and the profit motive to guide the process of managing resources economically, efficiently and effectively. However, not-for-profit organisations **cannot by definition be judged by profitability** and do not **generally have to be successful against competition,** so other methods of assessing performance have to be used.

3.2 As we have already said, a major problem with many non-profit seeking organisations, particularly government bodies, is that it is extremely **difficult to define their objectives** at all, let alone find one which can serve a yardstick function in the way that profit does for commercial bodies.

Question: objectives for non-profit seeking organisations

One of the objectives of a local government body could be 'to provide adequate street lighting throughout the area'.

(a) How could the 'adequacy' of street lighting be measured?

(b) Assume that other objectives are to improve road safety in the area and to reduce crime. How much does 'adequate' street lighting contribute to each of these aims?

(c)   What is an excessive amount of money to pay for adequately lit streets, improved road safety and reduced crime? How much is too little?

Answer

Mull over these questions and discuss them in class or with colleagues if possible. It is possible to suggest answers, perhaps even in quantitative terms, but the point is that there are no **easy** answers, and no right or wrong answers.

3.3   You might consider (partly depending upon your political point of view) that it is therefore not necessary to measure performance in non-profit seeking organisations. However, **few would argue** that such bodies **should be given whatever amount of money they say they need to pursue their aims, with no check on** whether it is spent well or badly.

(a)   Without information about what is being achieved (outputs) and what it is costing (inputs) it is impossible to make **efficient resource allocations**. These allocation decisions rely on a range of performance measures which, if unavailable, may lead managers to allocate resources based on subjective judgement, personal whim or in response to political pressure.

(b)   Without performance measures managers will not know the **extent to which operations are contributing to effectiveness and efficiency;** when diagnostic interventions are necessary; how the performance of their organisation **compares** with similar units elsewhere; and how their performance has **changed** over time.

(c)   **Government** may require performance information to decide how much to spend in the public sector and where, within the sector, it should be allocated. In particular they will be interested to know what results may be achieved as a consequence of a particular level of funding, or to decide whether or not a service could be delivered more effectively and efficiently in the private sector. Likewise **people who provide funds for** other kinds of non-profit seeking organisations are entitled to know whether their money is being put to good use.

How can performance be measured?

3.4   Performance is usually judged in terms of **inputs and outputs** and this ties in with the 'value for money' criteria that are often used to assess non-profit seeking organisations (covered in Section 4).

- **Economy** (spending money frugally)
- **Efficiency** (getting out as much as possible for what goes in)
- **Effectiveness** (getting done, by means of the above, what was supposed to be done)

More formal definitions are as follows.

> **KEY TERMS**
>
> **Effectiveness** is the relationship between an organisation's outputs and its objectives.
>
> **Efficiency** is the relationship between inputs and outputs.
>
> **Economy** is attaining the appropriate quantity and quality of inputs at lowest cost.

We will look at these concepts in more depth in Section 4.

Problems with performance measurement of non-profit seeking organisations

3.5   (a) **Multiple objectives**

As we have said, they tend to have multiple objectives, so that even if they can all be clearly identified it is impossible to say which is the overriding objective.

(b) **Measuring outputs**

Outputs can seldom be measured in a way that is generally agreed to be meaningful. (For example, are good exam results alone an adequate measure of the quality of teaching?) Data collection can be problematic. For example, unreported crimes are not included in data used to measure the performance of a police force.

(c) **Lack of profit measure**

If an organisation is not expected to make a profit, or if it has no sales, indicators such as ROI and RI are meaningless.

(d) **Nature of service provided**

Many non-profit seeking organisations provide services for which it is difficult to define a cost unit. For example, what is the cost unit for a local fire service? This problem does exist for commercial service providers but problems of performance measurement are made simple because profit can be used.

(e) **Financial constraints**

Although every organisation operates under financial constraints, these are more pronounced in non-profit seeking organisations. For instance, a commercial organisation's borrowing power is effectively limited by managerial prudence and the willingness of lenders to lend, but a local authority's ability to raise finance (whether by borrowing or via local taxes) is subject to strict control by central government.

(f) **Political, social and legal considerations**

(i)   Unlike commercial organisations, public sector organisations are subject to strong political influences. Local authorities, for example, have to carry out central government's policies as well as their own (possibly conflicting) policies.

(ii)   The public may have higher expectations of public sector organisations than commercial organisations. A decision to close a local hospital in an effort to save costs, for example, is likely to be less acceptable to the public than the closure of a factory for the same reason.

(iii)   The performance indicators of public sector organisations are subject to far more onerous legal requirements than those of private sector organisations. We consider this point in more detail in Section 6.

(iv)   Whereas profit-seeking organisations are unlikely in the long term to continue services making a negative contribution, non-profit seeking organisations may be required to offer a range of services, even if some are uneconomic.

Solutions

Inputs

3.6   Performance can be judged in terms of inputs. This is very common in everyday life. If somebody tells you that their suit cost £750, you would generally conclude that it was an extremely well-designed and good quality suit, even if you did not think so when you first saw it. The drawback is that you might also conclude that the person wearing the suit had been cheated or was a fool, or you may happen to be of the opinion that no piece of clothing is worth £750. So it is with the inputs and outputs of a non-profit seeking organisation.

Judgement

3.7 A second possibility is to accept that performance measurement must to some extent be subjective. Judgements can be made by **experts** in that particular not-for-profit activity or by the **persons who fund the activity**.

Comparisons

3.8 We have said that most non-profit seeking organisations do not face competition but this does not mean that all are unique. Bodies like local governments, health services and so on can judge their performance **against each other** and **against the historical results of their predecessors**. And since they are not competing with each other, there is less of a problem with confidentiality and so **benchmarking** is easier.

Case example

The UK government's benchmarking website (www.benchmarking.gov.uk) provides a useful description of benchmarking.

'What is benchmarking?

There are numerous definitions of benchmarking, but essentially it involves learning, sharing information and adopting best practices to bring about step changes in performance. So, at its simplest, benchmarking means:

"Improving ourselves by learning from others"

Most organisations tailor definitions of benchmarking to suit their own strategies and objectives. Two examples are given below:

"Benchmarking is simply about making comparisons with other organisations and then learning the lessons that those comparisons throw up"

Source: The European Benchmarking Code of Conduct

"Benchmarking is the continuous process of measuring products, services and practices against the toughest competitors or those companies recognised as industry leaders (best in class)."

Source: The Xerox Corporation

For those approaching benchmarking for the first time the plethora of definitions can be confusing, so it can help to focus on the learning and sharing that goes on during the process.

In practice, benchmarking usually encompasses:

- regularly comparing aspects of performance (functions or processes) with best practitioners;
- identifying gaps in performance;
- seeking fresh approaches to bring about improvements in performance;
- following through with implementing improvements; and
- following up by monitoring progress and reviewing the benefits.

Although benchmarking involves making comparisons of performance, it is not:

• Merely competitor analysis	– Benchmarking is best undertaken in a collaborative way.
• Comparison of league tables	– The aim is to learn about the circumstances and processes that underpin superior performance.

• A quick fix, done once for all time	– Benchmarking projects may extend over a number of months and it is vital to repeat them periodically so as not to fall behind as the background environment changes.
• Copying or catching up	– In rapid changing circumstances, good practices become dated very quickly. Also, the fact that other are doing things differently does not necessarily mean they are better.
• Spying or espionage	– Openness and honesty are vital for successful benchmarking.'

Quantitative measures

3.9 **Unit cost measurements** like 'cost per patient day' or 'cost of borrowing one library book' can fairly easily be established to allow organisations to assess whether they are doing better or worse than their counterparts.

3.10 **Efficiency measurement of inputs and outputs** is illustrated in three different situations as follows.

Where input is fixed

$$\frac{\text{Actual output}}{\text{Maximum output obtainable for a given input}}$$

25/30 miles per gallon = 83.3% efficiency

Where output is fixed

$$\frac{\text{Minimum input needed for a given output}}{\text{Actual input}}$$

55/60 hours to erect scaffolding = 91.7% efficiency

Where input and output are both variable

Actual output ÷ actual input compared with standard output ÷ standard input

£9,030/7,000 meals = £1.29 per meal;
£9,600/7,500 meals = £1.28 per meal
Efficiency = 99.2%

3.11 As a further illustration, suppose that at a cost of £40,000 and 4,000 hours (inputs) in an average year two policemen travel 8,000 miles and are instrumental in 200 arrests (outputs). A large number of possibly meaningful measures can be derived from these few figures, as the table below shows.

	£40,000	4,000 hours	8,000 miles	200 arrests
Cost £40,000 (£)		£40,000/4,000 = £10 per hour	£40,000/8,000 = £5 per mile	£40,000/200 = £200 per arrest
Time 4,000 (hours)	4,000/£40,000 = 6 minutes patrolling per £1 spent		4,000/8,000 = ½ hour to patrol 1 mile	4,000/200 = 20 hours per arrest
Miles 8,000	8,000/£40,000 = 0.2 of a mile per £1	8,000/4,000 = 2 miles patrolled per hour		8,000/200 = 40 miles per arrest
Arrests 200	200/£40,000 = 1 arrest per £200	200/4,000 = 1 arrest every 20 hours	200/8,000 = 1 arrest every 40 miles	

3.12 These measures **do not necessarily identify cause and effect** (do teachers or equipment produce better exam results?) **or personal responsibility and accountability.** Actual performance needs to be compared as follows.

  (a) With standards, if there are any
  (b) With similar external activities
  (c) With similar internal activities
  (d) With targets
  (e) With indices
  (f) Over time, as trends

3.13 An article in *Management Accounting* in March 1995 included the following examples of measures that are being used in *Executive Agencies*.

Area	Measure	Agency
Efficiency		
(a) Monetary	Unit cost of HGV testing £41.69	Vehicle inspectorate
(b) Non-monetary	Target: to increase by at least 3% the number of research milestones achieved annually per scientist Actual: Achieved	National Physical Laboratory
Effectiveness		
(a) Monetary	Receipts from visitors: Target: £2.76m Actual: £2.659m	Welsh Historic Monuments
(b) Non-monetary	Number of students in the Enterprise in Higher Education initiative: Target: 2,700 Actual: 3,000	Training and Employment Agency (Northern Ireland)
(c) Quality	Target: to make all documents available for public inspection within a maximum of five working days of receipt Actual achievement: average of 5.8 working days	Companies House
	Target: to issue at least 90% of patent search reports within 12 weeks Actual achievement: 76% issued within 12 weeks	Patent Office

3.14 Non-profit seeking organisations are forced to use a **wide range** of indicators and can be considered early users of a **balanced scorecard** approach (covered in Chapter 14).

Non-profit seeking organisations and profit-seeking bodies

3.15   If it has struck you when reading the previous sections that the main issue in the performance measurement of non-profit seeking organisations is one of **quality**, you may be wondering whether the distinction between profit-seeking and non-profit-seeking in this context is worth making!

3.16   The answer, of course, is that increasingly it is not. The **commercial sector's new focus on customers and quality of service has much in common with the aims of non-profit seeking organisations.** Conversely **non-profit seeking organisations** (in particular government bodies) have increasingly been forced to **face up to elements of competition and market forces.**

3.17   The **distinctions** are thus **becoming blurred.** The problems of performance measurement in non-profit seeking organisations are to a great extent the problems of performance measurement generally.

Question: profit-seeking v non-profit seeking

Can you think of some issues which would impact on the different performance indicators used by an NHS hospital and a private sector hospital?

Answer

- The private sector hospital would be focused on maximising **profit**, the NHS hospital on **cost efficiency.**

- Managers within a private sector hospital are likely to have far greater autonomy than those working in the NHS.

- A private sector hospital has far greater **freedom in selecting its patients** and the types of **treatment** offered. It can choose to specialise in the most profitable areas. An NHS hospital, unless it is a specialist centre, must treat all patients and offer a huge range of treatments.

- Private sector hospitals can **market** their services.

Case example

'To reach a turnover of £105.6 billion the discerning beancounter would have to add together the annual sales of BT, Tesco, Unilever, Marks & Spencer and British Airways to come close. BP is the only British corporation to rival the NHS's proposed turnover, with some £119 billion of sales. It has just 110,000 people, who managed to make a profit of £9 billion last year.

NHS trusts mainly make a loss but are allowed to roll over the more embarrassing deficits until the next year, or share them with more profitable parts of the business.

The greatest difference between BP and the NHS is the level and expertise of the oil company's senior staff compared with the oversized management of the health service. The NHS has 419 trusts which are run by 9,000 managers, a ratio of 21.479 for each trust. BP has 126 business units looked after by 126 unit leaders. Just one each.'

The Times, April 2002

Comparing the performance of profit-seeking and non-profit seeking organisations

Exam focus point

Question 1 in the December 2001 paper required a comparison between a profit-seeking organisation and a non-profit seeking organisation in terms of operational and financial performance. The topic was also examined in June 2004.

3.18 A valid comparison between such organisations may **require adjustments** to be made to data provided for analysis purposes. Here are some examples.

(a) If the non-profit seeking organisation does not **charge for services**, a hypothetical amount may need to be included in profit calculations, possibly based on the number of customers who would be willing to pay.

(b) The non-profit seeking organisation may have no debt (perhaps because it has been paid off by a governing body, a local authority and so on). Any **interest paid on debt** by the profit-seeking organisation may therefore need to be removed from profit calculations.

(c) Any **loss attributable to uneconomic sections/divisions/services** of the non-profit seeking organisation (which it may be required to continue for social or legal purposes), may need to be removed for comparison purposes.

4 VALUE FOR MONEY

KEY TERM

Value for money means providing a service in a way which is economical, efficient and effective.

4.1 Although much has been written about value for money (VFM), there is no great mystique about the concept. The term is common in everyday speech and so is the idea.

To drive the point home, think of a bottle of Fairy Liquid. If we believe the advertising, Fairy is good 'value for money' because it washes half as many plates again as any other washing up liquid. Bottle for bottle it may be more expensive, but plate for plate it is cheaper. Not only this but Fairy gets plates 'squeaky' clean. To summarise, Fairy gives us VFM because it exhibits the following characteristics.

- **Economy** (more clean plates per pound)
- **Efficiency** (more clean plates per squirt)
- **Effectiveness** (plates as clean as they should be)

4.2 The assessment of economy, efficiency and effectiveness should be a part of the normal management process of any organisation, public or private.

(a) Management should carry out **performance reviews** as a regular feature of their control responsibilities.

(b) Independent assessments of management performance can be carried out by 'outsiders', perhaps an internal audit department, as **value for money audits (VFM audits)**.

4.3 **Public sector organisations** are now under considerable **pressure** to prove that they operate economically, efficiently and effectively, and are encouraged from many sources to draw up **action plans** to achieve value for money as part of the continuing process of good management.

4.4 Value for money is important **whatever level of expenditure** is being considered. Negatively it may be seen as an approach to spreading costs in public expenditure fairly across services but positively it is necessary to ensure that the desired impact is achieved with the minimum use of resources.

Economy

4.5 Economy is concerned with the cost of inputs, and it is achieved by **obtaining those inputs at the lowest acceptable cost**. Economy **does not mean straightforward cost-cutting,** because resources must be acquired which are of a suitable **quality** to provide the service to the desired standard. Cost-cutting should not sacrifice quality to the extent that service standards fall to an unacceptable level. Economising by buying poor quality materials, labour or equipment is a 'false economy'.

Efficiency

4.6 Efficiency means the following.

(a) **Maximising output for a given input**, for example maximising the number of transactions handled per employee or per £1 spent.

(b) **Achieving the minimum input for a given output**. For example, the Department of Social Security is required to pay Unemployment Benefit to millions of people. Efficiency will be achieved by making these payments with the minimum labour and computer time.

Effectiveness

4.7 Effectiveness means ensuring that the **outputs** of a service or programme have the **desired impacts**; in other words, finding out whether they **succeed in achieving objectives**, and if so, to what extent.

Studying and measuring the three Es

4.8 Economy, efficiency and effectiveness can be studied and measured with reference to the following.

(a) **Inputs**

(i) Money
(ii) Resources - the labour, materials, time and so on consumed, and their cost

For example, a VFM audit into state secondary education would look at the efficiency and economy of the use of resources for education (the use of schoolteachers, school buildings, equipment, cash) and whether the resources are being used for their purpose: what is the pupil/teacher ratio and are trained teachers being fully used to teach the subjects they have been trained for?

(b) **Outputs,** in other words the **results of an activity**, measurable as the services actually produced, and the quality of the services.

In the case of a VFM audit of secondary education, outputs would be measured as the number of pupils taught and the number of subjects taught per pupil; how many examination papers are taken and what is the pass rate; what proportion of students go on to further education at a university or college.

(c) **Impacts,** which are the **effect that the outputs** of an activity or programme have in terms of achieving policy objectives.

Policy objectives might be to provide a minimum level of education to all children up to the age of 16, and to make education relevant for the children's future jobs and careers. This might be measured by the ratio of jobs vacant to unemployed school leavers. A VFM audit could assess to what extent this objective is being achieved.

4.9 As another example from education, suppose that there is a programme to build a new school in an area. The **inputs** would be the **costs of building** the school, and the resources used up; the **outputs** would be the **school building** itself; and the **impacts** would be the **effect that the new school has on education in the area** it serves.

VFM audits and objectives

4.10 In a VFM audit, the objectives of a particular programme or activity need to be specified and understood in order for the auditor to make a proper assessment of whether value for money has been achieved.

(a) In a **profit seeking organisation**, objectives can be expressed financially in terms of target profit or return. The organisation, and profit centres within it, can be judged to have operated **effectively** if they have **achieved a target profit** within a given period.

(b) In **non-profit seeking organisations**, effectiveness cannot be measured this way, because the organisation has non-financial objectives. The **effectiveness** of performance in such organisations could be measured in terms of whether **targeted non-financial objectives have been achieved**, but as we have seen there are several problems involved in trying to do this.

4.11 EXAMPLE: ASSESSING ACHIEVEMENT OF VFM

An example which has been cited is a decision by the government that hill farmers should be paid an allowance or subsidy. The allowances or subsidies could be paid economically and efficiently, but an auditor in a VFM audit would need to know why the allowance or subsidy was being paid to decide whether VFM had been achieved.

Suppose that the purpose of the subsidy was to encourage farmers to continue farming in hill areas so as to provide employment for the rural population. Farmers might use their allowance to buy labour–saving machinery, with the 'impact' that jobs were lost in hill farming.

In such a situation a VFM audit would reveal that **VFM had not been achieved** because the objective of the program of allowances/subsidies **had not achieved the stated objective** and even had the opposite effect.

5   POLITICS, PERFORMANCE MEASUREMENT AND UNDESIRABLE SERVICE OUTCOMES

Exam focus point

Public service performance measurement was examined in the June 2003 exam.

Performance measurement in the public sector

5.1   Performance measurement in the public sector has traditionally been perceived as presenting **special difficulties.**

5.2   **Problem 1**

With public sector services, there has **rarely been any market competition** and **no profit motive.** In the private sector, these two factors help to guide the process of fixing proper prices and managing resources economically, efficiently and effectively. Since most public sector organisations cannot be judged by their success against competition nor by profitability, other methods of assessing performance have to be used.

5.3   **Problem 2**

Different stakeholders hold different expectations of public sector organisations. For example, parents, employers, the community at large and central government might require different things from the education sector. And even within groups of stakeholders, such as parents, there might be a mix of requirements. Priorities of all the groups might change over time. Schools have to reconcile the possibly conflicting demands made on them but to make explicit statements of objectives might show that they are favouring one group of stakeholder at the expense of another.

5.4   **Problem 3**

Given the **role of government** in public sector organisations, **long-term organisational objectives** are sometimes **sacrificed** for **short-term political gains.**

5.5   **Problem 4**

In the public sector, **performance measures are difficult to define.** Measures of output quantity and output quality themselves provide insufficient evidence of, for example, a local authority's success in serving the community.

5.6   **Ways in which these problems could be managed/overcome**

(a) Set up systems for regional benchmarking (making allowances for known regional differences).

(b) Change the way in which such organisations are controlled to restrict political interference.

(c) Carry out cost-benefit-analyses in an attempt to place a financial value on services being provided.

(d) Use independent agencies (of experts) to make subjective decisions based upon their experience and information provided.

Performance indicators

5.7 During the 1980s, however, the increased availability of information technology led to a dramatic reduction in the cost of collecting data. This fuelled the practice of publishing information (**performance indicators**) about the performance of public sector bodies. This aimed to **overcome** the traditional **problems** of public sector performance measurement and enable various interested parties to **secure control** of public sector resources.

5.8 Whether within central government, local government or the NHS, public sector bodies are required to produce and publish key indicators on a variety of fronts.

Citizens' Charter

5.9 Many performance indicator schemes have been put in place, the most infamous of which is probably the Citizens' Charter. This was published in 1991 and **aims to hold public services to account** by publishing information about their activities and achievements.

   (a) **Standards** are set and published in service **charters**.

   (b) **Quality** is delivered by **privatising** or **contracting out** services.

   (c) Services are monitored and compared by compiling **league tables** of performance and making them public.

   (d) **Individuals** have **rights of redress** through complaints procedures.

5.10 The aim of the Charter is therefore to **turn the user into a consumer** operating in a public services marketplace, with **competing providers** to choose between and the **power to punish** them when performance falls below standard.

5.11 **Parents' Charter**

   This contains a number of measures intended to make schools more sensitive to the demands of parents.

   (a) Published **league tables** of public examinations results, truancy rates and destinations of pupils leaving school

   (b) The right of **parents** to **express a preference** for the school their child should attend, offering parents some **sanction against poor performance**

5.12 **Patients' Charter**

   (a) **Publication of performance data** including waiting times for outpatients' appointments and waiting times for ambulance services

   (b) **Patients' rights**, includes guaranteed admission for inpatient treatment within a specified number of years of being placed on a waiting list

Clarity of objectives

5.13 The Citizens' Charter attempts to specify **consistent** and **unambiguous** quality of service standards as clearly and **succinctly** as possible in an attempt to overcome the traditional difficulty of measuring performance against unclear or multiple objectives.

   (a) Quality of service standards can be specified in terms of problems like late trains in the same sort of way as in private sector airlines.

(b) The introduction of a national curriculum in schools has established a uniform standard of output for the whole country (although inputs in terms of students' abilities and prior education are uneven).

Examples of indicators

5.14 To assess **overall performance** of a public service (ie those areas/issues generally considered to be important), indicators can be usefully divided into three groups.

(a) **Financial indicators to measure efficiency**

(i) Cost per unit of activity (eg cost per arrest/bed-night in a hospital/pupil)

(ii) Variance analysis

(iii) Comparisons with benchmark information

(iv) Cost component as a proportion of total costs (eg administration costs as a proportion of total costs)

(v) Costs recovered as a proportion of costs incurred (eg payment received from householders requesting collection of bulky/unusual items of refuse)

(b) **Non-financial (quantifiable) indicators to measure effectiveness**

(i) Quality of service/output measures (eg exam results, crime rates)
(ii) Utilisation of resources (eg hospital bed occupancy ratios, average class sizes)
(iii) Flexibility/speed of response (eg hospital waiting lists)

(c) **Qualitative indicators to measure effectiveness**

(i) Workplace morale

(ii) Staff attitude to dealing with the public (eg can they provide the correct information in a helpful and professional manner)

(iii) Public confidence in the service being provided (eg will a pupil be well educated, a patient properly cared for)

We will be looking in more detail at various indicators in Chapter 14.

Undesirable service outcomes

5.15 The publication of league tables, such as those for schools, has been said to encourage **dubious comparisons**, however, and/or to lead to a **competitiveness which does not fit** with the nature of many of the services being provided.

5.16 For example, extra effort and expenditure on disruptive pupils may represent the **best way for a society as a whole** to deal with them, but a **school's best managerial strategy** is to exclude such pupils (and there has been a sharp rise recently in such exclusions) so as to improve performance for league table purposes.

5.17 Hospitals are under increasing pressure to **compete on price and delivery** in areas such as elective (in other words postponable) surgery such as hip and knee replacements. Although this **reduces waiting lists**, it may represent a **shift of resources from other, less measurable areas** such as emergency services. In attempting to reach a target of ensuring that no patient waits more than a certain number of years for an operation, patients awaiting serious surgery are said to have suffered longer waiting times as hospitals have concentrated on reducing the longer waiting times of those in need of relatively minor surgery. (This is an example of the problem of **measure fixation**, covered in Chapter 15.)

Case examples

(a) 'Fresh doubt on government claims that it has improved the NHS will be cast by an independent report out tomorrow disclosing the widespread distortion of waiting list figures.

Spot checks by the Audit Commission at dozens of hospitals have shown that at least three deliberately 'cooked the books' as they tried to meet Department of Health targets. Many others inadvertently published misleading or incomplete statistics.

Figures can be manipulated by moving patients to a suspended list or by offering appointments to patients only on days when they were known to be on holiday. Managers have also delayed adding patients to lists and medical records have been altered.'

(The Times, 4 March 2003)

(b) 'A housing association repair depot in Wallsend doesn't seem the most likely place to find a do-it-yourself primer on how to reform the public sector.

... Step one – both critical and brave – is to switch off, at least mentally, the apparatus of government-imposed targets and Best Value Performance Indicators and think systems instead. This is critical because the targets don't just interfere with improvement, they prevent it ...

In theory, repairs were a straightforward process. The tenant rang the call centre to report a broken window. The call centre arranged access and raised a works order, which it sent to the supervisor. The supervisor allocated the job to tradesmen, who collected materials and did the repair. Simple. But the reality experienced by tenants was anything but. Why? Because most of the effort was going into juggling organisational requirements to reach targets and pay tradesmen a decent wage, rather than improving the response to householder needs.

For a start, what for the tenant was one repair job, for example a broken window, for the organisation comprised four work orders: inspect, change window, make good, paint. Doing them sequentially could take months (without missing the targets) even if each bit was done properly the first time.

In fact, it usually wasn't. Rigidities in the system meant that communication between the call centre and the tradesman, through supervisors, was abysmal. This resulted in disagreement about what the job entailed (which determined tradesmen's bonuses) and led to 95 per cent of work orders being cancelled or changed and 40 per cent of appointments being missed. In turn, this sparked a fresh round of calls to the call centre (40 per cent of calls were re-calls) to complain or demand a new repair.

To meet the targets, staff simply closed existing work orders and opened new ones. This was entirely reasonable, given that the likelihood of first-time correct diagnosis and action was minimal. 'We were an organisation for opening and closing work orders, not for doing repairs,' says Deena Stephens, a core team member......

... The unit had implemented two significant changes in an attempt to improve performance: it had brought in new supervisors to ensure targets were met and set up a call centre to handle inquiries. But both of these moves made the system more unstable. The average (real) end-to-end time for repairs increased from 21 to 31 and then 51 days by January 2002. ...

... Central to this was to develop measures that helped rather than hindered the underlying purpose: doing more repairs quicker. ...

For the repairs unit, these measures were end-to-end repair time, whether it was fixed the first time, the number of repairs done (including unreported ones done on the spot), and whether the job was well done. ...

... now the call centre routes queries to a tradesman working on the estate, who arranges access directly with the tenant and, if possible, does the repair immediately. The tradesman has his own order book and carries enough stocks to cover most jobs without having to return to the base every day. Supervisors are there to help rather than police pay and targets. ...

... Within weeks of adopting the new ways of working, average end-to-end repair times fell from 51 to 9 days, with 83 per cent done first time (and a significant number of unreported ones carried out there and then). The impact on quality, costs and tenant satisfaction can be imagined. Further indirect improvements came from phasing down the now-redundant stores and paperwork, with more to come.

(The Observer, 24 November 2002)

5.18 Another example of an undesirable service outcome in the NHS centres on the use of a performance indicator based on perinatal mortality rate for maternity departments. Research showed that ante-natal clinics and parentcraft classes were given inadequate priority when emphasis was placed on the perinatal mortality rate. Managers believed that the **lack of attention to such community activity** could **lead to an increase in perinatal complications** and more general adverse development of children after birth. (This is an example of myopia, also discussed in Chapter 15.)

6 GOVERNMENT REGULATION

6.1 **Types of organisations subject to government regulation**

Type	Detail/example
Business	The Post Office operates on a commercial basis but has some level of monopoly (such as on letters costing less than £1 to post)
Free at the point of delivery	National Health Service
'Public good'	Army
Privatised utility	Such organisations (Railtrack, water firms, buses in London) are still, effectively, monopolies
Privatised utility now facing competition	British Telecom, gas industry, electricity, bus services out of London

Stakeholders

6.2 Such organisations often have to deal with conflicting stakeholder objectives, especially those of shareholders and customers/clients. Privatised utilities, in particular, are frequently criticised for paying huge dividends while quality standards fall and/or prices rise.

Case example

At the beginning of 2001, California, arguably one of the wealthiest corners of the world, is facing power cuts.

(a) There is an ever increasing demand for power but no new and no spare capacity.
(b) For practical purposes, price controls on prices charged to end consumers are in place.
(c) There are no price controls on input costs, however, and so utilities are going bankrupt.

Purposes of regulation

6.3 • Promote competition (as in the gas and electricity industries)

• Protect and enhance customer welfare

• Tap into private sector cash in order to improve quality levels (such as EU targets for the quality of beaches)

• Reduce levels of public spending

• Ensure that government subsidies are well spent

Types of regulation

6.4 Regulation of supply

Case example

OFWAT (the water regulator) insists that all water companies give customers 24 hours notice of any interruptions in supply (for repair work) and must restore supplies with 24 hours. There is a £20 fine per customer affected if they fail to comply.

6.5 Regulation of quality

Quality targets are intended to ensure that minimum standards of quality are met.

Case example

The train regulator forced South West trains to cut their prices by 1.8% in 2000 because of poor reliability and punctuality.

6.6 Regulation of prices

Price caps are intended to avoid the abuse of monopoly or near-monopoly power and to encourage efficiency savings.

Case example

OFWAT forced Southern Water to cut their prices by 15.6% in 2000 because their prices were felt to be too high.

Impact of regulation

6.7　One of the principal ways in which performance is assessed in such organisations is with **non-financial performance indicators**. Their advantages and disadvantages in general terms have already been covered in depth. Whether use of such indicators has improved performance in regulated industries is open to question. What is clear, however, is that **regulation has forced the performance of such organisations into the public spotlight.**

Chapter roundup

- One possible definition of a **non-profit seeking organisation** is that its first objective is to be involved in non-loss operations to cover its costs, profits only being made as a means to an end.

- The range of **objectives** of non-profit seeking organisations is as wide as the range of non-profit seeking organisations.

- **Public sector organisations** have limited control over both the level of **funding** they receive and, to an extent, the objectives they can achieve.

- Non-profit seeking organisations tend to have **multiple objectives** which are **difficult to define.** There are a range of other problems in measuring performance.

- Performance is therefore judged in terms of inputs and outputs and hence the **value for money criteria.**
  - ° **Economy**
  - ° **Efficiency**
  - ° **Effectiveness**

- The combination of politics and the desire to measure public sector performance may result in **undesirable service outcomes.**

- **Government regulates** supply, quality and prices of certain organisations.

Quick quiz

1   What general objectives of non-profit seeking organisations are being described in each of the following?

   (a)   Maximising what is offered
   (b)   Satisfying the wants of staff and volunteers
   (c)   Equivalent to profit maximisation
   (d)   Matching capacity available

2   The public service funding system operates on the basis that performance against non-financial objectives leads to a reduction in the level of funding. *True or false?*

3   *Match the definition to the term.*

   Terms   *Definition*

   (a)   Economy   (1)   Ensuring outputs succeed in achieving objectives
   (b)   Efficiency   (2)   Getting out as much as possible for what goes in
   (c)   Effectiveness   (3)   Spending money frugally

4   Economy means cost cutting. *True or false?*

5   Six problems of measuring performance in non-profit seeking organisations were described in this chapter. Which two are missing from the list below?

   (a)   Multiple objectives   (c)   Lack of profit measure
   (b)   Measuring output   (d)   Nature of service provided

Answers to quick quiz

1   (a)   Budget maximisation
    (b)   Producer satisfaction maximisation
    (c)   Surplus maximisation
    (d)   Usage targeting

2   False

3   (a) (3); (b) (2); (c) (1)

4   False

5   Financial constraints
    Political/social/legal considerations

Now try the question below from the Exam Question Bank

Number	Level	Marks	Time
11	Exam	20	36 mins

Chapter 14

ALTERNATIVE VIEWS OF PERFORMANCE MEASUREMENT

Topic list	Syllabus reference
1 The balanced scorecard	3(b)
2 The performance pyramid	3(b)
3 Building blocks	3(b)

Introduction

This chapter considers three alternative views of performance measurement which offer a **contrast to the more traditional approaches** we have been looking at.

Study guide

Section 16 - Alternative views of performance measurement

- Discuss the 'balanced scorecard' as a way in which to improve the range and linkage of performance measures

- Discuss the 'performance pyramid' as a way in which to link strategy and operations

- Discuss the work of Fitzgerald and Moon that considers performance measurement in business services using building blocks for dimensions, standards and rewards

Exam guide

Look out for questions on service sector performance measurement in which you can usefully employ Fitzgerald and Moon's dimensions as a framework for your answer.

The issues covered in this chapter are useful background to the Oxford Brookes degree Research and Analysis Project Topic 1, which requires you to analyse the efficiency and/or effectiveness of a management accounting technique in an organisational setting.

1   THE BALANCED SCORECARD

1.1   Although segments of a business may be measured by a single performance indicator such as ROI, profit, or cost variances, it might be more suitable to use multiple measures of performance where each measure reflects a **different aspect of achievement**. Where multiple measures are used, several may be **non-financial.**

1.2   The most popular approach in current management thinking is the use of a '**balanced scorecard**' consisting of a variety of indicators both financial and non-financial.

KEY TERM

The **balanced scorecard** approach emphasises the need to provide management with a set of information which covers all relevant areas of performance in an objective and unbiased fashion. The information provided may be both financial and non-financial and cover areas such as profitability, customer satisfaction, internal efficiency and innovation.

1.3 The balanced scorecard focuses on **four different perspectives**, as follows.

Perspective	Question	Explanation
Customer	What do existing and new customers value from us?	Gives rise to targets that matter to customers: cost, quality, delivery, inspection, handling and so on.
Internal	What processes must we excel at to achieve our financial and customer objectives?	Aims to improve internal processes and decision making.
Innovation and learning	Can we continue to improve and create future value?	Considers the business's capacity to maintain its competitive position through the acquisition of new skills and the development of new products.
Financial	How do we create value for our shareholders?	Covers traditional measures such as growth, profitability and shareholder value but set through talking to the shareholder or shareholders direct.

1.4 **Performance targets** are set once the key areas for improvement have been identified, and the balanced scorecard is the main monthly report.

1.5 The scorecard is '**balanced**' as managers are required to think in terms of **all four** perspectives, to prevent improvements being made in one area at the expense of another.

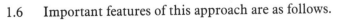

Case example

The fall from grace of Digital Equipment, in the past second only to IBM in the world computer rankings, was examined in a *Financial Times* article. The downfall is blamed on Digital's failure to keep up with the development of the PC, but also on the company's culture.

The company was founded on brilliant creativity, but was insufficiently focused on the bottom line. Outside the finance department, monetary issues were considered vulgar and organisational structure was chaotic. Costs were not a core part of important decisions - 'if expenditure was higher than budget, the problem was simply a bad budget'. Ultimately the low-price world of lean competitors took its toll, leading to huge losses.

1.6 Important features of this approach are as follows.

(a) It looks at both **internal and external** matters concerning the organisation.
(b) It is related to the key elements of a company's **strategy**.
(c) **Financial and non-financial** measures are linked together.

BPP
PROFESSIONAL EDUCATION

Case example

A number of benefits have materialised from the Royal Navy's implementation of the balanced scorecard (which began in 1997/98).

- Improved understanding of key issues and helped managers to focus resources and action more effectively

- Encouraged top managers to be more strategic

- Shorter and more effective board meetings as there is greater clarity and focus on the issues to be tackled

- Slimmer and more effective reporting processes

1.7 As with all techniques, problems can arise when it is applied.

Problem	Explanation
Conflicting measures	Some measures in the scorecard such as research funding and cost reduction may naturally conflict. It is often difficult to determine the balance which will achieve the best results.
Selecting measures	Not only do appropriate measures have to be devised but the number of measures used must be agreed. Care must be taken that the impact of the results is not lost in a sea of information.
Expertise	Measurement is only useful if it initiates appropriate action. Non-financial managers may have difficulty with the usual profit measures. With more measures to consider this problem will be compounded.
Interpretation	Even a financially-trained manager may have difficulty in putting the figures into an overall perspective.

1.8 The scorecard should be used **flexibly**. The process of deciding **what to measure** forces a business to clarify its strategy. For example, a manufacturing company may find that 50% - 60% of costs are represented by bought-in components, so measurements relating to suppliers could usefully be added to the scorecard. These could include payment terms, lead times, or quality considerations.

1.9 An example of how a balanced scorecard might appear is offered below.

Balanced Scorecard

Financial Perspective	
GOALS	**MEASURES**
Survive	Cash flow
Succeed	Monthly sales growth and operating income by division
Prosper	Increase market share and ROI

Customer Perspective	
GOALS	**MEASURES**
New products	Percentage of sales from new products
Responsive supply	On-time delivery (defined by customer)
Preferred supplier	Share of key accounts' purchases
	Ranking by key accounts
Customer partnership	Number of cooperative engineering efforts

Internal Business Perspective	
GOALS	**MEASURES**
Technology capability	Manufacturing configuration vs competition
Manufacturing excellence	Cycle time
	Unit cost
	Yield
Design productivity	Silicon efficiency
	Engineering efficiency
New product introduction	Actual introduction schedule vs plan

Innovation and Learning Perspective	
GOALS	**MEASURES**
Technology leadership	Time to develop next generation of products
Manufacturing learning	Process time to maturity
Product focus	Percentage of products that equal 80% sales
Time to market	New product introduction vs competition

Case example

An oil company (quoted by Kaplan and Norton, *Harvard Business Review*) ties 60% of its executives' bonuses to their achievement of ambitious financial targets on ROI, profitability, cash flow and operating cost, and 40% on indicators of customer satisfaction, retailer satisfaction, employee satisfaction and environmental responsibility.

2 THE PERFORMANCE PYRAMID

2.1 The performance pyramid derives from the idea that an **organisation operates at different levels,** each of which has **different concerns** which should nevertheless **support each other in achieving business objectives.** The pyramid therefore **links** the overall **strategic view** of management with **day to day operations.**

2.2 It includes a range of **objectives** for both **external effectiveness** (such as related to customer satisfaction) and **internal efficiency** (such as related to productivity), which are achieved through measures at the various levels.

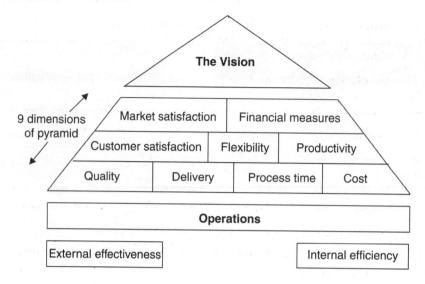

2.3 (a) At **corporate level,** financial and market objectives are set.

(b) At **strategic business unit** level, strategies are developed to achieve these financial and market objectives.

- **Customer satisfaction** is defined as meeting customer expectations.
- **Flexibility** indicates responsiveness of the business operating system as a whole.
- **Productivity** refers to the management of resources such as labour and time.

(c) These in turn are supported by more specific **operational** criteria.

(i) **Quality** of the product or service, consistency of product and fit for the purpose

(ii) **Delivery** of the product or service (the method of distribution, its speed and ease of management)

(iii) **Process time** of all processes from cash collection to order processing to recruitment

(iv) **Cost**, meaning the elimination of all non value added activities

2.4 The pyramid highlights the **links** running between the **vision for the company** and **functional objectives.** For example, a reduction in process time should lead to increased productivity and hence improved financial performance.

3 BUILDING BLOCKS

Question: services v manufacturing

In Chapter 5 we looked at five major characteristics of services that distinguish services from manufacturing. Can you relate them to the provision of a haircut?

Answer

(a) **Intangibility**. A haircut is intangible in itself, and the performance of the service comprises many other intangible factors, like the music in the salon, the personality of the hairdresser, the quality of the coffee.

(b) **Simultaneity/inseparability**. The production and consumption of a haircut are simultaneous, and therefore it cannot be inspected for quality in advance, nor can it be returned if it is not what was required.

(c) **Perishability**. Haircuts are perishable, that is, they cannot be stored. You cannot buy them in bulk, and the hairdresser cannot do them in advance and keep them stocked away in case of heavy demand.

(d) **Heterogeneity/variability**. A haircut is heterogeneous and so the exact service received will vary each time: not only will Justin and Nigel cut hair differently, but Justin will not consistently deliver the same standard of haircut.

(e) **No transfer of ownership.** A haircut does not become the property of the customer.

Question: characteristics of services

Consider how the factors intangibility, simultaneity, perishability, no transfer of ownership and heterogeneity apply to the various services that you use: public transport, your bank account, meals in restaurants, the postal service, your annual holiday and so on.

3.1 Performance measurement in service businesses has sometimes been perceived as difficult because of the five factors listed above, but the modern view is that if something is difficult to measure this is because it has not been clearly enough defined. Fitzgerald *et al* and Fitzgerald & Moon provide **building blocks** for **dimensions, standards** and **rewards** for performance measurement systems in service businesses.

Standards

3.2 These are **ownership, achievability** and **equity**.

(a) To ensure that employees take **ownership** of standards, they need to **participate** in the budget and standard-setting processes. They are then more likely to **accept** the standards, feel more **motivated** as they perceive the standards to be achievable and **morale** is improved. The disadvantage to participation is that it offers the opportunity for the introduction of **budgetary slack**.

(b) Standards need to be set **high enough** to ensure that there is some **sense of achievement** in attaining them, but **not so high** that there is a **demotivating** effect because they are unachievable. It is management's task to find a **balance** between what the organisation perceives as achievable and what employees perceive as achievable.

(c) **It is vital that equity is seen to occur when applying standards for performance measurement purposes. The performance of different business units should** not be measured against the same standards if some units have an inherent advantage unconnected with their own efforts. **For example, divisions operating in different countries should not be assessed against the same standards.**

Exam focus point

Standards were examined in December 2003.

Rewards

3.3 The reward structure of the performance measurement system should guide individuals to work towards standards. Three issues need to be considered if the performance measurement system is to operate successfully: **clarity, motivation** and **controllability**.

(a) The organisation's objectives need to be **clearly understood** by those whose performance is being appraised ie they need to know what goals they are working towards.

(b) Individuals should be **motivated** to work in pursuit of the organisation's strategic objectives. Goal clarity and participation have been shown to contribute to higher levels of motivation to achieve targets, providing managers accept those targets. Bonuses can be used to motivate.

(c) Managers should have a certain level of **controllability** for their areas of responsibility. For example they should not be held responsible for costs over which they have no control.

Dimensions

> ### Exam focus point
>
> Knowledge of Fitzgerald and Moon's dimensions of performance was required in a compulsory question in the December 2003 exam.

3.4 (a) **Competitive performance**, focusing on factors such as sales growth and market share.

(b) **Financial performance**, concentrating on profitability, capital structure and so on.

(c) **Quality of service** looks at matters like reliability, courtesy and competence.

(d) **Flexibility** is an apt heading for assessing the organisation's ability to deliver at the right speed, to respond to precise customer specifications, and to cope with fluctuations in demand.

(e) **Resource utilisation**, not unsurprisingly, considers how efficiently resources are being utilised. This can be problematic because of the complexity of the inputs to a service and the outputs from it and because some of the inputs are supplied by the customer (he or she brings their own hair, their own taste in coffee and so on). Many measures are possible, however, for example 'number of customers per hairdresser', 'waiting time to haircutting time' and so on. Performance measures can be devised easily if it is known what activities are involved in the service.

(f) **Innovation** is assessed in terms of both the innovation process and the success of individual innovations.

3.5 These dimensions can be divided into two sets.

- The **results** (measured by financial performance and competitiveness)
- The **determinants** (the remainder)

Focus on the examination and improvement of the determinants should lead to improvement in the results.

3.6 There is no need to elaborate on **competitive performance**, **financial performance** and **quality of service** issues, all of which have been covered already. The other three dimensions deserve more attention.

Flexibility

3.7 Flexibility has three aspects.

3.8 **Speed of delivery**

Punctuality is vital in some service industries like passenger transport: indeed punctuality is currently one of the most widely publicised performance measures in the UK, because organisations like railway companies are making a point of it. **Measures** include waiting time in queues, as well as late trains. In other types of service it may be more a question of **timeliness**. Does the auditor turn up to do the annual audit during the appointed week? Is the audit done within the time anticipated by the partner or does it drag on for weeks? These aspects are all easily measurable in terms of '**days late**'. Depending upon the circumstances, 'days late' may also reflect on inability to cope with fluctuations in demand.

3.9 Response to customer specifications

The ability of a service organisation to respond to **customers' specifications** is one of the criteria by which Fitzgerald *et al* distinguish between the three different types of service. Clearly a professional service such as legal advice and assistance must be tailored exactly to the customer's needs. Performance is partly a matter of customer perception and so **customer attitude surveys** may be appropriate. However it is also a matter of the diversity of skills possessed by the service organisation and so it can be measured in terms of the **mix of staff skills** and the amount of time spent on **training**. In **mass service** business customisation is not possible by the very nature of the service.

3.10 Coping with demand

This is clearly measurable in quantitative terms in a mass service like a railway company which can ascertain the extent of **overcrowding**. It can also be very closely monitored in service shops: customer **queuing** time can be measured in banks and retailers, for example. Professional services can measure levels of **overtime** worked: excessive amounts indicate that the current demand is too great for the organisation to cope with in the long term without obtaining extra human resources.

Resource utilisation measures

3.11 Resource utilisation is usually measured in terms of **productivity**. The ease with which this may be measured varies according to the service being delivered.

3.12 The main resource of a firm of accountants, for example, is the **time** of various grades of staff. The main output of an accountancy firm is **chargeable hours**.

3.13 In a restaurant it is not nearly so straightforward. Inputs are highly **diverse**: the ingredients for the meal, the chef's time and expertise, the surroundings and the customers' own likes and dislikes. A **customer attitude survey** might show whether or not a customer enjoyed the food, but it could not ascribe the enjoyment or lack of it to the quality of the ingredients, say, rather than the skill of the chef.

3.14 Here are some of the resource utilisation ratios listed by Fitzgerald *et al*.

Business	Input	Output
Andersen Consulting	Man hours available	Chargeable hours
Commonwealth Hotels	Rooms available	Rooms occupied
Railway companies	Train miles available	Passenger miles
Barclays Bank	Number of staff	Number of accounts

Innovation

3.15 In a modern environment in which product quality, product differentiation and continuous improvement are the order of the day, a company that can find innovative ways of satisfying customers' needs has an important **competitive advantage**.

3.16 Fitzgerald *et al* suggest that **individual innovations** should be measured in terms of whether they bring about **improvements in the other five 'dimensions'**.

3.17 The innovating **process** can be measured in terms of how much it **costs** to develop a new service, how **effective** the process is (that is, how innovative is the organisation, if at all?), and how **quickly** it can develop new services. In more concrete terms this might translate into the following.

(a) The amount of **R&D** spending and whether (and how quickly) these costs are recovered from new service sales

(b) The proportion of **new** services to **total** services provided

(c) The time between **identification** of the need for a new service and making it **available**

Question: competitiveness and resource utilisation

A service business has collected some figures relating to its year just ended.

		Budget	Actual
Customer enquiries:	New customers	6,000	9,000
	Existing customers	4,000	3,000
Business won:	New customers	2,000	4,000
	Existing customers	1,500	1,500
Types of services performed:	Service A	875	780
	Service B	1,575	1,850
	Service C	1,050	2,870
Employees:	Service A	5	4
	Service B	10	10
	Service C	5	8

Required

Calculate figures that illustrate competitiveness and resource utilisation.

Answer

Competitiveness can only be measured from these figures by looking at how successful the organisation is at converting enquiries into firm orders.

Percentage of enquiries converted into firm orders

	Budget	Actual
New customers (W1)	33%	44%
Existing customers (W1)	37.5%	50%

Resource utilisation can be measured by looking at average services performed per employee.

	Budget	Actual	Rise
Service A (W2)	175	195	+11.4%
Service B (W2)	157.5	185	+17.5%
Service C (W2)	210	358.75	+70.8%

Workings

1 For example 2,000/6,000 = 33%
2 For example 875/5 = 175

What comments would you make about these results? How well is the business doing?

3.18 There is some debate as to **how far the links between the financial results and the determinants** of those results **can be precisely identified.** Better quality will please customers, but there is a problem of **short-term versus long-term** benefits. Quality costs money now, while the benefits may take a long time to come through.

3.19 There is also the question of **how much quality** is enough: endless improvements that cost a lot of money, but are not necessarily sought by the customers (who may indeed be unwilling to pay for them) will harm long-term profitability.

Exam focus point

These six key areas of performance were examined in the June 2002 exam in one of the compulsory questions.

ATTENTION!

Be prepared to think up performance measures for different areas of an organisation's business. Remember to make the measures relevant to the organisation in question. There is little point in suggesting measures such as waiting times in queues to assess the quality of the service provided by an educational establishment. Try the following question, based in part on a December 2002 exam requirement.

Question: performance indicators

Suggest two separate performance indicators that could be used to assess each of the following areas of a fast food chain's operations.

(a) Food preparation department
(b) Marketing department

Answer

Here are some suggestions.

(a) Material usage per product
    Wastage levels
    Incidences of food poisoning

(b) Market share
    Sales revenue per employee
    Growth in sales revenue

Chapter roundup

- The **balanced scorecard** approach to performance measurement focuses on four different perspectives and uses financial and non-financial indicators.

- The **performance pyramid** highlights the links running between an organisation's vision and its functional objectives.

- Fitzgerald and Moon's **building blocks** for **dimensions, standards** and **rewards** attempt to overcome the problems associated with performance measurement of service businesses.

Quick quiz

1   Which of the following are the four perspectives of the balanced scorecard?

    A   Innovation and learning, customer, financial, competitive
    B   Financial, quality, innovation, internal
    C   Internal, financial, innovation and learning, customer
    D   Customer, quality, competitive, flexibility

2   *Label the performance pyramid below.*

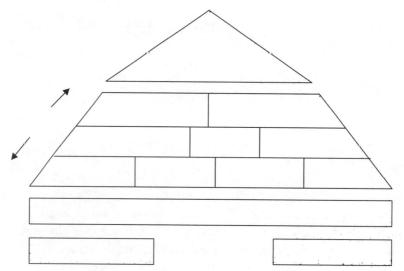

3   *Fill in the blanks.*

    The five characteristics of a service business are .... , ... , ... , ... and ....

4   Fitzgerald and Moon's standards for performance measurement systems are ownership, achievability and controllability. *True or false?*

5   *Fill in the gaps.*

    Fitzgerald and Moon's dimensions can be divided into the results (............................... and ....) and the determinants (............................... , ..., ... and ....) .

Answers to quick quiz

1   C

2

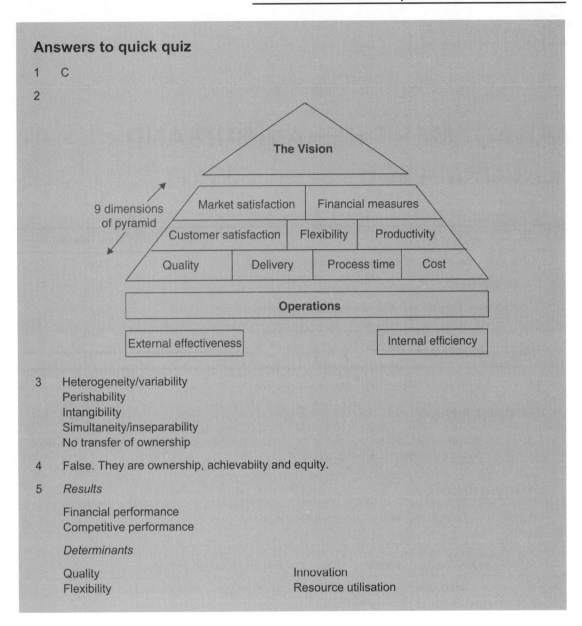

3   Heterogeneity/variability
Perishability
Intangibility
Simultaneity/inseparability
No transfer of ownership

4   False. They are ownership, achievabiity and equity.

5   *Results*

Financial performance
Competitive performance

Determinants

Quality   Innovation
Flexibility   Resource utilisation

Now try the question below from the Exam Question Bank

Number	Level	Marks	Time
12	Exam	20	36 mins

Chapter 15

MANAGEMENT BEHAVIOUR AND PERFORMANCE

Topic list	Syllabus reference
1 Performance measurement systems and behaviour	3(d)
2 Accountability	3(d)
3 Benefits and problems of performance measurement	3(d)
4 Reward schemes and performance measurement	3(d)
5 Management styles	3(d)

Introduction

The impact of **human behaviour** is a theme that runs throughout the syllabus for Paper 3.3. Here we see its **effect on performance measurement**.

Study guide

Section 17 – Management behaviour and performance

- Explain the relationship between performance measurement systems and behaviour

- Discuss how performance measurement systems can influence behaviour

- Consider the accountability issues arising from performance measurement systems

- Identify the ways in which performance measurement systems may send the 'wrong signals' and result in undesirable business consequences

- Comment on the potential beneficial and adverse consequences of linking reward schemes to performance measurement

- Explain how management style needs to be considered when designing an effective performance measurement system

Section 21 – Budgeting and budgetary control III

- Compare and contrast ways in which alternative management styles may affect the operation of budgetary planning and control systems

Exam guide

The examiner has highlighted the topic of 'differentiating managerial from business unit performance' as a potential issue for inclusion in the paper's compulsory questions.

The issues covered in this chapter are useful background to the Oxford Brookes degree Research and Analysis Project Topic 1, which requires you to analyse the efficiency and/or effectiveness of a management accounting technique in an organisational setting.

1 PERFORMANCE MEASUREMENT SYSTEMS AND BEHAVIOUR

1.1 If people **know** that their performance is being **measured** then this will **affect the standard** of their performance, particularly if they know that they will be **rewarded** for achieving a certain level of performance.

1.2 Ideally, performance **measures** will be devised that **reward behaviour** that **maximises the corporate good**. In practice, however, it is not quite so simple.

    (a) There is a danger that managers and staff will **concentrate** only upon what they know is **being measured**. This is not a problem if every important issue has a measure attached to it, but such a system is difficult to devise and implement in practice.

    (b) **Individuals** have their own goals, but good performance that satisfies their own sense of what is important will not necessarily work towards the **corporate good**.

1.3 Point (b) is the problem of **goal congruence**.

1.4 EXAMPLE: PERFORMANCE MEASUREMENT AND BEHAVIOUR

    (a) As we saw in Chapter 11, a divisional manager whose performance is assessed on the basis of his division's ROI might reject a proposal that produces an ROI greater than the group's target return if it reduces his division's overall return.

    (b) Traditional feedback control would seek to eliminate an adverse material price variance by requiring managers to source cheaper, possibly lower quality, suppliers. This may run counter to an organisational objective to implement a system of TQM with the aim of reducing quality costs.

Measuring managerial performance

1.5 One of the problems of measuring managerial performance is **segregating managerial performance from the economic performance of their department or division.** The distinction is very important. Horngren provides a good illustration (with BPP's emphasis).

> 'The most **skilful divisional manager is often put in charge of the sickest division in an attempt to change its fortunes**. Such an attempt may take years, not months. Furthermore the manager's efforts may merely result in bringing the division up to a minimum acceptable ROI. The division may continue to be a poor profit performer in comparison with other divisions. If top management relied solely on the absolute ROI to judge management, the skilful manager would be foolish to accept such a trouble-shooting assignment.'

1.6 It is difficult to devise performance measures that relate specifically to a manager to judge his or her performance as a manager. It is possible to calculate statistics to assess the manager as an employee like any other employee (days absent, professional qualifications obtained, personability and so on), but this is not the point. As soon as the issue of **ability as a manager** arises it is necessary to **consider him in relation to his area of responsibility.** If we want to know how good a manager is at marketing the only information there is to go on is the marketing performance of his division (which may or may not be traceable to his own efforts).

Uncontrollable factors

1.7 It is generally considered to be unreasonable to assess managers' performance in relation to matters that are beyond their control. Therefore **management performance measures** should **only include those items that are directly controllable by the manager** in question.

1.8 However, there is some research evidence that there may be good **reasons to hold managers accountable for factors that are beyond their control.**

(a) Motivating them to **pay attention** to cost and revenue **factors that are relevant** even if they are not controllable, such as interest expenses.

(b) Encouraging them to **respond to economic and competitive conditions** such as a rival's lower prices or higher quality.

1.9 In any case, there are **different degrees of controllability.**

(a) A divisional manager may have no control over the level of head office costs. It may seem unfair that X division, say, is allocated 10% of £1m = £100,000, when it is actually demands made by division Y that caused costs to be that high rather than £500,000 (10% × £500,000 = £50,000).

However, X division does have control over the relative demands it places on head office. If it placed fewer demands perhaps its percentage contribution could fall, say, to 5%.

(b) Likewise a division may not have control over the overall level of a group's interest charge, which will depend on the source of funds and on other division's activities. However, it may have control over its working capital requirements and perhaps over capital expenditure.

2 ACCOUNTABILITY

Agency theory

2.1 Agency theory considers the **relationship between a principal** (such as the owners of a company, the shareholders) **and an agent** (such as an organisation's managers and employees). George Brown, the examiner of the equivalent paper to 3.3 under the old syllabus, explains (with BPP's emphasis):

'The problem is "how can the agent be motivated and monitored?". The motivation may be achieved by the payment of ....a reward. The monitoring may be through the submission of regular accounts...(as a measure of performance). The key requirements are that:

- the **agent** must have to **give an account of performance** to the principal; and
- the **principal** must be able to **hold the agent to account**.'

('Accountability and performance measurement', *ACCA Student's Newsletter*, August 1998)

2.2 In the corporate sector, the identification of agents (managers and employees) and principals (shareholders) is comparatively straightforward. In public sector and non-profit seeking organisations there are likely to be multiple principals (such as the Government and students in the Higher Education sector), making identification more difficult.

2.3 The theory makes certain **assumptions about individuals as agents,** listed in Wilson and Chua, *Managerial Accounting: Method and Meaning* (1993) as follows.

(a) They behave rationally in seeking to maximise their own utility.

(b) They seek financial and non-financial rewards.

(c) They tend to be risk-averse and, hence, reluctant to innovate.

(d) Their individual interests will not always coincide with those of their principals.

(e) They prefer leisure to hard work.

(f) They have greater knowledge about their operating performance and actions than is available to their principals.

2.4 Key issues in agency theory are **attitudes to risk** and the **observability of effort**.

(a) Conventional management accounting assumes that principals protect agents from risk - it only makes managers responsible for things they can control. Agency theory suggests that if principals are risk averse then they should share the risk with agents and this can increase the utility of both parties. Making a large part of an executive's potential reward subject to some profit target is a simple example of such a contract.

(b) The principal may find it difficult to observe the agent's efforts. Alternatively the principal may not be able to evaluate the effort because he does not possess the information on which the decision to expend that much effort was based.

Accounting and accountability

2.5 Accountancy via the use of **management control systems** (budgeting and standard costing) has a key role to play in the development of regimes of accountability. Such control systems provide two forms of accountability.

2.6 **Hard accountability** involves consideration of financial and quantitative information and covers three areas.

(a) **Counting** (that is, **converting activities and outcomes into numbers**), such as the number and type of warranty claims

(b) **Ensuring that the numbers are accounted for** (in other words, **reporting on activities and outcomes** and providing a discussion of **how and why they have occurred**). The examiner's example is to report 'we achieved 20% new customers though promising a just-in-time delivery of orders (**how**) and 80% of complaints related to an inability to meet the JIT timetable because of internal failure of the 'pull-through' system due to lack of a synchronised manufacturing system (**why**)'.

(c) **Being held accountable for** accounting and also for the events and circumstances leading to the records, such as being held responsible for failing to meet unrealistic production schedules and for failing to take action such as implementing overtime working to try and meet the schedules.

2.7 **Soft accountability** involves consideration of the human input to the system and its role in shaping, evaluating and implementing goals. **Self accountability** achieved by employees, for example, will be affected by financial and non-financial rewards offered, training and developments programmes and the way in which employees are grouped in order to achieve specific business outcomes (such as multidisciplinary project teams and quality circles).

2.8 George Brown suggests that **accountability requires** the implementation of the following **steps**.

- 'choose and make public a range of accepted performance measures;
- ensure that the benefits of the performance measures have been identified;
- identify and understand possible problems in the use of performance measures;
- consider ways in which to counter perceived problems in the use of performance measures.'

3 BENEFITS AND PROBLEMS OF PERFORMANCE MEASUREMENT

Benefits of performance measures

3.1 Berry, Broadbent and Otley provide the following list.

- Clarify the objectives of the organisation
- Develop agreed measures of activity
- Greater understanding of processes
- Facilitate comparison of performance in different organisations
- Facilitate the setting of targets for the organisation and its managers
- Promote accountability of the organisation to its stakeholders

Problems

3.2 Here is their list of possible problems accompanying the use of performance measures.

- **Tunnel vision** (undue focus on performance measures to the detriment of other areas)

- **Sub-optimisation** (focus on some objectives so that others are not achieved)

- **Myopia** (short-sightedness leading to the neglect of longer-term objectives)

- **Measure fixation** (measures and behaviour in order to achieve specific performance indicators which may not be effective)

- **Misrepresentation** ('creative' reporting to suggest that a result is acceptable)

- **Misinterpretation** (failure to recognise the complexity of the environment in which the organisation operates)

- **Gaming** (deliberate distortion of a measure to secure some strategic advantage)

- **Ossification** (an unwillingness to change the performance measure scheme once it has been set up)

3.3 These problems highlight the issue of **congruence between the goals of individuals and the goals of the organisation.**

(a) We looked at organisational goals or objectives in Chapter 10.

(b) Individual goals may be financially or non-financially orientated and relate to remuneration, promotion prospects, job security, job satisfaction and self esteem.

3.4 Each **individual** may face a **conflict** between taking action to ensure organisational goals and action to ensure personal goals.

3.5 **Ways in which the problems may be reduced**

(a) **Involvement of staff** at all levels in the development and implementation of the scheme should help to reduce gaming and tunnel vision.

(b) A **flexible use** of performance measures should help to reduce measure fixation and misrepresentation.

(c) Keeping the performance measurement system under **constant review** should help to overcome the problems of ossification and gaming.

(d) Give careful consideration to the **dimensions of performance**. Quantifying all objectives should help to overcome sub-optimisation, while a focus on measuring customer satisfaction should reduce tunnel vision and sub-optimisation.

(e)   Consideration should be given to the **audit of the system**. Expert interpretation of the performance measurement scheme should help to provide an idea of the incidence of the problems, while a careful audit of the data used should help to reduce the incidence and impact of measure fixation, misinterpretation and gaming.

(f)   **Recognition of the key feature** necessary in any scheme (a long-term view/perspective amongst staff, a sensible number of measures, benchmarks which are independent of past activity) should help to overcome the range of problems listed above.

4   REWARD SCHEMES AND PERFORMANCE MEASUREMENT

4.1   In many organisations, senior management try to motivate managers and employees by offering organisational rewards (more pay and promotion) for the achievement of certain levels of performance. The **conventional theory of reward structures is that if the organisation establishes procedures for formal measurement of performance,** and **rewards individuals for good performance, individuals will be more likely to direct their efforts towards achieving the organisation's goals.**

4.2   **Beneficial consequences of linking reward schemes and performance**

(a)   There is some evidence that performance-related pay does give individuals an incentive to achieve a good performance level.

(b)   Effective schemes also attract and keep the employees valuable to an organisation.

(c)   By tying an organisation's key performance indicators to a scheme, it is clear to all employees what performance creates organisational success.

(d)   By rewarding performance, an effective scheme creates an organisation focused on continuous improvement.

(e)   Schemes based on shares can motivate employees/managers to act in the long-term interests of the organisation by doing things to increase the organisation's market value.

Case example

Chrysler Corporation gave many of its executives cash bonuses for performance during 1993. For the 200 most senior executives, the cash bonuses were about 100% of salary. For the next 100 executives, the bonuses amounted to about 80% of salary. Lower-level executives received much less.

The Chrysler bonus plan rewarded performance on the basis of three factors.

- Quality (measured by warranty claims)
- Customer satisfaction (measured by surveys)
- Profitability

The size of the bonus pool available for distribution reflected whether performance targets were met in all three areas. If performance targets were not met in some areas the pool was reduced proportionately. If goals were exceeded in all three areas, the bonus pool expanded to 125% of its original size.

The bonus pool for 1993 achieved its maximum amount.

4.3   On the other hand, a number of **problems** have been associated with their use.

(a)   A serious problem that can arise is that performance-related pay and performance evaluation systems can **encourage dysfunctional behaviour.** Many investigations have noted the tendency of managers to pad their budgets either in anticipation of cuts by superiors or to make subsequent variances more favourable.

(b) Perhaps of even more concern are the numerous examples of managers making **decisions that are contrary to the wider purposes of the organisation.**

(c) Schemes designed to **ensure long-term achievements** (that is, to combat short termism) **may not motivate** since efforts and reward are too distant in time from each other (or managers may not think they will be around that long!).

(d) It is questionable whether any performance measures or set of measures can provide a **comprehensive assessment of what a single person achieves** for an organisation. There will always be the old chestnut of lack of goal congruence, employees being committed to what is measured, rather than the objectives of the organisation.

(e) **Self-interested performance** may be encouraged at the **expense of team work**.

(f) High levels of output (whether this is number of calls answered or production of product X) may be achieved at the expense of **quality**.

(g) In order to make bonuses more accessible, **standards and targets may have to be lowered,** with knock-on effects on quality.

(h) They **undervalue intrinsic rewards** (which reflect the satisfaction that an individual experiences from doing a job and the opportunity for growth that the job provides) given that they promote extrinsic rewards (bonuses and so on).

Group schemes

4.4 Group schemes may **enhance team spirit and co-operation** as well as provide performance incentives, but they may also **create pressures within the group** if some individuals are seen to be 'not pulling their weight'.

Question: problems in the public sector

In addition to the problems outlined above, what particular problems could occur in the public sector?

Answer

(a) **Timescale**. Many projects (for example, environmental programmes) can only be assessed for effectiveness in the long term.

(b) **The political dimension**. A senior manager in the public sector may be set a goal which is highly undesirable from the point of view of opposition parties: if a change of power is imminent, the manager might later be rewarded for **not** achieving it.

5 MANAGEMENT STYLES

5.1 In a 1974 study, Hopwood identified three distinct management styles.

Style	Hopwood says ...
Budget-constrained style	'The manager's performance is primarily evaluated upon the basis of his ability to continually **meet the budget** on a short-term basis . . . stressed at the expense of other valued and important criteria and the manager will receive unfavourable feedback from his superior if, for instance, his actual costs exceed the budgeted costs, regardless of other considerations.'

Style	Hopwood says ...
Profit-conscious style	'The manager's performance is evaluated on the basis of his ability to **increase the general effectiveness** of his unit's operations in relation to the long-term purposes of the organisation'. '
Non-accounting style	'The budgetary information plays a **relatively unimportant** part in the superior's evaluation of the manager's performance.'

5.2 With the **profit-conscious** style of evaluation, budget reports are not dealt with in the rigid sense of analysing the size and direction of variances: the information in budget reports is supplemented with **information from other sources** and **interpreted in a wider sense**.

5.3 **Hopwood's summary of the effects of the three styles of evaluation**

	Style of evaluation		
Effects	**Budget-constrained**	**Profit-conscious**	**Non-accounting**
Involvement with costs	HIGH	HIGH	LOW
Job-related tension	HIGH	MEDIUM	MEDIUM
Manipulation of accounting reports	EXTENSIVE	LITTLE	LITTLE
Relations with the supervisor	POOR	GOOD	GOOD
Relations with colleague	POOR	GOOD	GOOD

5.4 The **profit-conscious style appears to be optimum** in terms of the variable examined but Hopwood pointed out this may **differ between organisations** and **between activities in the same organisation.**

5.5 **Otley** carried out a separate study and found **no significant difference** in job-related tension and so on, whichever managerial style was adopted. Otley's study considered managers who were comparatively independent, however, had a high degree of control over cash and resources and operated in a more predictable environment than the managers studied by Hopwood.

5.6 Otley's research indicates that the **context** in which budgetary control is used is as **important** as the style in which it is used. For example, some managers (like those studied by Hopwood) are highly interdependent and face a good deal of uncertainty, so that good performance depends upon others' co-operation and favourable external circumstances. Such situations do not match well with the budget-constrained style.

Exam focus point

Watch out for the topics covered in this chapter in exams in 2004, as they have yet to be examined in their own right.

BPP
PROFESSIONAL EDUCATION

Chapter roundup

- It is generally considered to be unreasonable to assess managers' performance in relation to matters that are beyond their control. Therefore **management performance measures** should **only include those items that are directly controllable by the manager** in question.

- **Hard accountability** involves consideration of financial and quantitative information. **Soft accountability** considers the human input to the system and its role in shaping, evaluating and implementing goals.

- Berry, Broadbent and Otley have described various **problems and benefits of performance measurement.**

- The conventional theory that **reward schemes** linked to the achievement of key performance measures will encourage goal congruence is open to question.

- Hopwood identified three distinct **management styles**.

Quick quiz

1   Which of the following is not an area of hard accountability?

   A   Ensuring that numbers are accounted for
   B   Counting
   C   Interaction with other employees
   D   Being held accountable

2   *Link the following terms (problems of performance measurement) to the correct definitions.*

   Terms

   (a)   Tunnel vision
   (b)   Sub-optimisation
   (c)   Myopia
   (d)   Measure fixation
   (e)   Misrepresentation
   (f)   Misinterpretation
   (g)   Gaming
   (h)   Ossification

   Definitions

   1   Deliberate distortion of a measure to secure some strategic advantage

   2   'Creative' reporting to suggest that a result is acceptable

   3   Undue focus on performance measures to the detriment of other areas

   4   Short-sightedness leading to the neglect of long-term objectives

   5   Focus on some objectives so that others are not achieved

   6   An unwillingness to change the performance measure scheme once it has been set up

   7   Failure to recognise the complexity of the environment in which the organisation operates

   8   Measures and behaviour in order to achieve specific performance indicators which may not be effective.

3   Complete the table below about management style.

| | Style of evaluation | | |
Effects	Budget-constrained	Profit-conscious	Non-accounting
Involvement with costs			
Job-related tension			
Manipulation of accounting reports			
Relations with the supervisor			
Relations with colleague			

4   Fill in the blanks.

Reward schemes undervalue .... rewards (which reflect the satisfaction that an individual experiences from doing a job and the opportunity for growth that the job provides) given that they promote .... rewards (bonuses and so on).

5   There is evidence to suggest there may be good reasons to hold managers accountable for factors that are beyond their control. *True or false?*

Answers to quick quiz

1   C

2   (a) 3
    (b) 5
    (c) 4
    (d) 8
    (e) 2
    (f) 7
    (g) 1
    (h) 6

3

| | Style of evaluation | | |
Effects	Budget-constrained	Profit-conscious	Non-accounting
Involvement with costs	HIGH	HIGH	LOW
Job-related tension	HIGH	MEDIUM	MEDIUM
Manipulation of accounting reports	EXTENSIVE	LITTLE	LITTLE
Relations with the supervisor	POOR	GOOD	GOOD
Relations with colleague	POOR	GOOD	GOOD

4   intrinsic
    extrinsic

5   True

Now try the question below from the Exam Question Bank

Number	Level	Marks	Time
13	Exam	20	36 mins

Part D
Planning and
control

Chapter 16

STRATEGIC PLANNING AND CONTROL

Topic list	Syllabus reference
1 Strategic versus operational planning and control	4(a)
2 Organisational survival and life cycle issues	4(a)
3 Strategic/corporate planning	4(a)
4 Strategic planning versus freewheeling opportunism	4(a)
5 SWOT analysis	4(a)
6 Risk and uncertainty	4(a)
7 Strategic management accounting in multinational companies	4(a)

Introduction

This chapter introduces the part of the text covering **different aspects of control**. It develops some of the topics covered in Chapter 1 and also describes the steps organisations take to ensure survival and growth, objectives described in Chapter 11.

Study guide

Section 1 – Strategic planning and decision making

- Contrast strategic planning with short term/operational planning (see also Chapters 1 and 2)

Section 18 – Strategic planning and control

- Compare strategic with operational planning and control (see also Chapters 1 and 2)

- Explain how organisational survival in the long term necessitates consideration of life cycle issues

- Identify the role of corporate planning in clarifying corporate objectives, making strategic decisions and checking progress towards the objectives

- Explain the structure of corporate planning

- Discuss the combining of strategic planning with freewheeling opportunism in a fast changing business environment

- Comment on the potential conflict between strategic plans and short term localised decisions

- Explain the principles of SWOT

- Explain how SWOT analysis may assist in the planning process

- Explain how risk and uncertainty play an especially important role in long term strategic planning that relies upon forecasts of exogenous variables

- Explain aspects of strategic management in the context of multinational companies

Exam guide

The topics covered in this chapter may provide the **context** for the company in an exam question. Performance measurement is conducted according to how an organisation meets its objectives, and these goals are set in the context of strategy.

The issues covered in this chapter are useful background to the Oxford Brookes degree Research and Analysis Project Topic 14, which requires you to investigate recent investment decisions by an organisations of your choice and how the use of different methods of risk and uncertainty analysis might affect such decisions.

1 STRATEGIC VERSUS OPERATIONAL PLANNING AND CONTROL

1.1 Chapters 1, 2 and 10 introduced the concepts of planning and control at different levels of the organisational hierarchy, and some of the main issues behind control systems.

1.2 To summarise, we can contrast briefly the **differences between planning and control** at corporate strategic and at operational levels.

Strategic	Operational
'Broad brush' targets	Detailed
Whole organisation	Departmental activities
External input	Mainly internal information
External focus	Internal focus, on actual procedures
Future-orientated feedforward control	More concerned with monitoring current performance against plan
Potential for double loop feedback, ie the opportunity to change the plan	Mainly single loop feedback; performance must change, not the plan

Linking strategy and operations

1.3 The former Paper 9 examiner wrote an **article** on this topic. The article includes a case study of a fictional company that adopts new management ideas like TQM, JIT and ABC as its strategy for dealing with a high level of customer complaints. The company is trying to improve **quality** and **speed of delivery** while **controlling costs**, but it faces a number of problems.

> 'The achievement of long-term goals will require strategic planning which is linked to short-term operational planning ... . If there is no link between strategic planning and operational planning the result is likely to be *unrealistic plans, inconsistent goals, poor communication and inadequate performance measurement.*'
>
> (George Brown, 'Management Accounting and Strategic Management', *ACCA Students' Newsletter*, March 1994)

Unrealistic plans

1.4 Unrealistic operational plans will force staff to **try too hard** with **too few resources**. Mistakes and failure are almost inevitable. This means poor quality products: costs include lost sales, arranging for returns, and time wasted dealing with complaints.

1.5 **Over-ambitious** plans may also mean that more stocks are produced than an organisation could realistically expect to sell (so costs of write-offs, opportunity costs of wasted resources, and unnecessary stock holding costs are incurred).

Inconsistent goals

1.6 Inconsistent strategic planning and operational planning goals may mean **additional costs** are incurred. An operational plan may require additional inspection points in a production process to ensure quality products are delivered to customers. The resulting extra costs will be at odds with the strategic planning goal of **minimum cost**.

Poor communication

1.7 **Poor communication** between senior management who set strategic goals and lower-level operational management could mean that operational managers are **unaware** of the strategic planning goal, say to sustain competitive advantage at minimum cost through speedy delivery of quality products to customers.

1.8 Some operational managers may therefore choose to focus on quality of product while others attempt to produce as many products as possible as quickly as they can; still others will simply keep their heads down and do as little as possible. This will lead to **lack of co-ordination**: there will be bottlenecks in some operational areas, needing expensive extra resources in the short term, and wasteful idle time in other areas.

Inadequate performance measurement

1.9 Inadequate performance measurement will mean that an organisation has little idea of which areas are performing well and which **need to improve**. If quality of product and speed of delivery are the main sources of competitive advantage a business needs to know how good it is at these things.

1.10 For example, if an organisation measures only **conventional accounting results** it will know how much stock it has and how much it has spent, say, on 'carriage out', but it will not know the **opportunity cost** of cancelled sales through not having stock available when needed, or not being able to deliver it on time. Equally the **quality** of products needs to be measured in terms not only of sales achieved, but also in terms of **customer complaints** and feedback: again the cost is the opportunity cost of lost sales.

Strategic control

1.11 Control at a strategic level means **asking** the question: **'is the organisation on target to meet its overall objectives and is control action needed to turn it around?'**

Case example

Ericsson is the world's third largest supplier of mobile phones. On 26 January 2001, the Financial Times carried the following report about control action Ericsson was taking.

By Christopher Brown-Humes in Stockholm, Dan Roberts in London and Richard Waters in New York.

Ericsson, the world's third biggest supplier of mobile phones, is today expected to announce it is **pulling out of handset manufacturing in a bid to stem huge losses** in its consumer products division...

The company will stress it remains committed to mobile phones. It will continue research and development and marketing activities, and phones will still carry the Ericsson brand.

Ericsson is believed to have ruled out any withdrawal from the handset market on the grounds that knowledge of the market is integral to its telecommunications infrastructure business – by far the biggest part of its operations – and is crucial to its ability to be able to offer telecoms operators a full service. But it has acknowledged that the need to restore profitability to its beleaguered handset division is paramount at a time when the market is deteriorating.

Other big handset makers, including Motorola, the biggest US producer, have **contracted out** some of their production…

The group has launched a range of measures to improve performance, including switching production from Sweden and the US to lower cost countries in Latin America and eastern Europe.

But analysts are not convinced the measures will be enough to get the group's handsets operations back into profit by the second half of this year, in line with the company's target. Some believe the groups may eventually pull out of mobile phones altogether.

Question: strategic control

What do you think the Ericsson case example above says about strategic control?

Answer

- In the long-term, the **control action focuses on** the **survival** of the firm, as losses of such magnitude cannot be sustained.

- Complicated **trade-offs** are needed. Ericsson will retain some handset activities to maintain competences needed for other business areas.

- It is in part **responding to external stimulus**, the declining handset market, as there is an element of **feedforward** control.

- The **control action** – withdrawal – is being taken to satisfy the overall company target of profitability.

For further context, in 2001 Ericsson has 10% of the global handset market, which has changed out of all recognition in recent years. **From being a specialist item, mobile phones are now a commodity driven by fashion and speed to market**, rather than a specialised technical activity.

'The company has improved its time to market and has produced some successful new models, such as the T20'. However this **single loop control** is not enough.

1.12 **Strategic control measures** might **require complicated trade-offs** between **current financial performance and longer-term competitive position**, and **between different desirable ways of building competitive strength**. The main task is to ensure that the **right things are measured**.

Gaps and false alarms

1.13 Many firms **measure the wrong things** and **do not measure the right things**.

(a) **False alarms** motivate managers to **improve areas** where there are **few benefits** to the organisation.

- Over-emphasis on direct costs is foolish when most costs are overheads

- Labour efficiency measures are easily manipulated and ignore labour effectiveness.

- Machine standard hours are irrelevant, as long as the firm has enough capacity.

(b) **Gaps** are important **areas** that are **neglected**.

- New product introduction
- Customer satisfaction
- Employee involvement

(c) **Different measures apply to different industries.** In continuous processes, such as chemicals, throughput time is not important as there will always be buffer stock. However, it is important in consumer electronics.

Strategic control systems

1.14 To **encourage** the **measurement of the right things,** firms can institute formal or informal systems of **strategic control**. There are four **influences on a strategic control system.**

- The **time-lag** between **strategic control** measures and **financial results**
- The **linkages** with the other businesses in a group
- The **risks** the business faces
- The **sources** of competitive advantage.

1.15 **Formal systems of strategic control**

Step 1. **Strategy review.** Review the progress of strategy.

Step 2. Identify **milestones of performance** (strategic objectives), both quantitative and qualitative (eg market share, quality, innovation, customer satisfaction).

- Milestones are identified **after** the business's **critical success factors** have been outlined.

- Milestones are **short-term steps** towards **long-term goals**.

- Milestones enable managers to monitor **actions** (eg whether a new product has been launched) and results (eg the success of the launch).

Step 3. **Set target achievement levels.** These need not be exclusively quantitative.

(i) Targets must be reasonably precise.
(ii) Targets should suggest strategies and tactics.
(iii) **Competitive benchmarks** are targets set **relative to the competition.**

Step 4. **Formal monitoring of the strategic process.** Reporting is less frequent than for financial reporting.

Step 5. **Reward.** For most systems, there is little relationship between the achievement of strategic objectives and the **reward system,** although some companies are beginning to use measures of strategic performance as part of the annual *bonus* calculations.

1.16 Many companies **do not** 'define explicit strategic objectives' or milestones that are regularly and formally monitored as part of the ongoing management control process'.

(a) Choosing one objective (eg market share) might encourage managers to ignore or downgrade others (eg profitability), or lead managers to ignore wider issues.

(b) Informality promotes flexibility.

(c) Openness of communication is necessary.

(d) Finite objectives overlook nuances especially in human resource management. In other words, an objective like 'employee commitment' is necessary for success, but hard to measure quantitatively.

1.17 Informal control does not always work because it enables managers to skate over important strategic issues and choices.

Guidelines for a strategic control system

1.18 The characteristics of strategic control systems can be measured on two axes.

(a) How **formal** is the process?

(b) How many **milestones** are identified for **review**?

1.19 As there is no optimum number of milestones or degree of formality, *Goold and Quinn* suggest these guidelines.

Guideline	Comment
Linkages	If there are linkages between businesses in a group, the formality of the process should be low, to avoid co-operation being undermined.
Diversity	If there is a great deal of diversity, it is doubtful whether any overall strategic control system is appropriate, especially if the critical success factors for each business are different.
Criticality	Firms whose strategic stance depends on decisions which can, if they go wrong, destroy the company as a whole (eg launching a new technology) need strategic control systems which, whether formal or informal, have a large number of milestones so that emerging problems in any area will be easily and quickly detected.
Change	Fashion-goods manufacturers must respond to relatively high levels of environmental turbulence, and have to react quickly. If changes are rapid, a system of low formality and few measures may be appropriate, merely because the control processes must allow decisions to be taken in changed contexts.
Competitive advantage	(a) Businesses with few sources of competitive advantage. Control can easily focus on perhaps market share or quality with high formality.
	(b) Businesses with many sources of competitive advantage. Success over a wider number of areas is necessary and the firm should not just concentrate on one of them.

1.20 EXAMPLE: STRATEGIC CONTROL REPORT

Date: March 20X4
Source: January 20X0 planning document
Mission: Market share

1. *Long-term targets, to be achieved by 20X9*

    (a) X% value of market share
    (b) Y% profitability over the decade

    Status: March 20X4. Market share lower than anticipated, owing to unexpected competition. Profits lower than expected because of loss of scale economies and increased marketing costs.

    Outlook. Profit will be improved thanks to cost-cutting measures. Market share target might be missed.

2. *Assumptions*

    The home market is growing only slowly, and is becoming mature. There are limited opportunities for segmentation.

    Overseas markets are likely to expand by Z% as some are reducing tariffs.

    Status March 20X4. The home market has matured more quickly than expected. Overseas market growth can compensate for this.

3. *Critical success factors*

    Although market share and hence profit are lower than expected, as a result of loss of scale economies, we have become more efficient. Defects per 1,000 have been reduced to 0.3, which allows us to bid for the Japanese contract.

4. *Key tasks*
    *   Launch of budget products for overseas markets
    *   Setting up of a computerised distribution system to enhance speedy response to demand and to cut warehousing costs
    *   Get BS EN ISO 9000 certification

1.21 **Desirable features of strategic performance measures**

Role of measures	Comment
Focus attention on what matters in the long term	Shareholder wealth?
Identify and communicate drivers of success	How the organisation generates shareholder value over the long term.
Support organisational learning	Enable the organisation to improve its performance.
Provide a basis for reward	Rewards should be based on strategic issues not just performance in any one year.

1.22 **Characteristics of strategic performance measures**

*   Measureable
*   Meaningful
*   Defined by the strategy and relevant to it

*   Consistently measured
*   Re-evaluated regularly
*   Acceptable

2   ORGANISATIONAL SURVIVAL AND LIFE CYCLE ISSUES

Exam focus point

The product life cycle and its impact on pricing (see Chapter 22) was examined in June 2004.

2.1 The **product life cycle model** suggests that a **product** goes through **stages** – launch, growth, maturity and decline - each of which has **different financial and operating characteristics**.

KEY TERM

Product life cycle. The period which begins with the initial product specification, and ends with the withdrawal from the market of both the product and its support. It is characterised by defined stages including research, development, introduction, maturity, decline and abandonment.

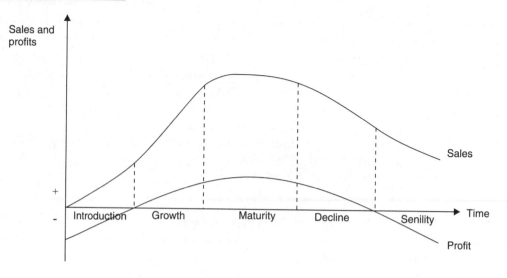

2.2 Introduction

- A new product takes time to find acceptance by would-be purchasers and there is a slow growth in sales. Unit costs are high because of low output and expensive sales promotion.

- There may be early teething troubles with production technology.

- The product for the time being is a loss-maker.

2.3 Growth

- If the new product gains market acceptance, sales will eventually rise more sharply and the product will start to make profits.

- Competitors are attracted. As sales and production rise, unit costs fall.

2.4 Maturity. The rate of sales growth slows down and the product reaches a period of maturity which is probably the longest period of a successful product's life. Most products on the market will be at the mature stage of their life. Profits are good.

2.5 Decline. Eventually, sales will begin to decline so that there is over-capacity of production in the industry. Severe competition occurs, profits fall and some producers leave the market. The remaining producers seek means of prolonging the product life by modifying it and searching for new market segments. Many producers are reluctant to leave the market, although some inevitably do because of falling profits.

Control measures

2.6 It is possible to summarise the different information and financial control needs of different stages of the product life cycle.

	Introduction	*Growth*	*Maturity*	*Decline*
Financial characteristics	High business risk. Negative net cash flow. DCF evaluation for overall investment	High business risk. Neutral net cash flow	Medium business risk. Positive cash flow	Low risk. Neutral-positive cash flow
Critical success factors	Increasing time to launch	Market share growth. Sustaining competitive advantage	Contribution per unit of limiting factor. Customer retention	Timely exit

	Introduction	Growth	Maturity	Decline
Information needs	Market research into demand	Market growth/ share. Diminishing returns. Competitor marketing strategies	Comparative competitor costs. Limiting factors	Rate of decline. Best time to leave. Reliable sale values of assets
Financial and other controls	Strategic 'milestones'. Physical evaluation. Mainly non-financial measures owing to volatility (eg rate of take up by consumers)	DCF Market share Marketing objectives	ROI Profit margin Maintaining market share	Free cash flow (for investment elsewhere)

The life cycle and long-term survival

2.7 The **returns** expected from a product will depend on where that product is in its life cycle.

Performance measure	Stage in the life cycle			
	Introduction	Growth	Maturity	Decline
Cash	Net user	Net user	Generator	Generator
Return on capital	Not important	Not important	Important	Important
Growth	Vital	Vital	Grow with new uses	Negative growth
Profit	Not expected	Important	Important	Very important

2.8 Ideally, firms should therefore have a **number of products at different stages** in the life cycle.

   (a) New products at the introduction and growth stages which, when mature, will generate cash.

   (b) Mature products which generate cash for new investment. Mature products generate most of the profits.

   (c) Products in decline to be harvested.

2.9 A product portfolio should also contain **products with life cycles of different lengths**.

2.10 A product's **life cycle** can be '**extended**' by the use of **technology.** Demand for recorded music has been met by vinyl, CD, DVD and internet downloads via MP3, different technological solutions to the same customer need.

3   STRATEGIC/CORPORATE PLANNING

KEY TERM

Strategic/corporate/long-range planning is the formulation, evaluation and selection of strategies for the purpose of preparing a long-term plan of action to attain objectives.

CIMA *Official Terminology*

BPP
PROFESSIONAL EDUCATION

Strategic planning model

3.1 To develop a business strategy, an organisation has to decide the following.

- What it is good at
- How the market might change
- How customer satisfaction can be delivered
- What might constrain realisation of the plan
- What should be done to minimise risk
- What actions should be put in place

To quote an article on strategy in the June 1998 issue of *Accountancy*, 'the real test of a good strategy is whether it enables the business to use its capabilities successfully in circumstances it cannot confidently predict'.

The structure of strategic planning

3.2 The **rational model** of strategic planning divides into a number of different stages: strategic **analysis**, strategic **choice** and **implementation**. This is illustrated in the diagram on the following page.

Strategic analysis

3.3

	Stage	Comment	Key tools, models, techniques
Step 1.	Mission and/or vision	Mission denotes values, the business's rationale for existing; vision refers to where the organisation intends to be in a few years time	• Mission statement
Step 2.	Goals	Interpret the mission to different stakeholders	• Stakeholder analysis
Step 3.	Objectives	Quantified embodiments of mission	• Measures such as profitability, time scale, deadlines
Step 4.	Corporate appraisal	Identify opportunities and threats, strengths and weaknesses	• SWOT analysis charts
Step 5.	Gap analysis	Compares outcomes of Step 4 with Step 3	• Gap analysis

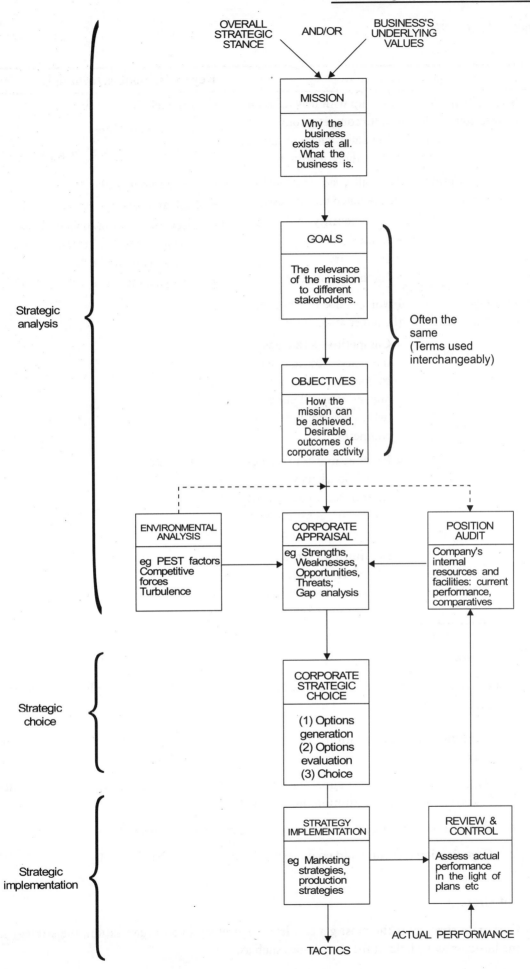

Strategic choice

3.4	Stage	Comment	Key tools, models, techniques
	Strategic options generation	Come up with new ideas on how to compete (competitive advantage), where to compete and method of growth	<ul><li>Value chain analysis</li><li>Scenario building</li><li>Acquisition vs organic growth</li></ul>
	Strategic options evaluation	Normally, each strategy has to be evaluated on the basis of<ul><li>Acceptability</li><li>Suitability</li><li>Feasibility</li><li>Environmental fit</li></ul>	<ul><li>Stakeholder analysis</li><li>Risk analysis</li><li>Decision-making tools such as decision trees, matrices, ranking and scoring methods</li><li>Financial measures (eg ROCE, DCF)</li></ul>
	Strategy selection	Involves choosing between the alternative strategies. • **Competitive strategies** are the generic strategies for competitive advantage an organisation will pursue (which determine **how you compete**). • **Product-market strategies** (which markets you should enter or leave) determine **where you compete** and the direction of growth. • **Institutional strategies** (ie relationships with other organisations) determine the **method of growth.**	

Strategy implementation

3.5 Strategy implementation is the **conversion** of the **strategy into detailed plans or objectives** for operating units.

3.6 The **planning of implementation** has several aspects. The strategic planning process is thus multi-layered.

(a) **Resource** planning (ie finance, personnel) involves assessing the key tasks that need to be carried out and determining the timing of them.

(b) **Operations** planning looks at the systems employed to manage the organisation.

(c) **Organisation** structure and control systems may need to be changed.

Types of strategy

3.7 **Corporate strategy** is the most general level of strategy in an organisation, the strategy for the business as a whole. It involves issues such as:

- Diversifying or limiting activities
- Investing
- Surviving

3.8 **Business strategy** is concerned with how an organisation approaches a particular market, or the activity of a particular business unit. An example of a business strategy is the decision by Mercedes-Benz to expand its product range to include four wheel drive vehicles.

3.9 **Operational and functional strategies** involve decisions which are made at operational level. These decisions include product pricing, investment in plant, personnel policy and so forth. The contributions of these different functions determine the success of the strategy.

4 STRATEGIC PLANNING VERSUS FREEWHEELING OPPORTUNISM

4.1 Advantages of a formal system of strategic planning

Advantages	Comment
Identifies risks	Strategic planning helps in managing these risks.
Forces managers to think	Strategic planning can encourage creativity and initiative by tapping the ideas of the management team.
Forces decision making	Companies cannot remain static - they have to cope with changes in the environment. A strategic plan draws attention to the need to change and adapt, not just to 'stand still' and survive.
Better control	Management control can be better exercised if targets are explicit.
Enforces consistency at all levels	Long-term, medium-term and short-term objectives, plans and controls can be made consistent with one another. Otherwise, strategies can be rendered ineffective by budgeting systems and performance measures which have no strategic content.
Public knowledge	*Drucker* has argued that an entrepreneur who builds a long-lasting business has 'a theory of the business' which informs his or her business decisions. In large organisations, the theory of the business has to become public knowledge, as decisions cannot be taken only by one person.
Time horizon	Some plans are needed for the long term.
Co-ordinates	Activities of different business functions need to be directed towards a common goal.
Clarifies objectives	Managers are forced to define what they want to achieve.
Allocates responsibility	A plan shows people where they fit in.

Case example

UK defence firms

The UK *defence industry* faces lower government spending and greater competition as contracts are put out to open tender. There is greater competition in export markets. Having failed to diversify into civil areas, companies are changing the way they work.

Planning

A number of assumptions can be made about the environment and customer demands.

(a)   Military needs are for mobile and flexible forces.

(b)   For economic reasons, reliability and maintainability are desired.

(c)   There should be military applications of civilian technology.

(d)   The Ministry of Defence has also tightened up on procurement, replacing cost-plus contracts with competitive tenders.

European defence is likely to consolidate, and defence firms are undertaking strategic management, perhaps for the first time. All firms are concerned with cash flow and productivity. Strategic planning departments have been set up to provide necessary inputs and analyses. The planners emphasise the threat from arms manufacturers in Russia, Germany and Japan. Analysts have identified that improvements in productivity and quality, to ensure the systems work, is of key importance.

4.2   The very notion that strategy making can be reduced to planning processes has come under attack from Henry Mintzberg, in his book *The Rise and Fall of Strategic Planning*.

Criticisms of strategic planning in practice (Mintzberg)

Problem	Comments
Practical failure	Empirical studies have not proved that formal planning processes ('the delineation of steps, the application of checklists and techniques') contribute to success.
Routine and regular	Strategic planning occurs often in an annual cycle. But a firm 'cannot allow itself to wait every year for the month of February to address its problems.'
Reduces initiative	Formal planning discourages strategic thinking. Once a plan is locked in place, people are unwilling to question it. Obsession with particular performance indicators means that managers focus on fulfilling the plan rather than concentrating on developments in the environment.
Internal politics	The assumption of 'objectivity' in evaluation ignores political battles between different managers and departments.
Exaggerates power	Managers are not all-knowing, and there are limits to the extent to which they can control the behaviour of the organisation.

No strategic planning: 'freewheeling opportunism'

4.3   The **freewheeling opportunism approach** suggests firms should **not bother with strategic plans** and should **exploit opportunities as they arise.**

(a)   **Advantages**

(i)   Good opportunities are not lost.

(ii)   A freewheeling opportunistic approach would **adapt to change** (eg a very steep rise in the price of a key commodity) more quickly.

(iii)   It might encourage a more **flexible, creative attitude**.

(b)   **Disadvantages**

(i)   There is **no co-ordinating framework** for the organisation, so that some opportunities get missed anyway.

(ii)   It emphasises the **profit motive** to the exclusion of all other considerations.

(iii)   The firm ends up **reacting** all the time rather than acting with a purpose.

Management accounting and freewheeling opportunism

4.4 A freewheeling opportunism approach eschews the careful routine of planning, and instead seizes such opportunities that arise. Not all 'opportunities' will work out, and there may be problems sustaining this policy.

4.5 The **management accountant's role** will be **investigative**.

   (a) What are the financial characteristics of the proposed strategy? For example, in an acquisition, what is the effect on cash flow?

   (b) How does the proposed strategy affect the firm's risk profile?

   (c) What new markets will the firm be entering by pursuing this strategy? If so, what is the likely response of competitors?

Combining the two approaches: flexibility

4.6 The **rational model** of strategic planning is a measured **framework** to **plan activities** in a **sequence** and to **programme the behaviour of the organisation**. **Freewheeling opportunism** implies that **plans only go so far** as the future cannot be known.

4.7 **Matching** formal strategic planning with freewheeling opportunism is **not impossible**, but it means deciding what aspects of organisational life are to be planned and identifying how potential opportunities are to be sought and evaluated.

4.8 **Focus for planning activities**

   (a) Running existing businesses effectively

   (b) Determining the resource capability of the organisation and its competences

   (c) Planning environmental scanning activities so that opportunities are actively hunted down and assessed for alignment with the company's mission, resource capability and management expertise.

4.9 A **freewheeling opportunistic approach** can then be adopted to **exploit a firm's competences**. These competences develop in a variety of ways.

   • Experience in making and marketing a product or service
   • The talents and potential of individuals in the organisation
   • The quality of co-ordination.

4.10 The **distinctive competence** of an organisation is what it does well, or better, than its rivals. Andrews says that, for a relatively undifferentiated product like cement, the ability of a maker to 'run a truck fleet more effectively' than its competitors will give it competitive strengths, since it can supply its product faster and more reliably.

4.11 Some competences are necessary to stay in business at all. For a restaurant, catering is a core competence; for a manufacturing firm it is not. As with all management jargon, some business people use the term to describe almost everything the organisation does.

4.12 **Tests for identifying a core competence**

   (a) **It provides potential access to a wide variety of markets**. GPS of France developed a core competence in 'one-hour' processing, enabling it to process films and build reading glasses in one hour.

(b) **It contributes significantly to the value enjoyed by the customer.** For example, for GPS, the waiting time restriction was very important.

(c) **It should be hard for a competitor to copy.** This will be the case if it is technically complex, involves specialised processes, involves complex interrelationships between different people in the organisation or is hard to define.

In many cases, a company might choose to combine competences.

4.13 This conveniently leads to SWOT analysis.

5 SWOT ANALYSIS

> ## KEY TERM
>
> **Corporate appraisal (SWOT analysis)** is a critical assessment of the strengths and weaknesses, opportunities and threats affecting an organisation to establish its condition before the long-term plan is prepared.

5.1 (a) **Strengths and weaknesses** analysis involves looking at the particular strengths and weaknesses of the organisation itself and its product/service range. It is an **internal appraisal**.

(b) An analysis of **opportunities and threats** is concerned with profit-making opportunities in the business environment, and with identifiable threats. It is therefore an **external appraisal**.

Case example

An example of a corporate appraisal is demonstrated by the following review of British Aerospace, as described in a corporate profile in *The Times*.

Opportunities: In 1997, BAe's defence sales were £6.4 billion, compared with £2.5 billion from commercial aerospace. The export prospects for the latest military aircraft are very significant. Chief among these is the 'Eurofighter', a joint project between the UK, Germany, Spain and Italy. BAe's 20% stake in Airbus is expected to yield higher profits and will give it a strong position when Airbus becomes a stand-alone company.

Threats: These come from cheaper and older models. The Eurofighter faces competition from the rest of Europe and the US. The United Arab Emirates recently chose the F16 in preference. The next big competition will be in Norway against the F18.

Strengths: The Chief Executive, John Weston, believes that BAe has the best product range in military aircraft. Analysts agree that its joint venture with Saab to sell the Gripen aircraft is an arrangement with lots of potential. The Hawk, probably BAe's most successful aircraft to date, continues to be sold, with strong sales prospects in South Africa.

With an emphasis on just-in-time delivery, BAe's lean manufacturing techniques are world class and push its profitability ahead of its partners in Airbus. This strength may enable it to negotiate a bigger slice of the profits.

Integrity Works, the consultant, gave BAe seven out of ten for 'ethical expression', saying it found a 'progressive array of policies aimed at promoting the interests of stakeholders'.

The total 'score' given to BAe by the review was 75/100. This covered areas ranging from its financial record and share performance to its attitude to employees, innovation and future prospects.

Strengths and weaknesses

5.2 In essence, an **internal appraisal** seeks to **identify** the following.

- **Shortcomings** in the company's present skills and resources
- **Strengths** which the company should seek to exploit

5.3 The precise content of the SWOT analysis will depend on the company.

Area	Issues
Marketing	Fate of new product launches
	Use of advertising
	Market shares and market sizes
	Growth markets
	Success rate of the sales team
	Level of customer/client service
Products and brands	Analysis of sales
	Margin and contribution
	Product quality
	Reputation of brands
	Age and future life of products
	Price elasticity of demand
Distribution	Service standards
	Delivery fleet facilities
	Geographical availability
Research and development	Relevance
	Costs
	Benefits
	Workload
Finance	Availability of funds
	Contribution
	Returns on investment
	Accounting ratios
Plant and equipment/ production	Production capacity
	Value of assets
	Land and buildings
	Economies of scale
Management and staff	Age
	Skills
	Industrial relations
	Training
	Recruitment
	Communications
Business management: organisation	Organisation structure
	Management style
	Communication links
	Information systems
	Strategic intelligence
Raw material and finished goods stocks	Sources of supply
	Turnover periods
	Storage capacity
	Obsolescence and deterioration

5.4 The appraisal should give particular **attention** to the following.

(a) **A study of past accounts and the use of ratios.** By looking at trends, or by comparing ratios with those of other firms in a similar industry, it might be possible to identify strengths and weaknesses.

(b) **Product position** and product-market portfolio.

(c) **Cash and financial structure.** If a company intends to expand or diversify, it will need cash or sufficient financial standing in order to acquire subsidiaries by issuing shares.

(d) **Cost structure.** If a company operates with high fixed costs and relatively low variable costs, it might be in a relatively weak position with regards to production capacity as this implies a high breakeven point.

(e) **Managerial ability.** Objective measurements should be sought.

Opportunities and threats

5.5 An **external appraisal** is required to **identify profit-making opportunities which can be exploited by the company's strengths** and also to **anticipate environmental threats** (a declining economy, competitors' actions, government legislation, industrial unrest etc) against which the company must protect itself.

5.6 **Opportunities**

• What opportunities exist in the business environment?

• What is the capability profile of competitors? Are they better placed to exploit these opportunities?

• What is the company's comparative performance potential in this field of opportunity?

5.7 **Threats**

• What threats might arise, to the company or its business environment?
• How will market players be affected?

5.8 **Areas to which opportunities and threats might relate**

Area	Detail
Economic	A recession might imply poor sales.
Political	Legislation may affect a company's prospects through the threats/ opportunities of pollution control or a ban on certain products, for example.
Competitors	They can threaten to 'steal' customers with better and/or cheaper products or services.
Technology	If technological changes are anticipated, there is a possibility of new products appearing, or cheaper means of production or distribution being introduced.
Social	Attitudes can be a threat.

Combining the elements of the SWOT analysis

5.9 The **internal and external appraisals** of SWOT analysis should be **brought together** so that **alternative strategies** will **emerge** from the identification of strengths, weaknesses, opportunities and threats.

   (a) Major **strengths** and profitable **opportunities** can be **exploited** especially if strengths and opportunities are matched with each other.

   (b) Major **weaknesses** and **threats** should be **countered**, or a contingency strategy or corrective strategy developed.

5.10 A **cruciform chart** is a table summarising significant strengths, weaknesses, opportunities and threats.

Strengths	Weaknesses
£10 million of capital available. Production expertise and appropriate marketing skills.	Heavy reliance on a small number of customers. Limited product range, with no new products and expected market decline. Small marketing organisation.
Threats Major competitor has already entered the new market.	Opportunities Government tax incentives for new investment. Growing demand in a new market, although customers so far relatively small in number.

5.11 In this simple example, it might be possible to identify that the company is in imminent danger of losing its existing markets and must diversify. The new market opportunity exists to be exploited and since the number of customers is currently few, the relatively small size of the existing marketing force would not be an immediate hindrance.

5.12 In practice, **a combination of individual strategies** covering product development, market development, diversification, resource planning, risk reduction and so on will be required. **Gap analysis** can then be carried out.

   • The gap between the current position of the firm and its planned targets is estimated.
   • One or more courses of action are proposed.
   • These are tested for their 'gap-reducing properties'.

5.13 It will help you to get used to the basic thinking that underlies strategic planning if you try a short exercise in SWOT analysis.

Question: SWOT

Hall Faull Downes Ltd has been in business for 25 years, during which time profits have risen by an average of 3% per annum, although there have been peaks and troughs in profitability due to the ups and downs of trade in the customers' industry. The increase in profits until five years ago was the result of increasing sales in a buoyant market, but more recently, the total market has become somewhat smaller and Hall Faull Downes has only increased sales and profits as a result of improving its market share.

The company produces components for manufacturers in the engineering industry.

In recent years, the company has developed many new products and currently has 40 items in its range compared to 24 only five years ago. Over the same five year period, the number of customers has fallen from 20 to nine, two of whom together account for 60% of the company's sales.

Give your appraisal of the company's future, and suggest what it is probably doing wrong.

Answer

A general interpretation of the facts as given might be sketched as follows.

(a) Objectives: the company has no declared objectives. Profits have risen by 3% per annum in the past, which has failed to keep pace with inflation but may have been a satisfactory rate of increase in the current conditions of the industry. Even so, stronger growth is indicated in the future.

(b)

Strengths	Weaknesses
Many new products developed.	Products may be reaching the end of their life and entering decline.
Marketing success in increasing market share	New product life cycles may be shorter. Reduction in customers. Excessive reliance on a few customers. Doubtful whether profit record is satisfactory.
Threats Possible decline in the end-product. Smaller end-product market will restrict future sales prospects for Hall Faull Downes.	*Opportunities* None identified.

(c) Strengths: the growth in company sales in the last five years has been as a result of increasing the market share in a declining market. This success may be the result of the following.

- Research and development spending.
- Good product development programmes.
- Extending the product range to suit changing customer needs.
- Marketing skills.
- Long-term supply contracts with customers.
- Cheap pricing policy.
- Product quality and reliable service.

(d) Weaknesses:

(i) The products may be custom-made for customers so that they provide little or no opportunity for market development.

(ii) Products might have a shorter life cycle than in the past, in view of the declining total market demand.

(iii) Excessive reliance on two major customers leaves the company exposed to the dangers of losing their custom.

(e) Threats: there may be a decline in the end-market for the customers' product so that the customer demands for the company's own products will also fall.

(f) Opportunities: no opportunities have been identified, but in view of the situation as described, new strategies for the longer term would appear to be essential.

(g) Conclusions: the company does not appear to be planning beyond the short-term, or is reacting to the business environment in a piecemeal fashion. A strategic planning programme should be introduced.

(h) Recommendations: the company must look for new opportunities in the longer-term.

(i) In the short term, current strengths must be exploited to continue to increase market share in existing markets and product development programmes should also continue.

(ii) In the longer term, the company must diversify into new markets or into new products and new markets. Diversification opportunities should be sought with a view to exploiting any competitive advantage or synergy that might be achievable.

(iii) The company should use its strengths (whether in R & D, production skills or marketing expertise) in exploiting any identifiable opportunities.

(iv) Objectives need to be quantified in order to assess the extent to which new long-term strategies are required.

5.14 Having constructed a matrix of strengths, weaknesses, opportunities and threats and carried out some level of evaluation, you can use the **matrix** to **guide strategy formulation**.

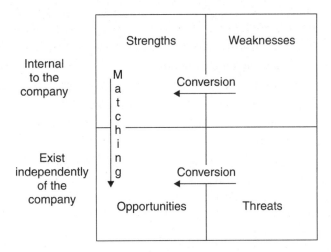

(a) **Matching**

This entails finding, where possible, a match between the strengths of the organisation and the opportunities presented by the market.

(b) **Conversion**

This requires the development of strategies which will convert weaknesses into strengths in order to take advantage of some particular opportunity.

6   RISK AND UNCERTAINTY

6.1 Strategies, by definition, deal with future events and the future cannot be predicted.

> **KEY TERMS**
>
> - **Risk** is sometimes used to describe situations where outcomes are not known, but their probabilities can be estimated. (This is the underlying principle behind insurance.)
>
> - **Uncertainty** is present when the outcome cannot be predicted or assigned probabilities. (Many insurance policies exclude 'war damage, riots and civil commotion'.)

6.2 **Types of risk and uncertainty**

Risk	Comment
Physical	Earthquakes, fire, flooding, and equipment breakdown. In the long-term, climatic changes: global warming, drought (relevant to water firms).
Economic	Assumptions about the economic environment might turn out to be wrong. Not even the government forecasts are perfect.
Business	Lowering of entry barriers (eg new technology); changes in customer/supplier industries leading to changed relative power; new competitors and factors internal to the firm (eg its culture or technical systems); management misunderstanding of core competences; volatile cash flows; uncertain returns; changed investor perceptions increasing the required rate of return.

Risk	Comment
Product life cycle	Different risks exist at different stages of the life cycle.
Political	Nationalisation, sanctions, civil war, political instability, can all have an impact on the business.
Financial	**Financial risk** has a **specific technical meaning: the risk to shareholders caused by debt finance**. The risk exists because the debt finance providers have first call on the company's profits. The need to pay interest might prevent capital growth or the payment of dividends, particularly when trading is difficult. The converse is that when business is buoyant, interest payments are easily covered and shareholders receive the benefit of the remaining profits.

Accounting for risk

6.3   A firm might require that all investments make a return of, say, 5%. This can be adjusted for risk.

(a)   **Return**. The target return could be raised to compensate for the risk.

(b)   **Payback**. To protect cash flows, it might be made a condition of all new investment projects that the project should pay back within a certain period of time.

(c)   **Finance**. It might be determined that the investment should be financed under strict conditions (eg only from profits).

6.4   Planners try to **quantify the risk**, so as to compare the estimated riskiness of different strategies.

(a)   **Rule of thumb** methods might express a range of values from worst possible result to best possible result with a best estimate lying between these two extremes.

(b)   **Basic probability theory** expresses the likelihood of a forecast result occurring. This would evaluate the data given by informing the decision maker that there is, for example, a 50% probability that the best estimate will be achieved, a 25% chance that the worst result will occur and a 25% chance that the best possible result will occur. This evaluation of risk might help the executive to decide between alternative strategies, each with its own risk profile.

(c)   One way of measuring the dispersion or **spread of values** with different possible outcomes from a decision is to calculate a **standard deviation** of the expected value (EV) of profit. The higher the standard deviation, the higher the risk, as the EV is more volatile.

6.5   **Decision rules** are useful in strategic planning because they embody managerial attitudes to uncertainty. The **maximax** approach is optimistic, while the **maximim** is pessimistic. Remember that these rules are used under conditions of **uncertainty**, as is the **minimax regret** rule. If risk can be quantified, probabilistic methods such as decision trees may be used.

6.6   In terms of strategic planning, **decision trees** can be used to assess which choices are mutually exclusive, and to try to give them some quantitative value. As such they are useful for three purposes.

- Clarifying strategic decisions when they are complex
- Using risk (in probability terms) as an input to quantifying the decision options.
- Ranking the relative costs and benefits of the options

6.7 That said, many of the options in a decision may not be mutually exclusive, and the decision tree may inhibit a creative approach to a problem by assuming that they are. Finally, it is often easy to forget that an **expected value is only useful for comparative purposes,** taking probability into account. It is **not a prediction** of an actual outcome. (If you toss a coin, there is a 50:50 chance of it turning heads; but in any one throw it will be either heads or tails, not a bit of both.)

Risk and managers

6.8 It is worth noting that shareholders and managers have different approaches to risk.

   (a) Shareholders can spread risk over a number of investments.

   (b) Managers' careers tend to be bound up with the success or failure of one particular company.

> **Exam focus point**
>
> Apart from the product life cycle, this chapter's topics have been conspicuous in their absence from exams to date. Will they appear in the exam you face?

7 STRATEGIC MANAGEMENT ACCOUNTING IN MULTINATIONAL COMPANIES

7.1 We looked at strategic management accounting in some depth in Chapter 1 and at performance comparison across different countries in Chapter 10. Here we need to briefly consider strategic management accounting in a multinational context.

What is a multinational organisation?

7.2 Multinational organisations have a **central headquarters in one country and subsidiaries in one or more other countries.**

Why might an organisation choose to set up a foreign subsidiary?

7.3 New markets may be sought for the following reasons.

   (a) An organisation might want to **extend the product life cycle** of a product.

   (b) Where there is **intense competition** in the home market, an organisation might want to escape to less competitive markets.

   (c) The domestic market might offer **low growth** prospects.

   (d) The domestic market might offer **significant risk,** and the organisation might wish to reduce its exposure.

7.4 In terms of **competitive strategy,** international activities can be justified on the following grounds.

   (a) **Cost leadership.** The domestic market may be too small for the organisation to reap the economies of scale which may be necessary for a cost leadership strategy.

(b) **Differentiation**. A differentiated product may appeal to a number of different overseas markets.

(c) **Focus**. Oddly enough, international marketing can be used to implement a *focus* strategy, which is a concentration on a core segment of consumers. The segment does not have to be defined in national or ethnic terms, but in terms of wealth, life-styles and so forth.

(d) To pre-empt competition from overseas producers. Organisations can expect incoming competition. They might have no alternative to competing abroad.

7.5 **Other reasons to market overseas**

- The market for a product is genuinely a global one.
- Overseas operations might be cheaper than manufacturing at home.
- Competitors are entering the overseas market.
- A company executive may recognise an opportunity while on a foreign trip.
- Profit margins may be higher abroad.
- Seasonal fluctuations may be levelled out.
- It offers an opportunity of disposing of excess production in times of low domestic demand.
- The organisation's prestige may be enhanced by portraying a global image.

7.6 Here are some reasons **why an organisation might choose to open up a foreign subsidiary**, in addition to the marketing issues identified above.

(a) **Natural resources strategy**. An organisation might wish to exploit the natural resources of a foreign country, such as coffee, cocoa, rubber or tobacco plantations, or mineral/oil deposits.

(b) **Manufacturing strategy**. An organisation with a technological lead in the manufacture of a product might decide to exploit this lead more widely and directly by opening a factory or distribution company in another country.

(c) **Commercial strategy**. This is a defensive strategy and the most common one. An organisation might decide to manufacture abroad in order to counter threats to its foreign markets from competition, or action by foreign governments and so on.

(d) **Investment strategy**. Foreign subsidiaries may be acquired as an investment rather than as a means of developing the manufacturing operations of the head office company. The contract between head office and the subsidiary is essentially that of consultant and client.

7.7 Before setting up an overseas subsidiary, an organisation must consider both strategic and tactical issues.

(a) **Strategic issues**

(i) Does the strategic decision to get involved overseas fit with the organisation's overall mission and objectives?

(ii) Does the organisation have (or can it raise) the resources necessary to exploit effectively the opportunities overseas?

(b) **Tactical issues**

(i) How can the organisation get to understand customers' needs and preferences in foreign markets?

(ii)   Does the organisation know how to conduct business abroad, and deal effectively with foreign nationals?

(iii) Are there foreign regulations and associated hidden costs?

(iv)   Does the organisation have the necessary management skills and experience?

Managing overseas subsidiaries

7.8   There are particular problems in the management of overseas subsidiaries.

(a) How much **control**? There is always a tension between autonomy and centralisation.

(b) **Staffing**. Ex-patriate managers are often expensive. Housing costs, school fees and so on often have to be paid. In addition there are cultural problems in adjusting to the country and the way of doing business.

Which markets should the company enter?

7.9   In most cases, it is better to start by selling in countries with which there is some familiarity and then expand into other countries gradually as experience is gained. Generally organisations should enter fewer countries in the following circumstances.

- Market entry and market control costs are high.
- Product and market communications modification costs are high.
- There is a large market and potential growth in the initial countries chosen.
- Dominant competitors can establish high barriers to entry.

7.10   The three major criteria for this decision should be as follows.

(a) **Market attractiveness**. This concerns such indicators as GNP per head and forecast demand.

(b) **Competitive advantage**. This is principally dependent on prior experience in similar markets, language and cultural understanding.

(c) **Risk**. This involves an analysis of political stability, the possibility of government intervention and similar external influences.

7.11   **Differences between domestic and international business**

Factor	Domestic	International
Cultural factors	Few language problems	Many language barriers
	Homogeneous market	Fragmented, diverse markets
	'Rules of the game' understood	Rules diverse, changeable and unclear
	Similar purchasing habits	Purchasing habits may vary by nation or region
Economic factors	National price	Diverse national prices
	Uniform financial climate	Variety of financial climates, ranging from very conservative to highly inflationary
	Single currency	Currencies differing in stability and real value
	Stable business environment	Multiple business environments, some unstable

Factor	Domestic	International
Competitive factors	Data available, usually accurate and easy to collect.	Formidable data collection problems
	Competitors' products, prices, costs and plans usually known	Many more competitors, but little information about their strategies
Political factors	Relatively unimportant	Often significant
Technological factors	Use of standard production and measurement systems	Training of foreign personnel to operate and maintain equipment
		Adaptation of parts and equipment
		Different measuring systems

7.12 **General policies** and **particularly financial policies** in multinational organisations are often **specifically designed to further the goals of the parent company**, and only incidentally those of subsidiaries or host countries.

7.13 Typical of such policies are the various schemes which are used to shift earnings from one country to another in order to avoid taxes, minimise risks or achieve other objectives. Examples of these schemes are discretionary pricing of inter-company transfers of goods and services. We look at this issue in more depth in Chapter 26.

7.14 Other multinationals allow more freedom of initiative to foreign subsidiaries. A factor is the **extent to which the different parts of the organisation are involved in international activity**. At one extreme a multi-domestic strategy treats each country as a separate market; at the other a global strategy treats the world as a single market. The following diagram describes the types of organisation structure which might arise.

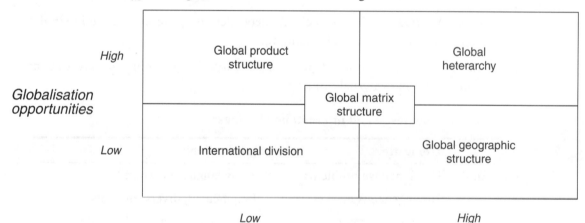

(a) The **international division**. The international division might be set up to co-ordinate all of an organisation's overseas activities. The international division is a separate department and is probably organised on an area basis.

(b) **Global matrix structure**. Individual business units report both on a country basis and on a product divisional (or functional) basis.

(c) **Global product structure**. The organisation is split into product divisions and further geographic divisions may be formed. This structure goes some way to maintaining overall market orientation by the demands of different geographic areas.

(d) **Global geographic structure**. Divisions comprising all the functions cover specific geographical areas such as Europe, the Middle East, the Far East and Australia. Sub-divisionalisation into, say, product or market divisions is possible within each division. Such a strategy ensures that long-term strategy rests with head office while operational decisions and co-ordination between functions occur within a manageable geographic area.

(e) **Global heterarchy**. The heterarchy is characteristic of large and very complex international firms: the matrix is simple in comparison.

Global organisations

7.15 The existence of the global organisation should not be taken for granted. An organisation will invest in many countries and will make decisions primarily with regard to its global ambitions without taking legal nationality into account. **Communications technology** makes boundaries irrelevant to knowledge based industries. In short, there is an **increasing number of 'stateless corporations', whose activities transcend national boundaries**, and **whose personnel come from any country**.

7.16 Against this view a number of research studies have raised the following **objections**.

(a) Most multinationals, other than those based in small nations, have less than half of their employees based abroad.

(b) Ownership and control of multinationals remain restricted. This is partly because of the way in which capital markets are structured. Few so-called global companies are quoted on more than two stock markets.

(c) Top management is rarely as multinational as the organisation's activities. This is particularly true of Japanese companies.

(d) National residence and status is important for tax reasons. Boundary-less corporations are not recognised as such by lawyers or tax officials.

(e) The bulk of a multinational's research and development is generally done in the home country, where strategic decisions are made.

(f) Where capital is limited, 'global' organisations stick to the home market rather than developing overseas ones.

(g) Finally, profits from a global organisation must be remitted somewhere.

Financial performance issues in multinational organisations

Objectives

7.17 The task of setting a financial objective within a multinational is complex, and several **problems** must be resolved.

(a) **Capital structure**. Where foreign subsidiaries are financed partly by loans, the differing rates of interest in each country might affect the relative profitability of subsidiaries.

(b) **Cost structure**. Overseas subsidiaries may have a different operational gearing.

(c) **Accounting policies**. In each country, the subsidiary may adopt a different rate of depreciation so that profits and asset values are not comparable. Profits can be transformed into losses by accounting policies.

(d) **Government policy** There will be differences in the levels of grants or concessions from the national government and in the rate of taxation and interest.

(e) **Transfer prices** for goods and services between the subsidiaries may be set in such a way as to improve the results of one subsidiary (or head office) at the expense of another (eg if goods are transferred from a subsidiary to head office at cost, the subsidiary will get no profit and the head office will obtain the goods at a low price).

(f) **Workforce.** A justification for expanding into developing countries is to take advantage of lower wages.

(g) **Exchange rate fluctuations** may turn profits into losses and vice versa.

(h) **Risk**. Some overseas operations may be a greater risk than others so that higher returns may be required from them.

(i) **Life cycle**. The same product may be at different stages in its product life cycle in each country, as we have seen.

(j) **Transport**. If a subsidiary in, say, the United Kingdom is performing much worse, and incurring higher unit costs of production than a comparable subsidiary in, say, Germany, it may still be uneconomic to switch production from the United Kingdom to Germany because the extra costs of transport to the UK may exceed the savings in the costs of production.

(k) **Domestic competition**. The market of the overseas subsidiary may face a unique configuration of Porter's five forces.

(l) **Different economic conditions**.

International comparisons

7.18 If the organisations being compared operate in different countries there will be certain **problems for performance measurement**.

(a) **Realistic standards**. It may be difficult to establish realistic standards for each different country. Performance standards should take account of local conditions, considering local opportunities as well as any restrictions on the activities of an operating unit in a particular country.

(b) **Controllable cash flows**. Care must be taken to determine which cash flows are controllable and to separate these from the cash flows which are outside the control of local management. In particular the distortions caused by local taxation laws should be eliminated.

(c) **Currency conversion**. Considerable friction and difficulty in measuring performance can be caused by the use of inappropriate currency conversion rates.

(d) **Basis for comparison**. Following on from the problem of setting realistic standards of performance, central management must exercise care when attempting to compare performance between the different countries.

Exchange rates

7.19 In practice many organisations have to **budget for exchange rate changes** which affect their plans. An organisation can lock itself into particular exchange rate by **hedging** or other financing. Jaguar used this when, as an independent British company, most of its sales were in the US. Hedging instruments were used to protect its profits from any fall.

7.20 As well as operational issues, such as the acquisition of funds, hedging contracts and so on, there is the obviously vexed problem of **performance assessment**.

7.21 We look at exchange rate later in this section.

Strategic options for multinationals

7.22 Being a multinational gives a group **many more strategic options** and alternatives in terms of the location of various element of its operations. This is not always the case, however,

7.23 Consider oil companies. A multinational oil company cannot choose where to find crude oil. It does have the choice between developing the field itself, selling it to another company or swapping it for another field in a better geographic position for the group, however. It can also decide where to locate its oil refineries in relation to its oil production fields and final product markets.

7.24 Such **decisions must be taken at group level** so that the interests of local mangers are not allowed to introduce bias. They must be based on the economic impact of each alternative on the group.

Diseconomies of scale

7.25 The **scale and spread** of a multinational should be justified because it **adds value** to shareholders **through increased economies of scale**. Some multinational organisations **can become too complex**, however, and the resulting problems of financial control and managerial motivation become so great that they outweigh the advantages of size and geographic spread. In such circumstances the multinational needs to simplify its structure or its span of business.

7.26 The sheer scale of the complexity problems of some multinationals makes it difficult for them to take advantage of the information technology solutions for coping with large data handling and processing issues.

Money and trade

7.27 International trade implies international remittances and therefore currency exchange. An **exchange rate is the rate at which one country's currency can be traded in exchange** for **another country's currency. Exchange rate risk** is the risk that future receipts in a foreign currency will exchange into a smaller amount than expected of the domestic currency.

7.28 A variety of **financial hedging devices** exist for the management of exchange rate risk. A company can also minimise its exposure to the risk associated with any given exchange rate by managing its affairs in such a way that it has money flowing in both directions between the countries concerned. If the flows are initially of equal value and the exchange rate changes, what is lost by exchange in one direction is gained by the opposite transaction. **Exchange rate risk thus motivates companies to both buy from and sell to the same countries if possible.**

7.29 Currencies can be **maintained** for quite long periods at **artificial rates by government intervention** in the market. Official exchange rates do not therefore always give a true indication of global resource costs. This is particularly the case when the countries concerned have different rates of inflation. Decisions relating to international operations may be more informed if they are made using **purchasing power parity exchange rates**. These rates attempt to **remove the distorting effects of inflation**. The purchasing power parity approach is to calculate an exchange rate based on the relative cost of purchasing the same basket of goods in the two countries. *The Economist* regularly publishes purchasing power parity exchange rates based on the price of McDonalds' Big Mac hamburger. This was chosen because of McDonald's well-known dedication to achieving standardisation of their product. The Economist Big Mac index indicates some quite wide discrepancies in official exchange rates.

Case example

The Big Mac Index

From the *Economist*, 20 December 2001

The Economist's Big Mac Index is based on the theory of 'purchasing-power parity'. Under PPP, exchange rates ought to adjust to equalise the price of a basket of goods and services across countries. Our basket is the Big Mac. Dividing the American price of a Big Mac, $2.59, by the British price, £1.99, implies a PPP exchange rate of $1.30. The market rate is $1.45, making sterling 12% overvalued. By this measure, the South African rand is undervalued by 68%.

Protectionism in international trade

7.30 Protectionism is the **discouraging of imports by government action.**

7.31 Some governments seek to protect their home producers from foreign competition by making it harder to import from overseas. A wide variety of methods is used.

- **Tariffs** or **customs duties**
- **Non-tariff barriers**
- **Exchange controls**
- **Exchange rate policy**

Tariffs or customs duties

7.32 A **tariff** is a **tax on imports.**

(a) The importer is required to pay either a percentage of the value of the imported good (an *ad valorem* **duty**) or per unit of the good imported (a **specific duty**).

(b) The **government raises revenue** and **domestic producers** may **expand sales,** but **consumers pay higher prices** if they buy imported goods. They may have to buy domestic goods of a lesser quality.

Non-tariff barriers

7.33

Type of barrier	Detail
Import quotas	**Restrictions** on the quantity of product allowed to be imported into a country. The restrictions can be imposed by **import licences** (in which case the government gets additional revenue) or simply by granting the **right to import only to certain producers**. **Prices will rise** because the supply of goods is artificially restricted. The consumer pays more.
Minimum local content rules	Related to quotas is a requirement that, to avoid tariffs or other restrictions, products should be made in the **country or region** in **which they are sold**. In the EU the product must be of a specified **minimum local content** (80% in the EU) to qualify as being 'home' or 'EU-made'. This is one of the reasons Japanese and Korean manufacturers have set up factories in Europe.
Minimum prices and anti-dumping action	The sale of a product in an **overseas market at a price lower** than **charged in the domestic market**. **Anti-dumping measures** include establishing quotas, minimum prices or extra excise duties.
Embargoes	An embargo on imports from one particular country is a **total ban**, a zero quota. An embargo may have a political motive, and may deprive consumers at home of the supply of an important product.
Subsidies for domestic producers	An enormous range of government **subsidies** and assistance for exporters is offered, such as **export credit guarantees** (insurance against bad debts for overseas sales), financial help and assistance from government departments in promoting and selling products. The effect of these grants is to make unit production costs lower. These may give the domestic producer a **cost advantage** over foreign producers in export as well as domestic markets.

Exchange controls and exchange rate policy

7.34 Many countries have **exchange control regulations** designed to make it **difficult** for **importers to obtain the currency they need to buy foreign goods**.

7.35 If a government allows its currency to depreciate, imports will become more expensive. Importers may cut their profit margins and keep prices at their original levels for a while, but sooner or later prices of imports will rise. A policy of exchange rate depreciation in this context is referred to as a **competitive devaluation**.

Case example

In the last several years whilst European countries were preparing to meet the criteria to establish a common currency, the Euro, there were considerable changes in the relative valuations of the individual country currencies. In particular, the pound sterling has strengthened making it more difficult for British exporters to sell their products abroad.

Unofficial non-tariff barriers

7.36 The governments of some countries are accused of establishing or tolerating **unofficial barriers to trade**. Here are some examples.

(a) Onerous **quality and inspection procedures** for imported products impose time and cost penalties on organisations selling them.

(b) **Packaging and labelling** requirements may be rigorous, **safety and performance** standards difficult to satisfy and **documentation procedures** very laborious.

(c) Restrictions may be imposed on **physical distribution**, such as the use of display facilities and transport systems.

Chapter roundup

- At **strategic and operational levels, planning and control** differ in terms of the nature of feedback (double loop versus single loop), orientation (future versus present) and scope (organisation as a whole versus limited set of processes within it).

- **Strategic control** depends on avoiding 'gaps' and 'false alarms' and on identifying milestones of performance.

- The **product life cycle** describes the financial and marketing life of a product from introduction, growth, maturity and decline.

- Assuming this pattern applies, in order to survive and prosper, firms need new products to take the place of declining ones. Different control measures are appropriate at different stages. The life cycle can be determined by technology or customer demand.

- The **rational model of strategic planning** involves strategic analysis, strategic choice and implementation. Such an approach can be too rigid and can result in opportunities being missed.

- A **freewheeling opportunistic approach** can result in opportunities being grasped but there may be a lack of focus.

- An **approach combining both** can include planning activities to nurture strengths and develop competences and environmental scanning activities to identify opportunities which are suitable for the company's competences.

- This can be modelled by the **SWOT** approach, which aims to identify strengths and weaknesses in the context of opportunities and threats.

- **Risk and uncertainty** must always be taken into account in strategic planning. Many areas of risk and uncertainty are **exogenous**, in other words outside the control of the organisation.

- **Strategic management accounting in a multinational context** requires consideration of a range of issues including exchange rates.

Quick quiz

1 *Place the words below in the correct columns.*

	Strategic	Operational
Whole organisation		
Mainly internal		
Future-orientated		
Procedures		
Single loop		
Double loop		

2 Customer satisfaction is likely to be a false alarm. *True or false?*

3   'Product X commands 50% in a market that is no longer growing. We are able to earn £Y per unit of scale resource, owing to economies of scale, and are pleased that our customer retention rate is increasing, reducing 'churn' costs.

What stage of the product life cycle is described above?

A   Introduction
B   Growth
C   Maturity
D   Decline

4   Which of the following is not an advantage of formal systems of strategic planning?

A   Public knowledge
B   Encourages strategic thinking
C   Allocation of responsibility
D   Identifies risks

5   Which of the following is not a feature of freewheeling opportunism?

A   Low level of risk
B   Adaptive to change
C   Opens new market opportunities
D   Focus on profit

6   *Fill in the blanks.*

A core competence provides potential access to a wide variety of ...., it contributes significantly to the value enjoyed by the .... and it should be hard for a .... to copy.

7   *Choose the appropriate words from those highlighted.*

(a)   Strengths and weaknesses analysis offers an **internal/external** appraisal.
(b)   Opportunities and threats analysis offers an **internal/external** appraisal.

Answers to quick quiz

1   *Strategic*
Whole organisation

Future orientated

Double loop

Operational

Mainly internal

Procedures
Single loop

2   False. It is likely to be a gap.

3   C

4   B   It discourages strategic thinking.

5   A   Some opportunities may be riskier than others. Higher levels of risk are acceptable with high returns.

6   markets
customer
competitor

7   (a)   internal
(b)   external

Now try the question below from the Exam Question Bank

Number	Level	Marks	Time
14	Exam	20	36 mins

Chapter 17

PLANNING AND BUDGETING

Topic list	Syllabus reference
1 Sources of planning information	4(b)
2 Short-term planning and budget preparation	4(b)
3 Uses of budgeting	4(b)
4 Budgetary control	4(b)
5 Alternative budget models	4(b)

Introduction

This is the first of three chapters which look at **budgeting and budgetary control.**

In fact, because you encountered budgeting, budgetary control, the behavioural implications of budgeting, quantitative aids to budgeting and alternative budgeting systems in Paper 2.4, albeit at an introductory level, you will **recognise** much of the material covered in this part of the Study Text.

This chapter provides an **introduction** to budgeting and budgetary control and examines the **place of budgets within the overall corporate plan**, the way in which their preparation helps to **co-ordinate activities** and their role as a **control device**. In the final section we take a look at some **alternative approaches to budgeting** and consider when they may or may not be appropriate.

In Chapter 18 we will be looking at various quantitative techniques which are useful in budgeting.

Study guide

Section 19 – Budgeting and budgetary control I

- Describe the internal and external sources of planning information for an organisation

- List the information used in the preparation of the master budget and in its functional components

- Explain and illustrate the use of budgeting as a planning aid in the co-ordination of business activity

- Explain and illustrate the relevance of budgeting in the co-ordination of business activities

- Explain and quantify the application of positive and negative feedback in the operation of budgetary control

- Explain and quantify the application of feedforward control in the operation of budgeting

- Contrast the information used in the operation of zero based budgeting and incremental budgeting

Section 20 – Budgeting and budgetary control II

- Identify the effects of flexible budgeting in reducing uncertainty in budgeting

Section 21 – Budgeting and budgetary control III

- Enumerate and evaluate the strengths and weaknesses of alternative budget models such as fixed and flexible, rolling, zero based and incremental

Exam guide

Topics covered in this chapter have **not been classified as core areas** of the syllabus and so are unlikely to be examined on their own. They could be required in conjunction with topics covered in Chapters 18 and 19, however.

The issues covered in this chapter are useful background to the Oxford Brookes degree Research and Analysis Project Topic 1, which requires you to analyse the efficiency and/or effectiveness of a management accounting technique in an organisational setting.

1 SOURCES OF PLANNING INFORMATION

1.1 Planning information has already been considered several times. We looked at strategic planning information in Chapter 1 and at sources of information in Chapter 8. In Chapter 16 we covered position audit/strategic analysis and SWOT analysis, information-gathering exercises carried out as part of an organisation's planning process.

1.2 **Factors that distinguish long-term planning information requirements from short-term planning information requirements**

Long-term planning information	Short-term planning information
Used by top management	Used at a lower level, by those who actually implement the plans
Broad in scope rather than deep in detail	More detailed
More external information is required for planning in the long term	Internal sources are more common
More descriptive in nature	Needs to be quantified to measure how well the plan is progressing
Looks to the future and lacks certainty	Forecasts need to be replaced, where possible, with definite information such as firm orders, agreed usage rates and so on

2 SHORT-TERM PLANNING AND BUDGET PREPARATION

2.1 **Short-term plans** attempt to **provide short-term targets within the framework of longer-term strategic plans.** This is generally done in the form of a budget.

> **KEY TERM**
>
> A **budget** is a plan expressed in financial terms, usually covering one year.

This one year period is then broken down into '**control periods**' of one month or four weeks.

2.2 You should have studied budget preparation in detail as part of your earlier studies. What follows should remind you of the key points.

Point	Detail
Long-term plan	The **starting point**, this will show **what the budget has to achieve** (the introduction of new production, the required return, and so on) and outline **how it is to be done**. It will also contain **general guidelines** on allowable price increases like wage rates. The **long-term policy** needs to be **communicated** to all managers responsible for preparing budgets so that they are aware of the context within which they are budgeting and how their area of responsibility is expected to contribute.
Limiting factor	The factor that **limits the scale of operations**, this is usually sales demand, but it may be production capacity where demand is high. Budgeting cannot proceed until the budget for the limiting factor has been prepared, since this affects all the other budgets. We shall assume that sales is the limiting factor.
Budget manual	Prepared to **assist functional managers**, this will show how figures and forecasts are to be arrived at and give any other information that is to apply across the organisation. It is likely to include **proformas** showing how the information is to be presented. If budgeting is done with spreadsheets, layouts and computations may be pre-programmed, requiring only the entry of the figures. It may include a **flow diagram** showing how individual budgets are interlinked and specify deadlines by which first drafts must be prepared.
Sales budget	This contains **information on the expected volume of sales** (based on estimates or market research), the **sales mix, and selling prices.** The total revenues indicated will be used to compile the cash budget, although this information needs to be adjusted to allow for the expected timing of receipts. The volume of sales indicates the level of production required and the extent of spending on distribution and administration. Preparation of the sales budget is covered in more detail below.
Production capacity	The level of sales anticipated is matched against opening stocks and desired closing stocks to establish the level of production. From this can be calculated the need for materials (again allowing for opening and closing stocks), labour and machine hours. In other words production budgeting is **done in terms of physical resources initially and costed afterwards**. At this stage, too, it is likely that needs for new capital expenditure will be identified. This information will be used in preparing the capital budget.
Functional budgets	Budgets **for other areas of the organisation** like distribution and administration take the anticipated sales level as their point of reference. Vehicle costs, carriage costs, stationery and communication costs, and above all staff costs feature in these budgets.
Discretionary costs	**Training and R&D** are known as 'discretionary costs' and have special features. Budgeting for such costs is discussed below.

Point	Detail
Consolidation and coordination	This can begin once all parts of the organisation have submitted their individual budgets. It is most **unlikely** that **all of the budgets will be in line with each other** at the first attempt. Areas of **incompatibility** must be identified and the **budgets modified** in consultation with individual managers. **Spreadsheets** are invaluable at this stage, both for the consolidation itself and to allow changes to be made quickly and accurately.
Cash budget	This can only be prepared at this stage because it **needs to take account of all of the plans of the organisation** and translate them into expected cash flows. Cash must be available when it is needed to enable the plans to be carried out. Overdraft facilities may need to be negotiated in advance, or some activities may need to be deferred until cash has been collected.
Master budget	The final stage, once all of the necessary modifications have been made, is to prepare a **summary** of all of the budgets in the form of a master budget, which generally comprises a **budgeted profit and loss account, a budgeted balance sheet and a budgeted cash flow statement.**

Sales budget

2.3   Before the sales budget can be prepared, a **sales forecast** has to be made. Sales forecasting is **complex** and **difficult** because it is **dependent** on the **actions of customers** rather than on internal processes and/or personnel and requires consideration of a number of factors.

- Past sales patterns
- Economic environment
- Market research results
- Anticipated advertising
- Competition
- Changing consumer tastes
- New and existing legislation
- Distribution
- Pricing policies and discounts offered
- Environmental factors

As well as bearing in mind the above factors, management can use a number of forecasting techniques (which we look at in Chapter 18).

3   USES OF BUDGETING

3.1   Budgeting is a multi-purpose activity. Here are some of the reasons why budgets are used.

Function	Detail
Ensure the achievement of the organisation's objectives	Quantified expressions of objectives are drawn up as targets to be achieved within the timescale of the budget plan.
Compel planning	Budgeting forces management to look ahead, to set out detailed plans for achieving the targets for each department, operation and (ideally) each manager and to anticipate problems.

Function	Detail
Communicate ideas and plans	A formal system is necessary to ensure that each person affected by the plans is aware of what he or she is supposed to be doing. Communication might be one-way, with managers giving orders to subordinates, or there might be a two-way dialogue.
Coordinate activities	The activities of different departments need to be coordinated to ensure maximum integration of effort towards common goals. This implies, for example, that the purchasing department should base its budget on production requirements and that the production budget should in turn be based on sales expectations. Coordination is remarkably difficult to achieve, however. We look at this issue in more detail below.
Resource allocation	The budgeting process involves identifying the resources required and those available for the forthcoming period. Budget holders may be asked to justify their resource requirements in the light of the expected level of activity for their budget centre. Managers will discuss the allocation of available resources in order to use them in the optimal way.
Authorisation	A formalised budget may act as an authorisation to budget managers to incur expenditure. As long as the expenditure item is included within the budget there may be no need to seek further approval before incurring the expenditure.
Provide a framework for responsibility accounting	Budgets require that managers of budget centres are made responsible for the achievement of budget targets for the operations under their personal control.
Establish a system of control	Control over actual performance is provided by the comparisons of actual results against the budget plan. Departures from budget can then be investigated and the reasons for the departures can be divided into controllable and uncontrollable factors.
Provide a means of performance evaluation	Budgets provide targets which can be compared with actual outcomes in order to assess employee performance.
Motivate employees to improve their performance	The interest and commitment of employees can be retained if there is a system which lets them know how well or badly they are performing. The identification of controllable reasons for departures from budget with managers responsible provides an incentive for improving future performance.

3.2   Communication of information, responsibility accounting and performance measurement are separate topics in this text. Our main interest in this part is in planning, co-ordination and control - deciding what to do, deciding who will do it and how, and seeing that it gets done.

3.3   A budget, since it has different purposes, might mean different things to different people.

What it might mean	Detail
Forecast	It helps managers to plan for the future. Given uncertainty about the future, however, it is quite likely that a budget will become outdated by the march of events and will cease to be a realistic forecast. New forecasts might be prepared that differ from the budget. (A **forecast** is **what is likely to happen;** a **budget** is **what an organisation wants to happen.** These are not necessarily the same thing.)
Means of allocating resources	It can be used to decide how many resources are needed (cash, labour and so on) and how many should be given to each area of the organisation's activities. Resource allocation is particularly important when some resources are in short supply. Budgets often set ceilings or limits on how much administrative departments and other service departments are allowed to spend in the period. Public expenditure budgets, for example, set spending limits for each government department.
Yardstick	By comparing it with actual performance, the budget provides a means of indicating where and when control action may be necessary (and possibly where some managers or employees are open to censure for achieving poor results).
Target	A budget might be a means of motivating the workforce to greater personal accomplishment, another aspect of control.

Question: coordination

Given the following information about a firm, what difficulties do you suspect may arise in the co-ordination of its activities? (No calculations are required.)

	Product X	Product Y
Market demand	150,000 units	250,000 units
Selling price	£4 per unit	£4 per unit

Production capacity (overall)	375,000 units
Capital expenditure requirements for the coming year	£110,000 (3 projects)
Average working capital required	£100,000 per 30,000 units

Cash collection trend	10% month 1; 20% month 2; 40% month 3; balance thereafter
Current overdraft	£40,000
Maximum overdraft facility	£75,000

Answer

Product X and product Y sales managers will compete for production time. Capacity is in any case inadequate to meet the full demand. All departments will compete for working capital and given the slowness of cash collection the overdraft facility may be exceeded without careful planning. Capital expenditure may have to be delayed, but this might hamper the ability of production to produce to meet demand.

Co-ordination

3.4   Let's look at this issue in more detail.

3.5   **Without guidance in the form of a budget, managers may make decisions in the belief that they are working in the best interests of the organisation.** For example, the marketing department may decide to run an advertising campaign which is intended to increase demand to a level in excess of the capacity of the production department. In other situations, the interests of individual managers may conflict: the purchasing manager may attempt to buy raw materials as cheaply as possible; the production manager is more concerned with quality materials that require no reworking and do not cause production to be interrupted.

3.6 One of the **aims of budgets** is to ensure that **decisions are taken for the good of the organisation as a whole,** rather than in the interests of particular areas. The preparation of a budget forces managers to **consider the relationships between their area of operations and sections of the organisation,** to identify any potential conflicts and resolve them.

3.7 When budgets are first prepared it is likely that some will be out of balance with others and will need **modifying so that they are compatible**. The **revision** of one budget may lead to the revision of others but finally, once they are all in agreement, the master budget can be prepared.

3.8 A system of budgeting therefore helps to co-ordinate the various activities of an organisation and ensures that all parts of the organisation are in mutual harmony.

4 BUDGETARY CONTROL

4.1 Suppose that a director tells a manager that he expects him to produce 100 units a day. On a particular day only 75 units are produced. When asked why, the manager says that production had to stop because a machine keeps breaking down. The director authorises the manager to buy a new machine. This is budgetary control in miniature.

> ## KEY TERM
>
> **Budgetary control** involves drawing up budgets for the areas of responsibility of individual managers and of regularly comparing actual results against expected results. The differences between actual results and expected results are called **variances** and these are used to provide a guideline for control action by individual managers.

4.2 **Main uses of budgetary control**

- To define the objectives of the organisation as a whole.
- To reveal the extent by which actual results have exceeded or fallen short of the budget.
- To indicate why actual results differ from those budgeted.
- As a basis for the revision of the current budget, or the preparation of future budgets.
- To ensure that resources are used as efficiently as possible.
- To see how well the activities of the organisation have been co-ordinated.
- To provide some central control where activities are decentralised.

Budgetary control as a control cycle

4.3 Budgetary control can be described as a **repetitive cycle: planning, activity and control** followed by more planning, activity, and control. Management accountants have the task of providing a feedback of control information within this budgetary control cycle.

Components of a budgetary control system

4.4

Component	Description	Examples
Standard	The targets at which the organisation is aiming	Budgeted/expected material costs or performance targets such as the number of claims under warranty
Sensor	Device or person by which information or data is collected and measured	Computer turn-around documents
Feedback	Measurement of differences between planned results and actual results	Management reports
Comparator	Means by which actual results of the system are measured against the predetermined plans	Managers. They are expected to make some judgement on the results of the calculation of the comparison, to decide whether any differences (variances) need to be investigated and then (after investigation) whether control action is required.
Effector or activator	The device or means by which control action is initiated	A managers instruction and a subordinate's action

4.5 The diagram below illustrates a control system. Notice how **corrective action impacts** on both **inputs and planned performance**.

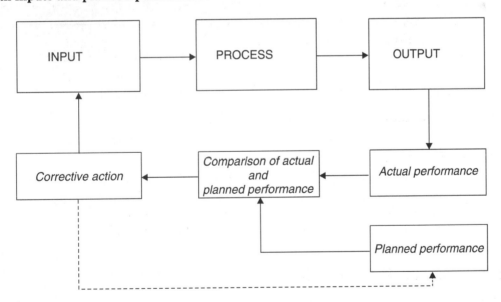

4.6 This example might help to make the idea of a control system easier to understand.

Component	Example
Standard	A sales budget or plan is prepared for the year.
Sensor	The costing system records actual results.
Feedback	At the end of each month, actual results (units sold, revenue and so on) are reported back to management.
Comparator	Managers compare actual results against the plan.
Effector	Where necessary, managers take corrective action to adjust the workings of the system, probably by amending the inputs to the system. For example, sales people might be asked to work longer hours or new price discounts might be decided. Where appropriate, the sales plan might be revised to take account of the results of control action.

Exam focus point

One of the optional questions in the June 2002 paper focused on the components of a budgetary control system listed above.

Feedback

4.7 We have already looked at feedback in terms of planning and control at different organisational levels. Here we consider it in terms of budgetary control.

KEY TERM

Feedback is a term used to describe the process of transmitting information about actual results to the people who are responsible for comparing them against a budget or standard, and initiating control action if required.

Feedback is also the control information itself. In a business organisation, it is information produced from within the organisation (for example, management control reports) with the purpose of helping management and other employees with control decisions.

4.8 **Examples** of feedback include profit reports (for profit centres), and variance analysis. Feedback may be required on a daily basis (by first-line supervisors) but variance reports to middle management are commonly prepared once every month or four weeks: thus annual budgets are usually divided into monthly or four-weekly control periods.

4.9 A feature of feedback is that it is information that is gathered by **measuring the outputs** of **the accounting system** itself. It has an 'internal' source, as distinct from 'environmental' information, which comes from outside the organisation.

4.10 Some form of internally generated feedback is essential if there is to be any effective control within an organisation, and the **most common types of control system** in businesses, such as budgetary control and stock control systems, are **all based on feedback** cycles.

Negative feedback

> ### KEY TERM
>
> **Negative feedback** indicates that targets were missed and this was not what was required. Control action is required to get back on target.

4.11 Thus, if the budgeted sales for June and July were £100,000 in each month, whereas the report of actual sales in June showed that only £90,000 had been reached, this negative feedback would indicate that control action was necessary to raise sales in July to £110,000 in order to get back on to the planned course.

Positive feedback

> ### KEY TERM
>
> **Positive feedback** means that actual results were better than target results. It leads to control action which causes actual results to maintain (or increase) their path of deviation from planned results. It indicates that the target should be moved.

4.12 Suppose that a company budgets to produce and sell 100 units of product each month, maintaining an average stock level of 40 units. If actual sales exceed the budget, and show signs of sustained growth, it will obviously be in the company's interests to produce and sell as much as possible (provided additional output earns extra contribution to profit).

   (a) Feedback in the first month might show that sales are above budget, selling costs are a little higher than budget and that stocks have been run down to meet demand.

   (b) Action should attempt to increase sales (in other words, to promote the deviation of actual results from the plan) even if this requires extra selling costs for advertising or sales promotion, maintaining the 'adverse' deviation of actual costs from budget.

   Additional production volumes would be required, although initially some extra sales might be made out of remaining stocks (resulting in further deviations from the production and finished goods stocks budgets).

Management accountant's role

4.13 The management accountant's role in an organisation is to **provide information to help with planning and control decisions by other managers** throughout the organisation. Management accounting **provides the feedback loop** for much control reporting.

   Step 1. By recording actual results

   Step 2. By analysing actual results and comparing them with the budget

   Step 3. By reporting actual results and the comparisons with plan to the managers who are responsible for whatever control action might be necessary

Feedforward control

4.14 Budgetary control usually entails a comparison of actual results and the budget. **Past events** are used as a means of **controlling or adjusting future activity**.

4.15 Consider a cash budget. This is used to identify likely peaks and troughs in cash balances, and if it seems probable, say, that a higher overdraft facility will be needed later in the year control action will be taken in advance of the actual need, to make sure that the facility will be available. This is an example of **feedforward control**.

> **KEY TERM**
>
> **Feedforward control** is control based on comparing original targets or actual results with a forecast of future results, and taking action that anticipates and makes allowance for future changes.

4.16 The 'information revolution' has **widened the scope for the use of this budgetary control technique.** Forecasting models can be constructed which enable regular revised forecasts to be prepared about what is now likely to happen in view of changes in key variables such as sales demand.

4.17 If regular forecasts are prepared, managers will have both the current forecast and the master budget to guide their action. The master budget, which is the original plan, may or may not be achievable in view of the changing circumstances. The current forecast indicates what is expected to happen in view of these new circumstances.

4.18 **Budgetary control comparisons which are then possible**

(a) **Current forecast v budget.** What action must be taken to get back to the budget plan, given the differences between the current forecast and the budget? Is any control action worthwhile?

(b) If control action is planned, the current forecast will need to be amended to take account of the effects of the control action and a revised forecast prepared. The next comparison should then be **revised forecast v budget** to determine whether the budget plan is now expected to be achieved.

(c) A comparison between the **first forecast and the revised forecast** will show what the expected effect of the control action will be.

(d) At the end of a control period, actual results will be analysed, and two comparisons may be made.

(i) **Actual results v the revised forecast.** Why did variances occur?

(ii) **Actual results so far in the year v the budget**

(e) At the same time, a **new current forecast** should be prepared, and the cycle of comparisons and control action may begin again.

> **Exam focus point**
>
> The identification and explanation of issues likely to cause problems in the operation of a budgetary control system was worth eight marks in the May 2002 exam. These are wide ranging and include uncontrollable external factors, goal congruence, 'good' information and internal politics – in fact, issues from across the Paper 3.3 syllabus.

5   ALTERNATIVE BUDGET MODELS

Incremental budgeting

> **KEY TERM**
>
> **Incremental budgeting** is the traditional approach to setting a budget and involves basing next year's budget on the current year's results plus an extra amount (an 'increment') for estimated growth or inflation next year.

5.1   Traditional incremental budgeting will be sufficient only if current operations are as effective, efficient and economical as they can be, without any alternative courses of action available to the organisation.

5.2   However, the planning process should take account of **alternative options**, and look for **ways of improving performance**: this is something that traditional incremental budgeting simply does not do.

5.3   Although administratively an incremental budget is fairly easy to prepare, it encourages **slack and wasteful spending** to creep into budgets and to become a normal feature of actual spending.

Slack

> **KEY TERM**
>
> **Slack** is the difference between the minimum necessary costs and the costs built into the budget or actually incurred.

5.4   In the process of preparing budgets, managers might be careful to **overestimate costs,** so that they will **not be blamed** in the future for overspending. 'The personal goals of managers (personal income, size of staff, esteem, power) will often lead to a "bargained" budget whereby managers intentionally create slack as a protective device.' (Horngren)

In controlling actual operations, managers must then ensure that their **spending rises to meet their budget,** otherwise they will be 'blamed' for careless budgeting.

5.5   A typical situation is for a manager to **waste money on non-essential expenses** so that he **uses all his budget allowances**. The reason behind his action is the fear that unless the allowance is fully spent it will be **reduced in future periods** thus making his job more difficult as the future reduced budgets will not be so easy to attain. Because inefficiency and slack are allowed for in budgets, achieving a budget target means only that costs have remained within the accepted levels of inefficient spending. One approach to the removal of slack is zero-based budgeting.

> **Exam focus point**
>
> You might be asked in your examination to compare the merits of newer approaches discussed in Chapter 4 with traditional incremental budgeting, or to suggest what the weaknesses of traditional incremental budgeting might be.

Zero based budgeting

> **KEY TERM**
>
> **Zero based budgeting** involves preparing a budget for each cost centre from 'scratch' (a 'zero base'). Every process or expenditure then has to be justified in its entirety in order to be included in the next year's budget.

5.6 In zero based budgeting (ZBB), there should be a positive attempt to **eliminate inefficiency and slack** from current expenditure, not merely to prevent future cost increases. ZBB rejects the idea that next year's budgeted activities should assume that last year's activities will continue at the same level or volume, and that next year's budget can be based on last year's costs plus an extra amount for expansion and inflation.

5.7 **The basic approach of zero-based budgeting**

Step 1. Managers within the organisation are asked to specify the **decision units** within their area of authority (programmes of work or capital expenditure programmes or areas of activity which can be individually evaluated).

Step 2. Each of the separate decision units is described in a **decision package** (a document which identifies and describes the specific activity in such a way that management can evaluate it and rank it in order of priority against other activities).

Step 3. Each decision package is evaluated and **ranked** by cost benefit analysis.

Step 4. Activities which would cost more than they are worth (in qualitative or quantitative terms) should be **dropped**.

Step 5. **Resources** in the budget are then **allocated** according to the funds available and the evaluation and ranking of the competing packages.

5.8 Packages involving small expenditures can be dealt with by junior managers but senior managers must make decisions involving larger amounts of expenditure. The ZBB process must, however, **run through the entire management structure.**

5.9 **Types of decision package**

(a) **Mutually exclusive packages**. Each of these contains an alternative method of getting the same job done. The best option among the packages must be selected by cost benefit analysis and the other packages are then discarded.

(b) **Incremental packages**. These divide one aspect of work or activity into different levels of effort. The 'base' package will describe the minimum amount of work that must be done to carry out the activity and the other packages describe what additional work could be done, at what cost and for what benefits.

5.10 EXAMPLE: ZBB

Suppose that a cost centre manager is preparing a budget for maintenance costs. He might first consider two mutually exclusive packages. Package A might be to keep a maintenance team of two men per shift for two shifts each day at a cost of £60,000 per annum, whereas package B might be to obtain a maintenance service from an outside contractor at a cost of £50,000. A cost-benefit analysis will be conducted because the quicker repairs obtainable from an in-house maintenance service might justify its extra cost. If we now suppose that package A is preferred, the budget analysis must be completed by describing the incremental variations in this chosen alternative.

(a) The **'base' package** would describe the **minimum requirement** for the maintenance work. This might be to pay for one man per shift for two shifts each day at a cost of £30,000.

(b) **Incremental package** 1 might be to pay for two men on the early shift and one man on the late shift, at a cost of £45,000. The extra cost of £15,000 would need to be justified, for example by savings in lost production time, or by more efficient machinery.

(c) **Incremental package** 2 might be the original preference, for two men on each shift at a cost of £60,000. The cost-benefit analysis would compare its advantages, if any, over incremental package 1.

(d) **Incremental package** 3 might be for three men on the early shift and two on the late shift, at a cost of £75,000; and so on.

Question: ZBB in 'real life'

Obtain your bank statements and credit card statements for the last three months, say, and identify as much of the expenditure as you can in as precise detail as possible.

(a) Identify the decision units ('accommodation', 'travel', 'food and drink', 'saving' etc).
(b) Identify mutually exclusive activities (eating out or in, driving to work or taking the bus etc).
(c) Identify 'incremental packages' (activities that you might spend more on if funds were available).
(d) Draw up a base package for these activities and several incremental packages.

What proportion of your total income do you spend per month on discretionary activities?

Uses of ZBB

5.11 (a) Budgeting for **discretionary cost items**, such as training costs. The priorities for spending money could be established by ranking activities and alternative levels of spending or service can be evaluated on an incremental basis. For example, is it worth spending £2,000 more to increase the numbers trained on one type of training course by 10%? If so, what priority should this incremental spending on training be given, when compared with other potential training activities?

(b) **Rationalisation** (a euphemism for cutting back on production and activity levels, and cutting costs). The need for service departments to operate above a minimum service level can be questioned, and ZBB can be used to make rationalisation decisions when an organisation is forced to make spending cuts. (This use of ZBB might explain any unpopularity it might have among managers.)

Advantages of ZBB

5.12 (a) It provides a budgeting and planning tool for management which **responds to changes** in the business environment; obsolete items of expenditure and activities are identified and ceased.

(b) It obliges an organisation to look very closely into its **cost behaviour** patterns in order to decide the effect of alternative courses of action.

(c) It should result in a more efficient **allocation of resources**.

(d) It adds a psychological impetus to employees to **avoid wasteful expenditure**.

(e) The **documentation** required makes a co-ordinated, in-depth knowledge of an organisation's operations available to all management.

Disadvantages of ZBB

5.13 The most serious drawback to ZBB is that it requires a lot of management **time** and paperwork (though computers help with this), and managers must be **trained** in ZBB techniques in order that they can apply them sensibly and properly. The organisation's **information systems** must also be capable of providing suitable incremental cost and incremental benefit analysis.

5.14 Zero-base budgeting requires the extensive involvement of managers and it will therefore **not be appropriate** in an organisation structure that is not conducive to participation in budgeting.

5.15 Frequently the disadvantages of the full version of ZBB will outweigh the benefits, but the approach is self-evidently preferable to traditional incremental budgeting and many organisations have adopted **less complex versions** of the ZBB approach.

Question: ZBB v incremental budgeting

An organisation used ZBB last year to prepare its budget and is now as efficient, effective and economical as it can possibly be. A manager has put it to the board that in view of this a further round of ZBB this year would itself be a wasteful activity and that the time could be more profitably spent on other matters. She proposes taking this year's results as the basis for next year's budget and adjusting the figures to allow for planned growth plus inflation at the rate currently indicated by the Retail Price Index, or other more appropriate indices where these are available.

The board has asked you for your opinion.

Answer

Provided that the organisation is indeed already as efficient, effective and economical as possible, and provided that the planned growth or other factors will not have an impact on this, then it would seem perfectly reasonable to use the proposed incremental approach in this case. In practice the conditions described will rarely apply, of course.

Exam focus point

ZBB was examined in June 2004.

Rolling budgets

KEY TERM

A **rolling budget** is a budget which is continuously updated by adding a further period (a month or quarter) when the earliest period has expired.

5.16 Rolling budgets are an attempt to prepare targets and plans which are **more realistic and certain**, particularly with a regard to price levels, by shortening the period between preparing budgets.

5.17 Instead of preparing a **periodic budget** annually for the full budget period, there would be budgets every one, two, three or four months. Each of these budgets would plan for the next twelve months so that the current budget is extended by an extra period as the current period ends: hence the name **rolling** budgets.

Advantages of rolling budgets

5.18 They may be advantageous in **larger businesses** operating in **unstable environments**.

(a) They reduce the element of **uncertainty** in budgeting because it is easier to predict what will happen in the short-term.

(b) Planning and control will be based on a **recent plan** which is **more realistic** than a fixed annual budget that might have been made many months ago. For example, a 12-month budget becomes outdated when there is rapid inflation; a rolling budget allows for more frequent reassessments and revisions in the light of inflationary trends.

(c) There will always be a budget which **extends for several months ahead.**

(d) They force managers to reassess the budget regularly, and to produce budgets which are **up to date** in the light of current events and expectations.

(e) Realistic budgets are likely to have a **better motivational influence** on managers.

Disadvantages of rolling budgets

5.19 In an organisation where the finance function is not fully developed or has limited time available, the **disadvantages** of rolling budgets can outweigh any benefits.

(a) They involve more **time, effort and money** in budget preparation, although computers and spreadsheets help considerably.

(b) Frequent budgeting might have an off-putting effect on **managers** who doubt the value of preparing one budget after another at regular intervals.

(c) If the business's environment is fairly **stable,** routine updating of the budget may be **unnecessary**. Instead the annual budget could simply be **updated** whenever changes become foreseeable. A budget might be updated once or twice during the course of the year.

Fixed and flexible budgeting

> **KEY TERMS**
>
> A **fixed budget** is one that is not adjusted to the actual volume of output or level of activity attained in a period. This is most unrealistic because the actual level will almost certainly be different from the level of activity originally planned.
>
> A **flexible budget**, however, recognises this uncertainty. It is designed to change so as to relate to the actual volumes of output.

5.20 Flexible budgets may be used in one of two ways.

Planning

5.21 At the **planning** stage when budgets are set, to reduce the effect of uncertainty. For example, suppose that a company expects to sell 10,000 units of output during the next year. A master budget (the fixed budget) would be prepared on the basis of this expected volume. However, if the company thinks that output and sales might be as low as 8,000 units or as high as 12,000 units, it may prepare contingency flexible budgets, at volumes of say, 8,000, 9,000, 11,000 and 12,000 units.

5.22 **Advantages of planning with flexible budgets**

(a) Finding out well in advance the **costs** of lay-off pay, idle time and so on if **output falls short** of budget

(b) Deciding whether it would be possible to find **alternative uses** for spare capacity if **output falls short** of budget

(c) Estimating the **costs** of overtime or sub-contracting work if sales **volume exceeds the fixed budget** estimate, and finding out if there is a **limiting factor** which would prevent high volumes of output and sales being achieved

5.23 It has been suggested, however, that since many cost items in modern industry are fixed costs, the value of flexible budgets in **planning** is dwindling.

(a) In many manufacturing industries, **plant costs** (depreciation, rent and so on) are a very large proportion of total costs, and these tend to be fixed costs.

(b) **Wages costs** also tend to be fixed, because employees are generally guaranteed a basic wage for a working week of an agreed number of hours.

(c) With the growth of **service industries,** fixed salaries and overheads will account for most costs, direct materials being only a relatively small proportion.

5.24 The advantages of flexible budgets for reducing uncertainty are clear. But the fact remains that **fixed budgets** are **more common in practice,** and in certain environments there is no reason why this should not be so. Some organisations, particularly **small specialised** ones, know exactly who their customers are, how much they intend to buy, how much, within a small margin, their costs are going to be and so forth. **If change occurs it is well understood** by the persons responsible for dealing with it and by the owners of the business – often because these people are one and the same.

5.25 When there is such a **high degree of stability** the administrative effort involved in flexible budgeting or rolling budgets produces little or no benefit and fixed budgets are perfectly adequate and appropriate.

Control

5.26 Flexible budgets are also used '**retrospectively**' at the end of each month (control period) or year, to compare actual results achieved with the results that would have been expected if the actual circumstances had been known in advance. Flexible budgets are an essential factor in **budgetary control** and **variance analysis.**

Chapter roundup

- This chapter is an **introduction** to budgeting, setting it in the context of long-term planning and viewing the budget as an **organisation-wide device for co-ordination and control.**

- **Long-term planning information** tends to be sourced **externally. Short-term planning information** tends to be sourced **internally**.

- Make sure that you are aware of the detail behind the following **points covered in your earlier studies.**

  - Long-term plan
  - Limiting factor
  - Budget manual
  - Sales budget
  - Production capacity

  - Functional budgets
  - Discretionary costs
  - Consolidation and co-ordination
  - Cash budget
  - Master budget

- Budgeting is a **multi-purpose activity**.

- A budget might be a **forecast**, a **means of allocating resources**, a **yardstick** or a **target**.

- **Budgetary control** recognises that business organisations are dynamic, especially when **feedforward control** is used to anticipate future threats to the achievement of the plan or opportunities to achieve it more efficiently.

- **Feedback** is the process of transmitting control information and the control information itself. It can be positive or negative.

- **Incremental budgeting** (which allows **slack** to creep into budgets) was contrasted with **zero based budgeting**.

- **Rolling budgets** are particularly useful for larger organisations operating in unstable environments.

- **Fixed budgets** were compared with **flexible budgets,** which can be used for planning or for control.

Quick quiz

1   An information-gathering exercise carried out to ensure that an organisation has a full understanding of where it is at present is known as a 'position analysis' or a 'strategic audit'. *True or false?*

2   Here are four characteristics of long-term planning information. List the corresponding characteristics of short-term planning information.

   (a) Used by top management
   (b) Broad in scope rather than deep in detail
   (c) External
   (d) Looks to the future and lacks certainty

3   List the ten purposes of using budgets.

4   Which of the following is not a use of budgetary control?

   A   To define the objectives of the organisation as a whole
   B   To ensure that resources are used as efficiently as possible
   C   To provide some central control when activities are centralised
   D   To provide the basis for the preparation of future budgets

5   What is the difference between the minimum necessary costs and the costs built into the budget?

6   *Match the description to the type of budget.*

   Budgets

   Incremental
   Rolling
   Zero based

Descriptions

(a) Next year's budget is based on the current year's results plus an extra amount for estimated growth or inflation.

(b) Each item in the budget is specifically justified, as though each activity were being undertaken for the first time.

(c) The budget is continuously updated by adding a further accounting period when the earliest accounting period has expired.

7   *Fill in the blanks.*

A flexible budget is a budget which, by recognising .... is designed to .... as the level of activity changes.

8   Training costs are an example of discretionary costs. *True or false?*

Answers to quick quiz

1   False. It is known as a 'position audit' or 'strategic analysis'.

2   (a) Used at a lower level by those who implement plans
    (b) Detailed
    (c) Internal
    (d) Definite

3   Ensure the achievement of the organisation's objectives
    Compel planning
    Communicate ideas and plans
    Co-ordinate activities
    Allocate resources
    Authorisation
    Provide a framework for responsibility accounting
    Establish a system of control
    Provide a means of performance evaluation
    Motivate employees to improve their performance

4   C   It should provide some central control when activities are decentralised.

5   Slack

6   Incremental   (a)
    Rolling   (c)
    Zero based   (b)

7   cost behaviour patterns
    change

8   True

Now try the question below from the Exam Question Bank

Number	Level	Marks	Time
15	Exam	20	36 mins

Chapter 18

BUDGETING TECHNIQUES

Topic list	Syllabus reference
1 Quantitative aids: cost analysis	4(b)
2 Forecasting techniques	4(b)
3 Sales forecasting	4(b)
4 Learning curve theory	4(b)
5 Budgets and uncertainty	4(b)

Introduction

To produce a budget calls for the preparation of sales forecasts and cost estimates, and the ability to formulate a plan of action within the framework of competing departmental claims for scarce resources. Modelling and quantitative techniques can assist with the 'number crunching' aspects of budgeting, and the application, usefulness and limitations of various quantitative methods could feature in the examination. A number of such techniques will be explained in this chapter.

We begin by looking at **methods of analysing costs into their fixed and variable components.** You have covered the methods in your earlier studies but, because the words quantitative techniques often strike terror into students' hearts (although they shouldn't), we will assume no prior knowledge in this instance.

Section 3 covers various **sales forecasting techniques. Time series analysis** is one technique which will be familiar to you from your earlier studies.

In some industries, budgeting must take account of the **learning curve effect.** Labour learns from experience and, in gaining this experience, the time required to complete a job lessens. This speeding up of a job with repeated performance is known as the learning effect or learning curve, and the reduction in the required direct labour time can be quantified. Learning curve theory is the subject of Section 4 of this chapter.

Budgeting is subject to **uncertainty** because it relies for its accuracy upon **factors which in reality are beyond control.**

- Customers may decide not to buy as much as has been forecast, or they may buy more.
- Competitors may 'steal' some of an organisation's expected customers, or some of the competitors' customers may change their buying allegiance to the organisation.
- The workforce may not work as hard as was hoped, or it may work harder
- Machines may break down unexpectedly.
- Suppliers may increase their costs, or lower them.
- Exchange rates, inflation or interest rates may change unpredictably.
- There may be political unrest (terrorist activity), social unrest (public transport strikes), or minor or major natural disasters (storms, floods).

Such factors make the task of setting realistic budgets in the first place extremely difficult, and as the budget period progresses they act to undermine the effectiveness of budgetary control. In the last section of this chapter we shall consider some ways in which **uncertainty in budgeting can be reduced or accommodated.**

In Chapter 19, we look at the behavioural aspects of budgeting.

> ## Study guide
>
> ### Section 20 – Budgeting and budgetary control II
>
> - Identify quantitative aids which may be used in budgetary planning and control
> - Discuss and evaluate methods for the analysis of costs into fixed and variable components
> - Give examples to demonstrate the use of forecasting techniques in the budgetary planning process
> - Explain the use of forecasting techniques in the budgetary planning process
> - Describe the use of learning curve theory in budgetary planning and control
> - Implement learning curve theory
> - Identify factors which may cause uncertainty in the setting of budgets and in the budgetary control process
> - Illustrate the use of probabilities in budgetary planning and comment on the relevance of the information thus obtained
> - Explain the use of computer based models in accommodating uncertainty in budgeting and in promoting 'what-if' analysis
>
> ## Exam guide
>
> This chapter's topics are not classified as a core syllabus area, but could easily appear in both quantitative and discursive questions in conjunction with other topics.
>
> The issues covered in this chapter are useful background to the Oxford Brookes degree Research and Analysis Project Topic 1, which requires you to analyse the efficiency and/or effectiveness of a management accounting technique in an organisational setting.

1 QUANTITATIVE AIDS: COST ANALYSIS

KEY TERM

Cost estimation is a term used to describe the measurement of historical costs with a view to providing estimates on which to base future expectations of cost.

Exam focus point

For your examination, you might be expected to assess the merits and weaknesses of various methods of estimating costs and apply one or more of these methods in practice.

1.1 Historical costs can be assumed to have a **'mixed cost'** behaviour pattern. Mixed costs can be **separated into their fixed and variable elements,** using a variety of techniques. Some techniques are more sophisticated than others, and are therefore likely to be more reliable, but in practice, the simpler techniques are more commonly found and might give estimates that are accurate enough for their purpose. The **techniques are dealt with in order of complexity in the following paragraphs.**

Using engineered costs

1.2 By this method (also called the **'account classification method'**) expenditure items are classified as **fixed, variable** or **semi-variable**. This allows managers to **determine the inputs required for a given level of output.**

1.3 This, in rough terms, is how the direct cost items (materials and labour costs) might be built-up when a budgeted direct cost per unit of output is estimated. The technique depends on **subjective judgement** and **skill and realism** in estimating costs, and so only an **approximate accuracy** can be expected from its use.

High-low method

1.4 The high low method involves reviewing records of production in previous periods and selecting the two with the **highest and lowest volume of output**. The **difference** between the total costs of the two periods is assumed to be the **total variable cost of the extra units produced**. For example, if the highest level of output were 8,000 units and the lowest 6,000, then the difference between the total costs for these two periods would equal the variable cost of 2,000 units. This allows the **variable cost per unit** to be calculated and, by **substitution**, the **total fixed costs** can be found. You should remember this method from earlier studies, so try a question.

Question: high-low method

A company has recorded the following total costs during the last five years.

Year	Output volume Units	Total cost £	Average price level index
20X0	65,000	145,000	100
20X1	80,000	179,000	112
20X2	90,000	209,100	123
20X3	60,000	201,600	144
20X4	75,000	248,000	160

What costs should be expected in 20X5 if output is 85,000 units and the average price level index is 180? (In other words do not ignore inflation!)

Answer

Price levels should be adjusted to a common basis, say index level 100.

(a)		Output Units	Total cost £	Cost at price level index = 100 £
	High level	90,000	209,100 × 100/123 =	170,000
	Low level	60,000	201,600 × 100/144 =	140,000
	Variable cost	30,000		30,000

Variable cost per unit = £30,000/30,000 = £1

(b) **Substituting**

	£
Total cost of 90,000 units (Index 100)	170,000
Variable cost of 90,000 units (× £1)	90,000
Fixed costs (Index 100)	80,000

(c) **Costs in 20X5 for 85,000 units will be:**

	£
Variable costs (Index 100)	85,000
Fixed costs (Index 100)	80,000
Total costs (Index 100)	165,000

At 20X5 price levels (index 180) = £165,000 × 180/100 = £297,000

1.5 The major **drawback** to the high-low method is that **only two historical cost records** from previous periods are used in the cost estimation. Unless these two records are a reliable indicator of costs throughout the relevant range of output, which is unlikely, only a 'loose approximation' of fixed and variable costs will be obtained.

1.6 The **advantage** of the method is its relative **simplicity**. It would be more appropriate than the engineering method for estimating total costs of a department, factory or business as it avoids the need to build up estimates for each cost item individually and is therefore quicker.

The scattergraph method

1.7 By this graphical method of cost estimation, **historical costs** from previous periods are **plotted,** and from the resulting scatter diagram, a **'line-of-best-fit'** can be drawn by visual estimation. Where necessary, costs should be **adjusted** to the same indexed price level to allow for inflation.

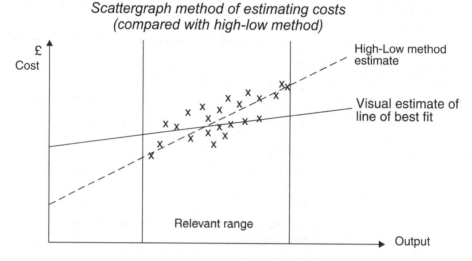

*Scattergraph method of estimating costs
(compared with high-low method)*

1.8 The **advantage** of the scattergraph over the high-low method is that a **greater quantity of historical data** is used in the estimation, but its **disadvantage** is that the cost line is drawn by **visual judgement** and so is a **subjective approximation**.

Linear regression analysis (least squares method)

KEY TERMS

Linear regression analysis is a statistical method of estimating fixed and variable costs using historical data from a number of previous accounting periods.

1.9 Linear regression analysis is used to derive a **linear cost function y = a + bx** where:

y, the dependent variable	=	total cost
x, the independent variable	=	the level of activity
a	=	the fixed cost
b	=	the variable cost per unit of activity

1.10 Historical data is collected from previous periods, and adjusted to a common price level to remove inflationary differences, so that a number of 'readings' exist for **output volumes (x)** and their **associated costs (y)**. The aim is to provide estimates of **fixed costs** (a) and **unit variable costs** (b) using these readings for x and y.

> **FORMULA TO LEARN**
>
> If $\quad y = a + bx$
>
> $\quad b = \dfrac{n\Sigma xy - \Sigma x\Sigma y}{n\Sigma x^2 - (\Sigma x)^2}$ and $a = \dfrac{\Sigma y}{n} - \dfrac{b\Sigma x}{n}$
>
> where n is the number of pairs of data for x and y.

1.11 EXAMPLE: LEAST SQUARES METHOD

The transport department of the Norwest Council operates a large fleet of assorted vehicles. These vehicles are used as the need arises by the various departments of the Council. Each month a statement is prepared for the transport department comparing actual results with budget. One of the items in the transport department's monthly statement is the cost of vehicle maintenance. This maintenance is carried out by the employees of the department. To facilitate his control the transport manager has asked that future statements should show vehicle maintenance costs analysed into fixed and variable costs.

Data from the six months from January to June 20X2 inclusive is given below.

20X2	Vehicle maintenance cost £	Vehicle running hours
January	13,600	2,100
February	15,800	2,800
March	14,500	2,200
April	16,200	3,000
May	14,900	2,600
June	15,000	2,500

Analyse the vehicle maintenance costs into fixed and variable costs, based on the data given, and utilising the least squares method.

1.12 SOLUTION

If $y = a + bx$, where y represent costs and x represents running hours, then

$$b = \frac{n\Sigma xy - \Sigma x\Sigma y}{n\Sigma x^2 - (\Sigma x)^2}$$

when n is the number of pairs of data, which is 6 in this problem.

x '000 hrs	y £'000	xy	x^2
2.1	13.6	28.56	4.41
2.8	15.8	44.24	7.84
2.2	14.5	31.90	4.84
3.0	16.2	48.60	9.00
2.6	14.9	38.74	6.76
2.5	15.0	37.50	6.25
15.2	90.0	229.54	39.10

$$\textbf{Variable cost per hour,} \quad b = \frac{6(229.54) - (15.2)(90.0)}{6(39.1) - (15.2)^2}$$

$$= \frac{1,377.24 - 1,368}{234.6 - 231.04} = \frac{9.24}{3.56} = £2.60$$

$$\text{Fixed costs (in } \pounds'000) \quad a = \frac{\Sigma y}{n} - \frac{b\Sigma x}{n} = \frac{90}{6} - \frac{2.6(15.2)}{6}$$

$$= \pounds 8.41 \text{ approx, say } \pounds 8,400$$

The conditions suited to the use of linear regression analysis

1.13 Linear regression analysis is an **alternative** technique to the **high-low method**, and it would be used in the following circumstances.

   (a) If the high-low method is thought to be too **unreliable** so that it might produce serious inaccuracies in the estimate of costs

   (b) If there is a **sufficient number of historical records** of cost at different activity levels to make it capable of providing a more reliable estimate of costs

1.14 **Conditions which should apply if linear regression analysis is to be used to estimate costs**

   (a) A **linear** cost function should be assumed.

   (b) There should be a **wide spread of activity levels** in the historical data used so that it covers the full normal range of business activity.

   (c) The historical data for cost and output should be adjusted to a **common price level** (to overcome cost differences caused by inflation) and the historical data should also be **representative of current conditions** (ie current technology, current efficiency levels, current operations (products made)).

   (d) Linear regression analysis is based on historical data. The estimates of variable and fixed costs will be used to predict costs in the future. Management must be confident that **conditions which have existed in the past will continue in the future** or the **estimates** of cost produced by linear regression analysis must be **amended to allow for expected changes** in the future (such as an improvement in labour productivity).

Multiple regression analysis

1.15 Unlike the techniques so far described multiple regression analysis recognises that **several different factors**, not just one, can affect costs. For example, total costs in a factory might be affected by the volume of output, the time of year, the size of batches, labour turnover, the age of machinery, and so on.

1.16 The **disadvantage** of multiple regression analysis is its relative complexity: a computer program would be needed to derive an estimation of the cost function. However, provided that past costs are a reliable guide to estimating future expected costs (if the use of historical data to predict the future is valid) multiple regression is likely to produce **more accurate estimates**. It should provide **better information** and its users can have more confidence in its cost predictions than with other methods.

Question: cost behaviour

Why should we want to analyse costs into fixed and variable components?

Answer

A knowledge of cost behaviour is fundamental to **planning**, where costs at various levels of activity help to determine what the organisation can and cannot attempt.

It is fundamental to **control**, because if the level of activity is not the expected level it is less meaningful to compare actual results with the budget without making allowance for this.

In **decision making** a knowledge of what costs will change as a result of a decision and which will remain the same is essential, because costs that will never be affected by the decision do not need to be considered when making it.

Cost analysis and budgeting

1.17 Once the estimates of fixed and variable costs have been established, budgeted costs can be set by adding the total variable cost at the budgeted activity level to the fixed cost.

2 FORECASTING TECHNIQUES

2.1 There are a number of different forecasting techniques which can be used for **budgeting and longer-term strategic planning**. Some of the techniques are mathematical and quantitative; others are based on human judgement.

2.2 The mathematical techniques usually take **historical records** as data which can be **analysed and extrapolated** to make forecasts. On the whole, however, the usefulness of historical records for forecasting decreases as the forecast period increases in length.

Long-term forecasting: scenario building (the Delphi model)

2.3 For long-term planning, forecasts will be needed about what the future state of an industry, its markets or its technology might be in a few years' time. **Scenario building** is a term used to describe the process of **identifying alternative futures** and predicting what might happen.

2.4 The **Delphi model** or technique is one method of scenario building, in which a **group of experts** are asked individually to **provide their views about what will happen in the future** (for example technological breakthroughs, changes over time and so on).

Econometric models

2.5 A variety of **forecasting models** might be used by an organisation. One type of model used for both short-term and medium-term forecasting is an econometric model. (**Econometrics** is the study of economic variables and how they are interrelated, using a computer model.)

2.6 Econometric models can be used to obtain **information about economic developments** which might be important for an organisation's future plans, such as the following.

- The likely rate of cost **inflation**
- The likely level of **interest rates**
- The expected **growth in the economy** and **consumer demand**
- Expected movements in **foreign exchange rates**

Short-term forecasts

2.7 Short-term forecasts are forecasts of sales, costs or resource requirements and so on for up to **about one year ahead**. They are usually prepared by **extrapolating** historical data, on the assumption that future operating trends and characteristics will, in the short term at least, be a continuation of recent trends and current operating characteristics.

KEY TERM

Extrapolation is the technique of determining a projection by statistical means.

2.8 It is usually done by some form of **time series analysis,** that is, by calculating how sales, costs and so on are likely to vary over time.

3 SALES FORECASTING

3.1 One of the most **important** forecasts for budgetary planning in a trading organisation is the sales forecast. How can an organisation estimate how much it is likely to sell?

3.2 **One approach** to sales forecasting is to obtain sales forecasts for each sales area or region from the area or regional **sales representatives.** Salespeople's forecasts will be based on their judgement of what they think they will be able to sell, and so could easily be too optimistic or too pessimistic, depending on the personal outlook of each person.

Mathematical techniques: time series analysis

3.3 Time series analysis was covered in detail in Paper 2.4. Here we provide a summary of the technique.

3.4 Suppose that sales of product X for the past four years have been as follows.

	Spring Units	Summer Units	Autumn Units	Winter Units
20X1	3,600	2,000	5,300	2,900
20X2	3,400	2,100	5,600	2,800
20X3	3,500	2,300	5,100	2,900
20X4	3,500	2,200	5,500	3,000

How might we forecast sales for 20X5?

3.5 Using the moving averages technique, we begin by **establishing what the seasonal cycle is.** Here it is obviously the four seasons of the year and a one year cycle. (In another situation, it might be a weekly cycle of seven days.)

3.6 Next, we **calculate the moving average of 12-monthly sales, and from this, the moving average of seasonal sales.** The idea behind calculating a moving average is to eliminate seasonal variations. The table below shows how this is done.

3.7 The first two columns need some explanation.

(a) **The first column**

Moving averages are matched against the mid-point of the time period to which they relate. Here, the 12-month moving averages do not relate to a specific season, but to the mid-point between two seasons.

The first figure is the sum of the sales for Spring to Winter 20X1 (3,600 + 2,000 + 5,300 + 2,900 = 13,800); the second is the sum of sales for Summer 20X1 to Spring 20X2 (2,000 + 5,300 + 2,900 + 3,400 = 13,600) and so on.

362

(b) **The second column.**

By **taking a further moving average** of each pair of total 12-monthly sales, a new moving average is obtained which **lines up** directly with a time period.

	Total 12-monthly sales	Centre and take average	Average seasonal sales (÷4) (a)	Actual sales (b)	Difference (b) – (a)
Spring 20X1					
Summer					
	13,800				
Autumn		13,700	3,425.0	5,300	1,875.0
	13,600				
Winter		13,650	3,412.5	2,900	(512.5)
	13,700				
Spring 20X2		13,850	3,462.5	3,400	(62.5)
	14,000				
Summer		13,950	3,487.5	2,100	(1,387.5)
	13,900				
Autumn		13,950	3,487.5	5,600	2,112.5
	14,000				
Winter		14,100	3,525.0	2,800	(725.0)
	14,200				
Spring 20X3		13,950	3,487.5	3,500	12.5
	13,700				
Summer		13,750	3,437.5	2,300	(1,137.5)
	13,800				
Autumn		13,800	3,450.0	5,100	1,650.0
	13,800				
Winter		13,750	3,437.5	2,900	(537.5)
	13,700				
Spring 20X4		13,900	3,475.0	3,500	25.0
	14,100				
Summer		14,150	3,537.5	2,200	(1,337.5)
	14,200				
Autumn					
Winter					

3.8   The **difference** (in the right hand column of the table) between the actual sales in each period and the moving seasonal average is the **seasonal variation** in actual sales from the average seasonal sales. To obtain a **best estimate** of the future variation in sales each season, we now **take the simple average** of these figures, as follows.

	Spring	Summer	Autumn	Winter	Total
Variation					
20X1			1,875.0	(512.5)	
20X2	(62.5)	(1,387.5)	2,112.5	(725.0)	
20X3	12.5	(1,137.5)	1,650.0	(537.5)	
20X4	25.0	(1,337.5)			
Total	(25.0)	(3,862.5)	5,637.5	(1,775.0)	
Average (÷ 3)	(8.0)	(1,288.0)	1,879.0	(592.0)	(9)
Reduce residual 9 to zero *	0.0	3.0	3.0	3.0	9
Revised average	(8.0)	(1,285.0)	1,882.0	(589.0)	0

* The total of seasonal variations around the average seasonal sales must, by definition, be 0. Rounding in our simple averaging technique has given us a residual amount of (9) which we can eliminate by sharing it out between the four seasons in a fairly arbitrary way. Here three units are added to each of the seasons where the variations are biggest.

This gives us our **estimated seasonal variations** in sales for each season, **above or below the 'average' seasonal sales.**

Question: time series analysis

(a) Where do the figures in the 'summer' column in Paragraph 3.7 come from?

(b) Why is it necessary to divide by 3?

3.9 If we now forecast the total sales for 20X5 to be, say 14,000 units, our sales forecast for inclusion in the budget for 20X5 would be as follows.

	Average per quarter Units	Seasonal variation Units	Sales forecast Units	
Spring	3,500	(8)	3,492, say	3,500
Summer	3,500	(1,285)	2,215, say	2,200
Autumn	3,500	1,882	5,382, say	5,400
Winter	3,500	(589)	2,911, say	2,900
	14,000	-		14,000

Mathematical techniques: exponential smoothing

3.10 Another sales forecasting technique is exponential smoothing. By this method, a new forecast for the next period's results is obtained by the following formula.

New forecast = old forecast + α (most recent observation – old forecast)

where α is the **smoothing factor** or **smoothing constant**

3.11 α **will be in the range 0 to 1,** but its actual value is chosen subjectively depending on which value would have been most suitable in the past. An example will help to make this clear.

3.12 EXAMPLE: EXPONENTIAL SMOOTHING (1)

Smooth Ltd uses the following formula to estimate future sales demand.

Demand $_{t+1}$ = forecast of demand $_{t0}$ + 0.2 (actual demand in t_0– forecast of demand in t_0)

The forecast of demand in 20X1 was 20,000 units, but actual demand was 21,500 units. What will be the forecast of demand for 20X2?

3.13 SOLUTION

Forecast of demand in 20X2 = old forecast for 20X1 + 0.2 × (difference between old forecast and actual results).

=   20,000 + 0.2 (21,500 – 20,000)

=   20,300 units.

Mathematical techniques: regression analysis

3.14 When sales are thought to be on an upward or declining trend, the **trend line** can be estimated from historical sales data using regression analysis. In the trend line y = a + bx, **y will be the sales level at a particular point in time (x), where x = 1 is the first period of time in the past data provided.** This trend line can then be **extrapolated** into the future to derive a sales forecast.

3.15 EXAMPLE: FORECASTING AND REGRESSION ANALYSIS

The trend in sales of product B can be described by the linear regression equation y = 18.23 + 0.56x, where x is the quarter of the year (with the third quarter of year 1 as x =1) and y is the volume of sales in the quarter, in thousands of units.

A forecast (y) for quarter 1 of year 4 would be

18.23 + 0.56x, where x = 11

$\therefore$ y = 18.23 + (0.56 × 11) = 24.39

$\therefore$ Forecast $-$ 24,390 units

3.16 If time series analysis had been applied to the past data and seasonal variations calculated, the above forecast could be amended by the appropriate seasonal variation.

4 LEARNING CURVE THEORY

> ### Exam focus point
>
> This topic was examined in June 2003.

4.1 Whenever an individual starts a job which is **fairly repetitive** in nature, and provided that his speed of working is not dictated to him by the speed of machinery (as it would be on a production line), he is likely to become **more confident and knowledgeable** about the work as he gains experience, to become **more efficient**, and to do the work **more quickly**.

4.2 **Eventually**, however, when he has acquired enough experience, there will be nothing more for him to learn, and so **the learning process will stop**.

> ### KEY TERM
>
> **Learning curve theory** applies to these situations, where the work force as a whole improves in efficiency with experience. The learning effect or learning curve effect describes the speeding up of a job with repeated performance.

Where does learning curve theory apply?

4.3 Labour time should be expected to get shorter, with experience, in the production of items which exhibit any or all of the following features.

- Made largely **by labour effort** (rather than by a **highly mechanised** process)
- Brand **new** or relatively **short-lived** (learning process does not continue indefinitely)

BPP
PROFESSIONAL EDUCATION

- **Complex** and made in **small quantities** for **special orders**

The learning rate: cumulative average time

4.4 In learning theory the **cumulative average time per unit** produced is assumed to **decrease** by a **constant percentage** every time **total output** of the product **doubles**.

4.5 For instance, where an 80% learning effect occurs, the cumulative average time required per unit of output is reduced to 80% of the previous cumulative average time when output is doubled.

(a) By **cumulative average time**, we mean the average time per unit for all units produced so far, back to and including the first unit made.

(b) The **doubling** of output is an important feature of the learning curve measurement.

4.6 Don't worry if this sounds quite **hard to grasp** in words, because it **is** hard to grasp (until you've learned it!). It is best explained by a numerical example.

4.7 EXAMPLE: AN 80% LEARNING CURVE

The first unit of output of a new product requires 100 hours. An 80% learning curve applies. The production times would be as follows.

Number of units produced	Cumulative avg time required per unit			Total time required		Incremental time for additional units	
1		100.0	(× 1)	100.0			
2★	(80%)	80.0	(× 2)	160.0	60.0	(for 1 extra unit)	
4★	(80%)	64.0	(× 4)	256.0	96.0	(for 2 extra units)	
8★	(80%)	51.2	(× 8)	409.6	153.6	(for 4 extra units)	

★ Output is being **doubled** each time.

4.8 This effect can be shown on a **graph**, as a learning curve either for **unit times** or **cumulative total times or costs**.

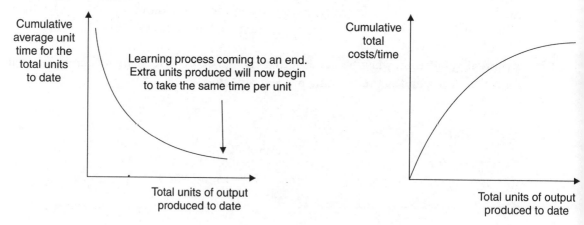

The curve and the formula

4.9 The curve on the left becomes horizontal once a sufficient number of units have been produced. At this point the learning effect is lost and production time should become a constant standard, to which a standard efficiency rate may be applied.

FORMULA TO LEARN

The formula for the learning curve is $\mathbf{y = ax^b}$

where   **y** is the cumulative average time per unit

x is the number of units made so far

a is the time for the first unit

b is the learning factor. With an 80% learning curve, b = -0.322.

(*Note.* 'b' may be taken from the logarithm of 0.8 divided by the logarithm of 2.)

4.10 EXAMPLE: THE LEARNING CURVE FORMULA

Captain Kitts Ltd has designed a new type of sailing boat, for which the cost and sales price of the first boat to be produced has been estimated as follows:

	£
Materials	5,000
Labour (800 hrs × £5 per hr)	4,000
Overhead (150% of labour cost)	6,000
	15,000
Profit mark-up (20%)	3,000
Sales price	18,000

It is planned to sell all the yachts at full cost plus 20%. An 80% learning curve is expected to apply to the production work. A customer has expressed interest in buying the yacht, but thinks £18,000 is too high a price to pay. He might want to buy 2, or even 4 of the yachts during the next six months. He has asked the following questions.

(a)   If he paid £18,000 for the first yacht, what price should be paid later for a second?

(b)   Could Captain Kitts Ltd quote the same unit price for two yachts, if the customer ordered two at the same time?

(c)   If the customer bought two yachts now at one price, what would be the price per unit for a third and a fourth yacht, if he ordered them separately later on?

(d)   If they were all ordered now, could Captain Kitts Ltd quote a single unit price for four yachts and eight yachts.

Assuming that there are no other prospective customers for the yacht, how would these questions be answered?

4.11 SOLUTION

Number of yachts		Cumulative average time per yacht Hours		Total time for all yachts to date Hours		Incremental time for additional yachts Hours
1				800.0		800.0
2	(× 80%)	640.0	(× 2)	1,280.0	(1,280 – 800)	480.0
4	(× 80%)	512.0	(× 4)	2,048.0	(2,048 – 1,280)	768.0
8	(× 80%)	409.6	(× 8)	3,276.8	(3,276.8 – 2,048)	1,228.8

(a) Separate price for a second yacht

	£
Materials	5,000
Labour (480 hrs × £5)	2,400
Overhead (150% of labour cost)	3,600
Total cost	11,000
Profit (20%)	2,200
Sales price	13,200

(b) A single price for the first two yachts

	£
Materials cost for two yachts	10,000
Labour (1,280 hrs × £5)	6,400
Overhead (150% of labour cost)	9,600
Total cost for two yachts	26,000
Profit (20%)	5,200
Total sales price for two yachts	31,200
Price per yacht (÷2)	£15,600

(c) A price for the third and fourth yachts

	£
Materials cost for two yachts	10,000
Labour (768 hours × £5)	3,840
Overhead (150% of labour cost)	5,760
Total cost	19,600
Profit	3,920
Total sales price for two yachts	23,520
Price per yacht (÷2)	£11,760

(d) A price for the first four yachts together and for the first eight yachts together

		First four yachts £		First eight yachts £
Materials		20,000		40,000
Labour	(2,048 hrs)	10,240	(3,276.8 hrs)	16,384
Overhead (150% of labour cost)		15,360		24,576
Total cost		45,600		80,960
Profit (20%)		9,120		16,192
Total sales price		54,720		97,152
Price per yacht	(÷4)	£13,680	(÷8)	£12,144

Question: learning curve theory

Bortamord Ltd anticipates that a 90% learning curve will apply to the production of a new item. The first item will cost £2,000 in materials, and will take 500 labour hours. The cost per hour for labour and variable overhead is £5.

You are required to calculate the total cost for the first unit and for the first 8 units.

Answer

	Units		Cumulative average time per unit Hours		Total time for all units produced to date Hours
	1		500.0		500
(double)	2	(90%)	450.0	(× 2)	900
(double)	4	(90%)	405.0	(× 4)	1,620
(double)	8	(90%)	364.5	(× 8)	2,916

	Cost of 1st unit £		Cost of 1st 8 units £
Materials	2,000		16,000
Labour and variable o/hd (500 hrs)	2,500	(2,916 hours)	14,580
	4,500		30,580
Average cost/unit	4,500		3,822.50

Incremental time model

4.12   The model described so far is the cumulative average time model and is the one most commonly encountered. An alternative is the incremental (**or marginal or direct**) model. This model uses the same formula as the cumulative average time model but y represents the time required to produce the final unit.

The practical application of learning curve theory

4.13   **What costs are affected by the learning curve?**

(a)   Direct labour time and costs

(b)   Variable overhead costs, if they vary with direct labour hours worked.

(c)   **Materials costs** are usually **unaffected** by learning among the workforce, although it is conceivable that materials handling might improve, and so wastage costs be reduced.

(d)   **Fixed overhead expenditure** should be **unaffected** by the learning curve (although in an organisation that uses absorption costing, if fewer hours are worked in producing a unit of output, and the factory operates at full capacity, the **fixed overheads recovered or absorbed per unit** in the cost of the output **will decline** as more and more units are made).

The relevance of learning curve effects in management accounting

4.14   **Situations in which learning curve theory can be used**

(a)   To **calculate the marginal (incremental) cost of making extra units** of a product.

(b)   To **quote selling prices for a contract**, where prices are calculated at cost plus a percentage mark-up for profit. An awareness of the learning curve can make all the difference between winning contracts and losing them, or between making profits and selling at a loss-making price.

(c)   To **prepare realistic production budgets** and more **efficient production schedules**.

(d)   To **prepare realistic standard costs** for cost control purposes.

4.15   **Considerations to bear in mind**

(a)   **Sales projections, advertising expenditure and delivery date commitments.** Identifying a learning curve effect should allow an organisation to plan its advertising and delivery schedules to coincide with expected production schedules. Production capacity obviously affects sales capacity and sales projections.

(b)   **Budgeting with standard costs.** Companies that use standard costing for much of their production output cannot apply standard times to output where a learning effect is taking place. This problem can be overcome in practice by:

      (i)   Establishing **standard times** for output, once the learning effect has worn off or become insignificant, and

      (ii)   Introducing a **'launch cost'** budget for the product for the duration of the learning period.

(c)   **Budgetary control.** When learning is still taking place, it would be unreasonable to compare actual times with the standard times that ought eventually to be achieved when the learning effect wears off. **Allowance should be made** accordingly when interpreting labour efficiency variances.

(d)   **Cash budgets.** Since the learning effect reduces unit variable costs as more units are produced, it should be allowed for in **cash flow projections**.

(e)   **Work scheduling and overtime decisions.** To take full advantage of the learning effect, **idle production time** should be avoided and work scheduling/overtime decisions should pay regard to the expected learning effect.

(f)   **Pay.** Where the workforce is paid a **productivity bonus**, the time needed to learn a new production process should be allowed for in calculating the bonus for a period.

(g)   **Recruiting new labour.** When a company plans to take on new labour to help with increasing production, the learning curve assumption will have to be reviewed.

(h)   **Market share.** The significance of the learning curve is that by increasing its share of the market, a company can benefit from shop-floor, managerial and technological 'learning' to achieve **economies of scale**.

Limitations of learning curve theory

4.16   (a)   The learning curve phenomenon is **not always present**.

      (b)   It assumes **stable conditions** at work which will **enable learning to take place**. This is not always practicable, for example because of **labour turnover**.

      (c)   It must also assume a certain degree of **motivation** amongst employees.

      (d)   Breaks between repeating production of an item must not be too long, or workers will **'forget'** and the learning process will have to begin all over again.

      (e)   It might be difficult to **obtain accurate data** to decide what the learning curve is.

      (f)   **Workers might not agree** to a gradual reduction in production times per unit.

      (g)   **Production techniques might change**, or product design alterations might be made, so that it takes a long time for a **'standard'** production method to emerge, to which a learning effect will apply.

5   BUDGETS AND UNCERTAINTY

Exam focus point

Budgeting under conditions of risk and uncertainty was examined in December 2003.

5.1   **Causes of uncertainty in the budgeting process**

    (a)   **Products/services.** In the modern business environment, organisations need to respond to customers' rapidly changing requirements.

(b) **Inflation** and movements in **interest and exchange rates**

(c) **Volatility** in the **cost of materials**

(d) **Competitors'** actions

5.2 **Rolling budgets** (covered in Chapter 17) are a way of trying to **reduce the element of uncertainty** in the plan. There are **other planning methods** which try to **analyse the uncertainty**. These methods are suitable when the **degree of uncertainty is quantifiable** from the start of the budget period and actual results are not expected to go outside the range of these expectations.

5.3 An analysis of uncertainty highlights the following.

(a) The **consequences of 'unforeseen' events** on expected results

(b) Those items in the budget which are **'critical' to the successful achievement** of budget goals

(c) The element of **risk** in different budget strategies. It might be thought better to adopt a budget which will achieve a lower expected profit but at a lower degree of risk, than to go for a high-risk budget where the expected value of profit is high.

5.4 **Methods of analysing uncertainty**

- Budgeting for worst-possible and best-possible outcomes (that is, planning with flexible budgets, as described in Chapter 17)

- Probability analysis

- Sensitivity analysis and the use of models

Budgets and probability

Knowledge brought forward from earlier studies

Probabilities and expected values

- If X, Y and Z are the mutually exclusive outcomes of an event (which means that no two outcomes can happen at the same time), P(X or Y or Z) = P(X) + P(Y) + (PZ) = 1.

- Suppose X and Y are independent events (which means that the occurrence of X in no way effects the occurrence of Y)

    ◦ Probability that both events occur (joint probability), P(X and Y) = P(X). P(Y)

    ◦ Probability that either or both events occur, P(X or Y) = P(X) + P(Y) – P(X and Y)

- If event Y is dependent upon/conditional upon event X taking place, the probability that both events will occur, P(X and Y)   = P(X). P(Y/X)

$$= P(Y).P (X/Y)$$

- The expected value (EV) of an opportunity is equal to the sum of (the probability (p) of an outcome occurring multiplied by the return (x) expected if its does occur)

$$EV = \Sigma px$$

KEY TERM

Probabilistic budgeting assigns probabilities to different conditions (most likely, worst possible, best possible) to derive an EV of profit. A standard deviation of the EV of profit can also be calculated as a measurement of risk. Management can then select, from among the alternatives which are being considered, the budget strategy which offers the 'best combination' of expected profit and risk.

5.5 A company, for example might make the following estimates of profitability for a given budget strategy under consideration.

	Profit/(loss)	*Probability*
	£'000	
Worst possible outcome	(220)	0.3
Most likely outcome	300	0.6
Best possible outcome	770	0.1

5.6 The EV of profit would be calculated as follows.

	Probability	*Profit*	*Expected value*
		£'000	£'000
Worst possible	0.3	(220)	(66)
Most likely	0.6	300	180
Best possible	0.1	770	77
Expected value of profits			191

5.7 Simple probabilistic income budgeting is not confined to a 'worst possible, most likely and best possible' analysis. For example, if the only uncertain elements in a budget are sales volume and unit variable costs, a probability tree analysis might be as follows.

Sales volume	Selling price £10 Variable cost per unit	Total contribution	Joint probability	EV of contribution
		£		£
6,000 units 0.2	£4 0.5	36,000	0.10	3,600
	£5 0.5	30,000	0.10	3,000
8,000 units 0.5	£5 0.4	40,000	0.20	8,000
	£6 0.6	32,000	0.30	9,600
10,000 units 0.3	£6 0.3	40,000	0.09	3,600
	£7 0.7	30,000	0.21	6,300
				34,100

5.8 EXAMPLE: A PROBABILISTIC BUDGET

PIB Ltd has recently developed a new product, and is planning a marketing strategy for it. A choice must be made between selling the product at a unit price of either £15 or £17.

Estimated sales volumes are as follows.

At price of £15 per unit		At price of £17 per unit	
Sales volume	Probability	Sales volume	Probability
Units		Units	
20,000	0.1	8,000	0.1
30,000	0.6	16,000	0.3
40,000	0.3	20,000	0.3
		24,000	0.3

(a) Sales promotion costs would be £5,000 at a price of £15 and £12,000 at a price of £17.

(b) Material costs are £8 per unit.

(c) Labour and variable production overhead costs will be £5 per unit up to 30,000 units and £5.50 per unit for additional units.

(d) Fixed production costs will be £38,000.

The management of PIB Ltd wish to allow for the risk of each pricing decision before choosing £15 or £17 as the selling price. They are considering the use of the formula 'desirability = WP + 2(EV)' to measure the 'desirability' value of each alternative, where WP is the worst possible outcome of profit and EV is the expected monetary value of profits.

Required

Determine which sales price would be preferred if the management selected the alternative which did the following.

(a) Minimised the worst possible outcome of profit

(b) Maximised the best possible outcome of profit

(c) Maximised the desirability value (which attempts to balance the separate considerations of profit maximisation and risk minimisation)

5.9 SOLUTION

The unit contribution will be as follows.

	Price per unit	
	£15	£17
Up to 30,000 units	£2	£4
Above 30,000 units	£1.50	N/A

Sales price £15

Units of sale '000	Unit contb'n £	Total contb'n £'000	Fixed costs £'000	Profit £'000	Probability	EV of profit £'000
20	2	40	43	(3)	0.1	(0.3)
30	2	60	43	17	0.6	10.2
40	30 @ £2 10 @ £1.50	75	43	32	0.3	9.6
						19.5

Sales price £17

Units of sale '000	Unit contb'n £	Total contb'n £'000	Fixed costs £'000	Profit £'000	Probability	EV of profit £'000
8	4	32	50	(18)	0.1	(1.8)
16	4	64	50	14	0.3	4.2
20	4	80	50	30	0.3	9.0
24	4	96	50	46	0.3	13.8
						25.2

(a) The price which minimises the worst possible outcome is £15 (with a worst-possible loss of £3,000).

(b) The price which maximises the best possible outcome is £17 (with a best-possible profit of £46,000).

(c) Desirability formula

   (i) *Price £15* (in £'000) Desirability = (3) + 2(19.5) = 36.0
   (ii) *Price £17* (in £'000) Desirability = (18) + 2(25.2) = 32.4

   Using this formula, a price of £15 would be preferred.

Sensitivity analysis and the use of models

5.10 **Sensitivity analysis tests the 'responsiveness' of profitability or cash flow to changes in one of the 'variables' in the budget.**

5.11 It would be possible to test a budget to see what happened if the following occurred.

   • An unforeseen 10% rise in material costs
   • An unforeseen 5% drop in productivity
   • A shortfall in sales volumes of, say, 10%
   • A labour strike of, say, one month's duration

5.12 Sensitivity analysis of this sort is commonly carried out, especially when an organisation uses a **computer spreadsheet model** or another **financial modelling package** for budgeting.

5.13 Although sensitivity analysis **provides answers to 'what if' questions** (what if labour costs are 4% higher?) it **does not analyse the likelihood of such a situation occurring**. In order to consider the likelihood of certain future happenings, or outcomes, we need to carry out probability analysis.

Data tables

> **KEY TERM**
>
> The term **data table** is used by some spreadsheet packages (for example Lotus 1-2-3 and Excel), and by the Paper 3.3 examiner, to refer to a group of cells that show the results of changing the value of variables.

5.14 Data tables can be produced when using spreadsheet packages and show the effect of changing the value of variables.

5.15 A **one-way** or **one-input data table** shows the effect of a range of values of one variable. For example it might show the effect on profit of a range of selling prices. A **two-way or two-input data table shows the results of combinations of different values of two key variables.** The effect on contribution of combinations of various levels of demand and different selling prices would be shown in a two-way data table.

5.16 **Any combination** of budget variable values can therefore be changed and the **effects monitored.**

5.17 EXAMPLE: A ONE-WAY DATA TABLE

Suppose a company has production costs which it would expect to be in the region of £5m were it not for the effects of inflation. Economic forecasts for the inflation rate in the coming year range from 2% to 10%. Profit before inflation is taken into account is expected to be £475,000.

By using a spreadsheet package and with three or four clicks of the mouse, the data table below is produced. This shows the effects of different levels of inflation on production costs and profit.

		Production costs	Profit
		£'000	£'000
	2%	5,100	375
	3%	5,150	325
Inflation rate	4%	5,200	275
	5%	5,250	225
	6%	5,300	175
	7%	5,350	125
	8%	5,400	75
	9%	5,450	25
	10%	5,500	(25)

So if inflation were to be 7%, the company could expect production costs to be in the region of £5,350,000 and profit to be about £125,000 (£(475,000 – (7% × £5m)).

5.18 EXAMPLE: TWO-WAY DATA TABLE

Suppose now that the company mentioned in the example above is not sure that its production costs will be £5m. They could alternatively be only £4.5m or else they could be up to £5.5m.

We therefore need to examine the effects of both a range of rates of inflation and three different production costs on profit, and so we need a two-way data table as shown below.

Two-way data table showing profit for a range of rates of inflation and production costs

		Production costs		
		£4,500,000	£5,000,000	£5,500,000
		£'000	£'000	£'000
	2%	385	375	365
	3%	340	325	310
Inflation rate	4%	295	275	255
	5%	250	225	200
	6%	205	175	145
	7%	160	125	90
	8%	115	75	35
	9%	70	25	(20)
	10%	25	(25)	(75)

So if production costs were £5,500,000 and the rate of inflation was 4%, the profit should be £255,000 (£(475,000 – (4% × £5,500,000)).

Other models

5.19 The development of computer models to aid management to reach budgeting decisions includes not only simulation models, but also simple cash flow models and mathematical programming models.

(a) **Cash flow models** are useful because they help management to determine the consequences to the forecast cash flow if, say, actual sales volumes fall short of budget, or efficiency levels decline.

(b) **Mathematical models** include linear programming models, which indicate the most profitable means of allocating scarce resources within a budget, and also inventory control models and network analysis models.

(c) **Discounted cash flow models** can be used to help with capital expenditure budgeting.

Question: budgeting with inflation

In Brazil the annual rate of inflation in the early 1990s was over 1,000%. The rate has been over 20% per month for the last 15 years and the annual rate consistently in four figures in recent years..

Interest rates often top 5% a month and bank account holders can invest their money for a day at a time. Cheques are cleared within one day. Retailers often sell products for less than they pay for them because if they can sell within 15 days but have 30 days to pay, the cash can be invested in the money markets. Some companies generate 80% of their profits from financial gains.

Periodically the Brazilian government imposes price freezes, and because companies fear being caught with their prices too low the longest price validity is 30 days. Companies such as ICI hold full scale price negotiations with unions and suppliers at least monthly. (*Financial Times*)

How might it be possible to budget in such conditions?

Answer

None of the techniques we have described above would cope very well with these conditions, although rolling budgets might help and 'what if' computer models would be a must for speed of reaction to change. Cash management is clearly crucial: the *FT* article notes that finance departments in Brazil are 40% larger than they would need to be in more stable conditions.

Probably the only sensible way of maintaining operational control is to abandon money as the unit of measurement, and budget in terms of physical quantities.

Chapter roundup

- In this chapter we have looked at a variety of different ways of manipulating data so as to produce the **information needed for budgeting**.

- Cost analysis may be carried out by the **engineering method (account classification method)**, the **high-low method**, the **scattergraph method**, **linear regression analysis** or **multiple regression analysis**.

- Forecasting may be done by means of the **Delphi model**, **econometric models**, **extrapolation and time series analysis**, or **exponential smoothing**.

- **Learning curve theory** may be useful for forecasting production time and labour costs in certain circumstances, although the method has many limitations.

- Uncertainty can be allowed for in budgeting by means of **flexible budgeting, rolling budgets, probabilistic budgeting** and **sensitivity analysis**.

Quick quiz

1   Put the following methods of cost analysis in order of increasing accuracy.

   (a)   Linear regression
   (b)   Account classification method
   (c)   Scattergraph method
   (d)   High-low method

2   In the linear cost function y = a + bx, which variable is used to represent the level of activity?

   A   a
   B   x
   C   b
   D   y

3   Econometric models are built up by a group of experts who are asked individually to provide their views about what will happen in the future. *True or false?*

4   *The sales of X Ltd have a six-week periodicity. Complete the following table to determine the trend.*

Week	Sales	Moving average	Centre and take average	Trend
1	150			
2	181			
3	190			
4	213			
5	161			
6	145			
7	152			

5   Explain each of the elements in the learning curve formula $y = ax^b$.

6   *Calculate the EV of revenue using the following information.*

Sales volume	Probability	Selling price £	Probability
10,000	0.2	3.00	0.1
12,000	0.7	3.50	0.1
13,000	0.1	4.50	0.8

BPP
PROFESSIONAL EDUCATION

Answers to quick quiz

1   (b), (d), (c), (a)

2   B

3   False. The Delphi model is being described.

4

Week	Sales	Moving average	Centre and take average	Trend
1	150			
2	181			
3	190			
		1,040		
4	213		1,041	173.5
		1,042		
5	161			
6	145			
7	152			

5   y = cumulative average time per unit
     x = number of units made so far
     a = time for first unit
     b = learning factor

6   EV = $((10{,}000 \times 0.2) + (12{,}000 \times 0.7) + (13{,}000 \times 0.1)) \times ((3 \times 0.1) + (3.5 \times 1) + (4.5 \times 0.8))$
        = $11{,}700 \times £4.25$
        = £49,725

Now try the question below from the Exam Question Bank

Number	Level	Marks	Time
16	Exam	20	36 mins

Chapter 19

BUDGETING FOR PEOPLE AND CONTINGENCIES

Topic list	Syllabus reference
1 Human behaviour and budgetary planning and control	4(b)
2 Budgeting and contingency theory	4(b)
3 Budgeting and change	4(b)

Introduction

This chapter completes our study of budgeting and budgetary control by considering two issues that are central to management accounting theory, the **behavioural aspects of budgeting** and **contingency theory**.

Many accountants find it hard to believe that anything as subjective as human behaviour can have an impact on budgeting systems since they see the operation of such a system as a purely technical, number-crunching process.

There has been a great deal of **research** into the behavioural implications of operating budgeting systems and, as in all studies of human behaviour, it is **difficult to draw concrete conclusions**. There is, however, one point which is agreed: budgeting and variance accounting are more than mathematical techniques.

How can control be simply a mathematical technique? Without the cooperation of its participants, the budgeting process is useless. If managers and employees make no attempt to achieve standards, if irresponsible estimates of figures are provided for inclusion in particular budgets, then the process is doomed.

This chapter will therefore begin by providing a more detailed consideration of some of the behavioural implications of operating budgeting systems.

The lack of consistency in the results of different observational studies into the link between accounting and human behaviour has led academics to the conclusion that a **contingency approach** should be adopted towards the design of accounting systems. We will therefore be studying contingency theory in Section 2.

Section 3 considers the **impact of change** on budgeting

Chapter 20 begins a new topic, decision making.

Study guide

Section 21 – Budgeting and budgetary control III

- Identify the factors which affect human behaviour in budgetary planning and control

- Explain budgeting as a bargaining process between people

- Explain the conflict between personal and corporate aspiration and its impact on budgeting

- Explain the application of contingency theory to the budgeting process

- Discuss the impact of political, social, economic and technological change on budgeting

- Critically review the use of budgetary planning and control
- Identify the effects on staff and management of the operation of budgetary planning and control

Exam guide

'Behavioural consequences' is a core syllabus area and so expect (usually discursive) questions on the topic on a regular basis.

The issues covered in this chapter are useful background to the following Oxford Brookes degree Research and Analysis Projects.

- Topic 1, which requires you to analyse the efficiency and/or effectiveness of a management accounting technique in an organisational setting
- Topic 6, which requires you to identify the key factors or indicators in the motivation of employees in an organisation of your choice

1 HUMAN BEHAVIOUR AND BUDGETARY PLANNING AND CONTROL

1.1 An important feature of control in business is that control is exercised by managers over **people**. Their **attitude and response to budgetary planning and control will affect the way in which it operates.**

1.2 A great deal has been written about the human behavioural factors at work in budgetary planning and control. Interest in the topic was stimulated by an article written in 1953 by Chris Argyris ('Human problems with budgets'). Argyris identified the following four perspectives.

Perspective	Comment
Pressure device	The budget is seen as a pressure device, used by management to force 'lazy' employees to work harder. The intention is to improve performance, but the unfavourable reactions of subordinates against it 'seems to be at the core of the budget problem'.
Budget men want to see failure	The accounting department is usually responsible for actual/ budget comparisons. Accountants are therefore budget men. Their success is to find significant adverse variances, and identify the managers responsible. The success of a 'budget man' is the failure of another manager and this failure causes loss of interest and declining performance. The accountant, on the other hand, fearful of having his budget criticised by factory management, obscures his budget and variance reporting, and deliberately makes it difficult to understand.
Targets and goal congruence	The budget usually sets targets for each department. Achieving the target becomes of paramount importance, regardless of the effect on other departments and overall company performance. This is the problem of goal congruence.
Management style	Budgets are used by managers to express their character and patterns of leadership on subordinates. Subordinates, resentful of their leader's style, blame the budget rather than the leader.

Bargaining

1.3 Budgeting may be seen as a **bargaining process** in two senses.

(a) In the sense that **managers will want to get a 'good bargain'**: a **share of resources** sufficient to enable them to achieve what they set out to achieve. This has been called 'political bargaining'.

(b) In a more general sense that a budget may either be **imposed from the top or agreed after negotiation** with those responsible for implementing it. This is the issue of the degree of **participation** that is desirable in setting budgets.

Political bargaining

1.4 Although **budgeting** might seem to be a technical process, it **depends heavily on the expectations, guesses, opinions and aspirations of managers because the future is always uncertain.** The **more uncertain** the future, the more valuable a budget will be for an organisation but there will also be **more scope for political bargaining over resource allocations.**

> 'Behind the essential technical facade of the budgetary procedures lies a prior and less formal bargaining process in which the managers compete for organisational resources. In practice, budget requests can vary from being a statement of a manager's anticipations to being one of his most optimistic aspirations. Since the amounts requested often have an important effect on the amounts received and hence on the subsequent control over organisational resources, the requests are themselves strategies in a bargaining process in which the issues transcend the immediate future state of the organisational economy to include personal motives for status, recognition and advancement' (Hopwood).

1.5 It is a widely-adopted practice for historical cost information to be used to estimate budget requirements and thus next year's budget is often based on last year's figures. Nevertheless, **managers use skill and cunning** to finalise their estimates. Reasons are found for increasing estimates, and **'padding'** is incorporated to allow for the expectation that top management will reduce budget expenditure levels by arbitrarily cutting x% from every manager's claim. The ability to **estimate 'what will go'** is thus regarded as a vital **skill**.

Participation in budgeting

Knowledge brought forward from earlier studies

Participation in budgeting

Budgets can be set from the **top down** (imposed) or from the **bottom up** (participatory).

- **Imposed budgets** can be effective.

  - During difficult economic conditions
  - If operational managers lack budgeting skills
  - If the organisation's units need very precise co-ordination
  - In very small businesses
  - In newly-formed organisations

- Imposed budgets may be more effective at incorporating **overall strategy** into operational plans.

- Imposed budgets may be **resented**. Operational managers may resent them or even go against them if they think they are unfair.

- **Participative budgets** are developed by lower-level managers, on the basis of what they think is achievable and the resources they need, and then submitted for approval to more senior managers.

- Participative budgets can be effective in the opposite set of circumstances to imposed budgets. Lower level managers have a clearer idea of the needs and limitations of their units. They are more likely to be committed to targets they set themselves.

- Participative budgets take longer to prepare and co-ordinate with other units' budgets and strategic plans. They risk **budgetary slack**.

1.6 **Conventional wisdom** about participation and the implementation of decisions is that when individuals **participate** in decision making, they will be **more satisfied** with their job and colleagues and they will be **more productive**: there will be fewer communication problems, and when circumstances change the individuals can adapt more quickly and readily to adjust their plans accordingly.

1.7 Research does not confirm this view, however. Effectiveness of participation may depend upon a number of factors

Factor	Detail
Nature of the task	'In highly programmed, environmentally and technologically constrained areas, where speed and detailed control are essential for efficiency, participative approaches may have less to offer from the point of view of the more economic aspects of organisational effectiveness ... In contrast, in areas where flexibility, innovation and the capacity to deal with unanticipated problems are important, participation in decision-making may offer a more immediate and more narrowly economic payoff than more authoritarian styles' (Hopwood).
Organisation structure	Where an organisation is decentralised managers perceive themselves to be participating more in the budgeting process and to be more satisfied with it than managers in centralised organisations. In centralised organisations a lack of participation is felt to be the more effective approach.
Personality	A participative approach has been found to be more effective when it involves people who feel that they have control over their destiny than with those who believe that their fortunes are dictated by 'luck'.

1.8 The **conclusion** that can be drawn from this is that there is **no one best way to deal with the problem of how much participation should be allowed.** 'It is ... necessary to identify those situations where there is evidence that participative methods are effective rather than to introduce universal application [of participation or non-participation] into organisations' (Drury). This is a **contingency approach,** a topic covered later in the chapter.

Question: participation

Most people have fairly strong opinions about the degree to which participation in decisions should be allowed, and a group discussion with fellow students or work colleagues would be fruitful. The following assertion may stimulate responses. 'It is impossible to gain any **satisfaction** from being **told** exactly what to do and given a specific amount of resources with which to do it.'

Discuss!

Motivation

1.9 If **'correct' management decisions are to be taken** in the organisation's best interests, it is necessary not only to provide good information for decision making, but also to ensure that **management and employees are motivated to work towards the goals of the organisation:** that they have the **same aspirations.**

1.10 To understand the conflict between personal and corporate aspirations we need first to consider **how individuals form their objectives,** that is, **what motivates people.**

1.11 **Motivation is what makes people behave in the way that they do.**

(a) It **comes from individual attitudes,** or **group attitudes.** Individuals will be motivated by personal desires and interests. These may be in line with the objectives of the organisation, and **some people 'live for their jobs'. Other individuals see their job as a 9 till 5 chore,** and their motivations will be unrelated to the objectives of the organisation they work for.

(b) Motivation can be **'positive'** - individuals might be trying to act in ways which help to achieve the objectives of the organisation; it can be **'negative'** - hostile to the objectives of the organisation; and it can be 'indifferent'.

(c) Motivating influences can be **weak or strong.** Strong influences are more likely to prod people into action than weaker influences.

1.12 Horngren defined motivation as 'the **need to achieve some selected goal and the resulting drive that influences action toward that goal',** and he suggested that motivation has **two aspects.**

(a) **Strength of purpose, or incentive.** 'Incentive is concerned with getting subordinates to run rather than walk toward the desired goals'. Accounting systems which evaluate the performance of managers (that is, of parts of the organisation under their control) are considered to be means of providing an incentive, just as wage bonus systems are sometimes considered to provide an incentive to employees to be more productive.

(b) **Direction, or goal congruence.** Goal congruence exists when managers working in their own best interests also act in harmony with the goals of the organisation as a whole. This is not easy to achieve and an accounting system can be designed in various ways to evoke the required behaviour.

The absence of motivation in budgeting

1.13 A poor attitude or hostile behaviour towards the budgetary control cycle can begin at the **planning stage.** If managers participate in preparing a budget in inappropriate circumstances then the following may happen.

(a) They **may complain that they are too busy** to spend much time on budgeting.

(b) They may **build in 'slack' to their expenditure estimates** and lobby for a high budget expenditure allowance.

(c) They may argue that **formalising a budget plan on paper is too restricting:** managers should be allowed flexibility and room for manoeuvre in the decisions they take.

(d) They may set budgets for their budget centre and **not co-ordinate** their own plans with those of other budget centres.

(e) They may **base future plans on past results,** instead of using the opportunity for formalised planning to look at alternative options and new ideas.

1.14 Problems will also occur if **managers are not involved in the budgeting process but should be.** It will be **hard for people to be motivated to achieve targets set by someone else.**

1.15 Poor attitudes can also arise when a **budget is implemented.**

(a) Managers might **put in only just enough effort** to achieve budget targets, without trying to beat targets.

(b) A formal budget might **encourage rigidity and discourage flexibility** in operational decision making.

(c) **Short-term planning** in a budget can **draw attention away from the longer-term consequences** of decisions.

(d) **Co-operation and communication** between managers might be **minimal**.

(e) Managers will often try to make sure that they **spend up to their full budget allowance, and do not overspend,** so that they will not be accused of having asked for too much spending allowance in the first place.

Motivation and the use of control information

1.16 The **attitude of managers towards the accounting control information they receive might reduce the information's effectiveness.**

(a) Management accounting control reports could well be seen as having a relatively **low priority** in the list of management tasks to be seen to. Managers might take the view that they have more pressing jobs on hand than looking at routine control reports.

(b) Managers might **resent the control information** that comes from the management accountant, seeing it as **part of a system of trying to find fault with their work**.

(c) If budgets are seen as **pressure devices** to push managers into doing better, control reports will be resented.

(d) Managers **may not understand the information** in the control reports, because they are unfamiliar with accounting terminology or principles.

(e) Managers might have a **false sense of what their objectives should be**. A production manager, for example, might consider it more important to maintain quality standards regardless of cost. They would then dismiss adverse expenditure variances as inevitable and unavoidable.

(f) If there are **flaws in the system of recording actual costs**, managers will dismiss **control information** as **unreliable**.

(g) Control **information** might be **received weeks after the end of the period to which it relates,** in which case managers might regard it as out-of-date and no longer useful.

Corporate aspirations and internal conflict

1.17 As we have seen, a **budget** is meant to be formulated so as to **achieve the overall objectives of the organisation,** at least within the short term. Organisational **objectives** are **very rarely clearly defined,** however (and one organisation is likely to **have a number of different objectives** anyway). Different managers will **perceive their objectives differently,** and so the budget demands of managers will frequently be **incompatible**.

1.18 The **conflicting demands** of different departments are **accentuated** by the following.

(a) The **lack of social interaction** between people in different departments.
(b) The different and often **conflicting sources of information** for each department.
(c) Different, or even competing, **reward structures**.

1.19 Although **budgeting** is still dominant as the **means of setting (short-term) goals in an organisation,** it has a severely **limited capacity** to do so, because it **emphasises profit to the exclusion of other goals** (as it is difficult for an accounting system of budgeting to incorporate non-financial or non-monetary goals successfully), and estimates of costs and revenues are subject to **political manipulation** by budget centre managers. Some managers have greater influence than others in the bargaining structure, but all management in turn is subject to the influence of trade union or government pressure, changing technology, changing markets and other environmental pressures.

Question: budgets and behaviour

Given the problems of accommodating personal motivations within a budgeting system on the one hand, and the difficulties of defining organisational goals by means of budgeting on the other, should budgeting even attempt to address these issues? Can you suggest another way of tackling the problem?

Answer

There is room here for a variety of views. It could be argued that the real problem is one of communication, in which case accountants have a good deal to answer for. It is more likely, however, that the budget is the wrong medium for the message. Many organisations have adopted **mission statements** to communicate their corporate aims and have successfully set about changing attitudes by encouraging philosophies like **total quality management.**

Expectations and aspirations

1.20 Budgets can motivate managers to achieve a high level of performance. But **how difficult** should targets be? And how might people react to targets of differing degrees of difficulty in achievement?

   (a) There is likely to be a **demotivating** effect where an **ideal standard** of performance is set, because adverse efficiency variances will always be reported.

   (b) A **low standard** of efficiency is also **demotivating**, because there is no sense of achievement in attaining the required standards. If the budgeted level of attainment is too 'loose', targets will be achieved easily, and there will be no impetus for employees to try harder to do better than this.

   (c) A budgeted level of attainment could be the **same** as the level that has been achieved in the past. Arguably, this level will be too low. It might encourage **budgetary slack**.

1.21 Academics have argued that each individual has a **personal 'aspiration level'**. This is a level of performance, in a task with which the individual is familiar, which the individual undertakes for himself to reach.

1.22 Individual aspirations might be much higher or much lower than the organisation's aspirations, however. The solution might therefore be to have **two budgets**.

   (a) A budget for **planning and decision making** based on **reasonable expectations**
   (b) A budget for **motivational purposes**, with more **difficult targets of performance**

   These two budgets might be called an 'expectations budget' and an 'aspirations budget' respectively.

Exam focus point

The behavioural implications of budgeting need to be considered in answering question 3 of the Pilot paper.

Conclusions

1.23 The foregoing discussion offers little in the way of conclusions; rather it draws attention to the **questions that need to be considered when designing management accounting systems.** It is, however, worth citing the five **conditions** that Dew and Gee (*Management Control and Information*) proposed for **an effective system of budgetary control.**

- Management's authority and responsibility must be clear.
- Managers must accept their budgets and consider them to be attainable.
- Budgetary control information must be understood by managers.
- Training in budgetary control must be effective.
- Managers must understand the aim of budgetary information.

1.24 This is not meant to be dogmatic. Dew and Gee suggest that accountants should think of themselves as **educators of management**, so that they will realise that budgetary information is meant to help them, not judge them, and as **translators of budgetary information** into forms that are most meaningful to management.

2 BUDGETING AND CONTINGENCY THEORY

2.1 Some researchers have argued that the **context** in which budgetary control is used is as important as the style in which it is implemented and used. As you should remember from Chapter 3, this is known as **contingency theory.**

Question: contingency theory and budgeting

Without looking back to the coverage of contingency theory in Chapter 3, comment on the impact of contingent factors (environment, technology and organisation) on the budgeting process.

Answer

Environment

(a) The sophistication of an accounting system is influenced by the intensity of competition faced.

(b) Budget information is evaluated by senior managers rigidly in 'tough' environments, but more flexibly in 'liberal' environments.

(c) The more dynamic the environment (the more rapidly it changes), the more frequently accounting control reports will be required.

(d) The larger the number of product markets an organisation is in, the more decentralised its control system will be, with quasi-independent responsibility centres.

Technology

(a) The more automated a production process is, the more formality there will be in the use of budget systems.

(b) The less predictable the production process is, the more likely production mangers are to create budgetary slack. (The proponent of this view admits evidence for this is weak.)

Organisation

(a) In larger organisations, a greater degree of decentralisation seems to lead to greater participation in budgeting.

(b) New control systems that threaten to alter existing power relationships may be thwarted by those affected.

3 BUDGETING AND CHANGE

3.1 Budgetary control systems are designed to cope with changes in the level of activity, without considering their cause. **Actual conditions may differ** from those anticipated when the budget was drawn up for a number of other reasons.

(a) **Political and economic conditions** may change: there may be a general recession, a war affecting supply or demand, or a change in government policy; the level of inflation may be different (higher or lower) than that anticipated.

(b) **Social changes** may occur within the organisation or because of outside influences.

   (i)   The adoption of new corporate cultures and philosophies such as Just-in-Time production and total quality management

   (ii) New agreements with the workforce about job demarcations, rest time or safety procedures, whether these are inspired within the organisation or through the influence of outside forces like the European Community

   (iii) The reallocation of responsibilities following, say, the removal of tiers of middle management and the 'empowerment' of workers further down the line

(c) **New technology** may be introduced to improve productivity, reduce labour requirements or enhance quality.

3.2 Any of these changes may make the original budget quite inappropriate, either in terms of the numbers expected, or the way in which responsibility for achieving them is divided, or both.

Chapter roundup

- This chapter has considered three issues central to budgeting.

  ° **Its impact upon people**
  ° **The impact of 'circumstances' upon it**
  ° **The impact of change**

- The **behavioural issues** identified include the following.

  ° Budgeting as a bargaining process
  ° Participation in budgeting
  ° Motivation
  ° The conflict between personal and corporate goals
  ° The difference between expectations and aspirations

- **Contingency theory** attempts to identify which aspects of an accounting system match with different circumstances and, in the course of a general evaluation of the strengths and weaknesses of alternative approaches to budgeting, it is possible to discern the influences of contingent factors such as the environment, organisational structure and technology.

- **Actual conditions may differ** from those anticipated when the budget was drawn up for a number of reasons.

  ° Political and economic conditions
  ° Social changes
  ° New technology

Quick quiz

1   What three factors are said to determine the effectiveness of participation?

A   Nature of the task, organisation structure, personality
B   Personality, technology, organisation structure
C   Nature of the task, production processes, personality
D   Personality, leadership style, aspirations

2   A budget for motivational purposes, with fairly difficult targets of performance, is an aspirations budget. *True or false?*

3   Provide four reasons why poor attitudes could arise when a budget is implemented.

4   *Fill in the blanks.*

The major contingent factors that have been identified are .... ,............................ , and ....

5   *Match the description to the correct term.*

Term		Description	
(a)	Motivation	1	Exists where managers working in their own interests also act in harmony with the interests of the organisation as a whole
(b)	Goal congruence		
(c)	Incentive	2	Comes from individual or group attitudes
		3	Concerned with getting subordinates to run rather than walk towards desired goals

Answers to quick quiz

1   A

2   True

3   (a)   Managers might put in only just enough effort to achieve budget targets, without trying to beat targets.

(b)   A formal budget might encourage rigidity and discourage flexibility in operational decision making.

(c)   Short-term planning in a budget can draw attention away from the longer-term consequences of decisions.

(d)   Cooperation and communication between managers might be minimal.

(e)   Managers will often try to make sure that they spend up to their full budget allowance, and do not overspend, so that they will not be accused of having asked for too much spending allowance in the first place.

4   environment
organisational structure
technology

5   (a) 2; (b) 1; (c) 3

Now try the question below from the Exam Question Bank

Number	Level	Marks	Time
17	Exam	20	36 mins

Part E
Decision making

Chapter 20

DECISION MAKING I

Topic list	Syllabus reference
1 Information for decision making	5(b)
2 Relevant and irrelevant information	5(b)
3 Qualitative factors in decision making	5(b)
4 Providing decision-making information	5(b)
5 The decision-making cycle	5(b)
6 Decision modelling	5(b)
7 Contribution and CVP analysis: a revision	5(b)
8 Further aspects of CVP analysis	5(b)

Introduction

This is the first chapter in the part of the Study Text that looks at **decision making** and it provides an **introduction** to the whole subject of decision making. We begin by focusing on the general **information requirements** for decision making, and the basic **decision-making cycle** for business decisions. We will also be looking at the **theory of model building** in anticipation of our study of **cost-volume-profit (breakeven) analysis models** in Sections 7 and 8, **resource allocation models** in Chapter 21 and **investment appraisal models** in Chapter 26.

Study guide

Section 22 – Short run decisions I

- Distinguish between relevant and irrelevant information using appropriate criteria

- Identify cost classification(s) in decision making

- Explain how quantitative and qualitative information is used in decision making

- Evaluate and assess the frequency, timing, format, and degree of accuracy in the provision of decision making information

- Describe the basic decision making cycle for business decisions

- Classify problems for the purpose of modelling into simple, complex and dynamic problems

- Explain the relevance of endogenous and exogenous variables, policies and controls, performance measures and intermediate variables in model building

- Explain the nature of CVP analysis and name planning and decision making situations in which it may be used

- Compare the accounting and economic models of CVP analysis

- Explain the assumptions of linearity and the principle of relevant range in the CVP model

- Prepare breakeven charts and profit-volume charts and interpret the information contained within each, including multi-product situations

- Comment on the limitations of CVP analysis for planning and decision making including multi-product situations

Section 23 – Short-run decisions II

- Explain the use of avoidable cost and incremental cost in decision making

Exam guide

'Decision-making techniques' has been classified as a core syllabus area by the examiner. Expect to see CVP analysis and relevant costing as major question topics. The other topics covered in this chapter may appear occasionally as parts of questions.

The issues covered in this chapter are useful background to the following Oxford Brookes degree Research and Analysis Projects.

- Topic 1, which requires you to analyse the efficiency and/or effectiveness of a management accounting technique in an organisational setting

- Topic 10, which requires you to analyse how management accounting techniques are used to support decision making in organisations

1 INFORMATION FOR DECISION MAKING

1.1 The accounting information required for decision making is different from the accounting information recorded in the books of financial accounts and conventional cost accounts. For cost accounting most UK companies still use **absorption costing** but this provides totally **misleading decision information**.

1.2 For example, suppose that a sales manager has an item of product which he is having difficulty in selling. Its historical full cost is £80, made up of variable costs of £50 and fixed costs of £30. A customer offers £60 for it.

(a) If there is no other customer for the product, **£60 would be better than nothing** and the product should be sold to improve income and profit by this amount.

(b) If the company has spare production capacity which would otherwise not be used, it would be profitable to continue making more of the same product, if customers are willing to pay £60 for each extra unit made. The additional costs are only £50 so that the profit would be increased marginally by £10 per unit produced.

(c) In **absorption costing terms**, the **product makes a loss of £20**, which would **discourage the sales manager from accepting a price of £60** from the customer. His decision would be a bad one.

    (i) If the product is **not sold** for £60, it will presumably be scrapped eventually, so the **choice** is really between making a **loss in absorption costing terms of £20, or a loss of £80 when the stock is written off,** whenever this happens.

    (ii) If there is **demand** for some extra units at £60 each, the absorption costing loss would be £20 per unit, but at the end of the year there would be an **additional contribution** to overheads and profit of £10 per unit. In terms of absorption costing the under-absorbed overhead would be reduced by £30 for each extra unit made and sold.

IMPORTANT POINT

Thus, for once-only decisions or decisions affecting the use of marginal spare capacity, absorption costing information about unit profits is irrelevant. On the other hand, since total contribution must be sufficient to cover the fixed costs of the business, marginal costing would be unsuitable as a basis for establishing long-term sales prices for all output.

2 RELEVANT AND IRRELEVANT INFORMATION

2.1 You covered relevant costs for your earlier studies. Make sure you still understand the following terms, which are just as important for Paper 3.3.

KEY TERMS

A **relevant cost** is a future cash flow arising as a direct consequence of a decision. Thus, only costs which differ under some or all of the available opportunities should be considered; relevant costs are therefore sometimes referred to as **incremental costs** or **differential costs**.

- **Avoidable costs** are usually associated with shutdown or disinvestment decisions and are defined as: 'those costs which can be identified with an activity or sector of a business and which would be avoided if that activity or sector did not exist'.

- An **opportunity cost** is the benefit forgone by choosing one opportunity instead of the next best alternative.

Non-relevant costs are irrelevant for decision-making because they are either not future cash flows or they are costs which will be incurred anyway, regardless of the decision that is taken.

- A **sunk cost** is used to describe the cost of an asset which has already been acquired and which can continue to serve its present purpose, but which has no significant realisable value and no income value from any other alternative purpose.

- A **committed cost** is a future cash outflow that will be incurred anyway, whatever decision is taken now about alternative opportunities. They may exist because of contracts already entered into by the organisation, which it cannot get out of.

- A **notional cost** or **imputed cost** is a hypothetical accounting cost to reflect the benefit from the use of something for which no actual cash expense is incurred. Examples include notional rent and notional interest.

- **Historical costs** are irrelevant for decision making.

The assumptions in relevant costing

2.2 Many of the assumptions that are typically made in relevant costing may be **dropped** in **Paper 3.3 questions**.

Assumption	Comment
Cost behaviour patterns are known	If a department closes, say, the attributable fixed cost savings would be known.
The amount of fixed costs, unit variable costs, sales price and sales demand are known with certainty	It is possible to apply risk and uncertainty analysis to decisions and so recognise that what will happen in the future is not certain.
The objective of decision making in the short run is to maximise 'satisfaction'	Satisfaction is often regarded as 'short-term profit'. However, there are many other qualitative factors or financial considerations which may influence a final decision.
The information on which a decision is based is complete and reliable	Decisions usually have to be based on imperfect information.

Imperfect information

2.3 All decision makers work with imperfect information.

(a) There may be some **uncertainty about objectives,** or an inclination to **settle for an acceptable or 'satisficing' performance** rather than maximum achievement.

(b) There may be **incomplete information** about alternative opportunities. For example, managers may face a choice between opportunities A and B, not realising that opportunities C, D and E exist as well.

(c) There is a **reluctance to go for radical changes,** and so managers have a tendency to reject opportunities that involve big changes or a step into the unknown.

(d) There is a **limit to the quantity of information that managers can digest**. One of the functions of the management accountant should be to filter information, and so avoid 'information overload' for the decision maker. Management accounting systems can also suffer information overload, receiving more data than can be adequately absorbed and analysed by the system.

2.4 Since managers cannot know everything there is to know that might be relevant to a decision, they should try to **take rational decisions within the limitations of the information available to them.** This is referred to as 'bounded rationality' in decision making.

Question: information for decision making

List five possible sources of information for decision making.

Answer

Financial transaction records; reference books; discussions with managers; suppliers' communications; market research. If you cheated, think of five more: there are plenty to choose from.

Exam focus point

Candidates in the June 2002 exam had to suggest information required to improve profit-maximising decisions for a particular organisation, whilst in the December 2002 exam they had to compile a list of information/data required to assess the financial consequences of a particular decision scenario.

3 QUALITATIVE FACTORS IN DECISION MAKING

3.1 Qualitative factors in decision making will inevitably vary with the circumstances and nature of the opportunity being considered. Here are some examples.

Factor	Comment
Availability of cash	An opportunity may be profitable, but there must be sufficient cash to finance any purchases of equipment and build-up of working capital. If cash is not available, new sources of funds must be sought.
Employees	Any decision involving the shutdown of plant, changes in work procedures and so on will require acceptance by employees, and ought to have regard to employee welfare.
Customers	Decisions about new products or product closures, the quality of output or after-sales service will inevitably affect customer loyalty and customer demand. A decision involving one product may have repercussions on customer attitudes towards a range of company products. The reliability of a customer and the risk of incurring a bad debt may be a factor in some decisions.
Competitors	Some decisions may stimulate a response from rival companies. The decision to reduce selling prices in order to raise demand may not be successful if all competitors take similar counter-action.
Suppliers	Suppliers' long-term goodwill may be damaged by a decision. Decisions to change the specifications for bought-out components, or to change stockholding policies so as to create patchy, uneven demand, might put a strain on suppliers. If a company is the supplier's main customer, a decision might drive the supplier out of business.
Feasibility	A proposal may look good on paper, but managers may have some reservations about their ability to carry it out in practice.
Unquantified opportunity costs	It may be useful to qualify a recommended decision by stating, for example, that 'Project X would appear to be viable on the assumption that there are no other more profitable opportunities available'.
Political pressures	Large companies must recognise that there might be political pressures applied by the government or society to influence their investment or disinvestment decisions. The Labour government's imposition of a windfall tax on privatised utilities like British Telecom is an example.
Legal constraints	A decision might occasionally be deferred or rejected because of doubts about the legality of the proposed action.

Exam focus point

Learn this list: it is invaluable as a source of ideas for written comments in exam questions.

Question: relevant costing and qualitative issues

A research project undertaken on behalf of a client has already incurred costs of £200,000. It is estimated that a further £280,000 will be charged to the project before its completion in one year's time.

The further costs have been calculated as follows.

	£
Materials	100,000
Staff costs	60,000
Overheads	120,000

The overheads comprise depreciation of plant and equipment (£40,000), and an allocation of general overheads incurred by the business based on 80% of material costs.

You have been asked to review the project because the project's total estimated costs of £480,000 exceed the contracted value of £350,000 for the completed research.

If the project is abandoned the client will receive £150,000 as compensation. You obtain the following information about the estimated cost to completion of the project.

Materials: contracts have already been exchanged for the purchase of £100,000 of materials. The material is highly specialised and has no alternative use on other projects. If not used on this project the material would have to be disposed of, incurring costs of £15,000.

Staffing: two highly skilled researchers each receive a salary of £25,000 pa. The other £10,000 is an allocation of part of the salary of a supervisor who is in overall charge of several projects.

If the project is abandoned, the research workers would be declared redundant, each receiving £10,000 in compensation.

Overheads: plant and equipment costing £80,000 was bought at the commencement of the project, and a second year's depreciation charge (£40,000) is included in the estimated costs. The plant and equipment is highly specialised and has no other use.

Estimated scrap values:	now	£10,000
	in one year	£4,000

Required

(a) Give your recommendation whether on financial grounds the project should be continued or abandoned.

Your calculations must be supported by clear statements of the reasons why a particular figure is included or excluded, and of any assumptions you make.

(b) Briefly explain any non-financial factors which need to be considered before finally deciding whether to abandon such a research project.

Answer

(a)

	Note	£	
Costs already incurred	(i)	0	
Materials	(ii)	(15,000)	saving
Staff costs	(iii)	30,000	
Overheads: plant and equipment	(iv)	6,000	
general overhead	(v)	0	
		21,000	
Contracted value		350,000	
Relevant future contribution from project		329,000	
Saving in compensation		150,000	
Total gain from continuing with project		479,000	

Therefore, on financial grounds the project should be continued.

Notes

(i) Costs already incurred are sunk and are not relevant to any future decision.

(ii) Contracts have already been exchanged and so the material must be paid for and the £100,000 cost is sunk. Using the material on this project would save the disposal costs.

(iii) The £10,000 allocated salary of the supervisor would not be affected by this project and so is not relevant. To continue to employ the skilled researchers would cost £15,000 more each than declaring them redundant.

(iv) The original cost of the equipment is a sunk cost. Depreciation is not a cash flow and is irrelevant. The relevant cost of using the equipment for this project is the £6,000 reduction in scrap value which would occur.

(v) General overheads are allocations of business overheads which are unaffected by this decision.

(b) **Non-financial factors** which would need to be considered are as follows.

(i) The effect on the company's reputation for completing projects once commenced.

(ii) The likelihood of further projects being received from the same customer.

(iii) The effect on the morale of the research staff.

(iv) Other opportunities for research projects which could use the facilities currently being employed on the project under consideration.

(v) The ease with which the skilled researchers could be replaced for future projects.

4   PROVIDING DECISION-MAKING INFORMATION

Frequency and timing

4.1   If a **decision has to be made every day** then **information needs to be available every day**.

(a) A treasury manager needs to know how much cash is in the bank, so that he can decide how much to invest overnight in what markets. He needs to know this daily, before the bank closes!

(b) A production manager needs to know early on how many staff he has available so that he can revise the production schedule if necessary.

4.2   **In other cases daily information may be quite inappropriate.** It may be meaningful to compare sales this March with sales last March, but quite meaningless to compare sales on March 7 this year with sales on March 7 last year. In this case monthly figures are what are needed to judge the trend and aid decisions about the need for extra marketing effort.

Format

4.3   The **format** in which decision-making information is provided will **depend upon the decision** being made.

(a) Many **operational decisions** will be made on the basis of information communicated by **word of mouth** or simply called up on **screen** from a computer database.

(b) **Tactical decisions** are likely to draw **information from wider sources;** but characteristically the information needed will **not need to be specially prepared,** because it will be available in the form of monthly reports and historical records. 'Providing' the information may be no more than telling the manager concerned which reports and records he needs, or at most responding to specific enquiries: 'Sales last March, £750,000'; 'Cost of full page advertisement: £2,500' and so on.

(c) For more **complex decisions,** particularly those at **strategic** level, a **specially prepared report** will usually be necessary. This is often the sort of information that is required in examination questions. The **principles of good report writing and good information apply.**

(i) The report should indicate its **purpose** clearly: 'Appraisal of options for replacing computer system', 'Proposals for cutting staff costs', and so on.

(ii) The report should be **addressed** to the person who has asked for it, and it should be in a **form that the user will understand**. Technical terms should be explained if necessary, and the rationale behind calculations (for example discounted cash flow) may need to be set out.

(iii) Ideally the decision to be made, the main argument of the appraisal, and the conclusions reached should be **summarised** on a single page. Detailed information and calculations should be included as necessary to back up any conclusions that are made, but they should be relegated to **appendices** at the end of the report rather than clogging up the main body.

(iv) If a **recommendation** is asked for, one should be made. If other alternatives are available, they should be identified.

(v) If there are **other factors** to be considered which fall outside the brief of the provider of the report, this should be made clear, and an indication should be given of the further information required.

Accuracy

4.4 The **degree of accuracy required** of a report again **depends upon the decision being made**. The treasury manager deciding how to invest the company's cash balance needs a precise figure: 'about £10 million' will not do if the actual figure is £10,250,000. The production director deciding on a site for a new factory with a limit of £5 million to spend, needs no more detail than 'Sites on the outskirts of London are likely to cost in excess of £10 million' to decide to look further afield.

4.5 An important point to remember in this context is that decision-making information **concerns the future** and so it is **often uncertain**. A report that concludes 'The cost of this option is £10,749.56' offers a degree of accuracy (and by implication, certainty) that may be quite spurious if it has been arrived at by making assumptions about such factors as future interest rates, the availability of materials at a certain price and so on. The apparent precision is in fact rather misleading.

Exam focus point

As well as being adept at the techniques covered in this Study Text, you need a basic level of mathematical proficiency. For example, in the December 2002 compulsory question 1, candidates had to use simultaneous equations.

5 THE DECISION-MAKING CYCLE

5.1 Decision making involves several steps.

Step 1. Identify **objectives.**

Step 2. Identify **alternative opportunities (strategies)** for achieving them.

Step 3. Collect and **analyse relevant data** about each alternative.

Step 4. **Make the decision**. State the **expected** outcome.

Step 5. **Implement** the decision.

Step 6. Obtain data about **actual results**.

Step 7. **Compare actual** results with the **expected** outcome.

Step 8. Evaluate achievements and **make further decisions** in this light.

5.2 Steps 3 to 8 will be dealt with as appropriate in the following chapters, but there are some points to be noted about Steps 1 and 2.

Identifying objectives

5.3 Objectives can be either long term or short term. In the **short term**, profit maximisation or cost minimisation (for example improved productivity) is often used as an objective towards which decision making should be aimed. However, alternative short-term objectives might be avoiding a loss, avoiding unnecessary risks or achieving a given growth in sales or profits compared with a previous year.

5.4 At the same time, some recognition might be given to **non-financial objectives** in the short term, such as maintaining or improving the **quality** of products or services, **employee welfare** (for example deciding to spend more money on health and safety at work) and **environmental considerations**.

5.5 The primary **long-term** objective of a profit-making organisation may be to maximise the return to shareholders, but without taking risks that shareholders might consider excessive.

Social and ethical objectives

5.6 In the long term as well as the short term, a commercial organisation ought to recognise its social and ethical obligations, and these ought to be considered in reaching decisions. They are **hard to quantify**, and it is therefore tempting (but wrong) to neglect them.

5.7 It is useful to be aware of a variety of ethical objectives. The following list is not comprehensive.

   (a) **Employees**

   - A minimum wage, perhaps with adequate differentials for skilled labour
   - Job security (over and above the protection afforded by legislation)
   - Good conditions of work
   - Job satisfaction

   (b) **Customers**

   - A product of a certain quality at a reasonable price
   - Products that should last a certain number of years

   (c) **Suppliers:** regular orders in return for reliable delivery and good service

   (d) **Society as a whole**

   - Controlling pollution, noise and smell
   - Providing financial assistance to charities, sports and community activities
   - Identifying and preventing health hazards in the products sold

Identifying alternative opportunities

5.8 The search for things to do which might help an organisation achieve its objectives is one of the major tests of good management. Decisions might not be taken, and opportunities might be missed, simply because managers failed to recognise that opportunities existed.

6 DECISION MODELLING

Classification of problems

6.1 **Managers construct models in order to foresee what might happen.** If you jot down a few figures to see whether you have enough cash in your pocket to last you until the end of the week you have built a model of your cash expenditure plans, to help you to decide whether or not to go to the cash point machine.

6.2 For modelling purposes, problems may be classified as simple, complex or dynamic.

Classification	Detail
Simple	A simple problem has only a few variables, perhaps only one output and a simple relationship between the two. For example, a CVP model at its most simple is $P = S - V - F$, where P is profit, S is sales revenue, V is total variable costs, F is total fixed costs.
Complex	A complex problem has more detail and complexities. An example is $P = (S_1 - V_1)q_1 + (S_2 - V_2)q_2 + ... (S_n - V_n)q_n - F$ where $S_1, S_2 ... S_n$ represent the sales price of product 1, product 2 ... product n in the sales mix V_1 etc represent the variable cost per unit of each product q_1 etc represent the sales quantities of each product
Dynamic	A dynamic problem is one in which the variables change and the relationships between them change and interact. The problem 'How much profit will be made' is a dynamic one in the real world. A dynamic model will therefore be continuously changing, either because new data is input to keep its parameters up to date or because new specifications are made to alter the model design.

6.3 The term '**simulation model**' is used to describe any model which somehow **represents a 'real' system.** The main type of simulation model used by management accountants is a symbolic or mathematical model, in which variables in the 'real' system are represented by mathematical symbols and equations.

6.4 **Elements of models**

Element	Detail
Exogenous variables	Literally variables 'growing or originating from outside' (from the Greek), these variables are determined **externally**, for example the cost of a raw material imposed by the supplier. These might be called **input variables.**
Endogenous variables	Literally, variables 'growing or originating from within', these are variables that are produced **within** the model by means of the interaction between other variables. To an extent they are controlled by the decision maker, who can influence the relationships between variables. They might alternatively be called **output variables.** For example, the **re-order level** for an item stock may be an endogenous variable, perhaps determined by means of the EOQ model, or simply an arbitrary percentage of the annual requirement of that item. (The formula or percentage is usually known as an intervening variable.) The term is sometimes used more simply to describe a variable whose value can be **decided by management**, for example the level of a bonus for employees. It is hard to think of universally applicable examples in modern business, where variables depend on customer needs.

Element	Detail
Policies	These are **general guidelines** for decision making. For example a company may have a positive discrimination policy that requires it to do business with third world organisations in preference to others, to encourage economic development. In a manufacturing decision this would place constraints on the sourcing of components. Policies may also be imposed from outside. For example a product may have to adhere to certain safety standards imposed as a policy of the government.
Performance measures	These are **standards** that the outputs arising from the decision must meet. They would generally derive from the overall objectives of a company's strategy.
Controls	In a model, these are **devices used to regulate the operation of the model**. For example the model might incorporate a control designed to reject an option in which labour costs exceed a certain figure. The control is the function of accepting or rejecting, not the figure itself: for instance the formula =IF(A5>B5, B5,A5) is a control in a spreadsheet which returns the value in cell B5 (the limit) if the value in A5 is over the limit.
Intermediate variables	The term (as mentioned in the Paper 3.3 Study Guide) may be taken literally to mean something that (actively) **comes between other things**, such as the EOQ formula mentioned above (an 'intervening variable'). They are used to **link endogenous** and **exogenous** variables to the performance measure. For instance the ranking technique in limiting factor analysis calculates **contribution per unit of limiting factor**, an intermediate variable which is then used to find the profit maximising production plan.

Question: models

Think of three 'real-world' business scenarios that could be modelled and identify some of the variables that would be used or would result.

Answer

Three suggestions are: a model of the launch of a new product; a model equating level of demand for public transport with level of service offered; a model of a commodity market to predict the availability of scarce resources. If you cannot think of any variables, Paragraph 3.1 may help.

7 CONTRIBUTION AND CVP ANALYSIS: A REVISION

7.1 Management accounting is concerned with the **provision of information which will help managers to make decisions for the future.** To forecast costs, accountants must know about the cost behaviour of all cost items. Cost behaviour refers to the way in which costs increase or fall, if at all, as a consequence of increases or decreases in the level of activity.

7.2 One way of providing information about expected future costs and revenues for management decision making is cost-volume-profit (CVP) (or breakeven) analysis.

7.3 CVP analysis was covered in your earlier studies; moreover, it is not a particularly difficult subject. We have therefore provided a **summary of the more straightforward areas** (breakeven arithmetic and breakeven charts) but do make sure that you know how the various charts are constructed. **The more complex or contentious areas we cover in full.**

> **Knowledge brought forward from earlier studies**
>
> *CVP (breakeven) analysis: arithmetic*
>
> - Breakeven point = activity level at which there is neither profit nor loss = activity level where total contribution equals fixed costs
>
> $$= \frac{\text{total fixed cost}}{\text{contribution per unit}} = \frac{\text{contribution required to break even}}{\text{contribution per unit}}$$
>
> - Contribution/sales (C/S) ratio = profit/volume (P/V) ratio = (contribution ÷ sales) × 100%
>
> - Sales revenue at breakeven point = fixed costs ÷ C/S ratio
>
> - Margin of safety = budgeted sales units – breakeven sales units
>
> - Total contribution required to achieve a target profit = fixed costs + target profit

Exam focus point

Note the **importance** of **contribution** in CVP analysis. It is a key consideration in many Paper 3.3 questions (being required in the June 2003 exam, for example) as you will see in the next chapter. So make sure you have a good grasp of the basics before continuing by doing the two questions which follow.

Question: contribution analysis

Tripod Ltd makes and sells three products, X, Y and Z. The selling price per unit and costs are as follows.

	X	Y	Z
Selling price per unit	£80	£50	£70
Variable cost per unit	£50	£10	£20
Fixed costs per month	£160,000		

The maximum sales demand per month is 2,000 units of each product and the minimum sales demand is 1,000 of each.

Required

(a) Comment on the potential profitability of the company.

(b) Suppose that there is a fixed demand for X and Y of 1,500 units per month, which will not be exceeded, but for which firm orders have been received. How many units of Z would have to be sold to achieve a profit of at least £25,000 per month?

Answer

(a) When there is no indication about whether marginal or absorption costing is in use, it is simpler (and more informative too) to assess profitability with contribution analysis and **marginal costing**. This is the requirement in part (a) of the problem. The obvious analysis to make is a calculation of the **worst possible** and **best possible** results.

	Best possible			Worst possible		
	Sales units	Cont'n per unit £	Total cont'n £	Sales units	Cont'n per unit £	Total cont'n £
X	2,000	30	60,000	1,000	30	30,000
Y	2,000	40	80,000	1,000	40	40,000
Z	2,000	50	100,000	1,000	50	50,000
Total contribution			240,000			120,000
Fixed costs			160,000			160,000
Profit/(loss)			80,000			(40,000)

The company's potential profitability ranges from a profit of £80,000 to a loss of £40,000 per month.

(b) The second part of the problem is a **variation of a 'target profit' calculation.**

	£	£
Required (minimum) profit per month		25,000
Fixed costs per month		160,000
Required contribution per month		185,000
Contribution to be earned from:		
product X 1,500 × £30	45,000	
product Y 1,500 × £40	60,000	
		105,000
Contribution required from product Z		80,000
Contribution per unit of Z		£50
Minimum required sales of Z per month		1,600 units

Question: CVP analysis

Lisbon Ltd achieved the following results in 20X1.

	£'000	£'000
Sales (200,000 units)		2,000
Cost of sales		
Direct materials	800	
Direct labour	400	
Overheads	600	
		1,800
Profit		200

Throughout 20X1, sales were £10 per unit, and variable overheads, which vary with the number of units produced, amount to £1 per unit.

Required

Using CVP analysis, calculate the sales volume necessary to achieve a profit of £330,000 in 20X2 if, at beginning of the year, the sales price is increased by £0.50 per unit, but the increases in costs above 20X1 levels are expected to be as follows. Comment on the result obtained.

Direct material	10%
Direct labour	15%
Variable overhead	10%
Fixed overhead	20%

Answer

In 20X1 sales were 200,000 units. **The variable cost per unit** is therefore as follows.

	20X1	20X2 prediction
	£	£
Direct materials	4	4.40
Direct labour	2	2.30
Variable overhead	1	1.10
	7 per unit	7.80 per unit

Fixed costs

	£
20X1 total overhead (fixed plus variable)	600,000
Variable overhead in 20X1 (200,000 × £1)5	200,000
Fixed overhead in 20X1	400,000
Add 20%	80,000
Estimated fixed overhead in 20X2	480,000

In 20X2, a **profit of £330,000 is required.**

	£
Required profit	330,000
Fixed costs	480,000
Required contribution	810,000

Contribution per unit in 20X2 (£10.50 - £7.80) = £2.70

Required sales $\dfrac{£810,000}{£2.70}$ = 300,000 units

This is an increase of 50% on 20X1 volumes. It is first of all questionable whether such a large increase could be achieved in one year. Secondly, given such an increase, it is likely that output will be outside the **relevant range** of output (see below). Thirdly, **estimates** of fixed costs and variable costs are **unlikely to be reliable.**

Knowledge brought forward from earlier studies

CVP (breakeven) analysis: charts

- **Breakeven charts** show levels of profit or loss at different levels of activity within a limited range.

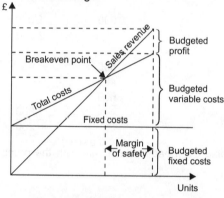

- **Contribution breakeven charts** show the contribution at different levels of activity.

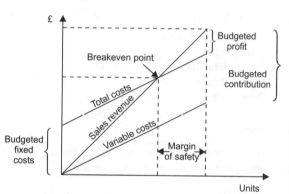

- **P/V (profit/volume) charts** provide a simple illustration of the relationship of costs and profits to sales, and of the margin of safety.

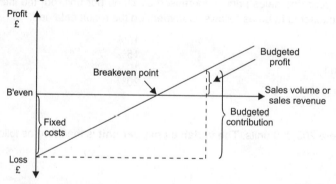

The gradient of the straight line is the contribution per unit (if the horizontal axis is measured in sales units) or the C/S ratio (if the horizontal axis is measured in sales value).

- **Multi-product charts** can be drawn if it is assumed that the output and sales mix of a number of products is fixed in certain proportions. Simply calculate **total** costs, **total** revenue and **total** contribution and proceed as for single-product charts.

Additional information about the contribution earned by each product individually, so that their performance and profitability can be compared, can be obtained from a multi-product P/V chart.

Knowledge brought forward from earlier studies (continued)

- ° Calculate the C/S ratio for each product at the budgeted output level.

- ° Beginning with the product with the highest C/S ratio and working from left to right, plot cumulative profit against cumulative sales.

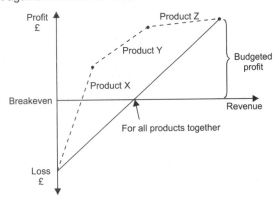

Question: multi-product CVP analysis

(a) What action should management take with regards the pricing of products X, Y and Z shown in the multi-product P/V chart in the 'knowledge brought forward' box?

(b) What information does a multi-product P/V chart provide?

Answer

(a) It may be apparent that since X is the most profitable in terms of C/S ratio, it might be worth considering an increase in the sales of X, even if there is a consequent fall in the sales of Z. Alternatively, the pricing structure of the products should be reviewed and a decision made as to whether the price of product Z should be raised so as to increase its C/S ratio (although an increase is likely to result in some fall in sales volume).

(b) The multi-product P/V chart is helpful in identifying firstly, the overall organisation breakeven point; secondly, which products should be expanded in output and which, if any, should be discontinued; and thirdly, what effect changes in selling price and sales volume will have on the organisation's breakeven point and profit.

Question: breakeven charts

What do you see as the value of breakeven charts?

Answer

Breakeven charts may be helpful to management in **planning the production and marketing** of **individual products, or the entire product range** of their company. A chart gives a **visual display** of how much output needs to be sold to make a profit and what the likelihood would be of making a loss if actual sales fell short of the budgeted expectations. Many managers who are not particularly numerate will find this **easier to understand** than the arithmetical approach, and many **spreadsheet packages** can produce a chart with ease once the model has been built.

Question: breakeven chart preparation

A company sells a product which has a variable cost of £2 per unit. Fixed costs are £15,000. It has been estimated that if the sales price is set at £4.40 per unit, the expected sales volume would be 7,500 units; whereas if the sales price is lower, at £4 per unit, the expected sales volume would be 10,000 units.

Required

Draw a breakeven chart to show the budgeted profit, the breakeven point and the margin of safety at each of the possible sales prices.

Answer

Workings	Sales price £4.40 per unit £		Sales price £4 per unit £
Fixed costs	15,000		15,000
Variable costs (7,500 × £2)	15,000	(10,000 × £2)	20,000
Total costs	30,000		35,000
Budgeted revenue (7,500 × £4.40)	33,000	(10,000 × £4)	40,000
Profit (£33,000 – £30,000)	3,000	(£40,000 – £35,000)	5,000

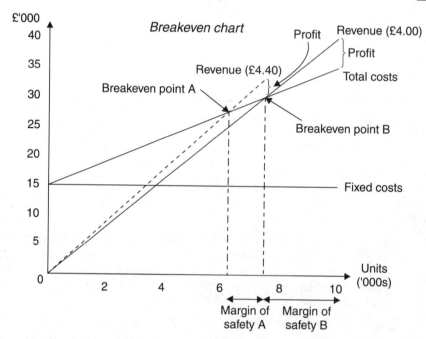

(a) **Breakeven point A** is the breakeven point at a sales price of £4.40 per unit, which is 6,250 units or £27,500 in costs and revenues.

$$\text{(check:} \quad \frac{\text{required contribution to break even}}{\text{contribution per unit}} = \frac{£15,000}{£2.40 \text{ per unit}} = 6,250 \text{ units)}$$

The **margin of safety (A)** is 7,500 units – 6,250 units = 1,250 units or 16.7% of expected sales.

(b) **Breakeven point B** is the breakeven point at a sales price of £4 per unit which is 7,500 units or £30,000 in costs and revenues.

$$\text{(check:} \quad \frac{\text{required contribution to break even}}{\text{contribution per unit}} = \frac{£15,000}{£2 \text{ per unit}} = 7,500 \text{ units)}$$

The **margin of safety (B)** = 10,000 units – 7,500 units = 2,500 units or 25% of expected sales.

Since a price of £4 per unit gives a higher expected profit and a wider margin of safety, this price will probably be preferred even though the breakeven point is higher than at a sales price of £4.40 per unit.

8 FURTHER ASPECTS OF CVP ANALYSIS

Accounting and economic models of CVP analysis and the relevant range

8.1 A **fundamental assumption** of CVP analysis is that **costs can be divided into a constant variable cost per unit and a constant total fixed cost.** However, there is a good **argument** that the **variable cost per unit,** which is the marginal cost per unit in the language of economics, **changes with the level of output.** This is because until a factory is working at a level approaching that for which it was designed it will be inefficient and the variable cost will be higher than it could be. Once it starts operating at a level beyond that for which it was designed it will become inefficient again and the variable cost will once more start to rise.

8.2 For the **economist,** therefore, the **marginal cost per unit** should be graphed as follows.

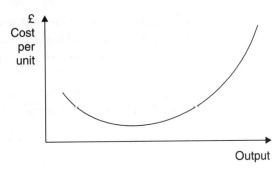

Total costs would therefore appear as a curved line as follows.

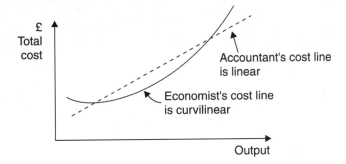

8.3 A **second fundamental assumption** of CVP analysis is that the **selling price is constant,** no matter how many units are sold. To the **economist** this is quite **inaccurate,** because in order to achieve higher sales it is usually necessary to charge lower selling prices. For the economist, therefore **total revenue** also stands in a **curvilinear** relationship to volume.

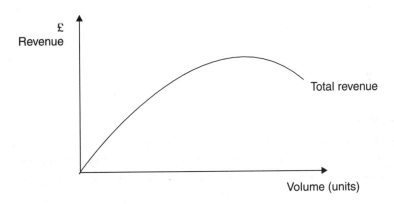

8.4 The **economist's breakeven chart therefore differs from the accountant's.**

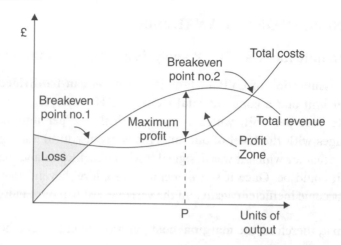

8.5 The shape of the total costs and total revenue lines means that there are **two breakeven points**. At the second, decreasing total revenue equals increasing total costs. The first is similar to the single breakeven point shown on an accountant's breakeven chart.

8.6 The accountant's breakeven chart is not intended to provide an accurate representation of total costs and total revenue behaviour in all ranges of output but rather to represent behaviour over the range of output in which the firm expects to be operating in the future (relevant range).

KEY TERM

The **relevant range** is the levels of activity at which the firm has had experience of operating in the past and for which cost information is available.

8.7 **Within the relevant range the economist's and accountant's charts are not too different.** The two types of chart are superimposed below.

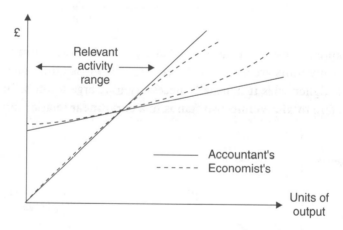

8.8 **Fixed costs** are also **assumed** to be **constant at all levels of output,** so that if there is no output at all, there will be a loss equal to the amount of fixed costs. It might be tempting to assume that this is true, but it could be a seriously **misleading assumption** because many 'fixed cost' items are step costs in nature over a wide range of activity. **Fixed cost** estimates should therefore only **apply within the relevant range** of activity.

Limitations of CVP analysis

8.9 Breakeven charts and breakeven arithmetic should be used carefully. The major limitations of breakeven analysis are as follows.

(a) A breakeven chart can only apply to **one single product** or a **single mix** (fixed proportions) of a group of products. This restricts its usefulness.

(b) It is **assumed** that **fixed costs are the same in total** and **variable costs are the same per unit at all levels of output**. This assumption is a great simplification.

   (i) Fixed costs will change if output falls or increases substantially (most fixed costs are step costs).

   (ii) The variable cost per unit will decrease where economies of scale are made at higher output volumes, and the variable cost per unit will also eventually rise where diseconomies of scale begin to appear at higher volumes of output (for example the extra cost of labour in overtime working).

   It is important to remember that although a **breakeven chart** is drawn on the assumption that fixed costs and the variable cost per unit are constant, this is only **correct within a normal range or relevant range of output**. It is generally assumed that both the budgeted output and also the breakeven point of sales lie within this relevant range.

(c) It is **assumed** that **sales prices will be constant at all levels of activity.** This may not be true, especially at higher volumes of output, where the price may have to be reduced to win the extra sales.

(d) **Production** and **sales are assumed** to be the **same**, therefore the consequences of any increase in stock levels (when production volumes exceed sales) or 'de-stocking' (when sales volumes exceed production levels) are ignored.

(e) **Uncertainty** in the estimates of fixed costs and unit variable costs is often **ignored** in breakeven analysis, and some costs (for example mixed costs and step costs) are not always easily categorised or divided into fixed and variable.

Multi-product situations

8.10 In a modern manufacturing environment a large proportion of total costs are incurred in relation to activities other than production itself, such as materials handling, setting up machinery and so on. Such costs are not volume related, but 'complexity-related': a wide variety of different versions of products are produced to customer demand, and this means that the management of the production environment is far more complex than in the traditional situation. **Complexity-related fixed costs do not change if the volume of production changes, but they will change if the range of products made is altered. CVP analysis cannot make allowance for this.**

8.11 CVP arithmetic should therefore be **used with a full awareness of its limitations.** In an appropriate environment it can usefully be applied to provide simple and quick estimates of breakeven volumes or profitability given variations in sales price, sales mix, variable and fixed costs and sales volumes, within a 'relevant range' of output/sales volumes.

Chapter roundup

- **Absorption costing** provides **misleading** decision information.

- Make sure that you understand and can explain the concepts of **incremental/differential** costs, **avoidable** costs and **opportunity** costs and can distinguish relevant from non-relevant (**sunk, committed, notional/imputed, historical**) costs.

- Many of the **assumptions** that are typically made in relevant costing may be dropped in Paper 3.3 questions.

- All decision makers work with **imperfect information.**

- You should learn the list of **qualitative factors** detailed in the chapter.

- The **frequency** and **timing, format** and **accuracy** of decision-making information is important.

- Do you know the eight steps of the **decision-making cycle?**

- Problems can be classified as **simple, complex** or **dynamic.**

- You need to be aware of the following **elements of models**.

  - Exogenous variables
  - Endogenous variables
  - Policies
  - Performance measures
  - Controls
  - Intermediate variables

- Despite its limitations it is very important to be fully conversant with **CVP arithmetic and charts** because CVP analysis is widely used in practice, being both quick and simple to perform and easy to understand - especially if it is conveyed in graphical form.

- Within the **relevant range**, the **economist's** and **accountant's charts** are not too different.

Quick quiz

1   *Choose the appropriate word(s) from those highlighted.*

   For once-only decisions, **absorption/marginal** costing information about unit profits is irrelevant.

   Marginal costing would be **unsuitable/suitable** as a basis for establishing long-term sales prices for all output.

2   *Match the correct definition to the appropriate term.*

   Terms

   (a) Sunk cost

   (b) Committed cost

   (c) Imputed cost

   Definitions

   1   A future cash outflow that will be incurred anyway, whatever decision is taken now

   2   A hypothetical accounting cost to reflect the benefit from the use of something for which no actual cost expense is incurred

   3   The cost of an asset which has already been acquired and which can continue to serve its present purpose, but which has no significant realisable value

3   List nine qualitative factors in decision making.

4   Decision-making information should strive for spurious accuracy. *True of false?*

5   *Put the following steps of the decision-making cycle in the correct order.*

Obtain data about actual results.
Identify objectives.
Collect and analyse relevant data about each alternative.
Evaluate achievements and make further decisions in this light.
Make the decision. State the expected outcome.
Implement the decision.
Compare actual results with the expected outcome.
Identify alternative opportunities (strategies) for achieving objectives.

6   *Match the correct definition to the appropriate term.*

Terms

(a)   Exogenous variables
(b)   Endogenous variables
(c)   Policies
(d)   Performance measures
(e)   Controls
(f)   Intermediate variables

Definitions

1   General guidelines for decision making
2   Variables determined externally
3   Devices used to regulate the operation of a model
4   Variables produced within the model
5   Standards that outputs from the decision must meet
6   Link endogenous and exogenous variables to a performance measure

7   *Sketch a P/V chart and mark on it the following.*

Breakeven point   Budgeted contribution
Fixed costs   Budgeted profit

8   Superimpose an economist's and an accountant's breakeven charts.

Answers to quick quiz

1   absorption
    unsuitable

2   (a) 3; (b) 1; (c) 2

3   Availability of cash
    Employees
    Customers
    Competitors
    Suppliers
    Feasibility
    Unquantified opportunity costs
    Political pressures
    Legal constraints

4   False. Apparent precision is misleading.

5   *Step 1.*   Identify objectives.
    Step 2.   Identify alternative opportunities (strategies) for achieving objectives.
    Step 3.   Collect and analyse relevant data about each alternative.
    Step 4.   Make the decision. State the expected outcome.
    Step 5.   Implement the decision.
    Step 6.   Obtain data about actual results.
    Step 7.   Compare actual results with the expected outcome.
    Step 8.   Evaluate achievements and make further decisions in this light.

6   (a) 2; (b) 4; (c) 1: (d) 5; (e) 3; (f) 6.

7

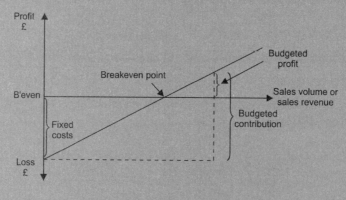

8

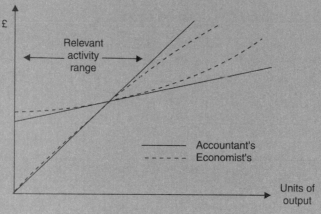

Now try the question below from the Exam Question Bank

Number	Level	Marks	Time
18	Exam	20	36 mins

Chapter 21

DECISION MAKING II

Topic list	Syllabus reference
1 Further cost classifications	5(b)
2 Identifying relevant costs	5(b)
3 Calculating relevant costs	5(a), 5(b)
4 Throughput accounting and decision making	5(b)
5 Limiting factors	5(b)
6 Discontinuance of products or departments	5(b)
7 Make or buy decisions	5(b)
8 Outsourcing	5(b)
9 Further processing decisions	5(b)
10 Product mix decisions	5(b)
11 Customer profitability analysis (CPA)	5(b)

Introduction

Chapter 20 served as an **introduction** to decision making. The concept of **relevant costs** was revisited and the **CVP model** was examined.

In **this chapter** we look in greater depth at **relevant costs** and at how they should be applied in decision-making situations.

We then turn our attention to a **variety of common short-run business decisions** and consider how they can be dealt with using relevant costs as appropriate.

Throughput accounting, a topic we covered in Chapter 4, is considered in conjunction with decision making in Section 4.

Study guide

Section 23 – Short run decisions II

- Explain the use of marginal cost and variable cost in decision making

- Describe the relationship between fixed cost and the time horizon used in a decision situation

- Explain how opportunity cost is used in making decisions

- Identify and calculate relevant costs for specific decision situations from given data

- Explain the meaning of throughput accounting and its use in decision making

- Explain and illustrate the impact of limiting factors in decision making

- Solve problems involving changes in product mix, discontinuance of products or departments

- Implement make or buy decisions using relevant costs

- Explain and demonstrate activity-based customer profitability analysis

- Make decisions as to whether to further process a product before sale using relevant costs and revenues

- Use relevant costs and revenues in decisions relating to the operation of internal service departments or the use of external services

Exam guide

Decision-making techniques is a core syllabus area and decision making in some form or another will no doubt appear in every paper.

The issues covered in this chapter are useful background to the following Oxford Brookes degree Research and Analysis Projects.

- Topic 1, which requires you to analyse the efficiency and/or effectiveness of a management accounting technique in an organisational setting

- Topic 10, which requires you to analyse how management accounting techniques are used to support decision making in organisations

1 FURTHER COST CLASSIFICATIONS

Variable costs and marginal costs

1.1 You should remember from your earlier studies that variable costs and marginal costs are usually relevant costs for decision making. They are **not always relevant costs,** however, and care is needed in analysing data.

1.2 Variable costs would include some non-relevant costs in the following circumstances.

(a) A labour cost might be accounted for as a variable cost item, when it is really a committed cost. For example, suppose that a new project requires 100 hours of labour time, which costs £5 per hour; however, the workforce is paid a fixed rate per man of £200 for a 40 hour week, there is a no-redundancies agreement and there is enough spare capacity to do the extra work. The relevant cost of the new project for direct labour would then be nil. The labour cost, although regarded as a variable cost of £5 per hour, is really a committed cost of £200 per man per week.

(b) A depreciation cost per hour might appear to be a variable cost item if the asset is depreciated at the rate of, say, £0.50 per hour. However, depreciation is never a relevant cost item because it is not a cash flow.

Fixed costs and the time horizon

1.3 **Most costs that are fixed in the short term are variable in the longer term.**

The concept of **attributable costs** was developed by Shillinglaw (1963) who argued that for many decisions, the **assumption that fixed costs will remain unchanged is invalid.** He distinguished between two types of fixed cost: divisible fixed costs and indivisible fixed costs.

(a) **A fixed cost is 'divisible' and hence attributable if it changes in line with a significant change in the volume of activity**. For example, if a company with one factory decides to double its capacity by opening an identical second factory, then all of the fixed costs associated with the first factory will also double. However, it is not possible to open a second factory overnight: it may take two years to build and equip it. This is why the **time horizon** is so important.

(b) A fixed cost is **indivisable** and hence **not attributable** if it is unaffected by any change in the volume of activity, no matter how large.

1.4 'Complexity-related costs' are the cost of support services that are **fixed in the short term** but vary, and therefore become relevant to a decision, **over a longer period of time** as the range and complexity of production changes.

Opportunity cost

1.5 We considered briefly the concept of opportunity cost in the previous chapter. Let us take a more detailed look.

> **KEY TERM**
>
> A **scarce resource** may be defined as a resource (materials, labour, machine time, cash and so on) which is in short supply, so that the total opportunities that exist for making profitable use of the resource exceed the amount of the resource available.

1.6 When a decision-maker is faced with an opportunity which would call for the **use of a scarce resource, the total incremental cost of using the resource will be higher than the direct cash cost of purchasing it.** This is because the resource could be used for **other purposes,** and so by **using it in one way, the benefits obtainable from using it another way must be forgone.**

1.7 If this seems a confusing explanation, a numerical example may help to clarify it. Suppose that a customer has asked whether your company would be willing to undertake a contract for him. The work would involve the use of certain equipment for five hours and its running costs would be £2 per hour. However, your company faces heavy demand for usage of the equipment which earns a contribution of £7 per hour from this other work. If the contract is undertaken, some of this work would have to be forgone.

1.8 The **contribution obtainable from putting the scarce resource to its alternative use is its opportunity cost** (sometimes referred to as its **'internal' opportunity cost**). Quite simply, since the equipment can earn £7 per hour in an alternative use, the contract under consideration should also be expected to earn at least the same amount. This can be accounted for by charging the £7 per hour as an opportunity cost to the contract and the total relevant cost of 5 hours of equipment time would be:

	£
Running costs (5 × £2))	10
Internal opportunity cost (5 × £7)	35
Relevant cost	45

It is important to notice that the variable running costs of the equipment are included in the total relevant cost.

1.9 **Rule for identifying the relevant cost of a scarce resource**

The total relevant cost of a scarce resource consists of the **sum** of the following.

- **The contribution/incremental profit forgone from the next-best opportunity for using the scarce resource**

- **The variable cost of the scarce resource,** that is, the cash expenditure to purchase the resource

2   IDENTIFYING RELEVANT COSTS

2.1   In this section we provide a fairly gentle introduction to the sort of thought processes that you will have to go through when you encounter a decision-making question. First some general points about machinery, labour, and particularly materials, that often catch people out.

2.2   **Machinery user costs**

Once a machine has been bought its cost is a **sunk** cost. **Depreciation** is not a relevant cost, because it is not a cash flow. However, **using** machinery may involve some incremental costs. These costs might be referred to as **user costs** and they include hire charges and any fall in resale value of owned assets, through use.

2.3   EXAMPLE: MACHINE USER COSTS

Bronty Ltd is considering whether to undertake some contract work for a customer. The machinery required for the contract would be as follows.

(a)   A special cutting machine will have to be hired for three months for the work (the length of the contract). Hire charges for this machine are £75 per month, with a minimum hire charge of £300.

(b)   All other machinery required in the production for the contract has already been purchased by the organisation on hire purchase terms. The monthly hire purchase payments for this machinery are £500. This consists of £450 for capital repayment and £50 as an interest charge. The last hire purchase payment is to be made in two months time. The cash price of this machinery was £9,000 two years ago. It is being depreciated on a straight line basis at the rate of £200 per month. However, it still has a useful life which will enable it to be operated for another 36 months.

The machinery is highly specialised and is unlikely to be required for other, more profitable jobs over the period during which the contract work would be carried out. Although there is no immediate market for selling this machine, it is expected that a customer might be found in the future. It is further estimated that the machine would lose £200 in its eventual sale value if it is used for the contract work.

What is the relevant cost of machinery for the contract?

2.4   SOLUTION

(a)   The **cutting machine** will incur an incremental cost of £300, the minimum hire charge.

(b)   The historical cost of the **other machinery** is irrelevant as a past cost; depreciation is irrelevant as a non-cash cost; and future hire purchase repayments are irrelevant because they are committed costs. The only relevant cost is the loss of resale value of the machinery, estimated at £200 through use. This 'user cost' will not arise until the machinery is eventually resold and the £200 should be discounted to allow for the time value of money. However, discounting is ignored here, and will be discussed in a later chapter.

(c) **Summary of relevant costs**

	£
Incremental hire costs	300
User cost of other machinery	200
	500

2.5 Labour

Often the labour force will be paid irrespective of the decision made and the costs are therefore **not incremental**. Take care, however, if the labour force could be put to an **alternative use**, in which case the relevant costs are the **variable costs** of the labour and associated variable overheads **plus** the **contribution forgone** from not being able to put it to its alternative use.

2.6 Materials

The relevant cost of raw materials is generally their current **replacement** cost, unless the materials have already been purchased and would not be replaced once used.

If materials have already been purchased but will not be replaced, then the relevant cost of using them is **either** (a) their current **resale** value **or** (b) the value they would obtain if they were put to an **alternative use**, if this is greater than their current resale value.

The **higher** of (a) or (b) is then the opportunity cost of the materials. If the materials have no resale value and no other possible use, then the relevant cost of using them for the opportunity under consideration would be nil.

2.7 The flowchart below shows how the relevant costs of materials can be identified, **provided that** the materials are **not in short supply**, and so have **no internal opportunity cost**.

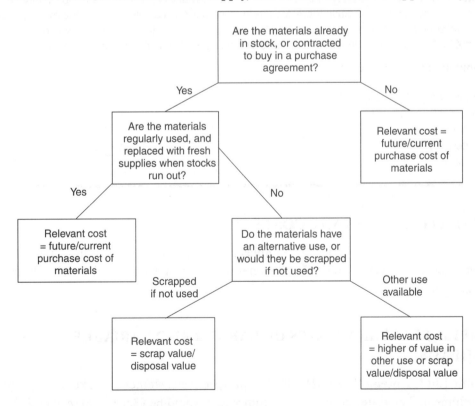

Question: relevant cost of materials

O'Reilly Ltd has been approached by a customer who would like a special job to be done for him, and who is willing to pay £22,000 for it. The job would require the following materials:

Material	Total units required	Units already in stock	Book value of units in stock £/unit	Realisable value £/unit	Replacement cost £/unit
A	1,000	0	-	-	6
B	1,000	600	2	2.5	5
C	1,000	700	3	2.5	4
D	200	200	4	6.0	9

(a)   Material B is used regularly by O'Reilly Ltd, and if units of B are required for this job, they would need to be replaced to meet other production demand.

(b)   Materials C and D are in stock as the result of previous over-buying, and they have a restricted use. No other use could be found for material C, but the units of material D could be used in another job as substitute for 300 units of material E, which currently costs £5 per unit (of which the company has no units in stock at the moment).

What are the relevant costs of material, in deciding whether or not to accept the contract?

Answer

(a)   **Material A** is not owned and would have to be bought in full at the replacement cost of £6 per unit.

(b)   **Material B** is used regularly by the company. There are existing stocks (600 units) but if these are used on the contract under review a further 600 units would be bought to replace them. Relevant costs are therefore 1,000 units at the replacement cost of £5 per unit.

(c)   **Material C:** 1,000 units are needed and 700 are already in stock. If used for the contract, a further 300 units must be bought at £4 each. The existing stocks of 700 will not be replaced. If they are used for the contract, they could not be sold at £2.50 each. The realisable value of these 700 units is an opportunity cost of sales revenue forgone.

(d)   **Material D:** these are already in stock and will not be replaced. There is an opportunity cost of using D in the contract because there are alternative opportunities either to sell the existing stocks for £6 per unit (£1,200 in total) or avoid other purchases (of material E), which would cost 300 × £5 = £1,500. Since substitution for E is more beneficial, £1,500 is the opportunity cost.

(e)   **Summary of relevant costs**

	£
Material A (1,000 × £6)	6,000
Material B (1,000 × £5)	5,000
Material C (300 × £4) plus (700 × £2.50)	2,950
Material D	1,500
Total	15,450

3   CALCULATING RELEVANT COSTS

3.1   In this section we look at a series of examples requiring the identification of the relevant costs for a decision. Try to identify the relevant costs of labour and overheads in the following example.

3.2   EXAMPLE: RELEVANT COSTS OF LABOUR AND VARIABLE OVERHEADS

Vanderbilt Ltd has been offered £21,000 by a prospective customer to make some purpose-built equipment. The materials cost of the equipment would be £3,000. There would also be a requirement for 2,000 labour hours. Labour wages are £4 per hour, variable overhead is £2 per hour and fixed overhead is absorbed at the rate of £4 per hour.

Labour, however, is in limited supply, and if the job is accepted, men would have to be diverted from other work which is expected to earn a contribution of £5 per hour towards fixed overheads and profit. Should the contract be undertaken?

3.3 SOLUTION

The **relevant costs of the scarce resource**, labour, are as follows.

(a) The **variable costs** of the labour and associated variable overheads
(b) The **contribution forgone** from not being able to put it to its alternative use

Fixed costs are ignored because there is no incremental fixed cost expenditure.

	£
Materials	3,000
Labour (2,000 hours @ £4)	8,000
Variable overhead (2,000 hours @ £2)	4,000
	15,000
Opportunity cost:	
Contribution forgone from other work (2,000 hours × £5)	10,000
Total costs	25,000
Revenue	21,000
Net loss on contract	(4,000)

The **contract should not be undertaken**.

3.4   At the risk of confusing this problem unnecessarily, it is worth thinking carefully about labour costs. The labour force will be paid £8,000 for 2,000 hours work, and variable overheads of £4,000 will be incurred no matter whether the men are employed on the new job or on other work. Relevant costs are future cash flows arising as a direct consequence of a decision, and the decision here will not affect the total wages paid. If this money is going to be spent anyway, shouldn't it therefore be ignored as an irrelevant cost?

3.5   The answer to this crucial question is 'no'. **The labour wages and variable overheads are relevant costs even though they will be incurred whatever happens**. The reason for this is that the **other work earns a contribution of £5 per hour, and contribution is stated after having covered labour and variable overhead costs. Work on the purpose-built equipment ought therefore to do at least the same.**

Minimum pricing

3.6   Opportunity costs of scarce resources might well feature in a broader examination question on relevant costs and as an exercise you should attempt a solution to the following problem. It is a minimum pricing problem, calling for a pricing decision, but the **minimum price for a one-off product or service contract is its total relevant costs**, in other words the **price at which the company would make no incremental profit and no incremental loss** from undertaking the work, but would just achieve an **incremental cost breakeven point**.

3.7   EXAMPLE: MINIMUM PRICING

A company has just completed production of an item of special equipment for a customer only to be notified that this customer has now gone into liquidation. After much effort, the sales manager has been able to interest a potential buyer, White Knight Ltd, which has indicated a willingness to buy the machine if certain conversion work could first be carried out.

(a) The sales price of the **machine** to the original buyer had been fixed at £138,600 and had included an estimated normal profit mark-up of 10% on total costs. The costs incurred in the manufacture of the machine were as follows.

	£
Direct materials	49,000
Direct labour	36,000
Variable overhead	9,000
Fixed production overhead	24,000
Fixed sales and distribution overhead	8,000
	126,000

(b) If the machine is **converted**, the production manager estimates that the cost of the extra work required would be:

Direct materials (at cost) £9,600

Direct labour: Dept X - 6 men for 4 weeks @ £210 per man/week

Dept Y - 2 men for 4 weeks @ £160 per man/week

(c) Variable overhead would be 20% of direct labour cost, and fixed production overhead would be absorbed at 83.33% of direct labour cost in Dept X and at 25% of direct labour cost in Dept Y.

(d) (i) In the original machine, there are three types of material. Type A could be sold for scrap for £8,000. Type B could be sold for scrap for £2,400 but it would take 120 hours of casual labour paid at £3.50 per hour to put it into a condition in which it would be suitable for sale. Type C would need to be scrapped, at a cost to the company of £1,100.

(ii) The direct materials required for the conversion are already in stock. If not needed for the conversion they would be used in the production of another machine in place of materials that would otherwise need to be purchased, and that would currently cost £8,800.

(iii) The conversion work would be carried out in two departments, X and Y. Department X is currently extremely busy and working at full capacity; it is estimated that its contribution to fixed overhead and profits is £2.50 per £1 of labour. Department Y, on the other hand, is short of work but for organisational reasons its labour force, which at the moment has a workload of only 40% of its standard capacity, cannot be reduced below its current level of 8 employees, all of whom are paid a wage of £160 per week.

(iv) The designs and specifications of the original machine could be sold to an overseas customer for £4,500 if the machine is scrapped.

(v) If conversion work is undertaken, a temporary supervisor would need to be employed for 4 weeks at a cost of £1,500. It is normal company practice to charge supervision costs to fixed overhead.

(vi) The original customer has already paid a non-returnable deposit to the company of 12.5% of the selling price.

Required

Calculate the minimum price that the company should accept from White Knight Ltd for the converted machine. Explain clearly how you have reached this figure.

3.8 SOLUTION

Note that the money received from the original customer should be ignored. Just as costs incurred in the past are not relevant to a current decision about what to do in the future, **past revenues** are also irrelevant.

Estimate of minimum price for the converted machine

	£	£
Opportunity cost of using the direct materials types A, B and C (W1)		8,880
Opportunity cost of additional materials for conversion (W2)		8,800
Opportunity cost of work in department X		
Labour (W3)	5,040	
Variable overhead (W3)	1,008	
Contribution forgone (W3)	12,600	
		18,648
Opportunity cost: sale of design and specifications (W4)		4,500
Incremental costs:		
Variable production overheads in department Y (W5)		256
Fixed production overheads (W6)		1,500
Minimum price		42,584

Workings

1   The **cost of the original machine** is a past cost and so is not relevant, and the £126,000 of cost incurred should be excluded from the minimum price calculation. It is necessary, however, to consider the alternative use of the direct **materials** (opportunity costs) which would be forgone if the conversion work is carried out.

	£
Type A: Revenue from sales as scrap (note (a))	8,000
Type B: Revenue from sales as scrap, minus the additional cash	
costs necessary to prepare it for sale (£2,400 – (120 × £3.50))	1,980
Type C: Cost of disposal if the machine is not converted	
(a negative opportunity cost)	(1,100)
Total opportunity cost of materials Types A, B and C	8,880

By agreeing to the conversion of the machine, the company would therefore lose a net revenue of £8,880 from the alternative use of these materials.

2   The cost of additional direct **materials** for conversion is £9,600, but this is an historical cost. The relevant cost of these materials is the £8,800 which would be spent on new purchases if the conversion is carried out. If the work goes ahead, the materials in stock would be unavailable for production of the other machine mentioned in item (d)(ii) of the question and so the extra purchases of £8,800 would then be needed.

3   **Direct labour** in Departments X and Y is a fixed cost and the labour force will be paid regardless of the work they do or do not do. The cost of labour for conversion in Department Y is not a relevant cost because the work could be done without any extra cost to the company. In Department X, however, acceptance of the conversion work would oblige the company to divert production from other profitable jobs. The minimum contribution required from using Department X labour must be sufficient to cover the cost of the labour and variable overheads and then make an additional £2.50 in contribution per £1 of labour.

Department X - costs for direct labour hours spent on conversion

6 men × 4 weeks × £210 =	£5,040
Variable overhead cost: £5,040 × 20% =	£1,008
Contribution forgone by diverting labour from other work:	
£2.50 per £1 of labour cost = £5,040 × 250% =	£12,600

4   If the machine is converted, the company cannot sell the designs and specifications. £4,500 is a relevant (**opportunity**) cost of accepting the conversion order.

5   **Variable overheads** in Department Y are relevant costs because they will only be incurred if production work is carried out. (It is **assumed** that if the workforce is idle, no variable overheads would be incurred.)

6   **Fixed overheads**, being mainly unchanged regardless of what the company decides to do, should be ignored because they are not relevant (incremental) costs. The additional cost of supervision should, however, be included as a relevant cost of the order because the £1,500 will not be spent unless the conversion work is done.

4   THROUGHPUT ACCOUNTING AND DECISION MAKING

4.1   We encountered throughput accounting back in Chapter 4. Here we look at its use in decision making.

Throughput measures

4.2   In a throughput environment, **production priority** must be given to the products best able to generate throughput, that is those **products that maximise throughput per unit of bottleneck resource** (which is similar in concept to maximising contribution per unit of limiting factor).

4.3   Products can be ranked according to the **TA ratio**.

TA ratio = return per factory hour/cost per factory hour

where   return per factory hour = throughput/time on bottleneck resource

cost per factory hour (for all products) = TFC/total time available on bottleneck resource

4.4   The **TA ratio** is **similar in concept to contribution per unit of limiting factor**. (In fact, if materials were the only variable cost, contribution and throughput would be identical and there would be no difference between traditional contribution analysis and throughput analysis.) The TA ratio can be **used to assess the relative earning capabilities of different products** and hence can help with decision making.

4.5   EXAMPLE: THROUGHPUT ACCOUNTING

Corrie Ltd produces three products, X, Y and Z. The capacity of Corrie's plant is restricted by process alpha. Process alpha is expected to be operational for eight hours per day and can produce 1,200 units of X per hour, 1,500 units of Y per hour, and 600 units of Z per hour.

Selling prices and material costs for each product are as follows.

Product	Selling price	Unit material cost	Throughput
	£	£	£
X	150	70	80
Y	120	40	80
X	300	100	200

Total factory cost (TFC) is £720,000 per day.

Required

(a) Calculate the profit per day if daily output achieved is 6,000 units of X, 4,500 units of Y and 1,200 units of Z.

(b) Determine the efficiency of bottleneck use.

(c) Calculate the TA ratio for each product.

(d) In the absence of demand restrictions for the three products, advise Corrie Ltd's management on the optimal production plan.

4.6 SOLUTION

(a) **Profit** = Throughput (sales revenue less direct material cost) – TFC = [(£80 × 6,000) + (£80 × 4,500) + (£200 × 1,200)] – £720,000 = £360,000

(b) **Efficiency of bottleneck use** = attributed TFC as % of actual TFC

TFC cost per unit = usage of bottleneck resource × TFC per unit of bottleneck resource

TFC per unit (minute) of bottleneck = £720,000/(8 hrs × 60 mins) = £1,500

TFC cost per unit is therefore as follows.

Product	Time in process alpha Minutes	× TFC per minute £	= TFC cost per unit £
X	60/1,200 = 0.05	1,500	75
Y	60/1,500 = 0.04	1,500	60
Z	60/600 = 0.10	1,500	150

TFC cost for the day is as follows.

Product	Output in day	TFC cost per unit £	TFC £'000
X	6,000	75	450
Y	4,500	60	270
Z	1,200	150	180
			900

Efficiency of bottleneck use = £900,000 ÷ £720,000 = 1.25 = 125%

Check. Equivalent hours produced X 6,000/1,200 = 5
Y 4,500/1,500 = 3
Z 1,200/600 = 2
10

Hours available 8, hours produced 10, ∴ 125% efficiency.

(c) **TA ratio** = return per factory hour/cost per factory hour

Return per factory hour = throughput/time on bottleneck resource
Cost per factory hour = TFC/availability of bottleneck resource = £720,000/8 = £90,000

Product	Return per factory hour	Cost per factory hour	TA ratio
X	(£80 ÷ 0.05 min) × 60	£90,000	1.07
Y	(£80 ÷ 0.04 min) × 60	£90,000	1.33
Z	(£200 ÷ 0.10 min) × 60	£90,000	1.33

(d) An attempt should be made to **remove the restriction** on output caused by the limited process alpha capacity. This will, of course, **result in another bottleneck** emerging elsewhere.

Extra capacity could possibly be obtained by overtime working, process improvements or product specification changes but until the volume of throughput can be increased, output should be **concentrated upon products Y and Z** (greatest TA ratios), unless there are good marketing reasons for continuing the current production mix.

5 LIMITING FACTORS

IMPORTANT POINT

Question 2 of the December 2001 exam contained a number of relatively straightforward decision-making scenarios but 'many [candidates] displayed a lack of understanding of basic management accounting techniques that should have been covered in prior examination papers' (Examiner's comments). In particular the examiner highlighted contribution and profit maximisation with limiting factors as areas where candidates showed little understanding. So don't skip this section, thinking that you know all about the subject already. Make sure that you do understand the difference between profit and contribution and that you can deal with a range of limiting factor scenarios.

KEY TERM

When sales demand is in excess of an organisation's production capacity, the scarce resources responsible for limiting output are known as **limiting factors.**

5.1 When an organisation provides a range of products or services to its markets, but has a restricted amount of resources available to it, then it will have to make a decision about what **product mix** (or mix of services) it will provide. Its volume of output and sales will be constrained by the limited resources rather than by sales demand, and so management faces a decision about **how scarce capacity should best be used**. The limiting factor might be material, machine time, cash or labour, for example.

5.2 From a management accounting point of view, the assumption would be that a firm faced with a problem of one or more limiting factors would select a product or service mix that would maximise overall profitability, and so **maximise** total **contribution**.

5.3 The technique for establishing the contribution-maximising product or service mix differs according to whether there is **just one** or **two or more** scarce resources.

Question: scarce resources

The word 'scarce' in this context is potentially misleading, because it does not necessarily mean that there is a worldwide shortage, it simply means that the firm cannot in the short-term obtain all the resources it needs to carry out a particular task. Consider the following cases.

(a) What resources would be scarce for a two-partner firm of certified accountants that wished to tender for the audit of Barclays Bank?

(b) What resources would be scarce for a small building firm that wished to build a football stadium?

As you probably realise yourself in practice, the commonest scarce resources are **time** and **money**.

Decisions involving one limiting factor

5.4 When there is just one limiting factor, the technique for establishing the contribution-maximising product mix or service mix is to **rank** the products or services in order of **contribution-earning ability per unit of the limiting factor**. You should have learned this technique of **limiting factor analysis** for your earlier studies, but it is still important for Paper 3.3. Here are a series of examples to illustrate this technique and the further considerations involved.

5.5 EXAMPLE: ONE LIMITING FACTOR

Spice Ltd makes two products, Posh and Ugly, for which there is unlimited sales demand at the budgeted sales price of each. A Posh takes 8 hours to make, and has a variable cost of £36 and a sales price of £72. An Ugly takes 5 hours to make, and has a variable cost of £24 and a sales price of £48. Both products use the same type of labour, which is in restricted supply. Which product should be made in order to maximise profits?

5.6 SOLUTION AND DISCUSSION

(a) There is no limitation on sales demand, but **labour** is in restricted supply, and so to determine the profit-maximising production mix, we must rank the products in order of **contribution-earning capability per labour hour**.

	Posh	Ugly
	£	£
Sales price	72	48
Variable costs	36	24
Contribution	36	24
Hours per unit	8 hrs	5 hrs
Contribution per labour hour	£4.50	£4.80
Ranking	**2nd**	**1st**

Although Posh units have the higher unit contribution, Ugly units are more profitable because they make a **greater contribution per unit** in each scarce hour of labour time worked. For instance, eight Ugly units (worth 8 × £24 = £192) can be made in the same time as five Posh (worth only 5 × £36 = £180).

(b) **Other considerations**

A profit-maximising budget would therefore be to produce Ugly units only, within the assumptions made. It is important to remember, however, that other considerations, so far excluded from the problem, might alter the decision entirely.

(i) Can the **sales price** of either product be **raised**, thereby increasing unit contribution, and the contribution per labour hour, without reducing sales demand? Since sales demand is apparently unlimited, it would be reasonable to suspect that both products are underpriced.

(ii) To what extent are sales of each product **interdependent**? For example, a manufacturer of knives and forks could not expect to cease production of knives without affecting sales demand for the forks.

   (iii)   Would a decision to cease production of Posh units really have no effect on fixed costs? The assumption that **fixed costs** are unaffected by limiting factor decisions is not always valid, and closure of either the Posh or Ugly production line might result in **fixed cost savings** (for example a reduction in production planning costs, product design costs, or equipment depreciation).

(c) **Qualitative factors**

   (i)   Would a decision to make and sell just Ugly units have a harmful effect on **customer loyalty** and sales demand?

   (ii)   Is the decision going to affect the long-term plans of the company as well as the short-term? If Posh units are not produced next year, it is likely that **competitors** will take over the markets vacated by Spice Ltd. **Labour** skilled in the manufacture of Posh units will be lost, and a decision in one year's time to reopen manufacture of Posh units might not be possible.

   (iii)   **Why is there a shortage of labour?** Are the skills required difficult to obtain, perhaps because the company is using very old-fashioned production methods, or is the company a high-tech newcomer located in a low-tech area? Or perhaps the conditions of work are so unappealing that people simply do not want to work for the company.

Question (c) (iii) should be asked whatever the limiting factor. If machine hours are in short supply is this because more machines are needed, or newer, more reliable and efficient machines? If materials are in short supply, what are competitors doing? Have they found an equivalent or better substitute? Is it time to redesign the product?

Limited sales demand

5.7   When there is a maximum **limit on sales demand** for an organisation's products or services, they should still be ranked in order of contribution-earning ability per unit of the limiting factor. However, the profit-maximising decision will be to produce the **top-ranked products** (or to provide the top-ranked services) **up to the sales demand limit.**

5.8 EXAMPLE: ONE LIMITING FACTOR AND LIMITED SALES DEMAND

Ferguson Ltd manufactures and sells three products, Beckham, Scholes and Neville, for which budgeted sales demand, unit selling prices and unit variable costs are as follows.

		Beckham		Scholes		Neville	
Budgeted sales demand		550 units		500 units		400 units	
		£	£	£	£	£	£
Unit sales price			16		18		14
Variable costs:	materials	8		6		2	
	labour	4		6		9	
			12		12		11
Unit contribution			4		6		3

The company has existing stocks of 250 units of Beckham and 200 units of Neville, which it is quite willing to use up to meet sales demand. All three products use the same direct materials and the same type of direct labour. In the next year, the available supply of materials will be restricted to £4,800 (at cost) and the available supply of labour to £6,600 (at cost). What product mix and sales mix would maximise the company's profits in the next year?

5.9 SOLUTION AND DISCUSSION

There appear to be **two** scarce resources, direct materials and direct labour. However, this is not certain, and because there is a limited sales demand as well, it might be that there is:

(a) no limiting factor at all, except sales demand - ie none of the resources is scarce;

(b) only one limiting factor preventing the full potential sales demand being achieved.

Step 1. Begin by establishing **how many limiting factors** there are, and if there are any, which one or which ones they are. In this example we have:

	Beckham Units	*Scholes* Units	*Neville* Units
Budgeted sales	550	500	400
Stock in hand	250	0	200
Minimum production to meet demand	300	500	200

	Minimum production to meet sales demand Units	*Required materials at cost* £	*Required labour at cost* £
Beckham	300	2,400	1,200
Scholes	500	3,000	3,000
Neville	200	400	1,800
Total required		5,800	6,000
Total available		4,800	6,600
(Shortfall)/Surplus		(1,000)	600

Materials are a limiting factor, but labour is not.

Step 2. The next step is to rank Beckham, Scholes and Neville in order of contribution earned per £1 of direct materials consumed.

	Beckham £	*Scholes* £	*Neville* £
Unit contribution	4	6	3
Cost of materials	8	6	2
Contribution per £1 materials	£0.50	£1.00	£1.50
Ranking	**3rd**	**2nd**	**1st**

Step 3. Neville should be manufactured up to the limit where units produced plus units in stock will meet sales demand, then Scholes second and Beckham third, until all the available materials are used up.

Ranking	Product	*Sales demand less units in stock* Units	*Production quantity* Units		*Materials cost* £
1st	Neville	200	200	(× £2)	400
2nd	Scholes	500	500	(× £6)	3,000
3rd	Beckham	300	175	(× £8)	* 1,400
		Total available			4,800

⋆ Balancing amount using up total available.

Step 4. The profit-maximising budget is as follows.

	Beckham Units	*Scholes* Units	*Neville* Units
Opening stock	250	0	200
Add production	175	500	200
Sales	425	500	400

	Beckham	*Scholes*	*Neville*	*Total*
	£	£	£	£
Revenue	6,800	9,000	5,600	21,400
Variable costs	5,100	6,000	4,400	15,500
Contribution	1,700	3,000	1,200	5,900

Question: qualitative issues

What other considerations should be taken into account by Ferguson Ltd?

Answer

Refer back to the previous example for suggestions if you cannot think of any for yourself.

Assumptions in limiting factor analysis: one scarce resource

5.10 In the previous examples, the following assumptions were made. If any of the assumptions are not valid, then the profit-maximising decision might be different.

(a) **Fixed costs will be the same** regardless of the decision that is taken, and so the profit maximising and contribution-maximising output level will be the same. This will not necessarily be true, since some fixed costs might be **directly attributable** to a product or service. A decision to reduce or cease altogether activity on a product or service might therefore result in some fixed cost savings, which would have to be taken into account.

(b) The **unit variable cost is constant**, regardless of the output quantity of a product or service. This has the following implications.

(i) The price of resources will be unchanged regardless of quantity; for example, there will be no bulk purchase discount of raw materials.

(ii) Efficiency and productivity levels will be unchanged; regardless of output quantity, the direct labour productivity, the machine time per unit, and the materials consumption per unit will remain the same.

(c) The **estimates** of sales demand for each product, and the resources required to make each product, are **known with certainty.** In the previous example, there were estimates of the maximum sales demand for each of three products, and these estimates were used to establish the profit-maximising product mix. **Suppose the estimates were wrong?** The product mix finally chosen would then either mean that some sales demand of the most profitable item would be unsatisfied, or that production would exceed sales demand, leaving some stock unsold. Clearly, once a profit-maximising output decision is reached, management will have to **keep their decision under continual review**, and adjust their decision as appropriate in the light of actual results.

(d) **Units of output are divisible**, and a profit-maximising solution might include fractions of units as the optimum output level. Where fractional answers are not realistic, some rounding of the figures will be necessary.

Exam focus point

A suitable adjustment will have to be made for any problem involving a scarce resource where one (or more) of the assumptions is invalid. A Paper 3.3 question might ask you to perform calculations that dropped one or more of the assumptions.

Scarce resources and opportunity costs: shadow prices

5.11 If there are scarce resources, there will be **opportunity costs** (the benefits forgone by using a scarce resource in one way instead of in the next most profitable way).

5.12 EXAMPLE: SHADOW PRICE

For example, suppose that a company manufactures two items X and Y, which earn a contribution of £24 and £18 per unit respectively. Product X requires 4 machine hours per unit, and product Y 2 hours. Only 5,000 machine hours are available, and potential sales demand is for 1,000 units each of X and Y. What should the product mix be?

5.13 SOLUTION (NO EXTRA RESOURCES)

Machine hours would be a limiting factor, and with X earning £6 per hour and Y earning £9 per hour, the profit-maximising decision would be:

	Units	Hours	Contribution £
Y	1,000	2,000	18,000
X (balance)	750	3,000	18,000
		5,000	36,000

Priority is given to Y because the opportunity cost of making Y instead of more units of X is £6 per hour (X's contribution per machine hour), and since Y earns £9 per hour, the incremental benefit of making Y instead of X would be £3 per hour.

5.14 SOLUTION WITH EXTRA RESOURCES

If extra machine hours could be made available, more units of X (up to 1,000) would be made, and an extra contribution of £6 per hour could be earned. Similarly, if fewer machine hours were available, the decision would be to make fewer units of X and to keep production of Y at 1,000 units, and so the loss of machine hours would cost the company £6 per hour in lost contribution.

5.15 This £6 per hour, the marginal contribution-earning potential of the scarce resource at the profit-maximising output level, is referred to as the **shadow price** (or **dual price**) of the scarce resource.

> **KEY TERM**
>
> The **shadow price** of a resource is the marginal contribution that can be earned for each unit of the scarce resource that is available.

6 DISCONTINUANCE OF PRODUCTS OR DEPARTMENTS

6.1 Discontinuance or shutdown problems involve the following decisions.

(a) **Whether or not to close down** a product line, department or other activity, either because it is making losses or because it is too expensive to run

(b) If the decision is to shut down, **whether the closure should be permanent or temporary**

6.2 **In practice,** shutdown decisions may often involve **longer-term considerations,** and **capital expenditures and revenues.**

(a) A shutdown should result in savings in **annual operating costs** for a number of years into the future.

(b) Closure will probably release **unwanted fixed assets for sale.** Some assets might have a small scrap value, but other assets, in particular property, might have a substantial sale value.

(c) **Employees** affected by the closure must be made redundant or relocated, perhaps after retraining, or else offered early retirement. There will be lump sum payments involved which must be taken into account in the financial arithmetic. For example, suppose that the closure of a regional office would result in annual savings of £100,000, fixed assets could be sold off to earn income of £2 million, but redundancy payments would be £3 million. The shutdown decision would involve an assessment of the net capital cost of closure (£1 million) against the annual benefits (£100,000 pa).

6.3 It is possible, however, for shutdown problems to be **simplified into short-run decisions,** by making one of the following assumptions.

(a) **Fixed asset sales and redundancy costs would be negligible.**

(b) **Income from fixed asset sales would match redundancy costs** and so these capital items would be self-cancelling.

In such circumstances the financial aspect of shutdown decisions would be based on **short-run relevant costs.**

6.4 EXAMPLE: ADDING OR DELETING PRODUCTS (OR DEPARTMENTS)

A company manufactures three products, Pawns, Rooks and Bishops. The present net annual income from these is as follows.

	Pawns £	Rooks £	Bishops £	Total £
Sales	50,000	40,000	60,000	150,000
Variable costs	30,000	25,000	35,000	90,000
Contribution	20,000	15,000	25,000	60,000
Fixed costs	17,000	18,000	20,000	55,000
Profit/loss	3,000	(3,000)	5,000	5,000

The company is concerned about its poor profit performance, and is considering whether or not to cease selling Rooks. It is felt that selling prices cannot be raised or lowered without adversely affecting net income. £5,000 of the fixed costs of Rooks are direct fixed costs which would be saved if production ceased (ie there are some attributable fixed costs). All other fixed costs, it is considered, would remain the same.

By **stopping production of Rooks,** the **consequences** would be a £10,000 fall in profits.

	£
Loss of contribution	(15,000)
Savings in fixed costs	5,000
Incremental loss	(10,000)

Suppose, however, it were possible to use the resources realised by stopping production of Rooks and **switch to producing a new item,** Crowners, which would sell for £50,000 and incur variable costs of £30,000 and extra direct fixed costs of £6,000. A new decision is now required.

430

	Rooks	Crowners
	£	£
Sales	40,000	50,000
Less variable costs	25,000	30,000
	15,000	20,000
Less direct fixed costs	5,000	6,000
Contribution to shared fixed costs and profit	10,000	14,000

It would be **more profitable to shut down production of Rooks and switch** resources to making Crowners, in order to boost profits by £4,000 to £9,000.

Qualitative factors

6.5 As usual the decision is not merely a matter of choosing the best financial option. Qualitative factors related to the impact on **employees, customers, competitors** and **suppliers** must once more be considered.

Question: shutdown decisions

How would the above decision change if Pawns, Rooks and Bishops were manufactured in different departments, variable costs could be split down into the costs of direct materials, labour and overheads, and fixed costs could be analysed into the costs of administrative staff and equipment and premises costs?

Answer

The decision would not change at all - unless perhaps activity based analysis of overheads were undertaken and unexpected cost patterns were revealed. The point of this exercise is to make you realise that problems that look complicated are sometimes very simple in essence even if the volume of calculations seems daunting.

Judging relative profitability

6.6 A common approach to judging the relative profitability of products is to calculate **C/S ratios**. The most profitable option is to concentrate on the product(s) with the highest C/S ratios.

7 MAKE OR BUY DECISIONS

7.1 A make or buy problem involves a decision by an organisation about **whether it should make a product or whether it should pay another organisation to do so**. Here are some examples of make or buy decisions.

(a) Whether a company should manufacture its own components, or else buy the components from an outside supplier

(b) Whether a construction company should do some work with its own employees, or whether it should sub-contract the work to another company

(c) Whether a service should be carried out by an internal department or whether an external organisation should be employed (discussed more fully later in this chapter)

7.2 The '**make**' option should give **management more direct control** over the work, but the '**buy**' option often has the benefit that the **external organisation** has a **specialist skill** and expertise in the work. Make or buy decisions should certainly **not be based exclusively on cost considerations**.

Make or buy decisions: no limiting factors

7.3 If an organisation has the freedom of choice about whether to make internally or buy externally and has no scarce resources that put a restriction on what it can do itself, the **relevant costs** for the decision will be the **differential costs** between the two options.

7.4 EXAMPLE: MAKE OR BUY WITH NO LIMITING FACTORS

Shellfish Ltd makes four components, W, X, Y and Z, for which costs in the forthcoming year are expected to be as follows.

	W	X	Y	Z
Production (units)	1,000	2,000	4,000	3,000
Unit marginal costs	£	£	£	£
Direct materials	4	5	2	4
Direct labour	8	9	4	6
Variable production overheads	2	3	1	2
	14	17	7	12

Directly attributable fixed costs per annum and committed fixed costs:

	£
Incurred as a direct consequence of making W	1,000
Incurred as a direct consequence of making X	5,000
Incurred as a direct consequence of making Y	6,000
Incurred as a direct consequence of making Z	8,000
Other fixed costs (committed)	30,000
	50,000

A sub-contractor has offered to supply units of W, X, Y and Z for £12, £21, £10 and £14 respectively. Should Shellfish Ltd make or buy the components?

7.5 SOLUTION

(a) The **relevant costs** are the differential costs between making and buying, and they consist of **differences in unit variable costs plus differences in directly attributable fixed costs**. Sub-contracting will result in some **fixed cost savings.**

	W	X	Y	Z
	£	£	£	£
Unit variable cost of making	14	17	7	12
Unit variable cost of buying	12	21	10	14
	(2)	4	3	2
Annual requirements (units)	1,000	2,000	4,000	3,000
	£	£	£	£
Extra variable cost of buying (per annum)	(2,000)	8,000	12,000	6,000
Fixed costs saved by buying	(1,000)	(5,000)	(6,000)	(8,000)
Extra total cost of buying	(3,000)	3,000	6,000	(2,000)

(b) The company would save £3,000 pa by sub-contracting component W (where the purchase cost would be less than the marginal cost per unit to make internally) and would save £2,000 pa by sub-contracting component Z (because of the saving in fixed costs of £8,000).

(c) In this example, relevant costs are the variable costs of in-house manufacture, the variable costs of sub-contracted units, and the saving in fixed costs.

(d) **Further considerations**

(i) If components W and Z are sub-contracted, the company will have **spare capacity**. How should that spare capacity be profitably used? Are there hidden benefits to be obtained from sub-contracting? Would the company's workforce resent the loss of work to an outside sub-contractor, and might such a decision cause an industrial dispute?

(ii) Would the sub-contractor be **reliable** with delivery times, and would he supply components of the same **quality** as those manufactured internally?

(iii) Does the company wish to be **flexible** and maintain better **control** over operations by making everything itself?

(iv) Are the **estimates** of fixed cost savings reliable? In the case of Product W, buying is clearly cheaper than making in-house. In the case of product Z, the decision to buy rather than make would only be financially beneficial if it is feasible that the fixed cost savings of £8,000 will really be 'delivered' by management. All too often in practice, promised savings fail to materialise!

Make or buy decisions and scarce resources

7.6 **One reason** for buying products or services from another organisation is **scarcity** of resources. A company might want to do more things than it has the resources for, and so its choice would be one of the following.

(a) To make the best use of the resources it has got, and **ignore the opportunities to buy help from outside**

(b) To **combine internal resources with buying externally** so as to do more and increase profitability further

7.7 Buying help from outside is justifiable if it adds to profits. However, a further decision is then how to split the work between internal and external effort. What parts of the work should be given to suppliers or sub-contractors so as to maximise profitability?

7.8 In a situation where a company must **sub-contract work to make up a shortfall in its own in-house capabilities**, its **total costs will be minimised** if those **units bought out from a sub-contractor have the lowest extra variable cost of buying out per unit of scarce resource**.

This basic principle can be made clearer with a simple example.

7.9 EXAMPLE: MAKE OR BUY DECISION WITH SCARCE RESOURCES

Mariner Ltd manufactures three components, S, A and T using the same machines for each. The budget for the next year calls for the production and assembly of 4,000 of each component. The variable production cost per unit of the final product, the CR is:

	Machine hours	Variable cost £
1 unit of S	3	20
1 unit of A	2	36
1 unit of T	4	24
Assembly		20
		100

Only 24,000 hours of machine time will be available during the year, and a sub-contractor has quoted the following unit prices for supplying components: S £29; A £40; T £34.

Advise Mariner Ltd.

7.10 DISCUSSION AND SOLUTION

The company's budget calls for 36,000 hours of machine time, if all the components are to be produced in-house. Only 24,000 hours are available, and there is a shortfall of 12,000 hours of machine time, which is therefore a **limiting factor**. The shortage can be overcome by **subcontracting the equivalent of 12,000 machine hours' output** to the subcontractor.

The **assembly costs are not relevant costs** because they are unaffected by the decision.

(a) It might be tempting to think that the company should minimise its internal costs first, and sub-contract what it cannot make itself. In this example, the **temptation might be to decide that the variable cost of making each product is as follows.**

Product	Variable cost	Machine hours per unit	Variable cost per machine hour
	£		£
S	20	3	6.67
A	36	2	18.00
T	24	4	6.00

and so in-house production would be cheapest by concentrating on T first, then S and finally A, giving a production and buying schedule as follows:

Product		Units	Hours		Variable costs
					£
Make:	T	4,000	16,000		96,000
	S	2,666	8,000	(balance)	53,320
			24,000		149,320
Buy:	S	1,334		(× £29)	38,686
	A	4,000		(× £40)	160,000
Total costs (excluding assembly)					348,006

This is not the cheapest option. Costs can be reduced still further by minimising the extra variable costs of sub-contracting per unit of scarce resource saved (ie per machine hour saved).

	S	A	T
	£	£	£
Variable cost of making	20	36	24
Variable cost of buying	29	40	34
Extra variable cost of buying	9	4	10
Machine hours saved by buying	3 hrs	2 hrs	4 hrs
Extra variable cost of buying per hour saved	£3	£2	£2.50

(b) **Correct conclusion.** It is cheaper to buy A than to buy T and it is most expensive to buy S. The priority for **making** the components in-house will be in the reverse order: S, then T, then A. There are enough machine hours to make all 4,000 units of S (12,000 hours) and to produce 3,000 units of T (another 12,000 hours). 12,000 hours' production of T and A must be sub-contracted.

The cost-minimising and so profit-maximising make and buy schedule is as follows.

Component	Machine hours used/saved	Number of units	Unit variable cost £	Total variable cost £
Make: S	12,000	4,000	20	80,000
T	12,000	3,000	24	72,000
	24,000			152,000
Buy: T	4,000	1,000	34	34,000
A	8,000	4,000	40	160,000
	12,000			
Total variable cost of components, excluding assembly costs				346,000

Question: make or buy decision with a scarce resource

In a make or buy situation involving a scarce resource should the problem be looked at from the point of view of making or the point of view of buying?

Answer

If you cannot answer this question you have not understood the preceding example and you should work through it again. Why should the company concentrate on S first?

Validity of analysis of costs

7.11 If a decision to 'buy' leads to a **significant change in internal production volumes**, the cost analysis used to make the decision may be invalid.

(a) The organisation's labour costs might vary: overtime work might no longer be required; efficiency levels might vary with length of production run.

(b) Material prices might incorporate quantity discounts or be subject to a fixed minimum charge.

Make or buy decisions with limiting factors: more than one scarce resource

7.12 When an organisation has more than one scarce resource restricting what it can make internally, the technique described so far cannot be used to establish the cost-minimising option. It might be possible to use **linear programming** to reach a decision.

8 OUTSOURCING

8.1 A significant trend in the 1990s has been for companies and government bodies to **concentrate on their core competences** – what they are really good at (or set up to achieve) – and **turn other functions over to specialist contractors.** A company that earns its profits from, say, manufacturing bicycles, does not also need to have expertise in, say, mass catering or office cleaning. **Facilities management companies** such as Rentokil have grown in response to this.

> **KEY TERM**
>
> **Outsourcing** is the use of external supplies for finished products, components or services. This is also known as **contract manufacturing** or **sub-contracting.**

8.2 **Reasons for this trend**

(a) Frequently the decision is made on the grounds that **specialist contractors** can offer **superior quality** and **efficiency**. If a contractor's main business is making a specific component it can invest in the specialist machinery and labour and knowledge skills needed to make that component. However, this component may be only one of many needed by the contractor's customer, and the complexity of components is now such that attempting to keep internal facilities up to the standard of specialists detracts from the main business of the customer.

(b) Contracting out manufacturing **frees capital** that can then be invested in core activities such as market research, product definition, product planning, marketing and sales.

(c) **Contractors** have the **capacity** and **flexibility** to start production very quickly to meet sudden **variations in demand**. In-house facilities may not be able to respond as quickly, because of the need to redirect resources from elsewhere.

Internal and external services

8.3 In administrative and support functions, too, companies are increasingly likely to use specialist companies. **Decisions** such as the following are now common.

(a) Whether the **design and development of a new computer system** should be entrusted to in-house data processing staff or whether an external software house should be hired to do the work

(b) Whether **maintenance and repairs** of certain items of equipment should be dealt with by in-house engineers, or whether a maintenance contract should be made with a specialist organisation

Even if you are not aware of specialist 'facilities management' companies such as Securicor, you will be familiar with the idea of office cleaning being done by contractors.

8.4 The **costs relevant** to such decisions are little different to those that are taken into account in a **'conventional' make or buy situation**: they will be the **differential costs between performing the service internally or using an external provider.**

> **Exam focus point**
>
> The major problem in examination questions is likely to be identifying whether existing staff will be made redundant or whether they will be redeployed, and whether there are alternative uses for the other resources made available by ceasing to perform the service internally. These, it hardly needs stating, are also likely to be the major problems in practice.

9 FURTHER PROCESSING DECISIONS

9.1 Suppose a manufacturing company carries out process operations in which two or more joint products are made from a common process. If the joint products can be sold either in their existing condition at the 'split-off' point at the end of common processing or after further separate processing, **a decision should be taken about whether to sell each joint product at the split-off point or after further processing.**

IMPORTANT POINT

Note that **joint (pre-separation) costs** are incurred regardless of the decision and are therefore **irrelevant**.

9.2 EXAMPLE: FURTHER PROCESSING

The Poison Chemical Company produces two joint products, Alash and Pottum from the same process. Joint processing costs of £150,000 are incurred up to split-off point, when 100,000 units of Alash and 50,000 units of Pottum are produced. The selling prices at split-off point are £1.25 per unit for Alash and £2.00 per unit for Pottum.

The units of Alash could be processed further to produce 60,000 units of a new chemical, Alashplus, but at an extra fixed cost of £20,000 and variable cost of 30p per unit of input. The selling price of Alashplus would be £3.25 per unit. Should the company sell Alash or Alashplus?

9.3 SOLUTION

The only relevant costs/incomes are those which compare selling Alash against selling Alashplus. Every other cost is irrelevant: they will be incurred regardless of what the decision is.

	Alash			*Alashplus*
Selling price per unit	£1.25			£3.25
	£		£	£
Total sales	125,000			195,000
Post-separation processing costs	-	Fixed	20,000	
		Variable	30,000	50,000
Sales minus post-separation (further processing) costs	125,000			145,000

It is £20,000 more profitable to convert Alash into Alashplus.

Question: further processing decision

A company manufactures four products from an input of a raw material to Process 1. Following this process, product A is processed in Process 2, product B in Process 3, product C in Process 4 and product D in Process 5.

The normal loss in Process 1 is 10% of input, and there are no expected losses in the other processes. Scrap value in Process 1 is £0.50 per litre. The costs incurred in Process 1 are apportioned to each product according to the volume of output of each product. Production overhead is absorbed as a percentage of direct wages.

Data in respect of the month of October

	Process					
	1	*2*	*3*	*4*	*5*	*Total*
	£'000	£'000	£'000	£'000	£'000	£'000
Direct materials at £1.25 per litre	100					100
Direct wages	48	12	8	4	16	88
Production overhead						66

	Product			
	A	B	C	D
	litres	litres	litres	litres
Output	22,000	20,000	10,000	18,000
	£	£	£	£
Selling price	4.00	3.00	2.00	5.00
Estimated sales value at end of Process 1	2.50	2.80	1.20	3.00

Required

Suggest and evaluate an alternative production strategy which would optimise profit for the month. It should not be assumed that the output of Process 1 can be changed.

Answer

During the month, the quantity of input to Process 1 was 80,000 litres. Normal loss is 10% =8,000 litres, and so total output should have been 72,000 litres of A, B, C and D. Instead, it was only 70,000 litres. In an 'average' month, output would have been higher, and this might have some bearing on the optimal production and selling strategy.

The **central question** is whether or not the output from Process 1 should be **processed further** in processes 2, 3, 4 and 5, or whether it should be **sold at the 'split-off' point**, at the end of Process 1. Each joint product can be looked at **individually**.

A further question is whether the **wages costs** in process 2, 3, 4 and 5 would be avoided if the joint products were sold at the end of process 1 and not processed further. It will be assumed that all the wages costs would be **avoidable**, but none of the **production overhead** costs would be. This assumption can be challenged, and in practice would have to be investigated.

	A	B	C	D
	£	£	£	£
Selling price, per litre	4.00	3.00	2.00	5.00
Selling price at end of process 1	2.50	2.80	1.20	3.00
Incremental selling price, per litre	1.50	0.20	0.80	2.00
Litres output	22,000	20,000	10,000	18,000
	£'000	£'000	£'000	£'000
Total incremental revenue from further processing	33	4	8	36
Avoidable costs from selling at split-off point (wages saved)	12	8	4	16
Incremental benefit/(cost) of further processing	21	(4)	4	20

This analysis would seem to indicate that **products A, C and D should be further processed** in processes 2, 4 and 5 respectively, but that **product B should be sold at the end of process 1**, without further processing in process 3. The saving would be at least £4,000 per month.

If **some production overhead** (which is 75% of direct wages) were also **avoidable**, this would mean that:

(a) selling product B at the end of process 1 would offer further savings of up to (75% of £8,000) £6,000 in overheads, and so £10,000 in total;

(b) the incremental benefit from further processing product C might fall by up to (75% of £4,000) £3,000 to £1,000, meaning that it is only just profitable to process C beyond the split-off point.

---

10 Product mix decisions

10.1 A process manufacturing company might be faced with a decision about whether to **alter the product mix** in its process, so as to **produce a greater proportion of one product and less of another**. For example, if a process produces joint products X and Y in the ratio 2:1, an alteration to the process might be possible, whereby the output ratio is changed to, say, 3:2. Deciding whether or not to change a product mix should be **based on the relevant costs and benefits of the change.**

10.2 EXAMPLE: PRODUCT MIX DECISION

Marchmeat produces two joint products P and Q in the proportion 2:1. After the split-off point the products can be sold for industrial use or they can be taken to the mixing plant for blending and refining. The latter procedure is normally followed.

For a typical week, in which all the output is processed in the mixing plant, the following profit and loss account can be prepared.

	Product P	Product Q
Sales (volume)	2,000 litres	1,000 litres
Price per litre	£35	£60
	£	£
Sales revenue	70,000	60,000
Joint process cost (apportioned using output volume)	30,000	15,000
Blending and refining costs	25,000	25,000
Other separable costs	5,000	1,000
	60,000	41,000
Profit	10,000	19,000

The joint process costs are 75% fixed and 25% variable, whereas the mixing plant costs are 40% fixed and 60% variable and all the 'other separable costs' are variable.

There are only 40 hours available per week in the mixing plant. Typically 30 hours are taken up with the processing of product P and Q (15 hours for each product line) and 10 hours are used for other work that generates (on average) contribution of £2,000 per hour. The manager of the mixing plant considers that he could sell all the plant's processing time externally at a price that would provide this rate of profit.

It has been suggested that it might be possible to change the mix of products achieved in the mixing plant. It is possible to change the output proportions to 3:2 at a cost of £5 for each additional litre of Q produced by the distillation plant.

Required

Compare the costs and benefits of this proposal.

10.3 SOLUTION

Assuming that output remains 3,000 litres per week, the change in product mix would result in output of 1,800 litres of P and 1,200 litres of Q, compared with the current 2,000 litres of P and 1,000 litres of Q.

Since blending and refining costs are the same for P and Q at the moment, one litre of Q takes twice as much time to blend and refine as one litre of P. (This is an example of a key assumption in decision accounting problems which needs to be identified from data given in the question.)

A **cost benefit analysis** of the proposal is shown below. The change in product mix would not be worthwhile, even though product Q seems more profitable per litre than product P!

	£	£
Additional sales revenue from extra 200 litres of Q (× £60)		12,000
Loss in revenue from 200 litres of P (× £35)		(7,000)
Extra joint processing costs (200 × £5)		(1,000)
Separable costs: all variable		
Extra cost of 200 litres of Q (× £1)	(200)	
Saving on 200 litres of P (× £2.5)	500	
Net saving		300
Blending and refining costs		
Extra cost of 200 litres of Q (200/1,000 × 60% of £25,000)	(3,000)	
Saving on 200 litres of P (200/2,000 × 60% of £25,000)	1,500	
		(1,500)

Extra blending and refining time needed for Q		
(200/1,000 × 15 hrs) =	3 hrs	
Less saving on time needed on P		
(200/2,000 × 15 hrs) =	1.5 hrs	
Net extra time = (3 – 1.5 hrs) =	1.5 hrs	
Opportunity cost of lost contribution from external work		
(1.5 × £2,000)		(3,000)
Net loss from change of product mix		(200)

11 CUSTOMER PROFITABILITY ANALYSIS (CPA)

11.1 **Traditionally, management accounting reports** have been analysed on a **product by product** basis. In the **modern business environment**, however, in which it is vital that organisations respond promptly to the demands of customers, **analysis on the basis of customers** can provide vital management information.

11.2 Profitability can vary widely between different customers because various **overhead costs** are, to some extent, **variable and customer driven**.

- Discounts
- Sales force (eg telesales are cheaper and more time-efficient than a field sales force)
- Quality control (some customers demand higher quality)
- Merchandising
- Distribution (full-pallet transactions are cheaper than breaking bulk)
- Promotions
- Financing costs
- Enquiries

11.3 Suppose a hotel offers a number of services such as a swimming pool, a gym and a nightly dinner dance.

- Older guests may attend the dinner dance.
- Families may use the swimming pool.
- People without children may appreciate the gym.

By charging services to the guests using them, a cost per bed night can be calculated for each guest group. **Strategies for attracting the most profitable guest group** can then be adopted.

11.4 Whether individual customers or groups of customers are costed largely depends on the number of customers.

(a) A manufacturing company supplying six companies would cost each customer separately.

(b) A supermarket or bank would cost groups of similar customers. UK banks divide their customers into categories such as single and 30ish, married with young children, older couples with spending money and so on, and give each category a colourful 'fruity' name such as plum or lemon.

11.5 Marketing departments should be aiming to **attract and retain profitable customers** but in order to do this they need to **know which customers are profitable** and **how much can be spent on retaining them**. The **costing system** should **provide the necessary answers**.

> **KEY TERM**
>
> **Customer profitability analysis (CPA)** is the analysis of both the revenue from and the costs of servicing specific customers or customer groups.

11.6 Customer profitability analysis (CPA) provides important information which allows an organisation to determine both **which classes of customers it should concentrate on** and the **prices it should charge for customer services**. Its use ensures that those customers **contributing sizeably to the profitability** of the organisation receive a **comparable amount of attention** from the organisation.

Customer revenues

11.7 **Customer revenues** are cash flows from customers. They are influenced by different factors, mainly **allowances and discounts**.

(a) Some types of customer **store and distribute goods** (eg wholesalers) or **promote** the goods in return for an **allowance**.

(b) By giving a **discount** a company may **encourage bulk orders**, which may be cheaper to provide and may result in higher sales volume. Studies on customer profitability have found large price discounting to be a key explanation for a group of customers being below expected profitability, however. Sales representatives may have given customers large price discounts unrelated to their current or potential value to the company, perhaps to meet bonuses dependant on sales volumes. Two customers may be purchasing the same volumes but the price discount given to one may make it unprofitable, while the other is profitable.

Case example

The USA company *General Electric*, which manufactures and sells refrigerators and so on, used to give substantial discounts to customers who placed large orders. This did not result in customers buying more products. Instead GE's sales orders bunched in particular weeks of the year. In turn this led to an uneven production and distribution flow, which increased costs. The company found that, by removing the discounts while at the same time guaranteeing swift delivery, order size decreased and profits increased.

Customer costs

11.8 The creation of cost pools for activities in **ABC** systems allows organisations to arrange costs in a variety of different ways. Because different customers use different amounts of activities, it is possible to **build up costs for individual customers or groups of customers** on an activity basis so that their **relative profitability** can be assessed.

11.9 **Examples of the build up of customer costs using an activity based system**

Activity	Cost driver
Order taking	Number of orders taken
Sales visits	Number of sales visits
Emergency orders	Number of rushed orders
Delivery	Miles travelled
Product handling	Number of pallets or part-pallets handled
After sales service and support	Number of visits
Product repairs and service	Number of repair visits

Case example

Drury cites the case of Kanthal, a Swedish company that sells electric heating elements. Customer-related selling costs represented 34% of total costs. In the past Kanthal had allocated these costs on the basis of sales value when customer profitability studies were carried out. The company then introduced an ABC system in order to determine the resources consumed by different customers.

An investigation identified two cost drivers for the resources used to service different customers.

(a) **Number of orders placed.** Each order had a large fixed cost, which did not vary with the number of items ordered. A customer ordering 10 items 100 times cost more to service than a customer placing a single order for 1,000 items.

(b) **Non-standard production items.** These cost more to manufacture than standard items.

A cost per order and the cost of handling standard and non-standard items were calculated and a CPA carried out on the basis of the previous year's sales. The analysis showed that only 40% of customers were profitable, and a further 10% lost 120% of the profits. In other words, 10% of customers incurred losses equal to 120% of Kanthal's total profits. Two of the most unprofitable customers were actually in the top three in terms of total sales volume but made many small orders of non-standard items.

11.10 **Unprofitable customers** identified by CPA should be persuaded to **alter their buying behaviour** so they become profitable customers. In the Kanthal example above, unprofitable customers should be discouraged from placing lots of small orders and/or from buying non-standard products.

11.11 The **activity based approach** also **highlights where cost reduction efforts should be focused**. Kanthal should concentrate on reducing ordering cost and the cost of handling non-standard items.

11.12 Activity-based CPA allows an organisation to adopt a more **market-orientated approach** to management accounting.

Question: CPA

B Ltd manufactures components for the heavy goods vehicle industry. The following annual information regarding three of its key customers is available.

	P	Q	R
Gross margin	£897,000	£1,070,000	£1,056,000
General administration costs	£35,000	£67,000	£56,000
Units sold	4,600	5,800	3,800
Orders placed	300	320	480
Sales visits	80	50	100
Invoices raised	310	390	1,050

The company uses an activity based costing system and the analysis of customer-related costs is as follows.

Sales visits	£420 per visit
Order processing	£190 per order placed
Despatch costs	£350 per order placed
Billing and collections	£97 per invoice raised

Using customer profitability analysis, how would the customers be ranked?

Answer

	P	Q	R
	£'000	£'000	£'000
Gross margin	897.00	1,070.00	1,056.00
Less: Customer specific costs			
Sales visits (80/50/100 × £420)	(33.60)	(21.00)	(42.00)
Order processing (300/320/480 × £190)	(57.00)	(60.80)	(91.20)
Despatch costs (300/320/480 × £350)	(105.00)	(112.00)	(168.00)
Billing and collections (310/390/1,050 × £97)	(30.07)	(37.83)	(101.85)
	671.33	838.37	652.95
Ranking	2	1	3

Customer profitability statement

11.13 There is no set format, but it would normally be similar to the one below. Note that financing costs have been included.

	£'000	£'000
Revenue at list prices		100
Less: discounts given		8
Net revenue		92
Less: cost of goods sold		50
Gross margin		42
Less: customer specific costs	28	
financing costs:		
credit period	3	
customer specific inventory	2	
		33
Net margin from customer		9

443

Question

Seth Ltd supplies shoes to Narayan Ltd and Kipling Ltd. Each pair of shoes has a list price of £50 and costs Seth Ltd £25. As Kipling buys in bulk it receives a 10% trade discount for every order for 100 pairs of shoes or more. Narayan receives a 15% discount irrespective of order size, because that company collects the shoes, thereby saving Seth Ltd any distribution costs. The cost of administering each order is £50 and the distribution cost is £1,000 per order. Narayan makes 10 orders in the year, totalling 420 pairs of shoes, and Kipling places 5 orders for 100 pairs. Which customer is the most profitable for Seth Ltd?

Answer

It can be shown that Seth Ltd earns more from supplying Narayan, despite the larger discount percentage.

	Kipling £	Narayan £
Revenue	25,000	21,000
Less: discount	2,500	3,150
Net revenue	22,500	17,850
Less: cost of shoes	(12,500)	(10,500)
customer transport cost	(5,000)	-
customer administration cost	(250)	(500)
Net gain	4,750	6,850

The difference on a unit basis is considerable.

Number of pair of shoes sold	500	420
Net gain per pair of shoes sold	£9.50	£16.31
Net gain per £1 of sales revenue	£0.19	£0.33

Costing customers

11.14 **Not all customers cost the same to serve even if they require the same products.** A customer will cost more to serve if based a long way from the factory (delivery costs increase), or places rush orders (production scheduling is interrupted, special transport is required), or requires a high level of after-sales service and technical assistance.

11.15 In order to analyse different customers it may therefore be useful to review **non-financial data.**

	Customer		
	X	Y	Z
Number of purchase orders	10	20	30
Number of sales visits	5	5	5
Number of deliveries	15	20	55
Distance per delivery	50	20	70
Number of emergency orders	1	0	4

Customer Y may be the cheapest to serve because of the number of deliveries per order, the lower distance travelled and the lack of emergency orders.

CPA and Pareto's rule

11.16 When a **customer profitability analysis** is first carried out it is often found that something close to **Pareto's rule** (or the **80/20 rule**) applies. This is illustrated in the following diagram where **20 of the 100** customers generate approximately **80%** of the company's total margin. As 50 of the 100 customers generate 100% of the total margin, resources appear to be wasted serving the remaining 50 customers.

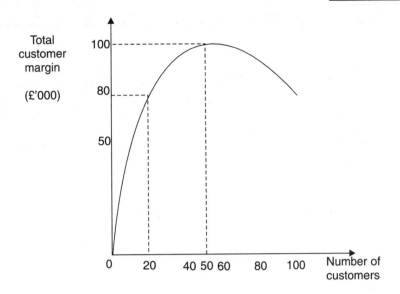

11.17 In order to produce a chart such as that above, customers need to be **ranked** according to their **relative profitability** to the company. A bar chart, such as that below, produces an alternative view and may prove more useful for the marketing department.

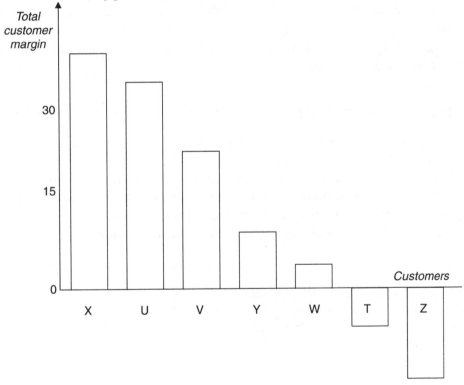

Categorising customers

11.18 It is not possible to 'cost' future dealings with customers accurately because the number and size of orders and rush orders is likely to be unpredictable. It is, however, possible to gain a broad idea of the amount of profit that can be expected from a particular category of customer. Customers can be categorised in the following grid.

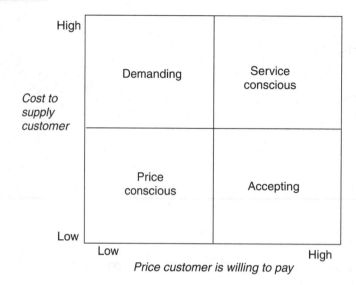

11.19 The aim is to **attract as many accepting customers as possible**. Such customers will have a low 'cost to supply' perhaps because they are located close by or do not place rush orders, and are prepared to accept a high price. **Many large retail organisations fall into the demanding category** because they expect the supplier to deal with rush orders, change production methods to suit them and so on. It is undesirable for a **small supplier to be tied to a large demanding customer** who has the power to threaten the withdrawal of its custom if the supplier does not acquiesce.

Customers and life cycle costing

11.20 **Customers** can also be **costed over their expected 'life cycle'** and expected future cash flows relating to the customer may be discounted. It is rarely possible to predict accurately the life cycle of a particular customer unless contracts are awarded for a specific time period. Nevertheless the information is valuable as **the longer the customer remains with the organisation** the **more profitable** the customer becomes. This is valuable information and may show the **importance of creating and retaining loyal customers**.

Exam focus point

CPA was the topic of question 2 in the June 2004 exam.

Chapter roundup

- Most costs that are fixed in the **short term** are variable in the **longer term.**

- The total **relevant cost of a scarce resource** is the sum of the contribution/incremental profit foregone from the next best opportunity for using the scarce resource and the variable cost of the scarce resource.

- Make sure that you can determine the **relevant cost of materials** based on the tree diagram in Section 2.

- The **minimum price** for a one-off product/service contract is its total relevant cost (the price at which the organisation would achieve an incremental cost breakeven point).

- The TA ratio (return per factory hour ÷ cost per factory hour) can be used to assess the relative earning capabilities of different products.

- With one **limiting factor**, rank products in order of contribution-earning ability per unit of limiting factor to determine the contribution-maximising product mix.

- When there is a **limit on sales demand**, produce the top-ranked products up to the sales demand limit.

- **Shutdown/discontinuance problems** can be simplified into short-run relevant cost decisions.

- In a **make or buy decision** with no limiting factors, the relevant costs are the differential costs between the two options.

- In a situation where a company must **sub-contract work to make up a shortfall in its own in-house capabilities**, its total costs will be minimised if those units bought out from a sub-contractor have the lowest extra variable cost of buying out per unit of scarce resource.

- The relevant costs/revenues in decisions relating to the **operating of internal service departments or the use of external services** are the differential costs between the two options.

- A joint product should be **processed further** past the split-off point if sales value minus post-separation (further processing) costs is greater than sales value at split-off point.

- Deciding whether or not to **change a product mix** should be based on the relevant costs and benefits of the change.

- **Activity-based customer profitability analysis** allows an organisation to adopt a more market-orientated approach to management accounting.

Quick quiz

1   *Fill in the relevant costs in the four boxes in the diagram below.*

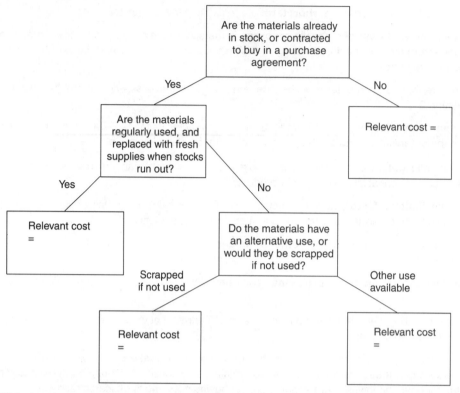

2   *Fill in the blanks using terms from those listed below.*

TA ratio = ... ÷ ....

Return per factory hour = ... ÷ ....

Cost per factory hour = ... ÷ ....

Terms

TFC	Equivalent hours produced
Time on bottleneck resource	Return per factory hour
Cost per factory hour	Total time available on bottleneck resource
Selling price	Throughput
Efficiency of bottleneck use	Material cost

3   *One of the key assumptions of limiting factor analysis is that units of output are indivisible. True or false?*

4   *Choose the correct word(s) from those highlighted.*

In a situation where a company must subcontract work to make up a shortfall in its own in-house capabilities, its total cost will be minimised if those units **bought out from a sub-contractor/made in-house** have the **lowest/highest** extra **variable/fixed** cost of **buying out/making in-house** per unit of **scarce resource/material**.

5   In a decision about whether or not to sell a joint product at the split-off point or after further processing, joint costs are relevant. *True or false?*

6   *Fill in the blanks.*

Most of the decisions considered in this chapter involve calculating .... obtained from various options after identifying .... They always involve .... issues, which depend upon the precise situation described.

Answers to quick quiz

1

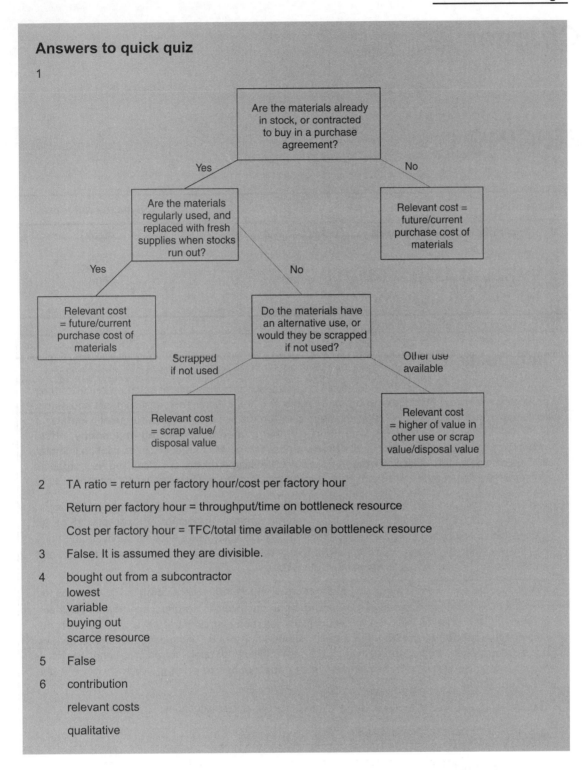

2   TA ratio = return per factory hour/cost per factory hour

   Return per factory hour = throughput/time on bottleneck resource

   Cost per factory hour = TFC/total time available on bottleneck resource

3   False. It is assumed they are divisible.

4   bought out from a subcontractor
   lowest
   variable
   buying out
   scarce resource

5   False

6   contribution

   relevant costs

   qualitative

Now try the question below from the Exam Question Bank

Number	Level	Marks	Time
19	Exam	40	72 mins

Chapter 22

PRICING I

Topic list	Syllabus reference
1 Pricing policy and the market	5(a)
2 Demand	5(a)
3 The optimum price/output level	5(a)
4 Traditional pricing bases	5(a)

Introduction

All profit organisations and many non-profit organisations face the task of setting a price for their products or services. **Price can go by many names**: fares, tuitions, rent, assessments and so on. Historically price was the single most important decision made by the sales department. However, it is as well that you should realise from the outset that in **modern marketing philosophy, price**, whilst important, is **not necessarily the predominant factor**. Modern businesses seek to interpret and satisfy consumer wants and needs by modifying existing products or introducing new products to the range. This contrasts with earlier production-oriented times when the typical reaction was to cut prices in order to sell more of an organisation's product.

Notwithstanding this change in emphasis, **pricing is very important**. Proper pricing of an organisation's products or services is essential to its profitability and hence its survival, and price has an important role to play as a competitive tool which can be used to differentiate a product and an organisation and thus exploit market opportunities.

In this chapter we will begin by looking at the **factors which influence pricing** policy. Perhaps the most important of these is the **level of demand** for an organisation's product and how that demand changes as the price of the product changes (its **elasticity of demand**). We will then turn our attention to a **model for determining a profit-maximising price**. This model, although supported by microeconomic theory, is (as we shall see) difficult to apply in practice and so many organisations use what are known as **cost-based approaches to pricing**, which we cover at the end of the chapter.

The following chapter deals with a variety of more specific pricing situations.

Study guide

Section 24 – Pricing I

- Identify and discuss market situations which influence the pricing policy adopted by an organisation
- Explain and discuss the variables (including price) which influence demand for a product or service
- Explain the price elasticity of demand
- Manipulate data in order to determine an optimum price/output level
- Calculate prices using full cost and marginal cost as the pricing base
- Compare the use of full cost pricing and marginal cost pricing as planning and decision-making aids

Exam guide

The use of decision-making techniques to enhance performance is a core area of the syllabus and so you can expect to see questions on pricing decisions on a regular basis.

The issues covered in this chapter are useful background to the following Oxford Brookes degree Research and Analysis Projects.

* Topic 1, which requires you to analyse the efficiency and/or effectiveness of a management accounting technique in an organisational setting

* Topic 10, which requires you to analyse how management accounting techniques are used to support decision making in organisations

Exam focus point

Decision-making techniques were required in three of the five Pilot paper questions.

1 PRICING POLICY AND THE MARKET

1.1   In practice in the **modern world** there are many more influences on price than the cost of a product or service.

Influence	Explanation/Example
Price sensitivity	Sensitivity to price levels will vary amongst purchasers. Those that can pass on the cost of purchases will be the least sensitive and will therefore respond more to other elements of perceived value. For example, a business traveller will be more concerned about the level of service in looking for an hotel than price, provided that it fits the corporate budget. In contrast, a family on holiday are likely to be very price sensitive when choosing an overnight stay.
Price perception	Price perception is the **way customers react to prices**. For example, customers may react to a price increase by buying more. This could be because they expect further price increases to follow (they are 'stocking up').
Quality	This is an aspect of price perception. In the absence of other information, customers tend to **judge quality by price**. Thus a price rise may indicate improvements in quality, a price reduction may signal reduced quality.
Intermediaries	If an organisation distributes products or services to the market through independent intermediaries, such intermediaries are likely to deal with a range of suppliers and **their aims** concern their own profits rather than those of suppliers.
Competitors	In some industries (such as petrol retailing) pricing moves in unison; in others, price changes by one supplier may initiate a price war. **Competition is discussed in more detail below.**
Suppliers	If an organisation's suppliers notice a price rise for the organisation's products, they may seek a rise in the price for their supplies to the organisation.
Inflation	In periods of inflation the organisation may need to change prices to reflect increases in the prices of supplies, labour, rent and so on.

Influence	Explanation/Example
Newness	When a **new product is introduced for the first time** there are **no existing reference points** such as customer or competitor behaviour; pricing decisions are most difficult to make in such circumstances. It may be possible to seek alternative reference points, such as the price in another market where the new product has already been launched, or the price set by a competitor.
Incomes	If **incomes are rising, price** may be a **less important** marketing variable than product quality and convenience of access (distribution). When income levels are falling and/or unemployment levels rising, price will be more important.
Product range	Products are often interrelated, being complements to each other or substitutes for one another. The management of the pricing function is likely to focus on the profit from the whole range rather than the profit on each single product. For example, a very low price is charged for a **loss leader** to make consumers buy additional products in the range which carry higher profit margins (eg selling razors at very low prices whilst selling the blades for them at a higher profit margin).
Ethics	Ethical considerations may be a further factor, for example whether or not to exploit short-term shortages through higher prices.

Porter's Five Forces Model

1.2 Porter's model suggests the importance of **pressure from five competitive forces on price.**

(a) **Threat of new entrants** (which will be affected by barriers to entry and expected reaction from existing firms).

(b) **Threat of substitutes** (which will be determined by the level of innovation of existing producers, the ability of existing competitors to finance responses to the threat and the propensity of buyers to substitute).

(c) **Bargaining power of buyers** (which will be linked to the number of buyers).

(d) **Bargaining power of suppliers** (supplier power and the impact on costs being greater when there are fewer of them).

(e) **Rivalry between existing competitors** (the strength of rivalry being determined by number of competitors, market power, brand identity, producer differences cost structure and so on).

Boston Consulting Group (BCG) Portfolio matrix

1.3 The BCG portfolio matrix provides a method of positioning products through their life cycles in terms of market growth and market share.

(a) **Stars** are products with a **high share** of a **high growth market.** In the short term, items require investment in excess of the cash they generate in order to maintain their market position, but promise high returns in the future.

(b) In due course, however, stars will become **cash cows,** with a **high share** of a **low growth** (mature) **market.** They require very little investment and generate high levels of cash income. The important strategic feature of cash cows is that they are already generating high cash returns, which can support the stars.

(c) **Question marks** are competitive products with a **low share** of a **high growth market.** They have the potential to become stars but a question mark hangs over their ability to achieve sufficient market retention to justify further investment.

(d) **Dogs** are products with a **low share** of a low growth market. They should be allowed to die, or be killed off.

1.4 The matrix must be managed so that an organisation's product range is balanced. Four basic strategies can be adopted.

(a) **Build.** This involves increasing the market share, even at the expense of short-term profits. A 'build' strategy might be to turn a question mark into a star. A penetration pricing policy (covered in the next chapter) and investment in stabilising quality and brand loyalty may be required.

(b) **Hold.** This involves preserving market share and ensuring that cash cows remain cash cows. Additional investment in customer retention through competitive pricing and marketing may be required.

(c) **Harvest.** This involves using funds to promote products which have the potential to become future stars or to support existing stars.

(d) **Divest.** This involves eliminating dogs and question marks which are under performing.

Markets

1.5 The price that an organisation can charge for its products will be determined to a greater or lesser degree by the **market** in which it operates. Here are some familiar economic terms that might feature as background for a question or that you might want to use in a written answer.

> **KEY TERMS**
>
> - **Perfect competition**: many buyers and many sellers all dealing in an identical product. Neither producer nor user has any market power and both must accept the prevailing market price.
>
> - **Monopoly**: one seller who dominates many buyers. The monopolist can use his market power to set a profit-maximising price.
>
> - **Monopolistic competition**: a large number of suppliers offer similar, but not identical, products. The similarities ensure elastic demand whereas the slight differences give some monopolistic power to the supplier.
>
> - **Oligopoly**: where relatively few competitive companies dominate the market. Whilst each large firm has the ability to influence market prices, the unpredictable reaction from the other giants makes the final industry price indeterminate. Cartels are often formed.

1.6 **Examples and barriers to entry**

Type of market	Examples	Barriers to entry
Perfect competition	Possibly financial markets	None
Monopoly	Central banks	High (economies of scale, legislation such as patents, high entry costs)
Monopolistic competition	Restaurants and hairdressers	None
Oligopoly	Cars, retail banking, oil	Yes

1.7 **Pricing policies**

Type of market	Pricing policy
Perfect competition	Price takers (sellers have no influence as the price is determined by market demand and market supply)
Monopoly	Price setters/makers
Monopolistic competition	Price setters/makers (using brand loyalty)
Oligopoly	Price setters (although constrained by interdependence)

Competition

1.8 In **established industries** dominated by a few major firms, it is generally accepted that a price initiative by one firm will be countered by a price reaction by competitors. In these circumstances, prices tend to be **fairly stable**, unless pushed upwards by inflation or strong growth in demand.

1.9 If a rival **cuts its prices** in the expectation of increasing its market share, a firm has several options.

(a) It will **maintain its existing prices** if the expectation is that only a small market share would be lost, so that it is more profitable to keep prices at their existing level. Eventually, the rival firm may drop out of the market or be forced to raise its prices.

(b) It may maintain its prices but respond with a **non-price counter-attack**. This is a more positive response, because the firm will be securing or justifying its current prices with a product change, advertising, or better back-up services.

(c) It may **reduce its prices**. This should protect the firm's market share so that the main beneficiary from the price reduction will be the consumer.

(d) It may **raise its prices** *and respond with a* **non-price counter-attack**. The extra revenue from the higher prices might be used to finance an advertising campaign or product design changes. A price increase would be based on a campaign to emphasise the quality difference between the firm's and the rival's products.

Question: pricing in the modern business environment

What technique might be used to relate prices to cost in the modern business environment?

Answer

The answer, of course, is **target costing,** which you met in Chapter 4. Price is determined by the market. Costs have to come below this price.

Pricing policy and price leadership

1.10 Given that price competition can have disastrous consequences in conditions of oligopoly, it is not unusual to find that **large corporations** emerge as **price leaders**. The operation of such price leadership brings about **relative price stability in otherwise unstable price dynamic oligopolies.**

1.11 A **price leader** will have the **dominant influence** on price levels for a class of products. Price increases or decreases by the price leader **provide a direction** to market price patterns. The price dominant firm may lead without moving at all. This would be the case if other firms sought to raise prices and the leader did not follow, so that the upward move in prices was halted. The price leader generally has a **large**, if not necessarily the largest, **market share**. The company will usually be an efficient low-cost producer that has a reputation for technical competence.

1.12 The role of price leader is also earned by a **track record of having initiated price moves that have been accepted by both competitors and customers.** This is frequently associated with a **mature, well established management group.**

2 DEMAND

The economic analysis of demand

2.1 **Economic theory** argues that the **higher the price of a good,** the **lower** will be the **quantity demanded.** We have already seen that in practice it is by no means as straightforward as this (some goods are bought *because* they are expensive, for example), but you know from your personal experience as a consumer that the theory is essentially true.

2.2 There are two extremes in the relationship between price and demand. A supplier can either **sell a certain quantity, Q, at any price** (as in graph (a)). Demand is totally unresponsive to changes in price and is said to be **completely inelastic.** Alternatively, **demand might be limitless at a certain price** P (as in graph (b)), but there would be no demand above price P and there would be little point in dropping the price below P. In such circumstances demand is said to be **completely elastic**.

(a)   (b)

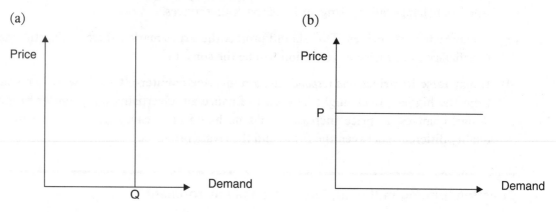

2.3   A more **normal situation** is shown below. The **downward-sloping** demand curve shows that demand will increase as prices are lowered. Demand is therefore **elastic**.

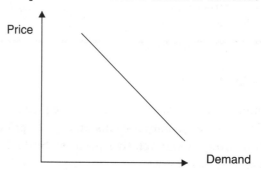

Price elasticity of demand (η)

> ### KEY TERM
>
> **Price elasticity of demand** (η) is a measure of the extent of change in market demand for a good in response to a change in its price. It is measured as:
>
> $$\frac{\text{The change in quantity demanded, as a \% of demand}}{\text{The change in price, as a \% of the price}}$$

2.4   Since the demand goes up when the price falls, and goes down when the price rises, the elasticity has a negative value, but it is usual to ignore the minus sign.

2.5   EXAMPLE: PRICE ELASTICITY OF DEMAND

The price of a good is £1.20 per unit and annual demand is 800,000 units. Market research indicates that an increase in price of 10 pence per unit will result in a fall in annual demand of 75,000 units. What is the price elasticity of demand?

2.6   SOLUTION

Annual demand at £1.20 per unit is 800,000 units.
Annual demand at £1.30 per unit is 725,000 units.

% change in demand   = $(75,000/800,000) \times 100\% = 9.375\%$

% change in price = (10p/120p) × 100% = 8.333%
Price elasticity of demand = (–9.375/8.333) = –1.125
Ignoring the minus sign, price elasticity is 1.125.

The demand for this good, at a price of £1.20 per unit, would be referred to as **elastic** because the **price elasticity of demand is greater than 1.**

Elastic and inelastic demand

2.7   The value of demand elasticity may be anything from zero to infinity.

> **KEY TERM**
>
> Demand is referred to as **inelastic** if the absolute value is less than 1 and **elastic** if the absolute value is greater than 1.

2.8   Think about what this means.

(a)   Where demand is **inelastic**, the **quantity demanded falls by a smaller percentage than the percentage increase in price**.

(b)   Where demand is **elastic, demand falls** by a **larger percentage than the percentage rise in price.**

Price elasticity and the slope of the demand curve

2.9   Generally, **demand curves slope downwards**. Consumers are willing to buy more at lower prices than at higher prices. In general, **elasticity** will **vary** in value **along the length of a demand curve**.

(a)   If a downward sloping demand curve becomes **steeper** over a particular range of quantity, then demand is becoming **more inelastic**.

(b)   A **shallower** demand curve over a particular range indicates **more elastic** demand.

2.10   The ranges of price elasticity at different points on a downward sloping straight line demand curve are illustrated in the diagram below.

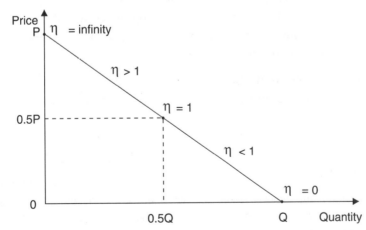

(a)   At **higher prices** on a straight line demand curve (the **top** of the demand curve), **small percentage price reductions** can bring **large percentage increases in quantity** demanded. This means that **demand is elastic** over these ranges, and **price reductions bring increases in total expenditure** by consumers on the commodity in question.

457

(b) At **lower prices** on a straight line demand curve (the **bottom** of the demand curve), **large percentage price reductions** can bring **small percentage increases in quantity**. This means that **demand is inelastic** over these price ranges, and **price increases** result in **increases in total expenditure**.

Special values of price elasticity

2.11 There are two special values of price elasticity of demand.

(a) **Demand is perfectly inelastic ($\eta = 0$). There is no change in quantity** demanded, **regardless of the change in price**. The demand curve is **a vertical straight line** (as in graph (a) in Paragraph 2.2).

(b) **Perfectly elastic demand ($\eta = \infty$).** Consumers will want to **buy an infinite amount**, but **only up to a particular price** level. Any price increase above this level will reduce demand to zero. The demand curve is a **horizontal straight line** (as in graph (b) in Paragraph 2.2).

Elasticity and the pricing decision

2.12 In practice, organisations will have only a rough idea of the shape of their demand curve: there will only be a limited amount of data about quantities sold at certain prices over a period of time *and,* of course, factors other than price might affect demand. Because any conclusions drawn from such data can only give an indication of likely future behaviour, management skill and expertise are also needed. Despite this limitation, an **awareness of the concept of elasticity can assist management with pricing decisions**.

(a) (i) In circumstances of **inelastic demand, prices should be increased** because revenues will increase and total costs will reduce (because quantities sold will reduce).

(ii) In circumstances of **elastic demand,** increases in prices will bring decreases in revenue and decreases in price will bring increases in revenue. Management therefore have to **decide** whether the **increase/decrease in costs will be less than/greater than the increases/decreases in revenue**.

(b) In situations of **very elastic demand,** overpricing can lead to a massive drop in quantity sold and hence a massive drop in profits whereas underpricing can lead to costly stock outs and, again, a significant drop in profits. **Elasticity must therefore be reduced by creating a customer preference which is unrelated to price** (through advertising and promotional activities).

(c) In situations of **very inelastic demand,** customers are **not sensitive to price. Quality, service, product mix and location** are therefore **more important** to a firm's pricing strategy.

Question: elasticity

Read the four statements below. Where the statement is expressed in layman's terms, rephrase it using the appropriate variant of the term *elasticity*. Where it is already phrased in terms of elasticity, translate it into layman's terms.

(a) We doubled sales of product A by dropping the price from £1.99 to £1.75.
(b) Price elasticity of product B is low.
(c) Demand for product C is highly inelastic.
(d) A large reduction in price will be necessary to stimulate further demand for product D.

Answer

Situation (a) is an example of elastic demand; (b) is a case of *inelasticity* and should be appropriately worded; (c) is the same as (b); (d) is also an example of inelasticity.

Variables which influence demand

2.13 **Variables which determine both the degree of elasticity and the volume of demand for a good in the market as a whole**

Variable	Detail
Price of other goods	For some goods the market demand is connected to the price of other goods Such goods are of two types. (a) **Substitutes,** so that an increase in demand for one version of a good is likely to cause a decrease in demand for others. Common examples are rival brands of the same commodity (like Coca-Cola and Pepsi-Cola), bus journeys versus car journeys, or different forms of entertainment. (b) **Complements,** so that an increase in demand for one is likely to cause an increase in demand for the other. Examples are cups and saucers, cars and components, audits and tax consultancy.
Income	A rise in income gives households more to spend and they will want to buy more goods. However this phenomenon does not affect all goods in the same way. (a) **Normal goods** are those for which a rise in income increases the demand. (b) **Inferior goods** are those for which demand *falls* as income rises, such as cheap wine. (c) For some goods demand rises up to a certain point and then remains unchanged, because there is a **limit to what consumers can or want to consume**. Examples are basic foodstuffs such as salt and bread.
Tastes or fashion	A change in tastes or fashion will alter the demand for a good, or a particular variety of a good. Changes in taste may stem from **psychological, social** or **economic** causes. There is an argument that tastes and fashions are **created by the producers** of products and services. There is undeniably some truth in this, but the **modern** focus on **responding to customers' needs and wants** suggests otherwise.
Expectations	If consumers have expectations that prices will rise or that shortages will occur they will attempt to stock up on the product, thereby creating excess demand in the short term.
Obsolescence	Many products and services have to be replaced periodically because of obsolescence. (a) In early 2001 there will be substantial demand for audits for the year ended 31 December 2000. Demand will dry up once the statutory time limit for filing audited accounts is passed. In other words many **services need to be bought repeatedly for reasons beyond the control of the consumer.** A haircut is another example. (b) **Physical goods** are literally **'consumed'**. Carpets become threadbare, glasses get broken, foodstuffs get eaten, children grow out of clothes.

Variable	Detail
	(c) **Technological developments** render some goods obsolete. Manual office equipment has been largely replaced by electronic equipment, because it does a better job, more quickly, quietly, efficiently and effectively.

Demand and the individual firm

2.14 We have looked at demand in the market as a whole. We also need to consider **factors that influence demand for one organisation's goods rather than another's.**

2.15 **Product life cycle**

To some extent this is an aspect of general demand and obsolescence: if you like we are talking about **built-in obsolescence** although this a rather cynical point of view. That aside, we can say that most products pass through the four phases described in Chapter 16.

2.16 **Different versions** of the same product may have **different life cycles,** and consumers are often aware of this. For example, the prospective buyer of a new car is more likely to purchase a recently introduced Ford than a Vauxhall that has been on the market for several years, even if there is nothing to choose in terms of quality and price.

2.17 **Quality**

One firm's product may be perceived to be better quality than another's, and may in some cases actually be so, if it uses sturdier materials, goes faster or does whatever it is meant to do in a 'better' way. Other things being equal, the **better quality good** will be **more in demand** than other versions.

2.18 **Marketing**

You may be familiar with the 'four Ps' of the marketing mix, all of which influence demand for a firm's goods.

(a) **Price**

(b) **Product**

(c) **Place** refers to the place **where a good can be purchased,** or is likely to be purchased.

    (i) If potential buyers find that a particular version of a good is difficult to obtain, they will turn to substitutes.

    (ii) Some goods have no more than local appeal.

(d) **Promotion** refers to the various means by which firms draw attention to their products and services.

    (i) A good **brand name** is a strong and relatively permanent influence on demand.

    (ii) Demand can be stimulated by a variety of **promotional tools,** such as free gifts, money off, shop displays, direct mail and media advertising.

2.19 In recent years, emphasis has been placed, especially in marketing, on the **importance of non-profit factors** in demand. Thus the roles of product quality, promotion, personal selling and distribution and, in overall terms, brands, have grown. Whilst it can be relatively easy for a competitor to copy a price cut, at least in the short term, it is much **more difficult to copy a successful brand image based on a unique selling proposition.** Successful branding can even imply premium pricing.

3 THE OPTIMUM PRICE/OUTPUT LEVEL

3.1 Some businesses enjoy a **monopoly** position in their market or something akin to a monopoly position, even in a competitive market. This is because they develop a unique marketing mix, for example a unique combination of price and quality, or a monopoly in a localised area.

3.2 The significance of a monopoly situation is as follows.

(a) The business has choice and flexibility in the prices it sets.

(b) Because the business has this freedom of choice in pricing, it will find that at **higher prices** demand for its products or services will be **less**. Conversely, at **lower prices**, demand for its products or services will be **higher**.

(c) There will be an **optimum** price/output level at which profits will be maximised.

Case example

A large public transport organisation might be considering an increase in bus fares or underground fares. The effect on total revenues and profit of the fares increase could be estimated from a knowledge of the demand for transport services at different price levels. If an increase in the price per ticket caused a large fall in demand (that is, if demand were price-elastic) total revenues and profits would fall; whereas a fares increase when demand is price-inelastic would boost total revenue and since a transport organisation's costs are largely fixed, would probably boost total profits too.

Deriving the demand curve

FORMULAE TO LEARN

When demand is linear the equation for the demand curve is:

$P = a - bQ/\Delta Q$

where P = the price
Q = the quantity demanded
a = the price at which demand would be nil
b = the amount by which the price falls for each stepped change in demand
ΔQ = the stepped change in demand

The constant a is calculated as follows.

$$a = \pounds(\text{current price}) + \left(\frac{\text{Current quantity at current price}}{\text{Change in quantity when price is changed by } \pounds b} \times \pounds b \right)$$

3.3 This looks rather complicated in words, but it is very easy once the numbers are substituted. **Note that you are not given these formulae in the exam.**

IMPORTANT POINT

Note that the coefficient of Q (b/ΔQ) is actually the price elasticity of demand.

3.4 EXAMPLE: DERIVING THE DEMAND CURVE

The current price of a product is £12. At this price the company sells 60 items a month. One month the company decides to raise the price to £14, but only 45 items are sold at this price. Determine the demand equation.

3.5 SOLUTION

Step 1. **Find the price at which demand would be nil**

Assuming demand is linear, each increase of £2 in the price would result in a fall in demand of 15 units. For demand to be nil, the price needs to rise from its current level by as many times as there are 15 units in 60 units (60/15 = 4) ie to £12 + (4 × £2) = £20.

Using the formula above, this can be shown as a = £12 + ((60/15) × £2)= £20

Step 2. **Extract figures from the question**

The **demand equation** can now be determined as P = a – bQ/ΔQ = 20 – 2Q/15

Step 3. **Check your equation**

We can check this by substituting £12 and £14 for P.

12 = 20 – (2 × 60/15) = 20 – 8 = 12
4 = 20 – (2 × 45/15) = 20 – 6 = 14

FORMULA TO LEARN

The equation can also be re-arranged as $Q = \dfrac{(a \times \Delta Q) - (\Delta Q \times P)}{b}$

Question: deriving the demand curve

The current price of a product is £30 and the producers sell 100 items a week at this price. One week the price is dropped by £3 as a special offer and the producers sell 150 items. Find an expression for the demand curve.

Answer

a   =   £30 + (100/50 × £3)   = £36
P   =   36 – 3Q/50   or   Q   = (1,800 – 50P)/3

Check

27   = 36 – 3Q/50   150 = (1,800 – 50P)/3
3Q/50 = 9   50P = 1,800 – 450
Q   = 150   P   = 27

Cost and revenue models

3.6   Determining the optimum price and output level requires that **cost and revenue behaviour** can be **modelled using equations**. These equations can range from simple to complex, although those you encounter in the exam will tend towards the 'simple' end of the range.

3.7 For example, an organisation's total costs (TC) might be modelled by the equation TC = 6,500 + 0.75Q, where Q is the number of units sold. Here the cost model is a simple linear equation of the form y = a + bx, where a (£6,500) represents the fixed costs and b (£0.75) represents the unit variable cost.

3.8 The format of the demand curve derived above (P = a – bQ/ΔQ) is also a linear equation of the form y = a + bx. (ΔQ is simply a number and so b in the standard form of the equation is b/ΔQ in the demand curve). This demand curve shows that the price must be lowered (from an initial price of £a) if demand is to increase from nil.

3.9 The demand curve provides the price (P) at level of demand Q. Revenue is the product of the price charged and the quantity sold and so we can write

Revenue (R) = PQ = (a – bQ/ΔQ)Q = aQ – bQ^2/ΔQ

3.10 An organisation with a demand curve P = 70 – 0.3x could therefore model revenue (R) as R = 70x – 0.3x^2.

Question: revenue models

An organisation's revenue model changed from R = 392x – 0.15x^2 to R = 450x – 0.27x^2, where x is the number of units sold.

Required

Explain the effect on revenue estimates of the change in model.

Answer

The revised model shows a higher price at which demand would be nil (£450 compared to £392), but a higher rate of decrease in price as the number of units sold increases. (The change in the coefficient of x from 0.15 to 0.27 shows that the price will decline at a faster rate for a given change in the number of units sold.) In other words, the revised model has a higher price elasticity of demand.

The revised model therefore generates higher revenue estimates at low levels of demand, but lower estimates at higher demand levels.

Exam focus point

Cost and revenue models were examined in December 2002.

3.11 There are a number of **problems** associated with using such models.

(a) The cost model assumes fixed costs remain unchanged over all ranges of output. (Think about the possibility of step costs, say.)

(b) The cost model assumes a constant unit variable cost over all ranges of output. (Think about the implications of economies and diseconomies of scale.)

(c) Should an allowance for inflation be incorporated?

(d) How accurate is the price elasticity of demand incorporated in the model?

(e) The revenue model assumes price is the only factor determining level of demand.

Profit maximisation

3.12 Microeconomic theory suggests that **as output increases**, the marginal cost per unit might rise (due to the law of diminishing returns) and whenever the firm is faced with a downward sloping demand curve, the **marginal revenue per unit will decline.**

Eventually, a level of output will be reached where the **extra cost** of making one extra unit of output is greater than the **extra revenue** obtained from its sale. It would then be unprofitable to make and sell that extra unit.

3.13 Profits will continue to be maximised only up to the output level where marginal cost has risen to be exactly equal to the marginal revenue.

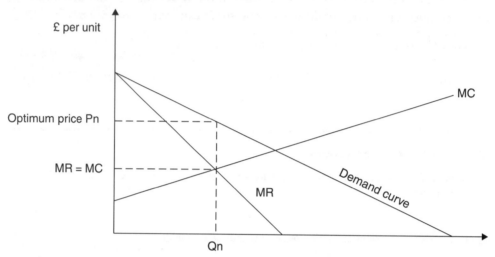

Profits are **maximised** at the point where **MC = MR**, ie at a volume of Qn units. If we add a demand curve to the graph, we can see that at an output level of Qn, the sales price per unit would be Pn.

3.14 It is important to make a clear **distinction** in your mind between the **sales price** and **marginal revenue**. In this example, the optimum price is Pn, but the marginal revenue is much less. This is because the 'additional' sales **unit** to reach output Qn has only been achieved by reducing the unit sales **price** from an amount higher than Pn for **all** the units to be sold, not just the marginal extra one. The increase in sales volume is therefore partly offset by a reduction in unit price; hence MR is lower than Pn.

Determining the profit-maximising selling price

Calculus/solving equations

3.15 Differential calculus (a topic outside your syllabus) can be used to determine equations for MC and MR. Alternatively, you might be provided with the equations (and the demand function) in the exam. Equating the two equations and solving will produce the level of demand at which profits are maximised.

3.16 EXAMPLE: SOLVING MC = MR

Suppose $MC = 3,500 + 15x$ and $MR = 4,000 - 10x$, where x = quantity sold.

Profits are maximised when MC = MR

∴ Profits are maximised when $3,500 + 15x = 4,000 - 10x$, ie when $x = 20$

If $P = 4,700 - 9x$, profit-maximising selling price when $x = 20$ is $(4,700 - (9 \times 20)) = £4,520$.

Visual inspection of a tabulation of data

3.17 (a) Work out the **demand curve** and hence the **price** and the **total revenue** (PQ) at various levels of demand.

(b) Calculate **total cost** and hence **marginal cost** at each level of demand.

(c) Finally calculate **profit** at each level of demand, thereby determining the price and level of demand at which profits are maximised.

Question: tabulation method

A firm operates in a market where there is imperfect competition, so that to sell more units of output, it must reduce the sales price of all the units it sells. The following data is available for prices and costs.

Total output Units	Sales price per unit (AR) £	Average cost of output (AC) £ per unit
0	-	-
1	504	720
2	471	402
3	439	288
4	407	231
5	377	201
6	346	189
7	317	182
8	288	180
9	259	186
10	232	198

The total cost of zero output is £600.

At what output level and price would the firm maximise its profits, assuming that fractions of units cannot be made?

Answer

Units	Price £	Total revenue £	Marginal revenue £	Total cost £	Marginal cost £	Profit £
0	0	0	0	600	-	(600)
1	504	504	504	720	120	(216)
2	471	942	438	804	84	138
3	439	1,317	375	864	60	453
4	407	1,628	311	924	60	704
5	377	1,885	257	1,005	81	880
6	346	2,076	191	1,134	129	942
7*	317	2,219	143	1,274	140	945
8	288	2,304	85	1,440	166	864
9	259	2,331	27	1,674	234	657
10	232	2,320	(11)	1,980	306	340

* Profit is maximised at 7 units of output where MR is most nearly equal to MC.

Graphical approach

3.18 The diagrams below show that **profits are maximised** at the point where the **vertical distance** between the total revenue curve and the total costs curve is at a **maximum** (which is fairly obvious if you think about it since profits are maximised when the difference between cost and revenue in maximised). This profit-maximising demand level also **corresponds** to the point at which the **MC and MR curves intersect,** as we would expect. Notice how the profit-maximising price can be read off from the demand curve.

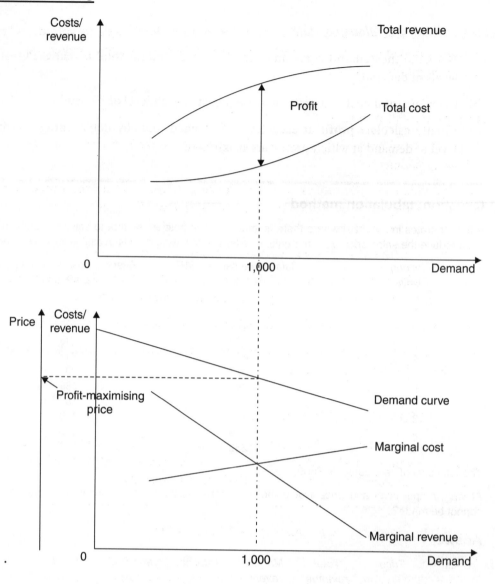

Using gradients

3.19 Suppose we were to draw **tangents** to the total revenue and total cost curves at the **points at which profit is maximised**. As you can see, the gradients of these tangents **are the same**.

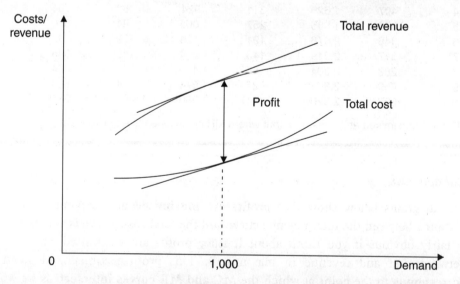

3.20 The **gradient of the total cost curve** is the **rate at which total cost changes with changes in volume**, which is simply **marginal cost**. Likewise, the **gradient of the total revenue**

curve is the **rate at which total revenue changes with changes in volume,** which is the **marginal revenue.** At the **point of profit maximisation,** the two gradients are **equal** and hence, once again, **MC = MR.**

Optimum pricing in practice

3.21 There are problems with applying the approach described above in practice for the following reasons.

(a) It assumes that the demand curve and total costs can be **identified with certainty.** This is unlikely to be so. And what about **inflation?** How, if necessary, should it be incorporated?

(b) It ignores the **market research costs** of acquiring knowledge of demand.

(c) It assumes the firm has **no production constraint** which could mean that the equilibrium point between supply and demand cannot be reached.

(d) It assumes the objective is **to maximise profits.** There may be other objectives.

(e) It assumes that **price is the only influence** on quantity demanded. We saw in Section 2 that this is far from the case.

4 TRADITIONAL PRICING BASES

4.1 You looked at traditional ideas about pricing for your earlier studies. Read the notes below and then try the questions, which will give you some practice on **basic techniques,** and also reinforce your understanding of how to deal with **uncertainty.**

Knowledge brought forward from earlier studies

Pricing

- With **full cost pricing** the sales price is determined by calculating the full cost of the product and then adding a percentage mark-up for profit.

  ○ This ensures that **all costs are covered.**
  ○ It is useful if prices have to be **justified** to customers.
  ○ However it takes **no account of market or demand** conditions.
  ○ It requires **arbitrary** decisions about **absorption** of costs.
  ○ There may be problems in determining the **profit mark up.**

- With **marginal cost pricing**, a profit margin is added on to either the marginal cost of production or the marginal cost of sales. This is sometimes called 'mark-up' pricing.

  ○ It draws management **attention to contribution**, and the effects of higher or lower sales volumes on profit. In this way, it helps to create a better awareness of the concepts and implications of marginal costing and cost-volume-profit analysis. For example, if a product costs £10 per unit and a mark-up of 150% is added to reach a price of £25 per unit, management should be clearly aware that every additional £1 of sales revenue would add 60 pence to contribution and profit.

  ○ It is convenient if there is a **readily identifiable variable cost** (eg in retail).

  ○ However, again it takes **no account of market or demand** conditions.

  ○ Pricing decisions **cannot ignore fixed costs** in the long term.

Question: full cost pricing

A product's full cost is £4.75 and it is sold at full cost plus 70%. A competitor has just launched a similar product selling for £7.99. How will this affect the first product's mark up?

Answer

The cost-plus percentage will need to be reduced by 2%.

Question: more complex full cost pricing

Markup Ltd has begun to produce a new product, Product X, for which the following cost estimates have been made.

	£
Direct materials	27
Direct labour: 4 hrs at £5 per hour	20
Variable production overheads: machining, ½ hr at £6 per hour	3
	50

Production fixed overheads are budgeted at £300,000 per month and because of the shortage of available machining capacity, the company will be restricted to 10,000 hours of machine time per month. The absorption rate will be a direct labour rate, however, and budgeted direct labour hours are 25,000 per month. It is estimated that the company could obtain a minimum contribution of £10 per machine hour on producing items other than product X.

The direct cost estimates are not certain as to material usage rates and direct labour productivity, and it is recognised that the estimates of direct materials and direct labour costs may be subject to an error of ± 15%. Machine time estimates are similarly subject to an error of ± 10%.

The company wishes to make a profit of 20% on full production cost from product X. What should the full cost based price be?

Answer

Even for a relatively 'simple' cost plus pricing estimate, some problems can arise, and certain assumptions must be made and stated. In this example, we can identify two **problems**.

(a) Should the opportunity cost of machine time be included in cost or not?
(b) What allowance, if any, should be made for the possible errors in cost estimates?

Using different assumptions, we could arrive at any of four different unit prices in the range £117.60 to £141.66.

(a) **Exclude machine time opportunity costs: ignore possible costing errors**

	£
Direct materials	27.00
Direct labour (4 hours)	20.00
Variable production o/hds	3.00
Fixed production o/hds (at £300,000/25,000 = £12 per direct labour hour)	48.00
Full production cost	98.00
Profit mark-up (20%)	19.60
Selling price per unit of product X	117.60

(b) **Include machine time opportunity costs: ignore possible costing errors**

	£
Full production cost as in (a)	98.00
Opportunity cost of machine time (contribution forgone (½ hr × £10))	5.00
Adjusted full cost	103.00
Profit mark-up (20%)	20.60
Selling price per unit of product X	123.60

(c) **Exclude machine time opportunity costs but make full allowance for possible under-estimates of cost**

	£	£
Direct materials	27.00	
Direct labour	20.00	
	47.00	
Possible error (15%)	7.05	
		54.05
Variable production overheads	3.00	
Possible error (10%)	0.30	
		3.30
Fixed production overheads (4 hrs × £12)	48.00	
Possible error (labour time) (15%)	7.20	
		55.20
Potential full production cost		112.55
Profit mark-up (20%)		22.51
Selling price per unit of product X		135.06

(d) **Include machine time opportunity costs and make a full allowance for possible under-estimates of cost**

	£
Potential full production cost as in (c)	112.55
Opp cost of machine time (potential contrib'n forgone (½ hr × £10 × 110%))	5.50
Adjusted potential full cost	118.05
Profit mark-up (20%)	23.61
Selling price per unit of product X	141.66

Exam focus point

Four very easy marks were available in the December 2002 exam for calculating full cost plus prices.

Full cost pricing versus marginal cost pricing

4.2 Perhaps the **most important criticism of full cost pricing** is that it **fails to recognise** that since sales demand may be determined by the sales price, there will be a **profit-maximising combination** of price and demand. A full cost based approach to pricing will be most unlikely, except by coincidence or 'luck', to arrive at the profit-maximising price. In contrast, a **marginal costing approach** to looking at costs and prices would be more likely to **help with identifying a profit-maximising price**.

4.3   EXAMPLE: FULL COST VERSUS PROFIT-MAXIMISING PRICES

Tigger Ltd has budgeted to make 50,000 units of its product, timm. The variable cost of a timm is £5 and annual fixed costs are expected to be £150,000.

The financial director of Tigger Ltd has suggested that a profit margin of 25% on full cost should be charged for every product sold.

The marketing director has challenged the wisdom of this suggestion, and has produced the following estimates of sales demand for timms.

Price per unit	Demand
£	Units
9	42,000
10	38,000
11	35,000
12	32,000
13	27,000

Required

(a) Calculate the profit for the year if a full cost price is charged.
(b) Calculate the profit-maximising price.

Assume in both (a) and (b) that 50,000 units of timm are produced regardless of sales volume.

4.4   SOLUTION

(a) (i)   The full cost per unit is £5 variable cost plus £3 fixed costs, ie £8 in total. A 25% mark-up on this cost gives a selling price of £10 per unit so that sales demand would be 38,000 units. (Production is given as 50,000 units.)

	£	£
Profit (absorption costing)		
Sales		380,000
Costs of production (50,000 units)		
Variable (50,000 × £5)	250,000	
Fixed (50,000 × £3)	150,000	
	400,000	
Less increase in stocks (12,000 units × 8)	(96,000)	
Cost of sales		304,000
Profit		76,000

(ii)   **Profit using marginal costing** instead of absorption costing, so that fixed overhead costs are written off in the period they occur, would be as follows. (The 38,000 unit demand level is chosen for comparison.)

	£
Contribution (38,000 × £(10 – 5))	190,000
Fixed costs	150,000
Profit	40,000

Since the company cannot go on indefinitely producing an output volume in excess of sales volume, this profit figure is more indicative of the profitability of timms in the longer term.

(b)   A **profit-maximising price** is one which gives the greatest net (relevant) cash flow, which in this case is the **contribution-maximising price**.

Price	Unit contribution	Demand	Total contribution
£	£	Units	£
9	4	42,000	168,000
10	5	38,000	190,000
11	6	35,000	210,000
12	7	32,000	224,000
13	8	27,000	216,000

The profit maximising price is £12, with annual sales demand of 32,000 units.

This example shows that a **cost based price** is **unlikely to be the profit-maximising** price, and that a **marginal costing approach**, calculating the total contribution at a variety of different selling prices, will be **more helpful** for establishing what the profit-maximising price ought to be.

Cost plus pricing versus target costing

4.5 As you should remember from Chapter 4, **target prices** are set in order to achieve a desired market share. Deduction of a desired profit margin produces the cost that has to be achieved. Design specifications and production methods are examined to establish ways in which the target cost can be met without reducing the value of the product to the customer.

4.6 Such an approach is likely to **offer greater competitive advantage** than cost plus pricing, being far more **strategically orientated** as it **takes account of the external environment**.

Chapter roundup

- In the modern world there are many more **influences on price** than cost (eg competitors, product range, quality).

- **Porter's Five Forces Model** suggests the importance of pressure from five competitive forces on price.

- The **BCG portfolio matrix** provides a method of positioning products through their life cycles in terms of market growth and market share.

- The price that an organisation can charge for its products will be determined to a greater or lesser degree by the **market** in which it operates.

- The **price elasticity of demand (PED)** is a measure of the extent of change in demand for a good in response to a change in its price.

- Most products pass through the four stages of the **product life cycle.**

- You need to be able to derive the **demand curve** $P = a - bQ/\Delta Q$.

- Cost and revenue behaviour can be **modelled** using equations.

- Microeconomic theory suggests that profits are maximised when **marginal cost = marginal revenue.**

- The **profit-maximising price** can be determined using equations, graphically or by tabulation of data.

- Traditional pricing approaches based on cost include **full cost pricing** and **marginal cost pricing**.

Quick quiz

1 *Match up the words from the two columns below to show the five competitive forces on price suggested by Porter.*

new entrants   threat of
suppliers   bargaining power of
substitutes   rivalry between
existing competitors threat of
buyers   bargaining power of

Part E: Decision making

2   Place the four types of product suggested by the BCG portfolio matrix on the diagram below.

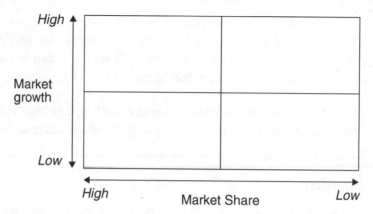

3   Monopolistic competition is when relatively few competitive companies dominate the market. *True or false?*

4   *Fill in the blanks.*

Demand is said to be elastic when a .... change in price produces a ....
change in quantity demanded. PED is .... than 1.

Demand is said to be inelastic when a .... change in price produces a ....
change in quantity demanded. PED is .... than 1.

5   What are the four phases of the product life cycle?

A   Birth, growth, maturity, death
B   Introduction, expansion, decline, death
C   Introduction, growth, maturity, decline
D   Birth, growth, expansion, saturation

6   *Fill in the blanks in the formula below for the variable 'a' in the equation for a demand curve.*

$$a = £(.............................) + \left(\frac{...}{...} \times £...... \right)$$

7   Sketch a graph showing how a profit-maximising price can be determined.

8   Cost-based approaches to pricing take more account of the external environment than target costing. *True or false?*

Answers to quick quiz

1   Threat of new entrants
    Threat of substitutes
    Rivalry between existing competitors

    Bargaining power of buyers
    Bargaining power of suppliers

2

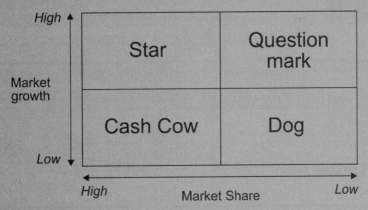

3   False. Oligopoly is being described.

4   (a)   Demand is said to be elastic when a **small change** in the price produces a **large change** in the quantity demanded. PED is **greater** than 1.

    (b)   Demand is said to be **inelastic** when a small change in the price produces only a **small change in the quantity** demanded. **PED is less than 1**.

5   C

6   $a = \text{(current price)} + \left(\dfrac{\text{Current quantity at current price}}{\text{Change in quantity when price is changed by £b}} \times £b \right)$

7

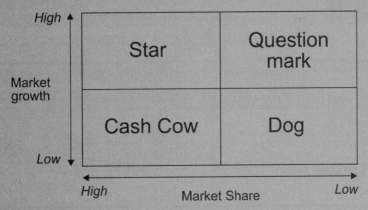

False

Now try the question below from the Exam Question Bank

Number	Level	Marks	Time
20	Exam	20	36 mins

Chapter 23

PRICING II

Topic list	Syllabus reference
1 Pricing and ABC	5(a)
2 Special orders	5(a)
3 New products	5(a)
4 Short-life products	5(a)
5 Differential pricing	5(a)

Introduction

In Chapter 22 we considered different approaches to pricing. In this chapter we will examine various **pricing decisions and policies** that can be taken and adopted in particular circumstances.

The chapter begins with a consideration of how **ABC** (covered in Chapter 3) can impact on pricing. We will then consider how to price **special orders**, **new products** and **short-life** products.

The last section of the chapter covers a particular pricing strategy, **differential pricing.**

Study Guide

Section 25 – Pricing II

- Calculate prices using activity based costing in the estimation of the cost element

- Contrast and discuss the implications of prices using the activity based costing technique with those using volume related methods in assigning costs to products

- Take informed pricing decisions in the context of special orders and new products

- Discuss pricing policy in the context of skimming, penetration and differential pricing

- Explain the process of pricing in the context of short-life products

Exam guide

Exam questions on the topics covered in this question could be computational (such as setting a price using ABC) or discursive (discuss the relevance of a particular strategy, for example).

The issues covered in this chapter are useful background to the following Oxford Brookes degree Research and Analysis Projects.

- Topic 1, which requires you to analyse the efficiency and/or effectiveness of a management accounting technique in an organisational setting

- Topic 10, which requires you to analyse how management accounting techniques are used to support decision making in organisations

1 PRICING AND ABC

1.1 As you know, under the ABC approach overheads are allocated to products on the basis of the activities that cause them to be incurred, rather than according to some arbitrary base like labour hours. The implication for pricing is that the **full cost** on which prices are based may be **radically different** if ABC is used.

1.2 EXAMPLE: ACTIVITY BASED COSTING AND PRICING

ABP Ltd makes two products, X and Y, with the following cost patterns.

	Product X	Product Y
	£	£
Direct materials	27	24
Direct labour at £5 per hour	20	25
Variable production overheads at £6 per hour	3	6
	50	55

Production fixed overheads total £300,000 per month and these are absorbed on the basis of direct labour hours. Budgeted direct labour hours are 25,000 per month. However, the company has carried out an analysis of its production support activities and found that its 'fixed costs' actually vary in accordance with non volume-related factors.

Activity	Cost driver	Product X	Product Y	Total cost
				£
Set-ups	Production runs	30	20	40,000
Materials handling	Production runs	30	20	150,000
Inspection	Inspections	880	3,520	110,000
				300,000

Budgeted production is 1,250 units of product X and 4,000 units of product Y.

Required

Given that the company wishes to make a profit of 20% on full production cost, calculate the prices that should be charged for products X and Y using the following.

(a) Full cost pricing
(b) Activity based cost pricing

1.3 SOLUTION

(a) The **full cost and mark-up** will be calculated as follows.

	Product X	Product Y
	£	£
Variable costs	50.00	55.00
Fixed prod o/hds (£300,000/25,000 = £12 per direct labour hr)	48.00	60.00
	98.00	115.00
Profit mark-up (20%)	19.60	23.00
Selling price	117.60	138.00

(b) Using **activity based costing**, overheads will be allocated on the basis of cost drivers.

	X	Y	Total
Set ups (30:20)	24,000	16,000	40,000
Materials handling (30:20)	90,000	60,000	150,000
Inspections (880:3,520)	22,000	88,000	110,000
	136,000	164,000	300,000
Budgeted units	1,250	4,000	
Overheads per unit	£108.80	£41.00	

The price is then calculated as before.

	Product X	Product Y
	£	£
Variable costs	50.00	55.00
Production overheads	108.80	41.00
	158.80	96.00
Profit mark-up (20%)	31.76	19.20
	190.56	115.20

(c) **Commentary**

The results in (b) are radically different from those in (a). On this basis it appears that the company has **previously been making a huge loss** on every unit of product X sold for £117.60. If the market will not accept a price increase, it may be worth considering ceasing production of product X entirely. It also appears that there is scope for a reduction in the price of product Y, and this would certainly be worthwhile if demand for the product is elastic.

The pricing implications of activity based costing

1.4 Consider a business that produces a **large volume** standard product and a number of **variants** which are more refined versions of the basic product and sell in low volumes at a higher price. Such companies are common in practice in the modern business environment. In practice, also, such companies absorb fixed overheads on a conventional basis such as direct labour hours, and price their products by adding a mark up to full cost.

1.5 In the situation described, the **majority of the overheads** would be allocated to the **standard** range, and only a small percentage to the up-market products. The result would be that the profit margin achieved on the standard range would be much lower than that on the up-market range.

1.6 Thus the traditional costing and pricing system indicates that the firm might be wise to concentrate on its high margin, up-market products and drop its standard range. This is **absurd,** however. Much of the overhead cost incurred in such an organisation is the cost of support activities like production scheduling: the more different **varieties** of product there are, the higher the level of such activities will become. The cost of marketing and distribution also increases disproportionately to the volume of products being made.

1.7 The bulk of the overheads in such an organisation are actually the '**costs of complexity**'. Their arbitrary allocation on the basis of labour hours gives an entirely **distorted** view of production line profitability; many products that appear to be highly profitable actually make a loss if costs are allocated on the basis of what activities cause them.

1.8 The problem arises with **marginal cost-plus** approaches as well as with absorption cost based approaches, particularly in a modern manufacturing environment, where a relatively small proportion of the total cost is variable. The implication in both cases is that conventional costing should be abandoned in favour of ABC.

Case example

In a survey reported in *Accountancy Age* ('The price is right... or is it?', June 2002), it was found that 'For many companies, pricing decisions are a seat-of-the-pants affair. There is generally low take-up of the analytical tools and techniques an accountant would expect to use in making financial decisions. The most extensively used technique was "face to face" research.' ABC was in third place, after competitive analysis but before breakeven analysis.

The survey also found that the leaders [most successful companies in the survey at using price management to achieve business objectives] ..."'focus on customer segments, differentiate products to serve them, pay attention to quality and deliver on customer care. This costs money but they see it as a way of reducing unit cost and delivering the economies of scale which lead to competitive prices and market leadership".

Significantly too, the leaders are more likely to use realistic cost allocation methodologies, such as activity-based costing, when they take pricing decisions. Some 62% of leaders ranked this either "very important" or "important" compared with just 23% of laggards.

"Confident - and profitable - pricing depends on knowing direct and indirect costs attributable to a particular product or service ... It's not surprising leader companies take better pricing decisions when they are more likely to have this information at their fingertips.'"

Exam focus point

Activity-based prices had to be calculated in the December 2002 exam (compulsory question 1) and then compared with and analysed against prices determined using absorption costing.

2 SPECIAL ORDERS

2.1 A special order is a **one-off** revenue earning opportunity. These may arise in the following situations.

(a) When a business has a regular source of income but also has some **spare capacity** allowing it to take on extra work if demanded. For example a brewery might have a capacity of 500,000 barrels per month but only be producing and selling 300,000 barrels per month. It could therefore consider special orders to use up some of its spare capacity.

(b) When a business has **no regular source of income** and relies exclusively on its ability to respond to demand. A building firm is a typical example as are many types of sub-contractors. In the service sector consultants often work on this basis.

2.2 The reason for making the distinction is that in the case of (a), a firm would normally attempt to cover its longer-term running costs in its prices for its regular product. Pricing for special orders need therefore take no account of unavoidable fixed costs. This is clearly not the case for a firm in (b)'s position, where special orders are the only source of income for the foreseeable future.

Exam focus point

Examination questions featuring pricing for special orders could present a scenario in which a firm has to decide whether to bid for a contract.

Minimum pricing

2.3 The basic approach in both situations is to determine the **price at which the firm would break even if it undertook the work,** that is, the **minimum price** that it could afford to charge.

2.4 A minimum price is the minimum price that would have to be charged so as to **cover the following two groups of cost.**

(a) The **incremental costs** of producing and selling the item
(b) The **opportunity costs** of the resources consumed in making and selling the item

A minimum price would leave the business no better or worse off than if it did not sell the item.

2.5 Two essential points to understand immediately about a minimum price are as follows.

   (a) It is **based on 'relevant costs'.** Relevant costs are the incremental costs plus the opportunity costs of making and selling the product or providing the service. We looked at this aspect in depth in Chapter 21.

   (b) It is **unlikely that a minimum price would actually be charged,** because if it were it would not provide the business with any incremental profit. However, the minimum price for an item shows the following.

   (i) An **absolute minimum** below which the price should not be set.

   (ii) The **incremental profit** that would be obtained from any price that is actually charged in excess of the minimum. For example, if the minimum price is £200 and the actual price charged is £240, the incremental profit on the sale would be £40.

2.6 If there are no **scarce resources,** and a company has **spare capacity,** the **minimum price** of a product would be an amount which equals the **incremental cost of making it.** Any price in excess of this minimum would provide an incremental contribution towards profit.

If there are **scarce resources** and a company makes **more than one product, minimum prices** would **include an allowance for the opportunity cost** of using the scarce resources to make and sell the product (instead of using the resources on the next most profitable product).

2.7 Where a firm also has to consider its **long-term costs** in the decision because it has no other way of recovering them it would have to **add a proportion of estimated unattributable costs to the price of each order.** This could be calculated on a time basis (if the job is expected to take one month, $^1/_{12}$ of unavoidable costs would be included), but this might lead to inconsistencies if, say, the unavoidable costs were all borne by one customer in one month and shared between several customers in another month.

Question: pricing

DDD Contracting Ltd refurbishes office buildings. As at 1 January it had won a number of contracts for the first three months of the year, as shown below.

Month	Contracts won
January	1
February	2
March	2

In February it won a further four firm orders, all of which are to be undertaken in April. It does not have the resources to carry out more than four jobs in one month. April to August are known to be the busiest months for this type of work.

Unavoidable fixed costs are expected to be £100,000 for the year.

Required

Given that prospective customers are aware of the prices charged to previous customers, what proportion of unavoidable fixed costs should be included in the price charged to the customer whose contract will be performed in January?

Answer

Not enough information is given to enable you to calculate a definite answer. You could have assumed that DDD Ltd will be working flat out from April to August (20 contracts) and might win, say 5 contracts in the final months of the year to give a total of 30, and hence $3^1/_3$% of the total overheads would be allocated to each customer. However, other assumptions would be equally valid.

Question: minimum pricing

DDD Ltd has decided to price its jobs as follows.

(a) It calculates the minimum price for the job using relevant costs.
(b) It adds £5,000 to cover fixed costs.
(c) It adds a 10% profit margin to the total cost.

A customer who has work to be performed in May says he will award the contract to DDD Ltd if its bid is reduced by £5,000. Should the contract be accepted?

Answer

Yes or no. Yes, if there is no other work available, because DDD will at least earn a contribution towards fixed costs of 10% of the minimum cost. But no, if by accepting this reduced price it would send a signal to other prospective customers that they too could negotiate such a large reduction.

2.8 The questions above illustrate the difficulties faced by firms with high overheads. Ideally some means should be found of **identifying the causes of such costs. Activity based analysis** might reveal ways of attributing overheads to specific jobs or perhaps of avoiding them altogether.

3 NEW PRODUCTS

3.1 The role of the management accountant in new product pricing might be to estimate the cash flows and return on investment that would be expected, given a particular sales price, and estimates of sales demand.

3.2 **Discounted cash** flow techniques could be used to estimate whether a new product will yield a satisfactory return at the proposed selling price, and which combination of sales price and sales volume would yield the best return for a product over its life cycle. In examination questions you would have to be given suitable information about the timing of cash flows and the cost of capital.

3.3 EXAMPLE: NEW PRODUCT PRICING

Novo plc is about to launch a new product with a variable cost of £10 per unit. The company has carried out market research (at a cost of £15,000) to determine the potential demand for the product at various selling prices.

Selling price £	Demand Units
30	20,000
25	30,000
20	40,000

Its current capacity is for 20,000 units but additional capacity can be made available by using the resources of another product line. If this is done the lost contribution from the other product will be £35,000 for each additional 10,000 units of capacity.

Senior management have asked you to analyse this information in a way that helps them to decide on the product's launch price.

3.4 SOLUTION

Tabulation is the approach to use with a problem of this type.

Selling price £	Demand Units ('000)	Variable costs £'000	Opportunity costs £'000	Total costs £'000	Sales revenue £'000	Contribution £'000
30	20	200	-	200	600	400
25	30	300	35	335	750	415
20	40	400	70	470	800	330

The optimum price to maximise short-term profits is £25.

3.5 The main **drawbacks** of the approach described above are that it only considers a limited range of prices (what about charging £27.50?) and it takes no account of the uncertainty of forecast demand. Allowance could be made for both situations, however, by collecting more information.

New product pricing strategies

3.6 A new product pricing strategy will depend largely on whether a company's product or service is the first of its kind on the market.

(a) If the **product is the first of its kind**, there will be **no competition** yet, and the company, for a time at least, will be a **monopolist**. Monopolists have more influence over price and are able to set a price at which they think they can maximise their profits. A monopolist's price is likely to be higher, and his profits bigger, than those of a company operating in a competitive market.

(b) If the new product being launched by a company is **following a competitor's product** onto the market, the pricing **strategy will be constrained** by what the competitor is already doing. The new product could be given a higher price if its quality is better, or it could be given a price which matches the competition. Undercutting the competitor's price might result in a price war and a fall of the general price level in the market.

3.7 Two alternative pricing strategies for new products are market penetration pricing and market skimming pricing.

Market penetration pricing

KEY TERM

Penetration pricing is a policy of low prices when a product is first launched in order to obtain sufficient penetration into the market.

3.8 A penetration policy may be appropriate in the cases below.

(a) The firm wishes to **discourage new entrants** into the market.

(b) The firm wishes to **shorten the initial period** of the product's life cycle in order to enter the growth and maturity stages as quickly as possible.

(c) There are significant **economies of scale** to be achieved from a high volume of output.

(d) Demand is **highly elastic** and so would respond well to low prices.

3.9 Penetration prices are prices which aim to secure a substantial share in a substantial total market. A firm might therefore deliberately build **excess production capacity** and set its prices very low. As demand builds up the spare capacity will be used up gradually and unit costs will fall; the firm might even reduce prices further as unit costs fall. In this way, early losses will enable the firm to dominate the market and have the lowest costs.

Market skimming pricing

> **KEY TERM**
>
> **Price skimming** involves charging high prices when a product is first launched in order to maximise short-term profitability. Initially there is heavy spending on advertising and sales promotion to obtain sales. As the product moves into the later stages of its life cycle (growth, maturity and decline) progressively lower prices are charged. The profitable 'cream' is thus skimmed off in stages until sales can only be sustained at lower prices.

3.10 The aim of market skimming is to gain **high unit profits** early in the product's life. High unit prices make it more likely that **competitors** will enter the market than if lower prices were to be charged.

3.11 Such a policy may be appropriate in the cases below.

(a) The product is **new and different,** so that customers are prepared to pay high prices so as to be one up on other people who do not own it.

(b) The strength of **demand** and the sensitivity of demand to price are **unknown**. It is better from the point of view of marketing to start by charging high prices and then reduce them if the demand for the product turns out to be price elastic than to start by charging low prices and then attempt to raise them substantially if demand appears to be insensitive to higher prices.

(c) High prices in the early stages of a product's life might generate **high initial cash flows**. A firm with liquidity problems may prefer market-skimming for this reason.

(d) The firm can identify **different market segments** for the product, each prepared to pay progressively lower prices. It may therefore be possible to continue to sell at higher prices to some market segments when lower prices are charged in others. This is discussed further below.

(e) Products may have a **short life cycle**, and so need to recover their development costs and make a profit relatively quickly.

3.12 **Products to which the policy has been applied**

- Calculators
- Video recorders
- Desktop computers

4   SHORT-LIFE PRODUCTS

4.1 A short-life product is one for which the demand is likely to cease a relatively short time after the product is launched. Examples include the following.

(a) Goods commemorating **special occasions**, like sporting events (the World Cup) or state ceremonies (the Golden Jubilee)

(b) Goods intended to **promote other products**, like T-shirts associated with a new film

(c) **'Limited editions'**, produced in very small numbers to give them a rarity value

(d) Goods which are of use for a **predetermined period**, after which a new version will be produced. Prime examples are **diaries and calendars**.

4.2 Such products have the characteristics of both special orders and new products. Short-life products are often **quite highly priced** so as to give the manufacturer a chance to recover his investment and make a worthwhile return. Market skimming pricing might be a useful strategy to adopt.

4.3 However, the main problem with short-life products is deciding **how many** to produce in order that demand will be fully satisfied and no unsold stocks will be left over when demand ceases. (This even applies to some extent to limited editions: how 'limited' should they be?) There is no easy answer to this question unless the level of demand can be predicted with absolute certainty. Given that such products are often one-offs, this can be extremely difficult.

Exam focus point

Be prepared for questions that ask you to determine the optimum pricing and production strategy given a range of possibilities.

5 DIFFERENTIAL PRICING

5.1 In certain circumstances the **same product** can be sold at different prices to **different customers**. There are a number of bases on which such discriminating prices can be set.

(a) **By market segment.** A cross-channel ferry company would market its services at different prices in England and France, for example. Services such as cinemas and hairdressers are often available at lower prices to old age pensioners and/or juveniles.

(b) **By product version.** Many car models have 'add on' extras which enable one brand to appeal to a wider cross-section of customers. The final price need not reflect the cost price of the add on extras directly: usually the top of the range model would carry a price much in excess of the cost of provision of the extras, as a prestige appeal.

(c) **By place.** Theatre seats are usually sold according to their location so that patrons pay different prices for the same performance according to the seat type they occupy.

(d) **By time.** This is perhaps the most popular type of price discrimination. Off-peak travel bargains, hotel prices and telephone charges are all attempts to increase sales revenue by covering variable but not necessarily average cost of provision. Railway companies are successful price discriminators, charging more to rush hour rail commuters whose demand is inelastic at certain times of the day.

5.2 Price discrimination can only be effective if a number of **conditions** hold.

(a) The market must be **segmentable** in price terms, and different sectors must show different intensities of demand. Each of the sectors must be identifiable, distinct and separate from the others, and be accessible to the firm's marketing communications.

(b) There must be little or **no** chance of a **black market** developing (this would allow those in the lower priced segment to resell to those in the higher priced segment).

(c) There must be little or **no** chance that **competitors** can and will undercut the firm's prices in the higher priced (and/or most profitable) market segments.

(d) The cost of segmenting and **administering** the arrangements should not exceed the extra revenue derived from the price discrimination strategy.

5.3 Try the following question which, although it has a few 'tricks', **looks more daunting than it is** if you keep your head and take care.

Question: differential pricing

Curltown Cinemas operates a chain of 30 cinemas. Standard admission price is £7 per person, but this is subject to certain discounts. Average attendance at a cinema per month on normal price days is 5,000 people, but this is expected to be subject to seasonal variation, as follows.

Month	J	F	M	A	M	J	J	A	S	O	N	D
%	+10	-2	0	+5	-5	-5	+10	+7	-4	-4	0	+12

In December, January, July and August audiences are made up of 60% under-14s, who pay half-price admission. For the rest of the year under 14s represent only 10% of the audience. One day per month all tickets are sold at a special offer price of £1, irrespective of the age of the customer. This invariably guarantees a full house of 200 customers.

Required

(a) What is Curltown Cinemas' total revenue from cinema admissions for a year?

(b) If Curltown puts up prices for over-14s (other than the £1 special offer price) to £8 what will its total revenue from cinema admissions be for the year?

(c) Should the special offer be continued?

Answer

(a) This is simply a matter of reading the question carefully and patiently tabulating the data using a **different layout** to the one given in the question. Note that you save yourself potential error if you convert percentages into decimals as you transfer the question information into your own table. Don't forget that there are 30 cinemas.

Month	Variation	Average no	Adjusted no	Full price	Revenue @ £7.00 £	Half price	Revenue @ £3.50 £
Jan	+0.10	5,000	5,500	0.4	15,400.00	0.6	11,550.00
Feb	-0.02	5,000	4,900	0.9	30,870.00	0.1	1,715.00
Mar	+0.00	5,000	5,000	0.9	31,500.00	0.1	1,750.00
Apr	+0.05	5,000	5,250	0.9	33,075.00	0.1	1,837.50
May	-0.05	5,000	4,750	0.9	29,925.00	0.1	1,662.50
Jun	-0.05	5,000	4,750	0.9	29,925.00	0.1	1,662.50
Jul	+0.10	5,000	5,500	0.4	15,400.00	0.6	11,550.00
Aug	+0.07	5,000	5,350	0.4	14,980.00	0.6	11,235.00
Sept	-0.04	5,000	4,800	0.9	30,240.00	0.1	1,680.00
Oct	-0.04	5,000	4,800	0.9	30,240.00	0.1	1,680.00
Nov	0.00	5,000	5,000	0.9	31,500.00	0.1	1,750.00
Dec	+0.12	5,000	5,600	0.4	15,680.00	0.6	11,760.00
					308,735.00		59,832.50

	£
Total normal price (£308,735.00 + £59,832.50)	368,567.50
Special offer (12 × £1 × 200)	2,400.00
Total per cinema	370,967.50
Total per 30 cinemas	11,129,025.00

(b) **There is no need to work out all the numbers again at the new prices.**

	£
Total as calculated above	11,129,025.00
Less: current adult normal price (£308,735 × 30)	(9,262,050.00)
Add: revised adult normal price (£308,735 × 30 × 8/7)	10,585,200.00
	12,452,175.00

(c) If the income of £200 per cinema on the twelve special offer days is compared with an average of, say, £368,567.50/(365 – 12 days) = over £1,000, then it is clearly not worthwhile. The cinemas get average attendances of (5000 × 12)/365 = about 164 people in any case, even without special offers. (You could do **rough calculations** to estimate the overall loss of revenue per annum. Try it, making any **assumptions** you need, if you haven't done so, but not at the expense of written comments.)

However, the offer is a **loss-leader** which probably has other benefits. It will be liked by customers, and if the film they see is a good one they will recommend it to their friends. It may help to encourage the cinema-going habit amongst potential new regular customers. You may have thought of other relevant comments, either in favour of the policy or against it.

Pricing for competitive advantage

5.4 Porter sites a number of strategies which an organisation can adopt with respect to its competitive position to provide competitive advantage.

(a) **Cost leadership**

(i) Cost-conscious approach to operations
(ii) Pursuit of technical advantages
(iii) Acknowledged lowest costs in the industry
(iv) Low costs ≠ cheap product philosophy
(v) Prices not necessarily low (but **can** lower prices if competition fierce)

(b) **Differentiation**

(i) Multiple products each branded and promoted
(ii) Competition must overcome brand loyalty through price cutting
(iii) Adds attributes valued by the customer and for which the customer will pay
(iv) Aims to maximise profit gap between price and cost

(c) **Focus (niche)**

(i) Focus on cost and differentiating factors in response to customer needs in a specific market segment
(ii) Higher profits in the short term

Target costing and pricing

5.5 Target costing, covered in Chapter 4, involves setting a target price at which an organisation is able to achieve a desired market share.

Chapter roundup

- **Activity based costing** provides an opportunity for organisations that use cost-based pricing to gain a greater understanding of their costs and so correct pricing anomalies that derive from the distorted view given by conventional volume-related costing.

- **Special orders** require a relevant cost approach to the calculation of the tender price.

- **New products** that are expected to have a long life will require management accounting techniques like discounted cash flow and risk analysis. New product pricing strategies include **market penetration pricing** and **market skimming**.

- **Short-life products** should be priced using relevant costs and risk analysis where possible. Accurately predicting demand is vital in such situations.

- The use of **differential pricing** means that the same product can be sold at different prices to different customers. This can be very difficult to implement in practice because it relies for success upon the continued existence of certain market conditions.

Quick quiz

1   The use of ABC tends to result in a lower profit margin on standard product ranges compared with that achieved on non-standard ranges. *True or false?*

2   *Fill in the gaps.*

The basic approach to pricing special orders is to set a .... price which would need to cover the following two groups of cost.

- The .... cost of producing and selling the item
- The .... cost of the resources consumed in making and selling the item

3   When would market skimming be a suitable pricing strategy?

A   If an organisation wished to discourage new entrants into the market
B   If demand is highly elastic
C   If there are significant economies of scale to be achieved from a high volume of output
D   If the product has a short life cycle

4   *Fill in the blanks.*

Discriminating prices can be set on the basis of .... , ... , ... or ....

5   What strategies does Porter suggest an organisation can adopt with respect to its competitive position to provide competitive advantage?

A   Cost leadership, differentiation, penetration
B   Skimming, differentiation, penetration
C   Cost leadership, differentiation, focus
D   Focus, premium, cost leadership

6   *Choose the correct words from those highlighted.*

Short-life products are often quite highly priced so as to give the manufacturer a chance to recover his investment and make a worthwhile return. **Market skimming/market penetration** pricing might be a useful strategy to adopt.

Answers to quick quiz

1   False. This is the result of using absorption costing.

2   minimum
    incremental
    opportunity

3   D

4   market segment   place
    product version   time

5   C

6   Market skimming

Now try the question below from the Exam Question Bank

Number	Level	Marks	Time
21	Exam	20	36 mins

Chapter 24

RISK AND UNCERTAINTY

Topic list	Syllabus reference
1 Risk and uncertainty	5(b)
2 Allowing for uncertainty	5(b)
3 Probabilities and expected values	5(b)
4 Decision trees	5(b)
5 Perfect information	5(b)

Introduction

Decision making involves making decisions now about what will happen in the future. Obviously, decisions can turn out badly, or actual results can prove to be very different from the estimates on which the original decision was made. **Ideally** the decision maker would **know with certainty** what the future consequences would be for each choice facing him. But the real world is not normally so helpful, and decisions must be made in the knowledge that their **consequences**, although probable perhaps, are **rarely 100% certain**.

Various **methods of bringing uncertainty and risk analysis** into the evaluation of decisions will be described in this chapter. You may well think that some methods are more sensible or practical than others but you should **judge** each method on its merits, and be able to **apply** it if necessary in an examination.

Study guide

Section 25 – Risk and uncertainty

- Define and distinguish between uncertainty and risk preference

- Explain ways in which uncertainty may be allowed for by using conservatism and worst/most likely/best outcome estimates

- Explain the use of sensitivity analysis in decision situations

- Explain the use of probability estimates and the calculation of expected value

- Explain and illustrate the use of maximin, minimax, maximax and minimin techniques in decision making

- Describe the structure and use of decision trees

- Apply joint probabilities in decision tree analysis

- Illustrate the use of decision tree analysis in assessing the range of outcomes and the cumulative probabilities of each outcome

Exam guide

Given that decision-making techniques are a core syllabus area, expect to see both computational and discursive questions on the topics covered in this chapter.

The issues covered in this chapter are useful background to the following Oxford Brookes degree Research and Analysis Projects.

> - Topic 1, which requires you to analyse the efficiency and/or effectiveness of a management accounting technique in an organisational setting
> - Topic 10, which requires you to analyse how management accounting techniques are used to support decision making in organisations
> - Topic 14, which requires you to investigate recent investment decisions by an organisation of your choice and how the use of different methods of risk and uncertainty analysis might affect such decisions.

1   RISK AND UNCERTAINTY

Uncertainty and risk

1.1   These terms were introduced in Chapter 16. Remember that in everyday usage the terms risk and uncertainty are not clearly distinguished. If you are asked for a definition, do not make the mistake of believing that the latter is a more extreme version of the former. It is not a question of degree, it is a question of whether or not **sufficient information** is available to allow the lack of certainty to be quantified. As a rule, however, the terms are used interchangeably.

Risk preference

> ### KEY TERMS
>
> A **risk seeker** is a decision maker who is interested in the best outcomes no matter how small the chance that they may occur.
>
> A decision maker is **risk neutral** if he is concerned with what will be the most likely outcome.
>
> A **risk averse** decision maker acts on the assumption that the worst outcome might occur.

1.2   This has clear implications for managers and organisations. A risk seeking manager working for an organisation that is characteristically risk averse is likely to make decisions that are **not congruent with the goals** of the organisation.

1.3   There may be a role for the management accountant here, who could be instructed to **present** decision-making information in such a way as to ensure that the manager considers **all** the possibilities, including the worst.

1.4   What is an **acceptable amount of risk** will of course **vary from organisation to organisation**. For large public companies it is largely a question of what is acceptable to the shareholders. A 'safe' investment like Tesco will attract **investors** who are to **some extent risk averse,** and the company will thus be obliged to **follow relatively 'safe' policies.** A company that is recognised as being an **innovator or a 'growth' stock in a relatively new market,** like Amstrad in the past or perhaps a dot.com at present, will attract **investors** who are looking for **high performance** and are prepared to accept some **risk** in return. Such companies will be expected to make **'bolder' (more risky) decisions.**

1.5 **Factors to consider when evaluating a strategy**

(a) Whether an individual strategy involves an **'unacceptable' amount of risk,** whatever that may be. If it does, it should be eliminated from further consideration in the planning process.

(b) However, the risk of an individual strategy should also be considered in the context of the **overall 'portfolio'** of investment strategies adopted by the company.

(i) If a strategy is risky, but its **outcome is not related to the outcome of other strategies,** then adopting that strategy will help the company to **spread** its risks. (Diversification, after all, is intended to 'put more eggs into different baskets'.)

(ii) If a strategy is risky, but it is **related to other adopted strategies**, so that if strategy A does well, other adopted strategies will do badly and vice versa, then adopting strategy A would actually **reduce** the overall risk of the company's investment portfolio.

2 ALLOWING FOR UNCERTAINTY

Conservatism

2.1 This approach simply involves estimating outcomes in a conservative manner in order to provide a built-in safety factor.

2.2 However, the method fails to consider explicitly a **range** of outcomes and, by concentrating only on conservative figures, may also fail to consider the **expected** or most likely outcomes.

2.3 Conservatism is associated with **risk aversion** and prudence (in the general sense of the word). In spite of its shortcomings it is probably the **most widely used** method in practice.

Worst/most likely/best outcome estimates

2.4 A more scientific version of conservatism is to measure the most likely outcome from a decision, and the worst and best possible outcomes. This will show the **full range of possible outcomes** from a decision, and might help managers to reject certain alternatives because the worst possible outcome might involve an unacceptable amount of loss. This requires the preparation of **pay-off tables.**

Pay-off tables

2.5 Pay-off tables **identify and record all possible outcomes (or pay-offs)** in situations where the action taken affects the outcomes.

2.6 EXAMPLE: WORST/BEST POSSIBLE OUTCOMES

Omelette Ltd is trying to set the sales price for one of its products. Three prices are under consideration, and expected sales volumes and costs are as follows.

Price per unit	*£4*	*£4.30*	*£4.40*
Expected sales volume (units)			
Best possible	16,000	14,000	12,500
Most likely	14,000	12,500	12,000
Worst possible	10,000	8,000	6,000

Fixed costs are £20,000 and variable costs of sales are £2 per unit.

Which price should be chosen?

2.7 SOLUTION

Here we need to prepare a pay-off table showing **pay-offs** (contribution) **dependant on different levels of demand and different selling prices.**

	£4	£4.30	£4.40
Contribution per unit	£2	£2.30	£2.40
Total contribution towards fixed costs	£	£	£
Best possible	32,000	32,200	30,000
Most likely	28,000	28,750	28,800
Worst possible	20,000	18,400	14,400

(a) The highest contribution based on **most likely** sales volume would be at a price of £4.40 but arguably a price of £4.30 would be much better than £4.40, since the most likely profit is almost as good, the worst possible profit is not as bad, and the best possible profit is better.

(b) However, only a price of £4 guarantees that the company would **not make a loss,** even if the worst possible outcome occurs. (Fixed costs of £20,000 would just be covered.) A risk averse management might therefore prefer a price of £4 to either of the other two prices.

Decision rules

The maximin decision rule

> ### KEY TERM
>
> The **maximin** decision rule suggests that a decision maker should select the alternative that offers the least unattractive worst outcome. This would mean choosing the alternative that *maxi*mises the *min*imum profits.

2.8 EXAMPLE: MAXIMIN DECISION RULE

A businessman is trying to decide which of three mutually exclusive projects to undertake. Each of the projects could lead to varying net profit which the businessman classifies as outcomes I, II, and III. He has constructed the following payoff table or matrix.

		Net profit in £'000s if outcome turns out to be		
		I (Worst)	*II (Most likely)*	*III (Best)*
	A	50	85	130
Project	B	70	75	140
	C	90	100	110

Which project should he undertake? Use the maximin decision rule.

2.9 SOLUTION

The maximin decision rule suggests that he should select the 'smallest worst result' that could happen. This is the decision criterion that managers should 'play safe' and either minimise their losses or costs, or else go for the decision which gives the higher minimum profits. If he selects project A the worst result is a net profit of 50. Similarly, the worst results for B and C are 70 and 90 respectively. The best worst outcome is 90 and project C would therefore be selected (because this is a better 'worst possible' than either A or B).

> **KEY TERM**
>
> The maximin decision rule is also known as the **minimax cost rule** - minimise the maximum costs or losses.

2.10 Criticisms of the maximin decision rule

(a) It is **defensive** and **conservative**, being a safety first principle of avoiding the worst outcomes without taking into account opportunities for maximising profits.

(b) It ignores the **probability** of each different outcome taking place. In the previous example, we ignored the fact that outcome II was the most likely outcome.

Maximax

> **KEY TERM**
>
> The **maximax** criterion looks at the best possible results. Maximax means 'maximise the maximum profit'. An alternative name that amounts to the same thing is **minimin cost rule** (minimise the minimum costs or losses).

2.11 EXAMPLE: MAXIMAX

Here is a payoff table showing the profits that will be achieved depending upon the action taken (D, E or F) and the circumstances prevailing (I, II or III).

		Profits *Actions*		
		D	*E*	*F*
	I	100	80	60
Circumstances	II	90	120	85
	III	(20)	10	85
Maximum profit		100	120	85

Action E would be chosen if the maximax rule is followed.

2.12 **Criticisms** of this approach would again say that it ignores probabilities and that it is over-optimistic.

Question: maximax and maximin

A company is considering which one of three alternative courses of action, A, B and C to take. The profit or loss from each choice depends on which one of four economic circumstances, I, II, III or IV will apply. The possible profits and losses, in thousands of pounds, are given in the following payoff table. Losses are shown as negative figures.

		Action		
		A	*B*	*C*
	I	70	60	70
Circumstance	II	-10	20	-5
	III	80	0	50
	IV	60	100	115

Required

State which action would be selected using each of the maximax and maximin criteria.

Answer

(a) The **best possible outcomes** are as follows.

A (circumstance III):	80
B (circumstance IV):	100
C (circumstance IV):	115

As 115 is the highest of these three figures, action C would be chosen using the maximax criterion.

(b) The **worst possible outcomes** are as follows.

A (circumstance II):	-10
B (circumstance III):	0
C (circumstance II):	-5

The best of these figures is 0 (neither a profit nor a loss), so action B would be chosen using the maximin criterion.

Minimax regret rule

> **KEY TERM**
>
> The **minimax regret** rule aims to minimise the regret from making the wrong decision. **Regret** is the opportunity lost through making the wrong decision.

This is cited by the examiner of Paper 9 (old syllabus) in an article entitled 'Quantitative Applications in Paper 9 – part 1' (*ACCA Students' Newsletter, April 2000*).

2.13 We first consider the extreme to which we might come to regret an action we had chosen.

Regret for any combination of action and circumstances	=	Profit for best action in those circumstances	–	Profit for the action actually chosen in those circumstances

The minimax regret decision rule is that the decision option selected should be the one which **minimises the maximum potential regret** for any of the possible outcomes.

2.14 EXAMPLE: MINIMAX REGRET

A manager is trying to decide which of three mutually exclusive projects to undertake. Each of the projects could lead to varying net costs which the manager calls outcomes I, II and III. The following payoff table or matrix has been constructed.

		Outcomes (Net profit)		
		I	*II*	*III*
		(Worst)	*(Most likely)*	*(Best)*
	A	50	85	130
Project	B	70	75	140
	C	90	100	110

Which project should be undertaken?

2.15 SOLUTION

A table of regrets can be compiled, as follows, showing the amount of profit that might be forgone for each project, depending on whether the outcome is I, II or III.

	Outcome			*Maximum*
	I	II	III	
Project A	40 ★	15 ★★★	10	40
Project B	20 ★★	25	0	25
Project C	0	0	30	30

★ 90 – 50   ★★ 90 – 70   ★★★ 100 – 85   etc

The **maximum regret** is 40 with project A, 25 with B and 30 with C. The lowest of these three maximum regrets is 25 with B, and so project B would be selected if the minimax regret rule is used.

Exam focus point

Pilot paper question 2 (question 21 in the Exam Question Bank) requires you to use the maximax, maximin and minimax regret decision rules. The rules were also examined in the June 2002 exam.

Contribution tables

Exam focus point

Contribution tables were required in both the pilot paper and the June 2002 paper.

2.16 Questions requiring application of the decision rules often incorporate a **number of variables, each with a range of possible values.** For example these variables might be:

- Unit price and associated level of demand
- Unit variable cost

Each variable might have, for example, three possible values.

2.17 Before being asked to use the decision rules, exam questions could ask you to **work out contribution** for each of the possible outcomes. (Alternatively profit figures could be required if you are given information about fixed costs.)

2.18 The **number of possible outcomes = number of values of variable 1 × number of values of variable 2** × number of values of variable 3 etc

So, for example, if there are **two variables, each with three possible values,** there are 3 × 3 = **9 outcomes.**

2.19 Perhaps the easiest way to see how to draw up contribution tables is to look at an example.

2.20 EXAMPLE: CONTRIBUTION TABLES

Suppose the budgeted demand for product X will be 11,500 units if the price £10, 8,500 units if the price is £12 and 5,000 units if the price is £14. Variable costs are estimated at either £4, £5, or £6 per unit.

Here is a contribution table showing the budgeted contribution for each of the nine possible outcomes.

Demand	Price	Variable cost	Unit contribution	Total contribution
	£	£	£	£'000
11,500	10	4	6	69.0
11,500	10	5	5	57.5
11,500	10	6	4	46.0
8,500	12	4	8	68.0
8,500	12	5	7	59.5
8,500	12	6	6	51.0
5,000	14	4	10	50.0
5,000	14	5	9	45.0
5,000	14	6	8	40.0

2.21 Once the table has been drawn up, the decision rules an be applied.

2.22 EXAMPLE: APPLYING THE DECISION RULES

Maximin

We need to maximise the minimum contribution.

Demand/price	Minimum contribution
11,500/£10	£46,000
8,500/£12	£51,000
5,000/£14	£40,000

Set a price of £12.

Maximax

We need to maximise the maximum contribution.

Demand/price	Minimum contribution
11,500/£10	£69,000
8,000/£12	£68,000
5,000/£14	£50,000

Set a price of £10.

Minimax

We need to minimise the maximum regret (lost contribution) of making the wrong decision.

Variable cost		Price	
£	£10	£12	£14
4	-	£1,000	£19,000
5	£2,000	-	£14,500
6	£5,000	-	£11,000
Minimax regret	£5,000	£1,000	£19,000

Minimax regret strategy (price of £12) is that which minimises the maximum regret (£1,000).

Sample working

At a variable cost of £4, the best strategy would be a price of £10. Choosing a price of £12 would mean lost contribution of £69,000 – £68,000, while choosing a price of £14 would mean lost contribution of £69,000 – £50,000.

Sensitivity analysis

> **KEY TERM**
>
> **Sensitivity analysis** is a term used to describe any technique whereby decision options are tested for their vulnerability to changes in any 'variable' such as expected sales volume, sales price per unit, material costs, or labour costs.

2.23 Here are three useful approaches to sensitivity analysis.

(a) To estimate by **how much costs and revenues would need to differ** from their estimated values before the decision would change.

(b) To estimate whether a decision would change **if estimated costs were x% higher** than estimated, or estimated revenues y% lower than estimated.

(c) To estimate by how much costs and/or revenues would need to differ from their estimated values before the decision maker **would be indifferent** between two options.

2.24 The essence of the approach, therefore, is to carry out the calculations with one set of values for the variables and then substitute other possible values for the variables to see how this affects the overall outcome.

(a) From your studies of information technology you may recognise this as **what if analysis** that can be carried out using a **spreadsheet**.

(b) From your studies of **linear programming** you may remember that sensitivity analysis can be carried out to determine over which ranges the various constraints have an impact on the optimum solution.

(c) **Flexible budgeting** can also be a form of sensitivity analysis.

(d) Sensitivity analysis is one method of analysing the risk surrounding a **capital expenditure project** and enables an assessment to be made of how responsive the project's NPV is to changes in the variables that are used to calculate that NPV.

> **Exam focus point**
>
> Sensitivity analysis was examined in the compulsory question of the June 2003 paper.

2.25 EXAMPLE: SENSITIVITY ANALYSIS

Sensivite Ltd has estimated the following sales and profits for a new product which it may launch on to the market.

		£	£
Sales	(2,000 units)		4,000
Variable costs:	materials	2,000	
	labour	1,000	
			3,000
Contribution			1,000
Less incremental fixed costs			800
Profit			200

Required

Analyse the sensitivity of the project.

2.26 SOLUTION

(a) If incremental **fixed costs** are more than 25% above estimate, the project would make a loss.

(b) If **unit costs of materials** are more than 10% above estimate, the project would make a loss.

(c) Similarly, the project would be sensitive to an **increase in unit labour costs** of more than £200, which is 20% above estimate, or else to a drop in the **unit selling price** of more than 5%.

(d) The **margin of safety**, given a breakeven point of 1,600 units, is (400/2,000) × 100% = 20%.

Management would then be able to judge more clearly whether the product is likely to be profitable. The **items to which profitability is most sensitive** in this example are the **selling price** (5%) and **material costs** (10%). Sensitivity analysis can help to **concentrate management attention on the most important forecasts**.

2.27 EXAMPLE: SENSITIVITY ANALYSIS

Kenney Ltd is considering a project. The 'most likely' cash flows associated with the project are as follows.

Year	0	1	2
	£'000	£'000	£'000
Initial investment	(7,000)		
Variable costs		(2,000)	(2,000)
Cash inflows (650,000 units at £10 per unit)		6,500	6,500
Net cash flows	(7,000)	4,500	4,500

The cost of capital is 8%.

Required

Calculate the increase/decrease in each of the variables affecting the project's NPV at which Kenney Ltd would be indifferent between accepting or rejecting the project. (*Note.* Consider each of the variables in turn, the other variables remaining unchanged.).

2.28 SOLUTION

Work carefully through this solution making sure you understand all the calculations, and noting how the figures are analysed (percentages, unit costs etc).

The PVs of the cash flow are as follows.

Year	Discount factor 8%	PV of initial investment £'000	PV of variable costs £'000	PV of cash inflows £'000	PV of net cash flow £'000
0	1.000	(7,000)			(7,000)
1	0.926		(1,852)	6,019	4,167
2	0.857		(1,714)	5,571	3,857
		(7,000)	(3,566)	11,590	1,024

The project has a positive NPV and would appear to be worthwhile. The changes in cash flows which would need to occur for the project to only just breakeven (and hence be on the point of being unacceptable) are as follows.

Variable		Increase/decrease to make Kenney indifferent
Initial investment	(W1)	+14.6%
Sales volume	(W2)	−12.7%
Selling price	(W3)	−8.8%
Variable costs	(W4)	+28.7%
Cost of capital	(W5)	+133.0%

Workings

1   **Initial investment**

The initial investment can rise by £1,024,000 before the investment breaks even. The initial investment may therefore increase by 1,024/7,000 = **14.6%**.

2   **Sales volume**

The present value of the cash inflows minus the present value of the variable costs is £8,024,000. This will have to fall to £7,000,000 for the NPV to be zero.

We need to find the net cash flows in actual values. The cumulative discount factor for 8% and year 2 is 1.783. If the discount factor is divided into the required present value of £7,000,000 we get an annual cash flow of £3,925,968. Given that the most likely net cash flow is £4,500,000, the net cash flow may decline by approximately £574,032 each year before the NPV becomes zero.

Net cash flow is 4,500/6,500 of sales, so sales = £574,032 × 6,500/4,500 = £829,157. At a selling price of £10 per unit this represents 82,916 units. Alternatively we may state that sales volume may decline by **12.7%** (82,916/650,000) before the NPV becomes negative.

3   **Selling price**

When sales volume is 650,000 units per annum, total sales revenue can fall to £5,925,968 (£(6,500,000 − £574,032 (W2)) per annum before the NPV becomes negative. This assumes that total variable costs and sales volume remain unchanged. This represents a selling price of £9.12 per unit (£5,925,968/650,000), an **8.8%** (£0.88/£10) reduction in the selling price.

4   **Variable costs**

The variable cost per year can increase by £574,032 (W3), or £0.88 per unit. This represents an increase of £574,032/2,000,000 = **28.7%**.

5   **Cost of capital**

We need to calculate the IRR. Let us try discount rates of 15% and 20%.

Year	Net cash flow	Discount factor	PV	Discount factor	PV
	£'000	15%	£'000	20%	£'000
0	(7,000)	0.870	(6,090)	0.833	(5,831)
1	4,500	0.756	3,402	0.694	3,123
2	4,500	0.658	2,961	0.579	2,606
			NPV = 273		NPV = (102)

IRR = 0.15 + [(273/(273 + 102)) × (0.20 − 0.15)] = 18.64%

The cost of capital can therefore increase by ((18.64 − 8)/8) = **133%** before the NPV becomes negative.

Question: sensitivity analysis

Nevers Ure Ltd is considering a project with the following 'most-likely' cash flows.

Year	Purchase of plant £	Running costs £	Savings £
0	(7,000)		
1		2,000	6,000
2		2,500	7,000

The cost of capital is 8%.

Required

Measure the sensitivity (in percentages) of the project to changes in the levels of expected costs and savings.

Answer

The **PVs of the cash flows** are as follows.

Year	Discount factor 8%	PV of plant cost £	PV of running costs £	PV of savings £	PV of net cash flow £
0	1.000	(7,000)			(7,000)
1	0.926		(1,852)	5,556	3,704
2	0.857		(2,143)	5,999	3,856
		(7,000)	(3,995)	11,555	560

The project has a **positive NPV** and would appear to be **worthwhile**. The **changes in cash flows** which would need to occur for the project to break even (NPV = 0) are as follows.

(a) Plant costs would need to increase by a PV of £560, that is by (560/7,000) × 100% = 8%
(b) Running costs would need to increase by a PV of £560, that is by (560/3,995) × 100% = 14%
(c) Savings would need to fall by a PV of £560, that is by (560/11,555) × 100% = 4.8%

Problems with this approach

2.29 (a) The method requires that **changes** in each key variable are **isolated** but management is more interested in the **combination** of the effects of changes in two or more key variables. Looking at factors in isolation is unrealistic since they are often interdependent.

(b) Sensitivity analysis does not examine the **probability** that any particular variation in costs or revenues might occur.

3 PROBABILITIES AND EXPECTED VALUES

3.1 Although the outcome of a decision may not be certain, there is some likelihood that probabilities could be assigned to the various possible outcomes from an analysis of previous experience.

Expected values

3.2 Where probabilities are assigned to different outcomes we can evaluate the worth of a decision as the **expected value**, or weighted average, of these outcomes. The principle is that when there are a number of alternative decisions, each with a range of possible outcomes, the optimum decision will be the one which gives the highest expected value.

3.3 EXAMPLE: EXPECTED VALUES

Suppose a manager has to choose between mutually exclusive options A and B, and the probable outcomes of each option are as follows.

	Option A			Option B	
Probability	Profit £		Probability	Profit £	
0.8	5,000		0.1	(2,000)	
0.2	6,000		0.2	5,000	
			0.6	7,000	
			0.1	8,000	

The expected value (EV) of profit of each option would be measured as follows.

Prob	Option A Profit £		EV of profit £	Prob	Option B Profit £		EV of profit £
0.8	×	5,000 =	4,000	0.1	×	(2,000) =	(200)
0.2	×	6,000 =	1,200	0.2	×	5,000 =	1,000
		EV =	5,200	0.6	×	7,000 =	4,200
				0.1	×	8,000 =	800
						EV =	5,800

In this example, since it offers a higher EV of profit, option B would be selected in preference to A, unless further risk analysis is carried out.

Question: EVs

A manager has to choose between mutually exclusive options C and D and the probable outcomes of each option are as follows.

	Option C		Option D	
Probability	Cost £	Probability	Cost £
0.29	15,000	0.03	14,000
0.54	20,000	0.30	17,000
0.17	30,000	0.35	21,000
		0.32	24,000

Both options will produce an income of £30,000. Which should be chosen?

Answer

Option C. Do the workings yourself in the way illustrated above. Note that the probabilities are for *costs* not profits.

Limitations of expected values

Exam focus point

The use of expected values as a guide to decision making was examined in December 2003.

3.4 The preference for B over A on the basis of expected value is marred by the fact that A's **worst possible** outcome is a profit of £5,000, whereas B might incur a loss of £2,000 (although there is a 70% chance that profits would be £7,000 or more, which would be more than the best profits from option A).

3.5 Since the decision must be made **once only** between A and B, the expected value of profit (which is **merely a weighted average** of all possible outcomes) has severe limitations as a decision rule by which to judge preference. The expected value will never actually occur.

3.6   Expected values are used to support a **risk-neutral attitude**. A risk-neutral decision maker will ignore any variability in the range of possible outcomes and be concerned only with the expected value of outcomes.

3.7   Expected values are more valuable as a guide to decision making where they refer to outcomes which will occur **many times over**. Examples would include the probability that so many customers per day will buy a can of baked beans, the probability that a customer services assistant will receive so many phone calls per hour, and so on.

EVs and elementary risk analysis

3.8   Where some analysis of risk is required when probabilities have been assigned to various outcomes, an **elementary**, but extremely **useful**, form of risk analysis is the **worst possible/best possible technique**.

3.9   EXAMPLE: RISK ANALYSIS

Skiver Ltd has budgeted the following results for the coming year.

Sales Units	Probability	EV of Sales Units
30,000	0.3	9,000
40,000	0.4	16,000
50,000	0.3	15,000
		40,000

The budgeted sales price is £10 per unit, and the expected cost of materials is as follows.

Cost per unit of output £	Probability	EV
4	0.2	0.8
6	0.6	3.6
8	0.2	1.6
		6.0

Materials are the only variable cost. All other costs are fixed and are budgeted at £100,000.

(a)   The **expected value** of profit is £60,000.

	£
Sales (EV 40,000 units) at £10 each	400,000
Variable costs (40,000 × £6)	240,000
Contribution	160,000
Fixed costs	100,000
Profit	60,000

(b)   However, the **worst possible outcome** would be sales of 30,000 units and material costs of £8 per unit.

    (i)   If sales are only 30,000 units, the total contribution would be:

        (1)   £180,000 at a material cost of £4 (contribution £6 per unit);
        (2)   £120,000 at a material cost of £6 (contribution £4 per unit);
        (3)   £60,000 at a material cost of £8 (contribution £2 per unit).

    Since there is a 20% chance that materials will cost £8, there is a 20% chance of making a loss, given fixed costs of £100,000. This applies only if sales are 30,000 units.

(ii) If materials cost £8 per unit, there would be a loss at sales volumes of both 30,000 and 40,000 units. The chance that one or other of these events will occur is 14%, as calculated below.

Sales	*Probability*	*Material cost*	*Probability*	*Joint probabilities*
30,000 units	0.3	£8	0.2	0.06
40,000 units	0.4	£8	0.2	0.08
			Combined probabilities	0.14

(c) However there is also a chance that sales will be 50,000 units and material will cost £4, so that contribution would be £300,000 in total and profits £200,000. This is the **best possible outcome** and it has a $0.3 \times 0.2 = 0.06$ or 6% probability of occurring.

More complex risk analysis and cumulative probability tables

Exam focus point

Candidates in the December 2003 exam had to draw up a cumulative probability table.

3.10 As we have seen, EVs can be used to compare two or more mutually exclusive alternatives. The alternative with the most favourable EV of profit or cost would normally be preferred. However, alternatives can also be compared by looking at the **spread of possible outcomes**, and the probabilities that they will occur. The technique of drawing up **cumulative probability tables** might be helpful, as the following example shows.

3.11 EXAMPLE: CUMULATIVE PROBABILITY

QRS Ltd is reviewing the price that it charges for a major product line. Over the past three years the product has had sales averaging 48,000 units per year at a standard selling price of £5.25. Costs have been rising steadily over the past year and the company is considering raising this price to £5.75 or £6.25. The sales manager has produced the following schedule to assist with the decision.

Price	£5.75	£6.25
Estimates of demand		
Pessimistic estimate (probability 0.25)	35,000	10,000
Most likely estimate (probability 0.60)	40,000	20,000
Optimistic estimate (probability 0.15)	50,000	40,000

Currently the unit cost is estimated at £5.00, analysed as follows.

	£
Direct material	2.50
Direct labour	1.00
Variable overhead	1.00
Fixed overhead	0.50
	5.00

The cost accountant considers that the most likely value for unit variable cost over the next year is £4.90 (probability 0.75) but that it could be as high as £5.20 (probability 0.15) and it might even be as low as £4.75 (probability 0.10). Total fixed costs are currently £24,000 pa but it is estimated that the total for the ensuing year will be £25,000 with a probability of 0.2, £27,000 with a probability of 0.6 or £30,000 with a probability of 0.2.

(Demand quantities, unit costs and fixed costs can be assumed to be statistically independent.)

Required

Analyse the foregoing information in a way which you consider will assist management with the problem, give your views on the situation and advise on the new selling price. Calculate the expected level of profit that would follow from the selling price that you recommend.

3.12 DISCUSSION AND SOLUTION

In this example, there are two mutually exclusive options, a price of £5.75 and a price of £6.25. Sales demand is uncertain, but would vary with price. Unit contribution and total contribution depend on sales price and sales volume, but total fixed costs are common to both options. Clearly, it makes sense to begin looking at EVs of contribution and then to think about fixed costs and profits later.

(a) A table of probabilities can be set out for each alternative, and an EV calculated, as follows.

(i) **Price £5.75**

Sales demand Units	Prob	Variable cost per unit £	Prob	Unit cont'n £	Total cont'n £'000	Joint prob	EV of cont'n £'000
35,000	0.25	5.20	0.15	0.55	19.25	0.0375	0.722
		4.90	0.75	0.85	29.75	0.1875	5.578
		4.75	0.10	1.00	35.00	0.0250	0.875
40,000	0.60	5.20	0.15	0.55	22.00	0.0900	1.980
		4.90	0.75	0.85	34.00	0.4500	15.300
		4.75	0.10	1.00	40.00	0.0600	2.400
50,000	0.15	5.20	0.15	0.55	27.50	0.0225	0.619
		4.90	0.75	0.85	42.50	0.1125	4.781
		4.75	0.10	1.00	50.00	0.0150	0.750
				EV of contribution			33.005

The EV of contribution at a price of £5.75 is £33,005. This EV could have been calculated more quickly and simply by calculating the EV of sales demand and the EV of variable cost, but an extended table of probabilities will help the risk analysis when the two alternative selling prices are compared.

(ii) **Price £6.25**

Sales demand Units	Prob	Variable cost per unit £	Prob	Unit cont'n £	Total cont'n £'000	Joint prob	EV of cont'n £000
10,000	0.25	5.20	0.15	1.05	10.50	0.0375	0.394
		4.90	0.75	1.35	13.50	0.1875	2.531
		4.75	0.10	1.50	15.00	0.0250	0.375
20,000	0.60	5.20	0.15	1.05	21.00	0.0900	1.890
		4.90	0.75	1.35	27.00	0.4500	12.150
		4.75	0.10	1.50	30.00	0.0600	1.800
40,000	0.15	5.20	0.15	1.05	42.00	0.0225	0.945
		4.90	0.75	1.35	54.00	0.1125	6.075
		4.75	0.10	1.50	60.00	0.0150	0.900
				EV of contribution			27.060

The EV of contribution at a price of £6.25 is £27,060.

(b) **Fixed costs**

The EV of fixed costs is £27,200.

Fixed costs	Probability	EV
£		£
25,000	0.2	5,000
27,000	0.6	16,200
30,000	0.2	6,000
		27,200

(c) **Conclusion**

On the basis of EVs alone, a price of £5.75 is preferable to a price of £6.25, since it offers an EV of contribution of £33,005 and so an EV of profit of £5,805; whereas a price of £6.25 offers an EV of contribution of only £27,060 and so an EV of loss of £140.

The disadvantages of point estimate probabilities

> **KEY TERM**
>
> A **point estimate probability** means an estimate of the probability of particular outcomes occurring.

3.13 In the previous example, there were point estimate probabilities for variable costs (£5.20 or £4.90 or £4.75) but in reality, the actual variable cost per unit might be any amount, from below £4.75 to above £5.20. Similarly, point estimate probabilities were given for period fixed costs (£25,000 or £27,000 or £30,000) but in reality, actual fixed costs might be **any amount between** about £25,000 and £30,000.

3.14 This is a disadvantage of using point estimate probabilities: they can be **unrealistic**, and can only be an **approximation** of the risk and uncertainty in estimates.

The advantages of point estimate probabilities

3.15 In spite of their possible disadvantages, point estimate probabilities can be very helpful for a decision maker.

   (a) They provide some estimate of risk, which is probably **better than nothing**.

   (b) If there are **enough** point estimates they are likely to be a **reasonably good** approximation of a continuous probability distribution.

   (c) Alternatively, it can be **assumed** that point estimate probabilities **represent a range** of values, so that if we had the probabilities for variable cost per unit, say, of £5.20, £4.90, and £4.75 we could assume that those actually represent probabilities for the ranges, say, £5.05 to £5.30, and £4.82 to £5.04 and £4.70 to £4.81.

   (d) The estimates are relatively easy to make, and so are **more practical** than attempting continuous probability distribution estimates.

Question: probabilities

In examination questions you are usually **told** the probability of various outcomes. Where would this information come from in practice and how reliable would you expect it to be?

Answer

Probabilities can be calculated from historical records. For example if your train was late four mornings out of five last week there is an 80% chance of your train being late. Obviously the larger the sample

BPP
PROFESSIONAL EDUCATION

the more reliable the information is likely to be - you may live on a particularly bad line, or there may have been engineering works last week.

As a further exercise, use your bank statements for the last year or so to calculate the probability that you will have over, say, £500 in the bank on the 20th day of a month. (Choose another amount if £500 is unrealistically high or low.)

---

4 DECISION TREES

> ## KEY TERM
>
> A **decision tree** is a pictorial method of showing a sequence of interrelated decisions and their expected outcomes. They can incorporate both the probabilities of, and values of, expected outcomes.

4.1 A probability problem such as 'what is the probability of throwing a six with one throw of a die?' is fairly straightforward and can be solved using the basic principles of probability.

More complex probability questions, although solvable using the basic principles, require a clear logical approach to ensure that all possible choices and outcomes of a decision are taken into consideration. **Decision trees** are a useful means of interpreting such probability problems.

4.2 Exactly how does the use of a decision tree permit a clear and logical approach?

- All the possible **choices** that can be made are shown as **branches** on the tree.
- All the possible **outcomes** of each choice are shown as **subsidiary branches** on the tree.

Constructing a decision tree

4.3 There are two stages in preparing a decision tree.

- Drawing the tree itself to show all the choices and outcomes
- Putting in the numbers (the probabilities, outcome values and EVs)

4.4 Every **decision tree starts** from a **decision point** with the **decision options** that are currently being considered.

(a) It helps to identify the **decision point**, and any subsequent decision points in the tree, with a symbol. Here, we shall use a **square shape**.

(b) There should be a **line**, or **branch**, for each **option** or **alternative**.

4.5 **It is conventional to draw decision trees from left to right**, and so a decision tree will start as follows.

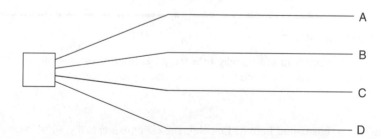

The **square** is the **decision point**, and A, B, C and D represent **four alternatives** from which a choice must be made (such as buy a new machine with cash, hire a machine, continue to use existing machine, raise a loan to buy a machine).

4.6 **If the outcome from any choice is certain, the branch of the decision tree for that alternative is complete.**

If the outcome of a particular choice is uncertain, the various possible outcomes must be shown.

4.7 We show the various possible outcomes on a decision tree by inserting an **outcome point** on the **branch** of the tree. Each possible outcome is then shown as a **subsidiary branch**, coming out from the outcome point. The probability of each outcome occurring should be written on to the branch of the tree which represents that outcome.

4.8 To distinguish decision points from outcome points, **a circle will be used as the symbol for an outcome point**.

In the example above, there are two choices facing the decision-maker, A and B. The outcome if A is chosen is known with certainty, but if B is chosen, there are two possible outcomes, high sales (0.6 probability) or low sales (0.4 probability).

4.9 **When several outcomes are possible, it is usually simpler to show two or more stages of outcome points on the decision tree.**

4.10 EXAMPLE: SEVERAL POSSIBLE OUTCOMES

A company can choose to launch a new product XYZ or not. If the product is launched, expected sales and expected unit costs might be as follows.

Sales		Unit costs	
Units	Probability	£	Probability
10,000	0.8	6	0.7
15,000	0.2	8	0.3

(a) The decision tree could be drawn as follows.

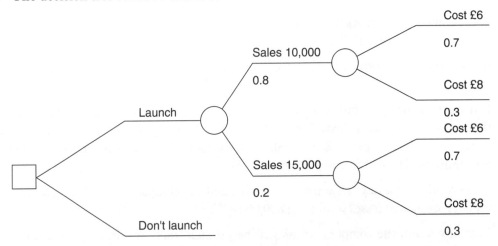

(b)   The layout shown above will usually be easier to use than the alternative way of drawing the tree, which is as follows.

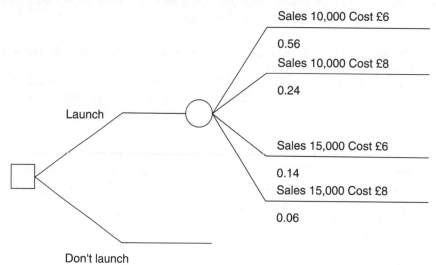

4.11   Sometimes, a **decision taken now** will lead to **other decisions to be taken in the future.** When this situation arises, the decision tree can be drawn as a **two-stage tree**, as follows.

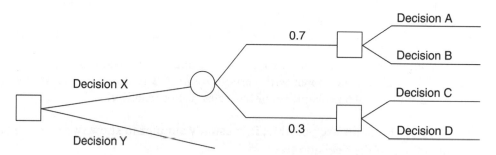

In this tree, either a choice between A and B or else a choice between C and D will be made, depending on the outcome which occurs after choosing X.

4.12   The decision tree should be in **chronological order** from **left to right**. When there are two-stage decision trees, the first decision in time should be drawn on the left.

4.13   EXAMPLE: A DECISION TREE

Beethoven Ltd has a new wonder product, the vylin, of which it expects great things. At the moment the company has two courses of action open to it, to test market the product or abandon it.

If the company test markets it, the cost will be £100,000 and the market response could be positive or negative with probabilities of 0.60 and 0.40.

If the response is positive the company could either abandon the product or market it full scale.

If it markets the vylin full scale, the outcome might be low, medium or high demand, and the respective net gains/(losses) would be (200), 200 or 1,000 in units of £1,000 (the result could range from a net loss of £200,000 to a gain of £1,000,000). These outcomes have probabilities of 0.20, 0.50 and 0.30 respectively.

If the result of the test marketing is negative and the company goes ahead and markets the product, estimated losses would be £600,000.

If, at any point, the company abandons the product, there would be a net gain of £50,000 from the sale of scrap. All the financial values have been discounted to the present.

(a) Draw a decision tree.

(b) Include figures for cost, loss or profit on the appropriate branches of the tree.

4.14 SOLUTION

The starting point for the tree is to **establish what decision has to be made now**. What are the options?

(a) To test market

(b) To abandon

The outcome of the 'abandon' option is known with certainty. There are two possible outcomes of the option to test market, positive response and negative response.

Depending on the outcome of the test marketing, another decision will then be made, to abandon the product or to go ahead.

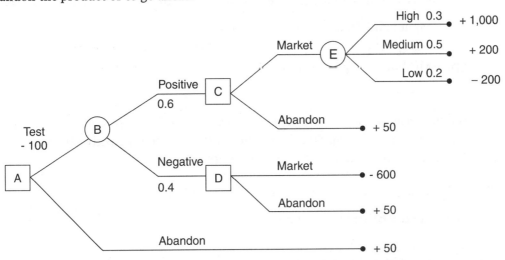

ATTENTION!

In an examination, remember to draw decision trees (and *all* diagrams) neatly, using a sharp pencil and ruler. Remember also to label decision points and branches as clearly as possible.

Evaluating the decision with a decision tree

4.15 The EV of each decision option can be evaluated, using the decision tree to help with keeping the logic properly sorted out. The basic rules are as follows.

(a) We start on the **right hand side** of the tree and **work back** towards the left hand side and the current decision under consideration. This is sometimes known as the **'rollback' technique**.

(b) Working from **right to left**, we calculate the **EV of revenue, cost, contribution or profit** at each outcome point on the tree.

4.16 In the above example, the right-hand-most outcome point is point E, and the EV is as follows.

	Profit	Probability	
	£'000		£'000
High	1,000	0.3	300
Medium	200	0.5	100
Low	(200)	0.2	(40)
		EV	360

This is the EV of the decision to market the product if the test shows positive response. It may help you to write the EV on the decision tree itself, at the appropriate outcome point (point E).

4.17 (a) **At decision point C,** the **choice** is as follows.

(i) Market, EV = + 360 (the EV at point E)
(ii) Abandon, value = + 50

The choice would be to market the product, and so the EV at decision point C is +360.

(b) **At decision point D,** the **choice** is as follows.

(i) Market, value = – 600
(ii) Abandon, value = +50

The choice would be to abandon, and so the EV at decision point D is +50.

The second stage decisions have therefore been made. If the original decision is to test market, the company will market the product if the test shows positive customer response, and will abandon the product if the test results are negative.

4.18 The evaluation of the decision tree is completed as follows.

(a) **Calculate the EV at outcome point B.**

```
    0.6 × 360   (EV at C)
+   0.4 ×  50   (EV at D)
=   216 +  20 = 236.
```

(b) **Compare the options at point A,** which are as follows.

(i) Test: EV = EV at B minus test marketing cost = 236 – 100 = 136
(ii) Abandon: Value = 50

The choice would be to test market the product, because it has a **higher EV of profit.**

Question: simple decision tree

Interpret the following diagram in words and figures.

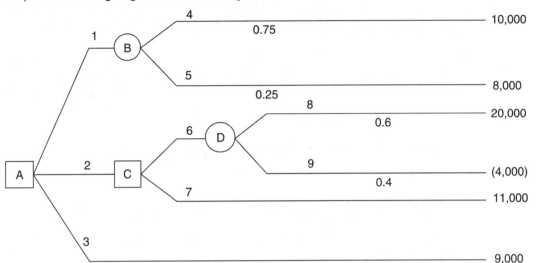

Answer

The square is a point at which a decision has to be made – here a choice between options 1, 2 and 3. A circle represents an event whose outcome is uncertain. Doubtful outcomes (4, 5, 8, 9) have probabilities assigned to them. To reach the decisions the various outcomes must be evaluated using expected values.

Point B: $(0.75 \times 10,000) + (0.25 \times 8,000) = 9,500$

Point D: $(0.6 \times 20,000) + (0.4 \times (4,000)) = 10,400$

Point C: Choice between 10,400 and 11,000

Point A: Choice between B (9,500), C (10,400 or 11,000) and choice 3 (9,000).

If we are trying to maximise the figure, option 2 and then option 7 are chosen to give 11,000.

If we are trying to minimise it, choice 3 is the one to go for.

4.19   Evaluating decisions by using **decision trees has a number of limitations.**

(a)   The time value of money may not be taken into account.

(b)   Decision trees are not very suitable for use in complex situations.

(c)   The outcome with the highest EV may have the greatest risks attached to it. Managers may be reluctant to take risks which may lead to losses.

(d)   The probabilities associated with different branches of the 'tree' are likely to be estimates, and possibly unreliable or inaccurate.

Exam focus point

A typical examination question on decision trees might require candidates to do the following.

*   Draw a decision tree for a problem given in the examination scenario
*   Analyse the tree
*   Comment on any limitations on evaluating decisions using decision trees

Alternatively, a decision tree may be provided and candidates could be required to explain (with calculations and logic) which decisions should be taken at various points and why.

Question: more complex decision tree

A software company has just won a contract worth £80,000 if it delivers a successful product on time, but only £40,000 if it is late. It faces the problem now of whether to produce the work in-house or to sub-contract it. To sub-contract the work would cost £50,000, but the local sub-contractor is so fast and reliable as to make it certain that successful software is produced on time.

If the work is produced in-house the cost would be only £20,000 but, based on past experience, would have only a 90% chance of being successful. In the event of the software *not* being successful, there would be insufficient time to rewrite the whole package internally, but there would still be the options of either a 'late rejection' of the contract (at a further cost of £10,000) or of 'late sub-contracting' the work on the same terms as before. With this late start the local sub-contractor is estimated to have only a 50/50 chance of producing the work on time or of producing it late. In this case the sub-contractor still has to be paid £50,000, regardless of whether he meets the deadline or not.

Required

(a) Draw a decision tree for the software company, using squares for decision points and circles for outcome (chance) points, including all relevant data on the diagram.

(b) Calculate expected values as appropriate and recommend a course of action to the software company with reasons.

Answer

(a) All values in £'000

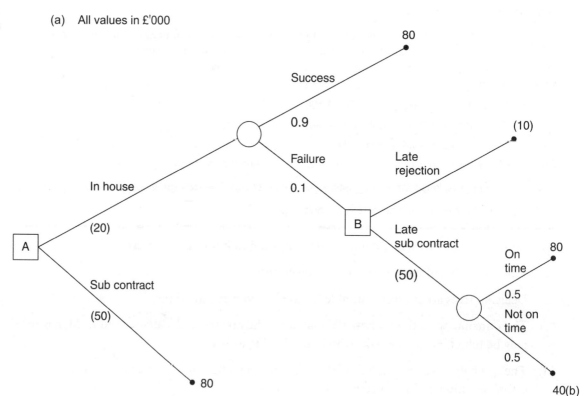

At decision point B

EV of late rejection = -10
EV of late sub-contract = (80 × 0.5) + (40 × 0.5) - 50 = 10
The optimum strategy at B is therefore to subcontract with EV = 10.

At decision point A

EV of sub-contract = 80 - 50 = 30
EV of in-house = (80 × 0.9) + (10* × 0.1) - 20 = 53
The optimum strategy at A is therefore to produce in-house with EV = 53.

*This is the optimum EV at decision point B.

Conclusions

The decisions which will maximise expected profits are to attempt initially to produce in-house and if this fails to sub-contract. The expected profit is £53,000.

Assuming that the probabilities have been correctly estimated, the company has a 90% chance of making a profit of £60,000, a 5% chance of making £10,000 and a 5% chance of making a £30,000 loss. If the company is not willing to risk making a loss, the initial option of subcontracting should be taken since this offers a guaranteed profit of £30,000.

Sensitivity analysis

4.20 In the previous question, the decision has been based on a 90% in-house success rate. Suppose a key member of the software development project team leaves the company, which puts into doubt the high success rate. The company might like to know the sensitivity of the decision to changes in the probability of in-house success from 90%. In other words, **by how much can this probability change before the decision changes.**

4.21 **Approach**

Step 1. Let the factor which is to vary be X.

Step 2. Replace the value of the factor in the original calculation with X.

Step 3. Rework the calculation algebraically to determine the value of X if the decision were to be reversed.

4.22 Let's apply this approach to the software example.

Let the probability of in-house success be X.
∴ The probability of failure = $1 - X$
EV at decision point B is still 10

Revised situation at decision point A

EV of subcontract = 30
EV of in-house = $80X + 10(1 - X) - 20 = 70X - 10$

The decision to produce in-house will therefore change if $70X - 10$ is less than 30 (the EV of the decision to subcontract).

ie if $70X - 10 < 30$
$70X < 40$
$X < 40/70$

∴ If the probability of in-house success is less than 40/70, the company should use the subcontractor.

5 PERFECT INFORMATION

5.1 Whenever a decision is made whose outcome is uncertain, there will always be some **doubt that the correct decision has been taken.** If a decision is based on selecting the option with the highest EV of profit, it can be assumed that in the long run (that is, with a sufficient repetition of the outcomes), the decision option so selected will give the highest average profit. But if the decision involves a once-only outcome, there will be a big risk that the outcome will be worse than the EV, and that in retrospect it will eventually be seen that the wrong decision was taken.

5.2 The uncertainty about the future outcome from taking a decision can sometimes be reduced by **obtaining more information** first about what is likely to happen. Information can be obtained from various sources, such as market research surveys, other surveys or questionnaires, conducting a pilot test or building a prototype model.

5.3   We can categorise information depending upon how reliable it is likely to be for predicting the future and hence for helping managers to make better decisions.

The value of perfect information

> ### KEY TERM
>
> **Perfect information** removes *all* doubt and uncertainty from a decision, and it would enable managers to make decisions with complete confidence that they have selected the most profitable course of action.

5.4   We can estimate a value of perfect information, based on expected values (EVs) as follows.

Step 1.   If we **do not have perfect information** and we must choose between two or more decision options, we would select the decision option which offers the **highest EV of profit**. This option will not be the best decision under all circumstances. There will be some probability that what was really the best option will not have been selected, given the way actual events turn out.

Step 2.   **With perfect information,** the **best decision option** will always be selected. Just what the profits from the decision will be must depend on the future circumstances which are predicted by the information; nevertheless, the EV of profit with perfect information should be higher than the EV of profit without the information.

Step 3.   The **value** of perfect information is the **difference** between these two EVs.

5.5   EXAMPLE: THE VALUE OF PERFECT INFORMATION

The management of Ivor Ore Ltd must choose whether to go ahead with either of two mutually exclusive projects, A and B. The expected profits are as follows.

	Profit if there is strong demand	*Profit/(loss) if there is weak demand*
Option A	£4,000	£(1,000)
Option B	£1,500	£500
Probability of demand	0.3	0.7

(a)   What would be the decision, based on expected values, if no information about demand were available?

(b)   What is the value of perfect information about demand?

5.6   SOLUTION

Step 1.   If there were **no information** to help with the decision, the project with the higher EV of profit would be selected.

Probability	Project A		Project B	
	Profit	*EV*	*Profit*	*EV*
	£	£	£	£
0.3	4,000	1,200	1,500	450
0.7	(1,000)	(700)	500	350
		500		800

Project B would be selected, and this is clearly the better option if demand turns out to be weak. However, if demand were to turn out to be strong, project A would be more profitable. There is a 30% chance that this could happen.

Step 2. **Perfect information** will indicate for certain whether demand will be weak or strong. If demand is forecast 'weak' project B would be selected. If demand is forecast 'strong', project A would be selected, and perfect information would improve the profit from £1,500, which would have been earned by selecting B, to £4,000.

Forecast demand	Probability	Project chosen	Profit £	EV of profit £
Weak	0.7	B	500	350
Strong	0.3	A	4,000	1,200
EV of profit with perfect information				1,550

Step 3.

	£
EV of profit without perfect information (that is, if project B is hosen)	800
EV of profit with perfect information	1,550
Value of perfect information	750

Provided the information does not cost more than £750 to collect, it would be worth having.

Question: perfect information

Watt Lovell Ltd must decide at what level to market a new product, the urk. The urk can be sold nationally, within a single sales region (where demand is likely to be relatively strong) or within a single area. The decision is complicated by uncertainty about the general strength of consumer demand for the product, and the following conditional profit table has been constructed.

			Demand	
		Weak £	Moderate £	Strong £
Market	nationally (A)	(4,000)	2,000	10,000
	in one region (B)	0	3,500	4,000
	in one area (C)	1,000	1,500	2,000
Probability		0.3	0.5	0.2

(a) What should the decision be, based on EVs of profit?
(b) What would be the value of perfect information about the state of demand?

Answer

(a) Without perfect information, the option with the highest EV of profit will be chosen.

	Option A (National)		Option B (Regional)		Option C (Area)	
Probability	Profit	EV	Profit	EV	Profit	EV
	£	£	£	£	£	£
0.3	(4,000)	(1,200)	0	0	1,000	300
0.5	2,000	1,000	3,500	1,750	1,500	750
0.2	10,000	2,000	4,000	800	2,000	400
		1,800		2,550		1,450

Marketing regionally (option B) has the highest EV of profit, and would be selected.

(b) If perfect information about the state of consumer demand were available, option A would be preferred if the forecast demand is strong and option C if the forecast demand is weak.

Demand	Probability	Choice	Profit £	EV of profit £
Weak	0.3	C	1,000	300
Moderate	0.5	B	3,500	1,750
Strong	0.2	A	10,000	2,000
EV of profit with perfect information				4,050
EV of profit, selecting option B				2,550
Value of perfect information				1,500

Part E: Decision making

Chapter roundup

- Management accounting directs its attention towards the **future** and the future is **uncertain**. For this reason a number of methods of taking **uncertainty** and **risk** into consideration have evolved.

- Decision makers might be **risk seekers, risk averse** or **risk neutral.**

- Approaches like **conservatism, worst/most likely/best outcome estimates** or **maximax/ maximin/minimax/minimin** are often used intuitively in practice. It may be that psychological factors (feelings of safety on the one hand or exhilaration at the risk on the other) need to be taken into account.

- **Sensitivity analysis** can be used in any situation so long as the relationships between the key variables can be established. Typically this involves changing the value of a variable and seeing how the results are affected.

- **Expected values** indicate what an outcome is likely to be in the long term with repetition. Fortunately, many business transactions do occur over and over again.

- A useful form of elementary **risk analysis** is the **worst possible/best possible technique.**

- **Cumulative probability tables** can be used for more complex risk analysis.

- **Decision trees** should be drawn from left to right using different symbols to distinguish decision points and outcome points. They are evaluated by 'rolling back' from right to left, calculating the EVs of each outcome point to enable the decision(s) to be made.

- Information is unlikely to be **perfect** in practice unless it is so general as to be of limited value. A theoretical value can be placed on it, however.

Quick quiz

1   *Match the terms to the correct definitions.*

Terms

(a)   Risk seeker
(b)   Risk neutral
(c)   Risk averse

Definitions

1   A decision maker concerned with what will be the most likely outcome

2   A decision maker interested in the best outcomes no matter how small the chance that they may occur

3   A decision maker who acts on the assumption that the worst outcome might occur

2   *Fill in the blanks.*

(a)   Maximin decision rule: choosing the alternative that .... the ....

(b)   Minimax decision rule: choosing the alternative that .... the ....

(c)   Maximax decision rule: choosing the alternative that .... the ....

(d)   Minimin decision rule: choosing the alternative that .... the ....

3   A project requires an initial investment of £1,780,000. Its NPV at 10% is £545,000. What is the percentage change in the investment at which the organisation will be indifferent between accepting and rejecting the project?

4   How is expected value calculated?

A Σpx
B $p\Sigma x$
C $e\Sigma px$
D $x\Sigma p$

5   (a)   A decision point in a decision tree is indicated by a square. *True or false?*

     (b)   Decision tree analysis requires one to work chronologically from right to left. *True or false?*

6   *Fill in the blanks.*

     Value of perfect information = ………………………… minus …………………………

Answers to quick quiz

1   (a) 2; (b) 1; (c) 3

2   (a)   Maximise, minimim profits
     (b)   Minimise, maximum costs/losses
     (c)   Maximise, maximum profits
     (d)   Minimise, minimum costs/losses

3   Initial investment can rise by £545,000 before breakeven point is reached and so it can increase by $(545/1,780) \times 100\% = 31\%$

4   A

5   (a)   True
     (b)   False

6   Value of perfect information = EV of profit with perfect information – EV of profit without perfect information

---

Now try the question below from the Exam Question Bank

Number	Level	Marks	Time
22	Exam	20	36 mins

Chapter 25

TRANSFER PRICING

Introduction

This chapter looks at transfer pricing, which is a system of **charging other divisions of your organisation when you provide them with your division's goods or services.**

In a **divisionalised organisation structure** of any kind, if one division does work that is used by another division, transfer pricing may be required. Do not be misled by the term 'price': there is **not necessarily any suggestion of profit** as there usually is with an external selling price. But as we shall see, transfer pricing is particularly appropriate where divisions are designated as **profit centres**.

Study guide

Section 27 – Transfer pricing I

- Describe the organisation structure in which transfer pricing may be required

- Explain divisional autonomy, divisional performance measurement and corporate profit maximisation and their link with transfer pricing

- Formulate the 'general rule' for transfer pricing and explain its application

- Describe, illustrate and evaluate the use of market price as the transfer price

- Assess where an adjusted market price will be appropriate for transfer business

- Assess the impact of market price methods on divisional autonomy, performance measurement and corporate profit maximisation

- Calculate an appropriate transfer price from given data

Section 28 – Transfer pricing II

- Describe the alternative cost based approaches to transfer pricing

- Identify the circumstances in which marginal cost should be used as the transfer price and determine its impact on divisional autonomy, performance measurement and corporate profit maximisation

- Illustrate methods by which a share of fixed costs may be included in the transfer price

- Comment on these methods and their impact on divisional autonomy, performance measurement and corporate profit maximisation

- Discuss the advantages which may be claimed for the use of standard cost rather than actual cost when setting transfer prices

- Explain the relevance of opportunity cost in transfer pricing

- List the information which must be centrally available in order that the profit-maximising transfer policy may be implemented between divisions where intermediate products are in short supply

- Illustrate the formulation of the quantitative model for a range of limiting factors from which the corporate profit maximising transfer policy may be calculated

- Analyse the concept of shadow price in setting transfer prices for intermediate products that are in short supply

- Illustrate the corporate maximising transfer policy where a single intermediate resource is in short supply and a limited external source is available and explain the information which must be available centrally in order that the transfer policy may be formulated

- Explain and demonstrate the issues that require consideration when setting transfer prices in multinational companies.

Exam guide

Expect entire questions, written or computational, on transfer pricing.

The issues covered in this chapter are useful background to the following Oxford Brookes degree Research and Analysis Projects.

- Topic 1, which requires you to analyse the efficiency and/or effectiveness of a management accounting technique in an organisational setting

- Topic 10, which requires you to analyse how management accounting techniques are used to support decision making in organisations

1   TRANSFER PRICING: BASIC PRINCIPLES

Divisionalisation

1.1   In general a large organisation can be **structured in one or two ways: functionally** (all activities of a similar type within a company, such as production, sales, research, are placed under the control of the appropriate departmental head) or **divisionally** (split into divisions in accordance with the products which are made or services which are provided).

1.2   Divisional managers are therefore responsible for all operations (production, sales and so on) relating to their product, the functional structure being applied to each division. It is quite possible, of course, that only part of a company is divisionalised and activities such as administration are structured centrally on a functional basis with the responsibility of providing services to *all* divisions.

Decentralisation

1.3 In general, a **divisional structure will lead to decentralisation** of the decision-making process and divisional managers may have the freedom to set selling prices, choose suppliers, make product mix and output decisions and so on. Decentralisation is, however, a matter of degree, depending on how much freedom divisional managers are given.

Advantages of divisionalisation

1.4 (a) Divisionalisation can **improve** the **quality of decisions** made because divisional managers (those taking the decisions) have good knowledge of local conditions and should therefore be able to make more informed judgements. Moreover, with the personal incentive to improve the division's performance, they ought to take decisions in the division's best interests.

(b) **Decisions should be taken more quickly** because information does not have to pass along the chain of command to and from top management. Decisions can be made on the spot by those who are familiar with the product lines and production processes and who are able to react to changes in local conditions quickly and efficiently.

(c) The authority to act to improve performance should **motivate divisional managers**.

(d) Divisional organisation **frees top management** from detailed involvement in day-to-day operations and allows them to devote more time to strategic planning.

(e) Divisions provide **valuable training grounds for future members of top management** by giving them experience of managerial skills in a less complex environment than that faced by top management.

(f) In a large business organisation, the **central head office will not have the management resources or skills to direct operations closely enough itself**. Some authority must be delegated to local operational managers.

Disadvantages of divisionalisation

1.5 (a) A danger with divisional accounting is that the **business organisation will divide into a number of self-interested segments, each acting at times against the wishes and interests of other segments**. Decisions might be taken by a divisional manager in the best interests of his own part of the business, but against the best interest of other divisions and possibly against the interests of the organisation as a whole.

A task of **head office** is therefore to try to **prevent dysfunctional decision making** by individual divisional managers. To do this, head office must reserve some power and authority for itself so that divisional managers cannot be allowed to make entirely independent decisions. A **balance** ought to be kept **between decentralisation** of authority to provide incentives and motivation, **and retaining centralised authority** to ensure that the organisation's divisions are all working towards the same target, the benefit of the organisation as a whole (in other words, **retaining goal congruence** among the organisation's separate divisions).

(b) It is claimed that the **costs of activities that are common** to all divisions such as running the accounting department **may be greater** for a divisionalised structure than for a centralised structure.

(c) **Top management**, by delegating decision making to divisional managers, may **lose control** since they are not aware of what is going on in the organisation as a whole.

(With a good system of performance evaluation and appropriate control information, however, top management should be able to control operations just as effectively.)

Exam focus point

The advantages and disadvantages of divisionalisation appeared in an optional question of the June 2002 paper. Transfer pricing also featured in the June 2004 compulsory question 1.

When transfer pricing is required

1.6 Where there are transfers of goods or services between divisions of a divisionalised organisation, the **transfers could be made 'free' or 'as a favour'** to the division receiving the benefit. For example, if a garage and car showroom has two divisions, one for car repairs and servicing and the other for car sales, the servicing division will be required to service cars before they are sold and delivered to customers. There is no requirement for this service work to be charged for: the servicing division could do its work for the car sales division without making any record of the work done.

1.7 Unless the cost or value of such work is recorded, however, management cannot keep a proper check on the amount of resources (like labour time) being used up on new car servicing. It is necessary for **control purposes** that some **record** of the inter-divisional services should be kept, and one way of doing this is **through the accounting system**. Inter-divisional work can be given a cost or charge: a transfer price.

KEY TERM

A **transfer price** is the price at which goods or services are transferred from one department to another, or from one member of a group to another.

---

2 THREE PROBLEMS WITH TRANSFER PRICING

Divisional autonomy

2.1 Transfer prices are particularly appropriate for **profit centres** because if one profit centre does work for another the size of the transfer price will affect the costs of one profit centre and the revenues of another.

2.2 However, a danger with profit centre accounting is that the business organisation will divide into a number of **self-interested segments,** each acting at times against the wishes and interests of other segments. Decisions might be taken by a profit centre manager in the best interests of his own part of the business, but against the best interests of other profit centres and possibly the organisation as a whole.

2.3 A task of head office is therefore to try to prevent dysfunctional decision making by individual profit centres. To do this, it must reserve some power and authority for itself and so profit centres **cannot** be allowed to make entirely **autonomous decisions**.

2.4 Just how much authority head office decides to keep for itself will vary according to individual circumstances. A **balance** ought to be kept between **divisional autonomy** to provide incentives and motivation, and retaining **centralised authority** to ensure that the organisation's profit centres are all working towards the same target, the benefit of the organisation as a whole (in other words, retaining **goal congruence** among the organisation's separate divisions).

Divisional performance measurement

2.5 Profit centre managers tend to put their own profit **performance** above everything else. Since profit centre performance is measured according to the profit they earn, no profit centre will want to do work for another and incur costs without being paid for it. Consequently, profit centre managers are likely to dispute the size of transfer prices with each other, or disagree about whether one profit centre should do work for another or not. Transfer prices **affect behaviour and decisions** by profit centre managers.

Corporate profit maximisation

2.6 When there are disagreements about how much work should be transferred between divisions, and how many sales the division should make to the external market, there is presumably a **profit-maximising** level of output and sales for the organisation as a whole. However, unless each profit centre also maximises its own profit at this same level of output, there will be inter-divisional disagreements about output levels and the profit-maximising output will not be achieved.

The ideal solution

2.7 Ideally a transfer price should be set at a level that overcomes these problems.

(a) The transfer price should provide an 'artificial' selling price that enables the transferring division to **earn a return** for its efforts, and the receiving division to **incur a cost** for benefits received.

(b) The transfer price should be set at a level that enables profit centre performance to be **measured 'commercially'** (that is, it should be a **fair** commercial price).

(c) The transfer price, if possible, should encourage profit centre managers to agree on the amount of goods and services to be transferred, which will also be at a level that is consistent with the organisation's aims as a whole such as **maximising company profits**.

In practice it is very difficult to achieve all three aims.

Question: problems with transfer pricing

(a) What do you understand by the term 'divisional autonomy'?

(b) What are the likely behavioural consequences of a head office continually imposing its own decisions on divisions?

Answer

(a) The term refers to the right of a division to govern itself, that is, the **freedom to make decisions without consulting a higher authority first and without interference from a higher body.**

(b) Decentralisation recognises that those closest to a job are the best equipped to say how it should be done and that people tend to perform to a higher standard if they are given responsibility. Centrally-imposed decisions are likely to **make managers feel that they do not really have any authority** and therefore that they **cannot be held responsible for performance**. They will therefore **make less effort** to perform well.

---

3 THE 'GENERAL RULE'

3.1 We shall see eventually that the **ideal transfer price** should **reflect the opportunity cost of sale to the supplying division and the opportunity cost to the buying division.** However, this 'general rule' requires extensive qualification, and you will need to work through the rest of this chapter before we return to it and you fully appreciate what it means. In the meantime, be content with Horngren's formulation of the problem:

'Is there an all-pervasive rule for transfer pricing that leads toward optimal decisions for the organisation as a whole? No. Why? Because the three criteria of goal congruence, managerial effort, and subunit autonomy must all be considered simultaneously.'

4 THE USE OF MARKET PRICE

Market price as the transfer price

4.1 If an **external market** price exists for transferred goods, profit centre managers will be aware of the price they could charge or the price they would have to pay for their goods on the external market, and so will **compare** this price with the internal transfer price.

4.2 EXAMPLE: TRANSFERRING GOODS AT MARKET VALUE

A company has two profit centres, A and B. Centre A sells half of its output on the open market and transfers the other half to B. Costs and external revenues in an accounting period are as follows.

	A £	B £	Total £
External sales	8,000	24,000	32,000
Costs of production	12,000	10,000	22,000
Company profit			10,000

Required

What are the consequences of setting a transfer price at market value?

4.3 SOLUTION

If the transfer price is at market price, A would be happy to sell the output to B for £8,000, which is what A would get by selling it externally instead of transferring it.

	A		B		Total
	£	£	£	£	£
Market sales		8,000		24,000	32,000
Transfer sales		8,000		-	
		16,000		24,000	
Transfer costs		-	8,000		
Own costs	12,000		10,000		22,000
		12,000		18,000	
Profit		4,000		6,000	10,000

The consequences, therefore, are as follows.

(a) A earns the same profit on transfers as on external sales. B must pay a commercial price for transferred goods, and both divisions will have their profit measured fairly.

(b) A will be indifferent about selling externally or transferring goods to B because the profit is the same on both types of transaction. B can therefore ask for and obtain as many units as it wants from A.

A **market-based** transfer price therefore seems to be the **ideal** transfer price.

Adjusted market price

4.4 However, internal transfers are often **cheaper** than external sales, with **savings** in selling and administration costs, bad debt risks and possibly transport/delivery costs. It would therefore seem reasonable for the buying division to expect a **discount** on the external market price.

4.5 The transfer price might be slightly less than market price, so that A and B could **share the cost savings** from internal transfers compared with external sales. It should be possible to reach agreement on this price and on output levels with a minimum of intervention from head office.

The merits of market value transfer prices

Divisional autonomy

4.6 In a decentralised company, divisional managers should have the **autonomy** to make output, selling and buying **decisions which appear to be in the best interests of the division's performance**. (If every division optimises its performance, the company as a whole must inevitably achieve optimal results.) Thus a **transferor division should be given the freedom to sell output on the open market,** rather than to transfer it within the company.

4.7 'Arm's length' transfer prices, which give profit centre managers the freedom to negotiate prices with other profit centres as though they were independent companies, will tend to result in a market-based transfer price.

Corporate profit maximisation

4.8 In most cases where the transfer price is at market price, **internal transfers** should be **expected**, because the **buying division** is likely to **benefit** from a better quality of service, greater flexibility, and dependability of supply. **Both divisions** may **benefit** from cheaper costs of administration, selling and transport. A market price as the transfer price would therefore **result in decisions which would be in the best interests of the company or group as a whole**.

Divisional performance measurement

4.9 Where a **market price exists,** but the **transfer price is a different amount** (say, at standard cost plus), divisional managers will **argue** about the volume of internal transfers.

4.10 For example, if division X is expected to sell output to division Y at a transfer price of £8 per unit when the open market price is £10, its manager will decide to sell all output on the open market. The manager of division Y would resent the loss of his cheap supply from X, and would be reluctant to buy on the open market. A wasteful situation would arise where X sells on the open market at £10, where Y buys at £10, so that administration, selling and distribution costs would have been saved if X had sold directly to Y at £10, the market price.

The disadvantages of market value transfer prices

4.11 Market value as a transfer price does have certain disadvantages.

(a) The market price may be a **temporary** one, induced by adverse **economic conditions**, or dumping, or the market price might depend on the volume of output supplied to the external market by the profit centre.

(b) A transfer price at market value might, under some circumstances, act as a disincentive to use up any **spare capacity** in the divisions. A price based on incremental cost, in contrast, might provide an incentive to use up the spare resources in order to provide a marginal contribution to profit.

(c) Many products **do not have an equivalent** market price so that the price of a similar, but not identical, product might have to be chosen. In such circumstances, the option to sell or buy on the open market does not really exist.

(d) The **external market** for the transferred item might be **imperfect**, so that if the transferring division wanted to sell more externally, it would have to **reduce** its price.

5 COST-BASED APPROACHES TO TRANSFER PRICING

5.1 Cost-based approaches to transfer pricing are often used in practice, because in practice the following conditions are common.

(a) There is **no external market** for the product that is being transferred.

(b) Alternatively, although there is an external market it is an **imperfect** one because the market price is affected by such factors as the amount that the company setting the transfer price supplies to it, or because there is only a limited external demand.

In either case there will not be a suitable market price upon which to base the transfer price.

Transfer prices based on full cost

5.2 Under this approach, the **full cost** (including fixed overheads absorbed) incurred by the supplying division in making the 'intermediate' product is charged to the receiving division. If a **full cost plus** approach is used a **profit margin** is also included in this transfer price.

> **KEY TERM**
>
> An **intermediate product** is one that is used as a component of another product, for example car headlights or food additives.

5.3 EXAMPLE: TRANSFERS AT FULL COST (PLUS)

Consider the example introduced in Paragraph 4.2, but with the additional complication of imperfect intermediate and final markets. A company has 2 profit centres, A and B. Centre A can only sell **half** of its maximum output externally because of limited demand. It transfers the other half of its output to B which also faces limited demand. Costs and revenues in an accounting period are as follows.

	A £	B £	Total £
External sales	8,000	24,000	32,000
Costs of production in the division	12,000	10,000	22,000
Profit			10,000

There are no opening or closing stocks. It does not matter here whether marginal or absorption costing is used and we shall ignore the question of whether the current output levels are profit maximising and congruent with the goals of the company as a whole.

Transfer price at full cost only

5.4 If the transfer price is at full cost, A in our example would have 'sales' to B of £6,000 (costs of £12,000 × 50%). This would be a cost to B, as follows.

	A £	A £	B £	B £	Company as a whole £
Open market sales		8,000		24,000	32,000
Transfer sales		6,000		-	
Total sales, inc transfers		14,000		24,000	
Transfer costs			6,000		
Own costs	12,000		10,000		22,000
Total costs, inc transfers		12,000		16,000	
Profit		2,000		8,000	10,000

The transfer sales of A are self-cancelling with the transfer costs of B so that total profits are unaffected by the transfer items. The transfer price simply spreads the total profit of £10,000 between A and B.

5.5 The obvious drawback to the transfer price at cost is that **A makes no profit** on its work, and the manager of division A would much prefer to sell output on the open market to earn a profit, rather than transfer to B, regardless of whether or not transfers to B would be in the best interests of the company as a whole. Division A needs a profit on its transfers in order to be motivated to supply B; therefore transfer pricing at cost is inconsistent with the use of a profit centre accounting system.

Transfer price at full cost plus

5.6 If the transfers are at cost plus a margin of, say, 25%, A's sales to B would be £7,500 (£12,000 × 50% × 1.25).

	A £	A £	B £	B £	Total £
Open market sales		8,000		24,000	32,000
Transfer sales		7,500		-	
		15,500		24,000	
Transfer costs			7,500		
Own costs	12,000		10,000		22,000
		12,000		17,500	
Profit		3,500		6,500	10,000

5.7 Compared to a transfer price at cost, **A gains some profit** at the expense of B. However, A makes a bigger profit on external sales in this case because the profit mark-up of 25% is less than the profit mark-up on open market sales. The choice of 25% as a profit mark-up was arbitrary and unrelated to external market conditions.

Divisional autonomy, divisional performance measurement and corporate profit maximisation

5.8 In the above case the transfer price **fails on all three criteria** for judgement.

(a) Arguably, it does not give A fair revenue or charge B a reasonable cost, and so their profit **performance** is distorted. It would certainly be unfair, for example, to compare A's profit with B's profit.

(b) Given this unfairness it is likely that the **autonomy** of each of the divisional managers is under threat. If they cannot agree on what is a fair split of the external profit a decision will have to be imposed from above.

(c) It would seem to give A an incentive to sell more goods externally and transfer less to B. This may or may not be in the best interests of the **company as a whole**.

Question: transfer pricing

Suppose, in the example, that the cost per unit of A's output is £9 in variable costs and £6 in fixed costs. B's own costs are £25 including a fixed element of £10. What is the minimum price that B should charge for its products to break even?

Answer

A produces £12,000/(£9 + £6) = 800 units and transfers half of them to B for £6,000. The cost for each unit that B buys is therefore £6,000/400 = £15. From B's perspective this is a **variable** cost. B's costs are as follows.

	Cost per unit £
Variable cost: transfers from A	15
Own variable costs	15
	30

From B's perspective it must charge more than £30 per unit to earn a contribution. However, from the overall perspective, £6 of the 'variable' cost of transfers is **fixed**. The variable cost is really £9 + £15 = £24, and any price above this will earn a contribution for the organisation as a whole.

Transfer price at marginal cost

5.9 A marginal cost approach entails charging the marginal cost that has been incurred by the supplying division to the receiving division. As above, we shall suppose that A's cost per unit is £15, of which £6 is fixed and £9 variable.

	A £	A £	B £	B £	Company as a whole £	Company as a whole £
Market sales		8,000		24,000		32,000
Transfer sales (£6,000 × 9/15)		3,600		-		
		11,600		24,000		
Transfer costs		-	3,600			
Own variable costs	7,200		6,000		13,200	
Own fixed costs	4,800		4,000		8,800	
Total costs and transfers		12,000		13,600		22,000
(Loss)/Profit		(400)		10,400		10,000

Divisional autonomy, divisional performance measurement and corporate profit maximisation

5.10 (a) This result is deeply unsatisfactory for the manager of division A who could make an additional £4,400 (£(8,000 – 3,600)) profit if no goods were transferred to division B.

(b) Given that the manager of division A would prefer to transfer externally, head office are likely to have to insist that internal transfers are made.

(c) For the company overall, external transfers only would cause a large fall in profit, because division B could make no sales at all.

5.11 The problem is that with a transfer price at marginal cost the **supplying division does not cover its fixed costs**.

6 FIXED COSTS AND TRANSFER PRICING

Ways in which this problem could be overcome

6.1 Each division can be given a **share** of the overall contribution earned by the organisation, but it is probably necessary to decide what the shares should be centrally, undermining **divisional autonomy**. Alternatively central management could impose a range within which the transfer price should fall, and allow divisional managers to **negotiate** what they felt was a fair price between themselves.

6.2 A second method is to use a **two-part charging system**: transfer prices are set at variable cost and once a year there is a transfer of a fixed fee to the supplying division, representing an allowance for its fixed costs. Care is needed with this approach. It risks sending the message to the supplying division that it need not control its fixed costs because the company will **subsidise any inefficiencies**. On the other hand, if fixed costs are incurred because spare capacity is kept available for the needs of other divisions it is reasonable to expect those other divisions to pay a fee if they 'booked' that capacity in advance but later failed to utilise it. The main problem with this approach once more is that it is likely to conflict with **divisional autonomy**.

6.3 A third possibility is a system of **dual pricing**. Be careful not to confuse this term with 'two-part' transfer pricing. Dual pricing means that two separate transfer prices are used.

(a) For the transfer of goods from the supplying division to the receiving division the transfer price is set at variable cost. This ensures that the receiving division makes optimal **decisions** and it leads to corporate profit maximisation.

(b) For the purposes of **reporting results** the transfer price is based on the *total* costs of the transferring division, thus avoiding the possibility of reporting a loss.

This method is not widely used in practice.

6.4 One final possibility that may be worth mentioning. Given that the problems are caused by the divisional structure, might it not be better to address the **structure**, for example by **merging the two divisions**, or ceasing to treat the transferring division as a profit centre. This may not be practical. Some would argue that the benefits of decentralisation in terms of motivation outweigh any costs that might arise due to slight inefficiencies.

7 STANDARD COST VERSUS ACTUAL COST

7.1 When a transfer price is based on cost, **standard cost** should be used, not actual cost. A transfer of actual cost would give no incentive to **control costs**, because they could all be passed on. Actual cost-*plus* transfer prices might even encourage the manager of A to overspend, because this would increase the divisional profit, even though the company as a whole (and division B) suffers.

7.2 Suppose, for example, that A's costs should have been £12,000, but actually were £16,000. Transfers (50% of output) would cost £8,000 actual, and the cost plus transfer price is at a margin of 25% (£8,000 × 125% = £10,000).

	A			*B*	*Total*
	£	£	£	£	£
Market sales		8,000		24,000	32,000
Transfer sales		10,000		-	
		18,000		24,000	
Transfer costs		-	10,000		
Own costs	16,000		10,000		26,000
		16,000		20,000	
Profit		2,000		4,000	6,000

A's overspending by £4,000 has reduced the total profits from £10,000 to £6,000.

7.3 In this example, B must bear much of the cost of A's overspending, which is clearly unsatisfactory for responsibility accounting. If, however, the transfer price were at standard cost plus instead of actual cost plus, the transfer sales would have been £7,500, regardless of A's overspending.

	A			*B*	*Total*
	£	£	£	£	£
Market sales		8,000		24,000	32,000
Transfer sales		7,500		-	
		15,500		24,000	
Transfer costs		-	7,500		
Own costs	16,000		10,000		
		16,000		17,500	26,000
Profit/(loss)		(500)		6,500	6,000

The entire cost of the overspending by A of £4,000 is now borne by division A itself as a comparison with the figures in Paragraph 7.2 will show.

Question: standard cost v actual cost

Why has A's profit fallen by £2,500, not £4,000?

Answer

A was already bearing 50% of its overspending. The fall in profit is £2,000 × 125% = £2,500, which represents the other 50% of its over spending and the loss of the profit margin on transfers to B.

---

8 COST-BASED APPROACHES WITH NO EXTERNAL MARKET

8.1 So far we have considered the use of cost-based approaches where the following factors applied.

(a) There was a **limit on the maximum output** of the supplying division.
(b) There was a **limit** to the amount that could be sold in the **intermediate market**.

8.2 We found that a **marginal cost** based approach led to the **best decisions** for the organisation overall, but that this was **beset with problems** in maintaining divisional autonomy and measuring divisional performance fairly.

8.3 We shall now consider whether this finding changes in different conditions. We shall remove the limit on output and demand for the final product, but assume that there is *no* intermediate market at all.

8.4 EXAMPLE: UNLIMITED CAPACITY AND NO INTERMEDIATE MARKET

Motivate Ltd has two profit centres, P and Q. P transfers *all* its output to Q. The variable cost of output from P is £5 per unit, and fixed costs are £1,200 per month. Additional processing costs in Q are £4 per unit for variable costs, plus fixed costs of £800. Budgeted production is 400 units per month, and the output of Q sells for £15 per unit. The transfer price is to be based on standard full cost plus. From what *range* of prices should the transfer price be selected, in order to motivate the managers of both profit centres to both increase output and reduce costs?

8.5 SOLUTION

Any transfer price based on **standard** cost plus will motivate managers to cut costs, because favourable variances between standard costs and actual costs will be credited to the division's profits. Managers of each division will also be willing to increase output above the budget of 400 units provided that it is profitable to do so; that is:

(a) In P, provided that the transfer price exceeds the variable cost of £5 per unit

(b) In Q, provided that the transfer price is less than the difference between the fixed selling price (£15) and the variable costs in Q itself (£4). This amount of £11 (£15 – £4) is sometimes called **net marginal revenue**

The range of prices is therefore between £5.01 and £10.99.

Let's do a check. Suppose the transfer price is £9. With absorption based on the **budgeted** output of 400 units what would divisional profits be if output and sales are 400 units or 500 units?

Overheads per unit are £1,200/400 = £3, so the full cost of sales is £(5 + 3) = £8 in division P. In division Q, full cost is £(4 + 2) = £6, plus transfer costs of £9.

At 400 units:

	P £	Q £	Total £
Sales	-	6,000	6,000
Transfer sales	3,600	-	
Transfer costs	-	(3,600)	
Own full cost of sales	(3,200)	(2,400)	(5,600)
	400	0	400
Under/over absorbed overhead	0	0	0
Profit/(loss)	400	0	400

At 500 units:

	P £	Q £	Total £
Sales	-	7,500	7,500
Transfer sales	4,500	-	-
Transfer costs	-	(4,500)	-
Own full cost of sales	(4,000)	(3,000)	(7,000)
	500	0	500
Over absorbed overhead (100 × £3; 100 × £2)	300	200	500
Profit/(loss)	800	200	1,000

Increasing output improves the profit performance of both divisions and the company as a whole, and so decisions on output by the two divisions are likely to be **goal congruent**.

Summary

8.6 To summarise the **transfer price should be set in the range** where:

Variable cost in supplying division $\leq$ **Selling price minus variable costs (net marginal revenue) in the receiving division**

8.7 In fact, if there is no external market, and if the transferred item is the major product of the transferring division, there is a strong argument for suggesting that profit centre accounting is a waste of time.

8.8 Profit centres cannot be judged on their commercial performance because there is no way of gauging what a fair revenue for their work should be. It would be more appropriate, perhaps, to treat the transferring 'division' as a cost centre, and to judge performance on the basis of cost variances.

> ### Exam focus point
>
> Question 4 of the Pilot paper (see question 22 of the Exam Question Bank) is on transfer pricing. One of the optional questions in the June 2002 paper was also on the topic.

9 OPPORTUNITY COSTS AND TRANSFER PRICES

9.1 Ideally, a transfer price should be set that enables the individual **divisions** to maximise their profits at a level of output that maximises profit for the **company as a whole**. The transfer price which achieves this is unlikely to be a market-based transfer price (if there is one) and is also unlikely to be a simple cost plus based price.

An opportunity cost approach

9.2 If optimum decisions are to be taken transfer prices should reflect **opportunity costs.**

(a) If profit centre managers are given sufficient autonomy to make their own output and selling decisions, and at the same time their performance is judged by the company according to the profits they earn, they will be keenly aware of all the commercial opportunities.

(b) If transfers are made for the good of the company as a whole, the commercial benefits to the company ought to be **shared** between the participating divisions.

9.3 Transfer prices can therefore be reached by:

(a) Recognising the levels of output, external sales and internal transfers that are best for the **company as a whole,** and

(b) Arriving at a transfer price that ensures that all divisions maximise their profits at this same level of output. The transfer price should therefore be such that there is **not a more profitable opportunity** for individual divisions. This in turn means that the opportunity costs of transfer should be covered by the transfer price.

10 TRANSFER PRICING WHEN INTERMEDIATE PRODUCTS ARE IN SHORT SUPPLY

10.1 When an intermediate resource is in short supply and acts as a limiting factor on production in the transferring division, the **cost of transferring** an item is the variable cost of production plus the contribution obtainable from using the scarce resource in its next most profitable way.

10.2 EXAMPLE: SCARCE RESOURCES

Suppose, for example, that division A is a profit centre that produces three items, X, Y and Z. Each item has an external market.

	X	Y	Z
External market price, per unit	£48	£46	£40
Variable cost of production in division A	£33	£24	£28
Labour hours required per unit in division A	3	4	2

Product Y can be transferred to division B, but the maximum quantity that might be required for transfer is 300 units of Y.

The maximum **external** sales are 800 units of X, 500 units of Y and 300 units of Z.

Instead of receiving transfers of product Y from division A, division B could buy similar units of product Y on the open market at a slightly cheaper price of £45 per unit.

What should the transfer price be for each unit if the total labour hours available in division A are 3,800 hours or 5,600 hours?

10.3 SOLUTION

Hours required to meet maximum demand:

External sales:	*Hours*
X (3 × 800)	2,400
Y (4 × 500)	2,000
Z (2 × 300)	600
	5,000
Transfers of Y (4 × 300)	1,200
	6,200

Contribution from external sales:

	X	Y	Z
Contribution per unit	£15	£22	£12
Labour hours per unit	3 hrs	4 hrs	2 hrs
Contribution per labour hour	£5.00	£5.50	£6.00
Priority for selling	3rd	2nd	1st
Total hours needed	2,400	2,000	600

(a) If only **3,800 hours** of labour are available, division A would choose, **ignoring transfers** to B, to sell:

	Hours
300 Z (maximum)	600
500 Y (maximum)	2,000
	2,600
400 X (balance)	1,200
	3,800

To transfer 300 units of Y to division B would involve forgoing the sale of 400 units of X because 1,200 hours would be needed to make the transferred units.

Opportunity cost of transferring units of Y, and the appropriate transfer price:

	£ per unit
Variable cost of making Y	24
Opportunity cost (contribution of £5 per hour available from selling X externally): benefit forgone (4 hours × £5)	20
Transfer price for Y	44

The transfer price for Y should, in this case, be less than the external market price.

(b) If **5,600 hours** are available, there is enough time to meet the full demand for external sales (5,000) and still have 600 hours of spare capacity, before consideration of transfers. However, 1,200 hours are needed to produce the full amount of Y for transfer (300 units), and so 600 hours need to be devoted to producing Y for transfer instead of producing X for external sale.

This means that the **opportunity cost** of transfer is:

(i) the variable cost of 150 units of Y produced in the 600 'spare' hours (£24/unit);

(ii) the variable cost of production of the remaining 150 units of Y (£24 per unit), plus the **contribution forgone** from the external sales of X that could have been produced in the 600 hours now devoted to producing Y for transfer (£5 per labour hour). An average transfer price per unit could be negotiated for the transfer of the full 300 units (see below), which works out at £34 per unit.

	£
150 units × £24	3,600
150 units × £24	3,600
600 hours × £5 per hour	3,000
Total for 300 units	10,200

In both cases, the opportunity cost of receiving transfers for division B is the price it would have to pay to purchase Y externally - £45 per unit. Thus:

Maximum labour hours in A	Opportunity cost to A of transfer £	Opportunity cost to B of transfer £
3,800	44	45
5,600	34 (average)	45

In each case any price between the two opportunity costs would be sufficient to persuade B to order 300 units of Y from division A and for division A to agree to transfer them.

Central information

10.4 The only way to be sure that a profit-maximising transfer policy will be implemented is to **dictate the policy from the centre**. This means that the following information must be available centrally.

(a) A precise **breakdown of costs in each division** at all levels of output

(b) **Market information** for each market, indicating the level of demand at a range of prices

(c) Perhaps most vitally, knowledge of the **likely reaction of divisional managers** to a centrally imposed policy that undermines their autonomy and divisional profits

10.5 OPTIMAL TRANSFER PRICES: AN EXTENDED EXAMPLE

A group of highly integrated divisions wishes to be advised as to how it should set transfer prices for the following inter-divisional transactions:

(a) Division L sells all its output of product LX to Division M. To one kilogram of LX, Division M adds other direct materials and processes it to produce two kilograms of product MX which it sells outside the group. The price of MX is influenced by volume offered and the following cost and revenue data are available:

Division L

The variable costs per kg of LX are £4 of direct materials and £2 of direct labour.

The following cost increases are expected at different levels of production per annum:

Direct materials	At 60,000 kg pa increase to £5.00 per kg
	At 90,000 kg pa increase to £5.50 per kg
	At 100,000 kg pa increase to £6.00 per kg
Direct labour	At 80,000 kg pa increases to £2.50 per kg
	At 100,000 kg pa increases to £3.00 per kg
Fixed overhead	Under 70,000 kg	£210,000 pa
	70,000 - 79,999 kg	£260,000 pa
	80,000 - 89,999 kg	£280,000 pa
	90,000 or more kg	£310,000 pa

Division M

To produce one kilogram of product MX, the variable cost incurred for each half-kilogram of LX used is made up of £1.50 of other direct materials and £3.50 processing cost.

The following cost increases are expected at different levels of production of MX per annum:

Other direct materials	At 140,000 kg pa increase to £1.75 per kg
	At 160,000 kg pa increase to £2.00 per kg
Processing	At 180,000 kg pa increases to £4.00 per kg

		£
Fixed overhead	Under 120,000 kg	250,000 pa
	120,000 - 139,999 kg	280,000 pa
	140,000 - 159,999 kg	290,000 pa
	160,000 - 199,999 kg	320,000 pa
	200,000 or more kg	360,000 pa
Selling price	Up to 199,999 kg	£16.00 per kg
	200,000 or more kg	£15.50 per kg

(b) Division N manufactures two products, NA and NB, whose variable production cost and selling prices per unit are:

Product	NA		NB	
	£	£	£	£
Direct materials	8		5	
Direct labour	<u>8</u>		<u>12</u>	
Production cost		16		17
Selling price		32		50

Direct labour is paid at £4.00 per hour. Fixed overhead is £72,000 per annum and total capacity is 960,000 man-hours per annum.

Division N sells product NA either to Division P or outside the group and Division P can buy from either source. Product NB is sold only outside the group. When NA and NB are sold outside the group, variable selling costs of £1.00 and £3.00 per unit respectively are incurred.

Required

(a) Recommend, with supporting calculations and explanations, the most appropriate narrow range of transfer price per kg for product LX between the two divisions; assume that any changes in output are in steps of 10,000 kg of product LX and 20,000 kg of product MX.

(b) Recommend, with supporting calculations and explanations:

    (i)   The most appropriate transfer price of product NA between Divisions N and P:

        (1)   on the assumption that Division N can just sell all of, but no more than, its capacity;

        (2)   on the assumption that Division N could sell more than its existing capacity, though the market price stays the same;

    (ii)   in the case of (i) (2) above, what quantities of NA Division P should buy from Division N.

10.6 DISCUSSION AND SOLUTION

Part (a) of the question is long and the calculations might easily be confusing. The **ratio** of 1 kg of LX to 2 kg of MX also complicates the figure-work. It is probably tempting to calculate **unit contribution** rather than **unit net profit**, but in this case it is probably easier to work out unit full costs, because of the stepped changes in fixed costs.

Step 1.   The first step in a solution is to work out **what is best for the group as a whole.**

          MX costs and profits can be calculated on a unit basis first and then total profitability at each level of output derived.

		Quantity of MX ('000 kg)						
	100	*120*	*140*	*160*	*180*	*200*	*220*	*240*
Division L cost								
(1 kg LX per 2 kg MX)								
	£	£	£	£	£	£	£	£
Direct materials	2.00	2.50	2.50	2.50	2.75	3.00	3.00	3.00
Direct labour	1.00	1.00	1.00	1.25	1.25	1.50	1.50	1.50
Fixed overhead	2.10	1.75	1.86	1.75	1.72	1.55	1.41	1.29
Total	5.10	5.25	5.36	5.50	5.72	6.05	5.91	5.79
Division M costs								
Other materials	1.50	1.50	1.75	2.00	2.00	2.00	2.00	2.00
Processing cost	3.50	3.50	3.50	3.50	4.00	4.00	4.00	4.00
Fixed overhead	2.50	2.33	2.07	2.00	1.78	1.80	1.64	1.50
Total	7.50	7.33	7.32	7.50	7.78	7.80	7.64	7.50
Full unit cost	12.60	12.58	12.68	13.00	13.50	13.85	13.55	13.29
Sales price	16.00	16.00	16.00	16.00	16.00	15.50	15.50	15.50
Unit profit	3.40	3.42	3.32	3.00	2.50	1.65	1.95	2.21
Total profit (£000)	340	410	465	480	450	330	429	530

Below 200,000 kg, profit is maximised at 160,000 kg of MX (£480,000) but this profit figure is exceeded when output rises to 240,000 kg and beyond, by which time profit is rising by £100,000 per extra 20,000 kg of MX. Division M ought to make 240,000 kg or more of MX, up to capacity output.

Step 2. So how do we calculate the **ideal transfer price**? First of all, the transfer price must be **higher than £5.79** per ½ kg of LX, but **not more than £(5.79 + 2.21) = £8** per ½ kg of LX. At the lower price, Division L would make no profit at 240,000 kg of MX and at the higher price, Division M would make no profit.

Step 3. The selection of a transfer price is further complicated by the **changing unit costs** at lower levels of output. The transfer price must give each division an incentive not to want to restrict output to less than 240,000 kg of MX.

(a) Left to its own devices Division M will produce **140,000 kg** because its unit costs are minimised at this level. So Division M will be willing to offer Division L a transfer price that persuades it to produce 70,000 kg and this must at least cover Division L's unit costs at this level of £5.36 per half kg.

(b) However, overall profit is maximised at the **240,000 kg** level, where unit costs for Division L are £0.43 (£5.79 - £5.36) higher.

$$240{,}000x \quad > \quad 140{,}000(x + 0.43)$$
$$100{,}000x \quad > \quad 60{,}200$$
$$x \quad > \quad 0.60$$

Our analysis suggests that unless Division L earns a unit profit of at least 60p, the division's manager will need a lot of persuading to increase output above 70,000 kg (enough for 140,000 kg of MX).

(c) In the case of Division M, a similar analysis can be applied. Unit costs are £0.18 per kg lower at 140,000 kg of output, and so if the unit profit at 240,000 kg is £y, we want a transfer price where:

$$240{,}000y \quad > \quad 140{,}000(y + 0.18)$$
$$100{,}000y \quad > \quad 25{,}200$$
$$y \quad > \quad 0.25$$

This suggests that unless Division M makes a profit per kg of at least 25p at 240,000 kg of output the division's manager might prefer to halt production and sales at 140,000 kg.

Step 4. The range of transfer prices per kg of MX is therefore narrower than the £5.79 to £8 range we began with. Division L should have a profit of at least £0.60 per kg of MX at 240,000 kg of output and so the minimum transfer price should be (£5.79 + £0.6) **£6.39** per kg of MX. Division M should have a profit of at least £0.25 and so the maximum transfer price should be (£8 – £0.25) **£7.75**.

Conclusion for Division L and Division M. The transfer price per kg of MX should be in the range £6.39 - £7.75, so that the transfer price range per kg of LX (2:1) is £12.78 - £15.50.

Let's now turn our attention to part (b). The situation facing Division N is probably a bit easier to understand.

(a) If Division N can sell all of its capacity but no more, the **opportunity cost** of transferring NA instead of selling it will be the external revenue per unit of NA less the variable selling costs - ie £(32 – 1) = £31 per unit.

(b) In part (2) of the question, N's existing capacity acts as a constraint on total output: labour hours become a scarce resource.

	NA	NB
	£	£
Contribution before variable selling costs	16	33
Variable selling costs	1	3
Net contribution	15	30
Labour hours per unit	2	3
Contribution per labour hour	£7.50	£10

Transferring NA to Division P (rather than making NB) would force Division N to forgo contribution of £10 per labour hour, and the transfer price of NA should reflect this opportunity cost:

	£
Variable cost of making NA	16
Opportunity cost of lost contribution on NB (2 hrs × £10)	20
Transfer price of NA, per kg	36

(c) Since the external market price of NA is only £32, Division P should buy all its supplies externally, and buy nothing from Division N. This would leave Division N free to make NB exclusively, and earn a contribution of £10 per labour hour on all its external sales.

11 TRANSFER PRICING AND A RANGE OF LIMITING FACTORS

11.1 One final production scenario that we have not yet covered is where the supplying division is subject to a **range of limiting factors** rather than just one.

11.2 In such circumstances the optimum production programme can be devised using a **linear programming model.**

11.3 EXAMPLE: TRANSFER PRICING WITH A RANGE OF LIMITING FACTORS

LP Ltd has two divisions, division 1 and division 2. Division 1 produces liquid A, all of which is transferred to division 2, and liquid B which can either be sold externally or transferred to division 2. Division 2 uses these liquids to produce its powdered products, X and Y.

Production of liquid A is restricted due to a shortage of skilled labour so that only 4,000 litres can be produced. Liquid B can also only be produced in limited numbers due to a scarcity of ingredients. Only 6,000 litres of liquid B can be made. Details of costs and revenues are as follows.

	A	B	X	Y
	£	£	£	£
Variable cost (division 1)	4	6	-	-
Variable cost (division 2)	-	-	7	5
Selling price	-	9	30	35

One sachet of powder X requires 1 litre of liquid A and 2 litres of liquid B.

One sachet of powder Y requires 2 litres of liquid A and 2 litres of liquid B.

Required

Formulate a linear programming model to determine the optimum production levels and transfer prices.

11.4 SOLUTION

Step 1. **Work out the contribution obtained from each product**

This needs to take account of the usage of A and B by X and Y.

	B	X	Y
Variable costs	6	7	5
Liquid A (1 litre/2 litres)	-	4	8
Liquid B (2 litres/2 litres)	-	12	12
	6	23	25
Selling price	9	30	35
Contribution	3	7	10

Step 2. **Formulate objective function**

The objective is to maximise the corporate contribution by producing the optimum quantities of products B, X and Y. Algebraically this is expressed as follows.

$$\text{Maximise } 3B + 7X + 10Y$$

Step 3. **Define constraints**

The constraints are as follows.

$$1X + 2Y \le 4{,}000 \text{ (labour shortage)}$$
$$B + 2X + 2Y \le 6{,}000 \text{ (ingredients shortage)}$$
$$B, X, Y \ge 0$$

IMPORTANT POINT

You are only required to be able to formulate the model, not solve it.

11.5 In practice, as you probably remember, where there are **more than two variables** in the objective function and more than a few constraints a **computer software package** is needed.

11.6 The **output** from the model will show **how many sachets of X and Y should be produced and how many litres, if any, of B should be sold externally.** The output also provides a means of calculating the ideal transfer price, because it indicates the shadow price of scarce resources.

12 SHADOW PRICE AND TRANSFER PRICES

> **KEY TERM**
>
> The **shadow price** is the maximum extra amount that it would be worth paying to obtain one extra unit of a scarce resource. To put it another way, the shadow price is the opportunity cost of the scarce resource, the amount of benefit forgone by not having the availability of the extra resources.

12.1 We know already that an **optimal transfer price** can be calculated by **adding together the variable cost of the intermediate product and the opportunity cost of making the transfer.** In our example, let us suppose that the shadow price of liquid A is £3 and of liquid B, £2.

	A	B
	£	£
Variable cost	4	6
Shadow price	3	2
Transfer price	7	8

12.2 This solution might be tested by the divisional manager of the supplying division by applying his own linear programming model attempting to maximise the contribution from external sales of B (which we shall call B1) and from transfers of A and B.

Maximise 3A + 2B + 3B1
Subject to

A	≤	4,000
B + B1	≤	6,000
A, B, B1	≥	0

This would give the same optimum production levels as the original linear programme, because it is derived from the same information.

12.3 For division 2, however, these transfer prices would result in each product yielding a contribution of nil. In effect this means that the **optimal solution must be centrally imposed,** otherwise the manager of division 2 will have no incentive to produce X and Y at all.

Question: transfer prices and shadow prices

In what circumstances are transfer prices calculated using shadow prices?

Answer

As earlier, this is to test how closely you followed the preceding paragraphs. Shadow prices replace opportunity cost in the transfer price formula when there are constraints on production.

13 NEGOTIATED TRANSFER PRICES

13.1 A transfer price based on opportunity cost is often **difficult to identify**, for lack of suitable information about costs and revenues in individual divisions. In this case it is likely that transfer prices will be set by means of **negotiation**. The agreed price may be finalised from a mixture of accounting arithmetic, politics and compromise.

13.2 The process of negotiation will be improved if **adequate information** about each division's costs and revenues is made available to the other division involved in the negotiation. By having a free flow of cost and revenue information, it will be easier for divisional managers to identify opportunities for improving profits, to the benefit of both divisions involved in the transfer.

13.3 A negotiating system that might enable **goal congruent plans** to be agreed between profit centres is as follows.

(a) Profit centres **submit plans** for output and sales to head office, as a preliminary step in preparing the annual budget.

(b) Head office **reviews these plans**, together with any other information it may obtain. Amendments to divisional plans might be discussed with the divisional managers.

(c) Once divisional plans are acceptable to head office and **consistent** with each other, head office might let the divisional managers arrange budgeted transfers and transfer prices.

(d) Where divisional plans are **inconsistent** with each other, head office might try to establish a plan that would maximise the profits of the company as a whole. Divisional managers would then be asked to negotiate budgeted transfers and transfer prices on this basis.

(e) If divisional managers fail to agree a transfer price between themselves, a head office **'arbitration' manager** or team would be referred to for an opinion or a decision.

(f) Divisions **finalise their budgets** within the framework of agreed transfer prices and resource constraints.

(g) Head office **monitors the profit performance** of each division.

14 MULTINATIONAL TRANSFER PRICING

Exam focus point

This topic was examined in June 2004.

14.1 **Globalisation,** the rise of the **multinational corporation** and the fact that more than **60% of world trade takes place within multinational organisations** mean that international transfer pricing is very important.

14.2 As we have seen, the level at which a transfer price should be set is not a straightforward decision for organisations. The situation is even less clear cut for **organisations operating in a number of countries**, when even more **factors need to be taken into consideration.** Moreover, the **manipulation of profits through the use of transfer pricing** is a common area of **confrontation between multinational organisations and host country governments.**

Factors to consider	Explanation
Exchange rate fluctuation	The value of a transfer of goods between profit centres in different countries could depend on fluctuations in the currency exchange rate.
Taxation in different countries	If taxation on profits is 20% of profits in Country A and 50% on profits in Country B, a company will presumably try to 'manipulate' profits (by means of raising or lowering transfer prices or by invoicing the subsidiary in the high-tax country for 'services' provided by the subsidiary in the low-tax country) so that profits are maximised for a subsidiary in Country A, by reducing profits for a subsidiary in Country B.
	Some multinationals set up marketing subsidiaries in countries with low tax rates and transfer products to them at a relatively low transfer price. When the products are sold to the final customer, a low rate of tax will be paid on the difference between the two prices.
Import tariffs	Suppose that Country A imposes an import tariff of 20% on the value of goods imported. A multi-national company has a subsidiary in Country A which imports goods from a subsidiary in Country B. In such a situation, the company would minimise costs by keeping the transfer price to a minimum value.
Exchange controls	If a country imposes restrictions on the transfer of profits from domestic subsidiaries to foreign multinationals, the restrictions on the transfer can be overcome if head office provides some goods or services to the subsidiary and charges exorbitantly high prices, disguising the 'profits' as sales revenue, and transferring them from one country to the other. The ethics of such an approach should, of course, be questioned.
Anti-dumping legislation	Governments may take action to protect home industries by preventing companies from transferring goods cheaply into their countries. They may do this, for example, by insisting on the use of a fair market value for the transfer price.
Competitive pressures	Transfer pricing can be used to enable profit centres to match or undercut local competitors.
Repatriation of funds	By inflating transfer prices for goods sold to subsidiaries in countries where inflation is high, the subsidiaries' profits are reduced and funds repatriated, thereby saving their value.

14.3 Tax authorities obviously recognise the **incentive to set transfer prices to minimise taxes and import tariffs. Many tax authorities** have the **power** to **modify transfer prices in computing tariffs or taxes on profit**, although a **genuine arms-length market price should be accepted.**

(a) Section 770 of the UK Income and Corporate Taxes Act restricts how far companies can declare their profits in a low taxation country. Some scope for profit apportionment between divisions clearly exists, however. The Inland Revenue has the power to adjust the taxable income of the UK party to a cross-border transaction to the figure that would have resulted if the **prices actually used had been between two unrelated parties** ('arm's length' price).

539

(b) In the USA, multinational organisations must follow an Internal Revenue Code specifying that transfers must be priced at 'arm's length' market values, or at the values that would be used if the divisions were independent companies. Even with this rule, companies have some leeway in deciding an appropriate 'arm's length' price.

14.4 EXAMPLE: ARM'S LENGTH TRANSFER PRICE

Suppose division A produces product B in a country where the income tax rate is 30% and transfers it to division C, which operates in a country with a 40% rate of income tax. An import duty equal to 25% of the price of product B is also assessed. The full cost per unit is £290, the variable cost £160.

Required

The tax authorities allow either variable or full cost transfer prices. Determine which should be chosen.

14.5 SOLUTION

Effect of transferring at £290 instead of £160

	£
Income of A is £130 higher and so A pays £130 × 30% more income tax	(39.0)
Income of C is £130 lower and so C pays £130 × 40% less income tax	52.0
Import duty is paid by C on an additional £130, and so C pays £130 × 25% more duty	(32.5)
Net effect (cost) of transferring at £290 instead of £160	(19.5)

14.6 **The pros and cons of different transfer pricing bases**

(a) A transfer price at **market value** is usually encouraged by the tax and customs authorities of both host and home countries as they will receive a fair share of the profits made but there are problems with its use.

    (i) Prices for the same product may vary considerably from one country to another.

    (ii) Changes in exchange rates, local taxes and so on can result in large variations in selling price.

    (iii) A division will want to set its prices in relation to the supply and demand conditions present in the country in question to ensure that it can compete in that country.

(b) A transfer price at **full cost** is usually acceptable to tax and customs authorities since it provides some indication that the transfer price approximates to the real cost of supplying the item and because it indicates that they will therefore receive a fair share of tax and tariff revenues.

(c) Transfer prices at **variable cost** are unlikely to be acceptable to the tax authorities of the country in which the supplying division is based as all the profits are allocated to the receiving division and the supplying division makes a loss equal to the fixed costs incurred.

(d) In a multinational organisation, **negotiated** transfer prices may result in overall sub-optimisation because no account is taken of factors such as differences in tax and tariff rates between countries.

14.7 To meet the multiple objectives of transfer pricing, companies may choose to maintain **two sets of accounting records, one for tax reporting and one for internal management reporting.** The tax authorities may interpret the use of two sets of records as **suggestive of profit manipulation,** however.

14.8 **Double taxation agreements** between countries mean that companies pay tax on specific transactions in one country only. If a company sets an unrealistically low transfer price, however, the company will pay tax in both countries (double taxation) if it is spotted by the tax authorities.

14.9 Most countries now accept the Organisation for Economic Co-operation and Development **(OECD) 1995 guidelines**. These aim to standardise national approaches to transfer pricing and provide guidance on the application of the 'arm's length' price. This can be determined in two main ways.

    (a) **Comparable price method** is the most widely used and involves setting the arm's length price on the basis of the prices of similar products. In other words, the market price or an approximation to one is used. It can be difficult to make meaningful comparisons, however, as most international trade is carried out between related companies.

    (b) **Gross margin method** involves an analysis of the gross margins in comparable transactions between unrelated companies.

14.10 These methods are of **little use** in determining arm's length prices for **intangible assets** such as a trade name, however, and much of the information required is not in the public domain. Setting transfer prices is therefore not straightforward.

14.11 **Many countries are tightening their regulations** in response to the OECD guidelines. In the UK, for example, it used to be up to the tax authorities to detect cases of inappropriate transfer pricing. Under self assessment, it is now the duty of the tax payer to provide the correct information. A penalty of 100% of any tax adjustment is payable for failing to demonstrate a reasonable attempt at using an arm's length price in a tax return. The taxpayer may enter into an Advanced Pricing Agreement (APA) with the two tax authorities involved. This is done in advance to avoid dispute, double taxation and penalties.

Question: multinational transfer pricing

RBN is a UK parent company with an overseas subsidiary. The directors of RBN wish to transfer profits from the UK to the overseas company. They are considering changing the level of the transfer prices charged on goods shipped from the overseas subsidiary to UK subsidiaries and the size of the royalty payments paid by UK subsidiaries to the overseas subsidiary.

Required

In order to transfer profit from the UK to the overseas subsidiary, explain very briefly what the directors of RBN should do.

Answer

They should increase both the transfer prices and royalty payments

To increase the overseas subsidiary's profit, the transfer price needs to be higher (since it is the overseas subsidiary doing the selling) and the royalty payments by the UK subsidiaries to the overseas subsidiary company should also be higher. Both would add to the overseas subsidiary's revenue without affecting its costs.

Question: more multinational transfer pricing

LL Multinational plc transferred 4,000 units of product S from its manufacturing division in the USA to the selling division in the UK in the year to 31 December.

Each unit of S cost $350 to manufacture, the variable cost proportion being 75%, and was sold for £600. The UK division incurred marketing and distribution costs of £8 per unit. The UK tax rate was 30% and the exchange rate £ = $1.5.

The market price for each unit of product S in the USA was $600. The USA's division's profit after tax for its sales to the UK division for the year just ended was $750,000.

Required

(a) If the transfers were at variable cost, calculate the UK division's profit after tax.
(b) Calculate the tax rate in the USA if product S was transferred at the USA market price.

Answer

(a)

	£
External sales (£600 × 4,000)	2,400,000
Variable cost (transfer price of ($350 × 75%/$1.5) × 4,000)	700,000
Marketing and distribution costs (£8 × 4,000)	32,000
Profit before tax	1,668,000
Tax at 30%	500,400
Profit after tax	1,167,600

(b)

	£
Transfer sales ($600 x 4,000)	2,400,000
Costs ($350 x 4,000)	1,400,000
Profit before tax	1,000,000
Tax	?
Profit after tax	750,000

Therefore tax = $(1,000,000 – 750,000) = $250,000

Therefore tax rate = ($250,000/1,000,000) = 25%

14.12 A study by Ernst and Young of 210 multinationals found that 49% were being investigated over transfer pricing, while 83% had been involved in a transfer pricing dispute at some time.

> 'Transfer pricing is big business ... The figures involved are sometimes huge. During the 1992 presidential campaign, Bill Clinton claimed that $45bn in tax revenue could be raised from foreign-based enterprises operating in the US which were unfairly allocating their profits by transfer pricing distortions.'
>
> (J Kelly, *Financial Times,* 23 November 1995)

Case examples

The following descriptions are taken from Christopher Pass's article 'Transfer Pricing in Multinational Companies' which appeared in the September 1994 edition of *Management Accounting*.

'In 1993 Nissan agreed to pay 'penalty taxes' of Y17bn (£106m) to the US Internal Revenue Services (IRS) following an IRS investigation which concluded that Nissan had avoided US taxes by transferring part of its US profits to Japan in the early 1990s. The IRS's main contention was that Nissan had set transfer prices on its passenger cars and trucks imported from Japan at 'unrealistically' high levels and as a result declared lower profits in the US than it should have done. What constitutes a 'fair' or 'realistic' transfer price is, as we have indicated above, open to question. In the USA, the common Japanese practice of charging relatively low prices to build market share over the longer term is viewed with some scepticism and hence has raised suspicions regarding 'unfair' transfer pricing practices.

The NTA alleged that many US and European concerns had deliberately under-recorded profits earned in Japan both by charging 'excessive' transfer prices to their local subsidiaries for materials imported from their parent companies, and by levying 'excessive' royalty payments on their Japanese subsidiaries.

The NTA imposed a penalty tax of Y15bn (£96m) on Cola-Cola for 'unfair' transfer pricing practices and for applying excessive brand and marketing royalty payments transferred to its US parent company over the period 1990-92; while Ciba-Geigy was charged a penalty tax of Y5.7bn (£38m) and Roche Y10bn (£64m) for engaging in manipulative transfer pricing over a similar three year period. Hoechst has been 'fined' an undisclosed amount which it is appealing against before a Japan-Germany inter-governmental tax authority.'

Chapter roundup

- There are advantages and disadvantages of **divisionalisation**.

- Transfer prices are a way of promoting **divisional autonomy**, ideally without prejudicing **divisional performance measurement** or discouraging overall **corporate profit maximisation**.

- They may be based on **market price** (or an **adjusted market price**) where there is a market.

- If not, problems arise with **cost-based** transfer prices because one party or the other is liable to perceive them as unfair.

- **Fixed costs** in the supplying division can be accounted for in a number of ways to ensure that it at least breaks even.

- **Standard costs** should be used for transfer prices to avoid encouraging inefficiency in the supplying division.

- With **no external market**, the transfer price should be set in the range where variable cost in the supplying division ≤ net marginal revenue in the receiving division.

- If a profit-maximising output level has been established, the transfer price should be set such that there is not a more profitable opportunity for individual divisions. In other words transfer prices should include **opportunity costs** of transfer.

- The problem with this approach is that it entails collecting all the relevant divisional **data** centrally and **imposing** a transfer price, undermining divisional autonomy.

- When an **intermediate resource is in short supply** and **acts as a limiting factor** on production in the supplying division, the cost of transferring an item is the variable cost of production plus the contribution obtainable from using the scarce resource in its next most profitable way.

- If a supplying division is subject to a range of limiting factors, the optimum production plan can be derived using a **linear programming model.**

- **Shadow prices** replace opportunity costs when determining transfer prices if there are constraints on production.

- In practice, **negotiated** transfer prices, **market-based** transfer prices and **full cost-based** transfer prices are the methods normally used.

- **Multinational transfer pricing** needs to take account of a range of factors.

  ○ Exchange rate fluctuations
  ○ Taxation in different countries
  ○ Import tariffs
  ○ Exchange controls
  ○ Anti-dumping legislation
  ○ Competitive pressures
  ○ Repatriation of funds

Quick quiz

1   To prevent dysfunctional transfer price decision making, profit centres must be allowed to make autonomous decisions. *True or false?*

2   Which of the following is not a disadvantage of using market value as a transfer price?

A   The market price might be a temporary one.
B   Use of market price might act as a disincentive to use up spare capacity.
C   Many products do not have an equivalent market price.
D   The external market might be perfect.

3   Dual pricing is the same as two-part transfer pricing. *True or false?*

4   *Fill in the blanks.*

Ideally, a transfer price should be set that enables the individual divisions to maximise their profits at a level of output that maximises ....

The transfer price which achieves this is unlikely to be a .... transfer price or a .... transfer price.

If optimum decisions are to be taken, transfer prices should reflect ....

5   *Choose the appropriate word(s) from those highlighted.*

When an intermediate resource is in short supply and acts as a **factoring limit/limiting factor** on production in the **transferring/receiving** division, the cost of transferring an item is the **variable/ fixed/opportunity** cost of production **plus/less** the **contribution obtainable/opportunity cost** from using the scarce resource in its next most profitable way.

6   *Fill in the action required at each step to formulate a linear programming model to determine optimum production levels and transfer prices.*

Step 1.   ....

Step 2.   ....

Step 3.   ....

7   Shadow price is not the same as the opportunity cost of a scarce resource. *True or false?*

Answers to quick quiz

1   False. They cannot be allowed to make entirely autonomous decisions.

2   D

3   False

4   profit for the company as a whole
       market-based
       cost-based
       opportunity costs

5   limiting factor
       transferring
       variable
       plus
       contribution obtainable

6   *Step 1.*   Work out the contribution obtainable from each product
       Step 2.   Formulate objective function
       Step 3.   Define constraints

7   False. It is the same.

Now try the question below from the Exam Question Bank

Number	Level	Marks	Time
23	Exam	20	36 mins

Chapter 26

LONG-TERM DECISIONS

Topic list	Syllabus reference
1 The time value of money	5(b)
2 Discounted cash flow techniques	5(b)
3 A choice of methods of investment appraisal	5(b)
4 NPV, RI and annuity depreciation	5(b)
6 Exam-standard application of DCF	5(b)

Introduction

Longer-term decisions (typically, related to a capital investment project) differ from short-run decisions in that they need to **take account of the time value of money:** the concept that £1 earned or spent sooner is worth more than £1 earned or spent later. You should know from your earlier studies that such decisions therefore involve the application of **discounted cash flow (DCF) techniques.**

Because DCF has been covered in some depth at earlier levels, we begin the chapter by **summarising** the more straightforward areas of the topic (the principles of discounting and simple net present value (NPV) and internal rate of return (IRR) calculations). Attempt the exercises to ensure that you are up to speed on these easier areas before moving on to the more complex areas covered in later sections of the chapter.

On completion of this chapter you have reached the end of the Study Text. **Congratulations.**

Now you need to work through all of the questions in the Exam Question Bank if you have not already done so.

Study guide

Section 29 – Long-term decisions

- Define and illustrate the concepts of net present value and internal rate of return

- Calculate the net present value and internal rate of return in the evaluation of an investment opportunity

- Explain the use of DCF techniques for decisions involving cash outlays over long periods

- Explain the relationship between net present value and residual income where annuity depreciation is used in the residual income calculations

- Compare and contrast net present value with payback and accounting rate of return in the evaluation of investment opportunities

Exam guide

DCF techniques could be required in any number of scenarios in both Section A and Section B questions.

The issues covered in this chapter are useful background to the following Oxford Brookes degree Research and Analysis Projects.

- Topic 1, which requires you to analyse the efficiency and/or effectiveness of a management accounting technique in an organisational setting

- Topic 10, which requires you to analyse how management accounting techniques are used to support decision making in organisations

- Topic 14, which requires you to investigate recent investment decisions by an organisation of your choice and how the use of different methods of risk and uncertainty analysis might affect such decisions.

1 THE TIME VALUE OF MONEY

1.1 DCF is a decision-making technique that is based on a concept known as the time value of money.

KEY TERM

The **time value of money** is the concept that £1 received today is not equal to £1 received in the future.

1.2 Given the choice between receiving £100 today, and £100 in one year's time, most people would **opt to receive £100 today because they could spend it or invest it** to earn interest. If the interest rate was 10%, you could invest £100 today and it would be worth (£100 × 1.10) = £110 in one year's time. A sum of **money received now** is therefore **worth more than the same amount of money received in the future.**

1.3 **Other reasons why a present £1 is worth more than a future £1**

(a) **Uncertainty.** The business world is full of risk and uncertainty and although there might be a promise of money to come in the future, it can never be certain that the money will be received until it has actually been paid.

(b) **Inflation.** It is common sense that £1 now is worth more than £1 in the future because of inflation. It should be noted that the time value of money concept applies even if there is zero inflation. Inflation obviously increases the discrepancy in value between monies received at different times but it is not the basis of the concept.

1.4 **Taking account of the time value of money** (by discounting) is one of the principal **advantages of the DCF technique.**

2 DISCOUNTED CASH FLOW TECHNIQUES

Knowledge brought forward from earlier studies

Discounted cash flow techniques

- *Discounting* involves determining the equivalent worth today (*present value (PV)*) of a future cash flow (FV).

  PV = FV × $1/(1+r)^n$, where $1/(1+r)^n$ = discount factor

Knowledge brought forward from earlier studies (continued)

- Example: the PV of £100,000 received in five years if r is 6%pa = £100,000 × $1/(1.06)^5$ = £74,726.

- Discount factors are shown in present value tables.

- DCF techniques look at the *cash flows* of a project, not accounting profits. The timing of cash flows is taken into account by discounting them.

- The *net present value (NPV) method* of using DCF to evaluate an investment is as follows.

  ○ Work out the PVs of all cash flows (income and expenditure) related to the investment using an organisation's cost of capital/target rate of return.

  ○ Work out a net total (a net present value (NPV)).

  ○ If the NPV is positive the investment is acceptable, but if it is negative the investment is unacceptable.

- The *internal rate of return (IRR) method* calculates the exact rate of return at which the investment's NPV = 0.

  ○ If IRR > target rate of return, the investment is acceptable.
  ○ If IRR < target rate of return, the investment is unacceptable.

- To determine the IRR of a one-or-two-year investment, equate the PV of costs with the PV of benefits.

- To determine the IRR of a more lengthy investment, use *interpolation*.

  ○ Calculate a rough estimate of the IRR using $^2/_3$ × (profit ÷ initial investment).

  ○ Calculate the NPV using the rough estimate of the IRR as r. If the NPV is negative, recalculate the NPV using a lower rate but if the NPV is positive, recalculate the NPV using a higher rate.

  ○ Calculate the IRR using $a\% + \left[\dfrac{A}{A-B} \times (b-a) \right]\%$ where

    a = one interest rate   b = the other interest rate
    A = NPV at rate a   B = NPV at rate b

- The following *timing of cash flow conventions* are used in DCF.

  ○ A cash flow at the beginning of an investment project (ie 'now') occurs in year 0, for which the discount factor is always 1.

  ○ Cash flows during the course of a time period are assumed to occur at the period end.

  ○ Cash flows at the beginning of a time period are assumed to occur at the end of the previous time period.

- An *annuity* is a constant sum of money each year for a given number of years. The PV of an annuity is calculated using cumulative PV factor tables.

  ○ *Approach 1.* The cumulative PV factor for years 3 to 6 = cumulative PV factor for years 1 to 6 minus cumulative PV factor for years 1 to 2.

  ○ *Approach 2.* Flows in years 3 to 6 mean cash will be received/paid for a total of four years. Had the flows occurred in years 1 to 4, we could use the four-year annuity factor to arrive at an equivalent lump sum at time 0. The flows are for years 3 to 6, however, and so are 'moved forward' by two years (from year 1 to year 3). Using the four-year annuity factor would therefore give the equivalent lump sum at time 2. To get back from time 2 to now (time 0), discount for two years.

    ∴ PV factor for years 3 to 6 = cumulative PV factor for years 1 to 4 × discount factor for year 2.

  ○ *Approach 3.* Use the annuity factor formula $1/r(1 - (1/r + r)^n)$

- A *perpetuity* is an annual cash flow (annuity) that lasts forever. The PV of £1 per annum in perpetuity is £1/r.

IMPORTANT POINT

If the contents of this knowledge brought forward box are **unfamiliar** we strongly recommend that you **revise** the topic using your Paper 2.4 Study Text.

Question: NPV

LCH Limited manufactures product X which it sells for £5 per unit. Variable costs of production are currently £3 per unit, and fixed costs 50p per unit. A new machine is available which would cost £90,000 but which could be used to make product X for a variable cost of only £2.50 per unit. Fixed costs, however, would increase by £7,500 per annum as a direct result of purchasing the machine. The machine would have an expected life of 4 years and a resale value after that time of £10,000. Sales of product X are estimated to be 75,000 units per annum. If LCH Limited expects to earn at least 12% per annum from its investments, should the machine be purchased?

Answer

Savings are 75,000 × (£3 - £2.50) = £37,500 per annum. **Additional costs** are £7,500 per annum. Net **cash savings** are therefore £30,000 per annum. (Remember, depreciation is not a cash flow and must be ignored as a 'cost'.)

The **first step** in calculating an NPV is to establish the **relevant costs** year by year. All future cash flows arising as a direct consequence of the decision should be taken into account.

It is **assumed** that the machine will be sold for £10,000 at the end of year 4.

Note. It is a **convention** of DCF that **receipts and payments** made during the course of a year are assumed to be **made at the year end**. Thus the net savings of £30,000 are assumed to occur at the end of year 1, year 2 etc.

Year	Cash flow £	PV factor (12%)	PV of cash flow £
0	(90,000)	1.000	(90,000)
1	30,000	0.893	26,790
2	30,000	0.797	23,910
3	30,000	0.712	21,360
4	40,000	0.636	25,440
		NPV	+7,500

The **NPV is positive** and so the project is **acceptable**: it will earn more than 12% pa.

Question: NPV and annuities

LC Ltd is considering the manufacture of a new product which would involve the use of both a new machine (costing £150,000) and an existing machine, which cost £80,000 two years ago and has a current net book value of £60,000. There is sufficient capacity on this machine, which has so far been under-utilised.

Annual sales of the product would be 5,000 units, selling at £32 per unit. Unit costs would be:

	£
Direct labour (4 hours @ £2)	8
Direct materials	7
Fixed costs including depreciation	9
	24

The project would have a 5 year life, after which the new machine would have a net residual value of £10,000. Because direct labour is continually in short supply, labour resources would have to be diverted from other work which currently earns a contribution of £1.50 per direct labour hour. The fixed overhead absorption rate would be £2.25 per hour (£9 per unit) but actual expenditure on fixed overhead would not alter. Working capital requirements would be £10,000 in the first year, rising to

£15,000 in the second year and remaining at this level until the end of the project, when it will all be recovered. The company's cost of capital is 20%.

Required

Assess whether the project worthwhile.

Answer

The relevant cash flows are as follows.   £

			£
(a)	**Year 0**	Purchase of new machine	150,000
(b)	**Years 1-5**	Contribution from new product	85,000
		5,000 units × £(32 – 15)	
		Less contribution forgone	
		(5,000 × 4) × £1.50	30,000
			55,000

(c) The project requires £10,000 of **working capital** at the beginning of year 1 and a further £5,000 at the start of year 2.

Increases in working capital reduce the net cash flow for the period to which they relate. When the working capital tied up in the project is 'recovered' at the end of the project, it will provide an extra cash inflow (for example debtors will eventually pay up).

(d) **All other costs**, which are past costs, notional accounting costs, or costs which would be incurred anyway without the project, are **not relevant** to the investment decision.

(e) The NPV is calculated as follows

Year	Equipment £	Working capital £	Contribution £	Net cash flow £	Discount factor at 20% cash flow	PV of net cash flow £
0	(150,000)	(10,000)		(160,000)	1.000	(160,000)
1		(5,000)		(5,000)	0.833	(4,165)
1-5			55,000	55,000	2.991	164,505
5	10,000	15,000		25,000	0.402	10,050
					NPV =	10,390

The **NPV** is **positive** and the project is **worthwhile**, although there is **not much margin for error**. Some **risk analysis** of the project is recommended.

Question: IRR

Find the IRR of the project given below and state whether the project should be accepted if the company requires a minimum return of 17%.

Time		£
0	Investment	(4,000)
1	Receipts	1,200
2	"	1,410
3	"	1,875
4	"	1,150

Answer

The total receipts are £5,635 giving a total profit of £1,635 and average profits of £409. The average investment is £2,000. The **ARR** is £409 ÷ £2,000 = 20%. **Two thirds of the ARR** is approximately 14%. The **initial estimate of the IRR** that we shall try is therefore 14%.

Time	Cash flow	Try 14% Discount factor at 14%	PV	Try 16% Discount factor at 16%	PV
	£		£		£
0	(4,000)	1.000	(4,000)	1.000	(4,000)
1	1,200	0.877	1,052	0.862	1,034
2	1,410	0.769	1,084	0.743	1,048
3	1,875	0.675	1,266	0.641	1,202
4	1,150	0.592	681	0.552	635
		NPV	+ 83	NPV	(81)

The **IRR must be less than 16%, but higher than 14%**. The NPVs at these two costs of capital will be used to estimate the IRR.

Using the **interpolation formula**:

$$IRR = 14\% + \left[\frac{83}{83 + 81} \times (16\% - 14\%) \right] = 15.01\%$$

The IRR is, in fact, exactly 15%.

The project should be **rejected** as the **IRR is less than the minimum return demanded.**

Replacement and annualised equivalents

2.1 Suppose a company is deciding whether to replace company cars after a three, four or five year cycle. The relevant cash flows might be as follows.

	Year	Three year cycle £	Four year cycle £	Five year cycle £
Capital cost	0	(6,000)	(6,000)	(6,000)
Running costs	1	(280)	(280)	(280)
Running costs	2	(1,090)	(1,090)	(1,090)
Running costs	3	(1,120)	(1,120)	(1,120)
Trade in value	3	1,000	-	-
Running costs	4	-	(1,590)	(1,590)
Trade in value	4	-	700	-
Running costs	5	-	-	(1,260)
Trade in value	5	-	-	300
NPV at 15% *		(7,147)	(8,313)	(9,190)

* The workings are not shown, but as an exercise you could check the NPV calculations yourself.

Try using a spreadsheet package if you have access to one.

2.2 **These NPVs cannot be compared directly** because they each relate to **a different number of years**. In order to make a comparison we must convert **each NPV to an annualised equivalent cost**. We do this by using **cumulative discount factors** as follows.

	Three year cycle	Four year cycle	Five year cycle
NPV at 15%	£(7,147)	£(8,313)	£(9,190)
Cumulative 15% discount factor	÷ 2.28	÷ 2.86	÷ 3.35
Annualised equivalent cost	£3,134	£2,907	£2,743

2.3 The **lowest annualised equivalent cost** results from a five year cycle, therefore the company should replace its cars every five years.

Now attempt this final exercise to help you revise an application of DCF techniques.

Question: lease or buy?

The management of a company has decided to acquire Machine X which costs £63,000 and has an operational life of four years. The expected scrap value would be zero.

Tax is payable at 33% on operating cash flows one year in arrears. Capital allowances are available at 25% a year on a reducing balance basis.

Suppose that the company has the opportunity either to purchase the machine or to lease it under a finance lease arrangement, at an annual rent of £20,000 for four years, payable at the end of each year. The company can borrow to finance the acquisition at 10%. Should the company lease or buy the machine?

Answer

Working

Capital allowances

Year		£
1	(25% of £63,000)	15,750
2	(75% of £15,750)	11,813
3	(75% of £11,813)	8,859
		36,422
4	(£63,000 – £36,422)	26,578

The financing decision will be appraised by discounting the relevant cash flows at the **after-tax cost of borrowing**, which is 10% × 67% = 6.7%, say 7%.

(a) **Purchase option**

Year	Item	Cash flow £	Discount factor 7%	Present value £
0	Cost of machine	(63,000)	1.000	(63,000)
	Tax saved from capital allowances			
2	33% × £15,750	5,198	0.873	4,538
3	33% × £11,813	3,898	0.816	3,181
4	33% × £8,859	2,923	0.763	2,230
5	33% × £26,578	8,771	0.713	6,254
				(46,797)

(b) **Leasing option**

Year	Item	Cash flow £	Discount factor 7%	Present value £
1-4	Lease costs	(20,000)	3.387	(67,740)
2-5	Tax savings on lease costs (× 33%)	6,600	3.165	20,889
				(46,851)

The **purchase option** is **marginally cheaper**, using a cost of capital based on the after-tax cost of borrowing.

On the assumption that investors would regard borrowing and leasing as equally risky finance options, the purchase option is recommended.

Risk and uncertainty

Use of probabilities

2.4 We saw in Chapter 24 how probabilities can be used to take account of risk and uncertainty in cash flows in short-term decisions. Likewise, probabilities can be applied to cash flows in long-term decisions.

2.5 For example, suppose the cash inflows of a project are affected by the state of the market.

State of market	Probability of occurrence	Change in cash flows
A	60%	+10%
B	30%	+17%
C	10%	−20%

If the cash inflow in year 1 was estimated at £100,000, the EV of the cash inflow would be £100,000 × ((0.6 × 1.1) + (0.3 × 1.17) + (0.1 × 0.8)) = £109,100.

This EV could be included in the NPV calculation.

Exam focus point

This technique was required in the December 2001 exam.

Best possible/worst possible/most likely outcomes

2.6 This approach was also covered in Chapter 24 and can be applied to projects (although contingency tables are not required).

Exam focus point

'Best outcome' and 'worst outcome' NPVs had to be calculated in the June 2003 exam.

3 A CHOICE OF METHODS OF INVESTMENT APPRAISAL

Knowledge brought forward from earlier studies

Other methods of investment appraisal

- The *accounting rate of return (ARR)*/return on investment (ROI)/return on capital employed (ROCE) method of appraising investments is to estimate the ARR of an investment and to undertake it if the ARR exceeds a target rate of return.

$$ARR = \frac{\text{Average annual profits}}{\text{Average net book value of investment}} \times 100\%$$

- The *payback method* of appraising investments is to estimate the time it will take the cash inflows of an investment to equal the cash outflows (the payback period). It should be a first screening process.

  ° The project with the shortest payback period should be selected from competing projects.
  ° A project with a payback period below a target payback period should be selected.

Question: ARR and payback

Calculate the ARR and the payback period of the following project.

Capital cost of asset	£80,000
Estimated life	4 years

Estimated profit before depreciation

Year 1	£20,000
Year 2	£25,000
Year 3	£35,000
Year 4	£25,000

The asset will be reduced by 25% of its cost each year and will have a nil residual value.

Answer

	£
Total profit before depreciation over four years	105,000
Total profit after depreciation over four years	25,000
Average annual profit after depreciation	6,250

Average net book value over four years $\dfrac{£(80,000 - 0)}{2}$ 40,000

$$ARR = \frac{£6,250}{£40,000} \times 100\% = 15.63\%$$

Year	Cash flow £	Cumulative cash flow £
0	(80,000)	(80,000)
1	20,000	(60,000)
2	25,000	(35,000)
3	35,000	-
4	25,000	25,000

The **payback period** is 3 years.

Contrast with DCF methods

3.1 **Disadvantages to the use of the payback method**

(a) It ignores any cash flows that occur after the project has paid for itself. Because of this a project that takes time to get off the ground but earns substantial profits once it is established might be rejected if the payback method is used.

(b) It fails to distinguish between projects which have the same payback period.

(c) It ignores project profitability.

3.2 **Disadvantages to the use of accounting rate of return**

(a) It is based on accounting profits rather than cash and it may therefore give too much emphasis to costs which are merely accounting conventions and not truly relevant to a project's performance.

(b) It ignores the length of the project and the size of the investment.

(c) There are differing views about the way in which ARR should be calculated.

3.3 Most importantly, **both methods ignore the time value of money**.

NPV or IRR?

3.4 None of these objections apply to DCF methods of investment appraisal. However, given that there are two methods of using DCF, the NPV method and the IRR method, the relative merits of each method have to be considered. **Which is better?**

3.5 The main advantage of the **IRR** method is that the **information** it provides is more **easily understood** by managers, especially non-financial managers. For example, it is fairly easy to understand the meaning of the following statement.

'The project will be expected to earn a yield of 25%, and have an initial capital outlay of £100,000. This is in excess of the target yield of 15% for investments.'

It is not so easy to understand the meaning of this statement.

'The project will cost £100,000 and have an NPV of £30,000 when discounted at the minimum required rate of 15%.'

3.6 In other respects, the **IRR** method has **serious disadvantages.**

(a) It might be tempting to confuse **IRR** and **accounting rate of return (ARR)**. The ARR and the IRR are two completely different measures. If managers were given information about both ARR and IRR, it might be easy to get their relative meaning and significance mixed up.

(b) It **ignores the relative size of investments**. Both the following projects have an IRR of 18%.

	Project A	Project B
	£	£
Cost, year 0	350,000	35,000
Annual savings, years 1 - 6	100,000	10,000

Clearly, project A is bigger (ten times as big) and so more 'profitable' but if the only information on which the projects were judged were to be their IRR of 18%, project B would be made to seem just as beneficial as project A, which is not the case.

(c) If the **cash flows** from a project are **not conventional** (with an outflow at the beginning resulting in inflows over the life of a project) it may have **more than one IRR**. This could be very difficult for managers to interpret. For example, the following project has cash flows which are not conventional, and as a result has two IRRs of approximately 7% and 35%.

Year	Project X
	£'000
0	(1,900)
1	4,590
2	(2,735)

(d) The IRR method should **not be used to select between mutually exclusive projects**. This follows on from point (b) and it is the most significant and damaging criticism of the IRR method, where the choice between mutually exclusive projects is made by **selecting the project with the highest IRR.**

Broader issues

3.7 As well as carrying out a financial analysis, broader issues must also be considered when deciding whether or not to proceed with a project.

(a) **Risk of the project.** Is it known? Can it be measured?

(b) The role of the individual project within the **corporate plan**. How does it 'fit' with existing and planned projects?

(c) Is the project an **integral part** of a wider plan? Does it have to commence now or could it be **postponed** if necessary?

(d) Will the project lower or increase the organisation's **overall level of risk** and hence affect the **corporate cost of capital**?

4   NPV, RI AND ANNUITY DEPRECIATION

4.1   As we have seen in Chapter 11, ROI and RI do not always point to the right decision and so, whenever possible, a DCF approach to decision making should be adopted. Two possible **refinements** to the normal approach to calculating ROI and RI exist, however, and these can be adopted if it is not possible to calculate an NPV or an IRR.

4.2   Suppose that Division M is considering an investment of £200,000 which will provide a net cash inflow (before depreciation) of £78,000 each year for the four years of its life. It is group policy that investments must show a minimum return of 15%.

4.3   As the working below shows, using net book value at the start of each year and **depreciating on a straight line basis** to a nil residual value, in year 1 the RI would be negative and the ROI below the target rate of return of 15%. If management were to take a short-term view of the situation, the **investment would be rejected** if either of the measures were to be used, despite the fact that the investment's NPV is positive and that in years 2 to 4 the RI is positive and the ROI greater than the target rate of return.

	Years			
	1	*2*	*3*	*4*
	£	£	£	£
NBV of investment at start of year	200,000	150,000	100,000	50,000
Cash flow (before depreciation)	78,000	78,000	78,000	78,000
Less depreciation	(50,000)	(50,000)	(50,000)	(50,000)
Net profit	28,000	28,000	28,000	28,000
Less inputed interest (at 15%)	(30,000)	(22,500)	(15,000)	(7,500)
RI	(2,000)	5,500	13,000	20,500
ROI	14.00%	18.67%	28.00%	56.00%

Net present value = (£200,000) + (£78,000 × 2.855) = £22,690.

Annuity depreciation method

4.4   However, if instead of using straight line depreciation we use what is known as **annuity depreciation** we get a different story.

4.5   To calculate annuity depreciation we need to determine an **annual equivalent cash flow** which represents the annual net cash inflow required so that, in present value terms, the investment would break even. This annual equivalent cash flow is calculated for our example as (initial investment/cumulative discount factor at 15% for 4 years) = £200,000/2.855 = £70,052.54.

4.6   As the annual equivalent cash flow is the annual cash inflow which ensures that the investment **breaks even**, it is the total of the 'costs' that the investment will cause, those 'costs' being interest and depreciation.

FORMULAE TO LEARN

Annual equivalent cash flow = depreciation + interest

Annuity depreciation = annual equivalent cash flow – imputed interest on capital employed

Year 1 annuity depreciation = £70,052.54 – (0.15 × 200,000) = £40,052.54

Year 2 annuity depreciation = £70,052.54 – (0.15 × (200,000 – 40.052.54)) = £46,060.42

and so on, the imputed interest depending on the NBV of the investment at the start of the year, which in turn depends on the annuity depreciation charged in the previous year.

	Years			
	1	*2*	*3*	*4*
	£	£	£	£
NBV of investment at start of year	200,000.00	159,947.46	113,887.04	60,917.56
Cash flow (before depreciation)	78,000.00	78,000.00	78,000.00	78,000.00
Less depreciation	(40,052.54)	(46,060.42)	(52,969.48)	(60,914.91)
Net profit	37,947.46	31,939.58	25,030.52	17,085.09
Less inputed interest (at 15%)	(30,000.00)	(23,992.12)	(17,083.06)	(9,137.63)
RI	7,947.46	7,947.46	7,947.46	7,947.46
ROI	18.97%	19.97%	21.98%	28.05%

Note that the use of annuity depreciation produces an increasing charge for depreciation but that the total depreciation charged still totals to £200,000 (with a small difference for rounding).

4.7 In the first year of the investment's life using annuity depreciation, the **ROI is in excess of the target rate of return** and the **RI is positive**. This means that the investment would be considered acceptable, even if management are taking a short-term view. The use of annuity depreciation therefore helps to make the ROI/RI and NPV measures **compatible**.

4.8 Moreover, this approach has **smoothed the ROI figures** reported each year compared with those reported when using straight-line depreciation and has produced a **constant RI** for each of the four years.

4.9 Note that if the RI were to be **discounted** in the same way as cash flows in the NPV approach, the overall discounted RI = £7,947.46 × 2.855 = £22,690 = the investment's NPV.

5 EXAM-STANDARD APPLICATION OF DCF

5.1 EXAMPLE: THE NPV METHOD

Due to the financial failure of an overseas competitor, a company sees the opportunity of taking up a new market for its product. At present this market would buy 325,000 tonnes of the product per annum, and this is forecast to rise at 9% per annum. Sales revenue is expected to be £8 per tonne ex plant.

The company proposes to go into this market immediately and considers methods of supply involving the import from elsewhere, the hiring of plant locally, and the construction of new plant.

Details are as follows.

(a) **Option A: Import from elsewhere**

It could import up to a maximum of 500,000 tonnes per annum of the product at an average cost of £7.50 per tonne at the plant.

(b) **Option B: Hire of plant locally**

It could hire plant capacity of 500,000 tonnes per annum at a nearby site. This is available immediately.

The terms of the hiring are £1.20 per tonne of capacity for a minimum of 12 years, with the plant owner being responsible for any variable operating costs. Direct material costs of £6 per tonne would be payable by the company.

(c) **Option C: Construction of new plant**

It could build up a plant with an effective capacity of 500,000 tonnes per annum which will be completed in three years. In the meantime, requirements may be imported.

Capital expenditure will be at £1.75 million, spent at the end of each year, as follows.

Year 1	£0.30 million
Year 2	£0.45 million
Year 3	£1.00 million

The expected life of the plant is 12 years and its salvage value is expected to be £0.30 million.

Direct material costs are expected to be £6 per tonne, variable operating costs £0.30 per tonne, and fixed operating costs £100,000 per annum. The company requires a cut-off rate of 20% DCF for projects involving capital expenditure.

Required

Recommend what action the company should take to achieve its objective. Support your recommendations with relevant calculations. Ignore taxation and inflation considerations.

5.2 DISCUSSION AND SOLUTION

There are three mutually exclusive options, and the preferred option will be the one with the highest NPV, provided that this is a positive value.

Step 1. **Determine evaluation period**

The three options must be compared on an equal basis, which means that the time period over which the projects are evaluated must be selected with care.

(a) **Option A** has no particular time period, and involves no capital outlay either.

(b) **Option B** has a minimum time period of 12 years, but again no capital outlay is involved.

(c) **Option C** involves capital expenditure with an equipment life of 12 years, but the equipment could not become operational until the end of year 3, and so with option C we are looking ahead up to 15 years.

To compare each option equally, we ought to look at each over a **15 year period.**

Step 2. **Estimate and discount cash flows**

The next step in the solution is to estimate the cash flows for each option, and discount them to an NPV at 20%. In this problem, there are no difficulties in distinguishing relevant and non-relevant cost items, but there are some snags in sorting out the logic of what would happen with each option. As in many other DCF problems, and decision-accounting problems generally, it is getting the logic sorted out that is half the battle.

(a) **Option A**

The company can import the exact quantity to meet the market demand. Demand will be 325,000 tonnes in year 1, rising by 9% per annum, but there is a constraint of 500,000 tonnes maximum that could be imported. The contribution is the net cash inflow, and is £0.50 per tonne.

Year	Sales demand Tonnes	Contribution £	Discount factor 20%	PV £
1	325,000	162,500	0.833	135,363
2	354,250	177,125	0.694	122,925
3	386,133	193,067	0.579	111,786
4	420,885	210,443	0.482	101,434
5	458,765	229,383	0.402	92,212
6 - 15	500,000 (max)	250,000 pa	1.684*	421,000
		Total PV of benefits		984,720

* PV of £1 pa for   Years 1 - 15   6.675

                 Years 1 - 5   (2.991)

                 Years 6 - 15   1.684

(b) Option B

A 15-year term is assumed to be feasible. The maximum capacity is 500,000 tonnes, and so what happens when demand exceeds 500,000 tonnes?

(i)   Does the plant capacity restrict sales to 500,000 tonnes?

(ii)   Or can the company top up the production shortfall by importing the difference?

Assumption (i) is chosen here, but you might prefer assumption (ii). If in doubt, state your assumptions clearly in your solution to any examination question.

The contribution per tonne is £2. The annual net cash flow is the total contribution minus the hire charge of £1.20 per tonne of *capacity*. A small trap here: capacity is fixed at 500,000 tonnes, and so the hire charge is an incremental fixed cost expenditure of £600,000; it is not a variable cost of £1.20 per tonne!

	Demand Tonnes	£	Fixed hire charge £	Net cash flow £	Discount factor 20%	£
1	325,000	650,000	600,000	50,000	0.833	41,650
2	354,250	708,500	600,000	108,500	0.694	75,299
3	386,133	772,266	600,000	172,266	0.579	99,742
4	420,885	841,770	600,000	241,770	0.482	116,533
5	458,765	917,530	600,000	317,530	0.402	127,647
6 - 15	500,000	1,000,000	600,000	400,000	1.684	673,600
				Total PV of benefits		1,134,471

(c) Option C

The snag here is working out what will happen in years 1-3. The equipment would not be operational for 3 years, but the company could not ignore the market until then. The question states this, in case you were doubtful. Presumably, the company would have to import what it needed for the first 3 years.

The second problem is the same as with Option B. Capacity is 500,000 tonnes, but would the company make up the shortfall by importing the difference? Again, to be consistent, the assumption here is that no, the maximum sales limit would be 500,000 tonnes.

The cash flows can be tabulated as follows, given the following.

(i)   A contribution of £0.50 per tonne in years 1 - 3

(ii)   A contribution of £(8 – 6 – 0.3) = £1.70 per tonne for years 4 - 15

Do not ignore the equipment's residual/scrap value of £300,000 at the end of year 15.

Year	Capital equipment £	Contribution £	Fixed costs £	Net cash flow £	Discount factor 20%	PV £
1	(300,000)	162,500 **	-	(137,500)	0.833	(114,538)
2	(450,000)	177,125 **	-	(272,875)	0.694	(189,375)
3	(1,000,000)	193,067 **	-	(806,933)	0.579	(467,214)
4		715,505	(100,000)	615,505	0.482	296,673
5		779,901	(100,000)	679,901	0.402	273,320
6 - 15		850,000	(100,000)	750,000	1.684	1,263,000
15	300,000			300,000	0.065	19,500
					NPV	1,081,366

** as for Option A

Step 3.   **Make decision**

The preference should be for option B, since it has a higher PV of benefits (or NPV) by £53,105 over Option C. (*Note*. There must be some allowance for rounding errors, and this figure is by no means 'exact'.)

Option A	NPV	£984,720
Option B	NPV	£1,134,471
Option C	NPV	£1,081,366

Exam focus point

The examiner has highlighted the **comparison of long-run and shot-run performance** as a potential issue for inclusion in the compulsory questions.

Chapter roundup

- The **time value of money** is the concept that £1 received today is not equal to £1 received in the future.

- Given the choice between receiving £100 today, and £100 in one year's time, most people would opt to receive £100 today because they could spend it or invest it to earn interest. If the interest rate was 10%, you could invest £100 today and it would be worth (£100 × 1.10) = £110 in one year's time. A sum of money received now is therefore worth more than the same amount of money received in the future.

- It is important that you are able to explain how **discounting** works and why DCF methods are superior for decision making to methods more likely to be used by the layman, like **ARR** and **payback**. You could well have to do so in practice at some stage.

- NPVs of projects over different numbers of years can be compared by converting each NPV to an **annualised equivalent cost**.

- Although the concept of IRR is more easily understood by managers, it has serious disadvantages when compared with NPV.

- The use of **annuity depreciation** helps to make the ROI/RI and NPV measures compatible.

- Examination questions sometimes tell you to ignore the time value of money or else say that all amounts are already stated at their present values. If a question is silent on this matter but seems to be a **long-run decision** you will have to decide whether DCF should be used or not. At the very least you should mention the time value of money in your list of **assumptions** or your note on 'other factors to be considered'.

Quick quiz

1   *Rearrange the following into a formula for present value.*

   n, (, FV, PV, x, +, /, 1, 1, =,), r

2   If an IRR is greater than a target rate of return, the investment is unacceptable. *True or false?*

3   *Fill in the blanks.*

   To determine the IRR of an investment, use ....

   - Calculate a rough estimate of the IRR using ....

   - Calculate the NPV using the rough estimate of the IRR as r. If the NPV is negative, recalculate the NPV using a .... rate but if the NPV is positive, recalculate the NPV using a ....rate.

   - Calculate the IRR using a% +................................. where

     a = ... rate   b = ... rate

     A = ...   B = ...

4   *Choose the appropriate word(s) from those highlighted.*

   The cumulative PV factor for years 7 to 11 = cumulative PV factors for years **1 to 7/7 to 11/1 to 11/1 to 6/6 to 11 minus/plus** cumulative PV factor for years **1 to 7/7 to 11/1 to 11/1 to 6/6 to 11**.

5   The principal disadvantage of the payback and ARR methods of appraisal is that they are based on accounting profits rather than cash. *True or false?*

6   *Fill in the blanks.*

   Annual equivalent cash flow = ... + ...

   Annuity depreciation = ... − ....

7   Which of the following is not a consequence of using annuity deprecation?

A   ROI figures are smoothed
B   A constant RI is reported
C   It makes the ROI/RI and NPV measures compatible
D   The discounted ROI = investment's NPV

8   The time value of money concept is that a present £1 is worth less than a future £1. *True or false?*

Answers to quick quiz

1    $PV = FV \times 1/(1+r)^n$

2   False

3   To determine the IRR of an investment, use interpolation.

- Calculate a rough estimate of the IRR using $^2/_3 \times$ (profit ÷ initial investment).

- Calculate the NPV using the rough estimate of the IRR as r. If the NPV is negative, recalculate the NPV using a lower rate but if the NPV is positive, recalculate the NPV using a higher rate.

- Calculate the IRR using $a\% + \left[\dfrac{A}{A-B} \times (b-a) \right]\%$ where

    a = one interest rate   b = the other interest rate
    A = NPV at rate a   B = NPV at rate b

4   1 to 11
     minus
     1 to 6

5   False. Both methods ignore the time value of money.

6   Annual equivalent cash flow = depreciation + interest

     Annuity depreciation = annual equivalent cash flow – imputed interest on capital employed

7   D

8   False

Now try the question below from the Exam Question Bank

Number	Level	Marks	Time
24	Exam	40	72 mins

Article by the examiner

environmental
management accounting
relevant to Professional scheme Paper 3.3

green

■ This article is intended to help students understand environmental management accounting, its increasing importance, and new developments.

The global profile of environmental issues has risen significantly during the past two decades, precipitated in part by major incidents such as the Bhopal chemical leak (1984) and the Exxon Valdez oil spill (1989). These events received worldwide media attention and increased concerns over major issues such as global warming, depletion of non-renewable resources, and loss of natural habitats.

This has led to a general questioning of business practices and numerous calls for change. These questions have not only been raised by organisations such as Friends of the Earth, Greenpeace, or groups of 'eco-warriors', but from the United Nations, the European Union, the UK government, the British Bankers Association, insurance companies and pension funds. Recognition that our current way of life poses a threat to us and our planet, has led to global agreements on action to prevent future environmental damage. Such agreements include the Montreal Protocol, the Rio Declaration, and the Kyoto Protocol.

Businesses have become increasingly aware of the environmental implications of their operations, products and services. Environmental risks cannot be ignored, they are now as much a part of running a

successful business as product design, marketing, and sound financial management. Poor environmental behaviour may have a real adverse impact on the business and its finances. Punishment includes fines, increased liability to environmental taxes, loss in value of land, destruction of brand values, loss of sales, consumer boycotts,

> Businesses have become increasingly aware of the environmental implications of their operations, products and services. Environmental risks cannot be ignored, they are now as much a part of running a successful business as product design, marketing, and sound financial management.

inability to secure finance, loss of insurance cover, contingent liabilities, law suits, and damage to corporate image.

Nearly all aspects of business are affected by environmental pressures, including accounting. From an accounting perspective, the initial pressures were felt in external reporting, including environmental disclosures in financial reports and/or the

production of separate environmental accounts. Much has been written about the nature and quality of these accounts (see Gray and Bebbington, 2001 for an introduction into this area). However, environmental issues cannot be dealt with solely through external reporting. Environmental issues need to be managed before they can be reported on, and this requires changes to management accounting systems.

ENVIRONMENTAL REVIEW OF CONVENTIONAL MANAGEMENT ACCOUNTING

In an ideal world, organisations would reflect environmental factors in their accounting processes via the identification of the environmental costs attached to products, processes, and services. Nevertheless, many existing conventional accounting systems are unable to deal adequately with environmental costs and as a result simply attribute them to general overhead accounts. Consequently, managers are unaware of these costs, have no information with which to manage them and have no incentive to reduce them (United Nations Division for Sustainable Development (UNDSD), 2003). It must be recognised that most management accounting techniques significantly underestimate the cost of poor environmental behaviour. Many overestimate the cost and underestimate the benefits of improving environmental practices.

Management accounting techniques can distort and misrepresent environmental issues, leading to managers making decisions that are bad for businesses and bad for the environment. The most obvious example relates to energy usage. A recent UK government publicity campaign reports that companies are spending, on average, 30% too much on energy through inefficient practices. With good energy management, we could reduce the environmental impact of energy production by 30% and slash 30% of organisations' energy expenditure. Frost and Wilmhurst (2000) suggest that by failing to reform management accounting practices to incorporate environmental concerns, organisations are unaware of the impact on profit and loss accounts and the balance sheet impact of environment-related activities. Moreover, they miss out on identifying cost reduction and other improvement opportunities, employ incorrect product/service pricing, mix and development decisions. This leads to a failure to enhance customer value, while increasing the risk profile of investments and other decisions with long-term consequences. If management accounting as a discipline is to contribute to improving the environmental performance of organisations, then it has to change. Environmental Management Accounting (EMA) is an attempt to integrate best management accounting thinking and practice with best environmental management thinking and practice.

ENVIRONMENTAL MANAGEMENT ACCOUNTING

EMA is the generation and analysis of both financial and non-financial information in order to support internal environmental management processes. It is complementary to the conventional financial management accounting approach, with the aim to develop appropriate mechanisms that assist in the identification and allocation of environment-

ENVIRONMENTAL MANAGEMENT ACCOUNTING (EMA)

	Monetary Environmental Management Accounting (MEMA)		Physical Environmental Management Accounting (PEMA)	
	Short-term focus	Long-term focus	Short-term focus	Long-term focus
Past orientated — Routinely generated information	Environmental cost accounting (e.g. variable costing, absorption costing, and activity-based costing)	Environmentally induced capital expenditure and revenues	Material and energy flow accounting (short-term impacts on the environment – product site, division and company levels	Environmental (or natural) capital impact accounting
Past orientated — Ad hoc information	Ex-post assessment of relevant environmental costing decisions	Environmental lifecycle (and target) costing Post-investment assessment of individual projects	Ex-post assessment of short-term environmental impacts (e.g. of a site or product)	Lifecycle inventories Post-investment assessment of physical environmental investment appraisal
Future orientated — Routinely generated information	Monetary environmental operational budgeting (flows) Monetary environmental capital budgeting (stocks)	Environmental long-term financial planning	Physical environmental budgeting (flows and stocks) (e.g. material and energy flow – activity-based budgeting)	Long-term physical environmental planning
Future orientated — Ad hoc information	Relevant environmental costing (e.g. special orders, product mix with capacity constraint)	Monetary environmental project investment appraisal Environmental lifecycle budgeting and target pricing	Relevant environmental impacts (e.g. given short run constraints on activities)	Physical environmental investment appraisal Lifecycle analysis of specific project

FIGURE 1: PROPOSED FRAMEWORK OF EMA ACCORDING TO BURRITT ET AL (2001)

related costs (Bennett and James (1998a), Frost and Wilmhurst (2000)). The major areas for the application for EMA are:
- ☐ in the assessment of annual environmental costs/expenditures
- ☐ product pricing
- ☐ budgeting
- ☐ investment appraisal
- ☐ calculating costs
and
- ☐ savings of environmental projects, or setting quantified performance targets.

EMA is as wide-ranging in its scope, techniques and focus as normal management accounting. Burritt et al (2001) stated: 'there is still no precision in the terminology associated with EMA'. They viewed EMA as being an application of conventional accounting that is concerned with the environmentally-induced impacts of companies, measured in monetary units, and company-related impacts on environmental systems, expressed in physical units. EMA can be viewed as a part of the environmental accounting framework and is defined as 'using monetary and physical information for internal management use'.

Burritt et al developed a multi-dimensional framework of EMA (**Figure 1**). Their framework considers the distinctions between five dimensions:

- ☐ internal versus external
- ☐ physical versus monetary classifications
- ☐ past and future timeframes
- ☐ short and long terms
and
- ☐ ad hoc versus routine information gathering in the proposed framework for the application of EMA.

Within this framework the different techniques of EMA – such as environmental lifecycle costing or environmental cost accounting – can be placed and assigned. The management of a company can choose appropriate tools on the basis of their information needs.

Similarly, in a series of publications (1997, 1998a, 1998b), Bennett and James describe the diverse range and scope of environmental management accounting. They provide a set of useful models, one of which is 'The Environment-Related Management Accounting Pyramid', to help evaluate environmental management accounting practices as well as to help in the design and implementation of new systems.

According to Bennett and James (1998a) (**Figure 2**), EMA is concerned with gathering data related to the environment (lowest levels), which are converted through techniques and processes (middle level) into information which is useful for managers (top). Key data is both non-financial and

financial in nature. Management accounting techniques such as performance measurement, operational budgeting, costing or pricing are used for the transformation.

EXAMPLES OF TECHNIQUES
Redefining Costs
A literature review reveals various approaches to the definition of environmental costs. In 1998, the US Environmental Protection Agency argued that the definition of environmental costs depended on how a company intends to use the information, for example in capital budgeting or product design. They introduced terminology that distinguishes between conventional costs, potentially hidden costs, contingent costs, and image and relationship costs.

Conventional costs are those raw material and energy costs having environmental relevance. Potentially hidden costs are those which are captured by accounting systems, but then lose their identity in 'overheads'. Contingent costs may be incurred at a future date – for example costs for cleaning up. They are also referred to as contingent liabilities. Image and relationship costs are intangible in nature and include, for example, the costs of producing environmental reports. However, such costs pale into insignificance when compared with the costs associated

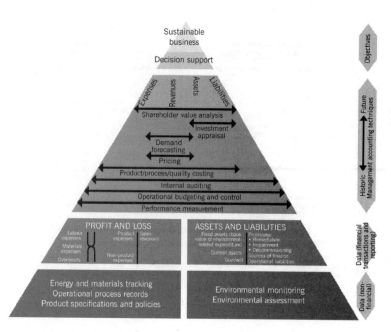

FIGURE 2: THE ENVIRONMENT-RELATED
MANAGEMENT ACCOUNTING PYRAMID,
BENNETT AND JAMES (1998A)

with being seen to behave in an irresponsible manner. The infamous Brent Spar incident that cost the Shell oil company millions of pounds in terms of lost revenues via the resultant consumer boycott, is an example of the powerful influence that environmental concern has in today's business environment. Shell learned the lesson, albeit somewhat belatedly, and as a result completely re-engineered its environmental management system.

ACCA has also published a research report outlining an agenda for action on full cost accounting (Bebbington, Gray, Hibbit and Kirk, 2001), which contains a detailed review of the business case for adopting full environmental costing. One example of the potential gains from using full costing (sometimes referred to as lifecycle costing, Bennett and James (1998b)) can be seen in the case of Xerox Limited.

Xerox Limited, a subsidiary of Xerox Corporation, introduced the concept of lifecycle costing for its logistic chain. The core business of Xerox Limited is manufacturing photocopiers, which are leased rather than sold. This means the machines are returned to Xerox Limited at the end of their lease. Previously, machines were shipped in a range of different types of packaging, which could rarely be re-used by customers to return the old copiers. The customer had to dispose of the original packaging and to provide new

packaging to return the machine at the end of its lease, which in turn could not be used to re-ship other machines. This meant Xerox lost the original costs and had to bear the costs of disposal of the packaging.

A new system was invented which used a standard pack (tote). Two types of totes were introduced to suit the entire range of products sold by Xerox. Totes can be used for both new machines delivery and return carcasses. The whole-chain cost analysis showed the considerably lower cost of the tote system, compared to the previously existing system and the supply chain became more visible. The tote system resulted not only in cost savings but also in reduced 'de-pack' times and improved customer relations (Bennett and James, 1998b).

UNDSD (2003) described total corporate environmental costs as environmental protection costs (emission treatment and pollution prevention) plus costs of wasted materials, plus costs of wasted capital and labour. Waste in this context means production inefficiency (purchase value of non-material output). UNDSD stated that wasted materials account for 40% to 90% of environmental costs according to a survey. One should recognise that environmental costs are not a separate type of cost; rather they are part of money flowing throughout a corporation.

The main difficulty associated with environmental costs is their identification

and allocation. According to UNDSD (2003), conventional accounting systems tend to attribute many of the environmental costs to general overhead accounts with the result that they are 'hidden' from management. Thus, management is often unaware of the extent of environmental costs and cannot identify opportunities for cost savings. EMA attempts to make all relevant, significant costs visible so that they can be considered when making business decisions (Jasch, 2003). UNDSD (2003) identified management accounting techniques which are useful for the identification and allocation of environmental costs as: input/output analysis, flow cost accounting, activity-based costing (ABC), and lifecycle costing.

Input/output analysis
The input/output analysis is a technique that can provide useful environmental information, sometimes referred to as mass balance (Envirowise, 2003). This technique records material flows with the idea that 'what comes in must go out – or be stored' (Jasch, 2003).

As shown in **Figure 3** on page 62, the purchased input is regarded as 100% and is balanced against the outputs – which are the produced, sold and stored goods and the residual (regarded as waste). Materials are measured in physical units and include energy

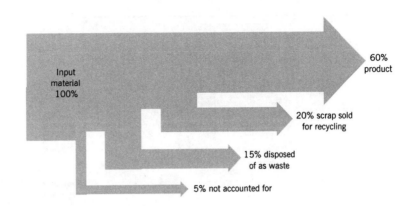

FIGURE 3: INPUT/OUTPUT ANALYSIS
ACCORDING TO ENVIROWISE (2003)

and water. At the end of the process, the material flows can be expressed in monetary units. Process flow charts can help to trace inputs and outputs, in particular waste. They demonstrate the details of the processes so that the relevant information can be allocated to main activities.

Process flow charts bring together technical information and cost accounting information (UNDSD, 2003). Flow cost accounting is a tool of a new management accounting approach – flow management. It aims to '...organise production end-to-end in terms of flows of materials and information – all structured in an efficient, objective-oriented manner' (UNDSD, 2003). It is more than a simple assessment of environmental costs, because it is focused on assessment of total costs of production.

Flow management involves not only material flows, but also the organisational structure. Classic material flows are recorded as well as material losses incurred at various stages of production. Flow cost accounting makes material flows transparent by using various data, which are quantities (physical data), costs (monetary data) and values (quantities x costs). The material flows are divided into three categories, material, system, and delivery and disposal, as shown in **Figure 4**. The material values and costs apply to the materials which are involved in the various processes. The system values and costs are the in-house handling costs, which are '...incurred inside the company for the purpose of maintaining and supporting material throughput, e.g. personnel costs or depreciation,' (UNDSD, 2003).

The delivery and disposal values and costs refer to the costs of flows leaving the company, for example transport costs or cost of disposing waste. EMA can benefit from

flow cost accounting because it aims to reduce the quantities of materials, which leads to increased ecological efficiency (UNDSD, 2003).

Environmental Activity-Based Accounting
Activity-based costing (ABC) '...represents a method of managerial cost accounting that allocates all internal costs to the cost centres and cost drivers on the basis of the activities that caused the costs,' (UNDSD, 2003). ABC applied to environmental costs distinguishes between environment-related costs and environment-driven costs. The former are attributed to joint environmental cost centres, for example incinerators or sewage plants. The latter are hidden in the general overheads and do not relate directly to a joint environmental cost centre, e.g. increased depreciation or higher cost of staff. Nevertheless they vary with the amount of throughput.

Schaltegger and Muller (1998) stated 'the choice of an adequate allocation key is crucial for obtaining correct information'. The four main allocation keys are:
☐ volume of emissions or waste
☐ toxicity of emission and waste treated
☐ environmental impact added (volume x input per unit of volume) volume of the emissions treated
 and
☐ the relative costs of treating different kinds of emissions.

LIFECYCLE COSTING
Environmental Management as part of Total Quality Management
The pursuit of environmental quality management via the development of an Environmental Management System (EMS) can only be achieved if 'environmental audit' is a concomitant feature of such a system. In

this respect the organisation becomes self-regulating and the undertaking of environmental audits on a regular basis provides the platform for organisations to adopt a self-critical and analytical posture as part of their routine organisational management processes. Organisations should be striving to achieve an integrated environmental strategy underpinned by the same type of culture that is required for the successful operation of a programme of total quality management (TQM).
It is arguable that the two are inextricably linked insofar as good environmental management is increasingly recognised as an essential component of TQM. In common with TQM, the focus is upon 'continuous improvement' and the pursuit of excellence. Such organisations pursue objectives that may include zero complaints, zero spills, zero pollution, zero waste and zero accidents. Information systems need to be able to support such environmental objectives via the provision of feedback – on the success or otherwise – of the organisational efforts in achieving such objectives. This approach to environmental quality management requires the development of environmental performance measures and indicators that will enable a comprehensive review of environmental performance to be undertaken. Many – if not all – total quality management accounting techniques can be modified and effectively adopted to help manage environmental issues.

CONCLUSION
It can be said that most companies do not know about the extent of their environmental costs and tend to underestimate them. This leads to distorted calculations of improvement options. For example, Amoco

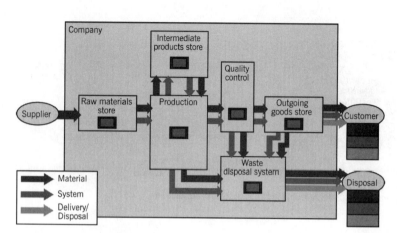

FIGURE 4: THE BASIC IDEA OF FLOW COST ACCOUNTING ACCORDING TO UNDSD (2003)

Yorktown Refinery estimated their environmental costs at 3% of non-crude operational costs. Actually they comprised 22% of non-crude operating costs as the case study of Ditz et al (1998) revealed. However, the study also discovered a large proportion of environmental costs were caused by other processes that had not been identified by Amoco.

EMA can solve these problems. The above-mentioned accounting techniques are useful for EMA to identify and allocate environmental costs. In addition, there are alternative techniques to estimate environmental costs such as the 'environmental cost decision tree' as described by Rimer (2000).

The most significant problem of EMA lies in the absence of a clear definition of environmental costs. This means it is likely that organisations are not monitoring and reporting such costs. The increase in environmental costs is likely to continue, which will result in the increased information needs of managers and provide the stimulus for the agreement of a clear definition. If a generally applicable meaning of environmental costs is established, the use of EMA will probably increase with positive effects for both organisations and the environment in which they operate. In the future it will not only be large companies which can afford to implement EMA but also small and medium-sized enterprises which have fewer available financial resources.

REFERENCES:

☐ Bebbington, J, Gray, R, Hibbitt, C and Kirk, E *Full Costs Accounting: An Agenda for Action* (ACCA Research Report No. 73, Certified Accountants Educational Trust, London, 2001)

☐ Bennett, M and James, P *Environment-Related Management Accounting Current Practice and Future Trends*, Greener Management International, Spring 97 (No.17, pp32-41, Business Source Premier, 1997)

☐ Bennett, M and James, P *The Green Bottom Line*, in: Bennett, M and James, P (Eds) *The Green Bottom Line – Environmental Accounting for Management: Current Practice and Future Trends* (Greenleaf Publishing, Sheffield, 1998a)

☐ Bennett, M and James, P *Life Cycle Costing and Packaging at Xerox Ltd*, in: Bennett, M and James, P (Eds) *The Green Bottom Line – Environmental Accounting for Management: Current Practice and Future Trends* (Greenleaf Publishing, Sheffield, 1998b)

☐ Burritt, L, Hahn, T and Schaltegger, S *Current Developments in Environmental Management Accounting – Towards a Comprehensive Framework for Environmental Management Accounting (EMA)* (Universitaet Lueneburg, 2001), http//:www.uni-lueneburg.de/eman/pdf_dateien/Burritt-Hahn.pdf

☐ Ditz, D, Ranganathan, J and Banks, R D *Green Ledgers – An Overview*, in: Bennett, M and James, P (Eds) *The Green Bottom Line – Environmental Accounting for Management: Current Practice and Future Trends* (Greenleaf Publishing, Sheffield, 1998)

☐ Envirowise *Increase your profits with environmental management accounting*, (Envirowise – Practical environmental advice for businesses, 2003, last update) http://www.envirowise.gov.uk/EnvirowiseV3.nsf/key/crod5hylhs

☐ Frost, G R and Wilmshurst, T D *The adoption of environment-related management accounting: an analysis of corporate environmental sensitivity* (Accounting Forum Vol 24, No 4, pp 344-365, Business Source Premier, 2000)

☐ Gray, R and Bebbington J *Accounting for the Environment (2nd edition)* (Sage Publications Ltd, 2001)

☐ Jasch, C *The use of Environmental Management Accounting (EMA) for identifying environmental costs, Journal of Cleaner Production*, http://www.sciencedirect.com

☐ Rimer, A E *Identifying, Reducing and Controlling Environmental Costs, Plant Engineering* (Vol 54, No 3, pp114-118, Business Source Premier, 2000)

☐ UNDSD – United Nations Division for Sustainable Development, *Environmental Management Accounting Procedures and Principles* (EMARIC Environmental Management Accounting Research and Information Center, 2003), http://www.emawebsite.org/documents/emaric_139.pdf

Further references:
http://www.accaglobal.com/sustainability

I wish to extend my thanks to Ian Thomson of Strathclyde University for reading the draft of this article and providing many helpful comments. ■

Shane Johnson is examiner for Paper 3.3

Mathematical tables

PRESENT VALUE TABLE

Present value of 1 ie $(1+r)^{-n}$

where r = discount rate

n = number of periods until payment

Periods	Discount rates (r)									
(n)	1%	2%	3%	4%	5%	6%	7%	8%	9%	10%
1	0.990	0.980	0.971	0.962	0.952	0.943	0.935	0.926	0.917	0.909
2	0.980	0.961	0.943	0.925	0.907	0.890	0.873	0.857	0.842	0.826
3	0.971	0.942	0.915	0.889	0.864	0.840	0.816	0.794	0.772	0.751
4	0.961	0.924	0.888	0.855	0.823	0.792	0.763	0.735	0.708	0.683
5	0.951	0.906	0.863	0.822	0.784	0.747	0.713	0.681	0.650	0.621
6	0.942	0.888	0.837	0.790	0.746	0.705	0.666	0.630	0.596	0.564
7	0.933	0.871	0.813	0.760	0.711	0.665	0.623	0.583	0.547	0.513
8	0.923	0.853	0.789	0.731	0.677	0.627	0.582	0.540	0.502	0.467
9	0.914	0.837	0.766	0.703	0.645	0.592	0.544	0.500	0.460	0.424
10	0.905	0.820	0.744	0.676	0.614	0.558	0.508	0.463	0.422	0.386
11	0.896	0.804	0.722	0.650	0.585	0.527	0.475	0.429	0.388	0.350
12	0.887	0.788	0.701	0.625	0.557	0.497	0.444	0.397	0.356	0.319
13	0.879	0.773	0.681	0.601	0.530	0.469	0.415	0.368	0.326	0.290
14	0.870	0.758	0.661	0.577	0.505	0.442	0.388	0.340	0.299	0.263
15	0.861	0.743	0.642	0.555	0.481	0.417	0.362	0.315	0.275	0.239

Periods										
(n)	11%	12%	13%	14%	15%	16%	17%	18%	19%	20%
1	0.901	0.893	0.885	0.877	0.870	0.862	0.855	0.847	0.840	0.833
2	0.812	0.797	0.783	0.769	0.756	0.743	0.731	0.718	0.706	0.694
3	0.731	0.712	0.693	0.675	0.658	0.641	0.624	0.609	0.593	0.579
4	0.659	0.636	0.613	0.592	0.572	0.552	0.534	0.516	0.499	0.482
5	0.593	0.567	0.543	0.519	0.497	0.476	0.456	0.437	0.419	0.402
6	0.535	0.507	0.480	0.456	0.432	0.410	0.390	0.370	0.352	0.335
7	0.482	0.452	0.425	0.400	0.376	0.354	0.333	0.314	0.296	0.279
8	0.434	0.404	0.376	0.351	0.327	0.305	0.285	0.266	0.249	0.233
9	0.391	0.361	0.333	0.308	0.284	0.263	0.243	0.225	0.209	0.194
10	0.352	0.322	0.295	0.270	0.247	0.227	0.208	0.191	0.176	0.162
11	0.317	0.287	0.261	0.237	0.215	0.195	0.178	0.162	0.148	0.135
12	0.286	0.257	0.231	0.208	0.187	0.168	0.152	0.137	0.124	0.112
13	0.258	0.229	0.204	0.182	0.163	0.145	0.130	0.116	0.104	0.093
14	0.232	0.205	0.181	0.160	0.141	0.125	0.111	0.099	0.088	0.078
15	0.209	0.183	0.160	0.140	0.123	0.108	0.095	0.084	0.074	0.065

ANNUITY TABLE

Present value of annuity of 1, ie

where   r = discount rate

          n = number of periods.

Periods					Discount rates (r)					
(n)	1%	2%	3%	4%	5%	6%	7%	8%	9%	10%
1	0.990	0.980	0.971	0.962	0.952	0.943	0.935	0.926	0.917	0.909
2	1.970	1.942	1.913	1.886	1.859	1.833	1.808	1.783	1.759	1.736
3	2.941	2.884	2.829	2.775	2.723	2.673	2.624	2.577	2.531	2.487
4	3.902	3.808	3.717	3.630	3.546	3.465	3.387	3.312	3.240	3.170
5	4.853	4.713	4.580	4.452	4.329	4.212	4.100	3.993	3.890	3.791
6	5.795	5.601	5.417	5.242	5.076	4.917	4.767	4.623	4.486	4.355
7	6.728	6.472	6.230	6.002	5.786	5.582	5.389	5.206	5.033	4.868
8	7.652	7.325	7.020	6.733	6.463	6.210	5.971	5.747	5.535	5.335
9	8.566	8.162	7.786	7.435	7.108	6.802	6.515	6.247	5.995	5.759
10	9.471	8.983	8.530	8.111	7.722	7.360	7.024	6.710	6.418	6.145
11	10.368	9.787	9.253	8.760	8.306	7.887	7.499	7.139	6.805	6.495
12	11.255	10.575	9.954	9.385	8.863	8.384	7.943	7.536	7.161	6.814
13	12.134	11.348	10.635	9.986	9.394	8.853	8.358	7.904	7.487	7.103
14	13.004	12.106	11.296	10.563	9.899	9.295	8.745	8.244	7.786	7.367
15	13.865	12.849	11.938	11.118	10.380	9.712	9.108	8.559	8.061	7.606

Periods										
(n)	11%	12%	13%	14%	15%	16%	17%	18%	19%	20%
1	0.901	0.893	0.885	0.877	0.870	0.862	0.855	0.847	0.840	0.833
2	1.713	1.690	1.668	1.647	1.626	1.605	1.585	1.566	1.547	1.528
3	2.444	2.402	2.361	2.322	2.283	2.246	2.210	2.174	2.140	2.106
4	3.102	3.037	2.974	2.914	2.855	2.798	2.743	2.690	2.639	2.589
5	3.696	3.605	3.517	3.433	3.352	3.274	3.199	3.127	3.058	2.991
6	4.231	4.111	3.998	3.889	3.784	3.685	3.589	3.498	3.410	3.326
7	4.712	4.564	4.423	4.288	4.160	4.039	3.922	3.812	3.706	3.605
8	5.146	4.968	4.799	4.639	4.487	4.344	4.207	4.078	3.954	3.837
9	5.537	5.328	5.132	4.946	4.772	4.607	4.451	4.303	4.163	4.031
10	5.889	5.650	5.426	5.216	5.019	4.833	4.659	4.494	4.339	4.192
11	6.207	5.938	5.687	5.453	5.234	5.029	4.836	4.656	4.486	4.327
12	6.492	6.194	5.918	5.660	5.421	5.197	4.988	4.793	4.611	4.439
13	6.750	6.424	6.122	5.842	5.583	5.342	5.118	4.910	4.715	4.533
14	6.982	6.628	6.302	6.002	5.724	5.468	5.229	5.008	4.802	4.611
15	7.191	6.811	6.462	6.142	5.847	5.575	5.324	5.092	4.876	4.675

BPP
PROFESSIONAL EDUCATION   574

Question bank

Exam standard questions have marks and time allocations.

1   **ELECTRICALLY-PROPELLED BABY CARRIAGES (20 marks)**   *36 mins*

It is May 20X8. X Ltd's directors are concerned that there is evidence of a declining trend in the sales of its lawn mowers and associated equipment. As the sale of equipment for estate maintenance is considered to be insufficiently rewarding, the marketing of an electrically-propelled baby carriage (pram) is being considered. None of the four firms making prams offers such a vehicle. Three of the firms are subsidiaries of the same international conglomerate. The other firm (K Ltd) has carved out its own up-market niche as a one-product company. Its cost structure, disclosed in accounts filed with the Department of Trade and Industry, is as follows.

	% of turnover	
	20X6	*20X7*
Cost of sales	85.4	85.2
Distribution costs	7.4	7.8
Administration costs	3.8	4.0
Operating profit	3.4	3.0
Labour (and associated) costs	11.5	11.7
Depreciation	0.7	0.5

It is believed that K Ltd's production overheads are approximately twice its labour (and associated) costs.

Relevant official statistics are available as follows.

	UK live births	UK pram sales (non-collapsible)	England and Wales median months marriage to first live birth	
Year			*Professionals***	*All***
	'000 pa	*£m*	*Months*	*Months*
20W1-20X1	736			
20X2	719	3.2	40	19
20X3	721	3.6	39	20
20X4	730	3.8	38	20
20X5	751	3.7	37	18
20X6	755	3.4		
20X3-20Y1	764 *			
20Y1-20Z1	808 *			

*   Projections
**   Class of father

X Ltd believes that an assisted vehicle could appeal to many families as a status symbol. A selling price of £500 + VAT is proposed, half of which will represent the retailer's margin.

X Ltd's actual and projected figures are as follows.

	20X6	*20X7*	*20X8*	*20X9*	*20Y0*
	£'000	*£'000*	*£'000*	*£'000*	*£'000*
Lawn mowers	750	650	600	500	350
Shopping trolleys	150	175	200	250	325
Hospital trolleys	850	860	875	900	950
Industrial trucks	50	75	80	90	95
Prams	-	-	-	10	50
	1800	1,760	1,755	1,750	1,770

Remember: 'Now' is May 20X8.

Required

(a)   Advise X Ltd, in the context of the above information and specifying what other information you would regard as appropriate, whether or not the proposed strategic development should be further investigated, explaining how information costs affect your recommendation.   (15 marks)

(b) Estimate the market share which should be included in X Ltd's projections and calculate the minimum output to break even. (5 marks)

2   OPERATIONAL AND STRATEGIC PLANNING

Explain what is meant by planning at operational level and at strategic level and list the notable traits of the planning process at each level.

3   ABC AND ABB (20 marks)   *36 mins*

The basic ideas justifying the use of activity based costing (ABC) and activity based budgeting (ABB) are well publicised, and the number of applications has increased. However, there are apparently still significant problems in changing from existing systems.

Required

(a) Explain which characteristics of an organisation, such as its structure, product range, or environment, may make the use of activity based techniques particularly useful. (8 marks)

(b) Explain the problems that may cause an organisation to decide not to use, or to abandon use of, activity based techniques. (12 marks)

4   JIT (20 marks)   *36 mins*

Many organisations believe that a key element of just-in-time (JIT) systems is JIT production.

(a) Discuss five main features of a JIT production system. (15 marks)

(b) State the financial benefits of JIT. (5 marks)

5   KLL (20 marks)   *36 mins*

KLL plc is a large health and fitness complex located in a capital city. Started seven years ago, the business has been profitable. The introduction of a much wider range of activities over the past few years has led to increased complexity of administration and difficulty in interpreting the rapidly growing basic data generated daily. This data remains largely unstructured and this in turn leads to uncertainty in decision making.

The present management information system (MIS) is able to produce monthly reports on the performance overall but can only break down the key indicators of turnover and gross profit into six broad categories: water sports, sports hall activities. fitness training, beauty treatments, squash courts and outdoor sports. Thus there is no detail on specific activities such as table tennis, sauna room, badminton or soccer. The managing director and the board cannot distinguish the profitable activities from the unprofitable ones. The managing director tells the board 'we must have a management information system that can cope with our complex business; there are so many variables it is becoming impossible to make decisions with confidence. Sometimes we have detail we cannot interpret and sometimes we simply do not have enough good information'. The finance director points out that 'the staff are doing their best but they have limited technical knowledge and the software support company is often slow to help'.

Recognising that it is important to build an MIS to serve the company well into the future, the board decides to ask you to submit a proposal to them for a new system.

Required

Prepare a memorandum to the Board explaining the main purposes of a new MIS and the benefits the company could expect such a system to bring.

6   BUSINESS PROCESS RE-ENGINEERING (20 marks)   *36 mins*

AB Ltd was established over a century ago and manufactures water pumps of various kinds. Until recently it has been successful, but imports of higher quality pumps at lower prices are now rapidly eroding its market share. The managing director feels helpless in the face of this onslaught from international competitors and is frantically searching for a solution to the problem. In his desperation, he consults a range of management journals and comes across what seems to be a wonder cure by the name of Business Process Re-engineering (BPR). According to the article, the use of BPR has already transformed the performance of a significant number of companies in the USA which were mentioned in the article, and is now being widely adopted by European companies. Unfortunately, the remainder of the article which purports to explain BPR is full of management jargon and he is left with only a vague idea of how it works.

Required

(a) Explain the nature of BPR and describe how it might be applied to a manufacturing company like AB Ltd. (10 marks)

(b) Describe the major pitfalls for managers attempting to re-engineer their organisations. (10 marks)

7 EXTERNAL INFORMATION (20 marks)   *36 mins*

JM Ltd is a private company which manufactures a range of packaging materials for customers in the fresh and frozen food industries. The company's chairman and founder has built up a vast network of contacts over a period of some twenty years and has always adopted a 'hands-on' management style, priding himself on the fact that he knows all his staff by name even though the company now has over 300 employees.

He is due to retire in about eighteen months' time and the other members of the board are concerned that they will lose an incredible 'database' of knowledge.

Required

Describe how JM Ltd could structure and implement formal methods and procedures for gathering information to monitor its external environment.

8 INFORMATION SYSTEMS (20 marks)   *36 mins*

'Considerable effort goes into the design of sophisticated information systems, many of which rely for their success on the quality of the data collection process that precedes the system, yet sometimes these collection processes are far from satisfactory. Why as trained accountants do we often close our eyes to the inadequacy of the data collection processes and still believe in the figures we report to management?'

Extract from article by T R Bentley, *Management Accounting*, January 1989

Required

(a) Describe typical problems and inadequacies encountered in data collection processes. (6 marks)

(b) Explain the key objectives of effective data collection with regard to the quantity of information, accuracy and timing. (6 marks)

(c) Describe how a decision maker's information needs could be reflected in the data collection process. (8 marks)

9 MISSION STATEMENTS (20 marks)   *36 mins*

The managing director of TDM plc has recently returned from a conference entitled 'Strategic planning beyond the year 2000'. Whilst at the conference, she attended a session on Corporate Mission Statements. She found the session very interesting but it was rather short and so has asked you the following questions.

'What does corporate mission mean? I don't see how it fits in with our strategic planning processes.'

'Where does our mission come from and what areas of corporate life should it cover?'

'Even if we were to develop one of these mission statements, what benefits would the company get from it?'

Required

Prepare a memorandum which answers the managing director's questions.

10   **ABBOTT AND BARTRAM (20 marks)**   *36 mins*

A company sells a large number of products that are accessories for a certain class of machine. For the United Kingdom it has nine salesmen, each of whom is responsible for sales in a separate territory.

Estimates of total market potential are £6.0 million and £7.1 million for 20X1 and 20X2 respectively.

Data for two individual salesmen and for the company as a whole is shown in the box below.

Required

(a)   For the average of all nine salesmen and for each of salesmen Abbott and Bartram for 20X2 do the following.

    (i)   Calculate the following.

        (1)   Sales potential
        (2)   Sales penetration percentages
        (3)   Sales potential per account

    (ii)   Calculate *eight* relevant measures that would help assess the performance of each salesman. These measures should be developed from the data given under the following five headings.

        (1)   Customers
        (2)   Gross margin
        (3)   Calls made
        (4)   Remuneration
        (5)   Expenses

    At least one measure should be calculated for each heading.   **(12 marks)**

(b)   Assess the performance of Bartram for 20X2 based on a combination of the data in (a) above plus any other data that you consider relevant.   **(8 marks)**

	Territory 1	Territory 2	Total UK(including territories 1 and 2)
Territory area ('000 sq km)	7.30	15.40	230.90
Number of machines in territory (millions)	1.65	0.83	12.80
Potential number of accounts	699	423	5,965
Salesmen	Abbott	Bartram	
20X1:			
Sales (£'000)	97	101	1,211
Customers (number of accounts)	412	323	3,318
Gross margin (£'000)	34	39	426
Calls made	1,410	1,163	10,901
20X2			
Sales (£'000)	112	123	1,460
Customers (number of accounts)	398	364	3,271
Gross margin	39	47	498
Calls made	1,450	1,220	11,030
Salary (£)	7,100	6,000	60,800
Commission (£)	1,680	1,845	21,585
Total remuneration (£)	8,780	7,845	82,385
Expenses (£)	1,940	3,200	28,060

11   **NON-PROFIT SEEKING ORGANISATIONS (20 marks)**   *36 mins*

(a)   The absence of the profit measure in non-profit seeking organisations causes problems for the measurement of their efficiency and effectiveness.

    Required

    (i)   Explain why the absence of the profit measure should be a cause of the problems referred to.   **(7 marks)**

    (ii)   Explain how these problems extend to activities within business entities which have a profit motive. Support your answer with examples.   (3 marks)

(b)   A public health clinic is the subject of a scheme to measure its efficiency and effectiveness. Amongst a number of factors, the 'quality of care provided' has been included as an aspect of the clinic's service to be measured. Three features of 'quality of care provided' have been listed.

    (i)   Clinic's adherence to appointment times
    (ii)   Patients' ability to contact the clinic and make appointment without difficulty
    (iii)   The provision of a comprehensive patient health monitoring programme

Required

    (i)   Suggest a set of quantitative measures which can be used to identify the effective level of achievement of each of the features listed.   (8 marks)

    (ii)   Indicate how these measures could be combined into a single 'quality of care' measure.   (2 marks)

12   BALANCED SCORECARD (20 marks)   *36 mins*

Recent articles have focused on summary information for running a business and on a 'balanced scorecard' approach, using a number of performance measures.

Required

Explain the following.

(a)   The arguments for using the profit measure as the all-encompassing measure of the performance of a business   (6 marks)

(b)   The limitations of this profit-measurement approach and of undue dependence on the profit measure   (8 marks)

(c)   The problems of using a broad range of non-financial measures for the short- and long-term control of a business   (6 marks)

13   PERFORMANCE RELATED REWARDS (20 marks)   *36 mins*

(a)   Explain the practical problems of implementing a scheme for rewarding divisional mangers in large companies on the basis of results of their divisions.   (10 marks)

(b)   A number of theories attempt to explain managerial motivation. How do they help in the design and evaluation of schemes for encouraging and rewarding improved managerial performance?   (10 marks)

14   CPP (45 marks)   *81 mins*

Introduction

CPP is a public service radio and television broadcasting organisation. Its Board of Directors stated the following main objectives of the organisation in its latest annual report.

- Remain a public service broadcaster

- Provide a comprehensive range of distinctive programmes and give excellence in providing a public broadcasting service

- Make and broadcast television and radio programmes which inform, educate and entertain

CPP is mainly funded through television licence fees which are paid by the residents of the country in which it is based. The television signal is currently broadcast through transmitters located on the surface of the land rather than via a remote satellite. The Board of Directors is held responsible by the government for ensuring that best value is obtained by the licence-fee payer.

Competition

The main competition for CPP comes from commercial broadcasters which are funded through advertising revenue. Some of these broadcasters use transmission media for both television and radio programmes which are earth-bound and others transmit via satellite. CPP has achieved an improvement in its market share of the viewing and listening audience in recent years despite this competition. One of the most distinguished services provided by CPP is its world radio service, which is renowned for its unbiased and uncensored news broadcasts relating to national and international events. None of its competitors is able to provide a parallel service of the same quality and reputation.

Accountability and editorial policy

CPP is accountable through its Board of Directors to the licence-fee payers and to the government. It regularly consults with representatives of its audience for both television and radio programmes and has established independent panels of viewers and listeners to review and advise on programmes.

In terms of editorial policy, the Board of Directors tries to ensure that there is as little interference as possible on the creativity of programme makers. Nevertheless, the Board aims to ensure that programmes are fair, accurate, impartial and meet the highest standards of good taste and decency.

New developments

Recently, CPP has introduced a 24-hour television news service. In addition, the organisation has entered a joint venture with a television subscription channel provider which allows the subscriber to access television programmes at any time to suit themselves rather than when they are broadcast. The additional income earned through subscriptions to this facility is re-invested by CPP in its main public service. Another potential development is the connection of the television to the telecommunications network, which would allow greater efficiency in the delivery of programmes.

Financial efficiency

The Board of Directors has entered a four-year licence-fee agreement with the government. The terms of this are that the licence fee will increase at a compound rate of 2% per annum both this year and next year. The licence fee will then remain at this level for the remaining two years of the agreement. The total licence fee income received in the last financial year as $2,147 million. The Board of Directors expects the number of licences sold to remain at the same level as last year for the full four-year period.

The Board of Directors is proud that CPP exceeded the efficiency savings target set by the government by 2% in each of the last three years. Over this period, CPP has out-sourced its financial processing functions and sold its transmission service to an independent company which has guaranteed the maintenance of a high-quality service at a reduced cost. The Board of Directors has placed much emphasis on the elimination of duplication of effort and reduction in waste from surplus capacity or over-staffing. An internal market has been introduced into CPP with programme-makers given the freedom to buy from producers who may be employed by the organisation or who may be external and completely independent of it. The savings achieved have been re-invested in programmes and services.

Despite these efficiency measures, CPP has experienced a steady average compound rate of growth of 3.7% in its expenditure over the last five years, and this is expected to continue at the same level over the next four-year period.

The following estimated levels of income and expenditure for the four-year period of the licence fee agreement are as follows:

	Income $ million	Expenditure $ million
Year 1	2,190	2,114
Year 2	2,234	2,192
Year 3	2,234	2,273
Year 4	2,234	2,357

Future targets and developments

The government has congratulated the Board of Directors on its record of achieving efficiency savings and has set a Return on Capital Employed (ROCE) target of 6% per annum. Its current ROCE is 9%, and has been calculated as follows:

$$\frac{\text{Excess of income over expenditure} \times 100}{\text{Average capital employed}} = \frac{\$108\text{million}}{£1,195\text{million}}$$

with average capital employed here equalling $\dfrac{\$1,250 + \$1,140m}{2}$

It is assumed that the value of capital employed by CPP will change only by adjustments in its operating reserve.

There has been continuing debate on the funding mechanism used for CPP through the licence fee. Some members of the government have questioned the fairness of this. They argue that commercial broadcasters cannot rely on a regular and guaranteed source of income and that the licence itself is a form of tax giving no discretion to the fee payer. One suggestion being considered by the government, to reduce CPP's dependence on the licence fee, is to separate the radio and television services. The radio services may then be financed by advertising revenue but would remain within the overall group alongside the television service. The rationale for this is that the licence fee is charged only on television receivers and therefore CPP does not obtain any direct income to support its radio services.

Financial extracts

Extracts from CPP's accounts reveal an increase in the overall surplus transferred to the operating reserve in the last financial year. Comparative extracts from the accounts over the last two years are as follows:

	Last year $ million	Previous year $ million
Income and expenditure account		
Excess of income over expenditure	108	82
Balance sheet		
Total assets less current liabilities	1,355	1,240
Long-term creditors and provisions	105	100
	1,250	1,140
Represented by:		
Capital reserve	700	698
Operating reserve	550	442
	1,250	1,140

CPP's total expenditure in the last financial year was $2,039 million, compared with $1,700 million five years ago. The breakdown of these costs in the last financial year was as follows:

	Last year $ million
Broadcast expenditure:	
Television services	1,265
Radio services	423
Non-broadcast expenditure	351
	2,039

Required

(a) Summarise the contents of a rational planning model which should be applied by CPP when formulating its strategic plan. (6 marks)

(b) CPP's major stakeholders are the public, the government, its employees and management. Explain how the Board of Directors can obtain the views of CPP's major stakeholders in determining the future strategic development of the organisation. (6 marks)

(c) (i) Calculate CPP's ROCE for each of the four years of the licence fee agreement.
    (ii) In the light of your findings, discuss what action CPP's management could take. (15 marks)

(d) Discuss the implications for CPP's objectives if the television and radio services are separated. (9 marks)

(e) Explain what financial and non-financial information should be provided to the Board of Directors of CPP on the performance of the radio subsidiary following its separation from the television service. (9 marks)

15   ZBB LTD (20 marks)   *36 mins*

ZBB Ltd has two service departments - material handling and maintenance, which are in competition for budget funds which must not exceed £925,000 in the coming year. A zero base budgeting approach will be used whereby each department is to be treated as a decision package and will submit a number of levels of operation showing the minimum level at which its service could be offered and two additional levels which would improve the quality of the service from the minimum level.

The following data have been prepared for each department showing the three possible operating levels for each.

Material handling department

Level 1. A squad of 30 labourers would work 40 hours per week for 48 weeks of the year. Each labourer would be paid a basic rate of £4 per hour for a 35 hour week. Overtime hours would attract a premium of 50% on the basic rate per hour. In addition, the company anticipates payments of 20% of gross wages in respect of employee benefits. Directly attributable variable overheads would be incurred at the rate of 12p per man hour. The squad would move 600,000 kilos per week to a warehouse at the end of the production process.

Level 2. In addition to the level 1 operation, the company would lease 10 fork lift trucks at a cost of £2,000 per truck per annum. This would provide a better service by enabling the same volume of output as for level 1 to be moved to a customer collection point which would be 400 metres closer to the main factory gate. Each truck would be manned by a driver working a 48 week year. Each driver would receive a fixed weekly wage of £155.

Directly attributable overheads of £150 per truck per week would be incurred.

Level 3. A computer could be leased to plan the work of the squad of labourers in order to reduce their total work hours. The main benefit would be improvement in safety through reduction in the time that work in progress would lie unattended. The computer leasing costs would be £20,000 for the first quarter (3 months), reducing by 10% per quarter cumulatively thereafter.

The computer data would result in a 10% reduction in labourer hours, half of this reduction being a saving in overtime hours.

Maintenance department

Level 1. Two engineers would each be paid a salary of £18,000 per annum and would arrange for repairs to be carried out by outside contractors at an annual cost of £250,000.

Level 2. The company would employ a squad of 10 fitters who would carry out breakdown repairs and routine maintenance as required by the engineers. The fitters would each be paid a salary of £11,000 per annum.

Maintenance materials would cost £48,000 per annum and would be used at a constant rate throughout the year. The purchases could be made in batches of £4,000, £8,000, £12,000 or £16,000. Ordering costs would be £100 per order irrespective of order size and stock holding costs would be 15% per annum. *The minimum cost order size would be implemented.*

Overheads directly related to the maintenance operation would be a fixed amount of £50,000 per annum.

In addition to the maintenance squad it is estimated that £160,000 of outside contractor work would still have to be paid for.

Level 3. The company could increase its maintenance squad to 16 fitters which would enable the service to be extended to include a series of major overhauls of machinery. The additional fitters would be paid at the same salary as the existing squad members.

Maintenance materials would now cost £96,000 per annum and could be used at a constant rate throughout the year. Purchases could be made in batches of £8,000, £12,000 or £16,000. Ordering costs would be £100 per order (irrespective of order size) and stock holding costs would now be 13.33% per annum. In addition, suppliers would now offer discounts of 2% of purchase price for orders of £16,000. The minimum cost order size would be implemented.

Overheads directly related to the maintenance operation would increase by £20,000 from the level 2 figure.

It is estimated that £90,000 of outside contractor work would still have to be paid for.

Required

(a) Determine the incremental cost for each of levels 1, 2 and 3 in each department. (16 marks)

(b) In order to choose which of the incremental levels of operation should be allocated the limited budgeted funds available, management have estimated a 'desirability factor' which should be applied to each increment. The ranking of the increments is then based on the 'incremental cost x desirability factor' score, whereby a high score is deemed more desirable than a low score. The desirability factors are estimated as:

	Material handling	*Maintenance*
Level 1	1.00	1.00
Level 2 (incremental)	0.60	0.80
Level 3 (incremental)	0.50	0.20

Use the above ranking process to calculate which of the levels of operation should be implemented in order that the budget of £925,000 is not exceeded. (4 marks)

16   LEARNING CURVE EFFECT (20 marks)   *36 mins*

Z plc experiences difficulty in its budgeting process because it finds it necessary to quantify the learning effect as new products are introduced. Substantial product changes occur and result in the need for retraining.

An order for 30 units of a new product has been received by Z plc. So far, 14 have been completed; the first unit required 40 direct labour hours and a total of 240 direct labour hours has been recorded for the 14 units. The production manager expects an 80% learning effect for this type of work.

The company uses standard absorption costing. The direct costs attributed to the centre in which the unit is manufactured and its direct material costs are as follows.

Direct material	£30.00 per unit
Direct labour	£6.00 per hour
Variable overhead	£0.50 per direct labour hour
Fixed overhead	£6,000 per four-week operating period

There are ten direct employees working a five-day week, eight hours per day. Personal and other downtime allowances account for 25% of the total available time.

The company usually quotes a four-week delivery period for orders.

Required

(a) Determine whether the assumption of an 80% learning effect is a reasonable one in this case, by using the standard formula $y = ax^b$

where y = the cumulative average direct labour time per unit (productivity)
         a = the average labour time per unit for the first batch
         x = the cumulative number of batches produced
         b = the index of learning (which is –0.322 for 80%)   (5 marks)

(b) Calculate the number of direct labour hours likely to be required for an expected second order of 20 units. (5 marks)

(c) Use the cost data given to produce an estimated product cost for the initial order, examining the problems which may be created for budgeting by the presence of the learning effect. (10 marks)

17   RESTRICT AND ENHANCE (Pilot paper, 20 marks)   *36 mins*

One of the most critical challenges facing a company today is the choice of performance measures.

Required

Explain how budgetary planning and control systems can result in business performance being restricted or enhanced.

18   ALTERNATIVE CHOICE DECISION-MAKING CYCLE (20 marks)   *36 mins*

(a) Enumerate and explain the relevance of the steps in an alternative choice decision-making cycle. (10 marks)

(b) Using increase in market share as the objective, give a detailed illustration of the alternative choice decision-making steps explained in (a). (10 marks)

19 AB LTD (40 marks)   *72 mins*

AB Ltd produces a consumable compound X, used in the preliminary stage of a technical process that it installs in customers' factories worldwide. An overseas competitor, CD, offering an alternative process which uses the same preliminary stage, has developed a new compound, Y, for that stage which is both cheaper in its ingredients and more effective than X.

At present, CD is offering Y only in his own national market, but it is expected that it will not be long before he extends its sales overseas. Both X and Y are also sold separately to users of the technical process as a replacement for the original compound that eventually loses its strength. This replacement demand amounts to 60% of total demand for X and would do so for Y. CD is selling Y at the same price as X (£64.08 per kg).

AB Ltd discovers that it would take 20 weeks to set up a production facility to manufacture Y at an incremental capital cost of £3,500 and the comparative manufacturing costs of X and Y would be as follows.

	X £ per kg	Y £ per kg
Direct materials	17.33	4.01
Direct labour	7.36	2.85
	24.69	6.86

AB Ltd normally absorbs departmental overhead at 200% of direct labour: 30% of this departmental overhead is variable directly with direct labour cost. Selling and administration overhead is absorbed at one-half of departmental overhead.

The current sales of X average 74 kgs per week and this level (whether of X or of Y if it were produced) is not expected to change over the next year. Because the direct materials for X are highly specialised, AB Ltd has always had to keep large stocks in order to obtain supplies. At present, these amount to £44,800 at cost. Its stock of finished X is £51,900 at full cost. Unfortunately, neither X nor its raw materials have any resale value whatsoever: in fact, it would cost £0.30 per kg to dispose of them.

Over the next three months AB Ltd is not normally busy and, in order to avoid laying off staff, has an arrangement with the trade union whereby it pays its factory operators at 65% of their normal rate of pay for the period whilst they do non-production work. AB Ltd assesses that it could process all its relevant direct materials into X in that period, if necessary.

There are two main options open to AB Ltd.

(a) Continue to sell X until all its stocks of X (both of direct materials and of finished stock) are exhausted, and then start sales of Y immediately afterwards;

(b) Start sales of Y as soon as possible and then to dispose of any remaining stocks of X and/or its raw materials.

Required

(a) Recommend with supporting calculations, which of the two main courses of action suggested is the more advantageous from a purely cost and financial point of view.   (20 marks)

(b) Identify three major non-financial factors that AB Ltd would need to consider in making its eventual decision as to what to do.   (10 marks)

(c) Suggest one other course of action that AB Ltd might follow, explaining what you consider to be its merits and demerits when compared with your answer at (a) above.   (10 marks)

20 GARBO LTD (20 marks)   *36 mins*

Garbo Ltd is about to begin operations to produce two products, P and Q. The senior management of the company have already decided that the new factory will work at maximum capacity in its first year of operations. Cost and production details for the first year are as follows.

			Variable cost per unit			
Product	Labour hours per unit	Machine hours per unit	Direct labour £	Direct materials £	Directly attributable fixed overheads £'000	Maximum production units
P	2	8	5	6	120	40,000
Q	16	4	28	16	280	10,000

General fixed production overheads which are not directly attributable to either product are estimated to amount to £720,000 per annum.

Both products P and Q are new, and nothing comparable is sold in the market; therefore Garbo Ltd can set its own sales price.

The sales manager has estimated that sales demand in the first year will depend on the price charged, as follows.

Product P		Product Q	
Sales price per unit	Sales volume	Sales price per unit	Sales volume
£	'000	£	'000
Up to 24	36	Up to 96	11
Above 24, up to 30	32	Above 96, up to 108	10
Above 30, up to 36	18	Above 108, up to 120	9
Above 36, up to 42 *	8	Above 120, up to 132	8
		Above 132, up to 144	7
		Above 144, up to 156*	5

* maximum price.

The board of directors of Garbo Ltd have a sales policy that the selling price must be full cost plus 20%. The determination of the full cost per unit depends on the apportionment of fixed overheads.

(a)   Directly attributable costs are to be charged to the product.

(b)   General fixed overheads will be apportioned between the products on the basis of either direct labour hours or machine hours. The choice between labour hours and machine hours is considered to be the only problem, and that a minor one - in setting a first year sales price.

Required

(a)   Show for each overhead apportionment method, what would be the amount of the following.

   (i)   Unit costs
   (ii)   Closing stock values
   (iii)   Disclosed profit for the first year of operations   (12 marks)

(b)   Comment briefly on the results in (a) and advise the managing directors on the validity of using the per unit cost figures produced for pricing decisions.   (8 marks)

---

21   **PRL (20 marks)**   *36 mins*

The Isle of Hamilton is a major centre for tourism and leisure pursuits. British Rail closed the railway line serving the Isle of Hamilton in 1971 but within five years various interests were calling for its reconstruction.

The old railway line passed through scenic countryside. It was felt that a reconstructed railway could itself be a tourist attraction.

Reconstruction of the line started in 1987 and was completed in 1994.

Permance Railway Ltd (PRL) has use of the line and offers journeys along it during summer weekends in trains pulled by steam engines, to be patronised by tourists and railway enthusiasts.

You have been engaged as a consultant by PRL to advise on its fares strategy for operations.

PRL is allowed to run four return train journeys per day along the line, each train having a capacity of 600 passengers. Initial market research has indicated that all trains will be filled to capacity if a fare of £2.00 per passenger for a one-way journey is charged. If this fare structure is adopted, then a significant number of passengers will have to be turned away from trains leaving at the most popular times.

Required

(a)   Explain how you would identify the 'profit maximising fare', assuming PRL is determined to adopt a uniform fare for each passenger making a single journey. You should state the information you would need, how you would acquire it and how you would analyse it.   (10 marks)

(b)   Explain how PRL might use 'price discrimination' (the practice of charging each customer what he is individually prepared to pay) in devising its fare structure. You should state the practical means by which price discrimination might be used and explain its benefit to PRL.   (10 marks)

22 **STOW HEALTH CENTRE (Pilot paper, 20 marks)**   *36 mins*

Stow Health Centre specialises in the provision of sports/exercise and medical/dietary advice to clients. The service is provided on a residential basis and clients stay for whatever number of days suits their needs.

Budgeted estimates for the year ending 31 June 20X1 are as follows.

(a) The maximum capacity of the centre is 50 clients per day for 350 days in the year.

(b) Clients will be invoiced at a fee per day. The budgeted occupancy level will vary with the client fee level per day and is estimated at different percentages of maximum capacity as follows.

Client fee per day	Occupancy level	Occupancy as percentage of maximum capacity
£180	High	90%
£200	Most likely	75%
£220	Low	60%

(c) Variable costs are also estimated at one of three levels per client day. The high, most likely and low levels per client day are £95, £85 and £70 respectively.

The range of cost levels reflects only the possible effect of the purchase prices of goods and services.

Required

(a) Prepare a summary which shows the budgeted contribution earned by Stow Health Centre for the year ended 30 June 20X1 for each of nine possible outcomes.   (6 marks)

(b) State the client fee strategy for the year to 30 June 20X1 which will result from the use of each of the following decision rules.

(i)   Maximax
(ii)   Maximin
(iii) Minimax regret

Your answer should explain the basis of operation of each rule. Use the information from your answer to (a) as relevant and show any additional working calculations as necessary.   (9 marks)

(c) The probabilities of variable cost levels occurring at the high, most likely and low levels provided in the question are estimated as 0.1, 0.6 and 0.3 respectively.

Using the information available, determine the client fee strategy which will be chosen where maximisation of expected value of contribution is used as the decision basis.   (5 marks)

23 **TRANSFER PRICING (Pilot paper, 20 marks)**   *36 mins*

(a) The transfer pricing system operated by a divisional company has the potential to make a significant contribution towards the achievement of corporate financial objectives.

Required

Explain the potential benefits of operating a transfer pricing system within a divisionalised company.   (6 marks)

(b) A company operates two divisions, Able and Baker. Able manufactures two products, X and Y. Product X is sold to external customers for £42 per unit. The only outlet for product Y is Baker.

Baker supplies an external market and can obtain its semi-finished supplies (product Y) from either Able or an external source. Baker currently has the opportunity to purchase product Y from an external supplier for £38 per unit. The capacity of division Able is measured in units of output, irrespective of whether product X, Y or combination of both are being manufactured. The associated product costs are as follows.

	X	Y
Variable costs per unit	32	35
Fixed overheads per unit	5	5
Total unit costs	37	40

Required

Using the above information, provide advice on the determination of an appropriate transfer price for the sale of product Y from division Able to division Baker under the following conditions.

(i) When division Able has spare capacity and limited external demand for product X

(3 marks)

(ii) When division Able is operating at full capacity with unsatisfied external demand for product X

(4 marks)

(c) The design of an information system to support transfer pricing decision making necessitates the inclusion of specific data.

Identify the data that needs to be collected and how you would expect it to be used.   (7 marks)

---

24   MANCASTLE CITY (40 marks)   *72 mins*

Mancastle City Football Club intends to sell its present stadium in five years time. In the interim the directors face a decision about the stadium's pitch. A number of experts in the property market have been consulted and most agree that an all-weather pitch will enable the stadium to be sold for £90,000 more (at the end of year 5) than would otherwise be the case. The payment will be received in six years time.

The directors therefore have three options.

(a) They can retain the present natural grass pitch.

(b) They can replace the grass pitch with Astroturf (a sort of plastic grass).

(c) They can replace the grass pitch with a new synthetic material called 'I Can't Believe It's Not Grass', but nicknamed ICING.

The decision also needs to take account of the club's cost of capital (8%) and incorporate inflation, which industry commentators have predicted will show the following pattern.

20X0	(ie year 0)	100
20X1		103
20X2		103
20X3		105
20X4		105
20X5		107

(a) Upkeep of the present *natural grass pitch* entails the following expenditure.

(i)	Fertiliser, grass seed, chemicals, etc	£53,000
(ii)	Groundspersons' salaries (proportion)	£42,000

The groundspersons also look after the seating area, leisure areas, and offices of the stadium. The above proportion is an allocation of total salary costs on the basis of time spent.

The club built up a store of chemicals some time ago in anticipation of price rises: if bought today the club would have to pay 15% more for its chemicals. These have no alternative uses or sales value, but there are enough chemicals to last for another three years, so actual costs in this category will be £10,000 per annum less than that stated above for this period.

(b) As for the *all-weather* options, Astroturf costs £29 per square metre while Icing is sold in units of 5 square metres and costs £800 per unit. The pitch (and its surrounding verge) will measure 110m by 90m. If either option is chosen, payment will be made *now* (ie the end of 20X0).

If either type of all-weather pitch is introduced it will become possible to use the main stadium for practice purposes some of the time. This in turn will enable the use of the current practice pitch to be reduced. Last year Mancastle City paid a fixed flat fee of £25,000 for the use of a practice ground and a further £78,000 in 'session' fees, chargeable at a rate per training session (3 hours). Astroturf will enable the number of sessions at the practice ground to be cut by 55%. If the slightly more delicate Icing is used the number of sessions will be reduced by 45%.

Upkeep of an all-weather pitch (of either type) entails the following annual expenditure.

(i)	Replacement of damaged 'turfs' (year 1 price)	£23,000
(ii)	Groundspersons' salaries (proportion) (year 1 price level)	£25,000

It is estimated that the cost of replacement turfs will be 10% greater in year 2 and a further 5% greater in each of years 3 to 5. (This is in addition to general inflation.)

No change in overall groundsperson's salaries is anticipated.

Required

(a) Identify the costs, revenues or cashflows that are *not* relevant to the decision, and explain why not.

(4 marks)

(b) Perform calculations so as to advise the club's board of directors whether it is worthwhile to replace the natural grass pitch and if so with which of the two alternative all-weather pitches.

(20 marks)

(c) One expert's forecast of the likely improvement in the disposal value of the stadium in five years time would leave the club indifferent between keeping the present pitch and replacing it with an Astroturf pitch. How much of an improvement did this expert forecast?

(4 marks)

(d) The directors have expressed dissatisfaction with the information they have been given to help them reach their decision.

(i)   A lot of estimates have been used.

(ii) There may be other matters that have not been taken into account.

Required

Explain how the first problem could be overcome and give examples of other information that may affect the calculations.

(12 marks)

---

25   MIS DESIGN (Pilot paper, 20 marks)   *36 mins*

Your manager has asked for some help in preparing a report entitled 'How to design an effective management information system'. The report should incorporate references to specific environment(s)/organisation type(s) and examples of the management accounting tools that would be of use.

Required

Prepare a draft report as requested by your manager.

> You're helping the manager prepare the report

> This is what the report should cover

Approaching the answer

Look for key words and ask questions of the information given to you. This is illustrated here.

Your manager has asked for some help in preparing a report entitled 'How to design an effective management information system'. The report should incorporate references to specific environment(s)/organisation type(s) and examples of the management accounting tools that would be of use.

Required

Prepare a draft **report** as requested by your manager.

> So this is not the only content

> Think of things like ABC, benchmarking

> Need to be specific, not general

> Format

Answer plan

- Correct headings at beginning of report (draft)

- What is an MIS?

- Information provided by an MIS

- Sources of data   - for strategic planning and control
                     - for tactical and operational planning and control

- Recording and processing methods   - type of entity
                                       - volume of info required
                                       - uses for the info
                                       - IT systems

- Format of reports
  - type
  - accuracy/detail/speed
  - management structure
  - controllability
  - security and access
  - systems compatibility
  - users' skills

- Other issues

26 AQUA HOLDINGS (Pilot paper, 40 marks) *72 mins*

Water Supply Services (WSS) and Enterprise Activities (EA) are two wholly owned subsidiaries of Aqua Holdings. You have recently qualified as an accountant and have joined the finance team of Aqua Holdings at headquarters. Your finance director is not satisfied with the performance of these two subsidiaries and has asked you to prepare a report covering the following issues.

(a) The profitability of the two subsidiaries
(b) The competence of the Enterprise Activity manager to make financial decisions
(c) The consequences of having a common management information system serving both companies

The finance directors has also provided you with the following background information on the two companies.

Water Supply Services

The company holds a licence issued by the government to be the sole supplier of drinking water to a large town. The business necessitates a considerable investment in infrastructure assets and is therefore highly capital intensive. To comply with the licence the company has to demonstrate that it is maintaining guaranteed service standards to its customers. WSS is extensively regulated requiring very detailed annual returns concerning costs, prices, profits and service delivery standards. The government enforces a price-capping regime and therefore the company has limited freedom in tariff determination - the government will normally only sanction a price increase following a demonstrable rise in costs.

Enterprise Activities

In contrast to Water Supply Services, Enterprise Activities operate in a very competitive market offering a plumbing service to domestic properties. The business has the following characteristics.

- Rapidly changing market conditions
- A high rate of new entrants and business failures
- Occasional shortages of skilled plumbers
- Fluctuating profits

In addition to this background information you also have the following.

(a) Summarised profit and loss accounts and balance sheets for the last two years for both companies

(b) Service contract costing information from Enterprise Activities

(c) Notes from a meeting that you have had with the manager responsible for the profitability of the three service contracts offered by Enterprise Activities

Water Supply Services
Summary profit and loss account

		20X0 £m		20W9 £m
Turnover		31		30
Less: Staff costs	3		2	
General expenses	2		2	
Depreciation	12		9	
Interest	5		5	
		(22)		(18)
		9		12

591

Summary balance sheet

	20X0 £m	20W9 £m
Fixed Asset	165	134
Current Assets	5	6
Total Assets	170	140
Current liabilities	(3)	(6)
Debentures	(47)	(47)
Net Assets	120	87
Shareholders' Equity	120	87

Enterprise Activities
Summary profit and loss account

	20X0 £m		20W9 £m	
Turnover		20		35
Less: Staff costs	5		6	
General expenses	10		10	
Materials	3		6	
Depreciation	1		1	
		(19)		(23)
Profit		1		12

Summary balance sheet

	20X0	20W9
Fixed Asset	22	22
Current Assets	12	12
	35	34
Current liabilities	(4)	(4)
Net Assets	31	30
Shareholders equity	31	30

Enterprise Activities
Service contract costing data

The Company offers three service contracts, standard, super and economy.

You have been provided with the following information.

	Standard	Super	Economy
Budgeted demand for contracts	1,000	800	2,000
Raw material cost per contract	£100	£150	£80
Direct labour hours per contract (£10 per hour)	5	8	2

Fixed overheads are allocated to the contracts at 150% of total direct costs.
The selling price is arrived at by adding 50% to the total costs.

Notes of meeting

(a) The manager states that his prime objective 'is to maximise the total profit that the three service contracts earn'.

(b) You discover that there is currently an unavoidable shortage of labour that has resulted in the available hours being limited to 80% of those originally planned in the budget.

(c) The manager responds to the shortfall in labour hours by 'concentrating sales on our most profitable service contracts, surely this is the obvious thing to do'.

(d) The manager is provided with the fixed overhead figure (150% of direct costs) from the finance department and assumes that it remains 'fixed' irrespective of the contract volume and contract mix. This overhead arises only as a consequence of operating the service contract business.

(e) The manager would never knowingly 'supply a service contract that did not cover the total cost, otherwise the company's profits would decline'.

(f)   The manager estimates the volume of contracts for budgetary purposes and provides these figures to the finance team. You have compared his past estimates with the actual sales and conclude that he is very accurate with the sales forecast - you can assume that the actual number of contracts sold for any of the three contract types will not be exceeded.

Required

(a)   Prepare a report on the comparative financial performance of Water Supply Services and Enterprise Activities from the above financial statements. Your report should incorporate an assessment of the potential limitations of undertaking such a comparison.   (16 marks)

(b)   Your finance director has asked you to provide a consultancy service to the newly appointed profit centre manager responsible for the service contract business.

       Describe the advice you would give him to assist the achievement of his financial target.
                                                                                                        (10 marks)

(c)   Calculate the maximum profit that the service contract business could earn if only 80% of the budgeted labour hours were available.   (10 marks)

(d)   Identify the likely differences in the two companies' management information needs.   (4 marks)

Approaching the answer

Look for key words and ask questions of the information given to you. This is illustrated here.

Water Supply Services (WSS) and Enterprise Activities (EA) are two wholly owned subsidiaries of Aqua Holdings. You have recently qualified as an accountant and have joined the finance team of Aqua Holdings at headquarters. Your finance director is not satisfied with the performance of these two subsidiaries and has asked you to prepare a report covering the following issues.

(a)   The profitability of the two subsidiaries
(b)   The competence of the Enterprise Activity manager to make financial decisions
(c)   The consequences of having a common management information system serving both companies

The finance directors has also provided you with the following background information on the two companies.

> *Not* non-profit making

> Government sets service levels

> WSS's market - monopoly

> How is this financed?

Water Supply Services

The company holds a licence issued by the government to be the sole supplier of drinking water to a large town. The business necessitates a considerable investment in infrastructure assets and is therefore highly capital intensive. To comply with the licence the company has to demonstrate that it is maintaining guaranteed service standards to its customers. WSS is extensively regulated requiring very detailed annual returns concerning costs, prices, profits and service delivery standards. The government enforces a price-capping regime and therefore the company has limited freedom in tariff determination - the government will normally only sanction a price increase following a demonstrable rise in costs.

> Important

> Areas of regulation

> Implication of regulation

Enterprise Activities

> EA's market

In contrast to Water Supply Services, Enterprise Activities operate in a very competitive market offering a plumbing service to domestic properties. The business has the following characteristics.

- Rapidly changing market conditions
- A high rate of new entrants and business failures
- Occasional shortages of skilled plumbers
- Fluctuating profits

> Risky!

> Information for two years

In addition to this background information you also have the following.

(a)   Summarised profit and loss accounts and balance sheets for the last two years for both companies

(b)   Service contract costing information from Enterprise Activities

(c)   Notes from a meeting that you have had with the manager responsible for the profitability of the three service contracts offered by Enterprise Activities

Question bank

Water Supply Services
Summary profit and loss account

Stable turnover – feature of regulated monopolies

		20X0	20W9
		£m	£m
Turnover		31	30
Less: Staff costs	3		2
General expenses	2		2
Depreciation	12		9
Interest	5		5
		(22)	(18)
Profit		9	12

Increase in depreciation

Decrease in profits

Summary balance sheet

	20X0	20W9
	£m	£m
Fixed Asset	165	134
Current Assets	5	6
Total Assets	170	140
Current liabilities	(3)	(6)
Debentures	(47)	(47)
Net Assets	120	87
Shareholders' Equity	120	87

Increased assets

Decrease

Take note of what figures are provided – what ratios can be calculated?

Debt

Increased equity

Enterprise Activities
Summary profit and loss account

Drop in turnover

		20X0	20W9
		£m	£m
Turnover		20	35
Less: Staff costs	5		6
General expenses	10		10
Materials	3		6
Depreciation	1		1
		(19)	(23)
Profit		1	12

Summary balance sheet

Drop in profit

	20X0	20W9
Fixed Asset	22	22
Current Assets	12	12
	35	34
Current liabilities	(4)	(4)
Net Assets	31	30
Shareholders equity	31	30

No debt – WSS has debt

Enterprise Activities
Service contract costing data

The Company offers three service contracts, standard, super and economy.

You have been provided with the following information.

	Standard	Super	Economy
Budgeted demand for contracts	1,000	800	2,000
Raw material cost per contract	£100	£150	£80
Direct labour hours per contract (£10 per hour)	5	8	2

Take note – will have to calculate price?

Fixed overheads are allocated to the contracts at 150% of total direct costs. The selling price is arrived at by adding 50% to the total costs.

Notes of meeting — With the manager responsible for EA contracts

His target

(a) The manager states that his prime objective 'is to maximise the total profit that the three service contracts earn'.

BPP PROFESSIONAL EDUCATION

(b) You discover that there is currently an unavoidable shortage of labour that has resulted in the available hours being limited to 80% of those originally planned in the budget.

> Limiting factor analysis?

(c) The manager responds to the shortfall in labour hours by 'concentrating sales on our most profitable service contracts, surely this is the obvious thing to do'.

> Appropriate

(d) The manager is provided with the fixed overhead figure (150% of direct costs) from the finance department and assumes that it remains 'fixed' irrespective of the contract volume and contract mix. This overhead arises only as a consequence of operating the service contract business.

> Under-standing of costs/ profits/ activity?

(e) The manager would never knowingly 'supply a service contract that did not cover the total cost, otherwise the company's profits would decline'.

(f) The manager estimates the volume of contracts for budgetary purposes and provides these figures to the finance team. You have compared his past estimates with the actual sales and conclude that he is very accurate with the sales forecast - you can assume that the actual number of contracts sold for any of the three contract types will not be exceeded.

Required

> Format

> What should be included?

(a) Prepare a report on the comparative financial performance of Water Supply Services and Enterprise Activities from the above financial statements. Your report should incorporate an assessment of the potential limitations of undertaking such a comparison. (16 marks)

> Don't forget limitations

(b) Your finance director has asked you to provide a consultancy service to the newly appointed profit centre manager responsible for the service contract business.

Describe the advice you would give him to assist the achievement of his financial target.

> Experience in industry?

> Refer to the meeting notes above

> Advice should relate to this

> What is this?

(10 marks)

(c) Calculate the maximum profit that the service contract business could earn if only 80% of the budgeted labour hours were available. (10 marks)

> Limiting factor analysis

(d) Identify the likely differences in the two companies' management information needs. (4 marks)

Answer plan

Not all the points you notice will necessarily be relevant and you may also find that you do not have time to mention all the points in your answer. Now you should prioritise your points in a more formal answer plan and then write your answer.

(a) **Calculation of ratios for each subsidiary for each of the two years**

- Profit margin
- ROCE
- Asset turnover
- Current ratio
- Gearing ratio – not for EA

Analysis of each subsidiary's ratios

Limitations of comparison

- Different markets ⇒ different levels of financial and business risk
  different levels of regulation
  different ways of setting quality standards

- Focuses on the short term

(b) What is his target?

What does he need to understand?

- Relationship between costs/profit/activity level
- Environment

What advice does he need?

- Pricing policy
- Budget preparation
- Limiting factor analysis
- General business/management eg TQM

(c) **Limiting factor analysis**

Calculate total cost and hence selling price
Calculate contribution per unit of limiting factor
Rank
Work out available resource
Determine optimal production plan and maximum possible profit

(d) **Differences in management information needs**

WSS -   on fixed assets
        non monetary
        for regulatory reporting
        prices/costs

EA -   for 'on the spot' decisions
      external
      for limiting factor analysis

Answer bank

1 **ELECTRICALLY-PROPELLED BABY CARRIAGES**

> **Tutor's hint**. This is a fairly **general** question in that you can **draw on** your studies for **papers at lower levels** and for **other papers at this level** – which is helpful given that you have only worked through one chapter of this Study Text!
>
> It is important to note that the company's directors have already decided that the decline in lawn mower sales cannot be reversed and so **any discussion** in your answer of how to improve **lawn mower sales** would be totally **irrelevant**!
>
> **Use the statistics** given in the question to analyse X Ltd's situation. **Market share** is particularly important. Other comments made in our solution are based on **common sense** (such as the implications of a rising trend in UK live births).
>
> In particular you should have had no great difficulty in **analysing the cost and revenue data** in order to estimate a C/S ratio for pram sales and resulting breakeven point in (b). You must state your **assumptions** about cost behaviour, however.
>
> You might like to try this question again once you have worked through all the chapters in this Study Text, as you should have a far wider understanding of the issues facing X Ltd.

(a) **Items of information that are not given in the data, but would be appropriate**

    (i)   Does the company have targets of profit growth and sales growth over the next few years; and if it does, what are they?

    (ii)   What are the current and projected profitability and cash flows from the existing product lines? Even if electrically-propelled baby carriages are eventually successful, it will take time before they can contribute towards profit and cash flow.

    (iii)   What will the development costs be for the new product, and will the anticipated profits/cash flows over the product's life provide an adequate return on investment?

    (iv)   What eventual market share does X Ltd hope to achieve for its new product? More information is needed about projected births among wealthier families.

Features of the situation apparent on the basis of the information given

    (i)   X Ltd's existing product range faces declining sales, no growth or slow growth. A new addition to the product range seems to be essential for future growth.

    (ii)   The electrically-propelled baby carriage will have unique features, and so the company can try to exploit a unique selling proposition (USP) to establish its product in the market.

    (iii)   UK live births appear to be on a rising trend, and so although UK sales of prams have declined since 20X4, there might be good prospects for future market growth. Professionals are likely to be a target market segment, and the shortening of the period between marriage and first live birth amongst this group adds support to the belief that there could be a good and growing market for the new product in the twenty-first century.

    (iv)   Assuming total UK pram sales in 20Y0 to be about £3.4 million (the same as in 20X6) X Ltd will be hoping to have won about 1.5% of the total market by 20Y0. There are only four other firms in the market, and so this market share is low, even allowing for the fact that X Ltd's pram will be aimed at a particular market segment. Presumably, it will be expected to rise in subsequent years.

    (v)   This share of the market amounts to £50,000 in 20Y0, and with a selling price to retailers of £250, sales in units would be just 200 prams.

    (vi)   The cost structure of K Ltd might provide some indication of the cost structure that X Ltd would have for its own prams, although the comparison is not a direct one. If we assume that distribution costs, administration costs and production overhead costs are all fixed cost items, the contribution margin on prams would be as follows.

	%	%
Sales		100.0
Cost of sales (20X7)	85.2	
Less production overhead (2 × 11.7)	(23.4)	
Less depreciation	(0.5)	
Estimate variable cost of sales		61.3
Estimated C/S ratio		38.7

(Labour is assumed to be a variable cost).

This suggests that a contribution margin of about 35% - 40% of sales might be achievable, with a resulting contribution for X Ltd in 20Y0 from pram sales in the order of £17,500 - £20,000.

Recommendation

Provided that the company expects to achieve a reasonable market share for its prams in due course of time, the strategic development is worth developing further, subject to the reservation about costs of entry which is discussed below. Production cost synergy should be achievable, to help X Ltd to obtain a reasonably good contribution margin on sales.

However, not enough information is available about future prospects for the pram market, especially amongst wealthier families. Market research information is also needed into whether an electrically-propelled pram would be a success in the market. Research and development costs might also be substantial. These information costs could be substantial, and if the costs of gaining entry into the new market are high, the project might be too risky to pursue further.

(b) It was estimated in part (a) that the **projected market share** for X Ltd's prams in 20Y0 is about 1.5%, although a bigger market share should be a target for subsequent years.

It was also estimated in part (a) that the **contribution/sales** ratio from the prams might be around 35% to 40%. Based on K Ltd figures **fixed costs as a % of sales** would be approximately:

	% of sales
Fixed production overhead (20X7 figures)	23.4
Distribution costs	7.8
Administration costs	4.0
Depreciation	0.5
	35.7

For sales of £50,000 in 20Y0, this might suggest **fixed costs** in the order of ($\times$ 35.7%) £17,850.

The **breakeven point** in 20Y0 would be (fixed costs $\div$ C/S ratio) as follows.

(I)	With a C/S ratio of 35%	=	£17,850 $\div$ 35%
		=	£51,000
	At £250 revenue per carriage	=	204 prams
(ii)	With a C/S ratio of 40%	=	£17,850 $\div$ 40%
		=	£44,625
		=	179 prams

2 OPERATIONAL AND STRATEGIC PLANNING

> **Tutor's hint.** After asking you to attempt an exam-standard question at the end of working through the first chapter in this Study Text, we thought we'd be a bit kinder to you and so have given you a **very straightforward** question here.
>
> It is vital that, having worked through the first two chapters, you have a full understanding of the **distinction between operational and strategic level planning**, however, so don't underestimate the importance of this introductory question.
>
> If you struggle with providing a decent answer if might be worth skimming through your notes, BPP's passcards or doing the quick quizzes again, as you do need to get the distinctions completely clear in your mind.

Operational planning works out what specific tasks need to be carried out in order to achieve the strategic plan. For example a strategy may be to increase sales by 5% per annum for at least five years, and an operational plan to achieve this would be sales reps' weekly sales targets. (*Note.* We use the words 'strategic' and 'operational' in the senses implied in the well known work of Robert Anthony.)

Notable characteristics of operational planning are the speed of response to changing conditions, and the use and understanding of non-financial information such as data about customer orders or raw material input.

Strategic planning is the process of setting or changing the long-term objectives or strategic targets of an organisation. These would include such matters as the selection of products and markets, the required levels of company profitability, the purchase and disposal of subsidiary companies or major fixed assets, and so on.

Notable characteristics of strategic planning are as follows.

(a) It will generally be formulated in writing, and only after much after discussion by committee (the Board).

(b) It will be (or should be) circulated to all interested parties within the organisation, and perhaps even to the press.

(c) It will trigger the production not of direct action but of a series of lesser plans for sales, production, marketing and so on.

3 ABC AND ABB

> **Tutor's hint.** This question is **typical** of what you could expect to encounter in the 3.3 exam in that you are asked to **criticise** the use of a management accounting technique rather than to use the technique in a somewhat simplistic, artificial exam scenario.
>
> The question gives you the opportunity to present **both sides of the argument** about the value of activity based techniques: part (a) requires an explanation of the circumstances in which they might be useful; part (b) asks for an explanation of the potential problems associated with their use.
>
> Make sure that you cover the characteristics suggested in (a) but don't be afraid to **cover other issues if you have time** – provided you **keep to the point!**
>
> The fact that the implementation of activity-based techniques can be time consuming and expensive may seem obvious but is perhaps the main obstacle for many organisations in setting-up activity-based systems. Don't forget to **state the obvious**.

(a) The usefulness of activity-based techniques will depend on the characteristics of an organisation, in particular its cost structure, product range and environment.

Cost structure

Activity-based techniques are particularly useful in organisations where **overheads account for a significant proportion of total costs**. The allocation of material costs and direct labour costs to cost objects is fairly straightforward but the traditional methods used to apportion and absorb overheads can often produce misleading product cost information. The higher the level of overheads, the less accurate the product costs are likely to be.

If an organisation has **introduced new technology** (leading to a large reduction in direct labour and a significant increase in overheads) or **business process re-engineering,** for example, an investigation is required into whether or not the existing cost system still provides a reasonable estimate of product or service costs as its cost structure is likely to be affected. Activity-based techniques can be used to review the cost allocation process.

Product range and diversity

If an organisation produces only a small number of products, product mix decisions for example can be made on a relevant cost basis. If a **vast number of products** are produced, however, the number of individual products and the number of combinations of products would make relevant cost analysis impossible. A general-purpose activity-based system is required that reports long-run product costs. The product costs reported are not designed to be used directly for decision making; instead they should provide attention-directing information and highlight problem areas that need more detailed analysis and the attention of management.

With the current focus on satisfying the customer, many organisations produce a **huge range of diverse products**. ABC is useful if increased product diversity means that an organisation produces **both high-volume standard products and low-volume variant products**. A more sophisticated costing system is required because, as the level of diversity increases, so does the level of distortion reported by absorption costing systems (which tend to allocate too high a proportion of overheads to high-volume products and too low a proportion of overheads to low-volume products).

Likewise, if an organisation's **customer base is wide**, ABC can provide information for customer profitability analysis. Costs such as those associated with travelling to call on a customer, after-sales service and special delivery methods are revealed, thereby assisting with the identification of profit-making/loss-making customers.

Environment

Increased **competition** may occur if other organisations recognise a particular product or service's profit potential, if the product or service has become feasible in terms of cost to make or perform, or if an industry has been deregulated. Organisations operating in a more competitive environment have a greater need for the more accurate cost information produced by activity-based techniques, since competitors are more likely to take advantage of any errors arising from the use of distorted cost information.

(b)   Despite the many advantages claimed by researchers and writers, there are a number of reasons why an organisation might decide not to use, or even to abandon the use of, activity-based techniques.

(i)   The implementation of activity-based techniques is a **time-consuming** and **expensive** process. Activities and cost drivers have to be identified, involving data collection, interviews and observation. Management may feel that the possible benefits are outweighed by the associated costs.

(ii)   The introduction of any new technique will be met with **resistance from those employees** who feel threatened by a change to the status quo or who feel that the current system is more than adequate. Such resistance can be reduced if employees are kept fully informed of the reasons for, and the process of, the techniques' introduction, however.

(iii)   Any change to the established way of doing things is unlikely to succeed unless the change has a **powerful champion** within the organisation. The champion of any activity-based techniques is likely to be the finance director. If the finance director is not supportive of their introduction or he/she is replaced by another director who is not supportive, their introduction and implementation is likely to fail.

(iv)   Even if overheads make up a significant proportion of an organisation's costs, if those **overheads cannot be traced easily to products and services** because cost driver identification is difficult (perhaps if the majority of them are administration costs), the introduction of activity-based techniques might not increase the accuracy of product cost information and hence will not be welcomed by management.

(v)   If the techniques appear to be part of a **policy of overhead cost reduction,** employees may worry about possible redundancies and **resist** their introduction. It is therefore vital that a detailed explanation of the reasoning behind any decision to introduce ABC, ABB, ABM and so on is given to affected members of the workforce.

(vi)   An organisation may decide not to use activity-based techniques if it becomes clear that they will not **provide additional information** for management planning and control decisions. If managers are not going to use the techniques to control non-value-added activities, for example, it would be much easier to stick with a simpler absorption costing system.

4   JIT

> **Tutor's hint**. What a nice, straightforward question. No ambiguities in the requirements, simply discuss features and state benefits. In the exam you would probably only need to provide five (relevant) financial benefits in part (b) to gain the full five marks. Make sure that you cover also list limitations of JIT.

(a)   JIT production systems will include the following features.

Multiskilled workers

In a JIT production environment, production processes must be shortened and simplified. **Each product family is made in a workcell based on flowline principles**. The variety and complexity of work carried out in these work cells is increased (compared with more traditional processes), necessitating a group of dissimilar machines working within each work cell. **Workers must therefore be more flexible and adaptable, the cellular approach enabling each operative to operate several machines.** Operatives are trained to operate all machines on the line and **undertake routine preventative maintenance**.

Close relationships with suppliers

JIT production systems often go hand in hand with JIT purchasing systems. **JIT purchasing** seeks to **match the usage of materials with the delivery of materials** from external suppliers. This means that **material stocks can be kept at near-zero levels**. For JIT purchasing to be successful this requires the organisation to have confidence that the supplier will deliver on time and that the supplier will deliver materials of 100% quality, that there will be no rejects, returns and hence no consequent production delays. The **reliability of suppliers is of utmost importance** and hence the company must **build up close relationships** with their suppliers. This can be achieved by doing **more business with fewer suppliers** and placing **long-term orders** so that the supplier is assured of sales and can produce to meet the required demand.

Machine cells

With JIT production, factory layouts must change to reduce movement of workers and products. Traditionally machines were grouped by function (drilling, grinding and so on). A part therefore had to travel long distances, moving from one part of the factory to the other, often stopping along the way in a storage area. All these are non-value-added activities that have to be reduced or eliminated. **Material movements between operations are therefore minimised by eliminating space between work stations and grouping machines or workers by product or component** instead of by type of work performed. Products can flow from machine to machine without having to wait for the next stage of processing or returning to stores. **Lead times and work in progress are thus reduced.**

Quality

Production management within a JIT environment seeks to both **eliminate scrap and defective units during production and avoid the need for reworking of units**. Defects stop the production line, thus creating rework and possibly resulting in a failure to meet delivery dates. Quality, on the other hand, reduces costs. Quality is assured by **designing products and processes with quality in mind, introducing quality awareness programmes** and **statistical checks on output quality**, providing **continual worker training** and implementing **vendor quality assurance programmes** to ensure that the correct product is made to the appropriate quality level on the first pass through production.

Set-up time reduction

If an organisation is able to **reduce manufacturing lead time** it is in a better position to **respond quickly to changes in customer demand**. Reducing set-up time is one way in which this can be done. Machinery set-ups are non-value-added activities which should be reduced or even eliminated. **Reducing set-up time** (and hence set-up costs) also makes the manufacture of **smaller batches more economical and worthwhile**; managers do not feel the need to spread the set-up costs over as many units as possible (which then leads to high levels of stock). Set-up time can be reduced by the **use of one product or one product family machine cells**, by **training workers** or by the use **of computer integrated manufacturing (CIM)**.

(b) JIT systems have a number of financial **benefits**.

- Increase in labour productivity due to labour being multiskilled and carrying out preventative maintenance
- Reduction of investment in plant space
- Reduction in costs of storing stock
- Reduction in risk of stock obsolescence
- Lower investment in stock
- Reduction in costs of handling stock
- Reduction in costs associated with scrap, defective units and reworking
- Higher revenue as a result of reduction in lost sales following failure to meet delivery dates (because of improved quality)
- Reduction in the costs of setting up production runs
- Higher revenues as a result of faster response to customer demands

5   KLL

> **Tutor's hint.** We'll say this only once in the hints to the questions in this Text as it is advice that will have been drummed into you since you started your ACCA studies: always provide an answer in the **format requested**. Here you are asked to provide a memo, which is normally used for fairly informal situations, but note the recipients: board members will expect a certain level of **formality** in terms of both language and structure.
>
> You may find that your answer did not cover all the points mentioned in ours and that you needed to rely to a large extent on knowledge picked up in the *Information Systems* or *Business Information Management* papers. Don't worry at all if this is the case. By the time you have worked through Parts A and B of this text you will feel far more confident about discussing information systems in terms of the requirements of *this* paper.
>
> Notice the mention of **Anthony's hierarchy** (strategic, tactical and operational levels) in part (b). You will find that you will be able to refer to the different activities and information requirements at the three levels in many questions, as the distinctions represent one of the **key themes** of Paper 3.3.
>
> The **qualities of good information** (covered in earlier studies and revisited in Part B of this text) could have been used as a framework for an answer plan. By comparing the type of information provided by the existing MIS to the information actually required by employees and management in terms of the qualities, you could have covered part (b) in particular.

MEMORANDUM

To: All board members
From: Your name
Subject: Purposes and benefits of an Management Information System
Date: December 20X1

KLL requires a new Management Information System to provide more detailed information on the various activities of the company. The existing MIS is limited in the information that it can provide, and the directors have identified additional information that would help them control and develop the business. This memo summarises the purposes and benefits that can be obtained from a modern Management Information System.

(a)   **Purposes of a Management Information System**

A MIS is a system to convert data from internal and external sources into information and to communicate that information, in an appropriate form, to managers at all levels in all functions to enable them to make timely and effective decisions for planning, directing and controlling the activities for which they are responsible. The MIS is therefore established in a company to satisfy the information needs of management.

Within KLL, the directors will already be aware of this objective of a MIS because the company already has a MIS. The limitations of that MIS are now apparent, however, because activities cannot be split between those that are profit making and those that are loss making.

(b)   **Benefits of a MIS**

The benefits of a MIS are summarised below, focusing particularly on the requirements of KLL.

(i)   **Provision of financial information**

The existing MIS can provide some financial information, although the limitations of this information have been recognised by the directors. This limitation may well be a function of an older MIS being designed to produce specific reports rather than holding the data in some form of database and then different reports being generated from that data as required.

A new MIS should store data in a less rigorous format, enabling different reports to be produced as required. Details of profit and loss making sports can therefore be obtained.

(ii)   **Provision of more timely information**

The current MIS produces reports on a monthly basis. It is not clear whether this is a system limitation or whether reports have not been requested on a more frequent basis. However, monitoring the profitability of individual sports activities may benefit from more frequent provision of information. For example if a competitor starts pricing activities below the price charged by KLL, then an immediate response will be required, rather than waiting up to a month to amend prices.

A modern MIS should be able to provide information on a daily if not real time basis to enable the directors to make quicker and more effective decisions.

(iii) **Provision of summary information**

The managing director is concerned about the inappropriate level of detail being provided by the MIS. If the detail cannot be interpreted, (per the question) then it is likely that the MIS is producing information at an operational level, rather than a strategic or tactical level. The detail is available, but this has not been summarised appropriately. It is possible, for example, that income from individual games of squash can be seen, but not the total income for each court or for the sport squash itself for each week or month.

The new MIS will provide a summary of income initially, with the ability to provide more operational information as necessary using the 'drill down' ability of many information systems. Focusing the information at the strategic level first, rather than the operational, should provide the managing director with the appropriate level of detail.

(iv) **'Better' information**

The managing director is also concerned about the lack of 'good' information. This appears to be linked to the comment concerning the limited technical knowledge of staff and poor support from the software company. It is therefore possible that staff either have a lack of training in the use of the MIS or they are producing bespoke reports, and are not receiving the support from the supplier to help them do this. The board are not receiving good information because reports are not sufficiently focused on the activities of KLL.

Whether the situation actually needs a new MIS to resolve it remains unclear. It is possible that appropriate training or support would enable staff to provide the appropriate reports for the board. Alternatively, more recent MIS programs normally provide an easy-to-use report generator so staff should find it easier to produce the necessary reports.

Alternatively, data can be exported into a spreadsheet package for additional analysis and production of visual aids such as charts and graphs as necessary.

(v) **Staff morale**

Providing a new MIS will have other benefits for the company such as increased staff morale and a better working environment. Staff are likely to be more motivated because the company is providing the software that is needed to carry out their job.

6 BUSINESS PROCESS RE-ENGINEERING

> **Tutor's hint.** In Paper 3.3 you must be able to **consider** the pros and cons of the **application** of a **particular management accounting technique** in **particular circumstances**. The key to providing a good answer to this question is ensuring that you **refer** wherever possible to the **scenario** provided in the question. Here are the **key phrases** in the scenario that you should have highlighted for part (b) and associated comment.
>
> - **Rapidly eroding its market share/onslaught from international competitors** – but is another reaction more appropriate than the implementation of BPR?
>
> - **Helpless/frantically searching/desperation** – but BPR should not be implemented unless there is good reason.
>
> - **Management journals/wonder cure** – but the company needs to consider the value of using a consultant.

(a) **The nature of BPR and its application to AB Ltd**

A **process** is 'a collection of activities that takes one or more types of input and creates output that is of value to the customer'.

Part of this process is manufacture of goods, and so is relevant to AB Ltd. However, a process is more than just manufacturing, it involves the ordering and delivery of goods to the customer. Arguably, AB Ltd does not need to manufacture. All aspects of the process, from ordering to delivery, must be considered.

Key features of BPR

(i) Focus on the **outcome**, not the task.

(ii) **Ignore the current way** of doing business. For example, AB Ltd may be divided into departments. The current organisation structure is not relevant to the process. Indeed having a large number of departments may make the process harder to manage, as it is split between several different responsibilities. The same customer's order may be passed from department to department.

(iii) Carefully determine how to use **technology**. IT has often been used to automate existing processes rather than redesign new ones. This means that **AB Ltd must have an information strategy** for the company as a whole.

(iv) **Review job design**. Scientific management split jobs into their smallest components. BPR suggests that, in some cases, **enlarged jobs** are more efficient if they lead to fewer people being involved in the process.

(v) **Do the work where it makes most sense.** This might affect where sales order processing and credit controls are carried out.

(vi) Work must be done in **logical sequence**. This can affect factory layout but also the sequence of clerical activities.

(vii) **Those who perform the process should manage it**. The distinction between managers and workers should be eroded; decision aids such as expert systems should be provided.

(viii) **Information provision should be included in the work** that produces it.

(ix) The customer should have **a single point of contact** in the organisation.

In effect, BPR requires the asking of the fundamental question: 'If we were starting from scratch, what would we do?'

(b) **Pitfalls**

(i) BPR is an **all or nothing proposition**. It is thus expensive and risky, requiring major expenditure on consultancy, investment in IT systems and disruption. It is not worth doing unless there is a good reason.

(ii) AB Ltd is concerned about overseas competition. There may be other **competitive responses more appropriate than BPR**, such as improving quality, outsourcing, a focus strategy or a differentiation strategy.

(iii) **Implementation is difficult**, as organisations fail to think through what they are trying to achieve, and the process becomes captured by departmental interest groups. In AB Ltd, the production director, sales director and finance director may well conflict. The customer may deal with all three of them.

(iv) Managers take a **departmental view**, rather than the view of the business as a whole.

(v) BPR becomes **associated only with across the board cost cutting** rather than a fundamental re-evaluation of the business. Managers will fight very hard to avoid any threats to their position.

(vi) Management consultants responsible for the ideas often fail to come up with realistic strategies for implementation. Managers are thus left with a BPR formula that they may not fully understand and have to implement it in a hostile work environment.

7   EXTERNAL INFORMATION

> **Tutor's hint.** We think the requirement of this question sounds more complex than the information you actually need to provide! You may have got bogged down in the intricacies of designing information systems, but all that you really needed to do was **comment** on the **issues that needed to be considered**.
>
> - Aspects of the environment that need to be monitored
> - Sources of information
> - Who will collect the information
> - The way in which it will be disseminated.
>
> It was important to note that you were supposed to be commenting on **formal** methods and procedures. Informal methods such as discussions between employees should not have been covered.
>
> You could also have made mention of **security** of information systems and **controls** over distribution of information if you had time.

Some aspects of JM Ltd's **external environment** will be more important for the company than others. Just what the most important aspects are vary from organisation to organisation. The first step that should therefore be taken is for an individual or a committee to be appointed to establish (and subsequently review) what aspects of the external environment should be monitored by formal methods and procedures.

The aspects of the environment that might be monitored include the following.

(a) **Competitors**. Information should be gathered about what competitors are doing, how successful they are and how much of a threat they are. New contracts awarded by food companies will be of interest to JM Ltd.

(b) **Suppliers**. Information should be gathered about suppliers and potential suppliers, their prices, product or service quality and delivery dates etc.

(c) **Customers**. An organisation should always try to be aware of the needs of its customers, to identify changes in these needs, to recognise potential market segments, and to assess the size of a potential market. Customer awareness is vital for new product development and successful selling.

(d) **Legal changes**. Changes in the law might affect how an organisation operates, and any such changes should be monitored. For example, changes in data protection legislation.

(e) **Political changes**. Some organisations are affected by national or local politics. If politics can be important, the organisation should try to monitor political decisions at both national and local level.

(f) **Financial and economic conditions**. Most organisations have to monitor developments in financial and economic conditions. As just one example, a company's treasury department must be aware of current money market interest rates and foreign exchange rates. As another example, the general rate of inflation is significant for decisions about wage increases for employees.

(g) **Environmental pressures**. The use of CFCs in packaging has been identified as contributing to the hole in the ozone layer. Companies such as JM Ltd therefore need to find alternative materials to use in their products.

Once the main types of environmental information have been identified, JM Ltd should then establish the following.

(a) The most **appropriate sources** for obtaining this information. This will vary according to the nature of the information.

(b) The individuals or departments **whose task** it should be to gather the information, and where appropriate, disseminate it through the organisation to other people who might need it.

(c) The **form** in which the information should be disseminated through the organisation.

Sources of information

(a) **Suppliers'** price lists and brochures.

(b) **Published reports and accounts** (of competitors, suppliers and business customers).

(c)   **Government** reports (often, reports on specific topics. Economic and trade reports, for example, are frequently produced by central government).

(d)   Government statistics.

(e)   External databases, provided by specialist organisations and often available over the **Internet**. Treasury departments, for example, use external databases to obtain information about current interest rates and foreign exchange rates.

(f)   Newspaper and other **media** reports.

Individuals or departments should be made **responsible** for obtaining information about certain aspects of the environment. In some cases, the individual department will collect information that it wishes to use itself. In other cases, there will be a need to distribute information throughout the rest of the organisation, and procedures should be established for doing this. Methods of distributing information would include the following.

(a)   Routine reports or in-house circulars
(b)   The company magazine
(c)   A company database, to which access is via computer terminals
(d)   An executive information system
(e)   E-mail
(f)   An intranet

8   INFORMATION SYSTEMS

> **Tutor's hint**. More than likely you found **part (c)** of this question the **trickiest**, as parts (a) and (b) required little more than regurgitation of book knowledge.
>
> The **qualities of good information** could be used as a framework for an answer to (a): you could explain the way in which data collection processes might fail to deliver data that meets each of the qualities. The danger would be including in (a) commentary which would be more appropriately included in (b).
>
> An alternative answer to part (c) could have made reference to the different information requirements of decisions at **strategic, operational and tactical levels** (there's the hierarchy again!) and to the way in which the data collection process would need to account for this. For example, data would need to be collected from internal and external sources.

(a)   The following **typical problems and inadequacies** may be encountered in data collection processes.

  (i)   The data collection process may be slow with the result that the decision maker is working with information which is out of date.

  (ii)   The data collection process may not be complete and vital pieces of information may be omitted.

  (iii)   The procedures for collecting and inputting the data into the information system may be subject to human error such as mistakes in keying data or coding errors.

  (iv)   In contrast to (ii) above, the process might collect too much data to be manageable and useful, instead of concentrating only on the data which is needed by managers.

  (v)   The individual collecting the data may have no appreciation of the use to which the data will be put. As a result they may be unable to judge the completeness or relevance of the data, or the degree of accuracy which is required.

  (vi)   The data collection process may rely heavily on secondary data which was originally collected for a different purpose and which may not be entirely suitable for the current decision.

(b)   **The quantity of information**

  One of the objectives of effective data collection is to collect the correct quantity of data for the decision. If too much is supplied then the cost of the data collection process may be excessive. Also the quantity of data may be unmanageable and vital data may be overlooked by the decision maker.

  If too little data is supplied then the decision maker will be working with data which is unnecessarily incomplete. Most decision makers accept that data is rarely complete but they should be supplied with all the available data which is relevant to their needs. This will involve a thorough analysis of the decision maker's requirements.

The accuracy and timing of data collection

There is usually a trade off between accuracy and timeliness in the data collection process. The production of completely accurate data can be very time-consuming with the result that the value of the data may be diminished by its lateness.

It is also necessary to weigh up the extra cost of time spent improving the accuracy of data against the harm which could be done if incorrect decisions are made due to data inaccuracies. The ultimate objective of effective data collection in this respect is to ensure that data is sufficiently accurate for the decision maker's requirements.

(c) A decision maker's needs could be reflected in the data collection process by ensuring that they are taken into account in the **initial design** of the information system.

In his article in *Management Accounting* Bentley suggests that every decision should be analysed to obtain a clear picture of the **decision maker's information needs** and what the decision maker does with the information provided. This probably involves several different decisions for each individual decision maker. Bentley suggests that a 'decision information flow diagram' should be drawn for each decision, showing a decision being made and the data flowing to and from the decision.

The information needs can then be **prioritised** so that a system or systems can be developed to meet them.

A further factor to consider is the information that might be required for decisions to be made in the **future**, so that the data collection procedure can be capable of adapting to alterations in information requirements.

9   **MISSION STATEMENTS**

> **Tutor's hint.** If you have answered this question yourself and analysed our solution you should have no problem in answering a question on mission and mission statements in the exam.
>
> When defining mission, it is a good idea to include a description of the **four key elements** of **purpose**, **strategy**, **policies** and **standards of behaviour and values** as this will ensure you have covered all important aspects.
>
> Notice that our solution includes **hypothetical examples**, both general (service businesses) and specific (investment company). Try to do this in your answers.
>
> You could include and analyse you **own organisation's mission statement** or else include **one that you particularly admire** – not necessarily because of the purpose/strategy of the organisation but perhaps because it is punchy and/or easy to remember. What about Federal Express's 'Absolutely, Positively, Overnight'? This makes it clear to the customer the importance the company attaches to delivering packages as well as requiring staff to focus on making package delivery their number one priority.

To: Managing Director
From: Anne Accountant
Date: 29 February 20X1
Subject: **Mission Statements**

Introduction

A **mission** can be defined as a business's basic function in society. It is often visionary, open-ended and has no time limit for achievement. It is possible however to reach a more expanded definition of mission to include four elements.

(a) **Purpose**. Why does the company exist, or why do its managers and employees feel it exists?

   (i)   To create wealth for shareholders, who take priority over all other stakeholders.

   (ii)   To satisfy the needs of all stakeholders (including employees, society at large, for example).

   (iii) To reach some higher goal and objective ('the advancement of society' and so forth).

(b) **Strategy**. This provides the commercial logic for the company, and so defines:

   (i)   the business the company is in;
   (ii)   the competence and competitive advantages by which it hopes to prosper.

(c) **Policies and standards of behaviour**. Policies and strategy need to be converted into everyday performance. For example, a service industry that wished to be the best in its market must aim for standards of service, in all its operations, which are at least as good as those found in its competitors. In service businesses, this includes simple matters such as politeness to customers, speed at which phone calls are answered, and so forth.

(d) **Values**. These relate to the organisation's culture, and are the basic, perhaps unstated beliefs of the people who work in the organisation. For example, a firm's moral principle might mean not taking on an assignment if it believes the client will not benefit, even though this means lost revenue. An example of this can be found in the standards of professional ethics required of accountants.

Mission statements

A **mission statement** is a document embodying some of the matters noted above. A mission statement might be a short sentence, or a whole page. It is intentionally unquantified and vague, and is sometimes seen as a statement of the guiding priorities that govern a firm's behaviour. Mission statements are rarely changed, as otherwise they have less force, and become mere slogans.

Objectives, on the other hand, are the embodiment of a mission statement in a commercial context. They specify the meaning of a mission in a particular period, market, or situation.

Mission statements and strategic planning

The relationship between mission statements and strategic planning is an ambiguous one. In some cases, the mission statement is prepared after the strategic plan is drawn up as a sort of summary of it. However this would only be done if there was a major change in the company's direction.

Whilst the mission inspires corporate objectives, the strategy is a means for fleshing them out. The strategy also provides directions for specific context. The mission statement cannot institute particular strategies but it can indicate priorities. Say an investment company prided itself on investing funds in companies which it regarded as behaving ethically, and its mission statement contains a clause which says that the company is 'to invest clients' funds in companies whose products promote health'. It would be unlikely to invest in tobacco firms, but no indication is given as to which shares to buy, on which stock exchanges, when to sell, what returns to expect, and so forth.

Originating a mission statement

A mission statement originates at the highest levels of the organisation. It is possible that, given a mission statement is meant to inspire as well as direct, a process of consultation with employees should take place to determine what the mission statement should be, or to assess what would be laughed out of courts. A company which declared its commitment to customer service in a mission statement, but whose practices for years had been quite the opposite, would have problems in persuading employees to take it seriously. The fact that the employees were consulted about the current ethos in a formal procedure would make the mission statement more effective. The mission statement would be introduced as part of an attempt to change the culture of the organisation.

The scope of mission statements

All areas of corporate life can be covered by a mission statement. This is because it is broadly based, and as a statement of an organisation's values and objectives, it should affect everyone in the organisation. That means its scope is wide-ranging. If it did not affect everybody in each department, from managing director to clerk, then its power would be lessened, and its purpose poorly satisfied.

For example, if a company's mission highlights the provision of *good quality* products and services, then this does not only include the way in which products are made and services delivered, but the way in which commercial relationships are conducted. Given that a successful business requires, in the long term, good commercial relationships, 'quality' applies to these as well.

The benefits of mission statements

(a) Describe what the company is about

(b) Provide a guiding philosophy where there are doubts about the direction a company should take, or a decision an individual manager or employee should make

(c) Display the area in which the company is operating

(d) Enable the communication of a common culture throughout the whole organisation

(e) Stimulate debate as to how the mission can be implemented

10 ABBOTT AND BARTRAM

> **Tutor's hint.** Even if you do not get a question in the exam which concentrates to such an extent on the calculation of non-financial performance indicators, this question provides you with lots of practice in thinking up relevant NFPIs.
>
> It was important to note that **each of the company's territories was the responsibility of one salesman**, with Abbott being the salesman for territory 1 and Bartram being the salesman for territory 2. Once you had this clear in your mind it should have made part (a)(i) more straightforward.
>
> - **Total sales potential** is **allocated** to individual salesmen on **the basis of the proportion of the total number of machines requiring the accessories in each territory**. So, for example, Abbott should be able to achieve 1.65/12.8 of total sales potential.
>
> - **Sales penetration** is the **proportion of potential sales achieved**.
>
> We have suggested 11 indices in part (a)(ii), although only eight were required for your answer. Don't worry if you didn't get the same as us; others might have been equally acceptable. **Gross margin ((a)(ii)(2))** as a % of sales would **not be a suitable measure to evaluate the performance of salesmen**. Rather, it would be a measure of the profitability of the products sold and the performance of production (production costs).
>
> We have assessed the performance of Bartram in terms of the five headings in (a)(ii). It was not necessary to do this but it does ensure that you cover a wide range of performance.

(a) (i) Sales potential in total is £7.1 million for 20X2.

		Average of all nine salesmen	Abbott	Bartram
(1)	**Sales potential**	$\dfrac{£7.1\text{ m}}{9}$	$\dfrac{1.65}{12.80} \times £7.1\text{ m}$	$\dfrac{0.83}{12.80} \times £7.1\text{ m}$
		= £788,889	= £915,234	= £460,391
(2)	**Sales penetration**	$\dfrac{£1,460,000}{9 \times £788,889}$	$\dfrac{£112,000}{£915,234}$	$\dfrac{£123,000}{£460,391}$
		= 20.6%	= 12.2%	= 26.7%
(3)	**Sales potential per account**	$\dfrac{£788,889 \times 9}{5,965}$	$\dfrac{£915,234}{699}$	$\dfrac{£460,391}{423}$
		= £1,190	= £1,309	= £1,088

(ii)

		Average of all nine salesmen	Abbott	Bartram
(1)	**Customers**			
	• Number of accounts per salesman as a percentage of potential accounts	$\dfrac{3,271}{5,965}$	$\dfrac{398}{699}$	$\dfrac{364}{423}$
		54.8%	56.9%	86.1%

	Average of all nine salesmen	Abbott	Bartram
• Average sales per customer account	$\dfrac{£1,460,000}{3,271}$	$\dfrac{£112,000}{398}$	$\dfrac{£123,000}{364}$
	= £446	= £281	= £338
• Average sales per customer as a percentage of average sales potential per account	$\dfrac{£446}{£1,190}$	$\dfrac{£281}{£1,309}$	$\dfrac{£338}{£1,088}$
	= 37.5%	= 21.5%	= 31.1%

(2) Gross margin

	Average of all nine salesmen	Abbott	Bartram
• Gross margin per customer	$\dfrac{£498,000}{3,271}$	$\dfrac{£39,000}{398}$	$\dfrac{£47,000}{364}$
	= £152	= £98	= £129
• Gross margin per call	$\dfrac{£498,000}{11,030}$	$\dfrac{£39,000}{1450}$	$\dfrac{£47,000}{1220}$
	= £45	£27	£39

(3) Calls made

	Average of all nine salesmen	Abbott	Bartram
• Calls per customer	$\dfrac{11,030}{3,271}$	$\dfrac{1,450}{398}$	$\dfrac{1,220}{364}$
	= 3.4	= 3.6	= 3.4
• Sales per call	$\dfrac{£1,460,000}{11,030}$	$\dfrac{£112,000}{1,450}$	$\dfrac{£123,000}{1,220}$
	= £132	= £77	= £101

(4) Remuneration

	Average of all nine salesmen	Abbott	Bartram
• Remuneration as a % of sales	$\dfrac{£82,385}{£1,460,000}$	$\dfrac{£8,780}{£112,000}$	$\dfrac{£7,845}{£123,000}$
	= 5.6%	= 7.8%	= 6.4%
• Commission % (workings not shown)	1.5%	1.5%	1.5%

(5) Expenses

	Average of all nine salesmen	Abbott	Bartram
• Expenses as a % of sales	1.9%	1.7%	2.6%
• Expenses per call	£2.54	£1.34	£2.62

(b) Assessment of performance of Bartram for 20X2.

(i) General

Despite gaining 41 customers in the year, increasing calls made by 5%, and gross margin by £195 per customer, his results are below average, with net margin 18% below the average of the other salesmen.

However, the market potential of his area is relatively low.

(ii) Customers

Despite the low market potential he increased the number of his customers by 13% despite an overall fall in the UK of 1%. However, he is selling to 85% of potential by 20X2, which compares favourably with the 20X2 UK average of 55% and his own 20X1 figure of 75%. Consequently his sales penetration of 27% is well above the UK average of 21%.

(iii)   **Gross margin**

These were below the UK averages of £152 per customer, and £45 per call.

(iv)   **Calls made**

Sales per call were below the UK average although calls as a percentage of customers was around the average.

(v)   **Remuneration and expenses**

Both salary and total remuneration were below the UK average as were his remuneration per call. Expenses per call were average.

11   NON-PROFIT SEEKING ORGANISATIONS

Tutor's hints. Like many examination questions, part (a) can be answered by taking a **logical, structured approach** that is offered to you by the wording of the question itself. You can take (1) **efficiency** and (2) **effectiveness** in turn (this solution opts to deal with effectiveness first) and explain for each why the absence of a profit measure causes problems. This suggest that you need to explain why the **presence of a profit measure** helps with the assessment of efficiency and effectiveness.

Take note of the **examples about objectives** we have provided in part (a)(i) – they may prove **useful in your exam** as this requirement is perhaps one of the more likely to appear on the subject of non-profit seeking organisations.

Note the need to provide **examples** in part (a)(ii) – this means at least one! As well as the given similarity between profit-seeking and non-profit seeking organisations, don't forget that the **distinctions between the two types of organisation are becoming blurred**.

Part (b) relates to both Chapter 12 and Chapter 11. Remember that indicators need to be **compared against a yardstick** to be of any use for performance measurement purposes. The fact that 8% of appointments were cancelled is useless information. When considered in conjunction with a target of 5%, it becomes useful!

(a)   (i)   **Effectiveness** refers to the use of resources so as to achieve desired ends or objectives or outputs.

In a profit-making organisation, objectives can be expressed financially in terms of a target profit or return. The organisation, or profit centres within the organisation, can be judged to have operated effectively if they have achieved a target profit within a given period.

In non-profit seeking organisations, effectiveness cannot be measured in this way. The organisation's objectives cannot be expressed in financial terms at all, and non-financial objectives need to be established. The effectiveness of performance could be measured in terms of whether targeted non-financial objectives have been achieved, but there are several **problems** involved in trying to do this.

(1)   The organisation might have several **different objectives** which are difficult to reconcile with each other. Achieving one objective might only be possible at the expense of failing to achieve another. For example, schools have the objective of providing education. They teach a certain curriculum, but by opting to educate students in some subjects, there is no time available to provide education in other subjects.

(2)   A non-profit seeking organisation will invariably be **restricted in what it can achieve by the availability of funds**. The health service, for example, has the objective of providing health care, but since funds are restricted there is a limit to the amount of care that can be provided, and there will be competition for funds between different parts of the service.

(3)   The objectives of non-profit seeking organisations are also difficult to establish because the **quality** of the service provided will be a significant feature of their service. For example, a local authority has, amongst its various different objectives, the objective of providing a rubbish collection service. The effectiveness of this service can only be judged by establishing what standard or quality of service is required.

(4) With differing objectives, none of them directly comparable, and none that can be expressed in profit terms, **human judgement** is likely to be involved in deciding whether an organisation has been effective or not. This is most clearly seen in government organisations where political views cloud opinion about the government's performance.

Efficiency refers to the rate at which resources are consumed to achieve desired ends. Efficiency measurements compare the output produced by the organisation with the resources employed or used up to achieve the output. They are used to control the consumption of resources, so that the maximum output is achieved by a given amount of input resources, or a certain volume of output is produced within the minimum resources being used up.

In profit-making organisations, the efficiency of the organisation as a whole can be measured in terms of return on capital employed. Individual profit centres or operating units within the organisation can also have efficiency measured by relating the quantity of output produced, which has a **market value** and therefore a quantifiable financial value, to the resources (and their costs) required to make the output.

In non-profit seeking organisations, output does not usually have a market value, and it is therefore more difficult to measure efficiency. This difficulty is compounded by the fact that since these organisations often have **several different objectives**, it is difficult to compare the efficiency of one operation with the efficiency of another. For example, with the police force, it might be difficult to compare the efficiency of a serious crimes squad with the efficiency of the traffic police, because each has its own 'outputs' that are not easily comparable in terms of 'value achieved'.

In spite of the difficulties of measuring effectiveness and efficiency, control over the performance of non-profit seeking organisations can only be satisfactorily achieved by assessments of '**value for money**' (economy, efficiency and effectiveness).

(ii) The same problems extend to **support activities** within profit-motivated organisations, where these activities are not directly involved in the creation of output and sales. Examples include research and development, the personnel function, the accountancy function and so on.

(1) Some of the outputs of these functions **cannot be measured in market values**.
(2) The **objectives** of the functions are **not easily expressed** in quantifiable terms.

Examples

(1) Within the personnel department, outputs from activities such as training and some aspects of recruitment can be given market price values by estimating what the same services would cost if provided by an external organisation. Other activities, however, do not have any such market valuation. Welfare is an example. Its objective is to provide support for employees in their personal affairs, but since this objective cannot easily be expressed as quantifiable targets, and does not have a market price valuation, the effectiveness and efficiency of work done by welfare staff cannot be measured easily.

(2) Within the accountancy department, outputs from management accountants are management information. This does not have an easily-measured market value, and information's value depends more on quality than quantity. The contribution of management accounting to profitability is difficult to judge, and so the efficiency and effectiveness of the function are difficult to measure.

(b) (i) To measure effectiveness, we need to establish objectives or targets for performance. Since these cannot be expressed financially, **non-financial targets** must be used. The effective level of achievement could be measured by comparing actual performance against target.

Adherence to appointment times

(1) Percentage of appointments kept on time
(2) Percentage of appointments no more than 10 minutes late
(3) Percentage of appointments kept within 30 minutes of schedule
(4) Percentage of cancelled appointments
(5) Average delay in appointments

A **problem** with these measures is that there is an implied assumption that all patients will be at the clinic by their appointed time. In practice, this will not always be the case.

Patients' ability to contact the clinic and make appointments

(1) Percentage of patients who can make an appointment at their first preferred time, or at the first date offered to them

(2) Average time from making an appointment to the appointment date

(3) Number of complaints about failure to contact the clinic, as a percentage of total patients seen

(4) If the telephone answering system provides for queuing of calls, the average waiting-for-answer times for callers and the percentage of abandoned calls

Comprehensive monitoring programme

Measures might be based on the definition of each element or step within a monitoring programme for a patient, It would then be possible to measure the following.

(1) Percentage of patients receiving every stage of the programme (and percentage receiving every stage but one, every stage but two, and so on)

(2) If each stage has a scheduled date for completion, the average delay for patients in the completion of each stage

(ii) A **single quality of care** measure would call for subjective judgements about the following.

(1) The key **objective**/objectives for each of the three features of service
(2) The relative **weighting** that should be given to each

The objectives would have to be measured on comparable terms, and since money values are inappropriate, an index based on percentage or a points-scoring system of measurement might be used. A target index or points score for achievement could then be set, and actual results compared against the target.

12   BALANCED SCORECARD

> **Tutor's hint.** Although the **balanced scorecard** is mentioned in the introduction to this question, you will notice that we have made **no mention of it in our answer**. Did you? Did you see the term and proceed to write down everything you know about the subject? Hopefully not!
>
> This question is related to the ideas behind the development of the balanced scorecard, however. One of these was to overcome the **problems of reliance on profit** as the principal measure of performance, an issue you need to cover in part (b). Of course there are arguments in favour of using **profit**, indeed it **cannot be ignored**, and it is these arguments that you need to cover in part (a).
>
> **Part (c)** is unusual in that you are asked to look at the **problems** of using a broad range of **non-financial performance measures**: questions more often focus on the advantages of such an approach. Hopefully you answered the question set and not the question you hoped had been set. It is important to note that the requirement specifically mentions non-financial performance measures. The balanced scorecard uses both financial and non-financial measures and so you were not being asked to provide a critique of it.

(a) High profits or massive losses make headlines, and it is perfectly apparent from scanning the business pages of any newspaper that **profitability** remains the **principal measure by which the success or failure of a business is judged**.

There are a number of **arguments in favour of this**.

(i) The use of a **single criterion** reduces all arguments to the effect on profit.

(ii) It makes **quantitative analysis possible.** With one single, clear objective, proposals can be evaluated for their effect on profit in terms of relevant costs and revenues. This contrasts with the imprecision of cost/benefit analysis used in the pubic sector.

(iii) Profit is a **broad performance measure:** managing profit assumes ability to balance costs and revenues.

    (iv)   It **enables decentralisation**.

    (v)   Profitability measures (such as ROI) can be used to **compare all profit-making operations** (although this argument ignores the difficult balance between risk and return).

    (vi)   Bonuses based on simple profit targets can be **highly effective motivators.**

    (vii)   The techniques of measuring profit are extremely **well established** and **codified** in standards of accounting practice. Even where different approaches are possible the issues are well publicised.

    (viii)   Profit is the **net result** of the success of marketing activities and the control of costs: as such it measures the two principal areas of concern for most commercial organisations.

    (ix)   It can be **applied to any profit-seeking activity**, whatever the nature of goods or services being produced and/or sold.

    (x)   It can be **related to aspects of output** (for example sales) or **input** (profit per machine/per employee etc), or (in the form of ROI) to **overall investment** in a business.

    (xi)   It is helpful for management in **deciding** which parts of a business should be **allocated resources**, and to investors in deciding **where their capital should be placed**.

(b)   In spite of its widespread use as a performance measure, profitability does have a number of **limitations**.

    (i)   **Not all organisations have profitability as their main objective**; for example government bodies and charities. Most organisations have subsidiary objectives of varying degrees of importance, and success or failure in achieving these may not be reflected in the profit measure.

    (ii)   Unless supplemented by additional measures, profit **does not adequately indicate the impact of external factors** such as inflation, exchange rate movements and general economic conditions. The impact may vary widely between different types of business: a company that makes a loss in certain conditions may nevertheless have performed better than another that makes a profit, if viewed in the light of external conditions. This can affect the effectiveness of profit as a measure of managerial performance.

    (III)   Even for financial reporting purposes the profit figure is **subject to a certain amount of manipulation** that may mislead the financially unsophisticated. For internal reporting purposes there is the further problem of which profit figure to use - operating profit, trading profit, profit before or after interest and tax and so forth.

    (iv)   A company may be **profitable and yet have severe cashflow problems**: profitability is not necessarily an indicator of continued success.

    (v)   The profit measure may encourage both managers and investors to take a **short-term view**. Managers may cut essential costs like training or research in order to show a profit in the short term. Investors may demand that profits are paid out as dividends when long-term interests require that the money be reinvested to fund future growth.

    (vi)   Focusing on a bottom line figure which is perhaps satisfactory overall may **encourage complacency**. Areas where further improvements could be made may be neglected if other areas have performed better than expected, giving a satisfactory net result.

    (vii)   Profit is measured by accounting rules, but **accounting conventions** on the valuation of intangibles, for example, can lead managers to make decisions which **decrease economic income**.

    (viii)   Profit should be **related to risk as well as capital employed**.

    (ix)   Profit may motivate profit centre managers but **cost centre managers may need alternative measures**.

(c)   Many companies are discovering the usefulness of **non-financial performance indicators (NFPIs)** such as quality measures, numbers of complaints, non-productive hours, system down time and so on. However there are a number of problems associated with such measures.

    (i)   **Too many measures could be reported**, overloading managers with information that is not truly useful (or comes to be regarded as not useful) or that sends conflicting signals.

    (ii)   It is **difficult to judge which** non-financial measures **are the most important**.

    (iii)   The ultimate goal of commercial organisations remains the **maximisation** of profit. An over-concentration on non-financial measures may lead to the **neglect of this criterion**.

(iv)   Some non-financial aspects of performance are very **difficult to measure objectively**. For example a measure of customer complaints does not indicate that all customers who did not complain were entirely satisfied.

(v)   Measures may **conflict with each other**: achieving measure X can be at the expense of achieving measure Y (such as productivity and quality).

(vi)   If NFPIs are used as the basis of **managerial performance** evaluation, the areas **not covered by the measures used may be ignored**.

13   PERFORMANCE RELATED REWARDS

> **Tutor's hint.** We have started part (a) by explaining the **theoretical reason for such a reward scheme** in order to provide a **context** for the practical problems.
>
> You probably didn't make reference to **transfer pricing** as this is not covered in the text until **Chapter 24**. (Transfer pricing, if you are interested, can be used in a divisionalised structure of any kind and is a way of pricing the work that one division does for another.) Obviously, when it comes to the exam, you will be able to pull together information from all areas of the syllabus.
>
> **Part (b)** is the trickier of the two sections of the question and so don't worry if you struggled a little with it. The key issues to mention are **pay, personal satisfaction, participation** and **tendencies to achieve success/avoid failure**.

(a)   The chief problem in basing managerial rewards on divisional results is how those results are **measured**. Performance is usually measured in **accounting** terms (variances, profit, return on investment, residual income and so on). The conventional theory is that by establishing procedures for formal measurement of performance and rewarding individuals for good performance on these terms managers will be more likely to direct their efforts towards achieving the organisation's goals, even though the formal measure of performance will not fully reflect all of the organisations' goals.

However devising a scheme to meet these aims can give rise to a number of **problems**.

(i)   If the work of a division is **dependent** on work done in another division performance may be impaired, for example by mistakes that other people have made, or by transfer prices set in the interests of one division but against the interests of another. Especially where external factors are involved it is difficult or impossible to separate the controllable components of performance from the uncontrollable, making performance measurement to some extent unfair.

(ii)   Performance-related rewards are less effective for **long-term achievements**, since effort and rewards are too distant in time from each other. Also accounting reports tend to concentrate on short-term achievements to the exclusion of the long-term.

(iii) There is evidence that the effectiveness of incentive schemes **wears off over time** as acceptable 'norms' of working are established.

(iv)   Formal reward and performance evaluation systems can encourage **dysfunctional** behaviour: for example divisional managers might be reluctant to replace old equipment because this might reduce the ROCE of their division.

(v)   No accounting measures of performance can provide a **comprehensive** assessment of what a person has achieved for the organisation: not all achievements are quantifiable.

(b)   Theories of managerial motivation can be of assistance in the **design** of motivation schemes in that if it is understood what motivates managers then these features can be included in the scheme while demotivating factors can be avoided. The **value** of a scheme can be judged after the event in terms of whether it actually did improve managerial performance (although with all the attendant problems of measurement mentioned in the answer to part (a)). Theory can, however, be of assistance in evaluating a proposed scheme in terms of likelihood of success and in evaluating an ongoing scheme which does not appear to be working.

Many researchers agree that **pay** can be an important motivator when there is a formal link between higher pay (or other rewards such as promotion) and achieving budget targets. Individuals are likely to work harder if they know that they will be rewarded for their successful efforts. **Problems** to be avoided are linking the reward to some performance factor that is outside the control of the person who is or is not being rewarded (since these merely lead to frustration and demotivation), and ensuring that incentives do not come to be perceived as 'entitlements'.

Other theorists have drawn attention to the importance of **personal satisfaction** as a driving force and consequently argue that organisations should aim to make managers' personal targets match those of the organisation. Some argue that the key to achieving this is to allow **participation** in the setting of performance measures. Others have acknowledged that **participation** appears to raise morale but claim that it is by no means clear that it improves performance. Still others distinguish between managers' tendency to **achieve success** on the one hand and to **avoid failure** on the other: targets need to be set according to which is uppermost.

The diversity of opinion (of which the above is only a sample) indicates that while theories of managerial motivation can be useful they must not be applied blindly: what motivates one manager may fail entirely to motivate another.

14 CPP

> **Tutor's hint**. This question requires both **numerical analysis** and a **discursive** approach and, as well as covering strategic planning, requires application of knowledge from other **chapters** in the text.
>
> **Forty five marks** is the **maximum** possible for a **Section A question**.
>
> The planning model required in **part (a)** should have presented few problems, although it is very important to **relate the planning model** you describe **to CPP's own circumstances**. You may have chosen to draw a diagram, and that is an acceptable approach provided you discuss the model's application. We have divided our answer into a consideration of **strategic analysis, strategic choice and strategic implementation.**
>
> **Part (b)** is specific in its requirements, but do not lose sight of the fact that you need to comment on **strategic developments**. Asking employees for a report on their opinion of the staff canteen will not help CPP towards its strategic objectives.
>
> **Part (c)(i)** is a very **straightforward** exercise and the case study scenario virtually tells you how to perform the calculations. There is very little reason for you not to have scored highly here. Your answer to the second part of the question should focus on ways of improving ROCE. Quality implications of cost cutting should be mentioned.
>
> You may not have questioned the **validity of ROCE** as a suitable measure of performance for CPP, but do not worry. So long as you had some sensible suggestions on improving ROCE, this would be enough for a pass mark.
>
> The **second part of (c)** hinges on the fact that the organisation is going to fall short of its ROCE targets – **options** could have included reducing costs, increasing income, reviewing the asset base, quality considerations or demand generation.
>
> Make sure that you **focus on the objectives** of the organisation in **part (d)**. Its **public service** nature will always colour its thinking, and the **contrast** (and potential **conflict**) between commercial advertising revenue and public service objectives should have struck you. We have taken that line in our answer.
>
> **Part (e)** requires **specific application to CPP's situation** rather than general comments. How do the types and sources of information that you identify help management of the new radio subsidiary? What specific information might a radio service require?

(a) Strategic planning divides into a number of different stages: strategic **analysis**, strategic **choice** and **implementation**. Providing a structure to the process serves to focus CPP management attention and make sure that all relevant factors are considered.

Strategic analysis is a consideration of CPP's overall strategic stance and the organisation's underlying values. This encompasses **mission**, **goals** and **objectives**. For CPP, this includes providing an excellent public broadcasting service and committing to 'inform, educate and entertain'. These are qualitative objectives. The government as a relevant stakeholder is concerned with 'best value' for the licence payer and has set an ROCE target of 6% per annum. This is a quantitative objective, based largely upon efficiency savings being made wherever possible.

A further component of strategic analysis is an assessment of 'where are we now?' for CPP. This can be addressed by a **corporate appraisal** (SWOT analysis) via environmental analysis and a position audit.

Forecasting a likely future position for CPP after consideration of these factors will lead to identification of a **planning gap** that will need to be filled by appropriate courses of action. In other words, CPP will have to make **strategic choices**. Ideas have to be generated and evaluated for best fit with the organisation's objectives. The chosen strategy has to be **implemented** via appropriate marketing and production channels and ultimately **review and control** procedures must be in place.

(b)   In determining the future strategic development of the organisation, a public service organisation dependent on licence fee income like CPP is well advised to consult with its **stakeholders**, both internal and external. In this case we are concerned with the viewing public, the government, employees and management. Their views must be represented by the Board when deciding on future strategy.

The viewing and listening public

CPP already consults regularly with audience representatives and independent review panels to ensure accountability. These stakeholders are likely to have valuable information and opinions, and CPP could back them up with further research covering the wider viewing and listening public in all areas of the country and overseas. Reactions to a new radio service could be predicted by conducting an opinion poll, or chairing a public meeting. CPP must be careful that the views it canvasses are representative of the population as a whole.

The government

The government, and its relationship with public service broadcasters, is an important factor in determining strategic direction. Government policy is a significant element of CPP's environmental analysis. Links with government officials and other politicians will ensure that CPP is included in discussions of relevant policy. Issues on which CPP, as a public service broadcaster, could be expected to contribute, will be fully discussed. New regulations on broadcasting standards may be planned, for example, which CPP would need to be aware of.

Employees and management

Employees of CPP may be expected to contribute ideas both formally at meetings, and informally. Small working groups might be set up to look at different strategic initiatives, which then report to the whole organisation via newsletters or the company intranet. It is likely that senior management will have a greater role to play in strategy development than employees lower on the hierarchy, but no potential source of information or ideas should be rejected in the early stages of strategic analysis. It should be remembered that with jobs to defend, managers and employees often have negative power to impede implementation. Employees of the radio service may be concerned at the implications of separation of their division.

(c)   **ROCE**

(i)   The **calculations of ROCE** over the next four years of the licence fee agreement are as follows.

	Year 1 $m	Year 2 $m	Year 3 $m	Year 4 $m
(1) Excess/(deficit) of income over expenditure (W1)	76	42	(39)	(123)
(2) Average capital employed (W2)	1,288	1,347	1,348.5	1,267.5
$\frac{(1)}{(2)}$ =	5.9%	3.1%	(2.9)%	(9.7)%

Workings

1	Year 1	$2,190m - $2,114m = $76m
	Year 2	$2,234m - $2,192m = $42m
	Year 3	$2,234m - £2,273m = $(39)m
	Year 4	$2,234m - £2,357m = $(123)m

2   Year 1 $\dfrac{\$1,250m + \$1,326m}{2} = \$1,288$

Year 2 $\dfrac{\$1,326m + \$1,368m}{2} = \$1,347$

Year 3 $\dfrac{\$1,368m + \$1,329m}{2} = \$1,348.5$

Year 4 $\dfrac{\$1,329m + \$1,206m}{2} = \$1,267.5$

(ii)   It is clear from the figures in (i) that CPP is heading for significant difficulties. The government **target ROCE** of 6% **will not be met** at all after this year, and **in years 3 and 4** of the agreement CPP's expenditure will be in excess of expected income, generating a **negative ROCE**. As long as ROCE is the measure being used, **ways to improve it** will have to address one or more of the following.

- **Increasing income**
- **Decreasing expenditure**
- **Decreasing capital employed**

A **strategy combining all three elements is likely to be the most effective**

Increasing income

As it is unlikely that the government (or public) will countenance an increase in the licence fee, CPP will have to seek **alternative sources of income.** This may come from selling programmes and/or expertise to overseas organisations, merchandising, further subscription-based services (as described in the scenario) or educational services for schools and colleges. The **objectives** of the organisation in terms of 'excellence' and the vow to 'inform, educate and entertain' must also be kept in mind. The possible impact on comprehensiveness and **quality** of a rush to generate new sources of demand and therefore income must also be considered. Programmes must continue to be seen by the viewing public and the independent review panels as 'fair, accurate, impartial and [meeting] the highest standards of good taste and decency'.

Cutbacks in the asset base to improve ROCE (selling production facilities, for example) may also have adverse implications for quality. If quality is not maintained, a long term future for CPP could be unsustainable.

Cutting costs

Reduction in costs may offer the greatest scope, but again quality may become compromised, although from the scenario presented, much emphasis has been placed on maintaining quality while reducing waste, surplus capacity and duplication of effort. The establishment of an internal market is very likely to have had a beneficial effect on quality, as programme makers have a wider choice of possible sources. The Board of Directors has a successful recent history of **efficiency savings**. Estimated expenditure is forecast to increase at a flat rate of 3.7% each year. How much realistic **analysis** has been put into these rather general forecasts, and is there any room for cutting costs, especially in the years when licence fee income is static? These estimates may need to be revisited.

Cutting capital employed

Return on capital employed is a performance measure with some **drawbacks**. Capital employed is notoriously suspect as a financial measure, since a book value on the balance sheet will probably bear little or no comparison with the 'true' value (replacement cost, net realisable value or economic value). **Long-term** requirements for investment in CPP will be difficult to balance against **short-term** ROCE targets, since longer-term projects will take more time to generate a return. CPP should try to persuade the government that other targets, more in keeping with objectives related to the **needs of viewers**, should be considered.

(d) **Separation of television and radio services**

(i)   **Objectives.** If the radio and television service are separated, the **objectives** for CPP are likely to become separated into **two distinct streams**: one for television and one for radio services, although the indications are that the organisation wishes to continue to be a public services broadcaster and this will be possible. While CPP's overall objective of remaining a high quality public service broadcaster could continue, the basis for obtaining revenue will have changed.

(ii) **Funding. Different funding mechanisms are very likely to impact upon content,** and this is likely to impact on CPP's avowed public service objectives.

(iii) **Public resource.** The vast majority of households in the UK own a television set. Households that only own radios are likely to be comparatively rare, and furthermore the possibility of charging for radio services separately as a way of subsidising possible lower television licence fees is likely not to be very lucrative. Radio services have not been specifically charged for in the past and the imposition of a fee is likely to be strongly resisted.

Financing the radio services by **advertising revenue** is a big step and is likely to be met with concern by a public that equates high advertising revenue with **commercial**, rather than **public service** broadcasting, objectives. The licence fee could be said to provide a stable funding mechanism allowing the production of distinctive programmes, while advertising revenue is likely to lead to a less distinctive service. Programme makers might start chasing advertising revenue on the back of tried and tested programme formats.

> **Tutor's hint.** Here are some examples. We have seen in the UK a proliferation of television programmes based on veterinary practices, home improvements, garden 'make-overs', disastrous weather and dramatic rescues because if they prove popular once, they are likely to be produced and broadcast again and again.

Stakeholders in CPP, such as overseas listeners and politicians, may be concerned about the implication for editorial content if radio services are separated. Objective coverage of overseas events may be compromised if advertising revenue is to be sought. The **government** may be persuaded to provide some funding for this arm of the service.

It is unlikely that CPP's dependence on the licence fee as a stable source of funding can be reduced significantly. The opportunity to seek alternative sources of funding for the radio subsidiary, however, will open up CPP to **commercial pressures** that may have the positive effect of stimulating **innovative** ideas and services that could heighten its **reputation** and further its objectives of providing a comprehensive and distinctive service. Channel 4 in the UK could be said to have successfully met such a challenge. The licence fee as it stands will theoretically be able to 'go further' when producing television programmes, if radio services are attracting additional funding from previously untapped sources.

(e) **Information on the performance of the radio subsidiary**

Performance measures enable an organisation to assess how far objectives are being achieved.

Financial performance indicators concentrate on profitability, growth, liquidity, capital structure and market ratios.

(i) From the point of view of the radio subsidiary of CPP, the management accountant should provide the Board with regular details of cost and advertising revenues (assuming that this is the agreed funding mechanism for the new service) to assess **profitability** against budgets. This provides a basic measure of both advertising **sales growth** and **operating income**.

The directors will be concerned to see that the new division is meeting its targets, and that it compares well to similar radio services which operate from advertising revenue.

(ii) **Liquidity** is measured by **cash flow**. Cash flow statements will have to be prepared for the new subsidiary, because adequate cash flow is key to survival. The pricing policy of CPP will be relevant here because if revenues (and hence cash flows) prove inadequate, the pricing of advertising 'slots' may have to be reviewed.

(iii) **Return on capital employed** has already been discussed as performance measure. It has its drawbacks but the directors may wish to see how the subsidiary is performing against government target ROCE, and in comparison to television services. Direct **comparison** of the profitability of radio and television services may no longer be meaningful because licence fee income and advertising income are different in nature. **Return on investment** as a measure may be more directly comparable.

(iv) Managers in the television subsidiary will have no control over licence fee income (at least for the next four years) while radio managers can influence advertising revenue via

621

marketing initiatives. These initiatives will cost money, as will collecting the advertising revenue generally. New management accounting systems will have to be developed for the new funding system.

Non-financial indicators

(i)   Non financial measures may give a more timely indication of the level of performance achieved, and for CPP's radio subsidiary would probably concentrate on audience-related factors. These are most likely to be the ones that can help further CPP's **objectives** of public service excellence. These would include the outcome of audience surveys on quality and enjoyment of programmes, listener rates and trends and (possibly) complaints received.

(ii)   Details of the **market share** (both listening figures and share of advertising revenue) will also be highly relevant when assessing current performance and opportunities for future growth.

(iii)   Major advertisers using CPP could be reported and reviewed each month, and this information used to generate repeat business and investigate possible new advertising clients.

(iv)   Other performance measures may be **employee** related. The radio subsidiary will be highly 'people-based' and is likely to be characterised by highly autonomous production staff, so staff turnover, training costs and other personnel related matters will merit attention on a regular basis.

15   ZBB LTD

> **Tutor's hint.** This is an **unusual** question on ZBB because it requires **calculations**, most questions on the topic being discursive.
>
> The key to success in part (a) was to **look at incremental costs** between the various levels of provision and not at total costs at the different levels. Once you realised you had to do this, **careful layout** and **logical thought** would have been all you needed to earn very high marks as the calculations were not too difficult.
>
> The only tricky area in the calculations for the **material handling department** is the effect of the **hours saved at level 3**. You had to account for this in terms of **basic wages, overtime premium and variable overheads**. You may well have missed out one or more of these.
>
> **Levels 2 and 3 maintenance** required minimum cost order size to be implemented – in other words use of the **EOQ model**. At level 2 you were able to work out the EOQ and then had to calculate stock ordering and holding costs. The calculations were more complex at level 3 because you had to take account of the supplier discount; work out the EOQ and then compare the cost of the EOQ with the cost of a batch at which the discount applies.
>
> The maintenance materials of £96,000 at level 3 were not an incremental cost but a total cost so you needed to deduct the cost of the materials at level 2 to derive the correct figure.
>
> For **part (b)**, the **available** budget had to be **allocated** to the incremental levels of expenditure according to the calculated scores **until all funds had been allocated or until there were insufficient funds available for the next required increment of cost**.

(a)   **Material handling department**

Level 1

	£
Labourers' wages:	
Basic rate: 30 × 40 hours × £4 × 48 weeks	230,400
Overtime premium: 30 × 5 hours × £2 × 48 weeks	14,400
	244,800
Employee benefits 20% × £244,800	48,960
Variable overheads 30 × 40 × £0.12 × 48 weeks	6,912
Incremental cost	300,672

Level 2

	£
Incremental costs:	
Leasing costs 10 × £2,000	20,000
Drivers' wages 10 × £155 × 48 weeks	74,400
Overheads 10 × £150 × 48 weeks	72,000
Incremental costs	166,400

	£	£

Level 3
Incremental costs:
Computer leasing costs:

Quarter 1		20,000
2 (20,000 × 90%)		18,000
3 (18,000 × 90%)		16,200
4 (16,200 × 90%)		14,580
		68,780

Less savings in labour costs:

Hours saved	= 10% × 30 × 40 hrs × 48 = 5,760 hrs		
∴ Overtime hours saved	= 2,880		
∴ Savings in labourers' basic wages	= 5,760 × £4 =	23,040	
Savings in overtime premium	= 2,880 × £2	5,760	
Savings in employee benefits	= (23,040 + 5,760) × 20%	5,760	
Savings in variable overheads	= 5,760 × £0.12	691	
			35,251
Incremental cost			33,529

Maintenance department

Level 1		£
Engineer's salaries 2 × £18,000		36,000
Outside contractors' cost		250,000
Incremental cost		286,000

Level 2		£
Incremental costs:	
Fitters' salaries 10 × £11,000		110,000
Maintenance materials		48,000
Stock ordering and holding costs (W1)		1,200
Overheads		50,000
		209,200
Less: saving in outside contractors' cost £(250,000 – 160,000)		90,000
Incremental costs		119,200

Level 3	£	£
Incremental costs:	
Additional fitters' salaries 6 ×x £11,000		66,000
Additional maintenance materials £(96,000 – 48,000)	48,000
Less supplier discount (W3)	1,920
		46,080
Increase in stock ordering and holding costs (W2)		445
Increase in overheads		20,000
		132,525
Less saving in outside contractors' cost £(160,000 – 90,000)		70,000
Incremental cost		62,525

Workings

1 Economic order quantity $= \sqrt{2 \times £100 \times £48,000/0.15} = £8,000$

Stock ordering costs =	(£48,000/£8,000) orders per annum × £100 =	£600
Stock holding costs =	(£8,000/2) average stock × 15% =	£600
		£1,200

2 Economic order quantity $= \sqrt{2 \times £100 \times £96,000/0.1333} = £12,000$

A discount is available for orders of £16,000, therefore the total annual cost of purchasing in batches of £12,000 must be compared with the cost for batches of £16,000.

Total cost of ordering £12,000 per batch:		£
Ordering cost	= (£96,000/£12,000) order per annum × £100	800
Stock holding cost	= (£12,000/2) average stock × 13.33 %	800
Annual materials cost		96,000
Total cost		97,600

Total cost of ordering £16,000 per batch:

		£
Ordering cost	= (£96,000/£16,000) orders per annum × £100	600
Stockholding cost	= (£16,000/2) × 98% average stock value × 13.33	1,045
Annual materials cost (£96,000 × 98%)		94,080
Total cost		95,725

This is less than the cost of ordering £12,000 per batch, therefore orders should be placed for £16,000 per batch.

Increase in stockholding and ordering costs	£
Level 3 costs (600 + 1045)	1,645
Level 2 costs (W1)	1,200
Increase	445

3   Supplier discount of 2% will be obtained because the purchase value per batch will be £16,000 (W2). Supplier discount = £96,000 × 2% = £1,920.

(b)

	Material handling			Maintenance		
	Incremental	Desirability		Incremental	Desirability	
Level	*cost*	*factor*	*Score*	*cost*	*factor*	*Score*
	£			£		
1	300,672	1.00	300,672	286,000	1.00	286,000
2	166,400	0.60	99,840	119,200	0.80	95,360
3	33,529	0.50	16,765	62,525	0.20	12,505

Allocation of budget

	Level	*Cost*	*Cumulative cost*
		£	£
Material handling	1	300,672	300,672
Maintenance	1	286,000	586,672
Material handling	2	166,400	753,072
Maintenance	2	119,200	872,272
Material handling	3	33,529	905,801

Material handling should be operated at level 3, but maintenance should be operated at level 2 because the budget of £925,000 will be exceeded if level 3 is implemented.

16   LEARNING CURVE EFFECT

> **Tutor's hint.** In **part (a)**, the learning curve formula allows you to calculate the average time per unit. You needed to multiply this by the volume of output to find **budgeted total time**, which should then be **compared with actual total time**.
>
> In **part (b)**, the number of hours needed for the second order, after the first order of 30 units has been completed, will be **the time required to produce units 31 to 50**, assuming an 80% learning curve. This is the difference between the total time required to make the first 50 units, and the total time required to make the first 30 units.
>
> As you will see, we have made two **assumptions** in **part (c)**. Your figures will be slightly different if you did not come to the same conclusions about absorption basis and hourly rates as we did.

(a)   The first unit took 40 hours and so the **average time for the first 14 units** should be

$$y = ax^b = 40\,(14^{-0.322}) = 40\,(1 \div 14^{0.322}) = 17.1$$

If the average time per unit for the first 14 units is 17.1 hours, the **total time** for the units will be (14 × 17.1) = 239.4 hours.

Actual time was 240 hours.

Actual time is therefore consistent with an 80% learning curve effect, and is therefore reasonable to assume in this case.

(b)

	1st 30 units	**1st 50 units**
$y = ax^b$	= $40\,(30^{-0.322})$	$y = 40\,(50^{-0.322})$
	= $40\,(1 \div 30^{0.322})$ = 13.38 hours	= $40\,(1 \div 50^{0.322})$ = 11.35 hours

		Direct labour
Total time for first 50 units (50 × 11.35)		567.5
Total time for first 30 units (30 × 13.38)		401.4
Total time for 2nd order (units 31-50)		166.1

Tutor's hint. Due to rounding, your own solution might be *slightly* different from this.

(c) **Estimated cost for the initial order of 30 units**

	£
Direct material (30 × £30)	900.0
Direct labour (401.4 hours × £6) (see note (1))	2,408.4
Variable overhead (401.4 hours × £0.5)	200.7
Fixed overhead (see note (2)) (401.4 hours × £5)	2,007.0
	5,516.1

Cost per unit   £183.87, say, £184.

Notes

(1) The hourly rate which is given for labour is assumed to be the cost per productive hour: labour rate paid per hour = £4.50, cost of productive time = £6 per hour.

(2) Fixed overhead is assumed to be absorbed on a direct labour hour basis.

Budgeted fixed overhead per 4-week period		£6,000
Direct labour hours per 4-week period		
Gross (10 × 8 × 5 × 4)	1,600 hours	
less downtime allowance (25%)	400 hours	
		1,200 hours
Absorption rate per direct labour hour		£5

Problems

(i) A major problem with the learning effect is that unit costs of production fall considerably as extra units are produced, especially during the early period of a product's manufacture.

With a cost per hour of £11.50 for direct labour and overhead in this case, the actual average unit cost for the first 14 units was approximately (£30 material + (17.1 × £11.5)) = £227, which is much higher than the expected average cost of £184 per unit for the first 30 units.

The budgeting problems are the **assumptions that the learning curve effect will continue** and that there will be an **80% learning curve effect**. If either of these assumptions is incorrect, budgeted unit costs could be inaccurate.

In particular, there is a danger of **underestimating costs** (and if prices are based on a cost-plus formula, there will be a danger of losses on the contract).

(ii) A further problem with assumptions about the learning curve effect is budgeting for the **use of manufacturing capacity**. If estimates of learning rate are incorrect, actual capacity will be either higher or lower than budgeted, with the consequences that there will be either surplus idle capacity in the budget period or an inability to meet sales orders on schedule.

(iii) The company uses standard costing, but when there is a learning curve effect, **standard costs** can only be an expected average cost, based on budgeted output volume in the period and budgeted learning rate. There is consequently a strong possibility that actual costs will differ from standard costs due to variance in output volume and/or learning rate, thus *possibly* reducing the control value of variance analysis.

17 **RESTRICT AND ENHANCE**

> **Tutor's hint.** A wide variety of answers to this question are possible but it was vital that you **concentrated on budgetary planning and control systems** rather than provide a general essay on performance measures.
>
> We have broken down our answer to this pilot paper question into **four key areas**. The first provides an **introduction**, the second and third cover the **basic requirement of the question** (which had two parts), while the fourth notes the **importance of behavioural considerations** to budgetary planning and control systems. By the time you have finished working through this text you will appreciate the importance of behavioural issues to all areas of the syllabus and you should always consider their relevance in any answer to a 3.3 question.

Impact of performance measures

Performance measurement is a means of **communicating the objectives** of the organisation (by the provision of appropriate measures/standards/targets) and of **concentrating efforts towards those objectives** (by comparing actual results against the measures).

The measures used can have a significant impact on the organisation's success or otherwise in achieving its goals, however. They can send the **wrong signals** to managers with the result that management action moves the organisation off of its planned path.

How budgetary planning and control systems can restrict performance

Budgetary planning and control systems are mainly concerned with controlling **short-term** costs and revenues and in practice managers' performance is usually judged by short-term achievements. For example, middle and senior management are expected to achieve budge targets and are criticised if they do not.

Since performance is judged by short-term achievements, it is hardly surprising that the natural tendency for managers is to **sacrifice longer-term aims, goals and objectives** in order to achieve short-term performance measures. In some situations this might be the 'right' thing to do; in other it might be short sighted and ultimately a bad decision. Here are some examples.

(a) Postponing or abandoning capital expenditure projects, which would eventually contribute to longer-term growth and profits, in order to protect short-term cash flow and profits

(b) Reducing quality control to save operating costs, but in so doing adversely affecting regulation and goodwill

(c) Reducing the level of customer service to save operating costs, but sacrificing goodwill

It is therefore vital that any performance measurement system considers long-term financial, non-financial and even non-quantifiable measures as well.

How budgetary planning and control systems can enhance performance

A budgetary planning and control system therefore needs to be **linked to the strategic plans** that are driving the organisation in the long term. For example, suppose that an organisation is trying to improve speed of delivery while controlling costs. A budgetary planning and control system based on only conventional accounting results will provide information about how much stock an organisation holds and how much has been spent on 'carriage out'. It will not indicate the opportunity cost of cancelled sales through not having stock available when needed, or not being able to deliver on time.

A budgetary planning and control system can **therefore maximise its contribution towards an effective performance measurement system** as follows.

(a) Budget only after the corporate plan has been taken into consideration.

(b) Any interdepartmental conflicts should be identified and resolved.

(c) Short-term targets should be realistic. If budget targets are unrealistically tough, managers may be forced into making short-term/long-term trade offs.

(d) Managers should be committed to targets.

(e) A system of responsibility accounting should be in place and accountability issues identified.

(f) Control reports should be accurate and timely.

This should ensure that short-term decisions taken on the basis of the budget are congruent with the long-term aims of the organisation.

Behavioural consequences

No matter how well designed and implemented, all budgetary planning and control systems can have behavioural implications. Here are some examples.

(a) Managers will often try to make sure that they spend up to their full budget allowance, and do not overspend, so that they will not be accused of having asked for too much spending allowance in the first place. An effective system should discourage **wasteful spending**, not encourage it.

(b) Unless managers **participate** in the preparation of budgets, goal congruence is likely to be difficult to attain, levels of motivation will be low, communication of targets is difficult and targets are unlikely to be realistic.

18   ALTERNATIVE CHOICE DECISION-MAKING CYCLE

> **Tutor's hint. Part (a)** only requires **regurgitation of knowledge** from the Study Text, no application whatsoever is required, and so you should have been able to earn ten marks very easily. Don't be surprised if you don't come across such a straightforward ten-mark requirement in the exam – this question is at the **easy** end of the range of types of question that you could encounter!
>
> **Part (b)** is more indicative of the sort of question you can expect as it focuses on **application** of knowledge. Half of your work for this part of the question has already been done, however, in part (a)! As **additional practice** why not apply different objectives such as improvements in quality or reductions in staff turnover.

(a) The main stages involved in the decision-making cycle are as follows.

    (i)   **Identify goals and objectives**
        Effective decision making requires that the objective is defined clearly and unambiguously.

    (ii)   **Identify alternative opportunities which might contribute towards achieving the objectives**
        Management must attempt to consider all possible alternatives at this stage so that they can be sure that the eventual decision has been reached after due consideration has been given to all opportunities.

    (iii)   **Collect and analyse relevant data about each alternative**
        Both quantitative and qualitative factors must be considered at this stage.

    (iv)   **Compare the alternatives, make the choice/decision and state the expected outcome**
        The expected outcome must be stated so that management have a yardstick for control purposes and so that they can formally check that the expected outcome is in keeping with the overall goals and objectives.

    (v)   **Implement the decision**
        This may involve issuing detailed instructions and plans to appropriate parts of the organisation.

    (vi)   **Record the actual results and compare with the expected outcome**
        This stage completes the decision-making cycle and enables management to evaluate the success or otherwise of their decision. This type of feedback will enable them to refine the decision-making process in future.

(b) **Increase in market share as the decision objective**

    (i)   **Identify goals and objectives**
        The objective should be quantified clearly. For example, 'to increase the market share to 15% for product A'. There may also be a limitation placed on the objective, such as '... without sacrificing the level of profits'.

    (ii)   **Identify alternative opportunities which might contribute towards achieving the objectives**
        Opportunities can be many and varied, depending on each particular situation. Examples could include enhanced market research or improving the forecasting of future requirements.

(iii)   **Collect and analyse relevant data about each alternative**
Quantitative data must be collected, for example concerning the cost of forecasting systems. Qualitative data must not be overlooked - for example the effect of 'fashion' and 'qualitative' as opposed to 'quantitative' market research.

(iv)   **Compare the alternatives, make the choice/decision and state the expected outcome**
Many techniques exist for evaluating the alternatives, ranging from a DCF appraisal, to a cost-benefit analysis of the qualitative data.

(v)   **Implement the decision**
Anybody in the company who is to be affected by the decision to increase market share must be informed in advance, not only those who are to be directly involved in the implementation of the decision. Detailed plans may be necessary to ensure that each stage of the implementation is properly co-ordinated.

(vi)   **Record the actual results and compare with the expected outcomes**
The actual market share must be recorded and compared with the stated expected outcome.

19   AB LTD

> **Tutor's hint.** This question has four ingredients of a good and testing problem on decision making.
>
> - It tests your ability to grasp the **nature of a decision problem**, and think about the **assumptions** you may have to make. For example, the alternative course of action we have suggested seems the most obvious one, but you might think otherwise, and a sensible alternative would be equally acceptable as a solution.
>
> - It tests your knowledge of **relevant costs**. For example, the £3,500 capital cost of Y will be incurred whatever course of action is taken, although with the alternative recommendation we have made the spending could be deferred by 33 weeks. Selling and administration overhead has been assumed to be a fixed cost and so is irrelevant to the decision.
>
> - It includes a consideration of **non-financial factors**. We looked at the workforce, customers' interests and competition – you may have focused on different areas.
>
> - Part (c) of the question introduces the very **practical issue** of **searching for alternative opportunities**. Have all the possible courses of action been identified and considered? It is assumed that stock in hand of finished X, valued at £51,900 at full cost, is valued at the full cost of production and not at the full cost of sale. This would be in keeping with SSAP 9, although the wording of the question is ambiguous on this point.

(a)   **Full cost of production per kg of X**

	£
Direct materials	17.33
Direct labour	7.36
Production overhead (200% of labour)	14.72
	39.41

The **quantity of stock-in-hand** is therefore £51,900/£39.41 = 1,317 kg

At a weekly sales volume of 74 kg, this represents 1,317/74 = about **18 weeks of sales**

It will take 20 weeks to set up the production facility for Y, and so stock in hand of finished X can be sold before any Y can be produced. This **finished stock is therefore irrelevant** to the decision under review; it will be sold whatever decision is taken.

The problem therefore centres on the **stock in hand of direct materials**. Assuming that there is no loss or wastage in manufacture and so 1 kg of direct material is needed to produce 1 kg of X then **stock in hand** is £44,800/£17.33 = 2,585 kg.

This would be converted into 2,585 kg of X, which would represent **sales volume** for 2,585/74 = 35 weeks.

If AB Ltd sells its existing stocks of finished X (in 18 weeks) there are **two options**.

(i)   To produce enough X from raw materials for 2 more weeks, until production of Y can start, and then dispose of all other quantities of direct material - ie 33 weeks' supply.

(ii)   To produce enough X from raw materials to use up the existing stock of raw materials, and so delay the introduction of Y by 33 weeks.

The relevant costs of these two options must be considered.

(i)   **Direct materials**. The relevant cost of existing stocks of raw materials is £(0.30). In other words the 'cost' is a benefit. By using the direct materials to make more X, the company would save £0.30 per kg used.

(ii)   **Direct labour.** It is assumed that if labour is switched to production work from non-production work in the next three months, they must be paid at the full rate of pay, and not at 65% of normal rate. The *incremental* cost of labour would be 35% of the normal rate (35% of £7.36 = £2.58 per kg produced).

Relevant cost of production of X

	£
Direct materials	(0.30)
Direct labour	2.58
Variable overhead (30% of full overhead cost of £14.72)	4.42
Cost per kg of X	6.70

Relevant cost per kg of Y

	£
Direct materials	4.01
Direct labour	2.85
Variable overhead (30% of 200% of £2.85)	1.71
	8.57

(*Note*. Y cannot be made for 20 weeks, and so the company cannot make use of spare labour capacity to produce any units of Y.)

It is **cheaper** to use up the direct material stocks and make X (£6.70 per kg) than to introduce Y as soon as possible, because there would be a saving of (£8.57 – £6.70) = £1.87 per kg made.

AB Ltd must sell X for at least 20 weeks until Y could be produced anyway, but the introduction of Y could be delayed by a further 33 weeks until all stocks of direct material for X are used up. The **saving** in total would be about £1.87 per kg × 74 kg per week × 33 weeks = £4,567.

(b)   (i)   **The workforce**

If the recommended course of action is undertaken, the workforce will produce enough units of X in the next 13 weeks to satisfy sales demand over the next year, (with 18 weeks' supply of existing finished goods stocks and a further 35 weeks' supply obtainable from direct materials stocks). When production of Y begins, the direct labour content of production will fall to £2.85 per kg - less than 40% of the current effort per kg produced - but sales demand will not rise. The changeover will therefore mean a big drop in labour requirements in production. Redundancies seem inevitable, and might be costly. By switching to producing Y as soon as possible, the redundancies might be less immediate, and could be justified more easily to employees and their union representatives than a decision to produce enough X in the next 3 months to eliminate further production needs for about 9 months.

(ii)   **Customers' interests**

Product Y is a superior and 'more effective' compound than X. It would be in customers' interests to provide them with this improved product as soon as possible, instead of delaying its introduction until existing stocks of direct materials for X have been used up.

(iii)   **Competition**

CD is expected to start selling Y overseas, and quite possibly in direct competition with AB Ltd. CD has the advantage of having developed Y itself, and appears to use it in the preliminary stage of an alternative technical process. The competitive threat to AB Ltd is two-fold:

(1)   CD might take away some of the replacement demand for Y from AB Ltd so that AB Ltd's sales of X or Y would fall.

(2)   CD might compete with AB Ltd to install its total technical process into customers' factories, and so the competition would be wider than the market for compound Y.

(c) **Alternative course of action**

(i) Produce enough units of X in the next 13 weeks to use up existing stocks of direct materials.

(ii) Start sales of Y as soon as possible, and to offer customers the choice between X and Y. Since X is an inferior compound, it would have to be sold at a lower price than previously.

Merits of this course of action

(i) The work force would be usefully employed for the next 13 weeks and then production of Y would begin at once. Although redundancies would still seem inevitable, the company would be creating as much work as it could for its employees.

(ii) AB's customers would be made aware of the superiority of Y over X in terms of price, and of AB's commitment to the new compound. AB's marketing approach would be both 'honest' and would also give customers an attractive choice of buying the superior Y or, for a time, an inferior X but at a lower price. This might well enhance AB's marketing success.

Demerits of this course of action

(i) It is unlikely to be a profit-maximising option, because selling X at a discount price would reduce profitability.

(ii) Customers who get a discount on X might demand similar discounts on Y.

(iii) Some customers might query the technical differences between X and Y, and question why AB Ltd has been selling X at such a high price in the past - this might lead to some customer relations difficulties.

(iv) AB Ltd must decide when to reduce the price of X, given that Y cannot be made for 20 weeks. The timing of the price reduction might create some difficulties with customers who buy X just before the price is reduced.

20 GARBO LTD

Tutor's hint. Part (a) was very **easy** and there really is no excuse for not getting full marks (unless you made a silly arithmetical error!). The sales demand is dependent on the sales price, which is dependent on unit cost. Once you know the sales demand you can derive closing stocks (the difference between production and sales). We are dealing with budget data and so there is no under or over absorption of fixed overhead.

The point to make in **part (b)** is that a pricing approach based on cost takes no account of the **link between price and demand** for the products and so it highly unlikely to result in a profit-maximising position.

(a) **Absorption rates in first year**

	Product P		Product Q		Total	
Units of production	40,000	units	10,000	units	50,000	units
Direct labour hours	80,000	hours	160,000	hours	240,000	hours
Machine hours	320,000	hours	40,000	hours	360,000	hours

Since general fixed overheads are £720,000, the absorption rate would be either £3 per direct labour hour or £2 per machine hour.

	Labour hour recovery		Machine hour recovery rate	
	P	Q	P	Q
	£'000	£'000	£'000	£'000
Direct labour	200	280	200	280
Direct materials	240	160	240	160
Directly attributable overhead	120	280	120	280
Share of general overhead	240	480	640	80
Full cost	800	1,200	1,200	800
Units produced	40,000	10,000	40,000	10,000
Unit full cost	£20	£120	£30	£80
Sales price (plus 20%)	£24	£144	£36	£96
Sales demand, 1st year (units)	36,000	7,000	18,000	10,000

	Labour hour recovery rate		Machine hour recovery rate	
	P	Q	P	Q
	£'000	£'000	£'000	£'000
Production costs (as above)	800	1,200	1,200	800
Less closing stock	80	360	660	0
Full cost of sales	720	840	540	800
Sales	864	1,008	648	960
Profit	144	168	108	160

Summary

If the **labour hour absorption rate** is used.

		P	Q	Total
		£	£	£
(i)	Units costs	20	120	-
(ii)	Closing stock value	80,000	360,000	440,000
(iii)	Profit in first year	144,000	168,000	312,000

If the **machine hour absorption rate** is used.

		P	Q	Total
		£	£	£
(i)	Units costs	30	80	
(ii)	Closing stock value	660,000	0	660,000
(iii)	Profit in first year	108,000	160,000	268,000

(b) The figures in (a) reveal the following.

(i) Due to the **elasticity of demand** for each product, a sales price based on full cost at maximum capacity plus a fixed profit margin will be woefully inadequate for establishing an optimum (or profit-maximising) price.

(ii) The calculation of a full cost depends on both:

(1) the **budgeted volume of output.** If this were reduced to expected sales levels, unit costs would rise (and so, presumably, would the sales price, thereby depressing budgeted output even further and increasing unit costs further in a vicious circle); and also

(2) the way in which overheads are **apportioned** between products. Different bases of absorption, in this case, result in radically different costs and prices for P and Q.

21   PRL

> **Tutor's hint.** For part (a) it is a good idea to start by considering **how the profit-maximising price is determined (where marginal cost equals marginal revenue)** and then you need to make some **assumptions** and **calculations** in relation to marginal cost and marginal revenue.
>
> The next step is to set out how the **information** required can be **acquired** and then **analysed.** You may need to look back at **Chapter 7** for this part of the question.
>
> Provide a **conclusion** that summarises the way in which the price should be fixed.
>
> Ensure that you **relate** your answer to **part (b)** to the **scenario** set. You were not required to explain the theory of price discrimination in abstract terms but to apply it to PRL. So rather than listing general bases for setting discriminating prices such as by market segment, provide an example for PRL (such as by offering fare concessions to students). We started our answer with an **analysis of the current situation** to **show why price discrimination might be useful** (because demand outstrips supply at certain times).

(a) **The profit-maximising price is always at the point where marginal cost (the cost incurred in carrying one extra passenger) equals marginal revenue (the revenue obtained from carrying one extra passenger).**

Information needed

Although we are given no information as to the cost patterns faced by PRL, we know that demand for the service more than meets supply. This indicates that marginal revenue over a very wide range is likely to be £2, the number of passengers being carried before the next passenger would not pay £2 being very high.

The only way to increase profit is therefore to increase the ticket price above £2 since it is unlikely that a reduction in the number of passengers would dramatically affect marginal cost, the majority of costs facing PRL probably being fixed. Under current conditions the maximum revenue per train is 600 × £2 = £1,200. Suppose that the price was raised to £2.50. To receive the same revenue only 480 passengers per journey would need to be carried and any passenger over and above 480 would increase profit. If the fares were raised to £5 only 241 passengers would need to be carried in order to increase profit.

PRL therefore needs to acquire two sets of information, the first being about the **number of passengers who would be willing to travel at different fares** and the second relating **to any cost factors that would need to be taken into account if passengers numbers were to change.**

How to acquire the information

The information about the number of passengers would be obtained **from market research**.

(i)   Customers would be interviewed and asked to state the maximum fare they would be willing to pay.

(ii)   The fares/entrance fees of similar attractions and indeed any other attractions could be examined to ascertain what people will pay for summer diversions.

(iii)   The fare structure of other steam engine rides could be reviewed to find out what competitors are charging. Information on passenger numbers would also be useful.

The second set of information may well be internally produced.

How to analyse the information

Market research information would, of course, have to be analysed **with great care**. Passengers may not always react truthfully when asked if they would be prepared to pay a higher price. It is in passengers' self-interest to keep fares as low as possible. Any information gathered from competitors (other attractions and other steam trains) **may not be reliable** if the competitors are aware of the reason for its provision and, as such, it could well be slanted.

Conclusion

Since it is not possible to test market, a price will have to be fixed that is based on **management judgement and the best of the limited information that is available**. PRL should bear in mind that a **price can always be changed**. It is best in these circumstances to set a fare that may be too high since it can always be lowered if there is no demand. Raising a fare will do nothing to engender customer goodwill.

(b)   **The current situation**

PRL has more customers than it can transport and so it is likely that some (if not all customers) **might be willing to pay more than the current fare of £2.**

Passengers will have to be turned away from trains leaving at the most popular times if the price is set at £2. Let us assume that, of the four trains, two leave at the most popular times. PRL could therefore increase the fare on these two trains to, say, £3. If, at this fare, the number of customers willing to pay is still greater than the number of available spaces on the train, there will be some customers who will instead opt for the cheaper trains. These trains are, however, also filled to capacity and so PRL could raise the fare to, say, £2.50 on the off-peak trains. At this point supply of seats may well equal demand for seats since there may well be some passengers not willing to pay more than £2 and who will not use the service at all but opt for another tourist attraction.

Using price discrimination

PRL should therefore attempt to devise a fare structure such that the **price set for the popular time trains fills those trains to capacity and the price set for the unpopular time trains fills them to capacity with both the overflow from the more expensive trains and with those willing to pay the lower price.** Since revenue is calculated as fare charged multiplied by number of passengers, revenue will be maximised when the maximum possible number of passengers (ie four trains full to capacity) pay the maximum amount to ensure full trains.

Methods of price discrimination available

There are, of course, different methods of price discrimination which PRL could use.

(i)   A **high standard** fare could be charged **with concessions** for senior citizens, students, the unemployed and so on.

(ii)   **Discounts for block bookings** could be given against a higher standard fare.

(iii) **Fares for particular seats in the train** (for example window seats) **could attract a premium**.

(iv) **Each train during the day could be slightly different** and hence charge a slightly different fare. For example, passengers on the train running at around 4 o'clock could be served afternoon tea whereas those on the train at midday could be served lunch.

(v) Passengers could **reserve a particular seat by paying a higher price**.

(vi) Passengers could **pre-book and pre-pay** for seats thus **ensuring early cash flow** and **certainty of passengers in inclement weather**.

(vii) **Special trains with higher fares could be run in the evenings** for illuminations, barbecues and so on.

(viii) **Trains with fares at a premium could be run to coincide with events such as carnivals or for Christmas shopping**.

All of the above suggestions would increase PRL's revenue either by charging a **higher standard fare and then offering discounts to particular passengers or** by charging a **standard fare for a standard journey and an enhanced fare for a special journey**.

22   STOW HEALTH CENTRE

> **Tutor's hint** Did you get confused in part (a)? The occupancy level will vary with the client fee per day, while the variable cost per client day is independent. In other words, at each of the **three different levels of client fee** per day, there are **three possible levels of variable cost** per client and so 3 × 3 = **9 possible levels of contribution per client day**.
>
> The most tricky aspect of part (b) was dealing with the **minimax regret decision rule**. This rule involves choosing the strategy which will **minimise the maximum regret** (ie drop in contribution) from choosing one option instead of the best option. This requires you to draw up an **opportunity loss table**. This will show the **drop in contribution** at **each level of variable cost** from **choosing a level of client fee which is not the best option**. For example, at a variable cost of £95 per day, the best strategy would be a client fee of £200 per day. The opportunity loss from using a fee of £180 would be the difference between the contributions at the two fee levels.
>
> For part (c) you simply need to **calculate an EV of variable cost per day**. You are then faced with a situation of one level of client fee per day and one level of variable cost per day at each level of 'demand'.

(a) We need to calculate budgeted contribution and so the summary will need to show the various income (fee) and variable cost levels.

Number of client days (W1)	Client fee per day £	Variable cost per client day £	Contribution per client day £	Total contribution this year £ (W2)
15,750	180	95	85	1,338,750
15,750	180	85	95	1,496,250
15,750	180	70	110	1,732,500
13,125	200	95	105	1,378,125
13,125	200	85	115	1,509,375
13,125	200	70	130	1,706,250
10,500	220	95	125	1,312,500
10,500	220	85	135	1,417,500
10,500	220	70	150	1,575,000

Workings

1   Maximum capacity = 50 × 350 = 17,500
High occupancy level = 90% × 17,500 = 15,750
Most likely occupancy level = 75% × 17,500 = 13,125
Low occupancy level = 60% × 17,500 = 10,500

2   Number of client days × contribution per client day

(b) (i) The **maximax** decision rule involves choosing the outcome with the **best possible result**, in this instance choosing the outcome which **maximises contribution**. The decision maker would therefore choose a **client fee of £180 per day**, which could result in a contribution of £1,732,500.

(ii) The **maximin** decision rule involves choosing the outcome that offers the **least unattractive worst outcome,** in this instance choosing the outcome which **maximises the minimum contribution**. The decision maker would therefore choose a **client fee of £200 per day**, which has a lowest possible contribution of £1,378,125. This is better than the worst possible outcomes from client fees per day of £180 and £220, which would provide contributions of £1,338,750 and £1,312,500 respectively.

(iii) The **minimax regret** decision rule involves choosing the **outcome that minimises the maximum regret** from making the wrong decision, in this instance choosing the outcome which minimises the opportunity lost from making the wrong decision.

We can use the calculations performed in (a) to draw up an **opportunity loss table.**

Client fee per day	Variable cost per day			Maximum regret
	£95	£85	£70	
£	£	£	£	£
180	39,375 (W1)	13,125 (W4)	0 (W7)	39,375
200	0 (W2)	0 (W5)	26,250 (W8)	26,250
220	65,625 (W3)	91,875 (W6)	157,500 (W9)	157,500

The minimax regret decision strategy would be to **choose a client fee of £200** to minimise the maximum regret at £26,250.

Workings

1 At a variable cost of £95 per day, the best strategy would be a client fee of £200 per day. The opportunity loss from using a fee of £180 would be £(1,378,125 – 1,338,750) = £39,375.

2 The opportunity loss in this case is £(1,378,125 – 1,378,125) = £0.

3 The opportunity loss in this case is £(1,378,125 – 1,312,500) = £65,625.

4 At a variable cost of £85 per day, the best strategy would be a client fee of £200 per day. The opportunity loss from using a fee of £180 would be £(1,509,375 – 1,496,250)= £13,125.

5 The opportunity loss in this case is £(1,509,375 – 1,509,375) = 0.

6 The opportunity loss in this case is £(1,509,375 – 1,417,500) = £91,875.

7 At a variable cost of £70 per day, the best strategy would be client fee of £180 per day. The opportunity loss from using a fee of £180 would be £(1,732,500 – 1,732,500) = £0.

8 The opportunity loss in this case is £(1,732,500 – 1,706,250) = £26,250.

9 The opportunity loss in this case is £(1,732,500 – 1,575,000) = £157,500.

(c) **Expected value of variable costs** = (0.1 × £95) + (0.6 × £85) + (0.3 × £70) = £81.50.

We can now **calculate an expected value of budgeted contribution at each client fee per day level**.

Number of client days	Client fee per day	EV of variable cost per day	EV of contribution per client day	EV of total annual contribution
	£	£	£	£
15,750	180	81.50	98.50	1,551,375.00
13,125	200	81.50	118.50	1,555,312.50
10,500	220	81.50	138.50	1,454,250.00

If **maximisation of EV of contribution is used as the decision basis**, a **client fee of £200 per day** will be selected, with an EV of contribution of £1,555,312.50 (although this is *very* close to the EV of contribution which results from a client fee of £180).

23   TRANSFER PRICING

> **Tutor's hint.** Hopefully you feel quite confident about your ability to tackle Paper 3.3 questions having completed this one as it is from the **pilot paper** and **indicative** of the type of thing you will face in the exam. And it's not too difficult is it?
>
> **Part (a)** is **basic book knowledge** and so you should have been able to score at least four of the six marks available.
>
> If you can answer **part (b)** successfully then there is every chance that you really understand transfer pricing. The reasoning required is not at all difficult but goes to the very **heart of the topic**. If you couldn't answer part (b) yourself, work through our answer really carefully until you understand what's going on.
>
> **Part (c)** is a **lot more straightforward than it appears**. Just think logically about the data that you need to determine transfer prices.

(a)   **Potential benefits of operating a transfer pricing system within a divisionalised company**

(i)   It can lead to **goal congruence** by motivating divisional managers to make decisions, which improve divisional profit and improve profit of the organisation as a whole.

(ii)   It can prevent **dysfunctional decision making** so that decisions taken by a divisional manager are in the best interests of his own part of the business, other divisions and the organisation as a whole.

(iii)   Transfer prices can be set at a level that enables divisional performance to be measured 'commercially'. A transfer pricing system should therefore report a level of divisional profit that is a **reasonable measure of the managerial performance** of the division.

(iv)   It should ensure that **divisional autonomy** is not undermined. A well-run transfer pricing system helps to ensure that a balance is kept between divisional autonomy to provide incentives and motivation, and centralised authority to ensure that the divisions are all working towards the same target, the benefit of the organisation as a whole.

(b)   (i)   **Division Able has spare capacity and limited external demand for product X**

In this situation, the incremental cost to the company of producing product Y is £35. It costs division Baker £38 to buy product Y from the external market and so it is cheaper by £3 per unit to buy from division Able.

The transfer price needs to be fixed at a price above £35 both to provide some incentive to division Able to supply division Baker and to provide some contribution towards fixed overheads. The transfer price must be below £38 per unit, however, to encourage division Baker to buy from division Able rather than from the external supplier.

The transfer price should therefore be set in the range above £35 and below £38 and at a level so that both divisions, acting independently and in their own interests, would choose to buy from and sell to each other.

(ii)   **Division Able is operating at full capacity with unsatisfied external demand for product X**

If division Able chooses to supply division Baker rather than the external market, the **opportunity cost** of such a decision must be incorporated into the transfer price.

For every unit of product Y produced and sold to division Baker, division Able will lose £10 (£(42-32)) in contribution due to not supplying the external market with product X. The relevant cost of supplying product Y in these circumstances is therefore £45 (£(35 + 10)). It is therefore in the interests of the company as a whole if division Baker sources product Y externally at the cheaper price of £38 per unit. Division Able can therefore continue to supply external demand at £42 per unit.

The company can ensure this happens if the transfer price of product Y is set above £38, thereby encouraging division Baker to buy externally rather than from division Able.

(c) **Data to be collected for an information system to support transfer pricing decision making**

Type of data	How it would be used
Unit variable costs	To show the incremental cost of making various products/providing various services
External selling prices	To provide guidance as to market value transfer prices
	To indicate contribution that could be earned if products were sold externally rather than transferred internally
Capacity levels	To give guidance as to whether opportunity costs of lost sales need to be incorporated in transfer prices
Limiting factors	To highlight how capacity can be expanded
Shadow prices	To determine whether or not additional resources should be obtained
Availability/prices of external prices	To make or buy decisions

24 MANCASTLE CITY

> **Tutor's hint**. Note that **part (a)** asks you to identify **non-relevant** costs/revenues/cash flows – not the relevant ones. Hopefully you read the question carefully enough to notice this.
>
> At heart **part (b)** is a fairly standard incremental cash flows question, made far more complex by the need to **work out when cash flows occur for discounting purposes** and to take **inflation** into account. Read through our workings very carefully to ensure that you understand where all the figures come from. We have considered **net cash flows calculated by subtracting grass cash flows from the Icing cash flows and the Astroturf cash flows**. This shows the incremental cost/benefit of Astroturf or Icing compared with grass. Alternatively you could consider the three options separately and look at their cash flows in isolation.
>
> If the club is **indifferent** between keeping the present pitch and replacing it with an Astroturf pitch (part (c)), the **NPV of the incremental Astroturf cash flows would be nil**. The **NPV of the increase in the disposal income** would therefore need to be **£39,009**. Don't forget to **adjust** the improvement to **year 0 values**.
>
> Part (d)(ii) has a **wide variety of possible answers**: you may have other valid suggestions besides those we suggest. Note that you are asked about other matters that might **affect the calculations**, not about other matters in general.

(a) The **salaries of the groundspersons** are not relevant because they will be paid whatever decision is made.

The **cost of the stocks of chemicals** is a sunk cost and not relevant to the decision.

(b) The net cash flows are calculated by **subtracting the Grass cash flows from the Icing cash flows and the Astroturf cash flows respectively**, and then **discounting** by the relevant factor.

Year	Df	Grass (W3)	Icing (W3)	Net Icing	DCF	Astroturf (W3)	Net Astroturf	DCF
0	1.000	-	316,800	316,800	316,800	287,100	287,100	287,100
1	0.926	124,630	67,187	(57,443)	(53,192)	59,153	(65,477)	(60,632)
2	0.857	124,630	69,487	(55,143)	(47,258)	61,453	(63,177)	(54,143)
3	0.794	127,050	72,126	(54,924)	(43,610)	63,936	(63,114)	(50,113)
4	0.735	139,125	73,480	(65,645)	(48,249)	65,290	(73,835)	(54,269)
5	0.681	141,775	76,328	(65,447)	(44,569)	67,982	(73,793)	(50,253)
6	0.630		(90,000)	(90,000)	(56,700)	(90,000)	(90,000)	(56,700)
					23,222			(39,010)

Positive incremental cash flows are shown in brackets. The analysis indicates that **Astroturf** is the **best option** to choose: it has a positive discounted cash flow as compared with Grass of £39,009.

Workings

1   **Turf costs**

There is 110m × 90m to cover. This will require (110 × 90) 9,900 units of Astroturf or 9,900 ÷ 5m^2 = 396 units of Icing.

Astroturf:	9,900 × £29	£287,100
Icing:	396 × £800	£316,800

2   **Indexed cash flows**

Emboldened figures refer to W3.

Year	0	1	2	3	4	5
Index	100	103	103	105	105	107

Training session fees (W4)

Grass	78,000	**80,340**	80,340	81,900	81,900	83,460
Astroturf (As grass × (100 – 55)%)	35,100	36,153	**36,153**	36,855	36,855	37,557
Icing (As grass × (100 – 45)%)	42,900	44,187	44,187	**45,045**	45,045	45,903

Fertiliser, chemicals etc (W5)

Stock	-	-	-	-	12,075	12,305
Purchased	43,000	44,290	44,290	45,150	45,150	46,010
Total	43,000	**44,290**	44,290	45,150	57,225	58,315

Turf replacement (Astroturf and Icing) (W6)	23,000	**25,300**	27,081	28,435	30,425

3   **Summary of cash flows**

Emboldened figures here correspond with emboldened figures in W2 to indicate the derivation of totals.

Year	1	2	3	4	5
Grass	**124,630**	124,630	127,050	139,125	141,775
Astroturf	59,153	**61,453**	63,936	65,290	67,982
Icing	67,187	69,487	**72,126**	73,480	76,328

4   **Training session fees**

For grass the fee of £78,000 is increased by the index figure for each year. For example for year 1 the figure is £78,000 × 1.03 = £80,340.

The figures for Astroturf and Icing are the grass fees reduced by the appropriate percentage.

5   **Fertiliser, chemicals**

Purchases are reduced by £10,000 to £43,000 in year 0. In later years this figure is multiplied by the appropriate index number. For year 5: £43,000 × 1.07 = £46,010.

Stocks last for three years. In year 4 these have to be purchased. The price is adjusted to year 0 value (£10,000 × 1.15 = £11,500) and then indexed up to year 4 and year 5 values (£11,500 × 1.05 = 12,075; £11,500 × 1.07 = £12,305).

6   **Replacement turfs**

Turfs are quoted at year 1 prices. They need to be adjusted to year 0 prices before the general (103, 105 etc) and specific (10%, 5%) inflation indexes can be applied.

Year 2: (£23,000/1.03) × 1.1 × 1.03	= £25,300
Year 3: (£23,000/1.03) × 1.1 × 1.05 × 1.05	= £27,081

and so on.

(c)   For this to hold true the **NPV of the Astroturf option would need to be nil**. In other words the NPV of the increase in disposal income would need to be £39,010 less. Adjusted to year 0 values the improvement forecast was £(56,700 – 39,010)/0.630 = £28,079.

(d)   (i)   The problem of uncertainty can never be fully overcome, but allowances can be made for it in a variety of ways.

(1)   The data could be set up on a **spreadsheet** with an input section for all the variables as stated in the question and an output section consisting of formulae and cell references to represent the relationships between the variables. It would then be

possible to change any of the input variables that are uncertain and see the effect that this has on the output. This is known as 'what-if' analysis.

(2) **Probabilities** could be assigned to ranges of values for the uncertain variables and NPVs in the best and worst scenarios calculated.

(3) The club could seek the reassurance of further guidance from **experts** in the economy or the relevant industries.

(ii) Some of the other matters to be considered are as follows.

(1) The impact of the use of an all-weather pitch may affect the team's **performance** and that of their opponents. If the team performs well this will increase usage of the stadium and so the costs of wear and tear (both of the pitch and of other facilities).

(2) There may be opposition to the scheme on **environmental** grounds, which may cause adverse PR for the club and affect attendance levels and so income.

(3) It may be possible to **charge** spectators to watch the team training at the stadium.

(4) The club will lose the **skills of grass pitch maintenance**, which may be needed (and will therefore will cost money to acquire again) when they move to a new stadium.

25   MIS DESIGN

DRAFT REPORT

To: Manager
From: Accountant
Date: 23 February 20X1
Subject: Designing an effective management information system

Set out below are some issues which you might wish to consider when designing an effective management information system.

What is a management information system?

A management information system (MIS) **collects data** from various sources **and turns it into the type of information that managers need** to help them to run their business. An MIS cannot be bought off-the-shelf and installed overnight. It is the combination of both informal and formal data collection, information analysis and information dissemination which provides an organisation's managers with the information they require for strategic, tactical and operational planning and control.

The information provided by an MIS

In essence, a manager needs to know three things.

* What are his resources?
* At what rate are his resources being consumed?
* How well are the resources being used?

This is the content of the information that an MIS needs to provide, but decisions must also be made as to the level of **detail** that is provided and the **frequency** of its provision.

Sources of data

> **Tutor's hint.** In this section you might mention information that a particular organisation/industry might require. An organisation with high levels of imports/exports might need to know about exchange rate movements. Supermarkets regularly send staff to competitors' stores to record prices being charged.

(a) **Information for strategic planning and control**

This will tend to require **outwards-looking** information such as information on market requirements, competitors' plans, and developments in the local and wider economies. This can be sourced from **customers, suppliers, trade associations** and the **government**. It might be **formally** collected, perhaps by a market research manager, or **informally** collected by employees from newspapers, television and so on.

(b) **Information for tactical and operational planning and control**

    (i)   **Inwards-looking** information such as throughput rates, cycle times and capacity utilisation

    (ii)   **Forwards-looking** information such as cash flow forecasts, production plans and budgets

    (iii)   Backwards-looking information such as that provided by classic budgetary control systems and published accounts

This type of information can be sourced from **within the business**, either formally from reports of meetings, time sheets and so on, or informally such as by word of mouth or from the television.

Recording and processing methods

The methods adopted will need to consider a number of factors.

(a) **The type of business entity**

> **Tutor's hint.** Here you could refer to a particular type of business with which you have familiarity. For example, you could mention electronic point of sale equipment that a large retailer might like to use.

(b) **The volume of information required**

    (i)   A concertina file, a cash book and the owners' memory might be sufficient to record the transactions of a small business.

    (ii)   Large organisations might use a database or a collection of linked databases from which managers are able to select information using a networked communications system.

(c) **The uses to which the organisation wants to put the information**

An organisation's needs for information are influenced by the uses to which it wants to put the information. The system must be able to deliver the **information needs of the management accounting tools and techniques used** by the organisation. For example, if an organisation wishes to use activity based costing rather than marginal costing it will need to ensure that information is collected on activities, cost drivers and so on. If benchmarking is to be adopted, the MIS must be able to gather information on 'best in class' organisations.

> **Tutor's hint.** You could mention any number of management accounting tools and techniques here. If you are discussing a manufacturing organisation, think about the impact of JIT.

(d) **IT systems**

The level of information technology available will influence recording and processing methods. **Personal computers**, for example, have transformed the role of MIS and allow data to be stored, retrieved and processed into information and reported in a timely and ultimately cost-effective manner. Sophisticated **software packages** support modern management accounting techniques such as ABC and modern manufacturing methods such as JIT.

Format of reports

The design of an MIS needs to take into account the way in which information will be disseminated to users. This hinges on a number of factors.

(a) **Type of report**

    (i)   Scheduled reports are routinely prepared on a regular basis. The payroll report is an example.

    (ii)   Exception reports draw attention to deviations from plans.

    (iii)   Some reports are produced on demand, not as a matter of course.

    (iv)   Planning reports include forecasts.

(b) **Accuracy, detail and speed**

There will need to be some trade-off between the accuracy of the report, the level of detail reported and the speed with which it is prepared.

(c) **Management structure**

Each manager should be given information according to what his or her responsibilities are, and this is dictated by the management structure of the organisation.

(d) **Management style**

In a **hierarchical** organisation, the way in which information is provided must prevent human bias and procrastination. In a **democratic** organisation, the correct volume of information must be disseminated to maintain democracy and to limit politics.

> **Tutor's hint.** This might be particularly important if you are discussing an organisation type which has both private and public sector versions, such as hospitals.

(e) **Controllability**

The information individual managers require is information about their own areas of responsibility. Managers should not be made responsible for matters that are controlled by somebody else within the organisation.

(f) **Security and access**

Controls must be in place to ensure the security of highly confidential information that is not for external consumption. Passwords and so on need to be set up.

(g) **Systems compatibility**

If the organisation intends to use **electronic data interchange** with customers and suppliers, the MIS must be designed with compatibility in mind.

(h) **Skills and systems knowledge of users**

Because of the availability of spreadsheet packages, mangers can download data from a database via a network and manipulate it as they like. The speed, ease of use and capacity of PCs is such that, when combined with the power of the spreadsheet, most business analysis problems that a manger might wish to tackle can be dealt with. A workforce with extensive knowledge of systems and software packages may carry out their own investigations and analyses as and when they wish.

Other general issues

- Expected life of the system
- Developments in MIS
- Commissioning dates - resources and time constraints

If I can provide any further information please do not hesitate to contact me.

26 AQUA HOLDINGS

(a) **WSS**

		20X0	20W9
ROCE =	$\left(\dfrac{\text{profit before interest}}{\text{capital employed}} \times 100\%\right)$	$\dfrac{14}{167} \times 100\% = 8.4\%$	$\dfrac{17}{134} \times 100\% = 12.7\%$
Sales margin =	$\left(\dfrac{\text{profit before interest}}{\text{sales}} \times 100\%\right)$	$\dfrac{14}{31} \times 100\% = 45\%$	$\dfrac{17}{30} \times 100\% = 57\%$
Asset turnover =	$\dfrac{\text{sales}}{\text{capital employed}}$	$\dfrac{31}{167} = 0.19$	$\dfrac{30}{134} = 0.22$
Gearing ratio =	$\dfrac{\text{long-term debt}}{\text{long-term debt + equity}}$	$\dfrac{47}{120 + 47} = 0.28$	$\dfrac{47}{87 + 47} = 0.35$
Current ratio =	$\dfrac{\text{current assets}}{\text{current liabilities}}$	$\dfrac{5}{3} = 1.7$	$\dfrac{6}{6} = 1.0$

EA	20X0	20W9
ROCE	$\dfrac{1}{31} \times 100\% = 3.2\%$	$\dfrac{12}{30} \times 100\% = 40.0\%$
Sales margin	$\dfrac{1}{20} \times 100\% = 5.0\%$	$\dfrac{12}{35} \times 100\% = 34.3\%$
Asset turnover	$\dfrac{20}{31} = 0.65$	$\dfrac{35}{30} = 1.17$
Gearing ratio	0	0
Current ratio	$\dfrac{12}{4} = 3$	$\dfrac{12}{4} = 3$

Water Supply Services

WSS's **profits** have fallen both in absolute terms (due to the £3 million increase in depreciation) and in relative terms. The organisation's rate of **asset turnover** has also fallen, although this is to be expected as it often takes time for new assets to generate sales.

A fall in the level of the organisation's current liabilities has led to a marked increase in the current ratio and so the organisation's **liquidity** gives no immediate cause for concern.

The increase in **shareholders' equity** has lowered the **gearing ratio** but a significant proportion of the organisation's assets are funded by debt

Shareholders may not have been too impressed by the fall in profits given the increase in their holdings.

Enterprise Activities

In contrast with the relative stability of WSS's turnover (an established feature of a regulated monopoly), EA's **sales revenue** has dropped dramatically, with a consequent substantial decline in **profit** in relative and absolute terms.

Unlike WAS, EA has **no long-term debt**. This may be because EA management felt that fixed interest payments would be impossible, given the rapidly changing market and the volatility of profits.

Like WSS, EA appears to be able to meet its future commitments to pay off its current liabilities (as indicated by the **current ratio**).

Limitations of undertaking comparisons of financial performance

(i)   The markets in which the two organisations operate are completely different.

   (1)   The markets are subject to different levels of financial and business risk. This will have a significant impact on the expectations of shareholders and their required level of organisational performance and return.

   (2)   The highly-regulated nature of WSS's operating environment means that high profits resulting from effective management might lead to the imposition of price cuts if profits are subject to regulation and are deemed excessive. On the other hand, inefficiency and high levels of costs might be hidden if price increases are allowed and hence fairly constant levels of profit are reported. EA's financial performance is not subject to control in this way.

   (3)   A regulatory framework monitors service standards offered by WSS and requires it to maintain these at a certain level at prices which are to a large degree determined by government. The level of service provided to customers by EA and the price at which it is provided are set by the market.

   These differences make comparisons between the two organisations fraught with difficulties.

(ii)   Given that the above analysis concentrates on relatively short-term performance, it is not a particularly appropriate means of assessing long-term organisational success.

   (1)   The asset acquisitions of WSS should produce future profits.

   (2)   We have no indication of whether the widely-fluctuating profit levels of EA are part of a long-term trend or a one-off 'blip' in performance.

Such analysis does not therefore provide the full picture of how the organisations have performed.

(b) The manager's financial **target** is to maximise the total profit that the three service contracts earn.

Most importantly, to assist him in achieving this aim, the manager needs to have a **deeper understanding of the basic relationships between costs, profits and levels of activity**, especially in respect of the following.

- The overall cost structure of the organisation
- The nature of fixed and variable costs
- The difference between general fixed overheads and directly attributable fixed overheads
- The concept of contribution
- The way in which optimal resource allocation decisions should be made when there is a limiting factor
- Appropriate methods of allocating overheads

This understanding will improve the manager's decision-making skills

The manager should also attempt to gain a **greater understanding of the environment** in which Enterprise Activities operates. Knowledge of the current business environment, a review of possible future operating scenarios and assimilation of detail on competitors will assist the manager in making appropriate decisions in a rapidly-changing competitive environment.

The manager could also benefit from information and advice about a number of **management accounting methods** such as pricing policy and budget preparation.

Advice on the following **general business/management areas** would also be of use.

(i)   TQM programmes and the associated costs and benefits
(ii)   Methods of overcoming labour shortages
(iii) Diversification of services offered (to reduce profit volatility)

(c) We begin by calculating total cost in order to work out selling price.

	Standard	Super	Economy
	£	£	£
Raw material	100.00	150.00	80.00
Direct labour	50.00	80.00	20.00
Variable cost	150.00	230.00	100.00
Fixed overheads	225.00	345.00	150.00
Total cost	375.00	575.00	250.00
Profit (50% of total cost)	187.50	287.50	125.00
Selling price	562.50	862.50	375.00

Step 1. **Calculate contribution per unit of limiting factor and rank products in order of production**

	Standard	Super	Economy
Contribution per unit	£412.50	£632.50	£275.00
Labour hours per unit	5	8	2
Contribution per unit of limiting factor	£82.50	£79.06	£137.50
Priority for production	Second	Third	First

Step 2. **Work out available resource**

Budgeted hours = (1,000 × 5) + (800 × 8) + (2,000 × 2) = 15,400
Available hours = 15,400 × 80% = 12,320

Step 3. **Work out optimal production plan and maximum possible profit**

	Units	Hours used	Hours remaining	Contribution
				£
Economy	2,000	4,000	8,320	550,000.00
Standard	1,000	5,000	3,320	412,500.00
Super	415*	3,320	-	262,487.50
Total contribution				1,224,987.50
Fixed overheads**				801,000.00
Maximum profit				423,987.50

*3,320 / 8
**£((225 × 1,000) + (345 × 800) + (150 × 2,000))

(d) **Differences in the two organisations' information needs**

The differences in the business environments of the two organisations will have a significant impact on the information needs of the two organisations.

Water Supply Services

(i)   The information system will need to provide extensive detail on fixed assets.

(ii)   Non-monetary information is needed to show that guaranteed service standards for customers have been maintained.

(iii)   Information for regulatory reporting requirements must be readily available.

(iv)   Detailed price and cost information is required to demonstrate equity of prices adopted and/or to justify price increases.

Enterprise Activities

(i)   Information to make 'on-the-spot' decisions in response to rapidly-changing market conditions must be available.

(ii)   Externally-sourced information about competitors, their prices and activities will allow the organisation to compete effectively.

(iii)   Information is needed to allow profit-optimising allocations of scarce resources (skilled plumbers) to be made.

Index

Key Terms and the pages where the Key Terms are defined are shown in **bold**.

REVIEW FORM & FREE PRIZE DRAW

All original review forms from the entire BPP range, completed with genuine comments, will be entered into a draw on 31 January 2005 and 31 July 2005. The names on the first four forms picked out will be sent a cheque for £50.

Name: _____   Address: _____

_____

How have you used this Text?
(Tick one box only)

☐ Home study (book only)

☐ On a course: college _____

☐ With 'correspondence' package

☐ Other _____

Why did you decide to purchase this Text?
(Tick one box only)

☐ Have used complementary Kit

☐ Have used BPP Texts in the past

☐ Recommendation by friend/colleague

☐ Recommendation by a lecturer at college

☐ Saw advertising

☐ Other _____

During the past six months do you recall seeing/receiving any of the following?
(Tick as many boxes as are relevant)

☐ Our advertisement in *ACCA Student Accountant*

☐ Our advertisement in *Pass*

☐ Our advertisement in *PQ*

☐ Our brochure with a letter through the post

Which (if any) aspects of our advertising do you find useful?
(Tick as many boxes as are relevant)

☐ Prices and publication dates of new editions

☐ Information on Text content

☐ Facility to order books off-the-page

☐ None of the above

Which BPP products have you used?

Text ☑	Success CD ☐	i-Learn ☐
Kit ☐	Success Tape ☐	i-Pass ☐
Passcard ☐	Big Picture Poster ☐	Virtual Campus ☐

Your ratings, comments and suggestions would be appreciated on the following areas of this Text.

	Very useful	Useful	Not useful
Introductory section (Key study steps, personal study)	☐	☐	☐
Chapter introductions	☐	☐	☐
Key terms	☐	☐	☐
Quality of explanations	☐	☐	☐
Case examples and other examples	☐	☐	☐
Questions and answers in each chapter	☐	☐	☐
Chapter roundups	☐	☐	☐
Quick quizzes	☐	☐	☐
7Exam focus points	☐	☐	☐
Question bank	☐	☐	☐
Answer bank	☐	☐	☐
List of key terms and index	☐	☐	☐
Icons	☐	☐	☐

	Excellent	Good	Adequate	Poor
Overall opinion of this Text	☐	☐	☐	☐

Do you intend to continue using BPP Products?   ☐ Yes   ☐ No

Please note any further comments and suggestions/errors on the reverse of this page. The BPP author of this edition can be e-mailed at: alisonmchugh@bpp.com

Please return to: Catherine Watton, ACCA Range Manager, BPP Professional Education, FREEPOST, London, W12 8BR

REVIEW FORM & FREE PRIZE DRAW (continued)

TELL US WHAT YOU THINK

Because the following specific areas of the text contain new material and cover highly examinable topics etc, your comments on their usefulness are particularly welcome.

Please note any further comments and suggestions/errors below.

See overleaf for information on other
BPP products and how to order

ACCA Order

To BPP Professional Education, Aldine Place, London W12 8AW

Tel: 020 8740 2211
Fax: 020 8740 1184
email: publishing@bpp.com
website: www.bpp.com
Order online www.bpp.com

Mr/Mrs/Ms (Full name) _____

Daytime delivery address _____

Postcode _____

Daytime Tel _____

Date of exam (month/year) _____   Scots law variant Y / N

Occasionally we may wish to email you relevant offers and information about courses and products. Please tick to opt into this service. ☐

	6/04 Texts	1/04 Kits	1/04 Passcards	***Success CDs	Big Picture Posters	8/04 i-Learn	8/04 i-Pass	Virtual Campus
PART 1								
1.1 Preparing Financial Statements	£24.95 ☐	£10.95 ☐	£6.95 ☐	£14.95 ☐	£6.95 ☐	£34.95 ☐	£24.95 ☐	£90 ☐
1.2 Financial Information for Management	£24.95 ☐	£10.95 ☐	£6.95 ☐	£14.95 ☐	£6.95 ☐	£34.95 ☐	£24.95 ☐	£90 ☐
1.3 Managing People	£24.95 ☐	£10.95 ☐	£6.95 ☐	£14.95 ☐	£6.95 ☐	£34.95 ☐	£24.95 ☐	£90 ☐
PART 2								
2.1 Information Systems	£24.95 ☐	£10.95 ☐	£6.95 ☐	£14.95 ☐	£6.95 ☐	£34.95 ☐	£24.95 ☐	£90 ☐
2.2 Corporate and Business Law **	£24.95 ☐	£10.95 ☐	£6.95 ☐	£14.95 ☐	£6.95 ☐	£34.95 ☐	£24.95 ☐	£90 ☐
2.3 Business Taxation FA2003 (12/04 exams)	£20.95 ☐	£10.95 ☐	£6.95 ☐	£14.95 ☐	£6.95 ☐	£34.95 ☐	£24.95 ☐	£90 ☐
2.3 Business Taxation FA2004 (8/04 for 6/05 exams)†	£24.95 ☐				£6.95 ☐			£90 ☐
2.4 Financial Management and Control	£24.95 ☐	£10.95 ☐	£6.95 ☐	£14.95 ☐	£6.95 ☐	£34.95 ☐	£24.95 ☐	£90 ☐
2.5 Financial Reporting (7/04)	£24.95 ☐	£10.95 ☐	£6.95 ☐	£14.95 ☐	£6.95 ☐	£34.95 ☐	£24.95 ☐	£90 ☐
2.6 Audit and Internal Review (12/04 exams)	£24.95 ☐	£10.95 ☐	£6.95 ☐	£14.95 ☐	£6.95 ☐	£34.95 ☐	£24.95 ☐	£90 ☐
2.6 Audit and Internal Review (9/04 for 6/05 exams)†	£24.95 ☐	£10.95 ☐	£6.95 ☐	£14.95 ☐	£6.95 ☐	£34.95 ☐	£24.95 ☐	£90 ☐
PART 3								
3.1 Audit and Assurance Services	£24.95 ☐	£10.95 ☐	£6.95 ☐	£14.95 ☐	£6.95 ☐		£24.95 ☐	£90 ☐
3.2 Advanced Taxation FA2003 (12/04 exams)	£20.95 ☐	£10.95 ☐	£6.95 ☐	£14.95 ☐	£6.95 ☐		£24.95 ☐	£90 ☐
3.2 Advanced Taxation FA2004 (9/04 for 6/05 exams)†	£24.95 ☐							
3.3 Performance Management	£24.95 ☐	£10.95 ☐	£6.95 ☐	£14.95 ☐	£6.95 ☐		£24.95 ☐	£90 ☐
3.4 Business Information Management	£24.95 ☐	£10.95 ☐	£6.95 ☐	£14.95 ☐	£6.95 ☐		£24.95 ☐	£90 ☐
3.5 Strategic Business Planning and Development	£24.95 ☐	£10.95 ☐	£6.95 ☐	£14.95 ☐	£6.95 ☐		£24.95 ☐	£90 ☐
3.6 Advanced Corporate Reporting (7/04)	£24.95 ☐	£10.95 ☐	£6.95 ☐	£14.95 ☐	£6.95 ☐		£24.95 ☐	£90 ☐
3.7 Strategic Financial Management	£24.95 ☐	£10.95 ☐	£6.95 ☐	£14.95 ☐	£6.95 ☐		£24.95 ☐	£90 ☐
INTERNATIONAL STREAM								
1.1 Preparing Financial Statements	£24.95 ☐	£10.95 ☐	£6.95 ☐			£34.95 ☐	£24.95 ☐	
2.2 Corporate and Business Law	£24.95 ☐	£10.95 ☐	£6.95 ☐					
2.5 Financial Reporting	£24.95 ☐	£10.95 ☐	£6.95 ☐			£34.95 ☐	£24.95 ☐	
2.6 Audit and Internal Review	£24.95 ☐	£10.95 ☐	£6.95 ☐			£34.95 ☐	£24.95 ☐	
3.1 Audit and Assurance Services	£24.95 ☐	£10.95 ☐	£6.95 ☐					
3.6 Advanced Corporate Reporting	£24.95 ☐	£10.95 ☐	£6.95 ☐					
Success in Your Research and Analysis								
Project - Tutorial Text (10/04)	£24.95 ☐							
Learning to Learn (7/02)	£9.95 ☐							

SUBTOTAL £ _____

POSTAGE & PACKING

Study Texts

	First	Each extra	Online
UK	£5.00	£2.00	£2.00
Europe*	£6.00	£4.00	£4.00
Rest of world	£20.00	£10.00	£10.00

Kits

	First	Each extra	Online
UK	£5.00	£2.00	£2.00
Europe*	£6.00	£4.00	£4.00
Rest of world	£20.00	£10.00	£10.00

Passcards/Success Tapes/CDs

	First	Each extra	Online
UK	£2.00	£1.00	£1.00
Europe*	£3.00	£2.00	£2.00
Rest of world	£8.00	£8.00	£8.00

Grand Total (incl. Postage) £ _____

I enclose a cheque for _____
(Cheques to BPP Professional Education)

Or charge to Visa/Mastercard/Switch

Card Number ☐☐☐☐ ☐☐☐☐ ☐☐☐☐ ☐☐☐☐

Expiry date _____   Start Date _____

Issue Number (Switch Only) _____

Signature _____

We aim to deliver to all UK addresses inside 5 working days; a signature will be required. Orders to all EU addresses should be delivered within 6 working days. All other orders to overseas addresses should be delivered within 8 working days. * Europe includes the Republic of Ireland and the Channel Islands. † For 6/05 exam, New edition Kit, Passcard, i-Learn and i-Pass available 2005. ** For Scots law variant students, a free Scots Law Supplement is